Lecture Notes in Computer Science   14681

Founding Editors

Gerhard Goos
Juris Hartmanis

Editorial Board Members

The series Lecture Notes in Computer Science (LNCS), including its subseries Lecture Notes in Artificial Intelligence (LNAI) and Lecture Notes in Bioinformatics (LNBI), has established itself as a medium for the publication of new developments in computer science and information technology research, teaching, and education.

LNCS enjoys close cooperation with the computer science R & D community, the series counts many renowned academics among its volume editors and paper authors, and collaborates with prestigious societies. Its mission is to serve this international community by providing an invaluable service, mainly focused on the publication of conference and workshop proceedings and postproceedings. LNCS commenced publication in 1973.

Arie Gurfinkel · Vijay Ganesh
Editors

Computer Aided Verification

36th International Conference, CAV 2024
Montreal, QC, Canada, July 24–27, 2024
Proceedings, Part I

 Springer

Editors
Arie Gurfinkel
University of Waterloo
Waterloo, ON, Canada

Vijay Ganesh
Georgia Institute of Technology
Atlanta, GA, USA

ISSN 0302-9743   ISSN 1611-3349 (electronic)
Lecture Notes in Computer Science
ISBN 978-3-031-65626-2   ISBN 978-3-031-65627-9 (eBook)
https://doi.org/10.1007/978-3-031-65627-9

This Springer imprint is published by the registered company Springer Nature Switzerland AG
The registered company address is: Gewerbestrasse 11, 6330 Cham, Switzerland

If disposing of this product, please recycle the paper.

Preface

It was our privilege to serve as the program chairs for CAV 2024, the 36th International Conference on Computer-Aided Verification. CAV 2024 was held in Montreal, Canada, on July 24–27, 2024, and the pre-conference workshops were held on July 22–23, 2024.

CAV is an annual conference dedicated to the advancement of the theory and practice of computer-aided formal analysis methods for hardware and software systems. The primary focus of CAV is to extend the frontiers of verification techniques by expanding to new domains such as security, quantum computing, and machine learning. This puts CAV at the cutting edge of formal methods research. This year's program is a reflection of this commitment.

CAV 2024 received 317 submissions. We accepted 16 tool papers, 2 case-study papers, and 51 regular papers, which amounts to an acceptance rate of roughly 26% in each category. The accepted papers cover a wide spectrum of topics, from theoretical results to applications of formal methods. These papers apply or extend formal methods to a wide range of domains such as concurrency, machine learning and neural networks, quantum systems, as well as hybrid and stochastic systems. The program featured keynote talks by Noriko Arai (National Institute of Informatics, Japan), Leonardo de Moura (Amazon Web Services, USA), and Erika Abraham (RWTH Aachen University, Germany). In addition to the contributed talks, CAV 2024 also hosted the CAV Award ceremony, and a report from the Synthesis Competition (SYNTCOMP) chairs. Furthermore, we continued the tradition of Logic Lounge, a series of discussions on computer science topics targeting a general audience. This year's Logic Lounge speaker was Scott J. Shapiro (Yale Law School) who spoke about topics at the intersection of formal methods and the law.

In addition to the main conference, CAV 2024 hosted the following workshops: Verification Mentoring Workshop (VMW), Correct Data Compression (CoDaC), Workshop on Synthesis (SYNT), Workshop on Verification of Probabilistic Programs (VeriProP), Developing an Open-Source, State-of-the-Art Symbolic Model-Checking Framework for the Model-Checking Research Community (OSSyM), Formal Reasoning in Distributed Algorithms (FRIDA), Workshop on Hyperproperties: Advances in Theory and Practice (HYPER), Symposium on AI Verification (SAIV), Deep Learning-aided Verification (DAV), and International Workshop on Satisfiability Modulo Theories (SMT).

Organizing a flagship conference like CAV requires a great deal of effort from the community. The Program Committee for CAV 2024 consisted of 90 members—a committee of this size ensures that each member has to review only a reasonable number of papers in the allotted time. In all, the committee members wrote over 900 reviews while investing significant effort to maintain and ensure the high quality of the conference program. We are grateful to the CAV 2024 Program Committee for their outstanding efforts in evaluating the submissions and making sure that each paper got a fair chance.

Like recent years in CAV, we made artifact evaluation mandatory for tool paper submissions, but optional for the rest of the accepted papers. This year we received 54 artifact submissions, all of which received at least one badge. The Artifact Evaluation Committee consisted of 92 members who put in significant effort to evaluate each artifact. The goal of this process was to provide constructive feedback to tool developers and help make the research published in CAV more reproducible. We are also very grateful to the Artifact Evaluation Committee for their hard work and dedication in evaluating the submitted artifacts.

CAV 2024 would not have been possible without the tremendous help we received from several individuals, and we would like to thank everyone who helped make CAV 2024 a success. We would like to thank Mirco Giacobbe and Milan Ceska for chairing the Artifact Evaluation Committee. We also thank Temegshen Kahsai for chairing the workshop organization. Norine Coenen and Hadar Frenkel for leading publicity efforts, Eric Koskinen and Grigory Fedyukovich as the fellowship chairs, Grigory Fedyukovich as sponsorship chair, and John (Zhengyang) Lu as the website chair. Hari Govind V. K. helped prepare the proceedings. We also thank Grigory Fedyukovich, Eric Koskinen, Umang Mathur, Yoni Zohar, and Jingbo Wang for organizing the Verification Mentoring Workshop. Last but not least, we would like to thank the members of the CAV Steering Committee (Kenneth McMillan, Aarti Gupta, Orna Grumberg, and Daniel Kroening) for helping us with several important aspects of organizing CAV 2024.

We hope that you will find the proceedings of CAV 2024 scientifically interesting and thought-provoking!

June 2024   Arie Gurfinkel
                                                     Vijay Ganesh

Organization

Steering Committee

Aarti Gupta   Princeton University
Daniel Kroening   University of Oxford
Kenneth McMillan   University of Texas at Austin
Ornal Grumberg   Technion

Conference Co-chairs

Arie Gurfinkel   University of Waterloo
Vijay Ganesh   Georgia Institute of Technology

Artifact Evaluation Co-chairs

Mirco Giacobbe   University of Birmingham
Milan Ceska   Brno University of Technology

Local Chair

Xujie Si   University of Toronto

Area Chairs

Alexandra Silva   Cornell University
Anthony Widjaja Lin   Technical University of Kaiserslautern
Borzoo Bonakdarpour   Michigan State University
Corina Pasareanu   NASA
Kristin Yvonne Rozier   Iowa State University
Laura Kovacs   TU Wien

Workshop Chair

Temesghen Kahsai   Amazon

Fellowship Chairs

Grigory Fedyukovich   Florida State University
Eric Koskinen   Stevens Institute of Technology

Publicity Chairs

Norine Coenen   CISPA Helmholtz Center for Information Security
Hadar Frenkel   CISPA Helmholtz Center for Information Security

Publication Chair

Hari Govind V. K.   University of Waterloo

Website Chair

John (Zhengyang) Lu   University of Waterloo

Program Committee

Aditya Thakur   University of California, Davis
Ahmed Bouajjani   IRIF
Aina Niemetz   Stanford University
Akash Lal   Microsoft Research
Alan Hu   University of British Columbia
Alessandro Cimatti   Fondazione Bruno Kessler
Alexander Nadel   Technion & Intel
Alexandra Silva   Cornell University
Amir Goharshady   Hong Kong University of Science and Technology
Anastasia Mavridou   KBR Inc.
Andrew Reynolds   University of Iowa
Anna Slobodova   Intel

Anthony Widjaja Lin	Technical University of Kaiserslautern
Azadeh Farzan	University of Toronto
B. Srivathsan	Chennai Mathematical Institute
Benjamin Kaminski	Saarland University
Bernd Finkbeiner	CISPA Helmholtz Center for Information Security
Bettina Könighofer	Graz University of Technology
Bor-Yuh Evan Chang	University of Colorado
Borzoo Bonakdarpour	Michigan State University
Caterina Urban	Inria
Cezara Dragoi	Inria
Christopher Hahn	Google
Constantin Enea	Ecole Polytechnique
Corina Pasareanu	NASA
Deepak D'Souza	Indian Institute of Science
Dejan Jovanović	Amazon
Elizabeth Polgreen	University of Edinburgh
Elvira Albert	Universidad Complutense de Madrid
Erika Abraham	RWTH Aachen University
Eunsuk Kang	Carnegie Mellon University
Florin Manea	University of Göttingen
Gagandeep Singh	University of Illinois Urbana-Champaign
Grigory Fedyukovich	Florida State University
Guy Amir	Hebrew University of Jerusalem
Hadar Frenkel	CISPA Helmholtz Center for Information Security
Hongce Zhang	Hong Kong University of Science and Technology, China
Ichiro Hasuo	National Institute of Informatics
Isil Dillig	University of Texas at Austin
Jana Hofmann	Azure Research, Microsoft
Jianwen Li	East China Normal University
Jingbo Wang	University of Southern California
Jorge A. Navas	Certora
Ken McMillan	University of Texas at Austin
Kristin Yvonne Rozier	Iowa State University
Kshitij Bansal	Google
Kuldeep Meel	University of Toronto
Kumar Madhukar	Indian Institute of Technology Delhi
Laura Kovacs	TU Wien
Liana Hadarean	Amazon
Loris D'Antoni	University of Wisconsin-Madison
Mathias Preiner	Stanford University
Matthias Heizmann	University of Freiburg

Artifact Evaluation Committee

Abhinandan Pal	University of Birmingham
Adwait Godbole	UC Berkeley
Akshatha Shenoy	Tata Consultancy Services Ltd.
Alejandro Hernández-Cerezo	Complutense University of Madrid
Alvin George	IISc Bangalore
Ameer Hamza	Florida State University
Andreas Katis	KBR Inc. at NASA Ames Research Center
Anna Becchi	Fondazione Bruno Kessler
Benjamin Mikek	Georgia Institute of Technology
Bohua Zhan	Institute of Software, Chinese Academy of Sciences
Chenyu Zhou	University of Southern California
Daniel Dietsch	University Freiburg
Daniel Riley	Florida State University
Diptarko Roy	University of Oxford
Edoardo Manino	University of Manchester
Ennio Visconti	TU Wien
Enrico Magnago	Amazon Web Services
Filip Cano	Graz University of Technology
Filip Macák	Brno University of Technology
Florian Renkin	IRIF
Francesco Parolini	Sorbonne Université
Francesco Pontiggia	TU Wien
Gianluca Redondi	Fondazione Bruno Kessler
Giulio Garbi	University of Molise
Haoze Wu	Stanford University
Jacqueline Mitchell	University of Southern California
Jialuo Chen	Zhejiang University
Jie An	National Institute of Informatics
Jiong Yang	National University of Singapore
Julia Klein	University of Konstanz
Kartik Nagar	IIT Madras
Kaushik Mallik	Institute of Science and Technology Austria
Kazuki Watanabe	National Institute of Informatics, Tokyo
Kevin Cheang	Amazon Web Services
Konstantin Kueffner	Institute of Science and Technology Austria
Lelio Brun	National Institute of Informatics
Lorenz Leutgeb	Max Planck Institute for Informatics
Luca Arnaboldi	University of Birmingham
Lucas Zavalia	Florida State University

Malinda Dilhara	University of Colorado Boulder
Marcel Moosbrugger	TU Wien
Marck van der Vegt	Radboud University
Marco Casadio	Heriot-Watt University
Marco Lewis	Newcastle University
Marek Chalupa	Institute of Science and Technology Austria
Mário Pereira	NOVA University Lisbon
Marius Mikučionis	Aalborg University
Mathias Fleury	University of Freiburg
Matteo Marescotti	Meta Platforms
Matthias Schlaipfer	Amazon Web Services
Maximilian Weininger	Institute of Science and Technology Austria
Mertcan Temel	Intel Corporation
Mihir Mehta	University of Texas at Austin
N. Ege Saraç	Institute of Science and Technology Austria
Natasha Jeppu	Amazon Web Services
Neea Rusch	Augusta University
Neta Elad	Tel Aviv University
Nham Le	University of Waterloo
Oliver Markgraf	Max Planck Institute Kaiserslautern
Omar Inverso	Gran Sasso Science Institute
Omri Isac	Hebrew University of Jerusalem
Oyendrila Dobe	Michigan State University
P. Habeeb	Indian Institute of Science
Patrick Trentin	Amazon Web Services
Philippe Heim	CISPA Helmholtz Center for Information Security
Po-Chun Chien	LMU Munich
Ranadeep Biswas	Informal Systems
Remi Desmartin	Heriot-Watt University
Roman Andriushchenko	Brno University of Technology
Samuel Pastva	Institute of Science and Technology Austria
Sayan Mukherjee	Université libre de Bruxelles
Shengping Xiao	East China Normal University
Shubham Ugare	University of Illinois Urbana-Champaign
Shufang Zhu	University of Oxford
Shuo Ding	Georgia Institute of Technology
Siddharth Priya	University of Waterloo
Sidi Mohamed Beillahi	University of Toronto
Stefan Pranger	Graz University of Technology
Tobias Meggendorfer	Lancaster University Leipzig
Tobias Winkler	RWTH Aachen University
Tzu-Han Hsu	Michigan State University

Wael-Amine Boutglay   Université Paris Cité and Mohammed VI
                             Polytechnic University
Xidan Song   University of Manchester
Xindi Zhang   Institute of Software, Chinese Academy of
                             Sciences
Xiyue Zhang   University of Oxford
Yannan Li   Oracle
Yannik Schnitzer   University of Oxford
Yizhak Elboher   Hebrew University of Jerusalem
Yuzhou Fang   University of Southern California
Zhe Tao   University of California, Davis
Zhendong Ang   National University of Singapore
Zhiwei Zhang   Rice University

Additional Reviewers

Albarghouthi, Aws   Hsu, Tzu-Han
Amarilli, Antoine   Hunt, Warren
Ang, Zhendong   Hyvärinen, Antti
Antal, László   Ivrii, Alexander
Banerjee, Subarno   Karmarkar, Hrishikesh
Batz, Kevin   Koll, Charles
Becchi, Anna   Labbaf, Faezeh
Ben Shimon, Yoav   Lester, Martin Mariusz
Biagiola, Matteo   Lotan, Raz
Blicha, Martin   Luo, Ziyan
Bossut, Camille   Magnago, Enrico
Britikov, Konstantin   Metta, Ravindra
Campion, Marco   Metzger, Niklas
De Palma, Alessandro   Mikek, Benjamin
Ding, Shuo   Moosbrugger, Marcel
Dobe, Oyendrila   Morris, Jason
Eeralla, Ajay   Mover, Sergio
Elad, Neta   Mukhopadhyay, Diganta
Elboher, Yizhak   Nalbach, Jasper
Emmi, Michael   Otoni, Rodrigo
Frenkel, Eden   Pailoor, Shankara
Georgiou, Pamina   Patterson, Zachary
Gerlach, Carolina   Piskachev, Goran
Gürtler, Tobias   Promies, Valentin
Hartmanns, Arnd   Quatmann, Tim
Hoad, Stuart   Rappoport, Omer
Hong, Chih-Duo   Ravitch, Tristan

Rawson, Michael
Ritzert, Martin
Saatcioglu, Goktug
Shenoy, Akshatha
Shetty, Abhishek
Shi, Zheng
Tarrach, Thorsten
Trivedi, Ashutosh
Tunç, Hünkar Can
Verscht, Lena

Visconti, Ennio
Winkler, Tobias
Zhang, Minjian
Kaivola, Roope
Kaufmann, Daniela
Kolárik, Tomáš
Le, Nham
Li, Yong
Lu, Zhengyang
Löding, Christof

Invited Talks

How to Solve Math Problems Without Talent

Noriko Arai

National Institute of Informatics, Japan

The desire to solve mathematical problems without inherent talent has been a long-standing aspiration of humanity since ancient times. In this lecture, we delve into the complexity theory of proofs, examining the relationship between talent and the cost of proof. Additionally, we discuss the possibilities and limitations of using a fusion of computational methods, including computer algebra and natural language processing, to solve mathematical problems with machines. Join us as we explore the frontier of machine-enabled mathematical problem-solving, reflecting on its potential and boundaries in fulfilling this age-old human ambition.

Bridging Formal Mathematics and Software Verification

Leonardo de Moura

Amazon Web Services, USA

This talk will explore the dual applications of Lean 4, the latest iteration of the Lean proof assistant and programming language, in advancing formal mathematics and software verification. We begin with an overview of its design and implementation. We will detail how Lean 4 enables the formalization of complex mathematical theories and proofs, thereby enhancing collaboration and reliability in mathematical research. This endeavor is supported by a philosophy that promotes decentralized innovation, empowering a diverse community of researchers, developers, and enthusiasts to collaboratively push the boundaries of mathematical practice. Simultaneously, we will discuss software verification applications using Lean 4 at AWS. By leveraging Lean's dual capabilities as both a proof assistant and a functional programming language, we achieve a cohesive approach to software development and verification. Additionally, the talk will outline future directions for Lean 4, including efforts to expand its user community, enhance user experience, and further integrate formal methods into both academic research and industrial applications.

The Art of SMT Solving

Erika Ábrahám

RWTH Aachen University, Germany

Satisfiability Modulo Theories (SMT) solving [3, 4, 9] is a technology for the fully automated solution of logical formulas. SMT solvers can be used as general-purpose off-the-shelf tools. Due to their impressive efficiency, they are nowadays frequently used in a wide variety of applications [2]. A typical application encodes real-world problems as logical formulas, whose solutions can be decoded to solutions of the original real-world problem.

Besides its unquestionable practical impact, SMT solving has another great merit: it inspired truly elegant ideas, which do not only enable the construction of efficient software tools, but provide also interesting theoretical insights.

For *propositional logic* where each formula has a finite number of Boolean variables, we could enumerate and check all possible variable assignments, but due to its bad average complexity, this exploration approach is not applicable in practice. Alternatively, the proof system of Boolean resolution can be applied, but the applicability of this method is also restricted to rather small problems. However, in the 90s, *SAT solvers* succeeded to become impressively powerful due to an elegant combination of these two methods, where the proof construction is guided by an exploration of the assignment space equipped with a smart look-ahead mechanism [5, 6, 10].

The effectivity of SAT solvers gave motivation to extend the scope of solver technologies to formulas of *quantifier-free first-order logic over different theories*. On the one hand, *eager SMT solving* approaches have been proposed for certain theories to transform their formulas to propositional logic and use SAT solving to check the result for satisfiability. On the other hand, *(full/less) lazy SMT solving* uses SAT solving to explore the Boolean structure of the formula, and employs theory solvers to check the consistency of Boolean assignments in the theory domains.

Recently, the idea of symbiotic combination of exploration and proof construction has been also generalized to theories, most notably quantifier-free real algebra [7], in the framework of the *model constructing satisfiability calculus (MCSAT)* [11]. In this approach, exploration-guided proof construction is designed to run *both* in the Boolean space and in the theory domain, simultaneously in a consistent manner.

Both the SAT and the MCSAT approaches are based on the generalization of "wrong guesses", made during exploration, into pieces of a proof, which are collected and used to synthesize a global proof during the solving process. While being one of the currently best approaches, for large or complex formulas, a large number of "proof pieces" cause high effort for their processing and restrict scalability.

Thus the question comes up whether there are also other ways to store such information in a more structured way, allowing a less costly processing. This idea is taken up by the *cylindrical algebraic covering* method [1, 8], developed for the satisfiability check of conjunctions of polynomial constraints.

In this talk we give an introduction to the mechanisms of SAT and SMT solving, discuss the above ideas, and illustrate the usage of SMT solvers on a few application examples.

References

1. Ábrahám, E., Davenport, J.H., England, M., Kremer, G.: Deciding the consistency of non-linear real arithmetic constraints with a conflict driven search using cylindrical algebraic coverings. J. Log. Algebraic Methods Program. **119**, 100633 (2021). https://doi.org/10.1016/j.jlamp.2020.100633
2. Ábrahám, E., Kovács, J., Remke, A.: SMT: something you must try. In: Herber, P., Wijs, A. (eds) iFM 2023. LNCS, vol. 14300, pp. 3–18. Springer, Cham (2024). https://doi.org/10.1007/978-3-031-47705-8_1
3. Ábrahám, E., Kremer, G.: SMT solving for arithmetic theories: theory and tool support. In: Proceedings SYNASC 2017, pp. 1–8. IEEE (2017). https://doi.org/10.1109/SYNASC.2017.00009
4. Barrett, C., Sebastiani, R., Seshia, S.A., Tinelli, C.: Satisfiability modulo theories. In: Handbook of Satisfiability, Frontiers in Artificial Intelligence and Applications, vol. 185, chap. 26, pp. 825–885. IOS Press (2009)
5. Davis, M., Putnam, H.: A computing procedure for quantification theory. J. ACM **7**(3), 201–215 (1960)
6. Davis, M., Logemann, G., Loveland, D.W.: A machine program for theorem-proving. Commun. ACM **5**(7), 394–397 (1962). https://doi.org/10.1145/368273.368557
7. Jovanović, D., de Moura, L.: Solving non-linear arithmetic. In: Gramlich, B., Miller, D., Sattler, U. (eds.) IJCAR 2012. LNCS, vol. 7364, pp. 339–354. Springer, Heidelberg (2012). https://doi.org/10.1007/978-3-642-31365-3_27
8. Kremer, G., Ábrahám, E., England, M., Davenport, J.H.: On the implementation of cylindrical algebraic coverings for satisfiability modulo theories solving. In: Proceedings SYNASC 2021, pp. 37–39. IEEE (2021). https://doi.org/10.1109/SYNASC54541.2021.00018
9. Kroening, D., Strichman, O.: Decision Procedures: An Algorithmic Point of View. Springer, Heidelberg (2008). https://doi.org/10.1007/978-3-662-50497-0
10. Moskewicz, M., Madigan, C.F., Zhao, Y., Zhang, L., Malik, S.: Chaff: engineering an efficient SAT solver. In: Proceedings 38th Design Automation Conference (2001)
11. de Moura, L., Jovanović, D.: A model-constructing satisfiability calculus. In: Giacobazzi, R., Berdine, J., Mastroeni, I. (eds.) VMCAI 2013. LNCS, vol. 7737, pp. 1–12. Springer, Heidelberg (2013). https://doi.org/10.1007/978-3-642-35873-9_1

Contents – Part I

Software Verification

Contents – Part II

Case Studies and Tools

Machine Learning and Neural Networks

Contents – Part III

Cyberphysical and Hybrid Systems

Probabilistic Systems

Quantum Systems

Decision Procedures

Split Gröbner Bases for Satisfiability Modulo Finite Fields

Alex Ozdemir[1,2]($\boxtimes$), Shankara Pailoor[2], Alp Bassa[2], Kostas Ferles[2],
Clark Barrett[1], and Işil Dillig[2]

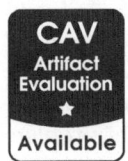

[1] Stanford University, Stanford, USA
aozdemir@cs.stanford.edu
[2] Veridise, Stanford, USA

Abstract. Satisfiability modulo finite fields enables automated verification for cryptosystems. Unfortunately, previous solvers scale poorly for even some simple systems of field equations, in part because they build a full Gröbner basis (GB) for the system. We propose a new solver that uses multiple, simpler GBs instead of one full GB. Our solver, implemented within the cvc5 SMT solver, admits specialized propagation algorithms, e.g., for understanding bitsums. Experiments show that it solves important bitsum-heavy determinism benchmarks far faster than prior solvers, without introducing much overhead for other benchmarks.

1 Introduction

Finite fields are critical to many cryptosystems. They underlie the AES-GCM cipher and ECDH key-exchange, which are used in over 80% of web requests [2,42]. They also underlie zero-knowledge proof systems (ZKPs) and multi-party computation protocols that are used in billion-dollar private cryptocurrencies [27,28,40,46], private DNS filters [34], agricultural auctions [8], discrimination studies [5], and US inter-agency data sharing [3].

Since (finite-)field-based cryptosystems are so prevalent, bugs in their implementations can have serious consequences. Furthermore, such bugs are not hypothetical. They routinely cause CVEs in OpenSSL [18,19,48] and compromise cryptocurrencies [1,57,62].

Motivated by this problem, recent research has explored automated verification for field-based computations [50,53]. However, these techniques inherit scalability challenges from the field-solving capabilities of current Satisfiability Modulo Theories (SMT) solvers. The best SMT solver [50] for fields of cryptographic size ($\approx 2^{256}$) uses Gröbner bases (GBs) [10]. A GB can answer many questions about a system of equations, but the GB itself must first be computed.

Unfortunately, computing a GB has high theoretical complexity: doubly exponential in the worst case [45]. In practice, computing a GB *can* be feasible for some systems [50], but it is intractable for others, even simple ones. For example, consider a prime field—representable as the integers modulo a prime p. Suppose that $p \geq 2^b$ and consider the following system in variables $X_1, \ldots, X_b, Z$:

© The Author(s) 2024
A. Gurfinkel and V. Ganesh (Eds.): CAV 2024, LNCS 14681, pp. 3–25, 2024.
https://doi.org/10.1007/978-3-031-65627-9_1

$$\bigwedge_{i=1}^{b} X_i(1 - X_i) = 0 \qquad \wedge \qquad X_1 + 2X_2 + 4X_3 + \cdots + 2^{b-1}X_b = 0 \qquad \wedge \qquad X_b Z = 1$$

In some sense, this system is simple: the first equation forces each X_i to be 0 or 1, and the second equation forces every X_i to be 0, which then contradicts the final equation. However, computing a GB for this system using current algorithms takes exponential time. We investigate systems like this in Sect. 3, but essentially there are two conclusions: first, a GB is hard to compute because of the *combination* of the bitsum $\sum_i 2^{i-1}X_i$ and the bit constraints $X_i(1-X_i) = 0$; second, bitsums and bit constraints are common when verifying systems that use ZKPs. So, the scalability of GB-based reasoning with bitsums is a real problem for ZKP verification.

To overcome this problem, we present a new approach for solving or refuting a system S of finite field equations. The key idea is that of a *split Gröbner basis*. If S is split into (possibly overlapping) subsystems $S_1 \wedge \cdots \wedge S_k = S$, and B_i is a GB for S_i, then we call the sequence $B_1, \ldots, B_k$ a split GB for S. A split GB approximates a full GB for S: it gives detailed information about each subsystem S_i, but more limited information about S. In exchange for this approximation, if each S_i is "small" or "simple," then the split GB might be easier to compute.

In this paper, we present a decision procedure for finite field arithmetic based on the idea of *iteratively refining* a split GB. It starts with some split of S and then refines it as necessary by sharing equations between the S_i's. We also add an extensible *propagation* algorithm for deducing new equations. Sharing equations increases the cost of computing the split basis but also improves the approximation that it offers. The key advantage is that the procedure can often solve or refute S before any S_i becomes too hard to compute a basis for.

We implement our approach as a solver for prime fields within the cvc5 SMT solver [4]. Our solver (a) splits bitsums and their bit constraints across two subsystems and (b) includes a specialized propagator for bitsum reasoning. This is particularly effective for important, bitsum-heavy verification problems related to ZKPs. For these problems, experiments show that our solver exponentially improves on prior work; for other problems, it has low overhead.

One application we consider is verifying field blaster ($\mathbb{F}$-blaster) rules in a ZKP compiler: these rules encode Boolean and bit-vector operations as (conjunctions of) field equations (see Sect. 2). We give a new SMT encoding for rule correctness, prove our encoding is correct, and show that combining it with our new solver improves the state of the art for $\mathbb{F}$-blaster verification [52]. To summarize, our key contributions are:

1. Split: an abstract decision procedure for field solving using a split Gröbner basis instead of a full Gröbner basis.
2. BitSplit: an instantiation of Split, optimized for bitsums and implemented in cvc5. It is exponentially faster than prior solvers on important benchmarks.
3. An application: a new encoding for $\mathbb{F}$-blaster verification conditions that improves the state of the art for $\mathbb{F}$-blaster verification by leveraging BitSplit.

The rest of the paper is organized as follows. First, we review related work (Sect. 1.1), give background (Sect. 2), and present a motivating example (Sect. 3). Then, we explain our abstract and concrete decision procedures (Sect. 4) and present experiments (Sect. 5). Last, we apply our solver to the problem of verified $\mathbb{F}$-blasting (Sect. 6).

1.1 Related Work

There are two prior finite field solvers for SMT: Hader et al. [36,38,39] use subresultant regular subchains [58], and Ozdemir et al. [50] use Gröbner bases. As we will see (Sect. 5), only the latter scales to large fields. Our work builds on it.

Other prior works propose verification and linting tools for ZKPs. QED^2 [53] checks whether an output variable Y in some system is uniquely determined by the values of input variables $X_1, \ldots, X_m$. Another project [52] verifies that a ZKP compiler's $\mathbb{F}$-blaster is correct. These both use satisfiability modulo finite fields and could benefit from our work. Other tools are purely syntactic [20,59,60].

Further afield, others consider finite fields in *interactive* theorem provers, applied to mathematics [9,16,31,41], to program correctness [25,26,54,55], and even to ZKPs [13,15,29,43]. In contrast, our work is fully automatic.

2 Background

Here we summarize necessary definitions and facts about finite fields [21, Part IV], computer algebra [17], satisfiability modulo finite fields (SMFF) [47,50], and applications of SMFF [52,53]. See the references for further details.

Finite Fields and Polynomials. For naturals $a \geq 1$, $[a]$ denotes $\{1, \ldots, a\}$. In general, $\mathbf{x}$ denotes a list of elements $x_1, \ldots, x_m$. Let p be a prime. $\mathbb{F}_p$ (abbreviated $\mathbb{F}$ when p is clear) denotes the unique finite field of order p, represented as $\{0, \ldots, p-1\}$ with addition and multiplication modulo p. A field of prime order is also called a *prime field*. Let $\mathbf{X}$ be a list of n variables: $(X_1, \ldots, X_n)$. $\mathbb{F}[\mathbf{X}]$ is the set of polynomials in $\mathbf{X}$ with coefficients from $\mathbb{F}$. For $f \in \mathbb{F}[\mathbf{X}]$, let $\deg(f)$ be its degree and $\mathsf{vars}(f)$ be the set of variables appearing in it.

Ideals and Their Zeros. Let $S = \{s_1, \ldots, s_m\}$ be a set of polynomials in $\mathbb{F}[\mathbf{X}]$. $\langle S \rangle$ denotes the *ideal* that is *generated* by S: the set $\{\sum_i f_i s_i : f_i \in \mathbb{F}[\mathbf{X}]\}$. Let $\mathbf{S} = (S_1, \ldots, S_k)$ be a list of *sets* of polynomials. Then, we define $\langle \mathbf{S} \rangle \triangleq \langle \cup_i S_i \rangle$.

Let $M : \mathbf{X} \to \mathbb{F}$ be a map from variables $\mathbf{X}$ to values in $\mathbb{F}$. For $f \in \mathbb{F}[X]$, denote the evaluation of f on M by $f[M]$; a *zero* of f is an M with $f[M] = 0$. The common zeros of S are denoted $\mathcal{V}_{\mathbb{F}}(S)$ (abbreviated $\mathcal{V}(S)$). Note that $\mathcal{V}(S) = \mathcal{V}(\langle S \rangle)$. When studying polynomial systems, one generally considers the system given by the ideal it generates, as it has more structure and has the same set of zeros. For any $f \in \mathbb{F}[\mathbf{X}]$, if $f \in \langle S \rangle$, then $\mathcal{V}(\{f\}) \supseteq \mathcal{V}(S)$. One implication of this is that $1 \in \langle S \rangle$ implies that $\mathcal{V}_{\mathbb{F}}(S)$ is empty. However, the converse does not hold: for example, the polynomial $X^2 + 1$ has no zero in $\mathbb{F}_3$, but $1 \notin \langle X^2 + 1 \rangle$.

Gröbner Bases. A Gröbner basis (GB) is a kind of polynomial set that is often used for solving polynomial systems. Two facts about GBs are relevant to this paper. First, there is an algorithm, GB, that for any polynomial set S, computes a GB B such that $\langle B \rangle = \langle S \rangle$. In this case, we say that B is a GB for S or for $\langle S \rangle$. (But: note that in this paper, B does not always refer to a GB!) Second, there is an algorithm $\mathsf{InIdeal}(f, B)$ that determines whether $f \in \langle B \rangle$ for polynomial f and GB B.[1] Thus, if $\mathsf{InIdeal}(1, \mathsf{GB}(S))$ returns true, this shows that $\mathcal{V}(S)$ is empty. Moreover, $\mathsf{InIdeal}(1, B)$ is computable in polytime if B is a GB since 1 reduces by B iff B contains a non-zero constant [17].

Satisfiability Modulo Finite Fields (SMFF). Previous work [38,50] defines the theory of finite fields, which we summarize here using the usual terminology of many-sorted first order logic with equality [24]. For every finite field $\mathbb{F}$, let the signature Σ include: sort $\mathsf{F}_\mathbb{F}$, binary function symbols $+_\mathbb{F}$ and $\times_\mathbb{F}$, constants $n \in \{0, \dots, |\mathbb{F}| - 1\} \subset \mathbb{N}$, and the inherited equality symbol $\approx_\mathbb{F}$. The theory of finite fields requires that any Σ-interpretation interprets $\mathsf{F}_\mathbb{F}$ as $\mathbb{F}$, n as the nth element of $\mathbb{F}$, and $+$, $\times$, and $\approx$ as addition, multiplication, and equality in $\mathbb{F}$. Previous work reduces the satisfiability problem for this theory to the problem of finding an element of $\mathcal{V}(S)$ given S or determining that there is no such element [50]. In this work, we consider the latter problem.

Applying SMFF to ZKPs. Prior work applies SMFF to verification for zero-knowledge proof systems (ZKPs) [50,52,53]. Practical ZKPs [11,30,33] allow one to prove knowledge of a solution to a system of *field equations* $\Phi(\mathbf{X}, \mathbf{Y})$, while keeping all or part of the solution secret. Since Φ is usually meant to encode a function from $\mathbf{X}$ to $\mathbf{Y}$, recent tools attempt to verify *determinism*: that the value of $\mathbf{X}$ uniquely determines the value of $\mathbf{Y}$ [53,56,59,60]. Determinism can be written as a single satisfiability query solved with SMFF:

$$\Phi(\mathbf{X}, \mathbf{Y}) \wedge \Phi(\mathbf{X}', \mathbf{Y}') \wedge \mathbf{X} = \mathbf{X}' \wedge \mathbf{Y} \neq \mathbf{Y}' \tag{1}$$

The formula (1) is satisfiable if and only if Φ is **non**deterministic. Determinism is important for two reasons. First, constructing (1) only requires identifying the inputs and outputs, making the specification task trivial and automatable. Second, determinism violations are frequent; one caused the Tornado Cash bug [57], and they are part of over half of the bugs in the ZK Bug Tracker [1]. Third, determinism violations cause real vulnerabilities. A recent survey of ZKP vulnerabilities concludes that insufficient constraints (which typically manifest as non-determinism) account for 95% of constraint-system-level vulnerabilities [12]. In Sect. 6, we give another reason why determinism is important: it can imply stronger properties.

3 Motivating Example

In this section, we explore a class of problems that is both important and challenging for existing SMFF solvers. First (Sect. 3.1), we explain the source

---

[1] The definition of GB and these algorithms depends on a *monomial order*. Throughout the paper, we use grevlex order. We discuss monomial orders in Appendix A.

```
1    template Num2Bits(b) { // split 'in' into 'b' bits.
2        signal input in;
3        signal output out[b];
4        var bitSum = 0;
5        for (var i = 1; i <= b; i++) {
6            out[i] * (out[i] -1 ) === 0; // 'out[i]' is 0 or 1
7            bitSum += out[i] * 2 ** (i - 1); // add a term to the accumulating bitsum
8        }
9        bitSum === in; // 'in' is the bitsum of 'out'
10   }
```

Fig. 1. `Num2Bits`: a widely-used circomlib library function. It converts a prime field element into an b-bit binary representation (assuming this is possible).

and prevalence of these problems—determinism queries with bit-splitting. Second (Sect. 3.2), we explore why they are hard for GB-based reasoning, and we present evidence that the core challenge is the combination of bitsums and bit-constraints. Third (Sect. 3.3), we sketch the design of a decision procedure that can meet this challenge.

3.1   Verifying the Determinism of `Num2Bits`

The circom language is used to synthesize field equations for ZKPs. Figure 1 shows a slice of the circom program `Num2Bits`. It relates an input signal in to its binary representation as an array of signals out. The code generates a set of field equations that encode this relationship. The === operator generates equations. Line 6 generates the equation forcing $out[i]$ to be either 1 or 0, line 7 adds $out[i]$ to the expression that is accumulating terms in the bitsum, and line 9 generates the equation equating the bitsum to in. Thus, the equations are:

$$\Phi(in, out) := \left(in = \sum_{i=1}^{b} 2^{i-1} out[i] \right) \wedge \bigwedge_{i=1}^{b} out[i](out[i] - 1) = 0 \qquad (2)$$

Here, b is constant. For any $j \in [b]$, the output $out[j]$ is deterministic if the following SMFF query is unsatisfiable:

$$\exists in, in', out, out'. \ \Phi(in, out) \wedge \Phi(in', out') \wedge in = in' \wedge out[j] \neq out'[j] \qquad (3)$$

Importance. Nearly every circom project uses `Num2Bits` or similar templates that bit-split field elements. This is because bit encodings are a natural way to encode common operations like range-checks ($x \in \{l, \ldots, u\}$) and comparisons ($<, >$) as field equations. In fact, in a crawl of all public circom Github projects, we found that 98% of projects use `Num2Bits` or other circuits with bitsums. Furthermore, bitsums are *very* common in many programs; for example, in circomlib's SHA2 implementation, 64% of the variables appear in some bitsum. We describe our methodology for these measurements in Appendix B.

Table 1. Different ideal families with bitsums and bit-constraints.

Ideal Family	Generators
$I_{2,\det}(b)$	$\mathsf{B\Sigma P}(Y,\mathbf{X}) \cup \mathsf{B\Sigma P}(Y',\mathbf{X}') \cup \{Y - Y'\} \cup \{(X_b - X'_b)Z - 1\}$
$I_2(b)$	$\mathsf{B\Sigma P}(Y,\mathbf{X}) \cup \mathsf{B\Sigma P}(Y',\mathbf{X}') \cup \{Y - Y'\}$
$I_1(b)$	$\mathsf{B\Sigma P}(Y,\mathbf{X})$
$I_{1,\mathrm{val}}(b)$	$\mathsf{B\Sigma P}(Y,\mathbf{X}) \cup \{Y\}$

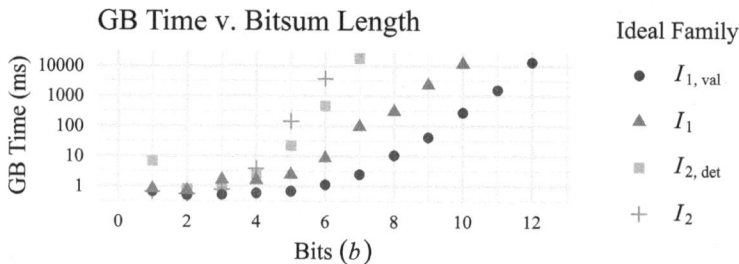

Fig. 2. GB computation time for different systems at different bitsum lengths.

3.2   The Challenge of Bit-Splitting

Unfortunately, state-of-the-art SMFF solvers struggle with (3). The solver of Hader et al. [38] scales poorly with field size (Sect. 5), and ZKP security typically requires $|\mathbb{F}| \approx 2^{255}$. It fails for (3), even when $b = 1$. The GB-based solver of Ozdemir et al. [50] scales better with $|\mathbb{F}|$, but poorly with b. It can handle many large-field benchmarks, but it cannot solve (3) for $b = 32$, even in a week.

To understand the problem, consider how a GB-based solver handles (3). First, it computes a polynomial set S such that $\mathcal{V}(S)$ encodes solutions to (3):

$$S = \{Y - Y', \qquad Y - \textstyle\sum_{i=1}^b 2^{i-1}X_i, \qquad Y' - \textstyle\sum_{i=1}^b 2^{i-1}X'_i,$$
$$X_1^2 - X_1, \ldots, X_b^2 - X_b, \qquad {X'}_1^2 - X'_1, \ldots, {X'}_b^2 - X'_b, \qquad (4)$$
$$(X'_j - X_j)Z - 1\}$$

In this system, *in*, *in'*, *out*, and *out'* are represented by variables Y, Y', $\mathbf{X}$, and $\mathbf{X}'$ respectively. The inequality $X_j \neq X'_j$ becomes the polynomial $(X'_j - X_j)Z - 1$ (for fresh Z) which can be zero only if $X_j \neq X'_j$. Next, the solver attempts to compute a GB for (4). But this takes time exponential in b, as we will see.

To empirically investigate the cause of the slowdown, we consider other families of ideals generated by sets similar to (4). Table 1 shows four ideal families of increasing simplicity that all include bit-splitting. The polynomials are in variables $(X_1, \ldots, X_b, X'_1, \ldots, X'_b, Y, Y', Z)$, and we define the set $\mathsf{B\Sigma P}(Y,\mathbf{X})$ as:

$$\mathsf{B\Sigma P}(Y, (X_1, \ldots, X_b)) \triangleq \{Y - \textstyle\sum_{i=1}^b 2^{i-1}X_i, X_1^2 - X_1, \ldots X_b^2 - X_b\}.$$

The first family, $I_{2,\det}(b)$, is exactly (4), for $j = b$. The second, I_2, removes the polynomial that enforces disequality. The third, I_1, removes one of the bitsum

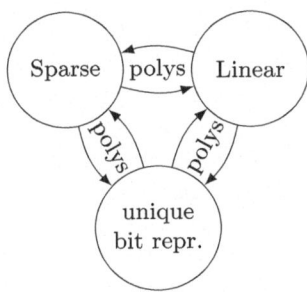

Fig. 3. High-level information flow in BitSplit: our concrete decision procedure.

and bit-constraint sets. The fourth, $I_{1,\text{val}}$, fixes the lone bitsum to a specific value ($Y = 0$). Computing a GB for *any of these families* takes time exponential in b.[2]

Figure 2 shows the times (using Singular [32]; others are similar). $I_{1,\text{val}}$ is easiest to compute a GB for, and I_2 is the hardest, but all take exponential time.

Interestingly, the singleton set of just the bitsum $\{Y - \sum_{i=1}^{b} 2^{i-1} X_i\}$ and the set of bit-constraints without the bitsum $\{X_1^2 - X_1, \ldots X_b^2 - X_b\}$ are both already GBs. It appears that the **combination** of the bitsum and the bit-constraints is what makes computing a GB hard.

Translation to Bit-Vectors: a Dead End. Since ZKPs process finite-field equations, the system (2) has coefficients in a *finite field*. Yet, the appearance of the bitsum pattern makes it tempting to attempt some kind of translation into the bit-vector domain. After all, in that domain, bit-decomposition is easy to reason about! However, this intuitive appeal is misleading. In practice, the approach is not trivial, since (in the general case) the system Φ includes other (non-bitsum) equations too. In fact, previous attempts to solve finite-field equations by translation to bit-vectors have been shown to be very ineffective [50]. Thus, performing some finite-field reasoning seems crucial.

3.3 Cooperative Reasoning: A Path Forward

We have seen that verifying Num2Bits is hard with only GBs. Yet, Num2Bits is easy to verify when we combine GBs with other kinds of reasoning. Consider the following inferences about $\langle S \rangle$ (Eq. 4): Since $\mathbf{X}, \mathbf{X}'$ are bit representations of Y, Y' respectively and $Y - Y'$ is in $\langle S \rangle$, every $X_i' - X_i$ must be too. This is the *congruence* rule for the function from a number to its bit representation. Then, since $f = X_j' - X_j$ and $g = (X_j' - X_j)Z - 1$ are both in $\langle S \rangle$ a GB shows that $1 = fZ - g$ is also in $\langle S \rangle$. But, if $1 \in \langle S \rangle$, then S can have no common zeros. So, (3) is UNSAT, and Num2Bits is deterministic. The key here is to use GB-based reasoning *and* non-GB-based reasoning (congruence for bit representations).

---

[2] For Fig. 2, we work in $\mathbb{F}_p$, where p is the smallest prime greater than $2^b - 1$. However, the results are similar for other values of p as well.

Our decision procedure BitSplit mixes GB-based and non-GB-based reasoning to understand the contents of an ideal $\langle S \rangle$. Figure 3 illustrates its architecture. There are three modules: each learns new polynomials in $\langle S \rangle$ and potentially shares them with other modules. The *sparse* module computes a GB for all polynomials except *bitsum polynomials* (or *bitsums*): those of form $Y - \sum_i 2^{i-1} X_i$. Its name refers to the fact that bitsums are dense: they have many terms. The *linear* module computes a GB for all linear polynomials (including all bitsums). The *unique bit representation* module infers bit equalities using congruence.

This architecture has three key features. First, it includes non-GB-based reasoning. Second, every polynomial is handled by *some* GB-based module (either the sparse or linear module); this will play a role in correctness. Third, by splitting bitsums (which go into the linear module) and bit-constraints (which go into the sparse module), it avoids computing a GB for both simultaneously.

4   Approach

In this section, we present our decision procedure. Given a set of polynomials G, our procedure either finds a common zero $M \in \mathcal{V}(G)$ or determines that none exists. Recall from Sect. 2 that satisfiability modulo $\mathbb{F}$ reduces to this problem.

To explain our decision procedure, we first introduce a *split Gröbner basis* (Sect. 4.1), which can be easier to compute than a full GB, but can also be less useful when deciding satisfiability. Next, we present our abstract decision procedure Split, which manipulates split Gröbner bases (Sect. 4.2). Split is parameterized by the number of bases k and also by some subroutines. We show that if the subroutines meet suitable conditions, then Split is sound and terminating (Theorem 3). Finally, we instantiate Split with $k = 2$ by defining the necessary subroutines (Sect. 4.3). The result is a concrete decision procedure BitSplit which is optimized for reasoning about bitsums.[3] We evaluate BitSplit experimentally in Sect. 5.

4.1   Split Gröbner bases

Definition 1 (Split Gröbner basis). *A **split Gröbner basis** for ideal I is a sequence $(B_1, \ldots, B_k)$ of Gröbner bases such that $I = \langle \mathbf{B} \rangle$.*

We make a few relevant observations about this definition.

1. A split GB generalizes a GB: that is, $(\mathrm{GB}(S))$ is always a split GB for $\langle S \rangle$.
2. Split GBs for an ideal I are not unique.
3. The split GB definition relaxes the GB definition: while GBs can be hard to compute, split GBs need not be. For example, the ideal $\langle f_1, \ldots, f_n \rangle$ has split GB $(\{f_1\}, \ldots, \{f_n\})$.

---

[3] We use the name "BitSplit" because the procedure is optimized for bitsums (used in bit-splitting) and because the name suggests an instantiation of the "Split" procedure.

1 Function Monolithic:	**1 Function Split:**
In: $G \subset \mathbb{F}[\mathbf{X}]$	**In:** $G \subset \mathbb{F}[\mathbf{X}]$
Out: A zero $M \in \mathcal{V}(G)$ or $\perp$	**Out:** A zero $M \in \mathcal{V}(G)$ or $\perp$
2	2 $\mathbf{G} \leftarrow (\{p \in G : \mathsf{init}(i,p)\})_{i=1}^{k}$;
3 $B \leftarrow \mathsf{GB}(G)$;	3 $\mathbf{B} \leftarrow \mathsf{SplitGB}(\mathbf{G})$;
4 **if** $1 \in \langle B \rangle$ **then return** $\perp$;	4 **if** $\exists i. \, 1 \in \langle B_i \rangle$ **then return** $\perp$;
5 **return** $\mathsf{FindZero}(B)$	5 **return** $\mathsf{SplitFindZero}(\mathbf{B})$
(a) The prior decision procedure [50].	(b) Our abstract procedure Split.

Fig. 4. The prior decision procedure (Monolithic) [50] and our framework (Split).

Informally, a split GB allows one to navigate a trade-off between the computational expense of computing GBs and the power of their ideal membership tests. Generally, a smaller split GB where each individual GB represents more of I makes $\mathsf{InIdeal}(\cdot, B_i)$ more informative. On the other hand, a bigger split GB where each GB represents less of I makes the split basis easier to compute. Section 3 gave an example of this: it is hard to compute a GB for $\langle \sum_{i=1}^{b} 2^{i-1} X_i, X_1^2 - X_1, \ldots, X_b^2 - X_b \rangle$, but $(\{\sum_{i=1}^{b} 2^{i-1} X_i\}, \{X_1^2 - X_1, \ldots, X_b^2 - X_b\})$ is *already* a split GB.

1 Function SplitGB:	
In: $\mathbf{G} = (G_i)_{i=1}^{k}$: a list of generator sets	
Out: $\mathbf{B} = (B_i)_{i=1}^{k}$: a split GB; initially each B_i is empty.	
2 **while** $\cup_i G_i$ is not empty **do**	
3 **for** $i \in [k]$ **do** $B_i \leftarrow \mathsf{GB}(G_i \cup B_i)$; $G_i \leftarrow \emptyset$;	
4 **for** $p \in (\cup_j B_j) \cup \mathsf{extraProp}(\mathbf{B}), i \in [k]$ **do**	
5 **if** $\mathsf{admit}(i,p) \wedge p \notin \langle B_i \rangle$ **then** $G_i \leftarrow G_i \cup \{p\}$;	
6 **return** $\mathbf{B}$	

Algorithm 1: SplitGB computes a split Gröbner basis, with propagation.

4.2 Abstract Procedure: Split

Our starting point is a prior solver based on Gröbner bases [50]. Figure 4a shows the prior procedure, which we call Monolithic, and Fig. 4b shows our new procedure, which is named Split. Monolithic begins by computing a GB B and returning $\perp$ if $1 \in \langle B \rangle$. Recall that $1 \in \langle B \rangle$ implies $\mathcal{V}(G)$ is empty, but the converse does not hold; thus, this is a sound but incomplete test for unsatisfiability. If the problem remains unsolved, then Monolithic proceeds to FindZero, which is a (complete) backtracking search over elements of $\mathbb{F}$.

The key difference in Split is that it works with a split GB $\mathbf{B}$ for $\langle G \rangle$. First (line 2), we split G into subsets $G_1 \cup \cdots \cup G_k = G$; these may overlap. Second (line 3), we compute a Gröbner basis B_i for each subset G_i (and perform additional propagations, discussed later). If some $\langle B_i \rangle$ contains 1, we return $\perp$. Third (line

5), we fall back to a (complete) backtracking search based on $\mathbf{B}$. We will now discuss each phase in more detail.

Splitting. Splitting is done with a function $\mathsf{init}(i, p)$ that decides whether polynomial p should initially be included in basis i. The function init is a parameter of Split. The only requirement of init is that no polynomial can be ignored:

Definition 2 (Covering init). *The function init is **covering** when for all $p \in \mathbb{F}[\mathbf{X}]$, there exists an $i \in [k]$ such that $\mathsf{init}(i, p) = \top$.*

Computing a Split GB and Propagating. In the second stage, we compute a split GB $\mathbf{B}$ using SplitGB (Algorithm 1). To start, SplitGB sets each B_i to be a GB for $\langle G_i \rangle$. However, SplitGB also adds to each B_i additional polynomials called *propagations*. Propagations can be *inter-basis* (from a different B_j) or *extra* (from a subroutine extraProp). Through extraProp, one can extend SplitGB with specialized reasoning (e.g., for bitsums). Whether a propagation p is admitted into B_i is controlled by a subroutine $\mathsf{admit}(i, p)$. Through admit, a basis can reject a polynomial p that would slow down future GB computations.

Now, we explain SplitGB in detail. In each iteration of the outer loop, B_i is a current basis and G_i is a set of polynomials that will be added in the next round. First, B_i is computed from the previous G_i and B_i. Then, polynomials from each B_j are added to each G_i if $\mathsf{admit}(i, \cdot)$ accepts them and $\langle B_i \rangle$ doesn't contain them already. Any propagations from extraProp($\mathbf{B}$) are added in the same way. The loop iterates until there are no new additions.

The correctness of SplitGB depends on extraProp, but not admit. As captured by Definition 3, extraProp($\mathbf{B}$) must only return polynomials in $\langle \mathbf{B} \rangle$. If extraProp obeys this requirement, then SplitGB terminates and preserves the generated ideal, as stated in Theorem 1. The proof is in Appendix C; correctness is straightforward, and termination follows from the same theory that guarantees termination for Buchberger's algorithm [10]. We discuss efficiency later.

Definition 3 (Sound extraProp). *The function extraProp is **sound** when for all $\mathbf{B} \in (2^{\mathbb{F}[\mathbf{X}]})^k$, extraProp($\mathbf{B}$) $\subseteq \langle \mathbf{B} \rangle$.*

Theorem 1. *If extraProp is sound, then SplitGB($\mathbf{G}$) terminates and returns a split Gröbner basis $\mathbf{B}$ such that $\langle \mathbf{B} \rangle = \langle \mathbf{G} \rangle$ and $\langle B_i \rangle \supseteq \langle G_i \rangle$ for all i.*

Backtracking Search. SplitFindZero (Algorithm 2) is our conflict-driven search. Given a split basis $\mathbf{B}$, it returns $M \in \mathcal{V}(\langle \mathbf{B} \rangle)$ if possible, and $\perp$ if $\mathcal{V}(\langle \mathbf{B} \rangle)$ is empty. It uses a subroutine SplitZeroExtend($\mathbf{B}$) which searches for an $M \in \mathcal{V}(\langle \mathbf{B} \rangle)$ by focusing on B_1, as we explain below. SplitZeroExtend returns one of three possibilities: an $M \in \mathcal{V}(\langle \mathbf{B} \rangle)$; $\perp$, indicating that $\mathcal{V}(\langle \mathbf{B} \rangle)$ is empty; or a *conflict polynomial* $p \in (\cup_i B_i) \setminus \langle B_1 \rangle$ that it failed to account for in its B_1-focused search. In the last case, SplitFindZero adds p to B_1 and tries SplitZeroExtend again. Each conflict is new information that is added to B_1 from some other B_i.

SplitZeroExtend is based on the FindZero algorithm of prior work [50]. FindZero is a backtracking search based on a GB B. In each recursive step, it assigns a single variable to a single value. Rather than doing an exhaustive case

```
1  Function SplitFindZero:
      In: B = (B_i)_{i=1}^{k}: a split GB
      Out: A zero M ∈ V(⟨B⟩) or ⊥
2     while conflict p ← SplitZeroExtend(B) do
3        | B ← SplitGB(B_1 ∪ {p}, B_2, …, B_k);
4     return SplitZeroExtend(B)
5  Function SplitZeroExtend:
      In: B = (B_i)_{i=1}^{k}: the current split GB
      In: G ⊂ F[X]: the original generators; if omitted, equal to ∪_i B_i
      In: A partial map M : X → F; if omitted, empty
      Out: A total map M or a conflict polynomial p or ⊥
6     if ∃i. 1 ∈ ⟨B_i⟩ then
7        | if ∃p ∈ G \ ⟨B_1⟩, vars(p) ⊆ vars(M) ∧ p[M] ≠ 0 then return p;
8        | else return ⊥;
9     if |M| = n then return M;
10    for (X_{j_i} ↦ z_i) ∈ ApplyRule(B_1, M) do
11       | r ← SplitZeroExtend(SplitGB((B_j ∪ {X_{j_i} − z_i})_{j=1}^{k}), G, M ∪ {X_{j_i} ↦ z_i});
12       | if r ≠ ⊥ then return r;
13    return ⊥
```

Algorithm 2: SplitFindZero finds zeros using split Gröbner bases.

split for each variable, a subroutine ApplyRule analyzes B and constructs a list (an implicit disjunction) of single-variable assignments $X_{j_1} \mapsto z_1, \ldots, X_{j_\ell} \mapsto z_\ell$ that *cover* $\mathcal{V}(B)$. That is, for each $M \in \mathcal{V}(B)$, there exists i such that $M[X_{j_i}] = z_i$. Thus, we know that if a solution exists, it must agree with at least one of these assignments. For example, with $B = \{X_1^2 - X_2, X_1(X_2 - 1)\}$, every solution must assign X_1 to 0 or X_2 to 1, so any set of assignments including these would do. ApplyRule might, for instance, return exactly $\{X_1 \to 0, X_2 \to 1\}$. For each i, FindZero recurses on $B \leftarrow \mathsf{GB}(B \cup \{X_{j_i} - z_i\})$. It backtracks if $1 \in \langle B \rangle$ and succeeds if every variable has been assigned.

SplitZeroExtend adapts FindZero to a split GB, essentially by running FindZero on B_1 and using SplitGB instead of GB. It also uses a limited notion of conflicts to prune the search space. It is given a split basis $\mathbf{B}$ (that changes in each recursion), a generator set G (that is fixed across recursions and is initially equal to $\cup_i B_i$), and a partial map M from variables to values. First (lines 6–8), it checks whether 1 is in any $\langle B_i \rangle$. There are two cases here. If some polynomial $p \in G \setminus \langle B_1 \rangle$ fully evaluates to a non-zero value, p is returned as a conflict. Otherwise, $\perp$ is returned. Second (line 9), if M is total, then it is returned as a common zero. Third (lines 10–12), SplitZeroExtend uses ApplyRule (from [50]) to obtain a list of single-variable assignments that cover $\mathcal{V}(B_1)$. For each assignment in the list, it attempts to construct a solution by adding that assignment to M and to each B_i and recursing. If no branch succeeds, it returns $\perp$.

For each conflict that SplitZeroExtend returns, SplitFindZero will call it again with a new starting split basis. Theorem 2 states the correctness of SplitFindZero. The correctness of Split (Theorem 3) is a corollary. The proofs are in Appendix D (Table 2).

Table 2. The functions that parameterize Split.

Function signature	Semantics
$\mathsf{init}(i \in [k], p \in \mathbb{F}[\mathbf{X}]) \rightarrow \{\top, \bot\}$	whether to initialize basis B_i with p
$\mathsf{admit}(i \in [k], p \in \mathbb{F}[\mathbf{X}]) \rightarrow \{\top, \bot\}$	whether to accept p into B_i during propagation
$\mathsf{extraProp}(\mathbf{B} \in (2^{\mathbb{F}[\mathbf{X}]})^k) \rightarrow 2^{\mathbb{F}[\mathbf{X}]}$	additional polynomials to propagate

Table 3. Which polynomials our bases accept. The linear basis accepts linear polynomials. The sparse basis accepts non-bitsums initially, and then equalities.

Basis # (i)	Name	$\mathsf{init}(i, p)$ definition	$\mathsf{admit}(i, p)$ definition
1	Sparse	$\neg\mathsf{isBitsum}(p)$	$\mathsf{isEq}(p)$
2	Linear	$\deg(p) \leq 1$	$\deg(p) \leq 1$

Theorem 2. *Let* $\mathbf{B}$ *be a split GB. If* $\mathsf{extraProp}$ *is sound then* $\mathsf{SplitFindZero}(\mathbf{B})$ *terminates and returns an element of* $\mathcal{V}_{\mathbb{F}}(\langle \mathbf{B} \rangle)$ *iff one exists.*

Theorem 3. *Let* G *be a polynomial set. If* $\mathsf{extraProp}$ *is sound and* init *is covering, then* $\mathsf{Split}(G)$ *terminates and returns an element of* $\mathcal{V}_{\mathbb{F}}(G)$ *iff one exists.*

4.3   Concrete Procedure: BitSplit

Bases. To construct BitSplit, we instantiate Split with $k = 2$. We call B_1 the *sparse* basis and B_2 the *linear* basis, and we define init and admit as shown in Table 3. We explain extraProp later.

We carefully avoid allowing a bitsum $X - \sum_{i=0}^{k} 2^i X_i$ and its bit constraints $(X_i^2 - X_i)_{i=1}^k$ in the same basis. Initially, the sparse basis rejects only bitsums (isBitsum(p) is defined as $\exists \ell > 1$, $\exists Y, X_1, \ldots X_\ell \in \mathbf{X}$, $p = Y - \sum_{i=0}^{\ell} 2^i X_i$). During propagation, the sparse basis accepts polynomials that encode equalities (isEq(p) is defined as $\exists X, Y \in \mathbf{X}$, $z \in \mathbb{F}$, $p = X - Y \vee p = X - z$). The linear basis accepts (in initialization and propagation) any linear polynomial. Our definition of admit is quite narrow (to accelerate calls to GB), but we ensure that both ideals accept equalities, since extraProp generates these. In our experiments, we consider some other definitions of admit, but they do not improve performance.

Extra Propagation. Our extraProp subroutine simply implements congruence for bitsums. That is, consider the following polynomials, with $m < \log_2 |\mathbb{F}|$:

$$Y - \sum_{i=1}^{m} 2^{i-1} X_i \qquad\qquad Y' - \sum_{i=1}^{m} 2^{i-1} X_i'$$

If all X_i and X_i' are known to have value zero or one (because $X_i^2 - X_i$ is in some $\langle B_j \rangle$) and Y and Y' are known to be equal ($Y - Y'$ is in some $\langle B_j \rangle$), then it propagates $X_i - X_i'$ for all i. Similarly, if Y is known to be a constant c ($Y - c$ is in some $\langle B_j \rangle$), then each X_i must be equal to the jth bit of c as an unsigned integer. Soundness for extraProp follows from bit representation uniqueness.

Inter-basis Interactions. SplitGB treats each B_i as a source of polynomials that might be added to other B_j. It does not use $\langle B_i \rangle$ as the source; this would be sound, but enumerating the infinite set $\langle B_i \rangle$ is impossible. The natural question is whether inter-basis propagation within SplitGB is nevertheless complete, that is, whether all polynomials $p \in \langle B_i \rangle$ that are admissible to B_j are in the ideal generated by the polynomials actually added to B_j.

We have both positive and negative results for BitSplit: Lemma 1 shows that propagation from the sparse basis to the linear basis **is** complete. The proof is in Appendix E. Example 1 shows that propagation from the linear basis to the sparse basis **is not** complete. There is a natural way to fix this: enumerate each variable pair X, Y, and propagate $X - Y$ to the sparse basis if $X - Y$ is in the ideal generated by the linear basis. However, our experiments (Sect. 5) show that this doesn't empirically improve solver performance for our benchmarks.

Lemma 1. *Let B be a Gröbner basis under a graded order (a degree compatible order, i.e., for all monomials p, q, $\deg(p) < \deg(q) \implies p < q$); then, every linear $p \in \langle B \rangle$ is in the ideal generated by the linear elements of B.*

Example 1. Consider $\mathbb{F}_5[W, X, Y, Z]$ in grevlex order. Then $B_1 = \{W - X - Y + Z, Y - Z\}$ is a GB. The only polynomial in B_1 that is admissible to the sparse basis is $Y - Z$. Now consider $W - X$. It is in $\langle B_1 \rangle$ (it is the sum of B_1's elements) and it is admissible to the sparse basis. However, it is not in $\langle Y - Z \rangle$; i.e., it **is not** generated by the subset of B_1 that is admissible to the sparse basis.

Connections. In some respects, our $\mathbb{F}$-solver resembles two prior SMT ideas: theory combination and portfolio solving with clause sharing. As in theory combination [6], we reduce a problem (a system of field equations) to sub-problems (subsets of the original system) that are handled by loosely-coupled sub-solvers (bases and propagators), each using different reasoning. As in portfolio solving with clause sharing [44,61], each sub-solver derives lemmas in a common language (not clauses, but polynomials) that they share with one another. Our work also resembles a prior combination of algebraic and propositional reasoning for preprocessing Boolean formulas by sharing $\mathbb{F}_2$ equations between algebraic and propositional modules [14]. However, our focus is on solving equations in a very large finite field with constraints of different structure.

Efficiency. In the worst case, BitSplit builds a GB for the full system (similar to Monolithic). A GB for degree-d polynomials in n variables can have size d^{2^n} [45], so the worst-case complexity of BitSplit (and Monolithic) is doubly exponential.

However, in the next section we will see that BitSplit is efficient on a number of problems of practical interest. For these problems it improves exponentially on Monolithic. Here, we give intuition for the source of the advantage. Consider a bitsum-heavy determinism problem. As discussed in Sect. 3, computing a full GB is hard, so Monolithic performs poorly. However, BitSplit can use extraProp to reason about the uniqueness of the bit-splitting and use its split GB to reason about other parts of the system. This might allow it to refute the system of equations without ever directly computing a GB for the full system.

5   Experiments

Now we present our experiments, which answer three empirical questions:

1. How does BitSplit perform when solving bitsum-heavy determinism queries? *(Exponentially better than the prior state of the art.)*
2. How does BitSplit perform when solving other queries? *(Similar to the prior state of the art.)*
3. How do BitSplit's components impact its performance? *(Propagation is key.)*

We implement BitSplit in cvc5 [4] as a solver for the theory of finite fields. This includes preprocessing that identifies bitsums in larger polynomials and isolates them for use in BitSplit. Our test bed is a cluster with Intel Xeon E5-2637 v4 CPUs. Each run gets one CPU, 8GB memory, and a time limit of 300 s. After presenting the benchmarks, we compare BitSplit to prior SMT $\mathbb{F}$-solvers ffsat [38][4] and Monolithic [50], and we compare BitSplit to variants of itself.

5.1   Benchmarks

Table 4 shows our benchmarks, most of which concern the correctness of ZK libraries (circomlib [7]) and compilers (ZoKrates [23] and CirC [49]). There are six families. The CirC-D benchmarks verify the determinism of operator encoding rules in CirC, at bitwidths up to 32. As we discuss in the next section (Sect. 6), these benchmarks are important to CirC's correctness, but are hard to solve. The Seq benchmarks verify the determinism of constraint systems with

Table 4. Our benchmark families. QED^2 [53], Small [38], TV [50], and CirC-S [52] are from prior work. CirC-D is a set of large determinism benchmarks based on prior work [52]; see Sect. 6. Seq is a set of determinism benchmarks for computations that perform a sequence of bit-splits; see Appendix F.

Family	#	Description
CirC-D	640	Determinism for CirC $\mathbb{F}$-blaster rules of bitwidth ≤ 32 (Sect. 6)
Seq	100	Determinism for sequenced bit-splits (Appendix F)
QED^2	100	Determinism for circomlib, generated by QED^2 [53]
CirC-S	100	Soundness for CirC $\mathbb{F}$-blaster rules of bitwidth ≤ 4 [52]
TV	100	Translation validation for ZKP compilers on boolean programs [50]
Small	100	Randomly generated with a small field: $|\mathbb{F}| \leq 211$ [38]

---

[4] At the time of our experiments, ffsat was a Sage-based Python tool for solving conjunctions of equations [35]. We wrapped it with a simple SMT-LIB parser that invokes ffsat if the query is sufficiently simple. Since then, ffsat has been reimplemented in Yices [22,37]; future work should compare against that implementation.

sequences of bit-splits. We discuss them further in Appendix F. The QED^2 benchmarks are determinism queries for circomlib generated by QED^2 [53]. The CirC-S benchmarks are soundness tests for CirC's operator rules, at bitwidths up to 4 [52]. The TV benchmarks are translation validation queries for ZoKrates and CirC, as applied to boolean functions [50]. Finally, the Small benchmarks are random, small-field (i.e., $|\mathbb{F}| < 2^8$) benchmarks from the evaluation of ffsat [38]. To keep the benchmark set from being too big, all families from prior work are sampled at random from that work's benchmarks.

5.2 Comparison to Prior Solvers

First, we compare BitSplit against prior solvers Monolithic [50] and ffsat [38]. Table 5 shows the number of solved benchmarks by family and result. ffsat is successful only when the field is small. BitSplit improves on Monolithic on families that test determinism (QED^2 and CirC-D) but suffers slightly on other benchmarks. BitSplit is slightly worse on SAT instances but better at UNSAT ones. Figure 5 presents the same results as cactus plots for the determinism families and the other families.

To better understand BitSplit's advantage, we focus on the CirC-D family. Each CirC-D benchmark tests the determinism of an operator rule at a specific bitwidth. We consider how the solve time scales with bitwidth. Figure 6 shows the results for arithmetic, shift, and comparison operators. Monolithic's solve time grows exponentially for all of these, while BitSplit's time is generally insignificant.

Table 5. Solved benchmarks, by family and result. BitSplit's gains are on determinism queries (the QED^2 and CirC-D families) and unsatisfiable benchmarks.

Solver	Solved	By Family						By Result	
		CirC-D	Seq	QED^2	CirC-S	TV	Small	SAT	UNSAT
BitSplit	**969**	**582**	**100**	**59**	92	70	66	88	**881**
Monolithic	475	191	13	38	**94**	**72**	**67**	**90**	385
ffsat	67	0	0	0	0	0	**67**	54	13

Comparison to prior solvers

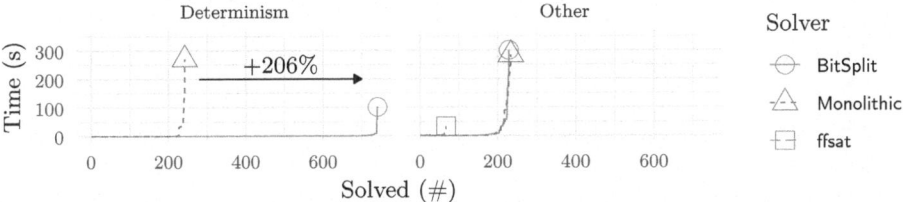

Fig. 5. On determinism benchmarks, BitSplit dominates Monolithic; on other benchmarks, they perform similarly.

BitSplit struggles only with division and remainder; verifying their determinism would require understanding that integer division is deterministic, as encoded in field constraints. We omit bitwise operators (e.g., bvor) from this experiment. Their operator rules assume that the input bit-vectors are *already represented as bits*, so their benchmarks do not include any bitsums. To summarize, BitSplit can verify many operators exponentially faster than Monolithic.

5.3   Comparison to Variants

To better understand BitSplit, we compare it against six variants of itself:

- BS-LinFirst: make the linear basis (not the sparse basis) B_1
- BS-NoIntProp disable inter-basis propagation
- BS-NoExtProp disable extraProp
- BS-FullIntProp: complete linear-to-sparse propagation (Sect. 4.3, fixes Example 1)
- BS-DenseProp for the sparse basis, use $\mathsf{admit}(p) = \deg(p) \le 1 \wedge |\mathsf{vars}(p)| \le 16$.
- BS-QuadProp for the linear basis, use $\mathsf{admit}(p) = \deg(p) \le 2$.

CirC-D: solve time v. bitwidth

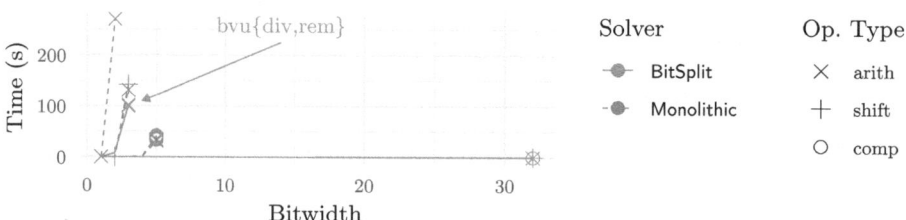

Fig. 6. Solve time for CirC-D benchmarks for different operators. Monolithic's solve time grows exponentially, while BitSplit's solve time usually does not.

Table 6. BitSplit v. variants of itself. Weaker propagation (BS-NoExtProp, BS-NoIntProp) gives worse results, but other changes have less impact.

Solver	Solved	By Family						By Result	
		CirC-D	Seq	QED^2	CirC-S	TV	Small	SAT	UNSAT
BitSplit	**969**	**582**	**100**	**59**	92	70	66	88	**881**
BS-LinFirst	959	576	**100**	58	92	69	64	84	875
BS-NoIntProp	877	576	24	58	86	70	63	84	793
BS-NoExtProp	344	131	0	34	45	69	65	85	259
BS-FullIntProp	953	576	97	56	92	69	63	83	870
BS-DenseProp	898	580	33	58	92	70	65	85	813
BS-QuadProp	898	580	32	**59**	92	71	64	86	812
Monolithic	475	191	13	38	**94**	**72**	**67**	**90**	385

Table 6 shows how many benchmarks each variant solves, with both BitSplit and Monolithic for comparison. First, changing the basis order (BS-LinFirst) has little effect. Second, disabling propagation (BS-NoIntProp and BS-NoExtProp) significantly hurts performance. Third, making inter-basis propagation complete (BS-FullIntProp) actually hurts performance slightly, perhaps because it takes quadratic time. Finally, defining admit more admissibly (BS-DenseProp and BS-QuadProp) makes little difference for many families, but significantly hurts performance on sequential bit-splits.

These results justify the key role that propagation plays in BitSplit. They also suggest that BitSplit would be a good choice for cvc5's default field solver.

6 Application

Prior work uses Monolithic to do bounded verification for a zero-knowledge proof (ZKP) compiler pass [52]. In this section, we improve their results using BitSplit. Thus, this section is a case study that shows the utility of BitSplit for a downstream verification task. Our improvement relies not just on a new solver (BitSplit), but also on a new verification strategy. First (Sect. 6.1), we give background on the verification task. Second (Sect. 6.2), we state our new strategy, prove it is correct, and show that it is more efficient—when using BitSplit.

6.1 Background on Verifiable Field-Blasting

We consider the *finite field blaster* in a ZKP compiler: its responsibilities include encoding bit-vector operations as field equations [52]. At a high level, the field blaster is a collection of *encoding rules.* Each rule is a small algorithm that is specific to some operator (e.g., bvadd). It is given field variables that encode the operator's inputs according to some *encoding scheme*. A rule defines new variables, creates equations, and ultimately returns a field variable that encodes the output of the rule's operator.

As an example, we describe an encoding scheme for bit-vectors and a rule for bit-vector addition. The scheme encodes a length-b bit-vector x as a field variable x' with value in $\{0, \dots, 2^b - 1\} \subseteq \mathbb{F}$ (assuming $|\mathbb{F}| \gg 2^b$). If x' and x have the same (unsigned) integer value, we say that $valid(x', x)$ holds. Suppose our rule applies to the addition of x and y, encoded as x' and y'. Our rule defines the following field variables. First, for each $i \in \{1, \dots, b+1\}$, it defines z_i' to 1 if the ith bit of the integer sum of the unsigned values of x' and y' is one, and zero otherwise. Second, it defines $z' = \sum_{i=1}^{b} 2^{i-1} z_i'$. Then, it enforces these equations:

$$x' + y' = \sum_{i=1}^{b+1} 2^{i-1} z_i' \quad \wedge \quad z' = \sum_{i=1}^{b} 2^{i-1} z_i' \quad \wedge \quad \bigwedge_{i=1}^{b+1} z_b'(z_b' - 1) = 0$$

Finally, it returns z'. Informally, the idea of this rule is to bit-decompose the sum $x' + y'$ and then use the bit-decomposition to reduce that sum modulo 2^b. For example, if $b = 2$, $x' = 3$, and $y' = 1$, then the unique solution for the z_i' is $z_1' = 0, z_2' = 0, z_3' = 1$, and then z' must be 0.

In general, an encoding rule for operator o maps a sequence of input encodings (field variables) $\mathbf{e}$ to three outputs: F, A, and e.[5] Each field variable e_i encodes some bit-vector variable t_i. The first output, $F = \{z_1 \mapsto s_1, \ldots z_\ell \mapsto s_\ell\}$, is a mapping that defines ℓ fresh field variables: $z_1, \ldots, z_\ell$. Variable z_i is mapped to a term s_i (in variables $\mathbf{e}$) that defines what value z_i is intended to take. The second output, A, is conjunction of field equations in variables $\mathbf{e}$ and $\mathbf{z}$. The final output is e: a distinguished variable that encodes the rule's output $o(\mathbf{t})$.

Prior work defines *correctness* for encoding rules as the conjunction of two properties: *completeness* and *soundness*. If all rules are correct, then they constitute a correct F-blaster [52]. Completeness says that if each e_i validly encodes t_i and the z_i take the values prescribed by F, then e validly encodes $o(\mathbf{t})$ and A holds. That is, completeness requires the following formula to be valid:

$$((\textstyle\bigwedge_i valid(e_i, t_i)) \implies (A \wedge valid(e, o(\mathbf{t})))) [F]$$

Soundness says that if each e_i validly encodes t_i and A holds, then e validly encodes $o(\mathbf{t})$. That is, the following must be valid:

$$(A \wedge \textstyle\bigwedge_i valid(e_i, t_i)) \implies valid(e, o(\mathbf{t}))$$

Verifier Performance. After fixing the sorts of the t_i (e.g., to bit-vectors of size 4), one can encode soundness and completeness as SMT queries. This enables automatic, bounded verification: one checks these properties up to some input bitwidth bound b using an SMT solver. However, the soundness query is especially challenging for the SMT solver. In prior work, some soundness queries for $b = 4$ could not be solved in 5 min with Monolithic. More generally, solving time grew exponentially with bit-width for most operators [52].

6.2   A New Strategy for Verifying Operator Rules

We propose a different strategy for automatically verifying operator rules. We define *determinism* for operator rules. It says that an operator rule applied to equal inputs should yield equal outputs. That is, if (A, e) and (A', e') are rule outputs for inputs $\mathbf{e}$ and $\mathbf{e}'$ respectively, then the following must be valid:

$$(A \wedge A' \wedge \mathbf{e} = \mathbf{e}') \implies e = e'$$

We prove the following theorem in Appendix G:

Theorem 4. *An operator rule that is deterministic and complete is also sound.*

---

[5] Actually, in prior work [52] and in our implementation, encodings are *type-tagged sequences* of field *terms*. In this paper we treat them as single variables to simplify the exposition. Generalization is straightforward, but notationally tedious.

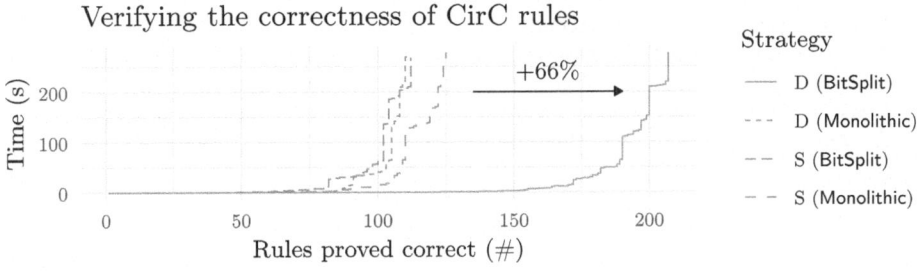

Fig. 7. The best way to verify that CirC rules are fully correct is to prove completeness using exhaust and prove determinism (D) using BitSplit.

Thus, to verify rule correctness, it suffices to verify completeness and **determinism**. This approach is promising because BitSplit is very effective on determinism queries (they were the CirC-D benchmarks in Sect. 5). So, a verification strategy comprises two choices: whether to prove soundness (S) or determinism (D) and whether to use BitSplit or Monolithic. In all cases, we prove completeness using exhaust (a specialized approach from prior work) [52]. For each strategy, we try to verify every bit-vector rule up to width 32. We limit SMT queries to 5 min each, using the same test bench as before.

Figure 7 shows verification time using different strategies. The best strategy is our new one. This approach verifies 66% more rule-bitwidth pairs than the next best strategy: proving soundness with Monolithic. More importantly, in our new strategy, verifying determinism (using BitSplit) is not the bottleneck: the bottleneck is proving completeness (using exhaust). Whereas, when proving soundness with Monolithic, Monolithic is the bottleneck. Further improvements will require new ideas for proving completeness.

7   Conclusion

We have presented a new approach for F-solving in SMT. Our contributions are three-fold. First, we proposed an abstract decision procedure Split that avoids computing a full Gröbner basis. Second, we described an instantiation of it (BitSplit) that is highly effective for bitsum-heavy determinism queries. Third, we applied BitSplit to a problem in ZKP compiler verification.

There are many directions for future work. First, we believe other instantiations of Split (beyond BitSplit) might be useful, for example, by considering other kinds of propagations (extraProp) and other conditions under which propagation is allowed (admit). Second, Split makes very limited use of CDCL(T) features that are known to improve performance: it acts only once a full propositional assignment is available; it constructs no theory lemmas; and it propagates no literals. Third, in this paper, we focus on applications of the theory of finite fields to ZKPs. Finite fields should also be relevant to many other kinds of cryptosystems, including algebraic multi-party computation and those based on elliptic curves. We leave these opportunities to future work.

Acknowledgements. We appreciate the help, support, and advice of Cesare Tinelli, Daniela Kaufmann, Haniel Barbosa, Mathias Preiner, Matthew Sotoudeh, Thomas Hader, the CAV reviewers, and all of the cvc5 developers.

This work was funded in part by NSF grant number 2110397, the Stanford Center for Automated Reasoning, and the Simons Foundation.

A   Additional Background

This appendix is available in the full version of the paper [51].

B   Computing Bitsum Usage in Real World Projects

This appendix is available in the full version of the paper [51].

C   Proof of Theorem 1

This appendix is available in the full version of the paper [51].

D   Proof of Theorems 2 and 3

This appendix is available in the full version of the paper [51].

E   Proof of Lemma 1

This appendix is available in the full version of the paper [51].

F   The Seq Benchmark Family

This appendix is available in the full version of the paper [51].

G   Proof of Theorem 4

This appendix is available in the full version of the paper [51].

References

1. 0xPARC. ZK bug tracker. https://github.com/0xPARC/zk-bug-tracker. Accessed 5 Sept 2023, via archive.org
2. Anderson, B., McGrew, D.: TLS beyond the browser: Combining end host and network data to understand application behavior. In: IMC (2019)
3. Archer, D., O'Hara, A., Issa, R., Strauss, S.: Sharing sensitive department of education data across organizational boundaries using secure multiparty computation (2021)
4. Barbosa, H., et al.: cvc5: a versatile and industrial-strength SMT solver. In: TACAS (2022)
5. Barlow, R.: Computational thinking breaks a logjam (2015). https://www.bu.edu/cise/computational-thinking-breaks-a-logjam/
6. Barrett, C., Tinelli, C.: Satisfiability modulo theories. In: Handbook of Model Checking, pp. 305–343. Springer, Cham (2018). https://doi.org/10.1007/978-3-319-10575-8_11
7. Bellés-Muñoz, M., Isabel, M., Muñoz-Tapia, J.L., Rubio, A., Baylina, J.: Circom: a circuit description language for building zero-knowledge applications. IEEE Trans. Dependable Secure Comput. (2022)
8. Bogetoft, P., et al.: Secure multiparty computation goes live. In: FC (2009)
9. Braun, D., Magaud, N., Schreck, P.: Formalizing some "small" finite models of projective geometry in coq. In: International Conference on Artificial Intelligence and Symbolic Computation (2018)
10. Buchberger, B.: A theoretical basis for the reduction of polynomials to canonical forms. SIGSAM Bulletin (1976)
11. Bünz, B., Bootle, J., Boneh, D., Poelstra, A., Wuille, P., Maxwell, G.: Bulletproofs: Short proofs for confidential transactions and more. In: IEEE S&P (2018)
12. Chaliasos, S., Ernstberger, J., Theodore, D., Wong, D., Jahanara, M., Livshits, B.: Sok: what don't we know? understanding security vulnerabilities in snarks (2024). https://arxiv.org/abs/2402.15293
13. Chin, C., Wu, H., Chu, R., Coglio, A., McCarthy, E., Smith, E.: Leo: a programming language for formally verified, zero-knowledge applications (2021). Preprint at https://ia.cr/2021/651
14. Choo, D., Soos, M., Chai, K.M.A., Meel, K.S.: Bosphorus: Bridging anf and cnf solvers. IEEE, In DATE (2019)
15. Coglio, A., McCarthy, E., Smith, E., Chin, C., Gaddamadugu, P., Dellepere, M.: Compositional formal verification of zero-knowledge circuits (2023). https://ia.cr/2023/1278
16. Cohen, C.: Pragmatic quotient types in coq. In: ITP (2013)
17. Cox, D., Little, J., OShea, D.: Ideals, varieties, and algorithms: an introduction to computational algebraic geometry and commutative algebra. Springer Science & Business Media (2013)
18. CVE-2014-3570. https://nvd.nist.gov/vuln/detail/CVE-2014-3570
19. CVE-2017-3732. https://nvd.nist.gov/vuln/detail/CVE-2017-3732
20. Dahlgren, F.: It pays to be Circomspect (2022). https://blog.trailofbits.com/2022/09/15/it-pays-to-be-circomspect/. Accessed 15 Oct 2023
21. Dummit, D.S., Foote, R.M.: Abstract algebra, vol. 3. Wiley Hoboken (2004)
22. Dutertre, B.: Yices 2.2. In: CAV (2014)
23. Eberhardt, J., Tai, S.: ZoKrates—scalable privacy-preserving off-chain computations. In: IEEE Blockchain (2018)

24. Enderton, H.B.: A mathematical introduction to logic. Elsevier (2001)
25. Erbsen, A., Philipoom, J., Gross, J., Sloan, R., Chlipala, A.: Systematic generation of fast elliptic curve cryptography implementations. Technical report, MIT (2018)
26. Erbsen, A., Philipoom, J., Gross, J., Sloan, R., Chlipala, A.: Simple high-level code for cryptographic arithmetic: With proofs, without compromises. ACM SIGOPS Operating Syst. Rev. **54**(1) (2020)
27. Y. Finance. Monero quote (2023). https://finance.yahoo.com/quote/XMR-USD/. Accessed 13 Oct 2023
28. Y. Finance. Zcash quote (2023). https://finance.yahoo.com/quote/ZEC-USD/. Accessed 13 Oct 2023
29. Fournet, C., Keller, C., Laporte, V.: A certified compiler for verifiable computing. In: CSF (2016)
30. Gabizon, A., Williamson, Z.J., Ciobotaru, O.: Plonk: permutations over lagrange-bases for oecumenical noninteractive arguments of knowledge (2019). https://ia.cr/2019/953
31. Gonthier, G., et al.: A machine-checked proof of the odd order theorem. In: ITP, pp. 163–179 (2013)
32. Greuel, G.-M., Pfister, G., Schönemann, H.: Singular-a computer algebra system for polynomial computations. In: Symbolic Computation and Automated Reasoning, pp. 227–233. AK Peters/CRC Press (2001)
33. Groth, J.: On the size of pairing-based non-interactive arguments. In: EUROCRYPT (2016)
34. Grubbs, P., Arun, A., Zhang, Y., Bonneau, J., Walfish, M.: Zero-knowledge middleboxes. In: USENIX Security (2022)
35. Hader, T.: Ffsat. https://github.com/Ovascos/ffsat, commit 67fecde
36. Hader, T.: Non-linear SMT-reasoning over finite fields (2022). MS Thesis (TU Wein)
37. Hader, T., Kaufmann, D., Irfan, A., Graham-Lengrand, S., Kovács, L.: Mcsat-based finite field reasoning in the yices2 smt solver (2024)
38. Hader, T., Kaufmann, D., Kovács, L.: SMT solving over finite field arithmetic. In: LPAR (2023)
39. Hader, T., Kovács, L.: Non-linear SMT-reasoning over finite fields. In: SMT (2022). Extended Abstract
40. Hopwood, D., Bowe, S., Hornby, T., Wilcox, N.: Zcash protocol specification (2013). https://raw.githubusercontent.com/zcash/zips/master/protocol/protocol.pdf
41. Komendantsky, V., Konovalov, A., Linton, S.: View of computer algebra data from coq. In: International Conference on Intelligent Computer Mathematics (2011)
42. Kotzias, P., Razaghpanah, A., Amann, J., Paterson, K.G., Vallina-Rodriguez, N., Caballero, J.: Coming of age: a longitudinal study of TLS deployment. In: IMC (2018)
43. Liu, J., et al.: Certifying zero-knowledge circuits with refinement types (2023). https://ia.cr/2023/547
44. Marescotti, M., Hyvärinen, A.E.J., Sharygina, N.: Clause sharing and partitioning for cloud-based SMT solving. In: Artho, C., Legay, A., Peled, D. (eds.) ATVA 2016. LNCS, vol. 9938, pp. 428–443. Springer, Cham (2016). https://doi.org/10.1007/978-3-319-46520-3_27
45. Mayr, E.W., Meyer, A.R.: The complexity of the word problems for commutative semigroups and polynomial ideals. Adv. Math. **46**(3), 305–329 (1982)
46. Monero technical specs (2022). https://monerodocs.org/technical-specs/

47. Nieuwenhuis, R., Oliveras, A., Tinelli, C.: Solving SAT and SAT Modulo Theories: From an abstract davis–putnam–logemann–loveland procedure to DPLL(T). J. ACM (2006)
48. OpenSSL bug 1953. https://www.mail-archive.com/openssl-dev@openssl.org/msg23869.html
49. Ozdemir, A., Brown, F., Wahby, R.S.: CirC: compiler infrastructure for proof systems, software verification, and more. In: IEEE S&P (2022)
50. Ozdemir, A., Kremer, G., Tinelli, C., Barrett, C.: Satisfiability modulo finite fields. In: CAV (2023)
51. Ozdemir, S., Pailoor, A., Bassa, A., Ferles, K., Barrett, C., Dillig, I.: Split Gröbner bases for satisfiability modulo finite fields (2024). https://ia.cr/2024/572. Full version
52. Ozdemir, A., Wahby, R.S., Brown, F., Barrett, C.: Bounded verification for finite-field-blasting. In: CAV (2023)
53. Pailoor, S., et al.: Automated detection of under-constrained circuits in zero-knowledge proofs. In: PLDI (2023)
54. Philipoom, J.: Correct-by-construction finite field arithmetic in Coq. Ph.D. thesis, Massachusetts Institute of Technology (2018)
55. Schwabe, P., Viguier, B., Weerwag, T., Wiedijk, F.: A coq proof of the correctness of x25519 in tweetnacl. In: CSF (2021)
56. Soureshjani, F.H., Hall-Andersen, M., Jahanara, M., Kam, J., Gorzny, J., Ahmadvand, M.: Automated analysis of halo2 circuits (2023). https://ia.cr/2023/1051
57. Tornado.cash got hacked. by us (2019). https://tornado-cash.medium.com/tornado-cash-got-hacked-by-us-b1e012a3c9a8. Accessed 13 Oct 2023
58. Wang, D.: Elimination methods. Springer Science & Business Media (2001)
59. Wang, F.: Ecne: automated verification of zk circuits (2022). https://0xparc.org/blog/ecne
60. Wen, H., et al.: Practical security analysis of zero-knowledge proof circuits (2023)
61. Wintersteiger, C.M., Hamadi, Y., de Moura, L.: A concurrent portfolio approach to SMT solving. In: Bouajjani, A., Maler, O. (eds.) CAV 2009. LNCS, vol. 5643, pp. 715–720. Springer, Heidelberg (2009). https://doi.org/10.1007/978-3-642-02658-4_60
62. Zcash counterfeiting vulnerability successfully remediated (2019). https://electriccoin.co/blog/zcash-counterfeiting-vulnerability-successfully-remediated/. Accessed 13 Oct 2023

Arithmetic Solving in Z3

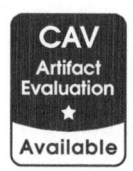

Nikolaj Bjørner[✉] and Lev Nachmanson

Microsoft, Redmond, USA
nbjorner@microsoft.com

Abstract. The theory of arithmetic is integral to many uses of SMT solvers. Z3 has implemented native solvers for arithmetic reasoning since its first release. We present a full re-implementation of Z3's original arithmetic solver. It is based on substantial experiences from user feedback, engineering and experimentation. While providing a comprehensive overview of the main components we emphasize selected new insights we arrived at while developing and testing the solver.

1 Introduction

The theory of arithmetic is among the most prolific theories used in SMT solvers. It is used across a wide set of applications, and they have a wide range of demands. Supporting efficient theory solvers for arithmetic requires balancing feature support, ranging from linear, difference logic, to linear real, linear integer, non-linear polynomial arithmetic and in cases transcendental functions such as exponentiation. The aim of this paper is to provide a high-level, yet self-contained, overview of internal ingredients of the arithmetic solver. It seeks to explain tool users what to expect of solving methodologies when using Z3 for arithmetic. We assume familiarity of basics of SMT solving using CDCL(T), e.g., [5]. While make an effort to cover all features for completeness, we devote attention to highlight a selection that to our knowledge are unique for arithmetic solvers. These highlights include (1) how the solver patches linear real programming solutions to find solutions to integer variables, (2) heuristics that are new in how the solver finds Gomory cuts, and (3) the solver's integration of Gröbner basis computation for solving non-linear constraints. User pain points around SMT have to our experience centered dominantly around quantifiers and non-linear arithmetic. A complete (for non-linear reals) solver that integrates with other theories and quantifier reasoning becomes relevant. The new arithmetic solver that we describe here was first integrated in version 4.8.8 of z3, turned on as default in the next release, and subjected to later significant revisions. To evaluate the contribution of each feature we use benchmarks drawn from SMTLIB benchmark sets [3] and benchmarks supplied by a user, Certora [12].

In overview, the arithmetic solver uses a waterfall model for solving arithmetic constraints. It is illustrated with additional details in Fig. 1.

- First, it establishes feasibility with respect to linear inequalities. Variables are solved over the rationals; Sect. 3.

© The Author(s) 2024

A. Gurfinkel and V. Ganesh (Eds.): CAV 2024, LNCS 14681, pp. 26–41, 2024.

https://doi.org/10.1007/978-3-031-65627-9_2

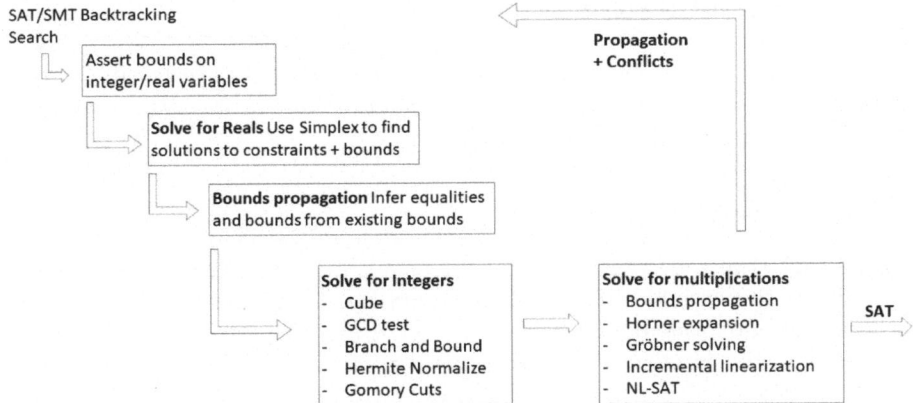

Fig. 1. Overview of Z3's Arithmetic Theory Solver

- Second, it establishes feasibility with respect to mixed integer linear constraints; Integer variables are considered solved if they are assigned integer values while satisfying linear inequalities; Sect. 4.
- Finally, it establishes feasibility with respect to non-linear polynomial constraints; Sect. 5.

The rest of the paper elaborates on the components of the solver. For completeness, we go through all relevant pieces. We highlight parts that to our knowledge are novel.

2   Design Goals and Implementation Choices

The SMT formalism for arithmetic in many cases subsumes formalisms used by mixed integer, MIP, solvers. However, there are several fundamental differences between the workloads we have tuned the arithmetic solver for compared to workloads seen by MIP solvers. Z3 uses infinite precision "big-num" numeral representations, in contrast to using floating points. The drawback is that the arithmetic solver is impractical on linear programming optimization problems, but the engine avoids having to compensate for rounding errors and numerical instability. The solver uses a sparse matrix representation for the Dual Simplex tableau. We also created a version that uses an LRU decomposition and floating point numbers but found that extending this version with efficient backtracking was not practical compared to the straight-forward sparse matrix format. Finally, the solver remains integrated within a CDCL engine that favors an eager case split strategy leaving it to conflict analysis to block infeasible branches. This contrasts mainstream MIP designs that favor a search tree of relatively few branches where the engine performs significant analysis before case splits.

3   Linear Real Arithmetic

The solver first determines whether arithmetic constraints are feasibility over the reals. It also attempts to propagate equalities eagerly for shared variables and infer stronger bounds of variables.

3.1   Linear Solving

Based on [21] the solver for real linear inequalities uses a dual simplex solver. It partitions the variables into *basic* and *non-basic* variables, and maintains a global set of equalities of the form $x_{bi} + \sum_j a_{ij} x_j = 0$, where i refers to the i'th row, x_{bi} is basic and x_j range over non-basic variables. It also maintains an evaluation β, such that $\beta(x_{bi}) + \sum_j a_{ij}\beta(x_j) = 0$ for each row i. Each variable x_j is assigned lower and upper bounds during search. The solver then checks whether $lo_j \leq \beta(x_j) \leq hi_j$, for bounds lo_j, hi_j that are dynamically added and removed by Boolean decisions $x_j \leq hi_j$, $x_j \geq lo_j$. If the bounds are violated, it updates the evaluation and pivots if necessary. We recall the approach using an example.

Example 1. For the following formula

$$y \geq 0 \wedge (x + y \leq 2 \vee x + 2y \geq 6) \wedge (x + y \geq 2 \vee x + 2y > 4)$$

the solver introduces auxiliary variables s_1, s_2 and represents the formula as

$$x + y - s_1 = 0, x + 2y - s_2 = 0, \; x \geq 0, (s_1 \leq 2 \vee s_2 \geq 6), (s_1 \geq 2 \vee s_2 > 4)$$

Only bounds (e.g., $s_1 \leq 2$) are asserted during search. The slack variables s_1, s_2 are initially basic (dependent) and x, y are non-basic. In dual Simplex tableaux, values of a non-basic variable x_j can be chosen between lo_j and hi_j. The value of a basic variable is a function of non-basic variable values. Pivoting swaps basic and non-basic variables and moves basic variables within their bounds to bounds violations. For example, assume we start with a set of initial values $x = y = s_1 = s_2 = 0$ and bounds $x \geq 0, s_1 \leq 2, s_1 \geq 2$. Then s_1 has to be 2 and it is made non-basic. Instead, y becomes basic: $y + x - s_1 = 0$, $s_2 + x - 2s_1 = 0$. The new tableau updates the assignment of variables to $x = 0, s_1 = 2, s_2 = 4, y = 2$. The resulting assignment is a model for the original formula.

3.2   Finding Equal Variables - Cheaply

It is useful to have the arithmetic solver propagate implied equalities when arithmetic is used in combination with other theories, or even when it solves non-linear arithmetic constraints. Equality propagation is disabled for pure arithmetic theories, such as QF_LIA, QF_LRA [3]. Z3 originally used a method based on storing *offset* equalities in a hash table. An offset equality is of the form $x_i = y + k$, where k is a numeric constant. Offset equalities are extracted from rows that contain x_i as a basic variable, and contains only one other non-fixed variable y, while other variables are fixed and their lower (upper) bounds add up to k. It turns out that computing k is expensive when the tableau contains large numeric constants. Hash table operations contribute with additional overhead. It turns out that neither the offset hash-table, nor computing k, is really necessary. We describe our new method, using an example. We first described the method for avoiding to compute offsets in [8]. The description there relies on building a tree data-structure for connecting variables and fails to leverage that the dual simplex tableau can be used directly.

Example 2. From equalities $x + 1 = y, y - 1 = z$ infer that $x = z$. Based on the tableau form, the solver is presented with the original equality atoms via slack variables

$$s_1 = x + u - y, s_2 = y - u - z, 1 \leq u \leq 1$$

The tableau can be solved by setting $x = 0, y = 0, z = 0, s_1 = 1, s_2 = -1, u = 1$. The slack variables are bounded when the equalities are asserted

$$s_1 = x + u - y, s_2 = y - u - z, 1 \leq u \leq 1, 0 \leq s_1 \leq 0, 0 \leq s_2 \leq 0$$

The original solution is no longer valid, the values for s_1, s_2 are out of bounds. Pivoting re-establishes feasibility using a different solution, for example

$$x = y - u - s_1, y = z - u - s_2, 1 \leq u \leq 1, 0 \leq s_1 \leq 0, 0 \leq s_2 \leq 0$$

with assignment $z = 0, x = y = -1$. The variables x and y have the same value, but must they be equal under all assignments? We can establish this directly by subtracting the right-hand sides $z - u - s_1$ and $z - u - s_2$ from another and by factoring in the constant bounds to obtain the result 0. But subtraction is generally expensive if there are many bounded constants in the rows. Such arithmetical operations are not required to infer that $x = y$.

Z3 uses the following conditions to infer an equality between variables x, y having the same values in the current assignment:

- x is basic, and the tableau has row $x - y + \alpha = 0$,
- x, y are connected through a non-basic variable z in a pair of the tableau rows in one of the following forms (1) $x - z + \alpha = 0, y - z + \alpha' = 0$, (2) $x + z + \alpha = 0, y + z + \alpha' = 0$,

where α, α' are linear combinations of fixed variables.

We experimented with generalizing the connection between equal variables to allow non-unit coefficients on z, but it did not result in measurable improvements.

3.3   Bounds Propagation

It is not uncommon that SMT formulas contain different bounds for the same variable, such as one atom $x \geq 2$ and another atom $x \geq 3$. When the atom $x \geq 3$

is assigned to true, the solver can directly propagate $x \geq 3$. Bounds can also be inferred indirectly. With a row $x - 2y = 0$ and bound $y \geq 1$, it follows that $x \geq 2$. To implement direct bounds propagation, the solver maintains an index that maps each variable to the set of bounds atoms where it occurs. To implement indirect bounds propagation, the solver queries updated rows for whether they imply bounds that are stronger than the currently asserted bounds. If so, these stronger bounds are used by the index for direct bounds propagation.

4   Integer Linear Arithmetic

The mixed integer linear solver consists of several layers that first attempt to *patch* integer variables form solutions over reals to solutions over integers. Then, if patching fails to correct all integer variables, it checks for integer infeasibility by checking light-weight Diophantine feasibility criteria and then resort to variants of Gomory Cuts and Branch and Bound.

4.1   Patching

In a feasible tableau we can assume that all non-basic variables are at their bounds and therefore if they have integer sort they are assigned integer values. Only the basic variables could be assigned non-integer values. Patching seeks changing values of non-basic values in order to assign integer values to basic variables. A related method, that diversifies values of variables using *freedom* intervals was described in [18], but we found it does not preserve integral assignments.

Thus, we patch rows with basic variables $x_b \notin \mathcal{Z}$. We use a process that seeks a δ, such that $|\delta|$ is minimal and the row with x_b is of the form $x_b + \alpha y + \alpha' x' = 0$, where $\alpha \notin \mathcal{Z}$, such that the update $\beta(y) := \beta(y) + \delta$ is within the bounds of y, x_b is assigned an integer value and such that x_b becomes integer without breaking any bounds in the tableau.

Example 3. Suppose we are given a tableau of the form $y - \frac{1}{2}x = 0$, $z - \frac{1}{3}x = 0$ where y, z are basic variables and x has bounds $[3, 10]$, y has bounds $[-3, 4]$, z has bounds $[-5, 12]$. The variable x is initially assigned at the bound $\beta(x) = 3$. Then $\beta(y) = \frac{3}{2}$ and $\beta(z) = 1$. But neither y nor z is close to their bounds. We can move x to 8 without violating the bound for y because of $y - \frac{1}{2}x = 0$. Thus, the freedom interval for x is the range $[3, 8]$ and within this range there is a solution, $x = 6$, where y, z are integers and within their bounds.

4.2   Cubes

An important factor in solving more satisfiable integer arithmetic instances is a method by Bromberger and Weidenbach [9,10]. It allows detecting feasible inequalities over integer variables by solving a stronger linear system. Their method relies on the following property: The inequalities $Ax \leq b$ are integer feasible, for matrix A and vectors x, b, if $Ax \leq b - \frac{1}{2}\|A\|_1$ has a solution over the reals. We use the 1-norm $\|A\|_1$ of a matrix as a column vector, such that each entry i is the sum of the absolute values of the elements in the corresponding row A_i.

Example 4. Suppose we have $3x + y \leq 9 \wedge -3y \leq -2$ and wish to find an integer solution. By solving $3x + y \leq 9 - \frac{1}{2}(3 + 1) = 7, -3y \leq -2 - \frac{1}{2}3 = -3.5$ we find a model where $y = \frac{7}{6}, x = 0$. After rounding y to 1 and maintaining x at 0 we obtain an integer solution to the original inequalities.

Z3 includes a twist relative to [10] that allows to avoid strengthening on selected inequalities [6]. First, we note that *difference* inequalities of the form $x - y \leq k$, where x, y are integer variables and k is an integer offset need not be strengthened: they have a solution over reals if and only if they have a solution over integers. For octagon constraints $\pm x \pm y \leq k$, there is a boundary condition: they need only require strengthening if x, y are assigned at mid-points between integral solutions. For example, if $\beta(x) = \frac{1}{2}$ and $\beta(y) = \frac{3}{2}$, for $x + y \leq 2$.

4.3 GCD Consistency

A basic test for integer infeasibility is by enforcing divisibility constraints.

Example 5. Assume we are given a row $5/6x + 3/6y + z + 5/6u = 0$, where x, y are fixed at $2 \leq x \leq 2, -1 \leq u \leq -1$, and z is the base variable. Then it follows that $5 + 3(y + 2z) = 0$ which has no solution over the integers: The greatest common divisor of coefficients to the non-fixed variables (3) does not divide the constant offset from the fixed variables (5).

The basic test is extended as follows. For each row $ax + by + c = 0$, where

- a, b, c and x, y are vectors of integer constants and variables, respectively.
- the coefficients in a are all the same and smaller than the coefficients in b
- the variables x are bounded

Let $l := a \cdot lb(x), u := a \cdot ub(x)$. That is, the lower and upper bounds for $a \cdot x$ based on the bounds for x. If $\lfloor \frac{u}{\gcd(b,c)} \rfloor > \lceil \frac{l}{\gcd(b,c)} \rceil$, then there is no solution for x within the bounds for x.

4.4 Branching

Similar to traditional MIP branch-and-bound methods, the solver creates somewhat eagerly case splits on bounds of integer variables if the dual simplex solver fails to assign them integer values. For example, Simplex may assign an integer variable x, the value $\frac{1}{2}$, in which case z3 creates a literal $x \leq 0$ that triggers two branches $x \leq 0$ and $\neg(x \leq 0) \equiv x \geq 1$.

4.5 Cuts

The arithmetic solver produces Gomory cuts from rows where the basic variables are non-integers after the non-basic variables have been pushed to the bounds. Z3 implements Chvátal-Goromy cuts described in [21]. It also implements algorithms from [13,20] to generate cuts after the linear systems have been transformed into Hermitian matrices. It is a long-standing and timely challenge [1] to harness the effectiveness of selecting cuts. While the solver takes [21] as starting point, it incorporates a few heuristics and enhancements.

Recall that a row $\sum_{j=0}^{k} a_j \cdot x_j + x_b = 0$ from the tableau is called a Gomory row, and is eligible for Gomory cut, if x_b is a basic variable and x_j are non-basic variables, x_b is an integral variable, but $\beta(x_b)$ is not integral, and for each x_j we have $\beta(x_j) = lo_j$ or $\beta(x_j) = hi_j$, and the bounds are not strict.

We use a relaxed definition of Gomory rows. For a non-basic integral variable x_j we allow for value $\beta(x_j)$ to be not at a bound when $\beta(x_j)$, and a_j are both integers: Let us call such x_j *row integral*.

To select a cut variable, our main heuristic sorts all Gomory rows from the tableau by the distance of $\beta(x_b)$ from the nearest integer, that is $\min\{\beta(x_b) - \lfloor \beta(x_b) \rfloor, \lceil \beta(x_b) \rceil - \beta(x_b)\}$, and pick a few of them having the minimal distance to produce the cuts. We break the ties by preferring the variables that are used in more terms. Heuristics used previously relied on distances to bounds.

We also look for the case when x_b is at an extremum. For example, if for all x_j we have $\beta(x_j) = lo_j$, and $a_j > 0$ then x_b is at the maximum, and we deduce $x_b \leq \lfloor \beta(x_b) \rfloor$. The explanations of the Gomory term do not include constraints on x_j for $j \in A$ from the relaxed definition, but in case of an extremum these constraints should be added.

Cuts are consequences of the current bounds. By default the solver adds new rows to the Dual Simplex tableau corresponding to cuts, but makes an exception when the new rows include large numerals. In analogy the solver avoids bounds propagation, Sect. 3.3, when computation of bounds relies on big-num arithmetic. Similarly, cuts that involve large coefficients are first added to a temporary scope where the tableau is checked for feasibility. The cuts are only re-added within the main scope if the temporary tableau is infeasible.

5 Non-linear Arithmetic

Similar to solving for integer feasibility, the arithmetic solver solves constraints over polynomials using a waterfall model for non-linear constraints. At the basis it maintains, for every monomial term $x \cdot x \cdot y$, a definition $m = x \cdot x \cdot y$, where m is a variable that represents the monomial $x \cdot x \cdot y$. The module for non-linear arithmetic then collects the monomial definitions that are violated by the current evaluation, that is $\beta(m) \neq \beta(x) \cdot \beta(x) \cdot \beta(y)$. It attempts to establish a valuation β' where $\beta'(m) = \beta'(x) \cdot \beta'(x) \cdot \beta'(y)$, or derive a consequence that no such evaluation exists.

5.1 Patch Monomials

A *patch* for a variable x is *admissible* if the update $\beta(x) := v$ does not break any integer linear constraints and x does not occur in monomial equations that are not already false under β.

- Set $\beta(m) := \beta(x) \cdot \beta(x) \cdot \beta(y)$ and check if the patch of m is admissible.
- Try to set $\beta(y) := \beta(m)/(\beta(x) \cdot \beta(x))$, provided βx is not 0, and check that the patch for x is admissible.
- When $\beta(m) = r^2$ for a rational and $m := x \cdot x$ try patching x by setting $\beta(x) := \pm r$.

5.2 Bounds Propagation

A relatively inexpensive step is to propagate and check bounds based on non-linear constraints. For example, for $y \geq 3$, then $m = x \cdot x \cdot y \geq 3$, if furthermore $x \leq -2$, we have the strengthened bound $m \geq 12$. Bounds propagation can also flow from bounds on m to bounds on the variables that make up the monomial, such that when $m \geq 8, 1 \leq y \leq 2, x \leq 0$, then we learn the stronger bound $x \leq -2$ on x. It uses an interval arithmetic abstraction, that understands bounds propagation over squares. Thus, if $-2 \leq x \leq 2$, then $0 \leq x^2 \leq 4$ instead of $-4 \leq x^2 \leq 4$.

The solver also performs Horner expansions of polynomials to derive stronger bounds. For example, if $x \geq 2, y \geq -1, z \geq 2$, then $y + z \geq 1$ and therefore $x \cdot (y + z) \geq 2$, but we would not be able to deduce this fact if combining bounds individually for $x \cdot y$ and $x \cdot z$ because no bounds can be inferred for $x \cdot y$ in isolation. The solver therefore attempts different re-distribution of multiplication in an effort to find stronger bounds.

5.3 Adding Bounds

Non-linear bounds propagation only triggers if all variables are either bounded from above or below or occur with an even power. The solver includes a pass where it adds a bound case split $x \geq 0$ to variables x where $lo_x = -\infty, hi_x = +\infty$. The added case split may help trigger bounds propagation, such as detecting conflicts on $xy > 0, xz > 0, y > 0 > z$.

5.4 Gröbner reduction

Z3 uses a best effort Gröbner basis reduction to find inconsistencies, cheaply, and propagate consequences. While Gröbner basis heuristics are not new to Z3, they have evolved and to our knowledge the integration is unique among SMT solvers. Recall that reduced Gröbner basis for a set of polynomial equations $p_1 = 0, \ldots, p_k = 0$ is a set $q_1 = 0, \ldots, q_m = 0$, such that every p_i is a linear sum of q_j's, and the leading monomials of every pair q_i, q_j, $i \neq j$, have no common factors. Since Z3 uses completion as a heuristic to make partial inferences, it does not seek to compute a basis. The Gröbner module performs a set of partial completion steps, preferring to eliminate variables that can be isolated, and expanding a bounded number of super-position steps (reductions by S-polynomials).

Z3 first adds equations $m = x_1 \ldots x_k$ for monomial definitions that are violated. It then traverses the transitive cone of influence of Simplex rows that contain one of the added variables from monomial definitions. It only considers rows where the basic variable is bounded. Rows where the basic variable is unbounded are skipped because the basic variable can be solved for over the reals. Fixed variables are replaced by constants, and the bounds constraints that fixes the variables are recorded as dependencies with the added equation. Thus, the equations handled by the Gröbner basis reduction are of the form $\langle p_i : xy + 3z + 3 = 0, d_i : \{3 \leq u \leq 3\}\rangle$, where p_i is a polynomial and d_i is a set of dependencies corresponding to fixed variables that were replaced by constants in p_i. In the example, we replaced u by 3 and the definition $\langle m = xy, \emptyset \rangle$ resolved m by xy. Dependencies are accumulated when two polynomials are resolved to infer a new derived equality. Generally, when $\langle xy + p_1 = 0, d_1 \rangle, \langle xz + p_2 = 0, d_2 \rangle$ are two polynomial equations, then $\langle zp_1 - yp_2 = 0, d_1 \cup d_2 \rangle$ can be derived accumulating the premises d_1, d_2.

Finally, equations are pre-solved if they are linear and can be split into two groups, one containing a single variable that has a lower (upper) bound, the other with more than two variables with upper (lower) bounds. This avoids losing bounds information during completion.

After (partial) completion, the derived equations are post-processed:

Constant Propagation. For equalities of the form $x = 0$ or $ax + b = 0$. If the current assignment to x does not satisfy the equation, then the equality is propagated as a lemma.

Linear Propagation. As a generalization of constant propagation, if the completion contains linear equations that evaluate to false under the current assignment, then these linear equations are added to the Simplex Tableau. Example 6 illustrates a use where this propagation is useful.

Factorization. Identify factors of the form $xyp \simeq 0$ where x, y are variables an p is linear. We infer the clause $xyp \simeq 0 \Rightarrow x \simeq 0 \vee y \simeq 0 \vee p \simeq 0$.

Example 6 (Combining Gröbner completion and Linear Solving). We include an example obtained from Yoav Rodeh at Certora. The instance was not solvable prior to adding simplex propagation. To solve it, Certora relied on treating multiplication as an uninterpreted function and including selected axioms for modular arithmetic and multiplication that were instantiated by E-matching. The distilled example is:

$$L \leq x \cdot y \leq U \wedge 1 \leq x \wedge m_r \leq U \wedge x \cdot y \neq m_r$$

where $L = N$ div $2, U = 1 + L$, $m_r = (x \cdot (ite(y \geq 0, y, N + y)))$ mod N. We assume N is even, such as $N = 2^{256}$. The solver associates a variable m with $x \cdot y$ and m' with $x \cdot y'$ and y' with $ite(y \geq 0, y, N + y)$ and includes the constraints $0 \leq m_r < N, m_q \cdot N + m_r = m'$, where m_q is an integer variable. The most interesting case is where $y < 0$, so $y' = y + N$. Gröbner basis completion then allows to derive $m_q N + m_r = m' = x(y + N) = xy + xN = m + xN$, which by integer linear arithmetic reasoning (the extended GCD test) contradicts $m \neq m_r$ because the absolute value of both variables is below N.

Our extraction of linear constraints represents a partial integration of linear programming and polynomial arithmetic, that favors only including linear inequalities over variables and monomials that are already present. Our implementation does not include any variables for new monomials produced by completion. In comparison, the approach in [25] proposes a domain for abstract interpretation that populates a linear solver with all equations produced by a completion. We have not experimented in depth with extending our approach with a full basis, or use it as a starting point for finding lemmas based on Positivstellensatz or other extension mechanisms [32,34].

We use an adaptation of ZDD (Zero suppressed decision diagrams [29,30]) to represent polynomials. The representation has the advantage that polynomials are stored in a shared data-structure and operations over polynomials are memorized. A polynomial over the real is represented as an acyclic graph, where nodes are labeled by variables and edges are labeled by coefficients. Figure 2 shows a polynomial stored in a polynomial decision diagram, PDD.

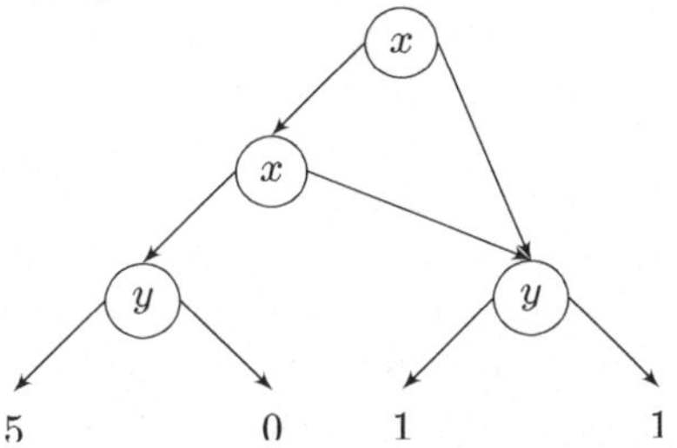

Fig. 2. PDD representation of $5x^2y + xy + y + x + 1$

The root node labeled by x represents the polynomial $x \cdot l + r$, where l is the polynomial of the left sub-graph and r the polynomial of the right sub-graph. The left sub-graph is allowed to be labeled again by x, but the right sub-graph may only have nodes labeled by variables that are smaller in a fixed ordering. The fixed ordering used in this example sets x above y. Then the polynomial for the right sub-graph is $y + 1$, and the polynomial with the left sub-graph is $5xy + (y + 1)$.

5.5   Incremental Linearization

Following [14] we incrementally linearize monomial definitions that currently evaluate to false. For example, we include lemmas of the form $x = 0 \rightarrow m = 0$ and $x = 1 \rightarrow m = y$, for $m = x^2y$. Incremental linearization proceeds by first applying linearizations that are considered cheap, such as case splitting on whether variables take values 0, 1, -1, when these boundary conditions are exhausted, instantiates lemmas based on monotonicity of multiplication and tangents. It is possible that there are overlapping monomial definitions, such as $m' = x \cdot y$. Then incremental linearization takes into account that the definition for m can be *factored* into $m' \cdot x$. It also uses specialized congruence closure reasoning, recognizing equalities modulo signs, such that when $m = x \cdot y, m' = z \cdot y$ and $x = -z$ in the current context, then $m \sim -m'$.

To find all factorizations of monomial $m = \prod_{i \in A} x_i$ as $m = m_0 \cdot m_1$, we choose $a \in A$ and enumerate over all proper subsets B of A containing a. For each B we check that $m_0 = \prod_{i \in B} x_i$ and $m_1 = \prod_{i \in A \setminus B} x_i$ are monomials.

To support floating point arithmetic reasoning we also include incremental linearization lemmas for special cases of exponentiation [15]. We also added rules for incremental linearization of divisibility operations. The front-end to the core arithmetic solver axiomatizes integer and real division operations using multiplication and addition, so that the solver does not have to reason about division. Nevertheless, we found use cases for instantiating axioms of the form $y > 0 \wedge x > z \Rightarrow x/y > z/y$ (when the input contains terms $x/y, z/y$) bypassing indirect reasoning around constraints created by axioms.

5.6   NLSat

As an end-game attempt, the solver attempts to solver the non-linear constraints using a complete solver for Tarski's fragment supported by the NLSat solver [24]. NLSAT is complete for non-linear arithmetic and includes branch-and-bound to handle cases of integer arithmetic. It can therefore sometimes be used to solve goals, bypassing the partial heuristics entirely. The solver therefore includes selected calls to NLSat with a small resource bound to close branches before attempting incomplete heuristics such as incomplete linearization. The results in Sect. 7 suggests that our use of NLSat with a resource bound currently incurs significant overhead on easy problems, but overall is an advantage. We found that it is sometimes the case that turning off NLSat all-together can speed up the solver significantly, but is overall a disadvantage.

6   Shared Equalities

Z3 uses model-based theory combination [18] for sharing equalities between theories. In the context of arithmetic it means that in a satisfiable state shared variables where $\beta(x) = \beta(y)$ it also holds that the literal $x \simeq y$ is assigned to true. For larger benchmarks we observed that there can be a significant overhead in checking whether a term occurs in a shared context because it relies on properties of which parent terms it occurs. We therefore introduced a way to cache the property of being shared in the E-nodes. The property gets invalidated when the a new parent E-node is added or the congruence class of the E-node is merged.

7   Evaluation

To get an idea of how the new solver compares and how the individual features of weigh on performance we conducted a set of measurements. They are based on three benchmark sets: QF_LIA, SMTLIB2 benchmarks for the theory of quantifier-free integer linear arithmetic, QF_NIA, SMTLIB2 benchmarks for the theory of quantifier-free non-linear integer arithmetic, and benchmark-submission, a smaller set of verification conditions obtained from Certora. Data associated with the measurements summarized in this Section are available from [7]. We ran the solvers for 600 s and measured how many problems are solved within 600 s. We compared default settings of the solvers with

CVC5 [2,17,26], MathSat5 [16,28], and Yices2 [22,37], and Z3's legacy arithmetic solver, which is available by setting the option smt.arith.solver=2. The advances relative to the legacy solver are noticable. Compared to other solvers, Yices2 and MathSat5 shine as fast out of the gates solving relatively more problems within 1 s. The are mainly limited by the set of supported features, such as lack of support for algebraic data-types. We compare how many instances the solvers handle within 1 s, within 1–10 s, 10–100 s, and 10–600 s. We also list timeouts and cases where the solver returns unknown because of incompleteness, and cases where benchmarks are unhandled, either because the solver runs out of allocated virtual memory set to 2 GB, or due to unsupported features. The version of Z3 used for the experiments corresponds to 4.12.5.

Figure 3 shows results of evaluating z3 when disabling selected features. It suggests that using NLSat to eagerly close branches comes with a steep cost for easy benchmarks. It can likely be tuned in future versions of Z3. The eager use of NLSat still provides an overall benefit. Z3 also uses *tactics* that run a few strategies with a 5 s resource bounds early on to find models using SAT encodings and selected branch-and-bound strategies. They are also a cause of relatively slow startup. The default tactics can be overridden. The feature with overall biggest impact is incremental linearization. While it is run after gcd tests, bounds propagation and Gröbner saturation, it has a significant effect. Other features have each a relative minor effect in isolation. The solver relies on their cumulative effect.

Solver	< 1s	1 to 10s	10 to 100s	100 to 600s	> 600s	unknown/unhandled	solved
CVC5	3082	4564	3578	1693	10959	0/0	12917
MathSat5	3304	6022	3894	2047	8607	0/2	15267
Yices2	6372	6284	2176	852	8192	0/0	15684
z3	4597	7440	4826	1504	5505	0/4	18367
z3legacy	3504	6881	4081	1577	6923	891/19	16043

(a) Comparison among solvers on QF_NIA

Solver	< 1s	1 to 10s	10 to 100s	100 to 600s	> 600s	unknown/unhandled	solved
CVC5	1540	1071	529	416	3391	0/0	3556
MathSat5	2995	1065	1124	1184	577	0/2	6368
Yices2	3638	2001	276	120	909	0/3	6035
z3	2840	1161	1521	754	669	0/2	6276
z3legacy	2714	1059	1619	702	851	0/2	6094

(b) Comparison among solvers on QF_LIA

Solver	< 1s	1 to 10s	10 to 100s	100 to 600s	> 600s	unknown/unhandled	solved
CVC5	11	23	54	33	183	4/0	121
MathSat5	147	17	19	32	70	0/23	215
Yices2	13	21	16	12	90	0/156	62
z3	26	88	86	17	91	0/0	217
z3legacy	36	69	55	8	133	7/0	168

(c) Comparison among solvers on Certora Benchmarks

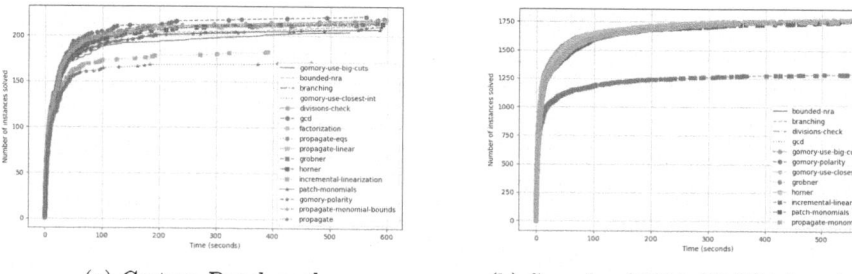

(a) Certora Benchmarks   (b) Sample of 2313 QF-NIA benchmarks

Fig. 3. Impact of selected features turned off

8   Summary and Discussion

We presented the architecture and a cross-cut of system innovations in a new arithmetic solver in Z3. It is shown to provide good advances relative to the legacy arithmetic solver, and our evaluation suggests it compares very well with other state-of-art SMT solvers. The new solver enabled us to addresses some design choices with the previous solver that limited extensibility. Notably, the new solver separates its representation of arithmetic constraints from terms shared by other solvers through an E-graph. We noticed that limitation of using shared terms is that the boundary for when to treat a sub-term as a variable or a polynomial is inherently ambiguous. The legacy solver is also highly incomplete for non-linear reasoning (over the reals).

Many avenues for further innovations and tuning remain. Another important aspect is trust. Implementing the many features of the arithmetic solver is inherently a complex task. Many bugs get uncovered by fuzzing [11,23,27,31,33,35,36] both in the legacy and new solver, bearing witness to the difficulty of creating a correct solver. The solver therefore supports a number of ways to validate results. The easiest validation is for satisfiable formulas, where the satisfiable formula is model checked against the returned model. The main difficulty with satisfiable models is to correctly track interpretations of under-specified operations, such as division by 0. To check that consequences produced by the solver are valid, there is a self-validator enabled by the `smt.arith.validate=true`. It uses the legacy arithmetic solver to check lemmas and propagations. There is also a mechanism for creating certificates that can be processed offline or online. With each theory axiom and propagation produced by the solver, it produces a certificate object that can be used to validate inferences by the arithmetic solver. The certificates are exposed in proof objects [19] and also as annotations in proof logs [4]. Z3 contains a built-in proof checker for proof logs. The proof checker for arithmetic certificates validates conflicts that can be justified by using Farkas lemma and bounds propagations that use cuts. It currently falls back to invoking Z3 on lemmas (using the legacy arithmetic solver) for non-linear lemmas and other cases not covered by the built-in checker. Certificates created for QF_LRA are fully handled, while self-contained or independent proof checking for more expressive fragments of arithmetic is future work.

References

1. Balcan, M.-F., Prasad, S., Sandholm, T., Vitercik, E. Structural analysis of branch-and-cut and the learnability of gomory mixed integer cuts. In: Koyejo, S., Mohamed, S., Agarwal, A., Belgrave, D., Cho, K., Oh, A. (eds.) Advances in Neural Information Processing Systems 35: Annual Conference on Neural Information Processing Systems 2022, NeurIPS 2022, New Orleans, LA, USA, November 28–December 9 2022 (2022)
2. Barbosa, H., et al.: cvc5: a versatile and industrial-strength SMT solver. In: TACAS 2022, Part I. LNCS, vol. 13243, pp. 415–442. Springer, Cham (2022). https://doi.org/10.1007/978-3-030-99524-9_24
3. Barrett, C., Fontaine, P., Tinelli, C.: The Satisfiability Modulo Theories Library (SMT-LIB) (2016)
4. Bjørner, N.: Proofs for SMT (2022). https://z3prover.github.io/slides/proofs.html
5. Bjørner, N., et al.: Z3 internals (2023). https://z3prover.github.io/papers/z3internals.html
6. Bjørner, N., Nachmanson, L.: Theorem recycling for theorem proving. In: Vampire (2017)
7. Bjørner, N., Nachmanson, L.: Supplementary data (2024). https://github.com/z3prover/doc/arithmetic
8. Bjørner, N., Nachmanson, L.: Navigating the universe of Z3 theory solvers. In: Carvalho, G., Stolz, V. (eds.) SBMF 2020. LNCS, vol. 12475, pp. 8–24. Springer, Cham (2020). https://doi.org/10.1007/978-3-030-63882-5_2
9. Bromberger, M., Weidenbach, C.: Fast cube tests for LIA constraint solving. In: IJCAR (2016)
10. Bromberger, M., Weidenbach, C.: New techniques for linear arithmetic: cubes and equalities. Formal Methods Syst. Des. **51**(3), 433–461 (2017)
11. Brummayer, R., Lonsing, F., Biere, A.: Automated testing and debugging of SAT and QBF solvers. In: Strichman, O., Szeider, S. (eds.) SAT 2010. LNCS, vol. 6175, pp. 44–57. Springer, Heidelberg (2010). https://doi.org/10.1007/978-3-642-14186-7_6
12. Certora: Certora Benchmarks (2023). https://github.com/jar-ben/benchmark-submission
13. Christ, J., Hoenicke, J.: Cutting the mix. In: CAV (2015)
14. Cimatti, A., Griggio, A., Irfan, A., Roveri, M., Sebastiani, R.: Experimenting on solving nonlinear integer arithmetic with incremental linearization. In: SAT (2018)
15. Cimatti, A., Griggio, A., Irfan, A., Roveri, M., Sebastiani, R.: Incremental linearization for satisfiability and verification modulo nonlinear arithmetic and transcendental functions. ACM Trans. Comput. Log. **19**(3), 19:1–19:52 (2018)
16. Cimatti, A., Griggio, A., Schaafsma, B.J., Sebastiani, R.: The MathSAT5 SMT solver. In: Piterman, N., Smolka, S.A. (eds.) TACAS 2013. LNCS, vol. 7795, pp. 93–107. Springer, Heidelberg (2013). https://doi.org/10.1007/978-3-642-36742-7_7
17. CVC5: CVC5 executable (2024). https://github.com/cvc5/cvc5/releases/. For the experiments we used the newest available version at the time https://cvc5.stanford.edu/downloads/builds/x86_64-win64-production/cvc5-2024-01-08-x86_64-win64-production.exe. It is no longer available for download, but would have

to be recreated from Git state. We reran experiments using the current release, March 2024 with degraded results

18. de Moura, L.M., Bjørner, N.: Model-based theory combination. Electron. Notes Theor. Comput. Sci. **198**(2), 37–49 (2008)
19. de Moura, L.M., Bjørner, N.: Proofs and refutations, and Z3. In: Rudnicki, P., Sutcliffe, G., Konev, B., Schmidt, R.A., Schulz, S. (eds.) Proceedings of the LPAR 2008 Workshops, Knowledge Exchange: Automated Provers and Proof Assistants, and the 7th International Workshop on the Implementation of Logics, Doha, Qatar, 22 November 2008, volume 418 of CEUR Workshop Proceedings. CEUR-WS.org (2008)
20. Dillig, I., Dillig, T., Aiken, A.: Cuts from proofs: a complete and practical technique for solving linear inequalities over integers. In: CAV (2009)
21. Dutertre, B., de Moura, L.: A fast linear-arithmetic solver for DPLL(T). In: CAV (2006)
22. Dutertre, B.: Yices 2.2. In: Biere, A., Bloem, R. (eds.) CAV 2014. LNCS, vol. 8559, pp. 737–744. Springer, Cham (2014). https://doi.org/10.1007/978-3-319-08867-9_49
23. Hwang, D.: Z3 Issue tracker (2024). https://github.com/z3prover/z3
24. Jovanovic, D., de Moura, L.M.: Solving non-linear arithmetic. In: IJCAR (2012)
25. Kincaid, Z., Koh, N., Zhu, S.: When less is more: consequence-finding in a weak theory of arithmetic. Proc. ACM Program. Lang. **7**(POPL), 1275–1307 (2023)
26. Kremer, G., Reynolds, A., Barrett, C., Tinelli, C.: Cooperating techniques for solving nonlinear real arithmetic in the cvc5 SMT solver (system description). In: Blanchette, J., Kovács, L., Pattinson, D. (eds.) IJCAR 2022. LNCS, vol. 13385, pp. 95–105. Springer, Cham (2022). https://doi.org/10.1007/978-3-031-10769-6_7
27. Mansur, M.N., Christakis, M., Wüstholz, V., Zhang, F.: Detecting critical bugs in SMT solvers using blackbox mutational fuzzing. In: Devanbu, P., Cohen, M.B., Zimmermann, T. (eds.) ESEC/FSE 2020: 28th ACM Joint European Software Engineering Conference and Symposium on the Foundations of Software Engineering, Virtual Event, USA, 8–13 November 2020, pp. 701–712. ACM (2020)
28. MathSat5: MathSat5 executable (2024). https://mathsat.fbk.eu/download.php?file=mathsat-5.6.10-win64-msvc.zip
29. Minato, S.: Zero-suppressed BDDs for set manipulation in combinatorial problems. In: Dunlop, A.E. (ed.) DAC (1993)
30. Nishino, M., Yasuda, N., Minato, S., Nagata, M.: Zero-suppressed sentential decision diagrams. In: AAAI (2016)
31. Park, J., Winterer, D., Zhang, C., Su, Z.: Generative type-aware mutation for testing SMT solvers. Proc. ACM Program. Lang. **5**(OOPSLA), 1–19 (2021)
32. Platzer, A., Quesel, J.-D., Rümmer, P.: Real world verification. In: Schmidt, R.A. (ed.) CADE 2009. LNCS (LNAI), vol. 5663, pp. 485–501. Springer, Heidelberg (2009). https://doi.org/10.1007/978-3-642-02959-2_35
33. Sun, M., Yang, Y., Wang, Y., Wen, M., Jia, H., Zhou, Y.: SMT solver validation empowered by large pre-trained language models. In: 2023 38th IEEE/ACM International Conference on Automated Software Engineering (ASE), pp. 1288–1300 (2023)
34. Tiwari, A.: An algebraic approach for the unsatisfiability of nonlinear constraints. In: Ong, L. (ed.) CSL 2005. LNCS, vol. 3634, pp. 248–262. Springer, Heidelberg (2005). https://doi.org/10.1007/11538363_18
35. Winterer, D., Zhang, C., Su, Z.: On the unusual effectiveness of type-aware operator mutations for testing SMT solvers. Proc. ACM Program. Lang. **4**(OOPSLA):193:1–193:25 (2020)

36. Winterer, D., Zhang, C., Su, Z.: Validating SMT solvers via semantic fusion. In: Proceedings of the 41st ACM SIGPLAN Conference on Programming Language Design and Implementation, pp. 718–730 (2020)
37. Yices2. Yices2 executable (2024). https://yices.csl.sri.com/releases/2.6.4/yices-2.6.4-x86_64-pc-mingw32-static-gmp.zip

Algebraic Reasoning Meets Automata in Solving Linear Integer Arithmetic

Peter Habermehl[2], Vojtěch Havlena[1], Michal Hečko[1], Lukáš Holík[1],
and Ondřej Lengál[1(✉)]

[1] Faculty of Information Technology, Brno University of Technology,
Brno, Czech Republic
lengal@fit.vutbr.cz
[2] Université Paris Cité, IRIF, Paris, France

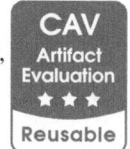

Abstract. We present a new angle on solving quantified linear integer arithmetic based on combining the automata-based approach, where numbers are understood as bitvectors, with ideas from (nowadays prevalent) algebraic approaches, which work directly with numbers. This combination is enabled by a fine-grained version of the duality between automata and arithmetic formulae. In particular, we employ a construction where states of automaton are obtained as derivatives of arithmetic formulae: then every state corresponds to a formula. Optimizations based on techniques and ideas transferred from the world of algebraic methods are used on thousands of automata states, which dramatically amplifies their effect. The merit of this combination of automata with algebraic methods is demonstrated by our prototype implementation being competitive to and even superior to state-of-the-art SMT solvers.

1 Introduction

Linear integer arithmetic (LIA), also known as *Presburger arithmetic*, is the first-order theory of integers with addition. Its applications include e.g. databases [60], program analysis [61], synthesis [59], and it is an essential component of every aspiring SMT solver. Many other types of constraints can either be reduced to LIA, or are decided using a tight collaboration of a solver for the theory and a LIA solver, e.g., in the theory of bitvectors [71], strings [19], or arrays [37]. Current SMT solvers are strong enough in solving large quantifier-free LIA formulae. Their ability to handle quantifiers is, however, problematic to the extent of being impractical. Even a tiny formula with two quantifier alternations can be a show stopper for them. Handling quantifiers is an area of lively research with numerous application possibilities waiting for a practical solution, e.g., software model checking [46], program synthesis [67], or theorem proving [49].

Among existing techniques for handling quantifiers, the complete approaches based on quantifier elimination [23,64] and automata [13,17,79] have been mostly deemed not scalable and abandoned in practice. Current SMT solvers use mainly incomplete techniques originating, e.g., from solving the theory of uninterpreted functions [66] and algebraic techniques, such as the *simplex* algorithm for quantifier-free formulae [25].

© The Author(s) 2024
A. Gurfinkel and V. Ganesh (Eds.): CAV 2024, LNCS 14681, pp. 42–67, 2024.
https://doi.org/10.1007/978-3-031-65627-9_3

This work is the first step in leveraging a recent renaissance of practically competitive automata technology for solving LIA. This trend that has recently emerged in string constraint solving (e.g. [2,7,8,18,20]), processing regular expressions [21,24,74], reasoning about the SMT theory of bitvectors [54], or regex matching (e.g. [40,53,62,78]). The new advances are rooted in paradigms such as usage of non-determinism and alternation, various flavours of symbolic representations, and combination with/or integration into SAT/SMT frameworks and with algebraic techniques.

We particularly show that the automata-based procedure provides unique opportunities to amplify certain algebraic optimizations that reason over the semantic of formulae. These optimizations then boost the inherent strong points of the automata-based approach to the extent that it is able to overcome modern SMT solvers. The core strong points of automata are orthogonal to those of algebraic methods, mainly due to treating numbers as strings of bits regardless of their numerical values. Automata can thus represent large sets of solutions succinctly and can use powerful techniques, such as minimization, that have no counterpart in the algebraic world. This makes automata more efficient than the algebraic approaches already in their basic form, implemented e.g. in [13,79], on some classes of problems such as the *Frobenius coin problem* [41].

In many practical cases, the automata construction, however, explodes. The explosion usually happens when constructing an intermediate automaton for a sub-formula, although the minimal automaton for the entire formula is almost always small. The plot in Fig. 1 shows that the gap between sizes of final and intermediate automata in our benchmark is always several orders of magnitude large, offering opportunities for optimizations. In this paper, we present a basic approach to breaching this gap by transferring techniques and ideas from the algebraic world to automata and using them to prune the vast state space.

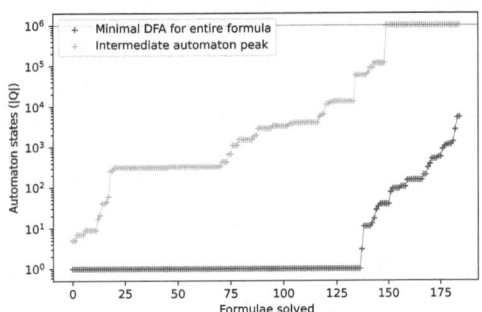

Fig. 1. Comparison of the peak intermediate automaton size and the size of the minimized DFA for the entire formula on the SMT-LIB benchmark (cf. Sect. 9).

To this end, we combine the classical inductive automata construction with constructing formula derivatives, similar to derivatives of regular expressions [3,15,74] or WS1S/WS*k*S formulae [32,45,77]. Our construction directly generates states of an automaton of a nested formula, without the need to construct intermediate automata for sub-formulae first. Although the derivative construction is not better than the inductive construction by itself, it gives an opportunity to optimize the state space *on the fly*, before it gets a chance to explode. The optimization itself is negotiated by the *fine-grained* version of the well-known *automaton-formula duality*. In the derivative construction, *every state* corresponds to a LIA formula. Applying equivalence-preserving formula rewriting on state formulae has the effect of merging or pruning states, similar to what DFA minimization could achieve after the entire automaton were constructed.

Our equivalence-preserving rewriting uses known algebraic techniques or ideas originating from them. First, we use basic formula simplification techniques, such as propagating true or false values or antiprenexing. Despite being simple, these simplifications have a large impact on performance. Second, we use *disjunction pruning*, which replaces $\varphi_1 \vee \varphi_2 \vee \cdots \vee \varphi_k$ by $\varphi_2 \vee \cdots \vee \varphi_k$ if φ_1 is entailed by the rest of the formula (this is close to the state pruning techniques used in [28,32,38]). We also adopt the principle of *quantifier instantiation* [26,36,68], where we detect cases when a quantified variable can be substituted by one or several values, or when a linear congruence can be simplified to a linear equation. We particularly use ideas from Cooper's quantifier elimination [23], where a quantifier is expanded into a disjunction over a finite number of values, and from Omega test [65], where a variable with a one-side unbounded range is substituted by the least restrictive value.

It is noteworthy that in the purely algebraic setting, the same techniques could only be applied once on the input formula, with a negligible effect. In the automata-based procedure, their power is amplified since they are used on thousands of derivative states generated deep within automata after reading several bits of the solution.

Our prototype implementation is competitive with the best SMT solvers on benchmarks from SMT-LIB, and, importantly, it is superior on quantifier-intensive instances. We believe that more connections along the outlined direction, based on the fine-grained duality between automata and formulae, can be found, and that the work in this paper is the first step in bridging the worlds of automata and algebraic approaches. Many challenges in incorporating automata-based LIA reasoning into SMT solvers still await but, we believe, can be tackled, as witnessed e.g. within the recent successes of the integration of automata-based string solvers [7,18,19].

2   Preliminaries

We use $\mathbb{Z}$ to denote the set of *integers*, $\mathbb{Z}^+$ to denote the set of *positive integers*, and $\mathbb{B}$ to denote the set of *binary digits* $\{0, 1\}$. For $x, y \in \mathbb{Z}$ and $m \in \mathbb{Z}^+$, we use $x \equiv_m y$ to denote that x is congruent with y modulo m, i.e., there exists $z \in \mathbb{Z}$ s.t. $z \cdot m + x = y$; and $x|y$ to denote that there exists $z' \in \mathbb{Z}$ s.t. $y = z' \cdot x$. Furthermore, we use $[x]_m$ to denote the unique integer s.t. $0 \leq [x]_m < m$ and $x \equiv_m [x]_m$. The following notation will be used for intervals of integers: for $a, b \in \mathbb{Z}$, the set $\{x \in \mathbb{Z} \mid a \leq x \leq b\}$ is denoted as $[a, b]$, the set $\{x \in \mathbb{Z} \mid a \leq x\}$ is denoted as $[a, +\infty)$, and the set $\{x \in \mathbb{Z} \mid x \leq b\}$ is denoted as $(-\infty, b]$. The *greatest common divisor* of $a, b \in \mathbb{Z}$, denoted as $\gcd(a, b)$, is the largest integer such that $\gcd(a, b)|a$ and $\gcd(a, b)|b$ (note that $\gcd(a, 0) = |a|$); if $\gcd(a, b) = 1$, we say that a and b are *coprime*. For a real number y, $\lfloor y \rfloor$ denotes the *floor* of y, i.e., the integer $\max\{z \in \mathbb{Z} \mid z \leq y\}$, and $\lceil y \rceil$ denotes the *ceiling* of y, i.e., the integer $\min\{z \in \mathbb{Z} \mid z \geq y\}$.

An *alphabet* Σ is a finite non-empty set of *symbols* and a *word* $w = a_1 \ldots a_n$ of length n over Σ is a finite sequence of symbols from Σ. If $n = 0$, we call w the *empty word* and denote it ϵ. Σ^+ is the set of all non-empty words over Σ and $\Sigma^* = \Sigma^+ \cup \{\epsilon\}$.

Finite Automata. In order to simplify constructions in the paper, we use a variation of finite automata with accepting transitions instead of states. A (*final transition acceptance-based*) *nondeterministic finite automaton* (FA) is a five-tuple $\mathcal{A} =$

$(Q, \Sigma, \delta, I, Acc)$ where Q is a finite set of *states*, Σ is an *alphabet*, $\delta \subseteq Q \times \Sigma \times Q$ is a *transition relation*, $I \subseteq Q$ is a set of *initial states*, and $Acc: \delta \to \{true, false\}$ is a transition-based acceptance condition. We often use $q \xrightarrow{a} p$ to denote that $(q, a, p) \in \delta$. A *run* of $\mathcal{A}$ over a word $w = a_1 \ldots a_n$ is a sequence of states $\rho = q_0 q_1 \ldots q_n \in Q^{n+1}$ such that for all $1 \le i \le n$ it holds that $q_{i-1} \xrightarrow{a_i} q_i$ and $q_0 \in I$. The run ρ is *accepting* if $n \ge 1$ and $Acc(q_{n-1} \xrightarrow{a_n} q_n)$ (i.e., if the last transition in the run is accepting)[1]. The language of $\mathcal{A}$, denoted as $\mathcal{L}(\mathcal{A})$, is defined as $\mathcal{L}(\mathcal{A}) = \{w \in \Sigma^* \mid$ there is an accepting run of $\mathcal{A}$ on $w\}$. We further use $\mathcal{L}_{\mathcal{A}}(q)$ to denote the language of the FA obtained from $\mathcal{A}$ by setting its set of initial states to $\{q\}$ (if the context is clear, we use just $\mathcal{L}(q)$).

$\mathcal{A}$ is *deterministic* (a DFA) if $|I| \le 1$ and for all states $q \in Q$ and symbols $a \in \Sigma$, it holds that if $q \xrightarrow{a} p$ and $q \xrightarrow{a} r$, then $p = r$. On the other hand, $\mathcal{A}$ is *complete* if $|I| \ge 1$ and for all states $q \in Q$ and symbols $a \in \Sigma$, there is at least one state $p \in Q$ such that $q \xrightarrow{a} p$. For a deterministic and complete $\mathcal{A}$, we abuse notation and treat δ as a function $\delta: Q \times \Sigma \to Q$. A DFA $\mathcal{A}$ is *minimal* if $\forall q \in Q: \mathcal{L}(q) \ne \emptyset \wedge \forall p \in Q: p \ne q \Rightarrow \mathcal{L}(q) \ne \mathcal{L}(p)$. Hopcroft's [51] and Brzozowski's [14] algorithms for obtaining a minimal DFA can be modified for our definition of FAs .

Linear Integer Arithmetic. Let $\mathbb{X} = \{x_1, \ldots, x_n\}$ be a (finite) set of integer variables. We will use $\vec{x}$ to denote the vector $(x_1, \ldots, x_n)$. Sometimes, we will treat $\vec{x}$ as a set, e.g., $y \in \vec{x}$ denotes $y \in \{x_1, \ldots, x_n\}$. A *linear integer arithmetic* (LIA) formula φ over $\mathbb{X}$ is obtained using the following grammar:

$$\varphi_{atom} ::= \quad \vec{a} \cdot \vec{x} = c \quad | \quad \vec{a} \cdot \vec{x} \le c \quad | \quad \vec{a} \cdot \vec{x} \equiv_m c \quad | \quad \perp$$

$$\varphi ::= \quad \varphi_{atom} \quad | \quad \neg\varphi \quad | \quad \varphi \wedge \varphi \quad | \quad \varphi \vee \varphi \quad | \quad \exists y(\varphi)$$

where $\vec{a}$ is a vector of n integer coefficients $(a_1, \ldots, a_n) \in \mathbb{Z}^n$, $c \in \mathbb{Z}$ is a constant, $m \in \mathbb{Z}^+$ is a *modulus*, and $y \in \mathbb{X}$ (one can derive the other connectives $\top, \to, \leftrightarrow, \forall, \ldots$ in the standard way)[2]. Free variables of φ are denoted as $fv(\varphi)$. Given a formula φ, we say that an assignment $v: \mathbb{X} \to \mathbb{Z}$ is a *model* of φ, denoted as $v \models \varphi$, if v satisfies φ in the standard way. Note that we use the same symbols $=, \le, \equiv_m, \neg, \wedge, \vee, \exists, \ldots$ in the syntactical language (where they are not to be interpreted, with the exception of evaluation of constant expressions) of the logic as well as in the meta-language. In order to avoid ambiguity, we use the style φ for a syntactic formula. W.l.o.g. we assume that variables in φ are unique, i.e., there is no overlap between quantified variables and also between free and quantified variables.

In our decision procedure we represent integers as non-empty sequences of binary digits $a_0 \ldots a_n \in \mathbb{B}^+$ using the two's complement with the *least-significant bit first* (LSBF) encoding (i.e., the right-most bit denotes the *sign*). Formally, the *decoding* of a binary word represents the integer

---

[1] Note that our FAs cannot accept the empty word ϵ, which corresponds in our use to the fact that in the two's complement encoding of integers, one needs at least one bit (the sign bit) to represent a number, see further.

[2] Although the modulo constraint $\vec{a} \cdot \vec{x} \equiv_m c$ could be safely removed without affecting the expressivity of the input language, keeping it allows a more efficient automata construction and application of certain heuristics (cf. Sect. 7.1).

$$Post(\vec{a} \cdot \vec{x} \le c, \sigma) \overset{\text{def}}{=} \vec{a} \cdot \vec{x} \le \lfloor \tfrac{1}{2}\kappa \rfloor \qquad \text{for } \kappa \overset{\text{def}}{=} c - \vec{a} \cdot \sigma$$

$$Post(\vec{a} \cdot \vec{x} = c, \sigma) \overset{\text{def}}{=} \begin{cases} \vec{a} \cdot \vec{x} = \tfrac{1}{2}\kappa & \text{if } 2|\kappa \\ \bot & \text{otherwise} \end{cases}$$

$$Post(\vec{a} \cdot \vec{x} \equiv_{2m} c, \sigma) \overset{\text{def}}{=} \begin{cases} \vec{a} \cdot \vec{x} \equiv_{m} \left[\tfrac{1}{2}\kappa\right]_m & \text{if } 2|\kappa \\ \bot & \text{otherwise} \end{cases}$$

$$Post(\vec{a} \cdot \vec{x} \equiv_{2m+1} c, \sigma) \overset{\text{def}}{=} \begin{cases} \vec{a} \cdot \vec{x} \equiv_{2m+1} \left[\tfrac{1}{2}\kappa\right]_{2m+1} & \text{if } 2|\kappa \\ \vec{a} \cdot \vec{x} \equiv_{2m+1} \left[\tfrac{1}{2}(\kappa + 2m + 1)\right]_{2m+1} & \text{otherwise} \end{cases}$$

$$Post(\bot, \sigma) \overset{\text{def}}{=} \bot$$

Fig. 2. Definition of the transition function *Post* for atomic formulae. Note that the right-hand sides contain constant expressions, so they will be evaluated.

$$\langle a_0 \dots a_n \rangle = \sum_{i=0}^{n-1} a_i \cdot 2^i - a_n \cdot 2^n. \tag{1}$$

For instance, $\mathsf{dec}(0101) = -6$ and $\mathsf{dec}(010) = 2$. Note that any integer has infinitely many representations in this encoding: the shortest one and others obtained by repeating the sign bit any number of times. In this paper, we work with the so-called *binary assignments*. A binary assignment is an assignment $v: \mathbb{X} \to \mathbb{B}^+$ s.t. for each $x_1, x_2 \in \mathbb{X}$ the lengths of the words assigned to x_1 and x_2 match, i.e., $|v(x_1)| = |v(x_2)|$. We overload the decoding operator $\langle \cdot \rangle$ to binary assignments such that $\langle v \rangle: \mathbb{X} \to \mathbb{Z}$ is defined as $\langle v \rangle = \{x \mapsto \langle y \rangle \mid v(x) = y\}$. A *binary model* of a formula φ is a binary assignment v such that $\langle v \rangle \models \varphi$. We denote the set of all binary models of a LIA formula φ as $[\![\varphi]\!]$ and we write $\varphi_1 \Rightarrow \varphi_2$ to denote $[\![\varphi_1]\!] \subseteq [\![\varphi_2]\!]$ and $\varphi_1 \Leftrightarrow \varphi_2$ to denote $[\![\varphi_1]\!] = [\![\varphi_2]\!]$.

3   Classical Automata-Based Decision Procedure for LIA

The following *classical decision procedure* is due to Boudet and Comon [13] (based on the ideas of [16]) with an extension to modulo constraints by Durand-Gasselin and Habermehl [29]. Given a set of variables $\mathbb{X}$, a symbol σ is a mapping $\sigma: \mathbb{X} \to \mathbb{B}$ and $\Sigma_{\mathbb{X}}$ denotes the set of all symbols over $\mathbb{X}$. For a symbol $\sigma \in \Sigma_{\mathbb{X}}$ and a variable $x \in \mathbb{X}$ we define the *projection* $\pi_x(\sigma) = \{\sigma' \in \Sigma_{\mathbb{X}} \mid \sigma'_{|\mathbb{X} \setminus \{x\}} = \sigma_{|\mathbb{X} \setminus \{x\}}\}$ where $\sigma_{|\mathbb{X} \setminus \{x\}}$ is the restriction of the function σ to the domain $\mathbb{X} \setminus \{x\}$.

For a LIA formula φ, the classical automata-based decision procedure builds an FA $\mathcal{A}_\varphi$ encoding all binary models of φ. We use a modification which uses automata with accepting edges instead of states. It allows to construct deterministic automata for atomic formulae, later in Sect. 4 also for complex formulae, and to eliminate an artificial final state present in the original construction that does not correspond to any arithmetic formula. The construction proceeds inductively as follows:

Base Case. First, an FA $\mathcal{A}_{\varphi_{atom}}$ is constructed for each atomic formula φ_{atom} in φ. The states of $\mathcal{A}_{\varphi_{atom}}$ are LIA formulae with φ_{atom} being the (only) initial state. $\mathcal{A}_{\varphi_{atom}}$'s structure is given by the transition function *Post*, implemented via a derivative $Post(\varphi_{atom}, \sigma)$ of φ_{atom} w.r.t. symbols $\sigma \in \Sigma_{\mathbb{X}}$ as given in Fig. 2 (an example will follow).

Intuitively, for $Post(\vec{a} \cdot \vec{x} = c, \sigma)$, the next state after reading σ is given by taking the least significant bits (LSBs) of all variables ($\vec{x}$) after being multiplied with the respective coefficients ($\vec{a}$) and subtracting this value from c. If the parity of the result is odd, we can reject the input word ($\vec{a} \cdot \vec{x}$ and c have a different LSB, so they cannot match), otherwise we can remove the LSB of the result, set it as a new c, and continue. One can imagine this process as performing a long addition of several binary numbers at once with c being the result (the subtraction from c can be seen as working with *carry*). The intuition for a formula $\vec{a} \cdot \vec{x} \leq c$ is similar. On the other hand, for a formula $\vec{a} \cdot \vec{x} \equiv_{2m} c$, i.e., a congruence with an even modulus, if the parity of the left-hand side ($\vec{a} \cdot \vec{x}$) and the right-hand side (c) does not match (in other words, $c - \vec{a} \cdot \vec{x}$ is odd), we can reject the input word (this is because the modulus is even, so the parities of the two sides of the congruence need to be the same). Otherwise, we remove the LSB of the modulus (i.e., divide it by two). Lastly, let us mention the second case for the rule for a formula of the form $\vec{a} \cdot \vec{x} \equiv_{2m+1} c$. Here, since κ is odd, we cannot divide it by two; however, adding the modulus ($2m + 1$) to κ yields an even value equivalent to κ.

The states of $\mathcal{A}_{\varphi_{atom}}$ are then all reachable formulae obtained from the application of *Post* from the initial state. The reachability from a set of formulae S using symbols from Γ is given using the least fixpoint operator μ as follows:

$$Reach(S, \Gamma) = \mu Z \colon S \cup \{Post(\psi, a) \mid \psi \in Z, a \in \Gamma\} \tag{2}$$

Lemma 1. *$Reach(\{\varphi_{atom}\}, \Sigma_{\mathbb{X}})$ is finite for an atomic formula φ_{atom}.*

Proof. The cases for linear equations and inequations follow from [13, Proposition 1] and [13, Proposition 3] respectively. For moduli, the lemma follows from the fact that in the definition of *Post*, the right-hand side of a modulo is an integer from $[0, m-1]$. □

Post is deterministic, so it suffices to define the acceptance condition for the derivatives only for each state and symbol, as given in Fig. 3. E.g., a transition from $2x_1 - 7x_2 = 5$ over $\sigma = \left[\begin{smallmatrix}1\\1\end{smallmatrix}\right]$ is accepting; the intuition is similar as for *Post* with the difference that the last bit is the sign bit (cf. Eq. (1)), so it is treated in the opposite way to

$$Fin(\vec{a} \cdot \vec{x} \leq c, \sigma) \overset{\text{def}}{\Leftrightarrow} c + \vec{a} \cdot \sigma \geq 0$$

$$Fin(\vec{a} \cdot \vec{x} = c, \sigma) \overset{\text{def}}{\Leftrightarrow} c + \vec{a} \cdot \sigma = 0$$

$$Fin(\vec{a} \cdot \vec{x} \equiv_m c, \sigma) \overset{\text{def}}{\Leftrightarrow} c + \vec{a} \cdot \sigma \equiv_m 0$$

$$Fin(\bot, \sigma) \overset{\text{def}}{\Leftrightarrow} \text{false}$$

Fig. 3. Acceptance for atomic formulae.

other bits (therefore, there is the "+" sign on the right-hand sides of the definitions rather than the "−" sign as in Fig. 2). If we substitute into the example, we obtain $2 \cdot (-1) - 7 \cdot (-1) = -2 + 7 = 5$. The acceptance condition *Acc* is then defined as $Acc(\varphi_1 \overset{\sigma}{\to} Post(\varphi_1, \sigma)) \overset{\text{def}}{=} Fin(\varphi_1, \sigma)$ and $\mathcal{A}_{\varphi_{atom}}$ is defined as the FA

$$\mathcal{A}_{\varphi_{atom}} = (Reach(\{\varphi_{atom}\}, \Sigma_{\mathbb{X}}), \Sigma_{\mathbb{X}}, Post, \{\varphi_{atom}\}, Acc). \tag{3}$$

Note that if an FA accepts a word w, it also accepts all words obtained by appending any number of copies of the most significant bit (the sign) to w.

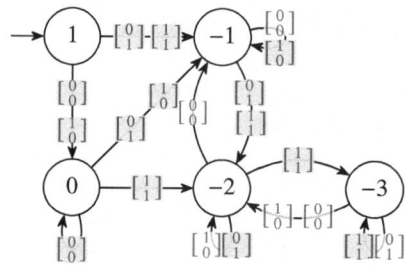 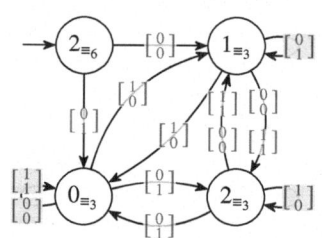

(a) The FA for $x + 2y \le 1$. A state $x + 2y \le c$ is represented by "c".

(b) The FA for $x + 2y \equiv_6 2$. A state $x + 2y \equiv_m c$ is represented by "$c_{\equiv_m}$".

Fig. 4. Examples of FAs for atomic formulae. The notation for symbols is $\left[\begin{smallmatrix} x \\ y \end{smallmatrix}\right]$; red background denotes accepting transitions. (Color figure online)

Example 1. Figure 4 gives examples of FAs for $x + 2y \le 1$ and $x + 2y \equiv_6 2$. For the case of the FA for $x + 2y \le 1$, consider for instance the state $x + 2y \le -1$ (denoted by the state "-1" in Fig. 4a). We show computation of the *Post* of this state over the symbol $\sigma = \left[\begin{smallmatrix} 1 \\ 0 \end{smallmatrix}\right]$. From the definition in Fig. 2, we have $Post(x + 2y \le -1, \left[\begin{smallmatrix} 1 \\ 0 \end{smallmatrix}\right]) = x + 2y \le k$ where $k = \lfloor \frac{1}{2}(-1 - (1,2) \cdot \left[\begin{smallmatrix} 1 \\ 0 \end{smallmatrix}\right]) \rfloor = \lfloor \frac{1}{2}(-2) \rfloor = -1$. Moreover, since $Fin(x + 2y \le -1, \left[\begin{smallmatrix} 1 \\ 0 \end{smallmatrix}\right]) \Leftrightarrow -1 + (1,2) \cdot \left[\begin{smallmatrix} 1 \\ 0 \end{smallmatrix}\right] = 0 \ge 0$, this transition is marked as accepting (cf. Fig. 3).

For the case of the second FA, consider for instance the state $x + 2y \equiv_3 0$ (denoted by the state "$0_{\equiv_3}$" in Fig. 4b). Similarly to the previous example, we show computation of *Post* of this state over the symbol $\sigma = \left[\begin{smallmatrix} 1 \\ 0 \end{smallmatrix}\right]$. From the definition in Fig. 2, we have $Post(x + 2y \equiv_3 0, \left[\begin{smallmatrix} 1 \\ 0 \end{smallmatrix}\right]) = x + 2y \equiv_3 \ell$ where $\ell = \left[\frac{1}{2}(0 - (1,2) \cdot \left[\begin{smallmatrix} 1 \\ 0 \end{smallmatrix}\right] + 3)\right]_3 = 1$. $Fin(\vec{x} + 2y \equiv_3 0, \left[\begin{smallmatrix} 1 \\ 0 \end{smallmatrix}\right]) \Leftrightarrow 0 + (1,2) \cdot \left[\begin{smallmatrix} 1 \\ 0 \end{smallmatrix}\right] \equiv_3 1$, so this transition is not accepting. $\square$

Inductive Case. The inductive cases for Boolean connectives are defined in the standard way: conjunction of two formulae is implemented by taking the intersection of the two corresponding FAs, disjunction by taking their union, and negation is implemented by taking the complement (which may involve determinization via the subset construction). Formally, let $\mathcal{A}_{\varphi_i} = (Q_{\varphi_i}, \Sigma_{\mathbb{X}}, \delta_{\varphi_i}, I_{\varphi_i}, Acc_{\varphi_i})$ for $i \in \{1, 2\}$ with $Q_{\varphi_1} \cap Q_{\varphi_2} = \emptyset$ be complete FAs. Then,

- $\mathcal{A}_{\varphi_1 \wedge \varphi_2} = (Q_{\varphi_1} \times Q_{\varphi_2}, \Sigma_{\mathbb{X}}, \delta_{\varphi_1 \wedge \varphi_2}, I_{\varphi_1} \times I_{\varphi_2}, Acc_{\varphi_1 \wedge \varphi_2})$ where
  - $\delta_{\varphi_1 \wedge \varphi_2} = \{(q_1, q_2) \xrightarrow{\sigma} (p_1, p_2) \mid q_1 \xrightarrow{\sigma} p_1 \in \delta_{\varphi_1}, q_2 \xrightarrow{\sigma} p_2 \in \delta_{\varphi_2}\}$ and
  - $Acc_{\varphi_1 \wedge \varphi_2}((q_1, q_2) \xrightarrow{\sigma} (p_1, p_2)) \overset{\text{def}}{\Leftrightarrow} Acc_{\varphi_1}(q_1 \xrightarrow{\sigma} p_1) \wedge Acc_{\varphi_2}(q_2 \xrightarrow{\sigma} p_2)$.
- $\mathcal{A}_{\varphi_1 \vee \varphi_2} = (Q_{\varphi_1} \times Q_{\varphi_2}, \Sigma_{\mathbb{X}}, \delta_{\varphi_1 \vee \varphi_2}, I_{\varphi_1} \times I_{\varphi_2}, Acc_{\varphi_1 \vee \varphi_2})$ where
  - $\delta_{\varphi_1 \vee \varphi_2} = \{(q_1, q_2) \xrightarrow{\sigma} (p_1, p_2) \mid q_1 \xrightarrow{\sigma} p_1 \in \delta_{\varphi_1}, q_2 \xrightarrow{\sigma} p_2 \in \delta_{\varphi_2}\}$ and
  - $Acc_{\varphi_1 \vee \varphi_2}((q_1, q_2) \xrightarrow{\sigma} (p_1, p_2)) \overset{\text{def}}{\Leftrightarrow} Acc_{\varphi_1}(q_1 \xrightarrow{\sigma} p_1) \vee Acc_{\varphi_2}(q_2 \xrightarrow{\sigma} p_2)$.
- $\mathcal{A}_{\neg \varphi_1} = (2^{Q_{\varphi_1}}, \Sigma_{\mathbb{X}}, \delta_{\neg \varphi_1}, \{I_{\varphi_1}\}, Acc_{\neg \varphi_1})$ where
  - $\delta_{\neg \varphi_1} = \{S \xrightarrow{\sigma} T \mid T = \{p \in Q_{\varphi_1} \mid \exists q \in S : q \xrightarrow{\sigma} p \in \delta_{\varphi_1}\}$ and

- $Acc_{\neg\varphi_1}(S \xrightarrow{\sigma} T) \overset{\text{def}}{\Leftrightarrow} \forall q \in S \, \forall p \in T : \neg Acc_{\varphi_1}(q \xrightarrow{\sigma} p).$

Existential quantification is more complicated. Given a formula $\exists x(\varphi)$ and the FA $\mathcal{A}_\varphi = (Q_\varphi, \Sigma_{\mathbb{X}}, \delta_\varphi, I_\varphi, Acc_\varphi)$, a word w should be accepted by $\mathcal{A}_{\exists x(\varphi)}$ iff there is a word w' accepted by $\mathcal{A}_\varphi$ s.t. w and w' are the same on all tracks except the track for x. One can perform projection of x out of $\mathcal{A}_\varphi$, i.e., remove the x track from all its transitions. This is, however, insufficient. For instance, consider the model $\{x \mapsto 7, y \mapsto -4\}$, encoded into the (shortest) word $\begin{bmatrix}1\\0\end{bmatrix}\begin{bmatrix}1\\0\end{bmatrix}\begin{bmatrix}1\\1\end{bmatrix}\begin{bmatrix}0\\1\end{bmatrix}$ (we use the notation $\begin{bmatrix}x\\y\end{bmatrix}$). When we remove the x-track from the word, we obtain $[0][0][1][1]$, which encodes the assignment $\{y \mapsto -4\}$. It is, however, not the shortest encoding of the assignment; the shortest encoding is $[0][0][1]$. Therefore, we further need to modify the FA obtained after projection to also accept words that would be accepted if their sign bit were arbitrarily extended, which we do by reachability analysis on the FA. Formally, $\mathcal{A}_{\exists x(\varphi)} = (Q_\varphi, \Sigma_{\mathbb{X}}, \delta_{\exists x(\varphi)}, I_\varphi, Acc_{\exists x(\varphi)})$ where

- $\delta_{\exists x(\varphi)} = \{q \xrightarrow{\sigma'} p \mid \exists q \xrightarrow{\sigma} p \in \delta_\varphi : \sigma' \in \pi_x(\sigma)\}$ and
- $Acc_{\exists x(\varphi)}(q \xrightarrow{\sigma} p) \overset{\text{def}}{\Leftrightarrow} \bigvee_{\sigma' \in \pi_x(\sigma)} Acc_\varphi(q \xrightarrow{\sigma'} p) \vee \exists r, s \in Reach(\{p\}, \pi_x(\sigma)): \bigvee_{\sigma' \in \pi_x(\sigma)} Acc_\varphi(r \xrightarrow{\sigma'} s).$

After defining the base and inductive cases for constructing the FA $\mathcal{A}_\varphi$, we can establish the connection between its language and the models of φ. For a word $w = a_1 \ldots a_n \in \Sigma_{\mathbb{X}}$ and a variable $x \in \mathbb{X}$, we define $w_x = a_1(x) \ldots a_n(x)$, i.e., w_x extracts the binary number assigned to variable x in w. For a binary assignment v of a LIA formula φ, we define its language as $\mathcal{L}(v) = \{w \in \Sigma_{\mathbb{X}}^* \mid \forall x \in \mathbb{X}: w_x = v(x)\}$. We lift the language to sets of binary assignments as usual.

Theorem 1. *Let φ be a LIA formula. Then $\mathcal{L}(\mathcal{A}_\varphi) = \mathcal{L}(\llbracket \varphi \rrbracket)$.*

Proof. Follows from [13, Lemma 5]. □

4 Derivative-Based Construction for Nested Formulae

This section lays down the basics of our approach to interconnecting automata with the algebraic approach for quantified LIA. We aim at using methods and ideas from the algebraic approach to circumvent the large intermediate automata constructed along the way before obtaining the small DFAs (cf. Fig. 1). To do that, we need a variation of the automata-based decision procedure that exposes the states of the target automata without the need of generating the complete

$$Post(\varphi_1 \wedge \varphi_2, \sigma) \overset{\text{def}}{=} Post(\varphi_1, \sigma) \wedge Post(\varphi_2, \sigma)$$

$$Post(\varphi_1 \vee \varphi_2, \sigma) \overset{\text{def}}{=} Post(\varphi_1, \sigma) \vee Post(\varphi_2, \sigma)$$

$$Post(\neg\varphi, \sigma) \overset{\text{def}}{=} \neg Post(\varphi, \sigma)$$

$$Post(\exists x(\varphi), \sigma) \overset{\text{def}}{=} \exists x \left(\bigvee_{\sigma' \in \pi_x(\sigma)} Post(\varphi, \sigma') \right)$$

$$Fin(\neg\varphi, \sigma) \overset{\text{def}}{\Leftrightarrow} \neg Fin(\varphi, \sigma)$$

$$Fin(\varphi_1 \wedge \varphi_2, \sigma) \overset{\text{def}}{\Leftrightarrow} Fin(\varphi_1, \sigma) \wedge Fin(\varphi_2, \sigma)$$

$$Fin(\varphi_1 \vee \varphi_2, \sigma) \overset{\text{def}}{\Leftrightarrow} Fin(\varphi_1, \sigma) \vee Fin(\varphi_2, \sigma)$$

$$Fin(\exists x(\varphi), \sigma) \overset{\text{def}}{\Leftrightarrow} \exists \psi \in Reach(\{\varphi\}, \pi_x(\sigma)): \bigvee_{\sigma' \in \pi_x(\sigma)} Fin(\psi, \sigma')$$

Fig. 5. *Post* and *Fin* for non-atomic formulae.

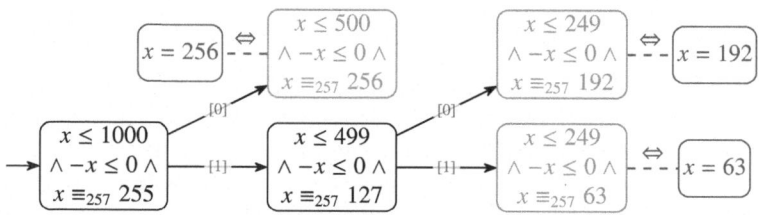

Fig. 6. Example of rewriting formulae in the FA for $x \leq 1000 \wedge -x \leq 0 \wedge x \equiv_{257} 255$.

state space of the intermediate automata first. To achieve this, we generalize the post-image function *Post* (and the acceptance condition *Fin*) from Sect. 3 to general non-atomic formulae using an approach similar to that of [32,45,76], which introduced derivatives of WS1S/WSkS formulae. Computing formula derivatives produces automata states that are at the same time LIA formulae, and can be manipulated as such using algebraic methods and reasoning about their integer semantics. We will then use basic Boolean simplification, antiprenexing, and also ideas from Cooper's quantifier elimination algorithm and Omega test [23,65] to prune and simplify the state-formulae. The techniques will be discussed in Sects. 5 to 7.

Example 2. In Fig. 6, we show an intuitive example of rewriting state formulae when constructing the FA for $0 \leq x \leq 1000 \wedge x \equiv_{257} 255$ (which is written in the basic syntax as $x \leq 1000 \wedge -x \leq 0 \wedge x \equiv_{257} 255$). After reading the first symbol [0], the obtained formula is a conjunction of the three following *Post*s:

- $Post(x \leq 1000, [0]) = x \leq \lfloor \frac{1}{2}(1000 - 1 \cdot 0) \rfloor = x \leq 500$,
- $Post(-x \leq 0, [0]) = -x \leq \lfloor \frac{1}{2}(0 + 1 \cdot 0) \rfloor = -x \leq 0$, and
- $Post(x \equiv_{257} 255, [0]) = x \equiv_{257} \left[\frac{1}{2}(255 - 1 \cdot 0 + 257) \right]_{257} = x \equiv_{257} 256$.

We can write the resulting formula as $0 \leq x \leq 500 \wedge x \equiv_{257} 256$, which is satisfied only by $x = 256$. We can therefore rewrite the formula into an equivalent formula $x = 256$. Similar rewriting can be applied to the state obtained after reading [1][0] and [1][1]. The rest of the automaton constructed from the rewritten states $x = 256$, $x = 192$, and $x = 63$ is then of a logarithmic size (each state in the rest will have only one successor based on the binary encoding of 256, 192, or 63 respectively, while if we did not perform the rewriting, the states would have two successors and the size would be linear).   □

In Fig. 5, we extend the derivative post-image function *Post* and the acceptance condition *Fin* (cf. Figs. 2 and 3) to non-atomic formulae. The derivatives mimic the automata constructions in Sect. 3, with the exception that at every step, the derivative (and therefore also the state in the constructed FA) is a LIA formula and can be treated as such. One notable exception is $Post(\exists x(\varphi), \sigma)$, which, since the *Post* function is deterministic, in addition to the projection, also mimics determinisation. One can see the obtained disjunction-structure as a set of states from the standard subset construction in automata. Correctness of the construction is stated in the following.

Lemma 2. *Let φ be a LIA formula and let $\mathcal{A}_\varphi$ be the FA constructed by the procedure in this section or any combination of it and the classical one. Then $\mathcal{L}(\mathcal{A}_\varphi) = \mathcal{L}(\llbracket \varphi \rrbracket)$.*

Proof. Follows from preservation of languages of the states/formulae.   □

Without optimizations, the derivative-based construction would generate a larger FA than the one obtained from the classical construction, which can perform minimization of the intermediate automata. The derivative-based construction cannot minimize the intermediate automata since they are not available; they are in a sense constructed on the fly within the construction of the automaton for the entire formula. Our algebraic optimizations mimic some effect of the minimization on the fly, while constructing the automaton, by simplifying the state formulae and detecting entailment between them.

In principle, when we construct a state q of $\mathcal{A}_\psi$ as a result of *Post*, we could test whether some state p was already constructed such that $\varphi_q \Leftrightarrow \varphi_p$ and, if so, we could merge p and q (drop q and redirect the edges to p). This would guarantee us to directly obtain the minimal DFA for ψ (no two states would be language-equivalent).

Solving the LIA equivalence queries precisely is, however, as hard as solving the original problem. Even when we restrict ourselves to quantifier-free formulae, the equivalence problem is **co-NP**-complete. Our algebraic optimizations are thus a cheaper and more practical alternative capable of merging at least some equivalent states. We discuss the optimizations in detail in Sects. 5 to 7 and also give a comprehensive example of their effect in Sect. 8.

5   Simple Rewriting Rules

The simplest rewriting rules are just common simplifications generally applicable in predicate logic. Despite their simplicity, they are quite powerful, since their use enables to apply the other optimizations (Sects. 6 and 7) more often.

1. We apply the propositional laws of *identity* ($\varphi \vee \bot = \varphi$ and $\varphi \wedge \top = \varphi$) and *annihilation* ($\varphi \wedge \bot = \bot$ and $\varphi \vee \top = \top$) to simplify the formulae.
2. We use *antiprenexing* [30,44] (i.e., pushing quantifiers as deep as possible using inverses of prenexing rules [69, Chapter 5]). This is helpful, e.g., after a range-based quantifier instantiation (cf. Sect. 7.2), which yields a disjunction. Since our formula analysis framework (Sect. 7) only works over conjunctions below existential quantifiers, we need to first push existential quantifiers inside the disjunctions to allow further applications of the heuristics.
3. Since negation is implemented as automaton complementation, we apply *De Morgan's laws* ($\neg(\varphi_1 \wedge \varphi_2) \Leftrightarrow (\neg\varphi_1) \vee (\neg\varphi_2)$ and $\neg(\varphi_1 \vee \varphi_2) \Leftrightarrow (\neg\varphi_1) \wedge (\neg\varphi_2)$) to push negation as deep as possible. The motivation is that small subformulae are likely to have small corresponding automata. As complementation requires the underlying automaton to be deterministic, complementing smaller automata helps to mitigate the exponential blow-up of determinization.

Moreover, we also employ the following simplifications valid for LIA:

4. We apply simple reasoning based on variable bounds to simplify the formula, e.g., $x \geq 0 \wedge x \leq 10 \wedge x \neq 0 \Leftrightarrow x \geq 1 \wedge x \leq 10$, and to prune away some parts of the formula, e.g., $x \geq 3 \wedge (\varphi \vee (x = 0 \wedge \psi)) \Leftrightarrow x \geq 3 \wedge \varphi$.

5. We employ rewriting rules aimed at accelerating the automata construction by minimizing the number of variables used in a formula, and, thus, avoiding constructing complicated transition relations, e.g., $\exists x_1, x_2 (ay + b_1 x_1 + b_2 x_2 \equiv_K 0) \Leftrightarrow \exists x (ay + bx \equiv_K 0)$ where $b = \gcd(b_1, b_2)$, or $\exists x (ay + bx = 0) \Leftrightarrow ay \equiv_{|b|} 0$.

6. We detect conflicts by identifying small isomorphic subformulae, i.e., subformulae that have the same abstract syntax tree, except for renaming of quantified variables, for example, $\exists x (x > 3 \wedge x + z \leq 10) \wedge \neg(\exists y(y > 3 \wedge y + z \leq 10) \Leftrightarrow \bot$. One can see this as a variant of DAGification used in MONA [57].

6   Disjunction Pruning

We prune disjunctions by removing disjunct implied by other disjuncts. That is, if it holds that $\varphi_2 \vee \cdots \vee \varphi_k \Rightarrow \varphi_1$, then $\varphi_1 \vee \varphi_2 \vee \cdots \vee \varphi_k$ can be replaced by just $\varphi_2 \vee \cdots \vee \varphi_k$. Testing the entailment precisely is hard, so we use a stronger but cheaper relation of

$$\vec{a_1} \cdot \vec{x_1} \leq c_1 \preceq_s \vec{a_2} \cdot \vec{x_2} \leq c_2 \overset{\text{def}}{\Leftrightarrow} \vec{a_1} = \vec{a_2} \wedge \vec{x_1} = \vec{x_2} \wedge c_1 \leq c_2$$

$$\bigwedge_{i=1}^{n} \varphi_i \preceq_s \bigwedge_{j=1}^{m} \psi_j \overset{\text{def}}{\Leftrightarrow} \forall 1 \leq j \leq m \; \exists 1 \leq i \leq n : \varphi_i \preceq_s \psi_j$$

$$\bigvee_{i=1}^{n} \varphi_i \preceq_s \bigvee_{j=1}^{m} \psi_j \overset{\text{def}}{\Leftrightarrow} \forall 1 \leq i \leq n \; \exists 1 \leq j \leq m : \varphi_i \preceq_s \psi_j$$

$$\neg \varphi \preceq_s \neg \psi \overset{\text{def}}{\Leftrightarrow} \psi \preceq_s \varphi$$

$$\exists x(\varphi) \preceq_s \exists x(\psi) \overset{\text{def}}{\Leftrightarrow} \varphi \preceq_s \psi$$

Fig. 7. Definition of the subsumption preorder $\preceq_s$ (we omit cases implied by reflexivity).

subsumption. Our subsumption is a preorder (a reflexive and transitive relation) $\preceq_s$ between LIA formulae in Fig. 7[3]. When we encounter the said macrostate and establish $\varphi_1 \preceq_s \varphi_2 \vee \cdots \vee \varphi_k$, we perform the rewriting. This optimization has effect mainly in formulae of the form $\exists x(\psi)$: their *Post* contains a disjunction of formulae of a similar structure.

Lemma 3. *For LIA formulae φ_1 and φ_2, if $\varphi_1 \preceq_s \varphi_2$, then $\varphi_1 \Rightarrow \varphi_2$.*

Example 3. In Fig. 8, we show an example of pruning disjunctions in the FA for the formula $\exists x(7x \leq 1000)$.   □

---

[3] The subsumption is similar to the one used in efficient decision procedures for WS1S/WSkS [32,45] with two important differences: (i) it can look inside atomic formulae and use semantics of states and (ii) it does not depend on the initial structure of the initial formula. (iii) Both of these make the subsumption relation larger.

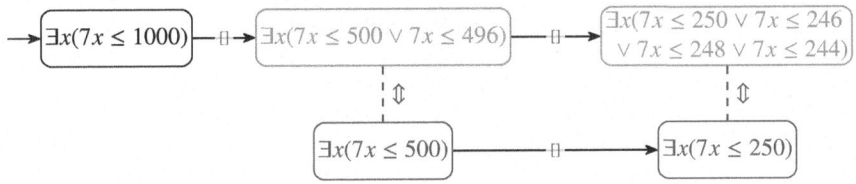

Fig. 8. Example of disjunction pruning in the FA for $\exists x(7x \leq 1000)$.

7 Quantifier Instantiation

The next optimization is an instance of quantifier instantiation, a well known class of algebraic techniques. We gather information about the formulae with a focus on the way a particular variable, usually a quantified one, affects the models of the whole formula. If one can find "the best" value for such a variable (e.g., a value such that using it preserves all models of the formula), then the (quantified) variable can be substituted with a concrete value. For instance, let $\varphi = \exists y(x - y \leq 33 \wedge y \leq 12 \wedge y \equiv_7 2)$. The variable y is quantified so we can think about instantiating it (it will not occur in a model). The first atom $x - y \leq 33$ says that we want to pick y as large as possible (larger y's have higher chance to satisfy the inequation), but, on the other hand, the second atom $y \leq 12$ says that y can be at most 12. The last atom $y \equiv_7 2$ adds an additional constraint on y. Intuitively, we can see that the best value of y—i.e., the value that preserves all models of φ—would be 9, allowing to rewrite φ to $x \leq 42$.

To define the particular ways of gathering such kind of information in a uniform way, we introduce the following *formula analysis* framework that uses the function FA to extract information from formulae. Consider a *meet-semilattice* $(\mathbb{D}, \sqcap)$ where $undef \in \mathbb{D}$ is the bottom element. Let atom be a function that, given an atomic formula φ_{atom} and a variable $y \in \mathbb{X}$, outputs an element of $\mathbb{D}$ that represents the behavior of y in φ_{atom} (e.g., bounds on y). The function FA then aggregates the information from atoms into an information about the behavior of y in the whole formula using the meet operator $\sqcap$ recursively as follows:

$$\mathsf{FA}(\varphi_{atom}, y, \mathsf{atom}, \sqcap) = \mathsf{atom}(\varphi_{atom}, y) \tag{4}$$

$$\mathsf{FA}(\varphi_1 \wedge \varphi_2, y, \mathsf{atom}, \sqcap) = \mathsf{FA}(\varphi_1, y, \mathsf{atom}, \sqcap) \sqcap \mathsf{FA}(\varphi_2, y, \mathsf{atom}, \sqcap) \tag{5}$$

(By default, a missing case in the pattern matching evaluates to *undef*.) We note that the framework is defined only for conjunctions of formulae, which is the structure of subformulae that was usually causing troubles in our experiments (cf. Sect. 9).

The optimizations defined later are based on substituting certain variables in a formula with concrete values to obtain an equivalent (simpler) formula. For this, we extend standard substitution as follows. Let $\varphi(\vec{x}, y)$ be a formula with free variables $\vec{x} = (x_1, \ldots, x_n)$ and $y \notin \vec{x}$. For $k \in \mathbb{Z}$, substituting k for y in φ yields the formula $\varphi[y/k]$ obtained in the usual way (with all constant expressions being evaluated). For $k = \pm\infty$, the resulting formula is obtained for inequalities containing y as

$$(\vec{a} \cdot \vec{x} + a_y \cdot y \leq c)[y/k] = \top \quad \text{if } a_y \cdot k = -\infty \tag{6}$$

and is undefined for all other atomic formulae.

7.1 Quantifier Instantiation Based on Formula Monotonicity

The first optimization based on quantifier instantiation uses the so-called *monotonicity* of formulae w.r.t. some variables (a similar technique is used in the Omega test [65]). Consider the following two formulae:

$$\varphi_1 = \exists y(\psi \wedge 3y - x \geq z) \quad \text{and} \quad \varphi_2 = \exists y(\psi \wedge 3y - x \geq z \wedge 5y \leq 42) \quad (7)$$

where ψ does not contain occurrences of y, and x, z are free variables in φ_1, φ_2. For φ_1, since y is existentially quantified, the inequation $3y - x \geq z$ can be always satisfied by picking an arbitrarily large value for y, so φ_1 can be simplified to just ψ. On the other hand, for φ_2, we cannot pick an arbitrarily large y because of the other inequation $5y \leq 42$. We can, however, observe, that $\lfloor \frac{42}{5} \rfloor = 8$ is the largest value that we can substitute for y to satisfy $5y \leq 42$. As a consequence, since the possible value of y in $3y - x \geq z$ is not bounded from above, we can substitute y by the value 8, i.e., φ_2 can be simplified to $\psi \wedge 24 - x \geq z$.

Formally, let $c \in \mathbb{Z} \cup \{+\infty\}$ and $y \in \mathbb{X}$. We say that a formula $\varphi(\vec{x}, y)$ is *c-best from below w.r.t.* y if (i) $[\![\varphi[y/y_1]]\!] \subseteq [\![\varphi[y/y_2]]\!]$ for all $y_1 \leq y_2 \leq c$ (for $c \in \mathbb{Z}$) or for all $y_1 \leq y_2$ (for $c = +\infty$) and (ii) $[\![\varphi[y/y']]\!] = \emptyset$ for all $y' > c$. Intuitively, substituting bigger values for y (up to c) in φ preserves all models obtained by substituting smaller values, so c can be seen as the most conservative limit of y (and for $c = +\infty$, this means that y does not have an upper bound, so it can be chosen arbitrarily large for concrete values of other variables). Similarly, $\varphi(\vec{x}, y)$ is called *c-best from above* (w.r.t. y) for $c \in \mathbb{Z} \cup \{-\infty\}$ if (i) $[\![\varphi[y/y_1]]\!] \subseteq [\![\varphi[y/y_2]]\!]$ for all $y_1 \geq y_2 \geq c$ (for $c \in \mathbb{Z}$) or for all $y_1 \geq y_2$ (for $c = -\infty$) and (ii) $[\![\varphi[y/y']]\!] = \emptyset$ for all $y' < c$. If a formula is *c-best from below or above, we call it *c-monotone* (w.r.t. y).

Lemma 4. *Let $c \in \mathbb{Z} \cup \{\pm\infty\}$ and $\varphi(\vec{x}, y)$ be a formula c-monotone w.r.t. y such that $\varphi[y/c]$ is defined. Then the formula $\exists y(\varphi(\vec{x}, y))$ is equivalent to the formula $\varphi[y/c]$.*

Moreover, the following lemma utilizes formula monotonicity to provide a tool for simplification of formulae containing a modulo atom.

Lemma 5. *Let $c \in \mathbb{Z}$ and $\varphi(\vec{x}, y)$ be a formula c-monotone w.r.t. y for $c \in \mathbb{Z}$. Then, the formula $\exists y(\varphi(\vec{x}, y) \wedge y \equiv_m k)$ is equivalent to the formula $\varphi[y/c']$ where (i) $c' = \max\{\ell \in \mathbb{Z} \mid \ell \equiv_m k, \ell \leq c\}$ if φ is c-best from below, and (ii) $c' = \min\{\ell \in \mathbb{Z} \mid \ell \equiv_m k, \ell \geq c\}$ if φ is c-best from above.*

In general, it is, however, expensive to decide whether a formula is c-monotone and find the tight c. Therefore, we propose a cheap approximation working on the structure of LIA formulae, which uses the formula analysis function FA introduced above. First, we propose the partial function $\mathsf{blw}_{atom}(\varphi, y)$ (whose result is in $\mathbb{Z} \cup \{+\infty\}$) estimating the c for atomic formulae c-best from above w.r.t. y:

$$\mathsf{blw}_{atom}(a \cdot y \leq c, y) = \left\lfloor \frac{c}{a} \right\rfloor \qquad \text{if } a > 0 \qquad (8)$$

$$\mathsf{blw}_{atom}(\vec{a} \cdot \vec{x} \leq c, x_i) = +\infty \qquad \text{if } a_i = 0 \vee \exists j : i \neq j \wedge a_j \neq 0 \wedge a_i < 0 \qquad (9)$$

Intuitively, if y is in an inequation $a \cdot y \leq c$ without any other variable and $a > 0$, then y's value is bounded from above by $\lfloor \frac{c}{a} \rfloor$. On the other hand, if $y = x_i$ is in an inequation $\vec{a} \cdot \vec{x} \leq c$ where $\vec{a}$ has at least two nonzero coefficients and y's coefficient is negative, or y does not appear in the inequation at all, then y's value is not bounded (larger values of y make it easier to satisfy the inequation). The value for other cases is undefined.

Similarly, $\mathsf{abv}_{atom}(\varphi, y)$ (with the result in $\mathbb{Z} \cup \{-\infty\}$) estimates the c for atomic formulae c-best from above:

$$\mathsf{abv}_{atom}(a \cdot y \leq c, y) = \left\lfloor \frac{c}{a} \right\rfloor \qquad \text{if } a < 0 \qquad (10)$$

$$\mathsf{abv}_{atom}(\vec{a} \cdot \vec{x} \leq c, x_i) = -\infty \qquad \text{if } a_i = 0 \vee \exists j: i \neq j \wedge a_j \neq 0 \wedge a_i > 0 \qquad (11)$$

Based on blw_{atom} and abv_{atom} and using the FA framework, we define the functions blw and abv estimating the c for general formulae c-best from below and above as

$$\mathsf{blw}(\varphi, y) = \mathsf{FA}(\varphi, y, \mathsf{blw}_{atom}, \min), \quad \mathsf{abv}(\varphi, y) = \mathsf{FA}(\varphi, y, \mathsf{abv}_{atom}, \max). \qquad (12)$$

For a formula $\psi = \exists y(\varphi(\vec{x}, y) \wedge y \equiv_m k)$, the simplification algorithm then determines whether φ is c-monotone for some c, which is done using the abv and blw functions. In particular, if $\mathsf{blw}(\varphi, y) = c$ for some $c \in \mathbb{Z} \cup \{\pm\infty\}$, we have that φ is c-best from below w.r.t. y (analogously for abv). Then, in the positive case and if $c \in \mathbb{Z}$, we apply Lemma 5 to simplify the formula ψ. If ψ is of the simple form $\exists y(\varphi(\vec{x}, y))$ where φ is c-monotone w.r.t. y, we can directly use Lemma 4 to simplify ψ to $\varphi[y/c]$.

Example 4. Consider the formula $\psi = \exists y(x - y \leq 1 \wedge y \leq -1 \wedge y \equiv_5 0)$. In order to simplify ψ, we first need to check if the formula $\varphi(x, y) = x - y \leq 1 \wedge y \leq -1$ is c-monotone. Using blw, we can deduce that $\mathsf{blw}(x - y \leq 1, y) = \infty$, $\mathsf{blw}(y \leq -1, y) = -1$, and hence $\mathsf{blw}(\varphi, y) = -1$ meaning that φ is (-1)-best from below w.r.t. y ($\mathsf{abv}(\varphi, y)$ is undefined). Lemma 5 yields that ψ is equivalent to $x \leq -4$ (using $c' = -5$). $\qquad \square$

7.2 Range-Based Quantifier Instantiation

Similarly as in Cooper's elimination algoroithm [23], we can compute the *range* of possible values for a given variable y and instantiating y with all values in the range. For instance, $\exists y(y \leq 2 \wedge 2y \geq 3 \wedge x + 3y = 42)$ can be simplified into $x = 36$.

To obtain the range of possible values of y in the formula φ, we use the formula analysis framework with the following function range_{atom} (whose result is an interval of integers) defined for atomic formulae as follows:

$$\mathsf{range}_{atom}(a \cdot y \leq c, y) = \left(-\infty, \left\lfloor \frac{c}{a} \right\rfloor \right] \qquad \text{if } a > 0 \qquad (13)$$

$$\mathsf{range}_{atom}(a \cdot y \leq c, y) = \left[\left\lceil \frac{c}{a} \right\rceil, +\infty \right) \qquad \text{if } a < 0 \qquad (14)$$

$$\mathsf{range}_{atom}(\vec{a} \cdot \vec{x} \leq c, x_i) = \left(-\infty, +\infty \right) \qquad \text{if } \exists j, k: j \neq k \wedge a_j \neq 0 \wedge a_k \neq 0 \qquad (15)$$

We then employ our formula analysis framework to get the range of y in φ using the function $\mathsf{range}(\varphi, y) = \mathsf{FA}(\varphi, y, \mathsf{range}_{atom}, \cap)$.

Lemma 6. *Let* $\psi = \exists y(\varphi(\vec{x}, y))$ *be a formula such that* $\mathsf{range}(\varphi, y) = [a, b]$ *with* $a, b \in \mathbb{Z}$. *Then* ψ *is equivalent to the formula* $\bigvee_{a \leq c \leq b} \varphi[y/c]$.

Proof. It suffices to notice that for all $c \notin [a, b]$ we have $[\![\varphi(\vec{x}, c)]\!] = \emptyset$. □

In our decision procedure, given a formula $\psi = \exists y(\varphi(\vec{x}, y))$, if $\mathsf{range}(\varphi, y) = [a, b]$ for $a, b \in \mathbb{Z}$ and $b - a \leq N$ for a parameter N (set by the user), we simplify ψ to $\bigvee_{a \leq c \leq b} \varphi[y/c]$. In our experiments, we set $N = 0$.

7.3   Modulo Linearization

The next optimization is more complex and helps mainly in practical cases in the benchmarks containing congruences with large moduli. It does not substitute the value of a variable by a constant, but, instead, substitutes a congruence with an equation.

Let $\varphi = \exists y \exists m(\psi \wedge y + m \equiv_{37} 12)$ such that ψ is 17-best from below w.r.t. y and $\mathsf{range}(\psi, m) = [1, 50]$. Since the modulo constraint $y + m \equiv_{37} 12$ contains two variables (y and m), we cannot use the optimization from Sect. 7.1. From the modulo constraint and the fact that ψ is 17-best from below w.r.t. y, we can infer that it is sufficient to consider y only in the interval $[-19, 17]$ (we obtained -19 as $17 - 37 + 1$). The reason is that any other y can be mapped to a y' from the same congruence class (modulo 37) that is in the interval and, therefore, gives the same result in the modulo constraint. This, together with the other fact (i.e., $\mathsf{range}(\psi, m) = [1, 50]$) tells us that it is sufficient to only consider the (possibly multiple) linear relations between y and m in the rectangle $[-19, 17] \times [1, 50]$ (cf. Fig. 9). The modulo constraint can, therefore, be substituted by the linear relations to obtain the formula

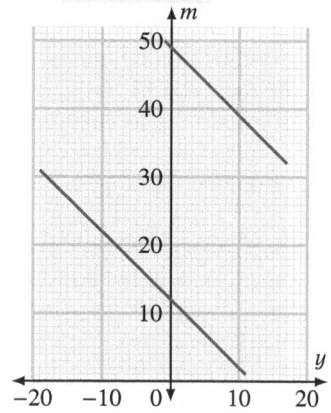

Fig. 9. Modulo linearization.

$$\exists y \exists m(\psi \wedge ((y \geq -19 \wedge y \leq 11 \wedge y + m = 12) \vee (y \geq -1 \wedge y \leq 17 \wedge y + m = 49))). \quad (16)$$

Although the formula seems more complex than the original one, it avoids the large FA to be generated for the modulo constraint (a modulo constraint with $\equiv_k$ needs an FA with k states) and, instead, generates the usually much smaller FAs for the (in)equalities.

The general rewriting rule can be given by the following lemma:

Lemma 7. *Let* $\psi(\vec{x}, y, m)$ *be a formula s.t.* $\mathsf{range}(\psi, m) = [r, s]$ *for* $r, s \in \mathbb{Z}$, *let* $\varphi = \exists y \exists m(\psi \wedge a_y \cdot y + a_m \cdot m \equiv_M k)$, *with* $a_y \neq 0 \neq a_m$, *and* $\alpha = \frac{M}{\gcd(a_y, M)}$. *If* ψ *is c-best from below w.r.t.* y, *then* φ *is equivalent to the formula*

$$\exists y \exists m \left(\psi \wedge \left(\bigvee_{i=0}^{N-1} a_y \cdot y + a_m \cdot m = k + (\ell_1 + i) \cdot \alpha\right)\right) \quad (17)$$

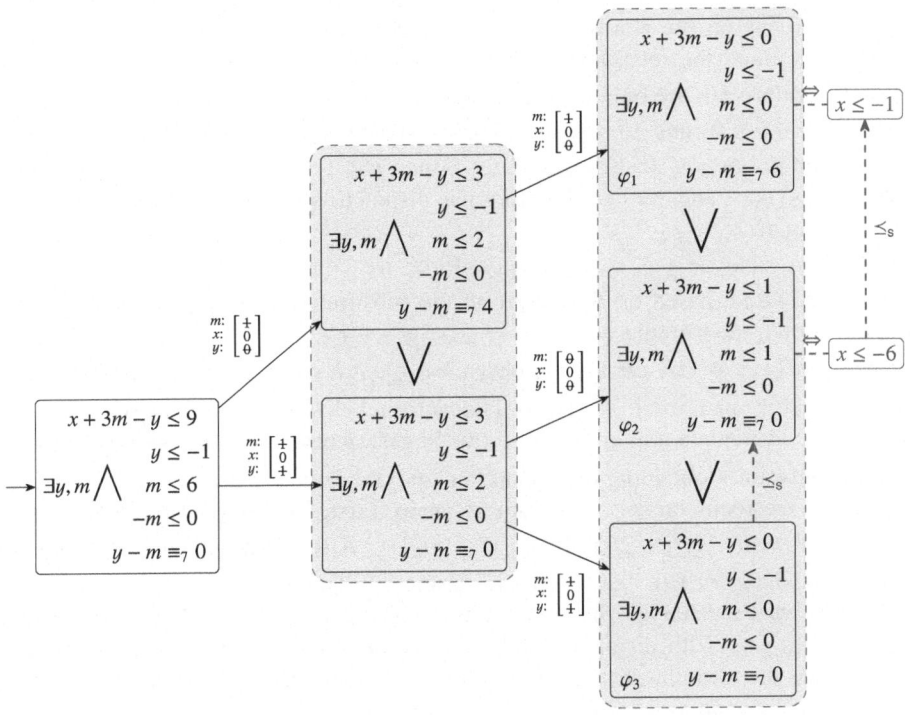

Fig. 10. Fragment of the generated space for the formula in the example.

where

$$\ell_1 = \begin{cases} \left\lceil \frac{a_y \cdot (c-\alpha+1) + a_m \cdot r - k}{\alpha} \right\rceil & for \ \frac{a_m}{a_y} > 0 \\ \left\lceil \frac{a_y \cdot (c-\alpha+1) + a_m \cdot s - k}{\alpha} \right\rceil & for \ \frac{a_m}{a_y} < 0 \end{cases}, y_1 = \begin{cases} \frac{k + \ell_1 \cdot \alpha - a_m \cdot r}{a_y} & for \ \frac{a_m}{a_y} > 0 \\ \frac{k + \ell_1 \cdot \alpha - a_m \cdot s}{a_y} & for \ \frac{a_m}{a_y} < 0 \end{cases}, \tag{18}$$

and

$$N = \left\lceil \frac{a_y(c - y_1) + a_m(s - r) + 1}{\alpha} \right\rceil. \tag{19}$$

Due to space constraints, we omit a similar lemma for the case when ψ is c-best from above. In our implementation, we use the linearization if the N from Lemma 7 is 1, which is sufficient with many practical cases with large moduli.

8   A Comprehensive Example of Our Optimizations

Consider the formula

$$\exists y, m(x + 3m - y \leq 9 \wedge y \leq -1 \wedge m \leq 6 \wedge -m \leq 0 \wedge y - m \equiv_7 0) \tag{20}$$

and see Fig. 10 for a part of the generated FA (for simplicity, we only consider a fragment of the constructed automaton to demonstrate our technique).

Let us focus on the configuration after reading the word x: [0][0]: $\varphi_1 \vee \varphi_2 \vee \varphi_3$. First, we examine the relation between φ_2 and φ_3. We notice that the two formulae look similar with the only difference being in two pairs of atoms: $x + 3m - y \le 1$ and $x + 3m - y \le 0$, and $m \le 1$ and $m \le 0$ respectively. Since $0 \le 1$ there are structural subsumptions $x + 3m - y \le 0 \preceq_s x + 3m - y \le 1$ and $m \le 0 \preceq_s m \le 1$, which yields $\varphi_3 \preceq_s \varphi_2$, and we can therefore use disjunction pruning (Sect. 6) to simplify $\varphi_1 \vee \varphi_2 \vee \varphi_3$ to $\varphi_1 \vee \varphi_2$.

Next, we analyze $\varphi_1 = \exists y, m(\psi_1)$. First, we compute $\mathsf{range}(\psi_1, m) = [0, 0]$ (cf. Sect. 7.2) and, based on that, perform the substitution $\psi_1[m/0]$, obtaining (after simplifications) the formula $\psi_1' = x - y \le 0 \wedge y \le -1 \wedge y \equiv_7 6$. Then, we analyze the behaviour of y in ψ_1' by computing $\mathsf{blw}(x - y \le 0 \wedge y \le -1, y) = -1$. Based on this, we know that $x - y \le 0 \wedge y \le -1$ is (-1)-best from below (cf. Sect. 7.1), so we can use Lemma 5 to instantiate y in ψ_1' with -5 (the largest number less than -1 satisfying the modulo constraint), obtaining the (quantifier-free) formula $x \le -1$.

Finally, we focus on $\varphi_2 = \exists y, m(\psi_2)$ again. First, we compute $\mathsf{range}(\psi_2, m) = [0, 1]$ and rewrite φ_2 to $\exists y(\psi_2[m/0] \vee \psi_2[m/1])$. After antiprenexing, this will be changed to $\exists y(\psi_2[m/0]) \vee \exists y(\psi_2[m/1])$. Using similar reasoning as in the previous paragraph, we can analyze the two disjuncts in the formula to obtain the formula $x \le -6 \vee x \le -8$. With disjunction pruning, we obtain the final result of simplification of φ_2 as the formula $x \le -6$. In the end, again using disjunction pruning (Sect. 6), the whole formula $\varphi_1 \vee \varphi_2 \vee \varphi_3$ can be simplified to $x \le -1$.

9 Experimental Evaluation

We implemented the proposed procedure in a prototype tool called AMAYA [48]. AMAYA is written in Python and contains a basic automata library with alphabets encoded using *multi-terminal binary decision diagrams* (MTBDDs), for which it uses the C-based SYLVAN library [27] (implementation details can be found in [42]). We ran all our experiments on Debian GNU/Linux 12 system with Intel(R) Xeon(R) CPU E5-2620 v3 @ 2.40 GHz and 32 GiB of RAM with the timeout of 60 s.

Tools. We selected the following tools for comparison: Z3 [63] (version 4.12.2), cvc5 [4] (version 1.0.5), PRINCESS [70] (version 2023-06-19), and LASH [80] (version 0.92). Out of these, only LASH is an automata-based LIA solver; the other tools are general purpose SMT solvers with the LIA theory.

Benchmarks. Our main benchmark comes from SMT-LIB [5], in particular, the categories LIA [72] and NIA (nonlinear integer arithmetic) [73]. We concentrate on formulae in directories UltimateAutomizer and (20190429-)UltimateAutomizer Svcomp2019 of these categories (the main difference between LIA and NIA is that LIA formulae are not allowed to use the modulo operator) and remove formulae from NIA that contain multiplication between variables, giving us 372 formulae. We denote this benchmark as SMT-LIB. The formulae come from verification of real-world C programs using Ultimate Automizer [46]. Other benchmarks in the categories, tptp and psyco, were omitted. Namely, `tptp` is easy for all tools (every tool finished within 1.3 s on each formula). The `psyco` benchmark resembles Boolean reasoning more than integer reasoning. In particular, its formulae contain simple integer constraints (e.g., $x = y + 1$ or just $x = y$) and complex Boolean structure with `ite` operators and quantified Boolean variables. Our prototype is not optimized for these features, but with a naive implementation of unwinding of `ite` and with encoding of Boolean variables in a special automaton track, AMAYA could solve 46 out of the 196 formulae in `psyco`.

Our second benchmark consists of the *Frobenius coin problem* [41] asking the following question: Given a pair of coins of certain coprime denominations a and b, what is the largest number not obtainable as a sum of values of these coins? Or, as a formula,

$$\varphi(p) \overset{\text{def}}{\Leftrightarrow} (\forall x, y\colon p \neq ax + by) \wedge (\forall r(\neg\exists u, v\colon r = au + bv) \Rightarrow r \leq p). \qquad (21)$$

Each formula is specified by a pair of denominations (a, b), e.g., $(3, 7)$ for which the model is 11. Apart from theoretical interest, the Frobenius coin problem can be used, e.g., for liveness checking of markings of conservative weighted circuits (a variant of Petri nets) [22] or reasoning about automata with counters [50,52,78]. We created a family of 55 formulae encoding the problem with various increasing coin denominations. We denote this benchmark as `Frobenius`. The input format of the benchmarks is SMT-LIB [5], which all tools can handle except LASH—for this, we implemented a simple translator in AMAYA for translating LIA problems in SMT-LIB into LASH's input format (the time of translation is not included in the runtime of LASH).

Results. We show the results in Table 1. For each benchmark we show the run time statistics together with the number of timeouts and the number of wins/losses for each competitor of AMAYA (e.g., the value "354 (40)" in the row for PRINCESS in SMT-LIB means that AMAYA was faster than PRINCESS on 354 SMT-LIB formulae and in 40 cases out of these, this was because PRINCESS timed out). Note that statistics about times tend to be biased in favour of tools that timed out more since the timeouts are not counted.

The first part of the table contains automata-based solvers and the second part contains general SMT solvers. We also measure the effect of our optimizations against AMAYA$_{\text{noopt}}$, a version of the tool that only performs the classical automata-based procedure from Sect. 3 without our optimizations.

Table 1. Comparison of solvers on formulae from the SMT-LIB and the Frobenius benchmark. Times are given in seconds. The columns **wins** and **losses** show numbers of formulae where AMAYA performed better and worse (wins/losses caused by timeouts are in parentheses).

solver	SMT-LIB (372)								Frobenius (55)							
	timeouts	mean	median	std. dev.	wins		losses		timeouts	mean	median	std. dev.	wins		losses	
AMAYA	17	1.12	0.26	3.58					5	11.79	3.54	16.03				
AMAYA$_{\text{noopt}}$	73	2.32	0.27	8.16	232	(56)	113	(0)	5	11.54	4.06	14.65	27	(0)	21	(0)
LASH	114	3.04	**0.01**	9.94	178	(98)	178	(1)	9	15.72	5.74	20.32	37	(5)	14	(0)
Z3	31	**0.11**	**0.01**	1.35	31	(28)	338	(14)	51	1.66	0.49	2.69	48	(46)	2	(0)
cvc5	28	0.20	0.02	2.42	32	(28)	340	(17)	54	**0.05**	**0.05**	—	49	(49)	1	(0)
PRINCESS	50	4.14	1.14	9.31	354	(40)	8	(7)	13	46.32	45.92	29.03	50	(8)	0	(0)

Discussion. In the comparison with other SMT solvers, from Table 1, automata-based approaches are clearly superior to current SMT solvers on Frobenius (confirming the conjecture made in [41]). cvc5 fails already for denominations $(3, 5)$ (where the result is 7) and Z3 follows suite soon; Princess can solve significantly more formulae than Z3 and cvc5, but is still clearly dominated by Amaya. Details can be found in [42].

On the SMT-LIB benchmark, Amaya can solve the most formulae among all tools. It has 17 timeouts, followed by cvc5 with 28 timeouts (out of 372 formulae). On individual examples, the comparison of Amaya against Z3 and cvc5 almost always falls under one of the two cases: (i) the solver is one or two orders of magnitude faster than Amaya or (ii) the solver times out. This probably corresponds to specific heuristics of Z3 and cvc5 taking effect or not, while Amaya has a more robust performance, but is still a prototype and nowhere near as optimized. The performance of Princess is, however, usually much worse. Amaya is often complementary to the SMT solvers and was able to solve 6 formulae that no SMT solver did.

Comparison with Amaya$_{\text{noopt}}$ (cf. Fig. 11) shows that the optimizations introduced in this paper have a profound effect on the number of solved cases (which is a proper superset of the cases solved without them). This is most visible on the SMT-LIB benchmark, where Amaya has 56 TOs less than Amaya$_{\text{noopt}}$. On the Frobenius benchmark, the results of Amaya$_{\text{noopt}}$ and Amaya are comparable. Our optimizations had limited impact here since the formulae are built only from a small number of simple atoms (cf. Eq. (21)). In some cases, Amaya takes even longer than Amaya$_{\text{noopt}}$; this is because the lazy construction explores parts of the state space that would be pruned by the classical construction (e.g., when doing an intersection with a minimized FA with an empty language). This could be possibly solved by algebraic rules tailored for lightweight unsatisfiability checking.

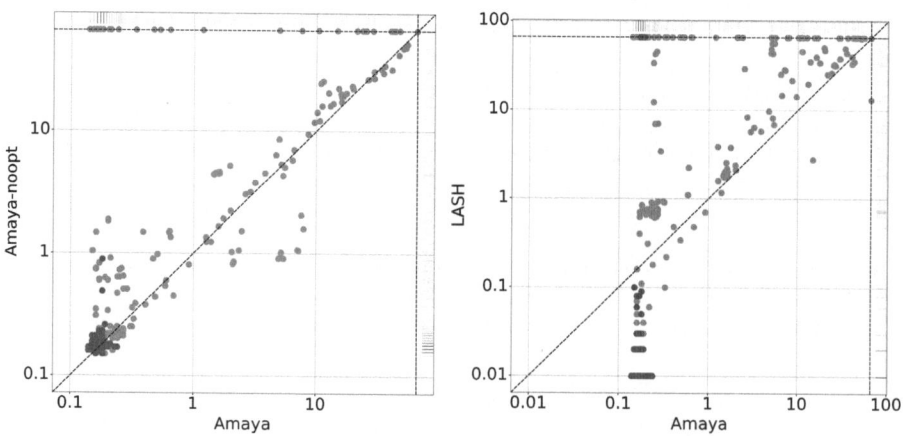

Fig. 11. Comparison of automata-based LIA solvers on formulae from SMT-LIB: •UltimateAutomizer (153), •UltimateAutomizerSvcomp2019 (219) and •Frobenius Coin Problem (55). Times are in seconds, axes are logarithmic. Dashed lines represent timeouts (60 s).

We also tried to evaluate the effect of individual optimizations by selectively turning them off. It turns out that the most critical optimizations are the *simple rewriting rules* (Sect. 5; when turned off, AMAYA gave additional 33 timeouts) and *quantifier instantiation* (Sect. 7; when turned off, AMAYA gave additional 28 timeouts). On the other hand, surprisingly, turning off *disjunction pruning* (Sect. 6) did not have a significant effect on the result. By itself (without other optimizations), it can help the basic procedure solve some hard formulae, but its effect is diluted when used with the rest of the optimizations. Still, even though it comes with an additional cost, it still has a sufficient effect to compensate for this overhead.

Comparing with the older automata-based solver LASH, AMAYA solves more examples in both benchmarks; LASH has 123 TOs in total compared to 22 TOs of AMAYA. The lower median of LASH on SMT-LIB is partially caused by the facts that (i) LASH is a compiled C code while AMAYA uses a Python frontend, which has a non-negligible overhead and (ii) LASH times out on harder formulae.

10 Related Work

The decidability of Presburger arithmetic was established already at the beginning of the 20th century by Presburger [64] via *quantifier elimination*. Over time, more efficient quantifier-elimination-based decision procedures occurred, such as the one of Cooper [23] or the one used within the Omega test [65] (which can be seen as a variation of Fourier-Motzkin variable elimination for linear real arithmetic [58, Section 5.4]). The complexity bounds of 2-**NEXP**-hardness and 2-**EXPSPACE** membership for satisfiability checking were obtained by Fischer and Rabin [35] and Berman [6] respectively. Quantifier elimination is often considered impractical due to the blow up in the size of the resulting formula. *Counterexample-guided quantifier instantiation* [66] is a proof-theoretical approach to establish (one-shot) satisfiability of LIA formulae, which can be seen as a lazy version of Cooper's algorithm [23]. It is based on approximating a quantified formula by a set of formulae with the approximation being refined in case it is found too coarse. The approach focuses on formulae with one alternation, but is also extended to any number of alternations (according to the authors, the procedure was implemented in CVC4).

The first *automata-based* decision procedure for Presburger arithmetic can be obtained from Büchi's decision procedure for the second-order logic WS1S [17] by noticing that addition is WS1S-definable. A similar construction for LIA is used by Wolper and Boigelot in [79], except that they avoid performing explicit automata product constructions by using the notion of *concurrent number automata*, which are essentially tuples of synchronized FAs.

Boudet and Comon [13] propose a more direct construction of automata for atomic constraints of the form $a_1 x_1 + \ldots + a_n x_n \sim c$ (for $\sim \in \{=, \leq\}$) over natural numbers; we use a construction similar to theirs extended to integers (as used, e.g., in [29]). Moreover, they give a direct construction for a conjunction of equations, which can be seen as a special case of our construction from Sect. 4. Wolper and Boigelot in [80] discuss optimizations of the procedure from [13] (they use the *most-significant bit first* encoding though), in particular how to remove some states in the construction for automata for inequations based on subsumption obtained syntactically from the formula representing the state (a restricted version of disjunction pruning, cf. Sect. 6). The works [9–12] extend the techniques from [80] to solve the mixed *linear integer real arithmetic* (LIRA) using weak Büchi automata, implemented in LASH [1].

WS1S [17] is a closely related logic with an automata-based procedure similar to the one discussed in this paper (as mentioned above, Presburger arithmetic can be encoded into WS1S). The automata-based decision procedure for WS1S is, however, of nonelementary complexity (which is also a lower bound for the logic), it was, however, postulated that the sizes of the obtained automata (when reduced or minimized) describing Presburger-definable sets of integers are bounded by a tower of exponentials of a fixed height. (3-**EXPSPACE**). This postulate was proven by Klaedtke [55] (refined later by Durand-Gasselin and Habermehl [29] who show that all automata during the construction do not exceed size 3-**EXP**). The automata-based decision procedure for WS1S itself has been a subject of extensive study, making many pioneering contributions in the area of automata engineering [31–34,39,44,45,47,56,57,75], showcasing in the well-known tool MONA [31,47,56,57].

Acknowledgments. This work has been supported by the Czech Ministry of Education, Youth and Sports ERC.CZ project LL1908, the Czech Science Foundation project 23-07565S, and the FIT BUT internal project FIT-S-23-8151.

Data Availability Statement. An environment with the tools and data used for the experimental evaluation in the current study is available at [43].

References

1. The Liège automata-based symbolic handler (LASH). https://people.montefiore.uliege.be/boigelot/research/lash/
2. Abdulla, P.A., et al.: Trau: SMT solver for string constraints. In: Bjørner, N.S., Gurfinkel, A. (eds.) 2018 Formal Methods in Computer Aided Design, FMCAD 2018, Austin, TX, USA, October 30 – November 2, 2018, pp. 1–5. IEEE (2018). https://doi.org/10.23919/FMCAD.2018.8602997
3. Antimirov, V.: Partial derivatives of regular expressions and finite automaton constructions. Theoret. Comput. Sci. **155**(2), 291–319 (1996). https://doi.org/10.1016/0304-3975(95)00182-4, http://www.sciencedirect.com/science/article/pii/0304397595001824
4. Barbosa, H., et al.: cvc5: a versatile and industrial-strength SMT solver. In: Fisman, D., Rosu, G. (eds.) ETAPS 2022, Part I. LNCS, vol. 13243, pp. 415–442. Springer (2022). https://doi.org/10.1007/978-3-030-99524-9_24
5. Barrett, C., Fontaine, P., Tinelli, C.: The Satisfiability Modulo Theories Library (SMT-LIB) (2016). www.SMT-LIB.org
6. Berman, L.: The complexity of logical theories. Theoret. Comput. Sci. **11**(1), 71–77 (1980). https://doi.org/10.1016/0304-3975(80)90037-7
7. Berzish, M., et al.: Towards more efficient methods for solving regular-expression heavy string constraints. Theor. Comput. Sci. **943**, 50–72 (2023). https://doi.org/10.1016/j.tcs.2022.12.009

8. Blahoudek, F., et al.: Word equations in synergy with regular constraints. In: Chechik, M., Katoen, J.P., Leucker, M. (eds.) FM 2023. LNCS, vol. 14000, pp. 403–423. Springer, Cham (2023). https://doi.org/10.1007/978-3-031-27481-7_23

9. Boigelot, B., Jodogne, S., Wolper, P.: On the use of weak automata for deciding linear arithmetic with integer and real variables. In: Goré, R., Leitsch, A., Nipkow, T. (eds.) IJCAR 2001. LNCS, vol. 2083, pp. 611–625. Springer, Heidelberg (2001). https://doi.org/10.1007/3-540-45744-5_50

10. Boigelot, B., Jodogne, S., Wolper, P.: An effective decision procedure for linear arithmetic over the integers and reals. ACM Trans. Comput. Log. **6**(3), 614–633 (2005). https://doi.org/10.1145/1071596.1071601

11. Boigelot, B., Rassart, S., Wolper, P.: On the expressiveness of real and integer arithmetic automata. In: Larsen, K.G., Skyum, S., Winskel, G. (eds.) ICALP 1998. LNCS, vol. 1443, pp. 152–163. Springer, Heidelberg (1998). https://doi.org/10.1007/BFb0055049

12. Boigelot, B., Wolper, P.: Representing arithmetic constraints with finite automata: an overview. In: Stuckey, P.J. (ed.) ICLP 2002. LNCS, vol. 2401, pp. 1–20. Springer, Heidelberg (2002). https://doi.org/10.1007/3-540-45619-8_1

13. Boudet, A., Comon, H.: Diophantine equations, Presburger arithmetic and finite automata. In: Kirchner, H. (ed.) CAAP 1996. LNCS, vol. 1059, pp. 30–43. Springer, Heidelberg (1996). https://doi.org/10.1007/3-540-61064-2_27

14. Brzozowski, J.A.: Canonical regular expressions and minimal state graphs for definite events. In: Proceedings of the Symposium Mathematics Theory of Automata (New York, 1962), Microwave Research Institute Symposia Series, Brooklyn, NY, vol. XII, pp. 529–561. Polytechnic (1963)

15. Brzozowski, J.A.: Derivatives of regular expressions. J. ACM **11**(4), 481–494 (1964). https://doi.org/10.1145/321239.321249

16. Büchi, J.R.: On a decision method in restricted second order arithmetic. In: Proceedings of International Congress on Logic, Method, and Philosophy of Science 1960. Stanford Univ. Press, Stanford (1962)

17. Büchi, J.R.: Weak second-order arithmetic and finite automata. Zeitscrift fur mathematische Logic und Grundlagen der Mathematik **6**, 66–92 (1960)

18. Chen, T., et al.: Solving string constraints with regex-dependent functions through transducers with priorities and variables. Proc. ACM Program. Lang. **6**(POPL), 1–31 (2022). https://doi.org/10.1145/3498707

19. Chen, Y.F., Chocholatý, D., Havlena, V., Holík, L., Lengál, O., Síč, J.: Solving string constraints with lengths by stabilization. Proc. ACM Program. Lang. **7**(OOPSLA2) (oct 2023). https://doi.org/10.1145/3622872

20. Chen, Y.F., Chocholatý, D., Havlena, V., Holík, L., Lengál, O., Síč, J.: Z3-noodler: an automata-based string solver (technical report). CoRR **abs/2310.08327** (2023). https://doi.org/10.48550/arXiv.2310.08327

21. Chocholatý, D., et al.: Mata: a fast and simple finite automata library (technical report). CoRR abs/2310.10136 (2023). https://doi.org/10.48550/arXiv.2310.10136, To appear at TACAS'23

22. Chrzastowski-Wachtel, P., Raczunas, M.: Liveness of weighted circuits and the diophantine problem of Frobenius. In: Ésik, Z. (ed.) FCT 1993. LNCS, vol. 710, pp. 171–180. Springer, Heidelberg (1993). https://doi.org/10.1007/3-540-57163-9_13

23. Cooper, D.: Theorem proving in arithmetic without multiplication. Mach. Intell. **7**, 91–99 (1972)

24. Cox, A., Leasure, J.: Model checking regular language constraints. CoRR abs/1708.09073 (2017)

25. Dantzig, G.B.: Inductive proof of the simplex method. IBM J. Res. Dev. **4**(5), 505–506 (1960). https://doi.org/10.1147/RD.45.0505

26. Detlefs, D., Nelson, G., Saxe, J.B.: Simplify: a theorem prover for program checking. J. ACM **52**(3), 365–473 (2005). https://doi.org/10.1145/1066100.1066102
27. van Dijk, T., van de Pol, J.: SYLVAN: multi-core framework for decision diagrams. Int. J. Softw. Tools Technol. Transf. **19**(6), 675–696 (2017). https://doi.org/10.1007/s10009-016-0433-2
28. Doyen, L., Raskin, J.-F.: Antichain algorithms for finite automata. In: Esparza, J., Majumdar, R. (eds.) TACAS 2010. LNCS, vol. 6015, pp. 2–22. Springer, Heidelberg (2010). https://doi.org/10.1007/978-3-642-12002-2_2
29. Durand-Gasselin, A., Habermehl, P.: On the use of non-deterministic automata for Presburger arithmetic. In: Gastin, P., Laroussinie, F. (eds.) CONCUR 2010. LNCS, vol. 6269, pp. 373–387. Springer, Heidelberg (2010). https://doi.org/10.1007/978-3-642-15375-4_26
30. Egly, U.: On the value of antiprenexing. In: Pfenning, F. (ed.) LPAR 1994. LNCS, vol. 822, pp. 69–83. Springer, Heidelberg (1994). https://doi.org/10.1007/3-540-58216-9_30
31. Elgaard, J., Klarlund, N., Møller, A.: MONA 1.x: new techniques for WS1S and WS2S. In: Hu, A.J., Vardi, M.Y. (eds.) CAV 1998. LNCS, vol. 1427, pp. 516–520. Springer, Heidelberg (1998). https://doi.org/10.1007/BFb0028773
32. Fiedor, T., Holík, L., Janků, P., Lengál, O., Vojnar, T.: Lazy automata techniques for WS1S. In: Legay, A., Margaria, T. (eds.) TACAS 2017. LNCS, vol. 10205, pp. 407–425. Springer, Heidelberg (2017). https://doi.org/10.1007/978-3-662-54577-5_24
33. Fiedor, T., Holík, L., Lengál, O., Vojnar, T.: Nested antichains for WS1S. In: Baier, C., Tinelli, C. (eds.) TACAS 2015. LNCS, vol. 9035, pp. 658–674. Springer, Heidelberg (2015). https://doi.org/10.1007/978-3-662-46681-0_59
34. Fiedor, T., Holík, L., Lengál, O., Vojnar, T.: Nested antichains for WS1S. Acta Informatica **56**(3), 205–228 (2019). https://doi.org/10.1007/s00236-018-0331-z
35. Fischer, M.J., Rabin, M.O.: Super-exponential complexity of Presburger arithmetic. In: Proceedings of the SIAM-AMS Symposium in Applied Mathematics, vol. 7, pp. 27—41 (1974)
36. Ge, Y., de Moura, L.: Complete instantiation for quantified formulas in satisfiabiliby modulo theories. In: Bouajjani, A., Maler, O. (eds.) CAV 2009. LNCS, vol. 5643, pp. 306–320. Springer, Heidelberg (2009). https://doi.org/10.1007/978-3-642-02658-4_25
37. Ghilardi, S., Nicolini, E., Ranise, S., Zucchelli, D.: Decision procedures for extensions of the theory of arrays. Ann. Math. Artif. Intell. **50**(3–4), 231–254 (2007). https://doi.org/10.1007/s10472-007-9078-x
38. van Glabbeek, R., Ploeger, B.: Five determinisation algorithms. In: Ibarra, O.H., Ravikumar, B. (eds.) CIAA 2008. LNCS, vol. 5148, pp. 161–170. Springer, Heidelberg (2008). https://doi.org/10.1007/978-3-540-70844-5_17
39. Glenn, J., Gasarch, W.: Implementing WS1S via finite automata. In: Raymond, D., Wood, D., Yu, S. (eds.) WIA 1996. LNCS, vol. 1260, pp. 50–63. Springer, Heidelberg (1997). https://doi.org/10.1007/3-540-63174-7_5
40. Google: RE2. https://github.com/google/re2
41. Haase, C.: A survival guide to Presburger arithmetic. ACM SIGLOG News **5**(3), 67–82 (2018). https://doi.org/10.1145/3242953.3242964
42. Habermehl, P., Havlena, V., Holík, L., Hečko, M., Lengál, O.: Algebraic reasoning meets automata in solving linear integer arithmetic (technical report). CoRR abs/2403.18995 (2024). https://doi.org/10.48550/arXiv.2403.18995
43. Habermehl, P., Havlena, V., Holík, L., Hečko, M., Lengál, O.: Artifact for the cav'24 paper "Algebraic reasoning meets automata in solving linear integer arithmetic" (2024). https://doi.org/10.5281/zenodo.10996343
44. Havlena, V., Holík, L., Lengál, O., Vales, O., Vojnar, T.: Antiprenexing for WSkS: a little goes a long way. In: Albert, E., Kovács, L. (eds.) LPAR 2020: 23rd International Conference

on Logic for Programming, Artificial Intelligence and Reasoning, Alicante, Spain, May 22–27, 2020. EPiC Series in Computing, vol. 73, pp. 298–316. EasyChair (2020). https://doi.org/10.29007/6bfc

45. Havlena, V., Holík, L., Lengál, O., Vojnar, T.: Automata terms in a lazy WSkS decision procedure. In: Fontaine, P. (ed.) CADE 2019. LNCS (LNAI), vol. 11716, pp. 300–318. Springer, Cham (2019). https://doi.org/10.1007/978-3-030-29436-6_18

46. Heizmann, M., Hoenicke, J., Podelski, A.: Software model checking for people who love automata. In: Sharygina, N., Veith, H. (eds.) CAV 2013. LNCS, vol. 8044, pp. 36–52. Springer, Heidelberg (2013). https://doi.org/10.1007/978-3-642-39799-8_2

47. Henriksen, J.G., et al.: Mona: monadic second-order logic in practice. In: Brinksma, E., Cleaveland, W.R., Larsen, K.G., Margaria, T., Steffen, B. (eds.) TACAS 1995. LNCS, vol. 1019, pp. 89–110. Springer, Heidelberg (1995). https://doi.org/10.1007/3-540-60630-0_5

48. Hečko, M.: AMAYA (2024). https://github.com/MichalHe/amaya

49. Hieronymi, P., Ma, D., Oei, R., Schaeffer, L., Schulz, C., Shallit, J.O.: Decidability for Sturmian words. In: Manea, F., Simpson, A. (eds.) 30th EACSL Annual Conference on Computer Science Logic, CSL 2022, February 14-19, 2022, Göttingen, Germany (Virtual Conference). LIPIcs, vol. 216, pp. 24:1–24:23. Schloss Dagstuhl - Leibniz-Zentrum für Informatik (2022). https://doi.org/10.4230/LIPICS.CSL.2022.24

50. Holík, L., Lengál, O., Saarikivi, O., Turoňová, L., Veanes, M., Vojnar, T.: Succinct determinisation of counting automata via sphere construction. In: Lin, A.W. (ed.) APLAS 2019. LNCS, vol. 11893, pp. 468–489. Springer, Cham (2019). https://doi.org/10.1007/978-3-030-34175-6_24

51. Hopcroft, J.: An n log n algorithm for minimizing states in a finite automaton. In: Theory of Machines and Computations (Proc. Internat. Sympos., Technion, Haifa, 1971), pp. 189–196. Academic Press, New York-London (1971)

52. Hu, D., Wu, Z.: String constraints with regex-counting and string-length solved more efficiently. In: Hermanns, H., Sun, J., Bu, L. (eds.) SETTA 2023. LNCS, vol. 14464, pp. 1–20. Springer, Cham (2023). https://doi.org/10.1007/978-981-99-8664-4_1

53. Hyperscan.io (2021). https://www.hyperscan.io/

54. Jonáš, M., Strejček, J.: Q3B: an efficient BDD-based SMT solver for quantified bit-vectors. In: Dillig, I., Tasiran, S. (eds.) CAV 2019. LNCS, vol. 11562, pp. 64–73. Springer, Cham (2019). https://doi.org/10.1007/978-3-030-25543-5_4

55. Klaedtke, F.: Bounds on the automata size for presburger arithmetic. ACM Trans. Comput. Log. 9(2), 11:1-11:34 (2008). https://doi.org/10.1145/1342991.1342995

56. Klarlund, N.: A theory of restrictions for logics and automata. In: Halbwachs, N., Peled, D. (eds.) CAV 1999. LNCS, vol. 1633, pp. 406–417. Springer, Heidelberg (1999). https://doi.org/10.1007/3-540-48683-6_35

57. Klarlund, N., Møller, A., Schwartzbach, M.I.: Mona implementation secrets. Int. J. Found. Comput. Sci. 13(4), 571–586 (2002)

58. Kroening, D., Strichman, O.: Decision Procedures - An Algorithmic Point of View, Second Edition. Texts in Theoretical Computer Science. An EATCS Series. Springer, Heidelberg (2016). https://doi.org/10.1007/978-3-662-50497-0

59. Kuncak, V., Mayer, M., Piskac, R., Suter, P.: Software synthesis procedures. Commun. ACM 55(2), 103–111 (2012). https://doi.org/10.1145/2076450.2076472

60. Kuper, G.M., Libkin, L., Paredaens, J. (eds.): Constraint Databases. Springer, Heidelberg (2000). https://doi.org/10.1007/978-3-662-04031-7

61. Monniaux, D.: Automatic modular abstractions for linear constraints. In: Shao, Z., Pierce, B.C. (eds.) Proceedings of the 36th ACM SIGPLAN-SIGACT Symposium on Principles of Programming Languages, POPL 2009, Savannah, GA, USA, January 21-23, 2009. pp. 140–151. ACM (2009). https://doi.org/10.1145/1480881.1480899

62. Moseley, D., et al.: Derivative based nonbacktracking real-world regex matching with backtracking semantics. Proc. ACM Program. Lang. **7**(PLDI), 1026–1049 (2023). https://doi.org/10.1145/3591262

63. de Moura, L., Bjørner, N.: Z3: an efficient SMT solver. In: Ramakrishnan, C.R., Rehof, J. (eds.) TACAS 2008. LNCS, vol. 4963, pp. 337–340. Springer, Heidelberg (2008). https://doi.org/10.1007/978-3-540-78800-3_24

64. Presburger, M.: Über die vollständigkeit eines gewissen systems der arithmetik ganzer zahlen, in welchem die addition als einzige operation hervortritt. In: Comptes Rendus du I congrès de Mathématiciens des Pays Slaves, pp. 92—101 (1929)

65. Pugh, W.W.: The omega test: a fast and practical integer programming algorithm for dependence analysis. In: Martin, J.L. (ed.) Proceedings Supercomputing '91, Albuquerque, NM, USA, November 18–22, 1991, pp. 4–13. ACM (1991). https://doi.org/10.1145/125826.125848

66. Reynolds, A., King, T., Kuncak, V.: Solving quantified linear arithmetic by counterexample-guided instantiation. Formal Methods Syst. Des. **51**(3), 500–532 (2017). https://doi.org/10.1007/s10703-017-0290-y

67. Reynolds, A., Kuncak, V., Tinelli, C., Barrett, C.W., Deters, M.: Refutation-based synthesis in SMT. Formal Methods Syst. Des. **55**(2), 73–102 (2019). https://doi.org/10.1007/S10703-017-0270-2

68. Reynolds, A., Tinelli, C., de Moura, L.: Finding conflicting instances of quantified formulas in SMT. In: Proceedings of the 14th Conference on Formal Methods in Computer-Aided Design. FMCAD '14, Austin, Texas, pp. 195-202. FMCAD Inc. (2014)

69. Robinson, J.A., Voronkov, A. (eds.): Handbook of Automated Reasoning (in 2 volumes). Elsevier and MIT Press (2001). https://www.sciencedirect.com/book/9780444508133/handbook-of-automated-reasoning

70. Rümmer, P.: A constraint sequent calculus for first-order logic with linear integer arithmetic. In: Cervesato, I., Veith, H., Voronkov, A. (eds.) LPAR 2008. LNCS (LNAI), vol. 5330, pp. 274–289. Springer, Heidelberg (2008). https://doi.org/10.1007/978-3-540-89439-1_20

71. Schuele, T., Schneider, K.: Verification of data paths using unbounded integers: automata strike back. In: Bin, E., Ziv, A., Ur, S. (eds.) HVC 2006. LNCS, vol. 4383, pp. 65–80. Springer, Heidelberg (2007). https://doi.org/10.1007/978-3-540-70889-6_5

72. SMT-LIB: LIA (2023). https://clc-gitlab.cs.uiowa.edu:2443/SMT-LIB-benchmarks/LIA

73. SMT-LIB: NIA (2023). https://clc-gitlab.cs.uiowa.edu:2443/SMT-LIB-benchmarks/NIA

74. Stanford, C., Veanes, M., Bjørner, N.: Symbolic Boolean derivatives for efficiently solving extended regular expression constraints. In: Proceedings of the 42nd ACM SIGPLAN International Conference on Programming Language Design and Implementation. PLDI 2021, New York, NY, USA, pp. 620–635. Association for Computing Machinery (2021). https://doi.org/10.1145/3453483.3454066

75. Topnik, C., Wilhelm, E., Margaria, T., Steffen, B.: jMosel: a stand-alone tool and jABC plugin for M2L(Str). In: Valmari, A. (ed.) SPIN 2006. LNCS, vol. 3925, pp. 293–298. Springer, Heidelberg (2006). https://doi.org/10.1007/11691617_18

76. Traytel, D.: A coalgebraic decision procedure for WS1S. In: Kreutzer, S. (ed.) 24th EACSL Annual Conference on Computer Science Logic, CSL 2015, September 7-10, 2015, Berlin, Germany. LIPIcs, vol. 41, pp. 487–503. Schloss Dagstuhl - Leibniz-Zentrum für Informatik (2015). https://doi.org/10.4230/LIPIcs.CSL.2015.487

77. Traytel, D., Nipkow, T.: Verified decision procedures for MSO on words based on derivatives of regular expressions. J. Funct. Program. **25** (2015). https://doi.org/10.1017/S0956796815000246

78. Turonová, L., Holík, L., Lengál, O., Saarikivi, O., Veanes, M., Vojnar, T.: Regex matching with counting-set automata. Proc. ACM Program. Lang. **4**(OOPSLA), 218:1–218:30 (2020). https://doi.org/10.1145/3428286

79. Wolper, P., Boigelot, B.: An automata-theoretic approach to Presburger arithmetic constraints. In: Mycroft, A. (ed.) SAS 1995. LNCS, vol. 983, pp. 21–32. Springer, Heidelberg (1995). https://doi.org/10.1007/3-540-60360-3_30
80. Wolper, P., Boigelot, B.: On the construction of automata from linear arithmetic constraints. In: Graf, S., Schwartzbach, M. (eds.) TACAS 2000. LNCS, vol. 1785, pp. 1–19. Springer, Heidelberg (2000). https://doi.org/10.1007/3-540-46419-0_1

Distributed SMT Solving Based on Dynamic Variable-Level Partitioning

Mengyu Zhao, Shaowei Cai[✉], and Yuhang Qian

Key Laboratory of System Software (Chinese Academy of Sciences) and State Key Laboratory of Computer Science, Institute of Software, Chinese Academy of Sciences, Beijing, China
{zhaomy,caisw,qianyh}@ios.ac.cn

Abstract. Satisfiability Modulo Theories on arithmetic theories have significant applications in many important domains. Previous efforts have been mainly devoted to improving the techniques and heuristics in sequential SMT solvers. With the development of computing resources, a promising direction to boost performance is parallel and even distributed SMT solving. We explore this potential in a divide-and-conquer view and propose a novel dynamic parallel framework with variable-level partitioning. To the best of our knowledge, this is the first attempt to perform variable-level partitioning for arithmetic theories. Moreover, we enhance the interval constraint propagation algorithm, coordinate it with Boolean propagation, and integrate it into our variable-level partitioning strategy. Our partitioning algorithm effectively capitalizes on propagation information, enabling efficient formula simplification and search space pruning. We apply our method to three state-of-the-art SMT solvers, namely CVC5, OpenSMT2, and Z3, resulting in efficient parallel SMT solvers. Experiments are carried out on benchmarks of linear and non-linear arithmetic over both real and integer variables, and our variable-level partitioning method shows substantial improvements over previous partitioning strategies and is particularly good at non-linear theories.

Keywords: Satisfiability Modulo Theories · Parallel Computing · Partitioning Strategy · Interval Constraint Propagation

1 Introduction

Satisfiability Modulo Theories (SMT) is a critical area of research focusing on the satisfiability of first-order logic formulas. The growth of SMT springs from the success of propositional Satisfiability (SAT) solving in the early 1960s. SMT aims to generalize the achievements of SAT solvers from propositional logic to fragments of first-order logic. The research in SMT has broadened the scope to include more complex logic, such as the theory of equalities and uninterpreted functions, array theory, bit-vector, floating-point arithmetic, difference logic, and linear and non-linear arithmetic.

Our research focuses on *Arithmetic Theories*, which comprise arithmetic atomic formulas of polynomial equations or inequalities over real or integer variables. Arithmetic Theories can be categorized into four distinctive sets based

© The Author(s) 2024
A. Gurfinkel and V. Ganesh (Eds.): CAV 2024, LNCS 14681, pp. 68–88, 2024.
https://doi.org/10.1007/978-3-031-65627-9_4

on the form of formulas and the domain of variable definitions, including *Linear Real Arithmetic* (LRA), *Linear Integer Arithmetic* (LIA), *Non-linear Real Arithmetic* (NRA), and *Non-linear Integer Arithmetic* (NIA). In widespread terms, considering all four subsets, the SMT problems of Arithmetic Theories are collectively denoted as SMT(Arithmetic). SMT(Arithmetic) is fundamental in numerous applications such as program verification [6], termination analysis [9], symbolic execution [11], test-case generation [26], program synthesis, optimization [23], and scheduling [31]. Formal verification of embedded software and hybrid systems [5] often requires deciding the satisfiability of quantifier-free first-order formulas involving arithmetic. For many users of SMT solvers, the solver's performance is a bottleneck for their application, so improving solver performance remains a top priority for solver developers.

Today, most state-of-the-art SMT solvers remain single-threaded, and previous efforts have been mainly devoted to improving the techniques and heuristics in sequential SMT solvers. In addition to enhancing the efficiency of the sequential solver, it is a natural idea to boost the solver performance by employing distributed SMT solving, considering the increasing availability of computational resources. Current research in distributed SMT solving can be divided into two main directions: *portfolio* and *divide-and-conquer*. Extensive investigations on partitioning strategies have been predominantly spearheaded by the OpenSMT2 team and are well-documented in [32]. A recent study in [32] has explored hybrid strategies that combine both methods and show improvements.

Portfolio solvers deploy multiple solvers or varying configurations of a single solver that attempt to solve identical or perturbed but equivalent SMT problems concurrently [33]. Portfolio solvers are limited by the best possible sequential performance. Consequently, the alternative divide-and-conquer method is a compelling approach. In this approach, the original problem is partitioned into sub-problems so that solving the sub-problems provides a solution to the original problem. The underlying assumption is that the smaller search spaces of the sub-problems allow for faster parallel solving than addressing the original problem in its entirety.

Our research focuses on the partitioning strategy for divide-and-conquer. While divide-and-conquer potentially outperforms the best sequential performance, it hinges heavily on discovering an effective partitioning algorithm, which still needs to be explored. Conventionally, a lookahead heuristic [21] is employed, opting for variables that reduce most exploration space, which is also studied in parallel MIP solving [29,30]. Most partitioning algorithms adopt a pre-partitioning approach, partitioning the problem into sub-problems before parallel solving [32]. This pre-partitioning approach inevitably leads to a waste of computational resources, although the *multijob* strategy [15] can alleviate this issue to some extent. Also, such partition-at-one-time strategies need to pay high costs to create sub-problems that are as balanced as possible. Beyond the pre-partitioning strategy, OpenSMT2 implements a dynamic partitioning method [1,24]. The parallel solver partitions the instance dynamically on-demand and allows clauses to be shared between solvers working on different instances.

Existing partitioning strategies for SMT mainly follow those for SAT, partitioning at the Boolean level (dividing the problem with different assignments to Boolean encoders), also known as the SMT term-level [20,32]. For formulas with complex logical structures, sufficient sub-problems can be generated by partitioning only at the term-level. However, these term-level partitioning strategies become futile for formulas with a simple Boolean structure, such as almost pure conjunction formulas, usually appearing in program verification and theorem-proving involving complex theories. Note that for the bit-vector theory, both bit-level and term-level partitioning have been studied in PBoolector [27].

In view of these shortcomings, we propose a dynamic parallel framework based on arithmetic variable-level partitioning. This framework ensures full utilization of computing resources, preventing idle core resources from lacking executable tasks. The dynamic parallel framework provides flexibility for parallel trees to grow. Thus, it can easily collaborate with other partitioning strategies — any sub-problem yielded previously by pre-partitioning strategies can be partitioned further. (Section 3)

What is more important, this is the first attempt to perform variable-level partitioning for arithmetic theories. Each time it picks a variable and partitions the problem by dividing the feasible domain of the variable, leading to (typically two) sub-problems, which can be further simplified via constraint propagation. Our proposed variable-level partitioning permits robust, comprehensive partitioning. Regardless of the Boolean structure of any given instance, our partitioning algorithm can keep partitioning to the last moment of the solving process. The variable-level partitioning strategy can be easily applied to other theories. (Section 4.2)

The effectiveness of our partition strategy is closely related to the underlying constraint propagation techniques to simplify the sub-problems. We propose an improved version of Interval Constraint Propagation (ICP) [22,28], named Boolean and Interval Constraint Propagation (BICP), and integrate it within our variable-level partitioning strategy. The BICP conducts arithmetic feasible interval reasoning and successfully integrates Boolean propagation, allowing stronger propagation. (Section 4.3)

We apply our techniques to three state-of-the-art SMT solvers as our base solvers, including CVC5 [2], OpenSMT2 [18] and Z3 [25]. Experiments are conducted to evaluate the resulting parallel solvers on four benchmarks, including QF_LRA, QF_LIA, QF_NRA, and QF_NIA instances from SMT-LIB[1]. Furthermore, we compare our variable-level partitioning strategy to the default partitioning strategies in CVC5 [32] and OpenSMT2 [19]. Overall, the experimental results show our techniques significantly improve the performance of the sequential SMT solvers, leading to a remarkable increase in total solved instances. Besides, our variable-level partitioning strategy exhibits superior performance and diversity compared to best term-level strategies, particularly in pure-conjunction instances.

---

[1] http://smtlib.cs.uiowa.edu.

2   Preliminaries

2.1   Definitions and Notations

A monomial m is an expression of the form $\prod_i x_i^{e_i}$ where $e_i \in \mathbb{N}$, x_i is a real (or integer) variable. A polynomial p is a linear combination of monomials, an arithmetic expression with $\sum_i a_i m_i$ where a_i are rational numbers and m_i are monomials. If all its monomials are linear in a polynomial, it is linear; otherwise, it is non-linear. A *quantifier-free arithmetic formula* is a first-order formula whose atoms are either propositional variables of equalities, disequalities, or inequalities of the form: $p \sim b$, where $\sim \in \{<, \leq, >, \geq, =\}$, $b \in \mathbb{R}$.

A Conjunctive Normal Form (CNF) formula is a conjunction of clauses $\bigwedge_i c_i$, each clause c_i being a disjunction of literals $\bigvee_j l_j$, and each literal l_j being either an quantifier-free arithmetic formula v or its negation $\bar{v}$. A clause containing only one literal is called a *unit clause*. The length of a clause is the number of literals in it. The length of a SMT formula is the sum of the length of the clauses in the formula. A key procedure in SAT and SMT solvers is the *unit clause rule*: if a clause is unit, then its sole unassigned literal must be assigned value *true* for the clause to be satisfied. The iterated application of the unit clause rule is referred to as *unit propagation* or *Boolean constraint propagation* (BCP).

2.2   Parallel SMT Solving with Partitioning

A typical parallel method is divide-and-conquer, which is based on partitioning. The satisfiability of a formula ϕ can be determined in parallel by dividing it into n independent sub-problems $\phi_1, \ldots, \phi_n$. Provided the disjunction $\phi_1, \ldots, \phi_n$ is equi-satisfiable with ϕ if any of the sub-problems are satisfiable, then the original problem is satisfiable, and if all of the sub-problems are unsatisfiable, then the original problem is unsatisfiable. No synchronization is necessary during solving in this simple scenario because the sub-problems are independent.

There are two main partitioning strategies, including cube-and-conquer and scattering. In the cube-and-conquer [15] partitioning strategy, a set of N atoms is selected, and each of the 2^N possible cubes using these atoms is used as a partitioning formula, resulting in 2^N partitions. Scattering [17] is an alternative strategy that differs from cube-and-conquer in that it creates partitioning formulas that are not cubes. Instead, scattering produces a series of N partitioning formulas as follows. The first partitioning formula is some cube C_1. The second is $\neg C_1 \wedge C_2$ for some new cube C_2. The next is $\neg C_1 \wedge \neg C_2 \wedge C_3$ for a new cube C_2, and so on. The Nth partitioning formula is simply $\neg C_1 \wedge \cdots \wedge \neg C_{N-1}$. The partitioning formulas by construction are disjoint, and the partitioning algorithm has considerable freedom in selecting cube variables.

2.3   Interval Constraint Propagation

Interval Constraint Propagation (ICP) is an efficient numerical method for finding interval over-approximations of solution sets of SMT formulas, and it is particularly beneficial for non-linear systems [3,12,28]. The fundamental principle of ICP is to maintain a feasible interval for every variable and shrink these intervals using relatively simple constraint propagation. This technique can effectively exclude extensive portions of the search space, sometimes proving unsatisfiability. ICP has been successfully implemented in various solvers such as dReal [13], HySAT [10], and SMT-RAT [7]. The primary method of using ICP is to quickly shrink the space of solution candidates and then exploit these additional bounds in the algebraic methods. We use a straightforward example to show how ICP works.

Example 1 (Interval constraint propagation).
    Case 1. Consider the constraint set $S = \{x > 1, \ x < 4, \ xy > 4, \ yz^2 \leq 4\}$. ICP contracts the feasible interval by the constraint set in the following way: Step 1. We derive $x \in (1, 4)$ from $x > 1 \wedge x < 4$. Step 2. By applying interval arithmetic, $y \in (1, \infty)$ is procured from $x \in (1, 4) \wedge xy > 4$. Step 3. We can further narrow the interval on z by maintaining its consistency with $y \in (1, \infty) \wedge yz^2 \leq 4$, and obtain $z \in (-2, 2)$. The resultant feasible intervals of variables after ICP are $x \in (1, 4)$, $y \in (1, \infty)$, and $z \in (-2, 2)$.
    Case 2. Consider the constraint set $S' = S \cup \{2xz + y^2 < -20\}$. As in case 1, ICP yields $x \in (1, 4)$, $y \in (1, \infty)$, and $z \in (-2, 2)$. We can obtain $2xz + y^2 = 2 \times (1, 4) \times (-2, 2) + (1, \infty)^2 \in (-15, \infty)$ by interval arithmetic. The intersection of $(-15, \infty)$ and $(-\infty, -20)$ results in an empty set. Thereby, ICP detects the unsatisfiability of the constraint set S'.

3   Dynamic Parallel Framework Based on Arithmetic Partitioning

This section introduces our dynamic parallel framework that leverages arithmetic variable-level partitioning. We first present the framework, including the main components and how they cooperate together. Two related techniques in the framework will also be introduced, followed by an illustration example. The partitioning algorithm will be introduced in Sect. 4.2.

3.1   The Framework

As illustrated in Fig. 1, in the parallel framework, there are three classes of threads, namely, the partitioner thread, the master thread, and worker threads. The master thread schedules tasks with a pivotal data structure: task buffer.
Partitioner. The partitioner generates sub-problems (also known as tasks) and puts them into the task buffer. It receives a formula from the task buffer and picks a variable (using heuristics and information from the master) to partition the formula. This would result in two sub-problems. The sub-problems are then simplified using constraint propagation techniques. Finally, the simplified sub-problems are put into the task buffer.
Master. The master plays a crucial role in task scheduling, including task assignments, on-demand terminations, and UNSAT propagation. It receives

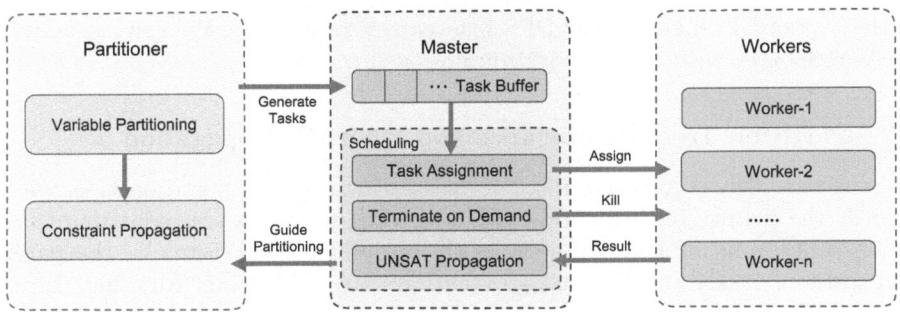

Fig. 1. Our dynamic parallel framework.

tasks generated by the partitioner, storing them in a task buffer for future assignments. The task buffer usually stores more tasks than the computation cores available. This strategy ensures the immediate task assignment by the master as soon as a computational resource is available, from the task buffer to worker threads. Simultaneously, worker threads keep the master informed of the status of running tasks. There are three possible statuses of ongoing tasks F:

- **UNSAT:** it does not necessarily mean the original problem is unsatisfied. Nonetheless, the master can perform UNSAT propagation (Sect. 3.2) if possible to speed up solving.
- **SAT:** the algorithm can confirm the original problem is SAT. A solution to the original SMT formula can be easily constructed by combining the solution of F and previous assignments to the variables being removed due to simplifications.
- **Running:** the master will analyze the information on tasks and send a termination signal to the workers that are solving problems that are unlikely to be resolved in the near future. The specific strategies and details of termination will be elaborated later in this section.

During the solving, if the root task is proven UNSAT, it marks the end of the algorithm, regardless of whether the UNSAT is the product of solving the problem by itself or UNSAT propagating upwards from sub-tasks.

Workers. The worker threads mainly call a base SMT solver to solve the problem assigned to it by the master. It communicates the result to the master when it succeeds in solving the problem. Additionally, a worker thread may also receive a termination signal from the master. In this case, it terminates the running task and releases its computational resources to make room for other tasks. Notably, worker threads have high flexibility in selecting and configuring their base solvers, thereby fostering diversified solving.

We would like to remark that the flexible task scheduling and partitioning strategy significantly enhance the capabilities of our framework. We can explore various scheduling heuristics when deciding which tasks require further partitioning. By designing the scheduling heuristic, we can extend the parallel tree in the way of BFS-like cube or DFS-like scattering strategy. We can also extend the parallel tree with dynamic scheduling.

3.2   Partition Tree Maintenance and UNSAT Propagation

To perform UNSAT propagation, the master maintains a partition tree, which records the history of formula partitioning. The partition tree consists of task nodes containing information such as the simplified SMT formula, the parent and children tasks, and the task's execution status (Waiting, Running, Terminated, SAT, UNSAT). Additionally, it keeps track of event timelines, including creation, execution, and termination times. As the solving progresses, the tree dynamically updates the state of its nodes. When the partitioner creates new subtasks through partitioning, they are added to the partition tree and subsequently updated with the related information.

When the master is notified of an UNSAT result of a task, it performs UNSAT propagation, if possible, to speed up solving. The UNSAT propagation can occur in two distinct directions: upward and downward.

- **The upward propagation:** if a task has a parent task and all the subtasks of the parent task are UNSAT, the master can infer the parent task as UNSAT and continue propagating this UNSAT upwards.
- **The downward propagation:** the master should terminate all of its subtasks since the parent task being proven UNSAT implies that all subtasks are UNSAT.

3.3   Terminate on Demand

In our framework, there are situations where a subtask and its parent task run concurrently. Allowing tasks with overlap to be solved simultaneously could inevitably result in exploring some identical search space, which we prefer to avoid. Furthermore, terminating these despairing tasks can help preserve available resources for more promising tasks. Based on these considerations, we propose a heuristic to determine if a running task should be terminated.

- If both subtasks of the task are in **waiting** states, the task is allowed a sufficient runtime duration.
- However, the task's runtime should be limited if both subtasks of the task have entered or been in a **running** state. Since the search space of the task entirely covers its descendant tasks, we should avoid unnecessary duplication of search wherever possible.
- The runtime limitation for the other scenarios should lie between these two situations.

3.4   A Running Example

Consider a running state in our framework as depicted in Fig. 2(a). In this scenario, the partitioner has generated 13 tasks with running statuses. With 5 computational cores, the size of the task buffer is set to 4.

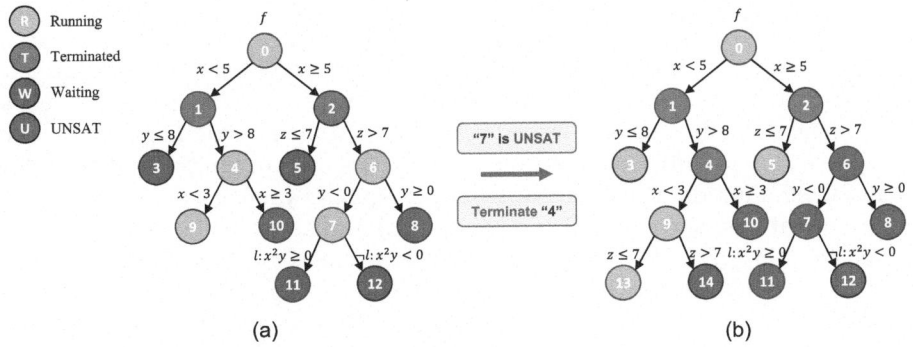

Fig. 2. A possible scheduling of our framework.

Step 1. Task 7 finishes with an UNSAT result and notifies the master. At this point, the computational resource previously allocated to task 7 is released, and the master performs both upward and downward propagation of the UNSAT result.

– During the upward propagation, the master determines that the status of task 6 is UNSAT by emerging the UNSAT result of its sub-tasks.
– With the downward propagation, the master updates the status of tasks 11 and 12 to UNSAT.

Step 2. The master sends a termination signal to task 4 according to the heuristic in Sect. 3.3, and task 4 is terminated, and the computational resource is released.

Step 3. Currently, the number of waiting tasks is fewer than the number of cores, prompting the partitioner to partition task 9 with variable z, subsequently adding new subtasks 13 and 14 to the task buffer.

Step 4. Recent result notification, UNSAT propagation, and task termination free up three computational cores. Subsequently, tasks 3, 5, and 13 are assigned to the worker threads based on the master's scheduling strategy. So, we arrive at the final running state shown in Fig. 2(b).

We omit these further task partitioning for clarity and brevity in our illustration. One may notice that the "SAT" label is missing from the tree. In fact, whenever any worker thread returns a SAT result, we know the answer to the original formula is SAT, and the model can be constructed easily.

4   Variable-Level Partitioning for Arithmetic Theories

Partitioning strategies are crucial in the paradigm of divide-and-conquer parallel solving and have a significant impact on the overall efficiency of parallel solving [16,19–21,32]. This section explores a variable-level partitioning strategy based on the BICP method, making a deeper and more comprehensive exploration of arithmetic theories.

4.1 Preprocessing

For convenience of constraint propagation, we preprocess the original formula to a standard form. Note that the preprocessing is performed only once for the original formula. All sub-formulas obtained from partitioning inherit this form. We utilize preprocessing techniques including but not limited to if-then-else operators elimination, constants elimination, equality propagation, flattening of nested operations, and normalizing polynomial formats.

As done in [8,12,28], we preprocess our formulas to maintain constraints in an easily-managed form of $x \sim b$. The preprocessing introduces two sets of auxiliary variables: polynomial and monomial. Whenever a monomial m_i first occurs, an associated monomial variable v_i^m is introduced. We substitute m_i with v_i^m, augmenting the original formula with the clause $v_i^m = m_i$. Likewise, for each non-monomial atomic formula $p_i \sim b_i$, a new variable v_i^p is defined. p_i is replaced by v_i^p in the formula, and the associated clause $v_i^p = p_i$ is added. Moreover, we performed an enhanced normalization as follows. For convenient notation, we assume that each constraint embeds constants and coefficients, which can be expressed as fractions. Consider a non-linear constraint c of the following form:

$$\sum_{i=1}^{|p|} \frac{a_i^n}{a_i^d} v_i^m \sim \frac{b^n}{b^d}, \ a_i^n, \ a_i^d, \ b^n \text{ and } b^d \in \mathbb{Z}.$$

To simplify and normalize the polynomial form, allowing shared variable boundaries that enhance efficiency in interval contraction, we transform the constraints into the standard form:

$$\sum_{i=1}^{|p|} a_i' v_i^m \sim b', \ a_i' \in \mathbb{Z}, \ b' \in \mathbb{Q} \text{ and } \gcd\left(a_1', \dots, a_{|p|}'\right) = 1.$$

This leads to $v^p = \sum_{i=1}^{|p|} a_i' v_i^m$ with the adjusted bound $v^p \sim b$. To summarize, for each distinctive non-linear monomial and linear left-hand side (excluding constants), a single v^m and v^p are introduced, respectively. This way, the procedures facilitate the construction of necessary equations for the ICP algorithm and generate bounds of introduced variables to express potential inequalities.

4.2 The Partitioning Algorithm

When the master notifies the partitioner to perform partitioning, the partitioner runs Algorithm 1 to generate two subtasks and sends them to the task buffer. The partition tree is then updated accordingly.

Choose a Formula to Partition. The partitioner thread maintains a partition tree as the master does. It iteratively chooses a leaf node from the tree and performs partitioning to the corresponding formula in the node, following the below heuristic:

- prefers a leaf node of the lowest level (that is, a leaf node closest to the root node)

Algorithm 1: Arithmetic Variable-level Partitioning

---

1   $\phi \leftarrow$ choose a leaf node from the *partition tree*

2   $x \leftarrow$ choose a partitioning variable for the node ϕ

3   $\{\phi_l, \phi_r\} \leftarrow$ perform interval partitioning on variable x within ϕ

4   $\{\mathcal{R}_l, \hat{\phi}_l\} \leftarrow$ perform the *BICP* on ϕ_l

5   **if** $\mathcal{R}_l \neq$ UNSAT **then**

6   Add node $\hat{\phi}_l$ into the *partition tree*

7   Send $\hat{\phi}_l$ to the *task buffer*

8   $\{\mathcal{R}_r, \hat{\phi}_r\} \leftarrow$ perform the *BICP* on ϕ_r

9   **if** $\mathcal{R}_r \neq$ UNSAT **then**

10   Add node $\hat{\phi}_r$ into the *partition tree*

11   Send $\hat{\phi}_r$ to the *task buffer*

– if there are more than one such leaf nodes, ties are broken by preferring the one with the most clauses, and further ties are broken by the length of the formula.

We would like to note that it is not mandatory for the partitioner to maintain the partition tree, as we already have the tree in the master. The reason we choose to also maintain the partition tree in the partitioner thread is mainly to reduce the communication cost and thus improve efficiency.

Choose an Arithmetic Variable for Partitioning. Given a formula, a specific variable is selected for partitioning. In the following, we discuss selecting partitioning variables and conducting our variable-level partitioning in arithmetic theories. The selection of arithmetic variables avoids auxiliary variables introduced in the preprocessing for ICP. When selecting the partitioning variable, we consider the following variable features in the formula. Our experimental validation has led us to prioritize these features based on their importance. We design a multi-tier heuristic, in which if the primary indicator is identical, the secondary indicator is considered, and so forth.

1. The highest degree of the variable in the constraints.
2. The occurrence frequency of the variable in the simplified formula.
3. The partitioning times of the variable.

With our implementation and evaluation, we rarely encounter variables that fall back to the third indicator, which means that the first two features are crucial indicators within our selection procedure.

Create Two Sub-Formulas via Interval Partitioning. Once the partitioning variable has been decided, creating partitions with reference to this variable is another pivotal aspect of the variable-level partitioning. In this context, *ub* and *lb* represent the existing upper bound and lower bound of the selected variable. The partitioner performs partitioning depending on the feasible interval of the variable as follows:

1. **Strictly containing** 0: A partitioning is made at the value 0.
2. **Both an upper and a lower bound:** Proportionate partitioning is performed in demand, usually at the midpoint $(lb + ub)/2$.
3. **Only an upper bound or a lower bound:** Partitioning at $(ub - penalty)$, *penalty* is a parameter. The case for the lower-bound-only variable is similar.
4. **No upper or lower bound:** Containing 0, thereby satisfying condition 1.

4.3   BICP in Arithmetic Partitioning

This section proposes an enhanced constraint propagation method called Boolean and Interval Constraint Propagation (BICP). Typically, the ICP is implemented within the theory solver in SMT, which is used for performing constraint propagation on conjunctive arithmetic constraints, sometimes leading to an UNSAT result.

We extend ICP to handle constraints with disjunctive structure by combining it with Boolean constraint propagation. This algorithm collects variable information from Boolean constraint propagation, including the feasible intervals of arithmetic variables, monomials, and polynomials, as well as the assignments of Boolean variables. BICP uses the feasible intervals of arithmetic variables to calculate the feasible intervals of monomials and polynomials encompassing these variables, which is straightforward. Additionally, the algorithm exploits the feasible intervals of monomials and polynomials to update the interval of variables within them. BICP involves both Boolean constraint propagation and numerical computation algorithms, a typical example being Newton's method for interval arithmetic [14]. During the propagation, BICP efficiently contracts the feasible interval of integer variables. Sometimes, BICP can lead to an UNSAT result, and in this case the task is directly discarded. An intuitive explanation is that BCP could lead to potential unit propagation and collect more arithmetic constraints, thus enhancing propagation ability. Without BCP, the ICP process may terminate early. Some examples of the techniques mentioned in BICP are listed in Table 1.

Table 1. Techniques implemented in BICP.

Technique	Example Input	Example Output
Unit Propagation	$x \in (1, 4)$, $(\neg a \vee x < -2)$	$\neg a$
	$\neg a$, $y = 4$, $(a \vee x^2 \geq 4 \vee y < 3)$	$x^2 \geq 4$
Interval Propagation	$x \in (1, 4)$, $y > 1$, $z \in (-2, 2)$	$2xz + y^2 > -15$
	$x \in (1, 4)$, $xy > 4$	$y > 1$
UNSAT Inference	$x \in (1, 4)$, $y \in (2, 3)$,	UNSAT
	$(x < -2 \vee y \geq 3)$	
Integer Contraction	$x \in \mathbb{Z}$, $x^2 < 5$	$x \in [-2, 2]$

Exhaustive propagation takes a lot of work due to the "slow convergence" of ICP [4]. In practice, the algorithm follows a predefined number of iterations or ignores the negligible improvement within a given threshold.

The SMT formula (i.e., a task) is then simplified according to the result of BICP, which may change the domains of the variables. The simplification procedure comprises three sub-procedures: clause reduction, feasible domain contraction of variables, and literal propagation.

- **Reduce Clauses.** We examine each clause of the original formula. This involves examining the truth value of the literals in the clause. For arithmetic literals, recalling that after preprocessing (Sect. 4.1), the polynomial in any arithmetic literal ℓ has been replaced with an auxiliary arithmetic variable x, we calculate the truth value of ℓ as follows: if the feasible interval of x is a subset of the feasible interval represented by the literal ℓ, then ℓ is **True**; if there is no intersection between these two domains, then literal ℓ is **False**; in other cases, we do not know the value of the literal. If a clause contains any literal whose value is **True** (due to propagation), the clause is satisfied, and thus it is removed. Conversely, we formulate a new clause from all literals with unknown status and add it to the task. If some clause becomes empty, it means the formula is UNSAT, and thus, the formula can be discarded.
- **Express Feasible Domains as Constraints.** We gather all assignments of Boolean variables and feasible intervals of arithmetic variables obtained from the constraint propagation. Each of them is expressed by a constraint and added to the formula.
- **Address Literals Assigned by BCP.** We avoid adding constraints about the feasible intervals of auxiliary variables, which stand for monomials and polynomials, into the task. To ensure that the simplified task has the same solution as the given formula, we need to collect the literals assigned by Boolean constraint propagation. This part could lead to redundancies within the task. So, we eliminate constraints dominated by others through a simple detection, ensuring the accuracy and conciseness of the task.

Example 2 (BICP and formula simplification). Consider the SMT formula $(x > 1) \wedge (x < 4) \wedge (xy > 4) \wedge (yz^2 \leq 4) \wedge (\neg a \vee x < -2) \wedge (y > 0 \vee x^2 z + y = 3) \wedge (a \vee x^2 \geq 4 \vee y > 5)$. From Example 1 in Sect. 2.3, we can derive $x \in (1, 4), y \in (1, \infty)$, and $z \in (-1, 1)$ by Boolean constraint propagation and interval arithmetic. Then, we infer $(x < -2) \mapsto$ False and propagate $\neg a$. After the BICP, the status of the given formula is:

$$(xy > 4 \wedge yz^2 \leq 4) \mapsto (\text{True} \wedge \text{True}),$$
$$(\neg a \vee x < -2) \mapsto (\text{True} \vee \text{False}),$$
$$(y > 0 \vee x^2 z + y = 3) \mapsto (\text{True} \vee \text{Unknown}),$$
$$(a \vee x^2 \geq 4 \vee y > 5) \mapsto (\text{False} \vee \text{Unknown} \vee \text{Unknown}).$$

So, the task after simplification is:

$$\underbrace{(x^2 \geq 4 \vee y > 5)}_{\text{Reduced Clauses}} \wedge \underbrace{(\neg a \wedge x \in (1,4) \wedge y \in (1,\infty) \wedge z \in (-2,2))}_{\text{Feasible Domain of Variables}} \wedge \underbrace{(xy > 4 \wedge yz^2 \leq 4)}_{\text{Propagated Literals}}.$$

5   Evaluation

5.1   Evaluation Preliminaries

In this work, we use our method to improve SMT solvers and conduct extensive experiments to evaluate the method's effectiveness. This subsection introduces the experiment setup, including implementation, benchmarks, base solvers, running environment, and reporting methodology.

Implementation: The partitioner is efficiently developed from the developing module of Z3 named "subpaving" in C++. We refined the code to support our variable-level partitioning and constraint propagation needs and fixed several bugs. Moreover, we implemented targeted adaptations and performance enhancements within the "subpaving" module to improve the capability of our method. The master is implemented by Python for task management and scheduling in parallel solving.

Benchmarks: The experiments are carried out on four non-incremental arithmetic benchmarks from SMT-LIB: 1753 instances from QF_LRA, 13226 instances from QF_LIA, 12134 instances from QF_NRA, and 25358 instances from QF_NIA.

Base Solvers: For the foundation of our research, we choose three state-of-the-art SMT solvers as the base solvers (i.e., the worker threads) for our studies, including CVC5 (v1.0.8) [2], OpenSMT2 (v2.5.2) [18], and Z3 (v4.12.1) [25]. CVC5 and Z3 have persistently demonstrated superior performance across numerous theories and tracks in the SMT-COMP over several consecutive years. Conversely, OpenSMT2 is a solver specifically oriented towards parallel and distributed solving and exhibits commendable efficacy in the theories of linear arithmetic. CVC5 and Z3 support all theories in benchmarks, and OpenSMT2 supports QF_LRA and QF_LIA of the four theories. As for comparisons, we also test the previous parallel versions of these solvers.

Experiment Setup: All experiments are conducted on servers running Ubuntu 20.04.4 LTS, each with 1T RAM and two AMD EPYC 7763 CPUs with 64 cores per CPU. Each solver performed one run for each instance with a cutoff time of 1200 CPU seconds. For each solver for each benchmark, we report our number of solved SAT/UNSAT instances, total failed instances, and total solved instances, denoted as "SAT", "UNSAT", "Failed", and "Solved". Furthermore, we present the penalized run-time "PAR-2", as used in SAT Competitions, where the run time of a failed run is penalized as twice the cutoff time, and the PAR-2 score improvement "Improve" compared to sequential solving. We use the PAR-2 score because it provides a single metric that incorporates both run time and the number of benchmarks solved. The CPU time consumed by the experiments is more than 20 CPU years. Our experiments primarily use sequential and parallel solving with 8 and 16 cores. Although our method supports parallelism for an arbitrary number of cores, we elected to use powers of 2 for our core number. This decision was made considering that some existing comparative strategies like cube-and-conquer can only accommodate parallelism for cores numbering to the powers of 2. Moreover, the choice of the core number aims to balance the advantage of the dynamic parallel framework against the practical time and equipment constraints. The framework's benefits might not be adequately exhibited in cases involving fewer cores, and employing a more significant number of cores may result in an unacceptable CPU time cost.

At last, we have provided our solver, evaluation scripts, and related experimental results in a GitHub repository[2]. For those interested, it is possible to utilize our solver and explore the experimental details further.

5.2 Comparison to Sequential Solving

This part of the evaluation focuses on testing the effectiveness of our variable-level partitioning in augmenting and accelerating the solving capabilities of different sequential solvers across various theories. The notation Solver(S) means sequential solving of the SMT solver "Solver", and Solver(AP-pX) is the notation for employing "Solver" within our method AP with X cores.

Table 2. Comparison to sequential solving in benchmarks of linear theories, where the solvers employing our partitioning method are denoted with "AP-p", followed by the number of cores.

	QF_LRA(1753)					QF_LIA(13226)				
	SAT	UNSAT	Failed	PAR-2	Improve	SAT	UNSAT	Failed	PAR-2	Improve
CVC5(S)	958	685	110	354714	0%	7046	3212	2968	7562277	0%
CVC5(AP-p8)	980	689	84	287256	19.02%	7321	3252	2653	6791509	10.19%
CVC5(AP-p16)	980	689	84	281524	20.63%	7350	3274	2602	6678936	11.68%
CVC5(AP-p32)	982	690	81	275957	22.20%	7365	3285	2576	6603235	12.68%
OpenSMT2(S)	991	700	62	173971	0%	7985	4645	596	1994585	0%
OpenSMT2(AP-p8)	1008	701	44	132925	23.59%	8116	4660	450	1629696	18.29%
OpenSMT2(AP-p16)	1008	701	44	133043	23.53%	8138	4663	425	1555190	22.03%
OpenSMT2(AP-p32)	1009	701	43	127489	26.72%	8160	4665	401	1489780	25.31%
Z3(S)	966	680	107	316097	0%	7862	3903	1461	4025347	0%
Z3(AP-p8)	995	683	75	235645	25.45%	8055	4152	1019	3031732	24.68%
Z3(AP-p16)	996	683	74	231738	26.69%	8066	4157	1003	2983526	25.88%
Z3(AP-p32)	998	684	71	225268	28.73%	8076	4160	990	2945091	26.84%

The results from different base solvers and their performance within our method are summarized in Table 2 and Table 3. From sequential to parallel

---

[2] https://github.com/shaowei-cai-group/AriParti.

Table 3. Comparison to sequential solving in benchmarks of non-linear theories.

	QF_NRA(12134)					QF_NIA(25358)				
	SAT	UNSAT	Failed	PAR-2	Improve	SAT	UNSAT	Failed	PAR-2	Improve
CVC5(S)	5485	5811	838	2100561	0%	9460	4803	11095	27485835	0%
CVC5(AP-p8)	5709	5864	561	1425236	32.15%	13030	5504	6824	17250199	37.24%
CVC5(AP-p16)	5731	5864	539	1372485	34.66%	13045	5513	6800	17186305	37.47%
CVC5(AP-p32)	5743	5864	527	1343006	36.06%	13691	5588	6079	15346228	44.17%
Z3(S)	5626	5375	1133	2770153	0%	13779	5836	5743	14636656	0%
Z3(AP-p8)	5744	5686	704	1741660	37.13%	14191	6785	4382	11225626	23.30%
Z3(AP-p16)	5766	5705	663	1637352	40.89%	14193	6789	4376	11206526	23.44%
Z3(AP-p32)	5789	5712	633	1561862	43.62%	14320	6884	4154	10610746	27.51%

solving with 8 cores by applying our parallel method for all base solvers, the number of solved instances is increased, and the PAR-2 scores are significantly improved. Specifically, the parallel solvers with 8 cores solve 25.3, 301, 353, and 2816 more instances compared to sequential versions on average for QF_LRA(1753), QF_LIA(13226), QF_NRA(12134) and QF_NIA(25358) theories respectively. Moreover, the PAR-2 scores are improved by 22.4%, 15.7%, 35.0%, and 32.4% on average. Overall, our parallel method with 8 cores solves 1211 additional instances (out of 6247) that any single solver could not solve without our partitioner, improving the solving ability essentially.

From 8 to 32 cores parallel solving results with our proposed method, we observed significant performance improvement. This preliminary evidence underscores the promising potential of our approach in terms of scalability. Time and computational resources, unavoidable constraints in our parallel experimentation, have limited us to exploring up to 32 cores. Nevertheless, our current experimental results do not display a solving performance saturation with the present number of cores. Extending the parallel cores beyond 32 would continue to improve the solving performance. In other words, the improvement is even worth the resource usage cost beyond 32 cores.

Further, we discover that the improvement across distinct theories varied considerably. The improvements are more significant in non-linear arithmetic instances than linear ones. This result aligns with the intention of ICP, which is mainly designed to speed up solving non-linear arithmetic constraints. For linear instances, the capacity of SAT instances is predominantly enhanced. For nonlinear instances, the improvement is also noticeable in UNSAT instances. From the standpoint of solvers, improvements using our method are evenly distributed in both instances in Z3, whereas in CVC5 and OpenSMT2, the enhancements are primarily evident within SAT instances.

5.3   Comparison to State-of-the-art Partitioning Strategies

We compare our variable-level partitioning strategy to state-of-the-art partitioning strategies evaluated in [32]: including decision-cube, the best strategy

Table 4. Comparison to state-of-the-art partitioning strategy.

	QF_LRA(1753)				QF_LIA(13226)			
	SAT	UNSAT	Solved	PAR-2	SAT	UNSAT	Solved	PAR-2
CVC5(p8)	964	677	1641	347087	7288	3199	10487	7004216
CVC5(AP-p8)	**980**	**689**	**1669**	**287256**	7321	3252	10573	6791509
OpenSMT2(p8)	998	**701**	1699	147360	**8169**	**4698**	**12867**	**1384618**
OpenSMT2(AP-p8)	1008	701	1709	132925	8116	4660	12776	1629696
CVC5(p16)	965	676	1641	346435	7316	3225	10541	6895797
CVC5(AP-p16)	**980**	**689**	**1669**	**281524**	**7350**	**3274**	**10624**	**6678936**
OpenSMT2(p16)	997	698	1695	157708	8097	4623	12720	1778020
OpenSMT2(AP-p16)	**1008**	**701**	**1709**	**133043**	**8138**	**4663**	**12801**	**1555190**
Z3(AP-p8)	995	683	1678	235645	8055	4152	12207	3031732
Z3(AP-p16)	996	683	1679	231738	8066	4157	12223	2983526
	QF_NRA(12134)				QF_NIA(25358)			
	SAT	UNSAT	Solved	PAR-2	SAT	UNSAT	Solved	PAR-2
CVC5(p8)	5559	5798	11357	1948280	12503	4480	16983	20716252
CVC5(AP-p8)	**5709**	**5864**	**11573**	**1425236**	**13030**	**5504**	**18534**	**17250199**
CVC5(p16)	5575	5796	11371	1920929	12821	4405	17226	20123111
CVC5(AP-p16)	**5731**	**5864**	**11595**	**1372485**	**13045**	**5513**	**18558**	**17186305**
Z3(AP-p8)	5744	5686	11430	1741660	14191	6785	20976	11225626
Z3(AP-p16)	5766	5705	11471	1637352	14193	6789	20982	11206526

in CVC5, and scattering, the best strategy in SMTS [1, 24], which is the parallel version of OpenSMT2. The notation CVC5(pX) refers to the decision-cube strategy in CVC5 with X cores. OpenSMT2(pX) stands for the scattering strategy in OpenSMT2 with X cores. Solver(AP-pX) is the notation for employing Solver within our method AP with X cores.

Our evaluation compares the results of our method with both best competitor strategies in Table 4, ensuring fairness by comparing both strategies with our strategy based on the same SMT solver. Considering that Z3 lacks an appropriate divide-and-conquer parallel strategy for testing, we have independently demonstrated the performance of employing Z3 within our method in the table for reference.

Overall, our method is obviously the best, outperforming all the other strategies, only except for 8-core execution on the QF_LIA theory. Our method performs particularly well for non-linear theories and shows significant improvements over the competitors. For example, when using 8 cores, CVC5 with our method solved 216 (out of 777 unsolved) and 1551 (out of 8375 unsolved) more instances for QF_NRA and QF_NIA theories than decision-cube strategy, respectively.

For the QF_LIA theory, our method shows competitive and complementary to OpenSMT2. This is indicated by 51 instances where OpenSMT2 fails, yet our method solves quickly, and there are 181 instances where our method solves more than 10 times faster. We discover the performance of OpenSMT2 degrades a little from 8 to 16 cores for the QF_LRA and QF_LIA benchmarks. A possible explanation is the lack of selection for parallel-friendly solving instances from the benchmark, resulting in performance decrement for specific instances.

5.4   Improvement on Pure-Conjunction Formulas

Lastly, we focus on pure-conjunction instances to empirically validate the effectiveness of our proposed variable-level partitioning strategy. Notably, the term-level partitioning strategies fall short of partition generation and parallel acceleration in these instances. We filter out instances where, after Z3 preprocessing and Boolean constraint propagation, all abstract Boolean variables have already been assigned. In other words, the propositional engine in SMT makes no or almost no decisions for the original formula during sequential solving.

For more details, pure-conjunction instances account for 22.8% (11957 out of 52471) of all across arithmetic theories, 19.2% (337 out of 1753) within QF_LRA, 30.7% (4066 out of 13226) with QF_LIA, a significant 49.7% (6034 out of 12134) within QF_NRA, and 6.0% (1520 out of 25358) within QF_NIA. Our forthcoming experiments compare the run time between our variable-level partitioning strategy and state-of-the-art strategies in CVC5 and OpenSMT2 on pure-conjunction instances.

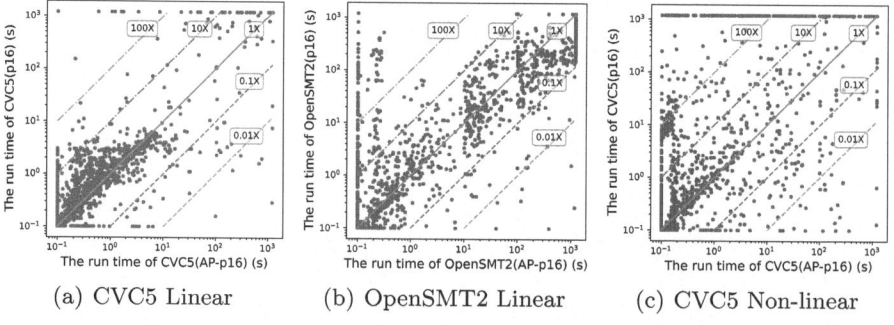

(a) CVC5 Linear   (b) OpenSMT2 Linear   (c) CVC5 Non-linear

Fig. 3. Run time comparison with partitioning strategies in pure-conjunction instances.

As displayed in Fig. 3(a), a comparison of run time for linear instances between our strategy and the best strategy in CVC5 indicates differences. We observe a speed-up of over 10X (10 times faster) on 92 instances and a slowdown of over 0.1X on 12 instances compared to our counterpart. For comparison with OpenSMT2, as presented in Fig. 3(b), our partitioning strategy is competitive with OpenSMT2 on linear instances. Our solution exceeds 10 times faster and slower in 152 and 12, respectively. Finally, our method significantly improves non-linear instances against CVC5, shown in Fig. 3(c). Our method succeeds in

265 instances where CVC5 fails, while it fails in only 11 instances where CVC5 succeeds. Performance improvement is impressive: the number of instances where the solving speed exceeds 100X, 10X, 0.1X, and 0.01X are 322, 533, 91, and 32, respectively.

In summary, the evaluation results confirm the potential of the variable-level partitioning strategy in pure-conjunction instances. Beyond pure-conjunction instances, our method also stands out in almost-pure-conjunction instances, which occupy a higher percentage in benchmarks.

6   Conclusion and Future Work

In this paper, we proposed the first variable-level partitioning strategy for parallel solving in arithmetic theories of SMT. Two main ideas include a dynamic parallel framework and a variable-level partitioning strategy with enhanced constraint propagation. We developed parallel solvers of 3 leading SMT solvers using our partitioning strategy. Extensive experiments showed that our variable-level partitioning strategy outperformed the best divide-and-conquer parallel strategies on all arithmetic theories and was significantly better on nonlinear arithmetic theories.

Our strategy can be extended to other theories within SMT with the need for customized specifics. Further research remains necessary to devise a comprehensive, variable-level partitioning strategy applicable across various SMT theories. Besides, it is interesting to combine our method with term-level partitioning to improve the performance of divide-and-conquer parallel further.

Acknowledgements. This work is generously supported by the NSFC under grant No. 62122078. We would like to thank Yiyuan Wang from Northeast Normal University for proofreading the paper and the artifact documents.

References

1. Asadzade, M., Blicha, M., Hyvärinen, A., Otoni, R., Sharygina, N.: The opensmt solver in SMT-COMP 2022. In: 17th International Satisfiability Modulo Theories Competition (SMT-COMP 2022) (2022)
2. Barbosa, H., et al.: cvc5: a versatile and industrial-strength SMT solver. In: TACAS 2022. LNCS, vol. 13243, pp. 415–442. Springer, Cham (2022). https://doi.org/10.1007/978-3-030-99524-9_24
3. Benhamou, F., Granvilliers, L.: Chapter 16 - continuous and interval constraints. In: Rossi, F., van Beek, P., Walsh, T. (eds.) Handbook of Constraint Programming, Foundations of Artificial Intelligence, vol. 2, pp. 571–603. Elsevier (2006)
4. Bordeaux, L., Hamadi, Y., Vardi, M.Y.: An analysis of slow convergence in interval propagation. In: Bessière, C. (ed.) CP 2007. LNCS, vol. 4741, pp. 790–797. Springer, Heidelberg (2007). https://doi.org/10.1007/978-3-540-74970-7_56
5. Cimatti, A., Mover, S., Tonetta, S.: SMT-based verification of hybrid systems. In: Proceedings of the AAAI Conference on Artificial Intelligence, vol. 26, pp. 2100–2105 (2012)

6. Cordeiro, L., Fischer, B.: Verifying multi-threaded software using SMT-based context-bounded model checking. In: 2011 33rd International Conference on Software Engineering (ICSE), pp. 331–340 (2011)
7. Corzilius, F., Kremer, G., Junges, S., Schupp, S., Ábrahám, E.: SMT-RAT: An Open Source C++ Toolbox for Strategic and Parallel SMT Solving. In: Heule, M., Weaver, S. (eds.) SAT 2015. LNCS, vol. 9340, pp. 360–368. Springer, Cham (2015). https://doi.org/10.1007/978-3-319-24318-4_26
8. Dutertre, B., de Moura, L.: A fast linear-arithmetic solver for DPLL(T). In: Ball, T., Jones, R.B. (eds.) CAV 2006. LNCS, vol. 4144, pp. 81–94. Springer, Heidelberg (2006). https://doi.org/10.1007/11817963_11
9. Esparza, J., Meyer, P.J.: An SMT-based approach to fair termination analysis. In: 2015 Formal Methods in Computer-Aided Design (FMCAD), pp. 49–56 (2015)
10. Fränzle, M., Herde, C.: HySAT: an efficient proof engine for bounded model checking of hybrid systems. Formal Methods Syst. Des. **30**, 179–198 (2007)
11. Franzén, A., Cimatti, A., Nadel, A., Sebastiani, R., Shalev, J.: Applying SMT in symbolic execution of microcode. In: Formal Methods in Computer Aided Design, pp. 121–128 (2010)
12. Gao, S., Ganai, M., Ivančić, F., Gupta, A., Sankaranarayanan, S., Clarke, E.M.: Integrating ICP and LRA solvers for deciding nonlinear real arithmetic problems. In: Formal Methods in Computer Aided Design, pp. 81–89 (2010)
13. Gao, S., Kong, S., Clarke, E.M.: dReal: an SMT solver for nonlinear theories over the reals. In: Bonacina, M.P. (ed.) CADE 2013. LNCS (LNAI), vol. 7898, pp. 208–214. Springer, Heidelberg (2013). https://doi.org/10.1007/978-3-642-38574-2_14
14. Herbort, S., Ratz, D.: Improving the efficiency of a nonlinear-system-solver using a componentwise newton method (1997)
15. Heule, M.J.H., Kullmann, O., Wieringa, S., Biere, A.: Cube and conquer: guiding CDCL SAT solvers by lookaheads. In: Eder, K., Lourenço, J., Shehory, O. (eds.) HVC 2011. LNCS, vol. 7261, pp. 50–65. Springer, Heidelberg (2012). https://doi.org/10.1007/978-3-642-34188-5_8
16. Huang, C., Kong, S., Gao, S., Zufferey, D.: Evaluating branching heuristics in interval constraint propagation for satisfiability. In: Zamani, M., Zufferey, D. (eds.) NSV 2019. LNCS, vol. 11652, pp. 85–100. Springer, Cham (2019). https://doi.org/10.1007/978-3-030-28423-7_6
17. Hyvärinen, A.E.J., Junttila, T., Niemelä, I.: A distribution method for solving SAT in grids. In: Biere, A., Gomes, C.P. (eds.) SAT 2006. LNCS, vol. 4121, pp. 430–435. Springer, Heidelberg (2006). https://doi.org/10.1007/11814948_39
18. Hyvärinen, A.E.J., Marescotti, M., Alt, L., Sharygina, N.: OpenSMT2: an SMT solver for multi-core and cloud computing. In: Creignou, N., Le Berre, D. (eds.) SAT 2016. LNCS, vol. 9710, pp. 547–553. Springer, Cham (2016). https://doi.org/10.1007/978-3-319-40970-2_35
19. Hyvärinen, A.E.J., Marescotti, M., Sharygina, N.: Search-space partitioning for parallelizing SMT solvers. In: Heule, M., Weaver, S. (eds.) SAT 2015. LNCS, vol. 9340, pp. 369–386. Springer, Cham (2015). https://doi.org/10.1007/978-3-319-24318-4_27
20. Hyvärinen, A.E., Wintersteiger, C.M.: Parallel satisfiability modulo theories. In: Handbook of Parallel Constraint Reasoning, pp. 141–178 (2018)
21. Hyvärinen, A.E.J., Marescotti, M., Sharygina, N.: Lookahead in partitioning SMT. In: 2021 Formal Methods in Computer Aided Design (FMCAD), pp. 271–279 (2021)

22. Kulisch, U.W.: Complete interval arithmetic and its implementation on the computer. In: Cuyt, A., Krämer, W., Luther, W., Markstein, P. (eds.) Numerical Validation in Current Hardware Architectures. LNCS, vol. 5492, pp. 7–26. Springer, Heidelberg (2009). https://doi.org/10.1007/978-3-642-01591-5_2

23. Li, Y., Albarghouthi, A., Kincaid, Z., Gurfinkel, A., Chechik, M.: Symbolic optimization with SMT solvers. SIGPLAN Not. **49**(1), 607–618 (2014)

24. Marescotti, M., Hyvärinen, A.E., Sharygina, N.: SMTS: Distributed, visualized constraint solving. In: LPAR, pp. 534–542 (2018)

25. de Moura, L., Bjørner, N.: Z3: an efficient SMT solver. In: Ramakrishnan, C.R., Rehof, J. (eds.) TACAS 2008. LNCS, vol. 4963, pp. 337–340. Springer, Heidelberg (2008). https://doi.org/10.1007/978-3-540-78800-3_24

26. Peleska, J., Vorobev, E., Lapschies, F.: Automated test case generation with SMT-solving and abstract interpretation. In: Bobaru, M., Havelund, K., Holzmann, G.J., Joshi, R. (eds.) NFM 2011. LNCS, vol. 6617, pp. 298–312. Springer, Heidelberg (2011). https://doi.org/10.1007/978-3-642-20398-5_22

27. Reisenberger, C.: PBoolector: a parallel SMT solver for QF_BV by combining bit-blasting with look-ahead. Ph.D. thesis, Master's thesis, Johannes Kepler Univesität Linz, Linz, Austria (2014)

28. Schupp, S., Ábrahám, E., Rossmanith, P., Loup, D.I.U.: Interval constraint propagation in SMT compliant decision procedures. Master's thesis, RWTH Aachen (2013)

29. Shinano, Y., Achterberg, T., Berthold, T., Heinz, S., Koch, T., Winkler, M.: Solving open MIP instances with paraSCIP on supercomputers using up to 80,000 cores. In: 2016 IEEE International Parallel and Distributed Processing Symposium (IPDPS), pp. 770–779 (2016). https://doi.org/10.1109/IPDPS.2016.56

30. Shinano, Y., Heinz, S., Vigerske, S., Winkler, M.: Fiberscip-a shared memory parallelization of scip. INFORMS J. Comput. **30**(1), 11–30 (2018)

31. Steiner, W.: An evaluation of SMT-based schedule synthesis for time-triggered multi-hop networks. In: 2010 31st IEEE Real-Time Systems Symposium, pp. 375–384 (2010)

32. Wilson, A., Noetzli, A., Reynolds, A., Cook, B., Tinelli, C., Barrett, C.W.: Partitioning strategies for distributed SMT solving. In: 2023 Formal Methods in Computer-Aided Design (FMCAD), pp. 199–208 (2023)

33. Wintersteiger, C.M., Hamadi, Y., de Moura, L.: A concurrent portfolio approach to SMT solving. In: Bouajjani, A., Maler, O. (eds.) CAV 2009. LNCS, vol. 5643, pp. 715–720. Springer, Heidelberg (2009). https://doi.org/10.1007/978-3-642-02658-4_60

Quantified Linear Arithmetic Satisfiability via Fine-Grained Strategy Improvement

Charlie Murphy[1]([envelope]) [ORCID] and Zachary Kincaid[2] [ORCID]

[1] University of Wisconsin-Madison, Madison,
WI 53706, USA
tcmurphy4@wisc.edu
[2] Princeton University, Princeton, NJ 08540, USA
zkincaid@cs.princeton.edu

Abstract. Checking satisfiability of formulae in the theory of linear arithmetic has far reaching applications, including program verification and synthesis. Many satisfiability solvers excel at proving and disproving satisfiability of quantifier-free linear arithmetic formulas and have recently begun to support quantified formulas. Beyond simply checking satisfiability of formulas, fine-grained strategies for satisfiability games enables solving additional program verification and synthesis tasks. Quantified satisfiability games are played between two players—SAT and UNSAT—who take turns instantiating quantifiers and choosing branches of boolean connectives to evaluate the given formula. A winning strategy for SAT (resp. UNSAT) determines the choices of SAT (resp. UNSAT) as a function of UNSAT's (resp. SAT's) choices such that the given formula evaluates to true (resp. false) no matter what choices UNSAT (resp. SAT) may make. As we are interested in both checking satisfiability *and* synthesizing winning strategies, we must avoid conversion to normal-forms that alter the game semantics of the formula (e.g. prenex normal form). We present fine-grained strategy improvement and strategy synthesis, the first technique capable of synthesizing winning fine-grained strategies for linear arithmetic satisfiability games, which may be used in higher-level applications. We experimentally evaluate our technique and find it performs favorably compared with state-of-the-art solvers.

Keywords: Quantified Satisfiability · SMT · Game Semantics · Strategy Improvement

1 Introduction

Checking satisfiability of quantified formulae modulo the theory of linear (integer or real) arithmetic (LA) has applications to a broad class of problems (e.g., program verification and synthesis). Satisfiability modulo theory (SMT) solvers excel at deciding satisfiability of the ground (quantifier free) fragment of first order theories (e.g., LA). Other techniques like first order theorem solvers work well for quantified formulae but have limited support for theories. Typically,

© The Author(s) 2024
A. Gurfinkel and V. Ganesh (Eds.): CAV 2024, LNCS 14681, pp. 89–109, 2024.
https://doi.org/10.1007/978-3-031-65627-9_5

SMT solvers either perform quantifier elimination, which is often computationally expensive, or heuristically instantiate quantifiers, which is sound but incomplete for deciding satisfiability [19]. Recently, decision procedures have been developed to check satisfiability of quantified LA formulae directly [4,5,8,18]. Notably, both Bjørner and Janota [4]'s and Farzan and Kincaid [8]'s decision procedures are based on the game semantics of first-order logic.

The game semantics of first-order logic gives meaning to a formula as a two player game [12]. Every (LA) formula induces a game between two players, SAT and UNSAT. SAT tries to prove the formula satisfiable, while UNSAT tries to prove it unsatisfiable. The players take turns instantiating quantifiers or choosing a sub-formula of boolean connectives. SAT controls existential quantifiers and disjunctions, while UNSAT controls universal quantifiers and conjunctions. SAT wins the game if the chosen model satisfies the chosen sub-formula; otherwise, UNSAT wins. A (LA) formula is satisfiable exactly when SAT has a winning strategy—a function determining how SAT should instantiate existential quantifiers and choose sub-formulae of disjuncts to prove the formula satisfiable—to the induced game.

The game-theoretic view of formulae suggests a variation of the satisfiability problem, in which the goal is not (just) to check satisfiability of a formula, but to synthesize a winning strategy for one of the two players. Strategy synthesis can be used as a decision procedure, but can also used for other tasks where a simple yes or no is insufficient (e.g., program synthesis, angelic symbolic execution, or invariant generation).

While the game semantics of first-order logic gives meaning to both quantifiers and connectives, both Bjørner and Janota [4]'s and Farzan and Kincaid [8]'s decision procedures only make use of the game semantics of quantifiers. To do so, both techniques require the input formula to be in prenex normal form—the formula is a sequence of quantifiers followed by a quantifier free formula. While any formula may be converted into a prenex normal form, doing so is undesirable for two reasons: (1) conversion to prenex normal form may increase the number of quantifier alternations within the formula and (2) conversion to prenex normal form may change the *game semantics* of the formula. Since prenex conversion does not preserve game semantics, it cannot be used in applications that rely on *strategy synthesis* rather than a yes/no answer.

Existing techniques for checking satisfiability of LA formulas are incapable of producing strategies for both quantifiers and Boolean connectives [4,5,8,18]. While both Bjørner and Janota [4]'s and Farzan and Kincaid [8,9] use the game semantics of LA formulas, they limit their scope to quantifiers via conversion to prenex normal form. Furthermore, the procedure by Bjørner and Janota does not produce an explicit term used to instantiate quantifiers. On the other hand, while the techniques of both Reynolds et al. [18] and Bonacina et al. [5] exploit the fine-grained (quantifier and Boolean connectives) structure of formulas, they do not produce a winning strategy.

This paper presents a decision procedure for checking satisfiability of quantified LA formulae that exploits the fine-grained structure of a formula to produce a winning strategy for SAT or UNSAT for both quantifiers and Boolean connectives. Our technique *Fine-grained Strategy Improvement* uses the fine-grained structure of LA formulas to formulate a recursive procedure that iteratively improves a candidate strategy via computing winning strategies to induced subgames. We generalize the notion of strategies and counter-strategy computation from Farzan and Kincaid [8] to handle quantifiers and connectives as well as allowing computing counter-strategies with a fixed prefix (to enable the recursive nature of fine-grained strategy improvement). Fine-grained strategy improvement improves upon existing techniques by (1) avoiding conversion to prenex normal form or (2) allowing extraction of a proof object (a winning strategy) that determines exactly how the formula is proven to be (un)satisfiable.

For simplicity, the remainder of this paper provides details for linear rational arithmetic (LRA); however, the algorithmic details and game semantics provided in this paper are directly applicable to any theory that admits an appropriate term-selection function (cf. Sect. 5.1) including linear integer arithmetic (LIA). In Sect. 2, we review the game semantics for linear arithmetic [12], and its relation with LRA satisfiability. Sections 3, 4, and 5 present the procedure to compute winning strategy skeletons, whose existence proves or disproves LRA satisfiability. Section 6 shows how to compute a winning strategy from a strategy skeleton. Sections 7 and 8 compares this work to others. The extended version[1] contains implementation details, proofs, and extended experimental results.

2 Fine-Grained Game Semantics for LRA Satisfiability

This section reviews the syntax (Sect. 2.1) of **Linear Rational Arithmetic** (LRA) and its game semantics (Sect. 2.2).

2.1 Linear Rational Arithmetic

The syntax of LRA is formed from two sets—Terms and Formulas. The grammar for terms and formulae parameterized over a set of variables X is as follows:

$$s, t \in \textbf{Term}(X) ::= c \in \mathbb{Q} \mid x \in X \mid s + t \mid c \cdot t$$
$$\varphi, \psi \in \textbf{Formula}(X) ::= t < 0 \mid t = 0 \mid \varphi \wedge \psi \mid \varphi \vee \psi \mid \forall x.\ \varphi \mid \exists x.\ \varphi$$

Without loss of generality, this paper considers negation free formulae and assumes that every variable bound by a quantifier within a formula to be distinct. For a formula φ, $FV(\varphi)$ denotes its free variables. Similarly, $FV(t)$ denotes the free variables of term t. A **sentence** is a LRA formula with no free variables. A **ground formula** is a quantifier-free formula which may contain free variables.

A **valuation**, $M : V \rightarrow \mathbb{Q}$, maps a finite set of variables, $V \subseteq X$, to the rationals. We use $[\![t]\!]^M$ to denote the value of t within the valuation M—assuming

---

[1] The extended version of this paper is available at https://pages.cs.wisc.edu/~tcmurphy4/docs/fine_grained_strategy_synthesis.pdf.

$FV(t) \subseteq dom(M)$—with the usual interpretation. $M \models \varphi$ denotes that M satisfies the formula φ (we say M is a model of φ).

For a valuation M, a variable x, and a rational constant c, $M\{x \mapsto c\}$ denotes the valuation M except with x mapped to c.

$$M\{x \mapsto c\} \triangleq \lambda y.\text{if } y = x \text{ then } c \text{ else } M(y)$$

For a formula φ, variable x, and term t, $\varphi[x \mapsto t]$ represents the formula obtained by substituting every free occurrence of x with t.

2.2   Fine-Grained Game Semantics

For a more thorough introduction, Hintikka describes the game semantics for first-order formulae [12]. Every LRA sentence defines a *satisfiability game*, which is played between two players: SAT and UNSAT. The players take turns choosing instantiations for quantifiers and sub-formulae of connectives. SAT controls the choices for existential quantifiers and disjunctions, while UNSAT controls universal quantifiers and conjunctions.

Formally, a state of a LRA-*satisfiability game* for a LRA-sentence φ is $G(\psi, M)$, where ψ is a sub-formula of φ and M is a valuation. The initial state of the satisfiability game for φ is $G(\varphi, \emptyset)$. Below gives the rules of the game with the assumption that $FV(\psi) \subseteq dom(M)$.

$G(t < 0, M)$ SAT wins if $M \models t < 0$. Otherwise, UNSAT wins.

$G(t = 0, M)$ SAT wins if $M \models t = 0$. Otherwise, UNSAT wins.

$G(\varphi \wedge \psi, M)$ UNSAT chooses to either play $G(\varphi, M)$ or $G(\psi, M)$.

$G(\varphi \vee \psi, M)$ SAT chooses to either play $G(\varphi, M)$ or $G(\psi, M)$.

$G(\forall x.\varphi, M)$ UNSAT picks $c \in \mathbb{Q}$ and then plays $G(\varphi, M\{x \mapsto c\})$.

$G(\exists x.\varphi, M)$ SAT picks $c \in \mathbb{Q}$ and then plays $G(\varphi, M\{x \mapsto c\})$.

A *strategy* for SAT or UNSAT determines that player's next move as a function of all the moves previously played. In the above definition of a LRA-satisfiability game, the state $G(\psi, M)$ implicitly represents the moves made so far. This is made explicit by representing a *play* of the game as a sequence of rational numbers (instantiating quantifiers) and the labels L and R (choosing the left or right branch of a disjunction or conjunction). For the formula φ and play π, we represent the sub-formula and valuation forming the state of the game after playing π as φ^π and m^π, respectively. Both are defined as follows:

$$\varphi^\epsilon \triangleq \varphi \quad (\forall x.\varphi)^{c \cdot \pi} \triangleq \varphi^\pi \qquad (\exists x.\varphi)^{c \cdot \pi} \triangleq \varphi^\pi$$
$$M^\epsilon \triangleq \emptyset \qquad M^{c \cdot \pi} \triangleq M^\pi\{x \mapsto c\} \qquad M^{c \cdot \pi} \triangleq M^\pi\{x \mapsto c\}$$

$$(\varphi \wedge \psi)^{L \cdot \pi} \triangleq \varphi^\pi \quad (\varphi \wedge \psi)^{R \cdot \pi} \triangleq \psi^\pi \quad (\varphi \vee \psi)^{L \cdot \pi} \triangleq \varphi^\pi \quad (\varphi \vee \psi)^{R \cdot \pi} \triangleq \psi^\pi$$
$$M^{L \cdot \pi} \triangleq M^\pi \qquad M^{R \cdot \pi} \triangleq M^\pi \qquad M^{L \cdot \pi} \triangleq M^\pi \qquad M^{R \cdot \pi} \triangleq M^\pi$$

If φ^π does not evaluate using the above rules, then π is an *illegal* play and φ^π is undefined. In the remainder of this paper, we use "play" to mean "legal play." A play π is **complete** when φ^π is an atom (neither player has any move to make). For any complete play π, SAT *wins* if and only if $M^\pi \models \varphi^\pi$. Similarly, UNSAT wins if and only if $M^\pi \not\models \varphi^\pi$.

For any formula φ, $\neg\varphi$ denotes the negation-free formula equivalent to the negation of φ. The sentence $\neg\varphi$, induces the dual satisfiability game of φ – a game played in the same manner as φ but with the roles of SAT and UNSAT swapped. This duality is used to define terminology and algorithms explicitly for SAT and implicitly for UNSAT as the corresponding SAT version for $\neg\varphi$.

Definition 1 (Strategy). *Let* $\mathcal{M} = \mathbb{Q} \cup \{L, R\}$ *be the set of all moves,* $f :$ $\mathcal{M}^* \to \mathcal{M}$ *be a partial function from sequences of moves to a move, and* π *a sequence of moves. The play* π **conforms** *to* f *exactly when* $\pi_i = f(\pi_1, \ldots, \pi_{i-1})$ *whenever* $f(\pi_1, \ldots, \pi_{i-1})$ *is defined.*

Let φ *be a LRA-sentence, a SAT* **strategy** *for* φ *is a partial function* $f :$ $\mathcal{M}^* \to \mathcal{M}$, *which has the property that for any play* π *that conforms to* f, *(1) if* φ^π *is* $F \vee G$ *then* $f(\pi)$ *is defined and* $f(\pi) \in \{L, R\}$ *and (2) if* φ^π *is* $\exists x.F$ *then* $f(\pi)$ *is defined and* $f(\pi) \in \mathbb{Q}$.

The SAT strategy f is **winning** if every complete play that conforms to f is won by SAT. It is well-known that φ is satisfiable if and only if SAT has a winning strategy.

3   Fine-Grained Strategy Skeletons

This section defines fine-grained SAT strategy skeletons that form the basis of our fine-grained strategy improvement algorithm (cf. Algorithm 1). A SAT strategy skeleton is an abstraction that represents multiple possible strategies that SAT may choose. Recall that in Sect. 2.2, we defined strategies to be a function that maps a play of a satisfiability game to the next move of the game. A *strategy skeleton* similarly maps a play of the satisfiability game to a finite set of *possible* moves to play next. At a high-level, the strategy improvement algorithm iteratively finds better and better strategy skeletons via the computation of counter-strategy skeletons (cf. Sect. 5).

Example 1. To illustrate fine-grained strategy skeletons and the algorithms presented in this paper consider the formula φ which we use as a running example throughout this paper:

$$\varphi \triangleq \forall x, z. \ (x = z \vee (\exists y. \ (x < y \wedge y < z) \vee (z < y \wedge y < x)))$$

The formula φ expresses the fact that for any pair of rational numbers x and z, either x and z are equal or there is some value y between x and z. To the right, we display a SAT strategy skeleton for φ which we call S. The two • symbols act as placeholders for the values chosen by UNSAT for the quantified variables x and z.

The skeleton encodes that no matter what values ($\bar{x}$ and $\bar{z}$) UNSAT chooses to instantiate x and y with, SAT chooses to play the left branch of the disjunction leading to the atom $x = z$—at the end of the path we display $\bar{x} = \bar{z}$, which is this atom after substituting the placeholder values for UNSAT's choice for the formally bound variables.

As seen in Examples 1 and 4, SAT skeletons are tree-like structures that follow the structure of φ. Formally, SAT strategy skeletons for a LRA-satisfiability game φ, are represented as a set of paths. We use $SKEL(\varphi, vars)$ to denote the set of SAT strategy skeletons for φ whose terms may range over the set of variables $vars$. For a sub-skeleton of a sentence, $vars$ represents the set of variables that in-scope in φ. The set of strategy skeletons for a sentence is thus $SKEL(\varphi, \emptyset)$. For a set of paths S, $\ell \cdot S = \{\ell \cdot \pi : \pi \in S\}$ denotes the set obtained by prepending each path in S with the label ℓ. Similarly, we define $\pi \Downarrow S = \{\pi' : \pi \cdot \pi' \in S\}$ to be the set of suffixes of π appearing in S. Formally, a skeleton is a subset of $(\mathbf{Term}(X) \cup \{\bullet, L, R\})^*$ (whose specific form depends on the formula φ). We define $SKEL$ as the least solution to the following set of rules:

$$\frac{\varphi \text{ is atomic}}{\{\epsilon\} \in SKEL(\varphi, vars)} \qquad \frac{S \in SKEL(\varphi, vars)}{L \cdot S \in SKEL(\varphi \vee \psi, vars)} \qquad \frac{S \in SKEL(\psi, vars)}{R \cdot S \in SKEL(\varphi \vee \psi, vars)}$$

$$\frac{S \in SKEL(\varphi, vars) \quad T \in SKEL(\psi, vars)}{(L \cdot S) \cup (R \cdot T) \in SKEL(\varphi \wedge \psi, vars)} \qquad \frac{S \in SKEL(\varphi, vars \cup \{x\})}{\bullet \cdot S \in SKEL(\forall x.\ \varphi, vars)}$$

$$\frac{t \in \mathbf{Term}(vars) \quad S \in SKEL(\varphi, vars \cup \{x\})}{(t \cdot S) \in SKEL(\exists x.\ \varphi, vars)} \qquad \frac{S, T \in SKEL(\varphi, vars)}{(S \cup T) \in SKEL(\varphi, vars)}$$

Just as strategies can be thought of as a collection of plays, strategy skeletons can be thought of as a collection of strategies. Similar to strategies and plays, we can determine when a strategy conforms to a strategy skeleton. We say a SAT strategy f conforms to a strategy skeleton S when every complete play π conforming to f conforms to S. A play π conforms to S, if there is some path $\rho \in S$ such that $|\pi| = |\rho|$ and for each i we have (1) $\varphi^{\pi_0, \ldots, \pi_{i-1}} = \exists x.\psi$ for some ψ and $[\![x]\!]^{M^\pi} = [\![\rho_i]\!]^{M^\pi}$, or (2) $\varphi^{\pi_0, \ldots, \pi_{i-1}}$ is a disjunctive or conjunctive formula and $\pi_i = \rho_i$, or (3) $\varphi^{\pi_0, \ldots, \pi_{i-1}}$ is a universally quantified formula and $\rho_i = \bullet$. A strategy skeleton is **winning** if there is a winning strategy that conforms to it.

In order to develop a decision procedure that produces a winning strategy skeleton, we first turn to the problem of determining if a SAT skeleton S for the LRA satisfiability game $G(\varphi, M)$ is winning. To determine if S wins the game $G(\varphi, M)$ we check if the *losing* formula $lose(S, \varphi)$ is not satisfied by M (i.e., S wins $G(\varphi, M)$ if $M \not\models lose(S, \varphi)$). This formulation results in a formula that is existentially quantified and can be easily Skolemized to a quantifier free formula and checked with an off-the-shelf SMT solver. Furthermore, we show in Sect. 5 that a model of the Skolemized formula can be used to construct an UNSAT strategy skeleton for φ that beats S. We define $\mathrm{lose}(S, \varphi)$ as follows:

$$\mathrm{lose}(\emptyset, \varphi) \triangleq true$$

$$\mathrm{lose}(\{\epsilon\}, \varphi) \triangleq \neg\varphi$$

$$\mathrm{lose}(S, \varphi \vee \psi) \triangleq \mathrm{lose}(L \Downarrow S, \varphi) \wedge \mathrm{lose}(R \Downarrow S, \psi)$$

$$\mathrm{lose}(S, \varphi \wedge \psi) \triangleq \mathrm{lose}(L \Downarrow S, \varphi) \vee \mathrm{lose}(R \Downarrow S, \psi)$$

$$\mathrm{lose}(S, \exists x.\varphi) \triangleq \bigwedge_{t \cdot \pi \in S} \mathrm{lose}(t \Downarrow S, \varphi)[x \mapsto t]$$

$$\mathrm{lose}(S, \forall x.\varphi) \triangleq \exists x.\mathrm{lose}(\bullet \Downarrow S, \varphi)$$

If M satisfies the losing formula $\mathrm{lose}(S, \varphi)$, then S is not a winning strategy skeleton for the game $G(\varphi, M)$. Intuitively, this implies that UNSAT can beat SAT if SAT plays according to any strategy conforming to S. We use the intuition to formalize when an UNSAT strategy skeleton U beats the SAT skeleton S.

Definition 2 (Counter Strategy). *Fix a LRA-satisfiability game φ, play π of φ, SAT skeleton S for φ^π, and UNSAT skeleton U for φ^π. U is a **counter-strategy** of S (U beats S), if there is some strategy g conforming to U such that for every strategy f conforming to S, UNSAT wins every complete play $\pi\pi'$ such that π' conforms to both f and g.*

Crucially, it cannot be the case that U beats S and S beats U. This asymmetry is ensures that the strategy improvement algorithm makes progress towards verifying or falsifying the formula φ.

Example 2. Recall the initial strategy S from Example 1, in which SAT always chose the branch with the atom $x = z$ no matter what values UNSAT chose for x and z. The losing formula of S is $lose(S) \triangleq \bar{x} \neq \bar{z}$ which summarizes the choices of $\bar{x}$ and $\bar{z}$ that UNSAT may make to falsify the atom $x = z$ SAT choose. The losing formula of S is satisfiable—e.g., with the model $M = \{\bar{x} \mapsto 0, \bar{z} \mapsto 1\}$. Since the losing formula is satisfiable, there must be some counter-strategy that beats S. One such counter-strategy U is depicted to the right—remember that the UNSAT strategy U is a SAT strategy to the for-

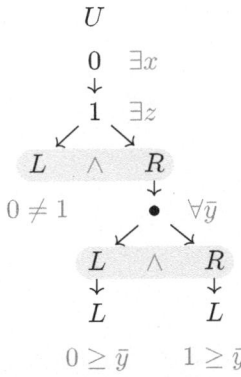

mula $\neg\varphi$. As in Example 1, U is annotated with additional labels: terms are labeled with the existential quantifier they are instantiating, each $\bullet$ is annotated with the corresponding Skolem constants from $lose(S, \varphi)$, and conjunctions are grouped and highlighted to visually distinguish conjunctive branches from disjunctive branches. Finally, each leaf of the skeleton is labeled with the atomic formula reached after substituting the terms and Skolem constants for each quantified variable.

The skeleton U states that UNSAT will always choose 0 to instantiate x and 1 to instantiate z. If SAT chooses the left branch, then the play is over and UNSAT wins. Otherwise, SAT chooses the right branch and a symbolic value $\bar{y}$ to instantiate y. Then SAT chooses to either play the left or right branch of the resulting sub-game. If SAT chose left then UNSAT will chose to play the left sub-game and the play ends in the atom $0 \geq \bar{y}$. Otherwise, when SAT plays the right sub-game, UNSAT chooses to play the resulting left sub-game and play ends in the atom $1 \geq \bar{y}$.

Proposition 1. *Let S be a SAT strategy for the game $G(\varphi, M)$. S is winning if and only if $M \models lose(S, \varphi)$.*

Algorithm 1: Satisfiability modulo LRA

Function Solve(φ,M^π,S)
  Input: LRA Formula $\varphi = \psi^\pi$ for
        some sentence ψ.
    Valuation $M^\pi : (x_0, \ldots, x_n) \to \mathbb{Q}$ such
    that $FV(\varphi) \subseteq dom(M^\pi)$.
    S a SAT skeleton for φ.
  switch has-counter-strategy(S, M^π, φ) do
    case *Counter-strategy U* **do**
      $\langle \pi', U' \rangle \leftarrow peel(\varphi, U)$;
      switch Solve($\neg\varphi^{\pi'}$, $M^\pi \cup M^{\pi'}$, U') do
        case *Sat U''* **do**
          return *Unsat $\pi' \cdot U''$*
        case *Unsat S'* **do**
          return Solve(φ, M^π, $S \cup (\neg\pi') \cdot S'$)
    case *default* **do**
      return *Sat S*

Function Strategy-Improvement(φ)
  Let $S \in SKEL(\varphi, \emptyset)$ be any skeleton
  for φ;
  switch Solve(φ, $\lambda x. \perp$, S) do
    case *Sat S'* **do**
      return *true*
    case *Unsat U* **do**
      return *false*

---

4   Fine-Grained Strategy Improvement

This section presents an algorithm for deciding LRA satisfiability (Algorithm 1). At a high level, the algorithm produces a winning strategy skeleton via fine-grained strategy improvement. Algorithm 1 iteratively improves the current player (SAT)'s strategy. Each iteration attempts to compute a counter-strategy for the opposing player (UNSAT), fixes the opposing player's initial moves and recursively solves the resulting sub-game. If the opposing player wins the sub-game, then they win the game, and a winning strategy can be constructed using the synthesized initial moves and the winning strategy for the subgame. If the opposing player loses the subgame, the current player's winning strategy for the subgame is used to improve their strategy. The algorithm then proceeds to the next iteration of the current game and repeats until a winning player can be determined.

Algorithm 1 assumes that UNSAT makes the first move in the game $G(\varphi, M)$. If SAT would instead play first, Algorithm 1 may be applied to $\neg\varphi$ and the result negated. The first step of the strategy improvement algorithm initializes a SAT skeleton. Any SAT skeleton $S \in SKEL(\varphi, \emptyset)$ may be used.

After initialization, the algorithm will check if a counter-strategy exists (cf. Sect. 5). If there is no counter-strategy, then necessarily SAT's current skeleton S must be winning. Otherwise, UNSAT has a counter-strategy U that beats S. The auxiliary function *peel* uses φ and U to compute π'—the leading universal and conjunctive moves—and U'—the remaining skeleton (i.e. $U = \pi' \cdot U'$). The algorithm continues by fixing the moves in π' and having the players swap places while solving the resulting sub-game $\neg\varphi^{\pi'}$. Formally, *peel* is defined as follows:

$$peel(\forall x.F, U) \triangleq \langle t \cdot \pi, U' \rangle \qquad \text{where } \langle \pi, U' \rangle = peel(F, U'') \text{ and } U = t \cdot U''$$

$$peel(F \wedge G, U) \triangleq \langle L \cdot \pi, U' \rangle \qquad \text{where } \langle \pi, U' \rangle = peel(F, U'') \text{ and } U = L \cdot U''$$

$$peel(F \wedge G, U) \triangleq \langle R \cdot \pi, U' \rangle \qquad \text{where } \langle \pi, U' \rangle = peel(G, U'') \text{ and } U = R \cdot U''$$

$$peel(\varphi, U) \triangleq \langle \epsilon, U \rangle \qquad \text{otherwise}$$

By construction, the leading UNSAT moves of a counter-strategy must form a single path—Algorithm 3 only chooses a single term or conjunct when constructing a counter-strategy. This ensures that *peel* is properly defined. After peeling off the leading universal and conjunctive moves from U, the algorithm recursively solves the resulting sub-game (from the point-of-view of UNSAT by recursing on $\neg\varphi^{\pi'}$ instead of $\varphi^{\pi'}$).

After the recursive call, either SAT or UNSAT has a winning skeleton to $G(\neg\varphi^{\pi'}, M^{\pi'})$. If SAT wins $G(\neg\varphi^{\pi'}, M^{\pi'})$ with the skeleton U'', then UNSAT must win $G(\varphi^{\pi'}, M^{\pi'})$ with the UNSAT skeleton U''. Since UNSAT controls the initial moves π', we may conclude that UNSAT wins the entire game $G(\varphi, M)$ and return the winning UNSAT skeleton $\pi' \cdot U''$.

Otherwise, UNSAT wins $G(\neg\varphi^{\pi'}, M^{\pi'})$ with the skeleton S'. The sub-skeleton S' can be extended to counter U by prepending every path of S' with the "negation" of π' the initial moves of UNSAT. Note that by construction, π' consists only of terms instantiating universal quantifiers or L or R denoting a choice of a conjunctive branch. We define the negation of π' as follows: each term in π' is replaced with a $\bullet$—i.e. $(\neg\pi')_i = \pi'_i$ if $\pi'_i \in \{L, R\}$, otherwise $(\neg\pi')_i = \bullet$. Technically, $(\neg\pi') \cdot S'$ is not a skeleton when π' contains conjunctive moves—the resulting set of paths only covers one of the branches, while a SAT skeleton must cover both branches of a conjunction—however, when unioned with S the initial skeleton for SAT, the final result is a skeleton that counters U.

Example 3.

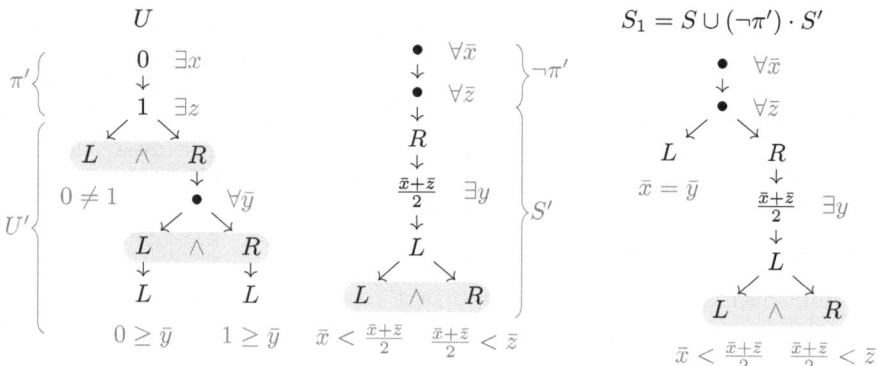

Continuing Example 1, let us suppose that we begin Algorithm 1 with the SAT strategy skeleton S depicted in Example 1 (which simply takes the left branch of the disjunction). S is not winning, since the UNSAT player may choose different values for x and z to invalidate the equality—one such counter-strategy U for S appears above. After using *peel* to construct π' and U', Algorithm 1 recursively solves the sub-game $\neg\varphi^{\pi'} \triangleq x \neq z \wedge \forall y. \ (x \geq y) \vee (y \geq z) \wedge (z \geq y) \vee (y \geq x)$ starting with U' and the model $M^{\pi'} = \{x \mapsto 0, z \mapsto 1\}$. The sub-game is played with the role of the two players switched—the recursive call uses the formula $\neg\varphi^{\pi'}$ rather than $\varphi^{\pi'}$—thus, U' is a SAT skeleton for the resulting sub-game *and* the assumption that the top-level connective of φ is controlled by UNSAT is maintained.

The recursive call returns that UNSAT won the game $G(\neg\varphi^{\pi'}, M^{\pi \cdot \pi'})$ with the skeleton S'. The skeleton S' will instantiate y with the average of x and z and chose the left disjunct $x < y < z$, which clearly beats U' when x is 0 and z is 1.

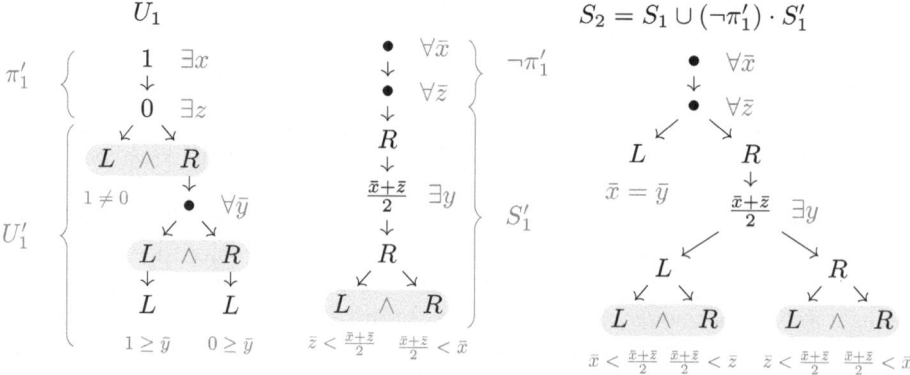

While S_1 counters U, it is not yet winning. SAT will lose any play where UNSAT instantiates x and z such that $z < x$. On the next iteration of the game the algorithm finds U_1 a counter-skeleton to S_1. Just as before the procedure splits apart U_1 and solves the induced sub-game. The procedure finds that SAT wins the sub-game with the skeleton S_1'. The new skeleton is extended and

---

Algorithm 2: Check if a given strategy skeleton has a counter-strategy

---

Function has-counter-strategy(S, M_0, φ)

Input: LRA formula φ.

Valuation $M_0 : (x_0, \ldots, x_n) \to \mathbb{Q}$ s.t.

$FV(\varphi) \subseteq dom(M_0)$

S a SAT strategy skeleton for φ

foreach π such that $\pi \bullet \pi' \in S$ for some π' **do**
　　$H[\pi\bullet] \leftarrow$ fresh rational variable

foreach π such that $\pi L \pi' \in S$ for some π' and
φ^π is a conjunction **do**
　　$H[\pi L] \leftarrow$ fresh Boolean variable
　　$H[\pi R] \leftarrow$ fresh Boolean variable

$lose \leftarrow true$

foreach $\pi \in S$ **do**
　　$win \leftarrow \varphi^\pi \{x \mapsto M_0(x) : x \in dom(M)\}$
　　$conds \leftarrow true$
　　for $i \leftarrow |\pi|$ to 1 **do**
　　　　$\pi' \leftarrow \pi_1, \ldots, \pi_{i-1}$
　　　　if $\varphi^{\pi'} = F \wedge G$ **then**
　　　　　　$conds \leftarrow conds \wedge (win \Rightarrow H[\pi' \cdot \pi_i])$
　　　　　　$win \leftarrow H[\pi' \cdot L] \wedge H[\pi' \cdot R]$
　　　　else if $\varphi^{\pi'} = \exists x.F$ **then**
　　　　　　$win \leftarrow win[x \mapsto \pi_i]$
　　　　　　$conds \leftarrow conds[x \mapsto \pi_i]$
　　　　else if $\varphi^{\pi'} = \forall x.F$ **then**
　　　　　　$win \leftarrow win[x \mapsto H[\pi'\bullet]]$
　　　　　　$conds \leftarrow conds[x \mapsto H[\pi'\bullet]]$
　　$lose \leftarrow lose \wedge (\neg win) \wedge conds$
　　if $lose$ is satisfiable **then**
　　　　Let M be an extension of M_0 satisfying $lose$
　　　　$\langle U, G \rangle \leftarrow \mathbf{CSS}(\varphi, M, M_0, \epsilon, S)$
　　　　return *Counter-strategy U*
　　return *None*

---

combined with S_1 to form S_2 and the current game φ continues starting from S_2; however, on the next iteration, the procedure determines that S_2 has no counter-strategy and is thus a winning SAT skeleton for the game φ.

Theorem 1. *Algorithm 1 is a decision procedure for LRA satisfiability.*

5   Computing Counter-Strategies

When a strategy skeleton is not winning—its losing formula is satisfiable—the opposing player must have a counter-strategy that beats every strategy that conforms to the strategy skeleton. Given a model of the losing formula, this section shows how to construct such a counter-strategy skeleton.

At a high level, Algorithm 1 uses Algorithm 2 to (1) determine if a strategy skeleton S is winning and (2) if S is not winning to return a counter-strategy U that beats S (and returning none if S is winning). Given a LRA satisfiability game $G(\varphi, M)$ and skeleton S, Algorithm 2 computes (a formula equisatisfiable to) lose(S, φ), then uses Algorithm 3 to synthesize a counter-strategy to S if lose(S, φ) is satisfied by M.

Algorithm 2 first constructs the losing formula. The first step of which introduces a new Herbrand constant for each path to a universal quantifier and a fresh Boolean variable for each path to a conjunct within φ. The produced formula is equisatisfiable to the losing formula described in Sect. 3. By existentially quantifying the introduced Boolean variables and Skolem constants *lose* becomes

---

Algorithm 3: Constructing a counter-strategy

Function CSS$(\varphi, M, M^\pi, \pi, S)$

Input: LRA formula φ.

Valuation $M : Image(H) \to (\mathbb{Q} \cup \mathbb{B})$
    with $M \models lose(\varphi^\pi, S)$

Valuation $M^\pi : (x_0, \ldots, x_n) \to \mathbb{Q}$ s.t.
    $FV(\varphi^\pi) \subseteq dom(M^\pi)$

π a path fixing SAT's initial moves

S the strategy skeleton for φ^π

Output: $\langle U, F \rangle$ where $M^\pi \models F$ and

U is an unsat skeleton that beats S on

$G(\varphi^\pi, M')$ for any M' satisfying F

if $S = \emptyset$ **then**
    return $\langle$Any $skel \in SKEL(\neg\varphi^\pi, dom(M^\pi)), \top\rangle$

else if φ^π is atomic **then**
    return $\langle\{\epsilon\}, \neg\varphi^\pi\rangle$

else if $\varphi^\pi = \varphi_l \wedge \varphi_r$ **then**
    if $\neg[\![H[\pi \cdot L]]\!]^M$ **then**
        $\langle U_l, F_l \rangle \leftarrow \mathbf{CSS}(\varphi_l, M, M^\pi, \pi \cdot L, L \Downarrow S)$
        return $\langle L \cdot U_l, F_l \rangle$
    else
        $\langle U_r, F_r \rangle \leftarrow \mathbf{CSS}(\varphi_r, M, M^\pi, \pi \cdot R, R \Downarrow S)$
        return $\langle R \cdot U_r, F_r \rangle$

else if $\varphi^\pi = \varphi_l \vee \varphi_r$ **then**
    $\langle U_l, F_l \rangle \leftarrow \mathbf{CSS}(\varphi_l, M, M^\pi, \pi \cdot L, L \Downarrow S)$
    $\langle U_r, F_r \rangle \leftarrow \mathbf{CSS}(\varphi_r, M, M^\pi, \pi \cdot R, R \Downarrow S)$
    return $\langle (L \cdot U_l) \cup (R \cdot U_r), F_l \wedge F_r \rangle$

else if $\varphi^\pi = \forall x.\varphi'$ **then**
    $M^{\pi\bullet} \leftarrow M^\pi\{x \mapsto [\![H[\pi\bullet]]\!]^M\}$
    $\langle U, F \rangle \leftarrow \mathbf{CSS}(\varphi', M, M^{\pi\bullet}, \pi\bullet, \bullet \Downarrow S)$
    $t \leftarrow \mathbf{select}(M^{\pi\bullet}, x, F)$
    return $\langle t \cdot U, F[x \mapsto t] \rangle$

else if $\varphi^\pi = \exists x.\varphi'$ **then**
    $U \leftarrow \emptyset$
    $G \leftarrow true$
    foreach t such that $t \cdot \pi' \in S$ for some π' **do**
        $M^{\pi \cdot t} \leftarrow M^\pi\{x \mapsto [\![t]\!]^{M^\pi}\}$
        $\langle U^+, F^+ \rangle \leftarrow \mathbf{CSS}(\varphi', M, M^{\pi \cdot t}, \pi \cdot t, t \Downarrow S)$
        $F \leftarrow F \wedge (F^+[x \mapsto t])$
        $U \leftarrow U \cup U+$
    return $\langle \bullet U, F \rangle$

---

logically equivalent to $lose(S, \varphi)$. The introduced Boolean variables enable an explicit encoding of UNSAT's choice of conjunct within the losing formula. This allows a model of the losing formula (if one exists) to explicitly track which branch UNSAT has a counter-strategy for. The algorithm computes the losing formula on a path-by-path basis. It does so by computing when SAT could win the given path and taking its negation (i.e., $(\neg win) \wedge conds$). We use win to denote if the path could be won by SAT—note that for conjunctions SAT must be able to win both of the conjuncts—and $conds$ to constrain the introduced Boolean variables (i.e., $H(\pi)$ represents if the sub-skeleton rooted at π is winning). After constructing $lose$, Algorithm 2 checks if the formula is satisfiable. If $lose$ is unsatisfiable, then S is a winning skeleton for the (sub-)game φ and has no counter-strategy. Otherwise, there is a model of $lose$, that can be used with Algorithm 3 to produce an UNSAT skeleton that beats S.

Algorithm 3 recursively decomposes S and φ to produce a counter-strategy. Before recursing, a model of the bound variables (M^π) and the path-prefix π is constructed. For universals, the valuation is extended using the model of $lose$, and for existentials the valuation is extended by evaluating the term instantiating the quantifier using the model of the previously bound variables. To ensure that the recursive call produces a counter-skeleton that beats the sub-skeleton of S, M must be a model of the losing formula of the sub-skeleton. Whenever φ is not conjunctive this is trivially true, as $lose(\varphi, S)$ is a conjunction of the losing formulae for the sub-skeletons. This ensures that the model of the parent formula is also a model of all sub-formulae. In the case when φ is a conjunction, the Boolean variables introduced to construct the losing formula determine which of the subformulae are also modeled by M. If the introduced Boolean variable for a given conjunct is false in the model M, then it must be that the given conjunct also evaluates to false in the given model. This condition ensures that M is also model of the losing formula of the sub-skeleton and thus that the recursive call computes a counter-strategy to the given sub-skeleton. The algorithm then goes back up and constructs a counter-strategy. For atomic formula, there is only one possible strategy, the empty strategy. For conjuncts, the counter-strategy simply extends a counter-strategy for the left or right branch of the conjunct depending on which branch has a counter-strategy in model M—it is possible both have a counter strategy in model M, taking either or both counter-strategies produces a counter-strategy. For disjunctions, a counter-strategy combines a counter-strategy for both the left and right disjuncts. If the strategy S only takes one of the two branches, then any skeleton for the disjunct may be returned. For universal quantifiers, we use model based term selection to select a term t to instantiate x such that t satisfies the same atoms of G within the given module $M^{\pi \bullet}$ (cf. Sect. 5.1). For existentials, we construct a counter-strategy as the union of a counter-strategy for each choice SAT had made.

5.1   Term Selection

When generating a counter-strategy, Algorithm 3 makes use of the auxiliary function **select** to select a term t to instantiate x. The function **select** is a (model-guided) term selection function [8].

Given a formula F, a variable $x \in FV(F)$ free in F, and a model $M \models F$ of F, we require $\mathbf{select}(M, x, F)$ to return a term t over the free variables of F excluding x (i.e., $FV(t) \subseteq FV(F) \setminus \{x\}$) such that M satisfies F when t is substituted for x (i.e., $M \models F[x \mapsto t]$). Furthermore, to ensure that Algorithm 1 is a decision procedure, we require that for any formula F and variable $x \in FV(F)$ **select** has finite image (i.e., the set $\{\mathbf{select}(M, x, F) : M \models F\}$ is finite).

For LRA, we define **select** as follows. Without loss of generality, we assume that any atom of F that contains x is written as $x = s$, $x < s$, or $x > s$ for some s. Let $EQ(M, x, F)$ contain the term s if and only if $x = s$ is an atom of F and $[\![x]\!]^M = [\![S]\!]^M$. Similarly $UB(M, x, F)$ contains the term s if and only if $x < s$ is an atom of F and $[\![x]\!]^M < [\![s]\!]^M$. Finally, let $LB(M, x, F)$ contain the term s if and only if $x > s$ is an aotm of F and $[\![x]\!]^M > [\![s]\!]^M$. Furthermore, if $EQ(M, x, F)$ is not empty, let $eq(M, x, F)$ be any $s \in EQ(M, x, F)$. If $UB(M, x, F)$ is not empty, then let $lub(M, x, F)$ be a term $s \in UB(M, x, F)$ such that for any other $s' \in UB(M, x, F)$, $[\![s]\!]^M \leq [\![s']\!]^M$. Similarly, if $LB(M, x, f)$ is not empty, then let $glb(M, x, F)$ be a term $s \in LB(M, x, F)$ such that for any other $s' \in LB(M, x, F)$, $[\![s]\!]^M \geq [\![s']\!]^M$.

$$\mathbf{select} = \begin{cases} eq(M, x, F) & \text{if } EQ(M, X, F) \neq \emptyset \\ \frac{1}{2}(lub(M, x, F) + glb(M, x, F)) & \text{if } UB(M, x, F) \neq \emptyset \text{ and } LB(M, x, F) \neq \emptyset \\ lub(M, x, F) - 1 & \text{if } UB(M, x, F) \neq \emptyset \\ glb(M, x, F) + 1 & \text{if } LB(M, X, F) \neq \emptyset \\ 0 & \text{otherwise} \end{cases}$$

For further details on model-guided term selection (including term selection for linear integer arithmetic), we refer the reader to Farzan and Kincaid [8]. While this paper so far has focused on satisfiability of LRA, we note that Algorithm 1 is a decision procedure for any theory that admits a term selection function with finite image. In fact, the only change required is to swap **select** with an appropriate term selection function for the desired theory.

6   Synthesizing Fine-Grained Strategies

Section 4 presents an algorithm that computes a winning strategy skeleton that either proves or refutes satisfiability of a LRA sentence. This section shows how to generalize the technique of [8] to compute a winning fine-grained strategy from a winning fine-grained strategy skeleton. As described in Sect. 2 a SAT strategy is a function from plays to either a rational number (for existential quantifiers) or the labels L and R (for disjunctions).

Strategies vs Skeletons. In Sects. 3, 4, and 5, our techniques and discussion focused on how to compute a *winning strategy skeleton*. While computing a winning strategy skeleton is sufficient to determine satisfiability of a formula, it may be insufficient for other tasks. For example for use in program verification and synthesis tasks (e.g., to determinize non-deterministic choices, synthesize safety conditions, etc.). By definition, a strategy skeleton S is winning if *some* strategy g that conforms to S is winning.

Computing Winning Strategies. This section focuses on how to extract a winning strategy from a winning strategy skeleton S for the game $G(\varphi, M)$. To do so, we construct a system of constrained horn clauses (CHCs) whose solution we use to produce a winning strategy from a winning skeleton. The produced CHC rules represent when the strategy skeleton is losing. Since the strategy skeleton is winning, the rules are satisfiable and a model satisfying the CHCs exists. The process starts by labeling each leaf of S with the atom reached, substituting each of the terms instantiating existential quantifiers. Formally, for any path π of S (from the root to a leaf), we label the leaf (rooted at π) with the formula $subst_\varphi(\neg\varphi^\pi, \pi)$. The function $subst_\varphi$ applies a substitution based on the given path in reverse order of the appearance of each existential quantifier.

$$
\begin{aligned}
subst_\varphi(G, \epsilon) &\triangleq G \\
subst_\varphi(G, \pi \cdot L) &\triangleq subst_\varphi(G, \pi) \\
subst_\varphi(G, \pi \cdot R) &\triangleq subst_\varphi(G, \pi) \\
subst_\varphi(G, \pi\bullet) &\triangleq subst_\varphi(G, \pi) \\
subst_\varphi(G, \pi \cdot t) &\triangleq subst_\varphi(G[x \mapsto t], \pi) \qquad \text{where } \varphi^\pi = \exists x.F
\end{aligned}
$$

For a strategy skeleton S, define its nodes $N = \{\pi : \exists \pi'. \; \pi\pi' \in S\}$ to be prefixes of paths in S. Furthermore, define $Succ : N \to 2^N$ to the set of immediate suffixes. For each node π of S, we introduce an uninterpreted relation $R_\pi(x_1, \ldots, x_n)$ where $x_1, \ldots, x_n = FV(\varphi^\pi)$ are the free variables of φ^π. We produce the following rules:

$$subst_\varphi(\neg\varphi^\pi, \pi) \Rightarrow R_\pi(\ldots) \text{ if } \varphi^\pi \text{ is atomic}$$

$$\left(\bigvee_{\pi' \in Succ(\pi)} R_{\pi'}(\ldots) \right) \Rightarrow R_\pi(\ldots) \text{ if } \varphi^\pi \text{ is conjunctive}$$

$$\left(\bigwedge_{\pi' \in Succ(\pi)} R_{\pi'}(\ldots) \right) \Rightarrow R_\pi(\ldots) \quad \text{otherwise}$$

$$R_\epsilon(x_1, \ldots, x_n) \Rightarrow x_1 \neq M(x_1) \vee \cdots \vee x_n \neq M(x_n)$$

For each $\pi \in N$, R_π represents the set of all M' such that $\pi \Downarrow S$ loses the game $G(\varphi^\pi, M')$. Of note, the last rule requires that R_ϵ does not contain M (i.e., that S must win the game $G(\varphi, M)$). Since the overall skeleton is winning, the rules are satisfiable. A solution for each relation R_π may be computed using an off-the-shelf CHC solver. Applying the negated solution as a guard for each path of the skeleton, produces a winning strategy. Technically, the guards should be determinized to produce a function; however, any such determinization will result in a winning strategy. Formally, for each node π such that φ^π is an existential or disjunctive formula, we produce the function:

$$f_\pi(x_1, \ldots, x_k) \text{ if } \neg R_{\pi'_1} \text{ then } l_1 \text{ elif } \ldots \text{ else } l_m$$

where $FV(\varphi^\varphi) \triangleq \{x_1, \ldots, x_k\}$, $Succ(\pi) \triangleq \{\pi'_1, \ldots, \pi'_m\}$, and where each child π'_i is reached with label l_i in S. Furthermore, for each path $\pi \in (\mathbb{Q} \cup \{L, R\})^*$ such that φ^π is an existential or disjunctive formula, define $f'(\pi)$ to be $f_\pi(c_1, \ldots, c_n)$ where each $c_i = M^\pi(x_i)$ for each free variable $x_i \in FV(\varphi^\pi)$. Finally define $f(\pi)$ to be $f'(\pi)$ if $f'(\pi) \in \{L, R\}$ and otherwise define $f(\pi)$ to be $[\![f'(\pi)]\!]^{M^\pi}$. The function f is a strategy conforming to S that wins the game $G(\varphi, M)$.

Consider the winning skeleton S_2 from Example 3. The left side of Example 4 shows the set of rules to label S_2, depicted as a tree (whose shape follows exactly from the shape of S_2). The graph should be interpreted as saying that a node's label is implied by the combination of each of its children's labels. For nodes 5 and 6, the labels of its children should be combined using disjunctive, otherwise, the label of its children should be combined conjunctively. For example, the rule for node 1, should be read as $R_2(\bar{x}, \bar{z}) \wedge R_3(\bar{x}, \bar{z}) \Rightarrow R_1()$, while the rule for node 5 should be read as $R_7(\bar{x}, \bar{z}) \vee R_8(\bar{x}, \bar{z}) \Rightarrow R_5(\bar{x}, \bar{z})$. The middle column of Example 4 shows a possible solution to the set of rules, and the left-hand side shows the winning strategy extracted from S_2 using the given solution. The strategy $f_{\bullet\bullet}$ states that given UNSAT's choices of $\bar{x}$ and $\bar{z}$ to instantiate x and z, if UNSAT chose equal values for x and y then SAT will chose the left branch—which results in SAT's immediate win—otherwise SAT will chose to play the right branch. $f_{\bullet\bullet R}$ and $f_{\bullet\bullet R\frac{\bar{x}+\bar{z}}{2}}$ are interpreted similarly.

Example 4.

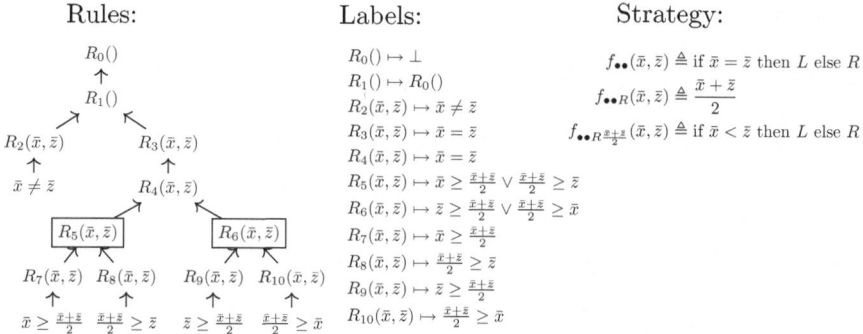

Rules:

Labels:

Strategy:

7   Experimental Evaluation

We extend the tool SimSat—a prototype implementation of the coarse-grained strategy improvement algorithm from Farzan and Kincaid [9]—with the fine-grained strategy improvement procedureSimSat is implemented in OCaml using Z3 [7] to handle ground formulas.

Our experiments aim to answer the following questions: (1) is fine-grained SimSat competitive with state-of-the-art SMT solvers? (2) how much of the difference between coarse-grained SimSat and fine-grained SimSat is driven by considering non-prenex normal form formulas and how much is due to the new strategy improvement algorithm? (3) what is the overhead of computing a winning fine-grained strategy after checking satisfiability of a formula?

We compare fine-grained SimSat to coarse-grained SimSat as well as to Z3 (version 4.11.2) [7], CVC5 (version 1.0.0) [1], and YicesQS [11]. Z3 implements the procedure from Bjørner and Janota [4], CVC5 implements the procedure from Reynolds et al. [18], and YicesQS implements the procedure from Bonacina et al. [5].

We evaluate each tool on three suites of benchmarks: SMT-LIB2, Termination, and Simulation. Each benchmark is described in detail below. All experiments were conducted on a desktop running Ubuntu 18.04 LTS equipped with a 4 core Intel(R) Xeon(R) processor at 3.2GHz and 12 GB of memory. Each experiment was allotted a maximum of five minutes to complete.

To answer (1), fine-grained SimSat is compared to coarse-grained SimSat, CVC5, YicesQS, and Z3. This section does not consider other solvers and methods (e.g. quantifier elimination) as Reynolds et al. [18], Bjørner and Janota [4], and Bonacina et al. [5] show that their methods outperform other existing solvers and methods for quantified LIA and LRA formulas. To answer (2) we consider three variants of fine-grained SimSat. The first variant, "prenex," first converts the input formula to prenex-normal form before running the decision procedure. The second variant, "miniscope," miniscopes (reduces the scope of quantifiers) the formula before running the decision procedure, and the final variant, "fine,"

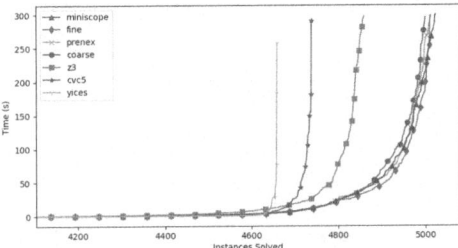 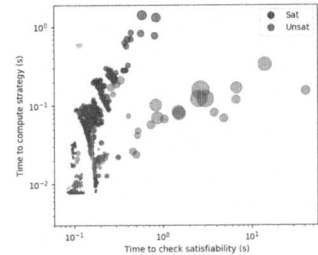

(a) A cactus plot showing x instances solved within y seconds per solver.

(b) Log-scale plot of strategy synthesis time (y-axis) vs satisfiability time (x-axis).

Fig. 1. (a) A cactus plot showing x instances solved within y seconds per solver. (b) Log scale plot of strategy synthesis time (y-axis) vs satisfiability time (x-axis) (Color figure online)

applies the decision procedure without modifying the input formula. Finally, to answer (3) we wish to measure the efficacy of our algorithm for strategy synthesis, but we know of no other algorithm capable of synthesizing strategies for fine-grained games with which to establish a baseline. Instead, we measure the overhead of synthesizing a strategy on top of synthesizing a strategy skeleton.

SMT-LIB2. This suite of benchmarks consists of 2419 LRA and 616 LIA benchmarks. All benchmarks come from SMT-LIB2 [3]. All LIA benchmarks come from industrial problems. The LRA benchmarks consists of 1800 randomly generated formulas in prenex normal form with varying quantifier depth (see Monniaux [15] for detailed descriptions) and 619 industrial benchmarks.

Termination. This suite of benchmarks consists of 200 LIA formulas. The formulas are derived from Zhu and Kincaid's [21] method for proving termination of programs (see Sects. 5 and 6 for details on how formulas are constructed). Each formula encodes a sufficient condition for which a program is terminating—the program terminates if the formula is valid. The suite of benchmark consists of a formula for each program in the "polybench" and "termination" benchmarks from Zhu and Kincaid's evaluation section [21].

Simulation. This suite of benchmarks consists of 2060 LIA formulas. The formulas represent when the state of two integer message passing programs are weakly similar for the next n instructions. For complete details see Chap. 4 of [16], which uses fine-grained strategy synthesis to determinize angelic choice when proving weak simulation between two integer message passing programs.

Results. Table 1 and Figs. 1a 1b summarize the results of the experiments. Figure 1a is a cactus plot. Each line represents a solver's performance. Each point (x, y) within the line for a solver represents that x instances were individually solved in under y seconds by the given solver. The closer the line is to the x-axis the better the solver performed. Table 1 breaks down the results a little further by (sub-)suite of benchmarks. Each entry shows the number of

Table 1. Number of instances solved per suite of benchmarks—UltimateAutomizer, psyco, tptp, Mjollnir, keymaera, and Scholl are sub-categories of SMT-LIB2.

Benchmarks	Miniscope	Fine	Prenex	Coarse	CVC5	YicesQS	Z3	Any	All	Total
Simulation	**2060**	**2060**	**2060**	2059	2059	1972	**2060**	2060	1972	2060
UltimateAutomizer	316	316	315	315	**345**	82	242	349	60	372
psyco	**189**	**189**	**189**	**189**	**189**	146	**189**	189	146	189
tptp (LIA)	**46**	**46**	**46**	**46**	**46**	42	**46**	46	42	46
Termination	**200**	**200**	**200**	196	195	0	166	200	0	200
All LIA	2811	2811	2810	2805	**2834**	2242	2703	2850	2220	2867
Mjollnir	1597	1584	1586	1578	1300	**1800**	1541	1800	1177	1800
keymaera	**222**	**222**	**222**	**222**	**222**	**222**	**222**	222	222	222
Scholl	372	373	372	373	362	**374**	372	374	359	374
tptp (LRA)	**23**	**23**	**23**	**23**	**23**	**23**	0	23	0	23
All LRA	2214	2202	2203	2196	1907	**2419**	2135	2419	1781	2419
All	**5025**	5013	5013	5001	4741	4661	4861	5269	4001	5286

instances from the given suite of benchmarks by the given solver. The "Any" column counts the number of instances solved by *any* of the solvers, while the "All" column counts the number of instances solved by every solver. The "total" column details the total number of instances (solved and unsolved) within the suite of benchmarks. For each suite of benchmark, bolded values highlight which solver(s) solved the most instances of that set of benchmarks.

Overall, all solvers performed well. In fact, Fig. 1a shows that all solvers solved the first 4200 instances in under a second. The Figure zooms into the x-axis after this point to highlight the differences between solvers. The experiments show that the SimSat variants all behaved similarly and out-performed CVC5, Z3, and YicesQS overall. Of the SimSat variants, the miniscoped variant performed best, followed by the normal fine-grained variant, then the fine-grained prenex variant and lastly the coarse-grained variant.

Looking into each suite of benchmarks further, Table 1 shows that while YicesQS solved the fewest instances overall, it actually solved all LRA formulas. Similarly, while CVC5 performed the worst on LRA, it was the best performer on LIA instances, solving 23 more LIA instances than the miniscoped SimSat variant—the next best performer. In both scenarios, the miniscoped SimSat variant placed a close second. CVC5 performed well on the industrial benchmarks; however, struggled with the randomly generated Mjollnir benchmarks, perhaps due to the bottom-up instantiation strategy of its implemented decision procedure [18]. YicesQS excelled at the LRA formulas but failed to solve many of the simulation and termination benchmarks. Overall, Z3 performed well but struggled more with the UltimateAutomizer and Termination benchmarks— benchmarks where conversion to prenex normal form increased quantifier alternations significantly.

Finally, Fig. 1b summarizes the cost of computing a winning fine-grained strategy after checking satisfiability of the given formula—i.e. how much time in seconds did it take to compute a winning strategy from a winning strategy skeleton. Figure 1b, plots a point for each formula within the Simulation benchmark. A point has four associated values: (1) its x position represents how much time is required to prove the formula Sat or Unsat (e.g. time to run "Fine" SimSat variant), (2) its y position represents the amount of time in seconds required to compute a winning strategy from a winning strategy skeleton, (3) its size visually quantifies the number of AST-nodes within the produced winning strategy, and (4) a node is blue if the formula is won by SAT and red if it is won by UNSAT. The smallest computed strategy consisted of a single node (move), while the largest strategy consisted of 448 nodes. Across all instances, the it took roughly 18.4% extra time to additionally compute a winning strategy over just determining satisfiability of a formula. The maximum time to compute a strategy is 1.4 s.

8   Discussion and Related Works

The closest techniques to Algorithm 1 are the QSMA algorithm of Bonacina et al. [5] and the coarse-grained strategy improvement algorithm of Farzan and Kincaid [8]. Fine-grained and course-grained strategy improvement algorithms are similar in that they both use model-based term selection to synthesize counter-strategies to find better and better strategies for each player; however, they differ in a few key ways. Fine-grained strategy synthesis works for formulae that are not in prenex normal form. Additionally, while the coarse-grained strategy improvement iterates between skeletons for the two players computing a counter-strategy to the previous player's most recent skeleton, the fine-grained strategy improvement algorithm chooses a sub-game to focus on and solve before returning to the current game. The coarse-grained algorithm iterates over "global" strategies, where the fine-grained algorithm builds up a strategy by recursively solving sub-games. While Algorithm 1 and QSMA share a similar high-level recursive structure and used model-based techniques, the method of solving sub-formulae differ. The QSMA algorithm uses over- and under-approximations to abstract quantified sub-formulae when determining satisfiability of the current formula whereas Algorithm 1 uses winning strategies of sub-games and model-based term selection to synthesize counter-strategies and ultimately yield a winning strategy to the current formula.

Algorithm 1 also shares some similarities with QSAT the quantified satisfiability algorithm of Bjørner and Janota [4] which is also based on the game semantics of FOL. For formulas in prenex normal form, QSAT and Algorithm 1 both fix a strategy for the first quantifier and then recursively compute a strategy for the remaining quantifiers and back-tracks if no winning strategy exists for the current player; however, the notion of strategy used differs. In QSAT, a strategy selects a subset of the literals in the formula—whose free variables belong to the prefix of quantifiers already explored—that constrains the possible strategies of the remaining quantifiers.

Finally, Algorithm 1 shares similarities with the counter-example instantiation method of Reynolds et al. [18]. Both methods work for formulas beyond prenex normal form and use model based projection techniques to instantiate quantifiers; however, Algorithm 1 uses a top-down approach to synthesize winning strategies, while counter-example instantiation uses a bottom-up technique to instantiate and eliminate quantifiers one quantifier block at a time.

Other methods for LRA/LIA formulas include heuristic instantiation and quantifier elimination. Heuristic instantiation is sound but incomplete and was traditionally the method of choice for many SMT solvers (e.g. CVC4 [2]). Traditional quantifier elimination methods (e.g. Fourier-Motzkin elimination [14], Ferrante-Rackoff [10], and Weispfenning [20] algorithms for LRA, and Cooper's algorithm [6], and Pugh's Omega test [17] for LIA) are sound and complete for LRA/LIA but are extremely costly. Monniaux developed a lazy quantifier elimination method for LRA based on polyhedral projection that performs better in practice [15]. However, Bjørner and Janota show that their algorithm dominates the use of Monniaux's method as a [4]. Finally, Komuravelli et al. [13] introduced model-based projection which under-approximates quantifier elimination for LA and is closely related to the model-based term selection function we use in Sect. 5.1.

Acknowledgements. This work was supported in part by the NSF under grant number 1942537. Opinions, findings, conclusions, or recommendations expressed herein are those of the authors and do not necessarily reflect the views of the sponsoring agencies.

References

1. Barbosa, H., et al.: cvc5: a versatile and industrial-strength SMT solver. In: TACAS 2022. LNCS, vol. 13243, pp. 415–442. Springer, Cham (2022). https://doi.org/10.1007/978-3-030-99524-9_24

2. Barrett, C., et al.: CVC4. In: Gopalakrishnan, G., Qadeer, S. (eds.) CAV 2011. LNCS, vol. 6806, pp. 171–177. Springer, Heidelberg (2011). https://doi.org/10.1007/978-3-642-22110-1_14

3. Barrett, C., Fontaine, P., Tinelli, C.: The Satisfiability Modulo Theories Library (SMT-LIB) (2016). www.SMT-LIB.org

4. Bjørner, N.S., Janota, M.: Playing with quantified satisfaction. LPAR (short papers) **35**, 15–27 (2015)

5. Bonacina, M.P., Graham-Lengrand, S., Vauthier, C.: Qsma: a new algorithm for quantified satisfiability modulo theory and assignment. In: International Conference on Automated Deduction, pp. 78–95. Springer (2023). https://doi.org/10.1007/978-3-031-38499-8_5

6. Cooper, D.C.: Theorem proving in arithmetic without multiplication. Mach. Intell. **7**(91–99), 300 (1972)

7. de Moura, L., Bjørner, N.: Z3: an efficient SMT solver. In: Ramakrishnan, C.R., Rehof, J. (eds.) TACAS 2008. LNCS, vol. 4963, pp. 337–340. Springer, Heidelberg (2008). https://doi.org/10.1007/978-3-540-78800-3_24

8. Farzan, A., Kincaid, Z.: Linear arithmetic satisfiability via strategy improvement. In: IJCAI, pp. 735–743 (2016)

9. Farzan, A., Kincaid, Z.: Strategy synthesis for linear arithmetic games. In: Proceedings of the ACM on Programming Languages 2(POPL), pp. 1–30 (2017)

10. Ferrante, J., Rackoff, C.: A decision procedure for the first order theory of real addition with order. SIAM J. Comput. **4**(1), 69–76 (1975)
11. Graham-Lengrand, S.: Yices-qs 2022, an extension of yices for quantified satisfiability (2022)
12. Hintikka, J.: Game-theoretical semantics: insights and prospects (1982)
13. Komuravelli, A., Gurfinkel, A., Chaki, S.: Smt-based model checking for recursive programs. Formal Methods Syst. Des. **48**, 175–205 (2016)
14. Kroening, D., Strichman, O.: Decision procedures. Springer (2016)
15. Monniaux, D.: Quantifier elimination by lazy model enumeration. In: Touili, T., Cook, B., Jackson, P. (eds.) CAV 2010. LNCS, vol. 6174, pp. 585–599. Springer, Heidelberg (2010). https://doi.org/10.1007/978-3-642-14295-6_51
16. Murphy, T.C.: Relational Verification of Distributed Systems Via Weak Simulations. Ph.D. thesis, Princeton University (2023)
17. Pugh, W.: The omega test: a fast and practical integer programming algorithm for dependence analysis. In: Supercomputing'91: Proceedings of the 1991 ACM/IEEE Conference on Supercomputing, pp. 4–13. IEEE (1991)
18. Reynolds, A., King, T., Kuncak, V.: Solving quantified linear arithmetic by counterexample-guided instantiation. Formal Methods Syst. Des. **51**(3), 500–532 (2017)
19. Reynolds, A., Tinelli, C., Goel, A., Krstić, S., Deters, M., Barrett, C.: Quantifier instantiation techniques for finite model finding in SMT. In: Bonacina, M.P. (ed.) CADE 2013. LNCS (LNAI), vol. 7898, pp. 377–391. Springer, Heidelberg (2013). https://doi.org/10.1007/978-3-642-38574-2_26
20. Weispfenning, V.: The complexity of linear problems in fields. J. Symb. Comput. **5**(1–2), 3–27 (1988)
21. Zhu, S., Kincaid, Z.: Termination analysis without the tears. In: Proceedings of the 42nd ACM SIGPLAN International Conference on Programming Language Design and Implementation, pp. 1296–1311 (2021)

From Clauses to Klauses*

Joseph E. Reeves(✉) ⓘ, Marijn J. H. Heule ⓘ, and Randal E. Bryant ⓘ

Carnegie Mellon University, Pittsburgh, Pennsylvania, United States
{jereeves,mheule,randy.bryant}@cs.cmu.edu

Abstract. Satisfiability (SAT) solvers have been using the same input format for decades: a formula in conjunctive normal form. Cardinality constraints appear frequently in problem descriptions: over 64% of the SAT Competition formulas contain at least one cardinality constraint, while over 17% contain many large cardinality constraints. Allowing general cardinality constraints as input would simplify encodings and enable the solver to handle constraints natively or to encode them using different (and possibly dynamically changing) clausal forms. We modify the modern SAT solver CADICAL to handle cardinality constraints natively. Unlike the stronger cardinality reasoning in pseudo-Boolean (PB) or other systems, our incremental approach with cardinality-based propagation requires only moderate changes to a SAT solver, preserves the ability to run important inprocessing techniques, and is easily combined with existing proof-producing and validation tools. Our experimental evaluation on SAT Competition formulas shows our solver configurations with cardinality support consistently outperform other SAT and PB solvers.

Keywords: Cardinality constraints · SAT solving · CNF Encoding

1 Introduction

Satisfiability (SAT) solvers have become remarkably effective automated reasoning engines in the last 25 years, with many applications in verification including bounded model checking [7] and automatic test generation [4]. Although many aspects of the solvers have changed, the top-tier solvers continue using conjunctive normal form (CNF) formulas as their input. There exist richer representations that allow for stronger reasoning techniques and make encoding problems much simpler. The most successful is Satisfiability Modulo Theories (SMT), which enables high-level reasoning (theory propagation). Higher-level reasoning is not always necessary, and for theories like strings [33] and bit vectors [39] a so-called eager SMT approach works well. This involves transforming the problem from SMT to SAT and using an off-the-shelf SAT solver.

Various groups have proposed a more modest deviation from CNF: a conjunction of cardinality constraints [20,34,43]. A cardinality constraint asserts that the sum of a

---

*Supported by the U.S. National Science Foundation under grant CCF-2108521, and in part by a fellowship award under contract FA9550-21-F-0003 through the National Defense Science and Engineering Graduate (NDSEG) Fellowship Program, sponsored by the Air Force Research Laboratory (AFRL), the Office of Naval Research (ONR) and the Army Research Office (ARO).

A. Gurfinkel and V. Ganesh (Eds.): CAV 2024, LNCS 14681, pp. 110–132, 2024.
https://doi.org/10.1007/978-3-031-65627-9_6

set of literals exceeds a given bound, e.g., $\ell_1 + \ell_2 + \cdots + \ell_s \geq k$. Note that cardinality constraints generalize clauses because a clause $\ell_1 \vee \ell_2 \vee \cdots \vee \ell_s$ is equivalent to $\ell_1 + \ell_2 + \cdots + \ell_s \geq 1$. Cardinality constraints appear frequently in problem descriptions, whether as at-most-one (AMO) constraints that may force some k-valued variable to be unique (e.g., the color of a vertex), or general at-least-k (ALK)/at-most-k (AMK) constraints that place a lower or upper bound on some resource, e.g., for optimization. In our evaluation of 5,354 SAT Competition formulas, we found that over 64% contained at least one cardinality constraint and over 17% contained at least 10 large cardinality constraints (see Section 7). There exist pseudo-Boolean (PB) solvers with stronger reasoning techniques than SAT solvers, but similar to strings and bit vectors, an eager approach transforming cardinality constraints into clauses is often desirable. SAT solvers work well across a wide range of problems and have a more developed verification toolchain. This work attempts to bridge the gap between cardinality constraints and clauses. We introduce an infrastructure for a cardinality-based input for SAT solving that makes encoding problems easier and significantly improves the performance on some problems with many cardinality constraints. These changes come without throwing away the well-developed verification toolchain and high-performance solving of modern SAT solvers.

Attempts to improve solver performance on problems with cardinality constraints have focused on either strengthening the underlying proof system, improving encodings, or natively propagating on constraints. Solvers can make use of stronger proof systems both on formulas with richer input structure and on formulas in CNF. The solver RoundingSAT [21] exploits the strength of the cutting planes proof system [16], allowing it to efficiently solve various problems that are hard for resolution. The solver SAT4J [5] implements cardinality extraction [10] and generalized resolution [26] in a preprocessing step to quickly solve formulas in CNF that contain cardinality constraints, with additional native handling for finding hamiltonian cycles [43]. Additionally, to make writing formulas simpler, solver engineers have provided support for cardinality-based representations. The solver MINISAT+ [20] supports cardinality-based input transforming the formula into clauses, and the solver package PYSAT [27] provides API calls for converting constraints into clauses. Lastly, the solver MiniCARD [34] substantially reduces the memory footprint and improves propagation by handling cardinality constraints natively. However, most of the recent work has focused on stronger proof systems or better encodings. This is partly because implementation details for cardinality-constraint propagation [34,47] came before the development of modern inprocessing, did not account for proof generation, and were only evaluated on some crafted formulas. We revisit native cardinality constraint handling in the context of modern CDCL, showing that performance can be improved on some problems without compromising the verification toolchain (assuming no cutting planes are used).

First, consider propagation, the well-known bottleneck of SAT solvers. Improving propagation speed can boost solver performance on both satisfiable and unsatisfiable formulas. Cardinality constraint propagation can be supported with limited overhead by generalizing the watch-pointer data-structure [34]. Moreover, with modest-sized changes a cardinality-based representation can work with some other reasoning techniques in modern solvers, ranging from learned clause minimization to vivification.

These important techniques can be kept because cardinality-based propagation does not alter the relevant properties of the implication graph during conflict analysis. These changes do not require cutting planes or a new proof checker such as VERIPB [45], and are compatible with standard DRAT proofs. This is in contrast to other forms of native reasoning in CDCL solvers such as XOR parity reasoning. For example, to communicate propagated units and conflicts between XOR clauses and a CNF formula, the solver CRYPTOMINISAT makes use of BDD packages [13] to generate checkable proofs [44], adding overhead to the solving and producing large proofs.

Second, a cardinality-based representation allows for alternative ways to encode and reencode constraints. The choice of encoding can have a large impact on performance [38]. Alternatively, handling cardinality constraints separately, or dynamically encoding partial constraints [2], may also improve performance through faster propagation on frequently visited constraints and the lack of propagation on unimportant constraints. Modern CDCL solvers constantly switch between a SAT and UNSAT mode with differing heuristics [40]. We implement a hybrid solver that maintains reencoded clauses throughout solving but only propagates on cardinality constraints natively during SAT mode. The solver has access to auxiliary variables in the reencoded clauses along with the capability to propagate on cardinality constraints, improving performance on both satisfiable and unsatisfiable formulas.

Contributions. We incorporated cardinality-constraint handling into the modern CDCL SAT solver CADICAL, while still allowing several important inprocessing techniques including clause vivification and local search. We ensure clause learning from propagation on cardinality constraints produces valid proof steps.

We implemented a tool to extract cardinality constraints with a "guess and verify" approach that heuristically identifies possible encoded cardinality constraints in CNF formulas and then uses BDDs to validate and characterize them. We provide three solver configurations: one that uses cardinality-based CDCL reasoning, one that reencodes the cardinality constraints into CNF, and a hybrid approach that combines the two former configurations via. mode-switching. This hybrid configuration (HYBRID) represents a novel approach for incorporating both encoded clauses that are useful for unsatisfiable formulas and native cardinality constraints that are useful for satisfiable formulas. Proofs generated from the three solving configurations are checked with DRAT-TRIM.

We evaluated the cardinality extractor and solving configurations on the SAT Competition Anniversary Track formulas, finding cardinality constraints in over half the formulas, and many large cardinality constraints in over 17% of formulas. On these formulas, CDCL solvers outperformed PB solvers and the cardinality constraint handling further improved the CDCL solver performance. Additionally, solvers were evaluated on the Magic Squares and Max Squares problems, highlighting the importance of a good reencoding and the power of native cardinality constraint propagation.

2   Background

We consider propositional formulas in *conjunctive normal form* (CNF). A CNF formula F is a conjunction of *clauses* where each clause is a disjunction of *literals*. A literal ℓ is either a variable x (positive literal) or a negated variable $\bar{x}$ (negative literal). The *phase* of a literal indicates whether it is positive or negative.

An *assignment* α is a mapping from variables to truth values 1 (*true*) and 0 (*false*). Assignment α *satisfies* a positive (negative) literal ℓ if α maps var(ℓ) to true (α maps var(ℓ) to false, respectively), and *falsifies* it if α maps var(ℓ) to false (α maps var(ℓ) to true, respectively). An assignment satisfies a clause if the clause contains a literal satisfied by the assignment, and satisfies a formula if every clause in the formula is satisfied by the assignment. A formula is *satisfiable* if there exists a satisfying assignment, and *unsatisfiable* otherwise. Two formula are *logically equivalent* if they share the same set of satisfying assignments. Two formulas are *satisfiability equivalent* if they are either both satisfiable or both unsatisfiable.

A *unit* is a clause containing a single literal. *Unit propagation* applies the following operation until a fixed point: take all units α in a formula F and remove from F clauses containing a literal in α, remove from clauses all literals negated in α. In cases where unit propagation yields the empty clause ($\bot$) we say it derived a *conflict*.

2.1 Cardinality Constraints

A cardinality constraint on Boolean variables has the form $\ell_1 + \ell_2 + \cdots + \ell_s \geq k$ and is satisfied by a partial assignment if the sum of the assigned literals is at least k. The size of the cardinality constraint is the number of literals (s) it contains. For this work, we do not permit duplicate literals in cardinality constraints as it would complicate the implementation of unit propagation seen in Section 5. Variables occurring in the cardinality constraint are *data variables*, and new variables added in a clausal encoding are *auxiliary variables*. The introduction of auxiliary variables is known to be beneficial to solvers for some problems, and has been studied in the context of the preprocessing technique bounded variable addition [35].

We refer to cardinality constraints as *klauses*, containing a bound k and the literals in the constraint. All clauses can be written as klauses with $k = 1$, corresponding to at-least-one (ALO) constraints. Throughout the rest of the paper, we refer to klauses with $k = 1$ as clauses. When $k = s - 1$, the klause can be viewed as an at-most-one (AMO) constraint by negating the literals, i.e., $\ell_1 + \ell_2 + \cdots + \ell_s \geq s - 1$ is equivalent to AMO($\bar{\ell}_1, \ldots, \bar{\ell}_s$). There are multiple ways to encode an AMO constraint into CNF.

Pairwise Encoding for an AMO constraint is given by a set of binary clauses with negative literals and no auxiliary variables. AMO($\ell_1, \ldots, \ell_s$) is encoded as the conjunction of $(\bar{\ell}_i \vee \bar{\ell}_j)$ with $1 \leq i < j \leq s$, resulting in $s(s-1)/2$ binary clauses.

Linear Encoding (an instance of the commander encoding [30]) for AMO($\ell_1, \ldots, \ell_s$) uses the pairwise encoding for $s \leq 4$ and splits on $s > 4$ using fresh auxiliary variables (y) according to the following recursion:

$$\text{Linear}(\ell_1, \ldots, \ell_s) : \text{Pairwise}(\ell_1, \ell_2, \ell_3, y) \wedge \text{Linear}(\bar{y}, \ell_4, \ldots, \ell_s) \qquad (1)$$

The encoding uses $(s-3)/2$ auxiliary variables and $3s - 6$ clauses. The cutoff of $s = 4$ (commonly used in practice) was selected as the "optimal" value to minimize the sum of the number of variables and the number of clauses.

For a general klause with $1 < k < s - 1$, an efficient encoding to CNF requires $\Theta(s \cdot k)$ auxiliary variables to keep track of the count of data variables that have been assigned. When $s - k + 1$ literals in the klause are falsified, unit propagation should lead to a conflict. For these klauses we use the sequential counter (or *Sinz*) encoding [42].

A clausal encoding of a klause $\ell_1 + \ell_2 + \cdots + \ell_s \geq k$ is *consistent* if assigning any $s - k + 1$ literals to false will always result in a conflict by unit propagation. It is *arc-consistent* [24] if it is consistent and unit propagation will assign all unassigned literals to true if exactly $s - k$ literals are assigned to false. There are many encodings for cardinality constraints [3,20,28]. We use the Linear and Sinz encodings as a proof of concept, but these could easily be substituted with other arc-consistent encodings.

2.2 Conflict-Driven Clause Learning and Proofs of Unsatisfiability

To evaluate the satisfiability of a formula, a CDCL solver [36] iteratively performs the following operations: First, the solver performs unit propagation and tests for a conflict. Two-literal watch pointers [37] enable efficient unit propagation. If there is no conflict and all variables are assigned, the formula is satisfiable. Otherwise, the solver chooses an unassigned variable through a variable decision heuristic [9,32], assigns a truth value to it through a phase selection heuristic, and performs unit propagation. The selected variables are *decision variables*, and the assignment including decision variables and propagated variables is called the *trail*. If, however, there is a conflict, the solver performs conflict analysis potentially learning a short clause. In case this clause is the empty clause, the formula is unsatisfiable. In case it is not the empty clause, the solver revokes some of its variable assignments ("backjumping") and then repeats the whole procedure. Additionally, modern solvers incorporate pre- and inprocessing techniques that change the formula in some way, usually reducing the number of variables and clauses or shrinking the sizes of clauses.

CDCL solvers produce satisfying assignments for satisfiable formulas and proofs of unsatisfiability for unsatisfiable formulas. A clause C is *redundant* w.r.t. a formula F if F and $F \cup \{C\}$ are *satisfiability equivalent*. The clause sequence $F, C_1, C_2, \ldots, C_m$ is a clausal proof of C_m if each clause C_i ($1 \leq i \leq m$) is redundant w.r.t. $F \cup \{C_1, C_2, \ldots, C_{i-1}\}$. The proof is a refutation of F if C_m is $\bot$. Clausal proof systems may also allow deletion.

The strength of a clausal proof systems is determined by the syntactic criterion it enforces when checking clause redundancy. The standard SAT solving paradigm CDCL learns clauses that are logically implied by the formula and fall under the *reverse unit propagation* (RUP) proof system. A clause is RUP if unit propagation on the falsified literals of the clause results in a conflict. The *Resolution Asymmetric Tautology* (RAT) proof system generalizes RUP. We make use of RAT proof steps in our derivations (see Section 6), but refer the reader to [29] for more details. Proofs are typically transformed to a format with hints, e.g. LRAT, before being passed to a formally-verified checker like CAKE-LPR [46].

3   At-Least-K Conjunctive Normal Form (KNF)

$$x_1 + x_2 + x_3 + \overline{x}_4 \geq 2 \qquad \text{k 2 x}_1 \text{ x}_2 \text{ x}_3 \text{ -x}_4 \text{ 0} \qquad (2)$$

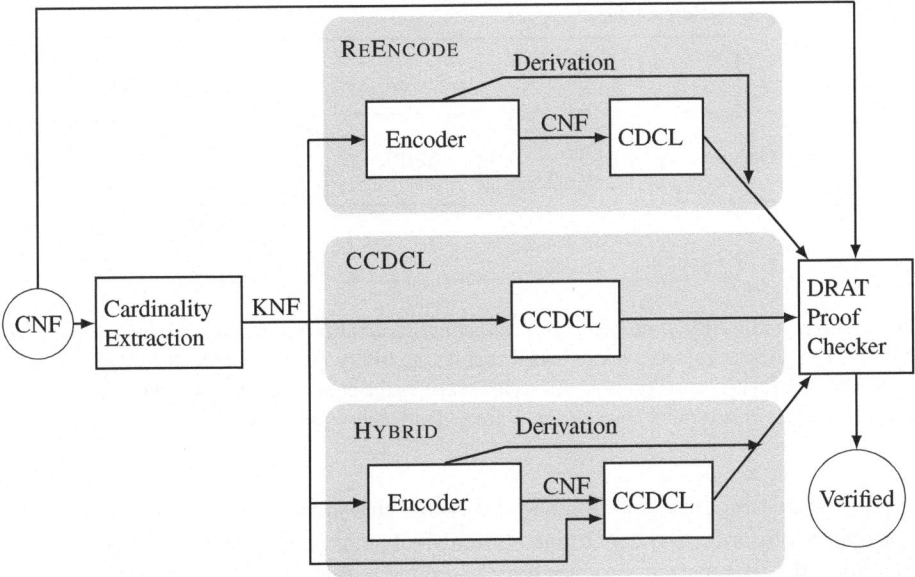

Fig. 1. Three configurations for solving a KNF formula extracted from an input CNF formula.

We propose enriching the input of SAT solvers and proof checkers to accept a conjunction of klauses (KNF). As an initial step, we provide backwards compatibility with CNF formulas, so KNF solvers can be used on existing benchmarks. Consistent AMO cardinality constraints can be extracted from the input CNF formula (see Section 4), then converted to klauses in the KNF format. In Equation (2) if the cardinality constraint on the left appears as clauses in a CNF formula, those clauses can be replaced by a single klause, shown on the right, in the corresponding KNF formula. Klauses with $k > 1$ are written with a 'k' followed by the bound and then the literals. All other clauses in the CNF formula can be placed directly in the KNF formula.

In Figure 1 we present three independent configurations for solving a KNF extracted from a CNF formula: REENCODE, CCDCL, and HYBRID. Each configuration produces a DRAT proof (or satisfying assignment) for the input CNF formula.

REENCODE, the encoder reencodes the klauses into clauses, and the resulting CNF formula is solved by a CDCL solver. Since the CDCL solver is using reencoded clauses that do not appear in the original CNF formula, a DRAT derivation for the clausal reencoding must be prepended to the solver's DRAT proof. This derivation explains how the reencoded clauses can be added to the original CNF formula.

CCDCL, cardinality-CDCL (CCDCL) seen in Section 5 is used to solve the formula in KNF directly by natively propagating on klauses. The DRAT proof generated by the CCDCL solver can be verified against the input CNF formula if the extracted constraints were arc-consistent (otherwise a derivation is added).

HYBRID, a CCDCL solver takes in both the formula in KNF along with a clausal reencoding of klauses as input. The reencoded clauses are kept throughout solving as irredundant formula clauses (never deleted by the solver). The klauses are only watched

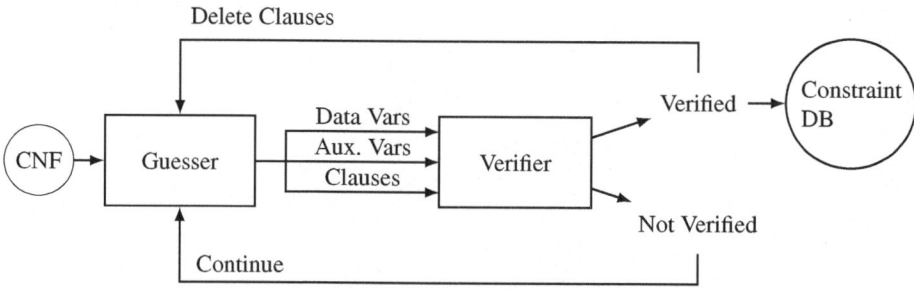

Fig. 2. Guess and verify framework for extracting cardinality constraints from an input CNF formula. The guesser selects a set of data variables, auxiliary variables, and clauses representing a candidate cardinality constraint. If the verifier verifies the constraint, it is added to the constraint database and the constraint's clauses are removed from subsequent guesses.

and propagated on during SAT mode. So, while the solver is in UNSAT mode when propagating on cardinality constraints it exclusively makes use of the reencoded clauses. This gives the solver access to auxiliary variables within the encoding and these variables can be extremely important for finding short proofs of unsatisfiable formulas. While the solver is in SAT mode it can propagate natively on klauses, allowing faster propagation that bypasses the auxiliary variables. This can be important for quickly solving satisfiable formulas. In general the solver moves back and forth between SAT and UNSAT modes with increasing limits, and will roughly spend half of its time in either mode. Clauses learned in either mode can be kept during the mode switch, but certain heuristics are modified for each mode. The proof requires a derivation as in REENCODE. Further details on verification are found in Section 6.

The three different solving configurations highlight the flexibility provided by the KNF format. In some cases, a smaller representation and fast propagation on klauses is beneficial. In other cases, reencoding klauses introducing auxiliary variables can lead to a much shorter proof. And a combination of the two approaches may work best for unknown problems. These configurations can be implemented with straightforward changes to a CCDCL solver, and the proof checker DRAT-TRIM is used as is.

4   Cardinality Constraint Extraction and Analysis

4.1   Extraction

Several researchers have devised techniques for automatically extracting cardinality constraints from CNF representations either as part of a preprocessing step [10] or dynamically within a pseudo-Boolean constraint solver [22]. We implemented our own preprocessor that detects cardinality constraints within a CNF file, converts these into klauses, and emits both these and the remaining clauses as a KNF file.

AMO constraints with pairwise constraints can be detected by finding cliques in the graph having a node for each literal and an edge between two literals if they occur in the same binary clause [10]. Although finding maximal cliques is NP-hard, simple greedy approaches work well for this task.

We use a "guess-and-verify" approach for detecting non-pairwise constraints, shown in Figure 2. Our method of guessing looks for patterns of clauses in the CNF representation that could be cardinality constraints, including classifying the variables in these clauses as either data or auxiliary variables. To do this it examines the binary clauses in the formula and classifies each variable as being either *unate*—always having the same phase, or *binate*—occurring with both phases. Data variables are assumed to be unate, while auxiliary variables must be binate. Starting with a binate variable, the extractor forms the transitive closure of all binate variables that occur in clauses with other variables in the set. It then selects as data variables all unate variables that occur in these clauses.

We have found this approach to guessing effective at detecting standard encodings of AMO constraints, including all of those handled by previous extractors [10]. It can fail when a data variable is used with one phase for some constraint and with some other phase for another. It will also find patterns that meet the phase requirements but do not encode cardinality constraints. Fortunately, these will be rejected in the "verify" stage. Although our verifier could determine whether a set of clauses encodes a non-AMO cardinality constraint, we have been unable to devise a reliable strategy for distinguishing these clauses from the other clauses in a file. We plan to extend the extraction to general cardinality constraints in the future.

4.2 Analysis with BDDs

We use a BDD-based analysis to verify that our guessed cardinality constraints are in fact cardinality constraints. Given a set of clauses and a classification of the variables into a set of data variables X and a set of auxiliary variables Y, we construct the representation of the associated Boolean function $f(X)$ as an Ordered Binary Decision Diagram (BDD) [12]. We generate the BDD for $f(X)$ using *bucket elimination*, a systematic way to perform conjunctions and quantifications [17,41]. That is, we create a total ordering of the data and auxiliary variables, described below, and use this ordering for the BDDs and as the *bucket ordering*. For each $y \in Y$, we associate a set B_y, which we refer to as the "bucket" for variable y. We also have a set B_d, which we refer to as the "data bucket". At each point in the processing, we maintain a set of *terms*, where each term T is a BDD depending on a set of variables $D(T) \subseteq X \cup Y$. Term T is placed in bucket B_y when $y = \min(D(T) \cap Y)$ and in the data bucket when $D(T) \cap Y = \emptyset$. The initial set of terms consists of the BDD representations of the clauses.

Bucket elimination processes the terms via conjunction and quantification operations until the only nonempty bucket is B_d. That is, let y be the maximum variable for which B_y is nonempty. While this bucket contains more than one element, we remove two, compute their conjunction, and place the result in the proper bucket. This must be in some bucket $B_{y'}$ such that $y' \leq y$ or in the data bucket B_d. When bucket B_y contains a single term, we form its existential quantification with respect to y and place the result in the proper bucket. This will either be in some bucket $B_{y'}$ for which $y' < y$ or in the data bucket. Eventually, the only terms will be in the data bucket. We form their conjunction to get the BDD representation of $f(X)$.

Building BDDs and performing bucket elimination requires defining a total ordering of all of the variables in $X \cup Y$. Our approach targets the layered structure that arises in many encodings of cardinality constraints. We start with the auxiliary variables in Y by building an undirected graph with a node for each variable y and an edge (y, y') of length 1.0 when some clause contains a literal of y and a literal of y'. In addition, we add an edge (y, y') with length 0.75 when there is some data variable x such that there is some clause containing literals of x and y and another clause containing literals of x and y'.

We identify a "source" node s and a "sink" node t and (conceptually) view the edges as elastic, enabling us to stretch the graph between these two endpoints into a single line and order the nodes according to where they lie on this line. The two edge types will tend to group the auxiliary variables first by their occurrence in clauses with matching data variables and second by their occurrence with each other. Our implementation of this idea starts by looking for endpoints s and t for which the shortest path between the two nodes is maximal. Starting with some random node, we jump to the most distant node (in terms of shortest path), and from there to the most distant node, iterating as long as the distance increases. We perform these iterations from multiple starting points and take the most distant pair as the graph endpoints. Then, we order the variables first in terms of their proximity to s and secondarily in terms of their distance from t. Finally, each data variable $x \in X$ is inserted into the ordering to be near the first variable y for which some clause contains a literal of x and a literal of y. For a layered graph, this approach will tend to find opposite corners as endpoints s and t and generate a layered ordering of the variables. For a graph having a tree structure, it will produce an ordering that approximates what would be obtained via an inorder traversal of the tree. Both of these make good BDD orderings.

Once the BDD for the function $f(X)$ has been constructed, detecting whether it encodes a cardinality constraint and the parameters of that constraint can readily be inferred from the structure of the BDD. Let us number the data variables as $x_1, x_2, \ldots, x_N$. For a set of literals $\{\ell_1, \ell_2, \ldots, \ell_N\}$, where each $\ell_i \in \{x_i, \overline{x}_i\}$, function f can encode both a lower bound L and an upper bound H, giving a *two-sided* constraint:

$$L \leq \ell_1 + \ell_2 + \cdots + \ell_N \leq H \tag{3}$$

Lower bound L can degenerate to $L = 0$, while upper bound H can degenerate to $H = N$. As examples, an at-most-one constraint has $L = 0$ and $H = 1$, while a clause has $L = 1$ and $H = N$.

Our task is to determine the two bounds and the phase of each literal, or to reject f as not encoding a cardinality constraint. The BDD encoding of the constraint (3) has a simple, layered structure [1, 13]. In detail, let us say that the pair of integers (i, j) is *feasible* if there is some satisfying assignment for the constraint where the first $i - 1$ variables have j literals assigned to true. More precisely, the following conditions must be satisfied for (i, j) to be feasible:

- i satisfies $1 \leq i \leq N + 1$
- j satisfies $0 \leq j \leq i - 1$
- There must be some value k such that $0 \leq k \leq N - i + 1$ and $L \leq j + k \leq H$.

Table 1. Detecting size 10 AMO constraints on the 9 PySAT exactly-one clausal encodings: pairwise, sequential counter, cardinality network, sorting network, totalizer, modulo totalizer, modulo k-totalizer, bitwise, and ladder. The table shows the number of data variables/auxiliary variables in the largest AMO constraint detected by the extraction tool on a given encoding. A 10/0 represents the full constraint on all of the data variables. No approach detected an AMO constraint in the bitwise encoding.

Tool	Pair	SCnt	CNet	SNet	Tot	mTot	mkTot	Bit	Lad
Guess-and-Verify	10/0	10/0	10/0	10/0	10/0	10/0	10/0	–	9/0
LINGELING (Syntactic)	10/0	1/2	2/1	2/1	2/1	2/1	2/1	–	1/2
RISS (Semantic)	10/0	3/2	4/2	4/1	3/2	3/2	3/2	–	3/2

The BDD will have a node $u_{i,j}$ for each feasible pair (i, j). This node can either be L_1, the leaf node representing Boolean constant 1, or it can be a nonterminal node labeled by variable x_i. When $u_{i,j}$ is nonterminal and $\ell_i = x_i$, then its positive (respectively, negative) child will be node $u_{i+1,j+1}$ (resp., $u_{i+1,j}$) if pair $(i+1, j+1)$ (resp., $(i+1, j)$) is feasible and leaf node L_0 (representing Boolean constant 0) otherwise. If $\ell_i = \overline{x}_i$, then the two children will be reversed. Starting with the root node, the literal assignments and values of L and H can be determined by examining the BDD level-by-level, while also determining whether or not the structure matches that of an cardinality BDD.

4.3 PySAT Encodings Experimental Evaluation

In this section we compare our Guess-and-Verify G&V tool against the two extraction techniques presented in [10]. LINGELING implements the static detection of pairwise constraints and RISS implements the static pairwise and two product encoding detection along with the merging operation and semantic detection. The merging operation involves taking two AMO constraints of the form $-x + \ell_1 + \ell_2 + \cdots + \ell_s \geq s$ and $x + j_1 + j_2 + \cdots + j_n \geq n$ and resolving on the opposing literal x to produce $\ell_1 + \ell_2 + \cdots + \ell_s + j_1 + j_2 + \cdots + j_n \geq n + s - 1$ (where duplicate literals are removed and the bound is updated appropriately). The semantic detection involves using unit propagation to detect AMK cardinality constraints with an arc-consistent encoding. In short, starting from a clause, unit propagation is used to determine if literals can extend the candidate cardinality constraint. This approach may be disrupted by auxiliary variables within the encoding such that the unit propagation produces only truncated versions of the cardinality constraints.

For this evaluation, we modified LINGELING and RISS to run cardinality detection, print the detected constraints, then exit. Neither solver provides command line options for this operation, or the ability to produce a formula in any format similar to KNF with clauses and auxiliary variables from the extracted cardinality constraints removed. PySAT [27] provides a Python API for encoding cardinality constraints into clausal form. It supports 9 different encodings, and these contain the most common AMO encodings. We performed unit propagation and pure literal elimination on the generated PySAT encodings, and added an ALO constraint on the data variables, making the constraint exactly-one. We add this clause because data variables will appear in both polarities in a typical formula (otherwise they would be propagated by pure literal elimination and removed from the AMO constraint). Table 1 shows a comparison between G&V, LINGELING, and RISS [10] on the PySAT encodings for AMO constraints of size 10. Our G&V tool found the the original AMO constraints for 7 of the PySAT encodings, and found the core of the original AMO constraint for the Ladder encoding (missing a single data variable). The other tools found small nested AMO constraints of sizes 3-6, but they could not find the core of the AMO constraint for any encoding other than pairwise. Finding many small AMO constraints is less useful, since the propagation power is weaker and a reencoding would only consider the sub constraints individually; whereas finding a larger AMO constraint on a majority of the data variables is far more effective for applying native cardinality constraint handling or reencoding.

The semantic detection from RISS detects some AMO2 constraints among the encodings, but they do not use a majority of the original data variables. The merge operation from RISS can generate constraints of size 4-6, but this operation is less helpful in our setting since it does not allow the deletion of the smaller constraints used in the merge. We plan to explore additional heuristics to encapsulate all commonly used encodings in subsequent iterations of the extraction tool.

In future work we plan to extend the G&V framework to general cardinality constraint extraction. The general case is much more difficult than the AMO case, and is relatively unexplored in the literature. Our tool would require more sophisticated heuristics for guessing since general cardinality constraint encodings may contain data variables in varying polarities as well as varying clause structures. The verifier would also require modifications. It is well-known that BDDs have size limitations, and this could be a factor for large general cardinality constraints. In addition, it would be important to have a verifier that could dynamically adapt the constraint it is characterizing so that the guessing algorithm could provide an under approximation of a given constraint (e.g., providing a set of clauses to the verifier that contains all of the clauses used in a cardinality constraint as well as other clauses not used in the cardinality constraint).

5   Cardinality Conflict-Driven Clause Learning

In this section we describe cardinality-CDCL (CCDCL), an extension of CDCL with propagation on klauses. For problems with many large klauses, handling them natively will significantly reduce the size of the formula and increase the speed at which cardinality constraints propagate.

$$K_1 : x_1 + x_2 + x_3 + \overline{x}_4 + x_5 \geq 3 \qquad\qquad C_1 : x_1 + x_2 + x_3 + \overline{x}_4 + x_5 \geq 1$$

Example 1. The partial assignment $\overline{x}_1 \, \overline{x}_2$ forces the extension $x_3 \, \overline{x}_4 \, x_5$ for K_1 to be satisfied. The partial assignment $\overline{x}_1 \, \overline{x}_2 \, \overline{x}_3 \, x_4$ forces the extension x_5 for C_1 to be satisfied. K_1 can propagate at most 3 literals, whereas C_1 can propagate at most 1 literal.

Example 1 shows the added propagation power of klauses over clauses, not to mention the many auxiliary variables that must be propagated in a clausal encoding. Klauses

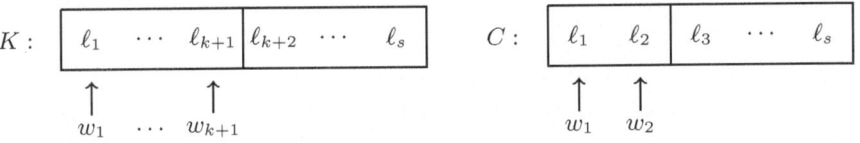

Fig. 3. Klause (left) of the form $\ell_1 + \cdots + \ell_s \geq k$ and clause (right) of the form $\ell_1 + \cdots + \ell_s \geq 1$, with watch pointers for the first $k + 1$ literals in the clause.

can be handled natively with minimal changes to a CDCL solver, and no changes to the proof logging.

CCDCL incurs a few tradeoffs. Some inprocessing techniques need to be restricted or disabled, and the propagation/analysis algorithms become more complicated. More importantly, the auxiliary variables in clausal encodings may be important for learning useful clauses. These limitations are further discussed in the experimental evaluation.

5.1   Implementation Details

A klause requires more watch pointers ($k + 1$) than a clause (Figure 3), since $s - k$ literals must be falsified in order to propagate the klause [34]. The invariant on a non-conflicting klause is that at least k watched literals are either unassigned or satisfied. If this is not the case, then at least $s - (k + 1)$ literals are falsified and therefore the klause is falsified.

Propagation on clauses is unchanged. For a klause, assuming the watch pointer in question is w_i for assigned literal $\overline{\ell_i}$, the first unassigned or satisfied literal starting from ℓ_{k+2} is swapped with ℓ_i, then w_i is released and a new watch is created for the swapped literal. If no such literal exists, then the watched literals $\ell_1, \ldots, \ell_{k+1}$ (not including ℓ_i) are assigned to true, and their *reason* is all of the literals $\ell_i, \ell_{k+2}, \ldots, \ell_s$ that are falsified. If any of the would-be propagated literals is already falsified, then there is a conflict and the propagation algorithm breaks. The conflict clause contains the reason literals, ℓ_i, and first falsified watched literal other than ℓ_i.

Conflict analysis works the same as in CDCL, where the implication graph is traversed backwards from the conflict clause to the first unique implication point in order to produce a learned clause. An *implication graph* is a data structure capturing the ordering and dependencies of decided or propagated literals, where each node is a literal assigned to true and incoming edges to a node are the reason literals for why the node was propagated. Intuitively, the clauses learned by CDCL are RUP because they represent a cut in the implication graph, from which unit propagation will derive a conflict. It is similar for CCDCL. Consider a literal propagated by a klause. In the implication graph, the reason for the literal is exactly the literals that propagated the klause. Since important properties of the implication graph are unchanged, clause minimization can be applied to learned clauses. We have not considered the effect of klauses on chronological backtracking, and therefore only allow backjumping.

5.2 Inprocessing Techniques

In order to support a selection of the most important inprocessing techniques, we split the klause database into clauses ($k = 1$) and klauses ($k > 1$). When one clause is a subset of another clause it can subsume (or replace) the other clause. This operation can be performed on all clauses, without considering klauses. We allow bounded variable elimination (BVE) [18] on all variables not occurring in klauses. Variables in klauses are frozen [19] so they are not selected as candidates for BVE. Variable elimination relies on resolving the clauses containing a variable with themselves. This would not work with klauses since we provide no corresponding inference rule for klausal resolution. We allow vivification [31] on all clauses. During the vivification procedure, the literals in a clause are falsified and propagated. If a conflict is derived, conflict analysis is used to strengthen the clause. We enable propagation on klauses during vivification.

We support Stochastic Local Search (SLS) for phase saving [8]. The SLS algorithm within CADICAL is simple and only relies on break values, i.e., the number of clauses falsified after flipping a literal. In our implementation, a falsified cardinality constraint adds additional weight to the break value of a literal depending on how many falsified literals are contained within the cardinality constraint.

There are additional inprocessing techniques that we plan to include in future work, but are less important than the implemented techniques. These include failed literal probing [23] and Equivalent Literal Substitution (ELS). While we do not allow duplicate literals in a klause, ELS could be performed by adding clauses for literal equivalence, then substituting literals in all clauses but not in klauses.

6 Proof Checking

A formula is transformed from CNF to KNF by iteratively detecting cardinality constraints and replacing the clauses encoding the constraint with a corresponding klause, leaving the remaining clauses unchanged. We only detect consistent clausal encodings to ensure correct proof generation. We did not encounter any non-consistent AMO constraints during extraction; however, if this were the case or if it occurred for general cardinality constraints, we could use a BDD to generate a derivation of a consistent constraint from the extracted constraint [14]. There are two possible results produced by the solver: a satisfying assignment or a clausal proof of unsatisfiability. And for each there are three cases to consider: propagating natively on the KNF, reencoding the klauses into clauses, or a hybrid approach.

6.1 Satisfying Assignments

It is possible that some variables from the original formula are removed when generating the KNF formula since certain extracted constraints use auxiliary variables that will not appear in the corresponding klause. This will not affect proof generation for unsatisfiable problems but will affect satisfying assignments. If a solver produces a satisfying assignment for the KNF formula, the auxiliary variables from the original CNF formula will be unassigned. Every partial assignment that satisfies a cardinality constraint must be extendable to an assignment that satisfies the clausal encoding of the constraint. So, calling a secondary SAT solver on the original CNF formula under the partial assignment given by the solver will produce a satisfying assignment that includes the auxiliary variables. For configurations where klauses are reencoded, the new clauses may contain auxiliary variables not appearing in the original CNF formula. These can simply be removed from the satisfying assignment produced by the solver, then the same procedure for calling a secondary SAT solver is followed.

6.2 Clausal Proofs

For configurations that make use of reencoded constraints, we must generate a derivation of these constraints proving they are redundant and can be added to the original CNF formula. To derive the pairwise encoding, we add the clauses from the encoding to the formula. Each binary clause is RUP since assigning two literals in the constraint to true must propagate a conflict. The derivation of the linear encoding is similar to its clausal encoding, with an additional clause for each auxiliary variable:

$$\mathrm{Deriv}(\ell_1, \ldots, \ell_s) = \mathrm{Pairwise}(\ell_1, \ell_2, \ell_3, y), (\ell_1 \vee \ell_2 \vee \ell_3 \vee y), \mathrm{Deriv}(\overline{y}, \ell_4, \ldots, \ell_s) \quad (4)$$

The Linear derivation makes use of so-called RAT proof steps since new auxiliary variables are being added to the formula. Then, the proof produced by the solver with reencoded clauses is appended to the derivation, and this serves as a complete proof for the original CNF formula.

For configurations that propagate natively on cardinality constraints, the clauses learned by the solvers are RUP with respect to an arc-consistent clausal encoding of the cardinality constraints. To see this, consider when a propagation on an AMO cardinality constraint occurs – exactly when one literal is set to true – and this will propagate the remaining literals to false for both the native propagation and an arc-consistent clausal encoding. So, for formulas with arc-consistent encodings (the vast majority), the proof produced by our natively propagating configurations can be checked against the original CNF formula as is. In the special case where the clausal encoding is consistent but not arc-consistent, a derivation is prepended to the proof.

6.3 Starting with KNF Input

Finally, we consider the case when the original formula is in KNF. A satisfying assignment can be verified by checking if each klause in the KNF is satisfied. If the formula is unsatisfiable, we can use any of the three solver configurations above to produce a DRAT proof. We then transform the KNF formula to a CNF formula using an arc-consistent encoding. The proof can be checked against this CNF formula. To increase trust, one can use a formally verified KNF to CNF encoder [15]. Alternatively, one could verify the transformation from KNF to CNF with a PB checker [25]. As a long-term solution, existing DRAT proof checkers can be modified to accept KNF formulas as input, with moderate changes to parsing and unit propagation. This approach would avoid the overhead required to check a KNF to CNF translation since propagation on klauses would be handled natively by the checker.

7   Experimental Evaluation

All experiments were performed in the Pittsburgh Supercomputing Center on nodes with 128 cores and 256 GB RAM [11]. We ran 64 experiments in parallel per node with 5,000 second timeouts. Therefore, each process held approximately 4GB of memory. This was not a limiting factor except for the only Java based solver SAT4J which failed from memory outs more than timeouts. We report the PAR-2 score for each solver. PAR-2 is the sum of completed runtimes added to the number of timeouts and memory outs multiplied by two times the timeout (10,000), averaged over the number of formulas solved by some configuration.

We implemented the CCDCL algorithm on top of the award winning CDCL solver CADICAL [6]. The base CADICAL is run with all default inprocessing enabled, in contrast with the CCDCL-based approaches that disable some reasoning techniques. Converting the KNF formulas to the pseudo-Boolean input format OPB format is purely syntactical. As such, we are able to run both ROUNDINGSAT [21] and SAT4J [5] (with cutting planes enabled) after extracting cardinality constraints. These two solvers provide a baseline for comparing stronger reasoning techniques against our resolution-based CDCL solvers. We use the following configurations, given an input CNF formula, an extracted KNF formula, and an OPB formula from the KNF formula:

- CADICAL : run CADICAL on the input CNF formula.
- REENCODE : run CADICAL on reencoded formula (Linear encoding for AMOs).
- CCDCL : run CCDCL on the extracted KNF formula.
- HYBRID : run CCDCL on the extracted KNF formula plus linearly encoded AMO constraints. Klauses are present during SAT mode.
- ROUNDINGSAT : run ROUNDINGSAT on the extracted KNF formula (converted to OPB).
- SAT4J : run SAT4J with combined cutting planes and resolution on the extracted KNF formula (converted to OPB).

The runtimes presented in the experimental evaluation include only each solver's runtime when given the proper input formula. We do not include the extraction time or translation time because we intend to compare solvers as if a user had generated the input formula in different formats. From our experience, when a user has a CNF formula generator, it is simple to modify the generator to output both KNF or OPB formulas. The repository containing our solver, experiment configurations, and experiment data can be found at https://github.com/jreeves3/Cardinality-CDCL.

7.1   SAT Competition Benchmarks

We evaluated solvers and the cardinality extraction tool on the SAT Competition Anniversary Track formulas. First we performed unit propagation, removing one from the set that was solved immediately, leaving 5,354 formulas. We applied cardinality extraction on each formula with a timeout of 1,000 seconds per AMO constraint type (pairwise or non-pairwise), producing a corresponding KNF formula. For the PB solvers, we translated the KNF formula into an OPB formula (a line-by-line syntactic translation).

Table 2. Statistics running the cardinality extractor with a 1,000 second timeout for pairwise and then non-pairwise constraints on the 5,354 competition formulas. Found is the number of formulas containing extracted cardinality constraints (64%), Pairwise is the count with exclusively pairwise encodings, Non-Pairwise is the count with exclusively non-pairwise encodings, and Both is the count with a mixture of encodings. $geq5$ is the percent of formulas with at least one constraint of at least size 5, and $\geq 10 \times 10$ is with at least 10 constraints of at least size 10. We show the average runtime and the percentage of these formulas that took ≤ 15 seconds.

Found	Pairwise	Non-Pairwise	Both	≥ 5	$\geq 10 \times 10$	Average. (s)	≤ 15 s
3,415	3,090	55	270	36%	17%	69.0	78.0 %

Table 2 shows that of the 3,415 formulas with cardinality constraints the vast majority contained pairwise encoded constraints and we extracted non-pairwise encoded constraints from only a few hundred formulas. While an expert may know that for many problems the pairwise encoding can be improved for unsatisfiable problems with more compact encodings, these results show that many formulas still implement the pairwise encoding. Furthermore, we log the sizes of constraints extracted, and found that 1,946 formulas contained a cardinality constraint of at least size 5, and 933 formulas contained at least 10 cardinality constraints of size 10 or more. A large fraction of formulas appearing in the SAT Competitions contained many large cardinality constraints, indicating our approach could impact many potential users. By breaking down the formula set in this way, we are able to gauge the performance of the various solving configurations on general formulas versus formulas with many large cardinality constraints. Cardinality constraint extraction was fast (less than 15 seconds) for the majority of formulas, but again, we expect it would be easy for benchmark authors to rewrite the problems in KNF.

Table 3 shows the performance of solvers on two increasingly more restrictive formula sets. It is expected that a reencoding approach or native cardinality propagation would work better on problems with many large cardinality constraints, where the difference between encodings or propagation is more pronounced. This motivated the curation of the formula sets.

At a high-level, the table shows the separation of our three cardinality-based configurations from the default CDCL and PB solvers. For each of the PAR-2 scores, a cardinality-based configuration has the best result. While there are some crafted instances in the formula set that SAT4J and ROUNDINGSAT can solve instantly, neither solver performs well over all formulas. As expected, for a general set of formulas with only AMO constraints extracted the CDCL solvers perform better. The PB solvers are more suited for special cases where formulas contain many general cardinality constraints.

REENCODE performs best for unsatisfiable formulas but does not perform as well as CADICAL on satisfiable formulas. Since many of the formulas originally use the pairwise encoding, this result suggests that for some satisfiable formulas the pairwise encoding outperforms the more compact Linear encoding. CCDCL and HYBRID solve the most satisfiable formulas. The cardinality-based propagation is more effective when the formula contains larger cardinality constraints, seen in the larger difference in PAR-

Table 3. From top to bottom, the first set of results are for the 1,946 (847 SAT, 716 UNSAT) formulas with at least one cardinality constraint of at least size 5. The second set of results are for the 933 (405 SAT, 345 UNSAT) formulas with at least 10 cardinality constraints of at least size 10. PAR-2 score is the sum of all completed solving times plus twice the timeout for each unsolved benchmark that was solved by another configuration, averaged over the number of solved formulas. Combined is both SAT and UNSAT formulas. Solving times do not include constraint extraction.

Configuration	SAT / UNSAT	SAT PAR-2	UNSAT PAR-2	Comb. PAR-2
At least one constraint of size 5				
CADICAL	790 / 619	931.68	1850.31	1352.5
CCDCL	789 / 593	953.19	2292.22	1566.59
HYBRID	**795** / 585	**897.54**	2427.31	1598.31
REENCODE	787 / **636**	965.55	**1560.70**	**1238.18**
ROUNDINGSAT	647 / 475	2592.14	3823.39	3156.17
SAT4J	373 / 240	5676.72	6720.69	6154.95
At least 10 constraints of size 10				
CADICAL	373 / 269	1062.52	2824.08	1872.84
CCDCL	**380** / 254	**928.64**	3315.55	2026.62
HYBRID	377 / 262	1017.63	3104.27	1977.49
REENCODE	372 / **282**	1108.04	**2297.03**	**1654.98**
ROUNDINGSAT	294 / 185	2975.97	4924.31	3872.21
SAT4J	166 / 103	5953.62	7065.07	6464.89

2 score between CADICAL and CCDCL at the bottom set of the table. HYBRID solves many more unsatisfiable formulas than CCDCL on the second formula set, showing the possible benefit of a configuration that targets both satisfiable and unsatisfiable formulas with many cardinality constraints.

Figure 4 presents the tradeoff between cardinality-based propagation and encodings. HYBRID implements mode-switching that trades approximately half the time between the cardinality-based propagation, leading to a slow down on average for solving unsatisfiable formulas. This is made clear by the $2\times$'s line in the scatter plot containing many of the unsatisfiable formulas. On the other hand, HYBRID is able to solve the satisfiable instances with many cardinality constraints much faster due to the native cardinality propagation. Our heuristic-based extraction only works for AMO constraints, so many general cardinality constraints may have been missed. If the problems were first encoded in KNF containing general cardinality constraints, we expect the results to improve significantly. We explore this possibility in the following section with two problems encoded directly in KNF.

7.2   Magic Squares and Max Squares

In this section we explore the Magic Squares and Max Squares problems. These problems demonstrate the effectiveness of cardinality-based propagation on satisfiable formulas with general cardinality constraints, as well as the importance of good encodings

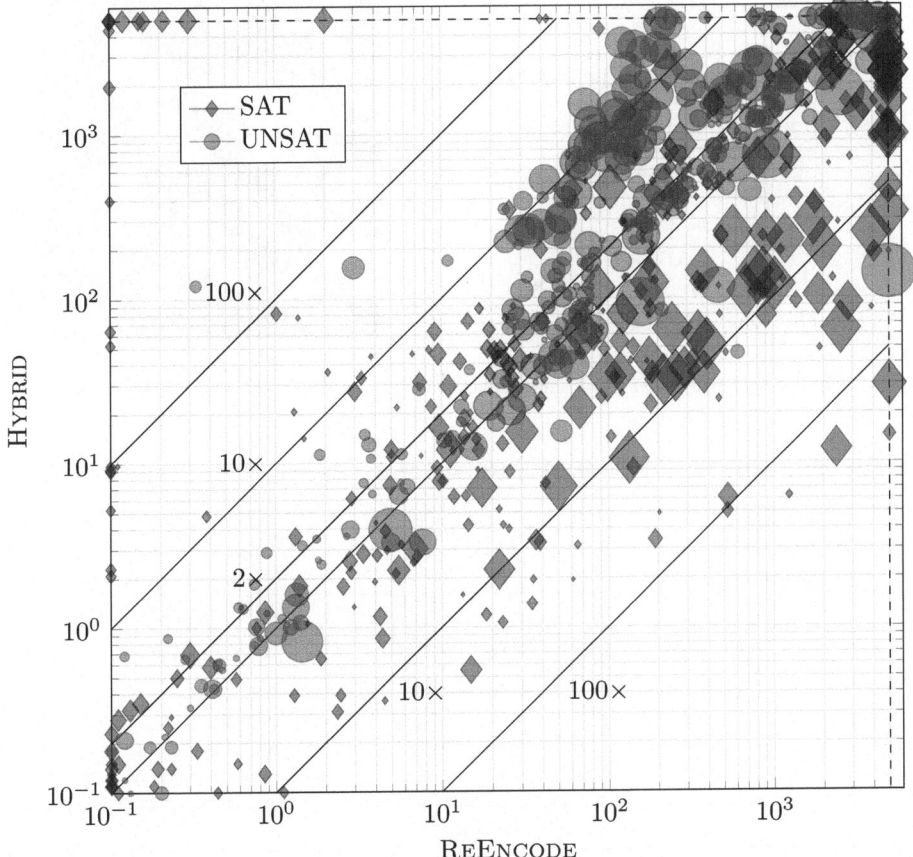

Fig. 4. Comparison between solver configurations on the 933 formulas with at least 10 extracted constraints of size 10 or more. The size of a mark is proportional to the number of extracted constraints of size 10 or more, i.e., formulas with many large AMO constraints have large marks.

for unsatisfiable formulas. Both problems were generated in KNF, so no cardinality extraction is necessary.

The **Magic Squares** problem asks whether the integers from 1 to n^2 can be placed on an $n \times n$ grid such that the sum of integers in each row, column, and diagonal all have the same value (a.k.a. the magic number M) see Table 5. Problem variables denote the integer value of a cell. We add a unary encoding of values such that the pop count of these encoded values in a row, column, or diagonal is the corresponding sum. We use the following constraints: (a) ALO constraints stating each cell is assigned to a value, (b) AMO constraints stating no two nodes can have the same value, (c) klausal constraints stating the sum of each row, column, and diagonal is at least M, (d) klausal constraints stating the difference between the total $n \times n$ and the sum of each row, column, and diagonal is at least the total $n \times n - M$.

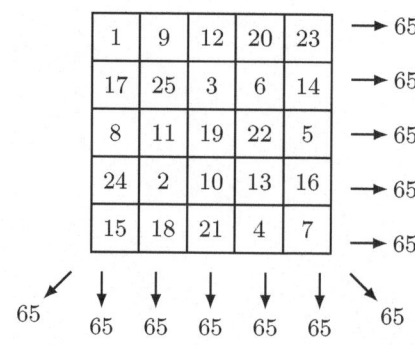

Fig. 5. Left a magic square ($n = 5$) and right an optimal solution of a max square ($n = 10$, $m = 61$).

Table 4. Solving times for Magic Squares (top) and Max Squares (bottom), timeout of 5,000 s.

	Magic Squares							
Configuration					n			
	5	6	7	8	9	10	11	12
CCDCL	**0.18**	**1.42**	**6.56**	**12.01**	46.37	**460.82**	**164.61**	**766.07**
HYBRID	2.54	37.04	1070.97	887.71	–	–	–	–
REENCODE	58.75	246.55	1099.65	4487.79	–	–	–	–
ROUNDINGSAT	3.88	8.24	4.41	264.83	631.46	4212.7	1150.16	–
SAT4J	0.78	8.3	5.31	23.45	**17.99**	958.56	247.94	3177.64

	Max Squares							
	SAT (n,m)				UNSAT (n,m)			
	(7,32)	(8,41)	(9,51)	(10,61)	(7,33)	(8,42)	(9,52)	(10,62)
CCDCL	0.12	15.01	539.88	660.25	217.62	–	–	–
HYBRID	0.02	0.92	**17.0**	101.42	1.07	1.27	58.53	–
REENCODE	**0.01**	**0.62**	57.83	**24.33**	**0.18**	**0.72**	22.82	–
ROUNDINGSAT	0.06	1582.62	–	–	2.31	1046.83	–	–
SAT4J	5.75	–	–	–	26.24	–	–	–

When encoding the problem with the correct magic number, it is satisfiable for any $n \times n$ grid. Table 4 shows the solving times on the Magic Squares formulas of increasing size. CCDCL configuration significantly outperforms the solvers, finding satisfying assignments for large values of n. Only the PB solvers SAT4J and ROUND-INGSAT get close to the performance of CCDCL. This shows that for some crafted instances with many cardinality constraints, improved propagation alone can perform better than a stronger reasoning system like cutting planes. Still, the addition of encoded constraints in REENCODE and HYBRID can significantly worsen the performance. The mode-switching of HYBRID gives it a slight edge over REENCODE.

The **Max Squares** problem [48] asks whether you can set m cells to true in an $n \times n$ grid such that no set of four true cells form the corners of a square. There exists an optimal value opt for each grid such that the Max Squares problem on opt is satisfiable and on $opt+1$ is unsatisfiable. Problem variables denote whether a cell is in the solution. We use the following constraints: (a) clauses with 4 literals blocking the 4 corners of each possible square in the grid, (b) a klausal constraint stating at least m cells are set to true.

The results in Table 4 show the solving times on several configurations with satisfiable formulas ($m = opt$) and unsatisfiable formulas ($m = opt + 1$). For these formulas, both cardinality-based propagation and PB reasoning are ineffective. The two configurations with encoded constraints, REENCODE and HYBRID are able to solve much larger unsatisfiable formulas. This problem is unique in that it contains one large cardinality constraint unlike Magic Squares with many cardinality constraints. This may explain the worse performance of CCDCL on even the satisfiable formulas.

The problems above highlight the main difficulty with handling klauses and reencodings: sometimes encoded constraints make the problem much easier, yet sometimes keeping the cardinality constraints abstract makes the problems easier. We attempt to address this dilemma with the combined configuration HYBRID that has access to auxiliary variables throughout solving, and klauses during SAT modes. For Magic Squares, HYBRID outperforms REENCODE, and for Max Squares HYBRID outperforms CCDCL. For future work, we plan to improve the combined approach HYBRID by modifying solver heuristics. For example, variable scores can be modified to prefer deciding on auxiliary variables at different stages of the search. With these and other changes, we believe HYBRID can get closer to the performance of a virtual portfolio of REENCODE and CCDCL.

8   Conclusion and Future Work

We argue the input format for SAT solvers and proof checkers should be enriched with klauses. In this work, we present several solver configurations that take as input KNF formulas extracted from CNF formulas. In an experimental evaluation we show that with modifications to the state-of-the-art solver CADICAL, our three cardinality-based configurations outperform default CDCL and PB solvers on SAT Competition and Magic/Max Squares formulas. The CCDCL configuration performs well on satisfiable formulas, the REENCODE configuration on unsatisfiable formulas, and HYBRID on a mixture of both. We plan to extend this further by incorporating partial encodings dynamically during runtime. By partially encoding the cardinality constraints as the solver runs, we can guide the solver to focus on cardinality constraints that appear more important, and provide auxiliary variables for those cardinality constraints in case the problem appears to be unsatisfiable.

This initial step opens many avenues for future work. We plan to incorporate more complex propagation-based cardinality constraint detection in the extractor in order to go beyond AMO constraints. We plan to modify a DRAT proof-checker to take KNF formulas as input and propagate on klauses, comparing the verification tool chain against corresponding pseudo-Boolean toolchains. And finally, we plan to explore the possibility of using KNF to enhance other paradigms including local search and parallel solving.

References

1. Abío, I., Nieuwenhuis, R., Oliveras, A., Rodríguez-Carbonell, E.: A new look at BDDs for pseudo-Boolean constraints. Journal of Artificial Intelligence Research **45**, 443–480 (2012)
2. Abío, I., Stuckey, P.J.: Conflict directed lazy decomposition. In: Principles and Practice of Constraint Programming (CP) (2012)
3. Bailleux, O., Boufkhad, Y.: Efficient CNF encoding of boolean cardinality constraints. In: Principles and Practice of Constraint Programming (CP). pp. 108–122. Springer (2003)
4. Becker, B., Drechsler, R., Eggersglüß, S., Sauer, M.: Recent advances in SAT-based ATPG: Non-standard fault models, multi constraints and optimization. In: Design and Technology of Integrated Systems in Nanoscale Era (DTIS). pp. 1–10 (2014)
5. Berre, D.L., Parrain, A.: The sat4j library, release 2.2. Journal on Satisfiability, Boolean Modeling and Computation **7**, 59–6 (2010)
6. Biere, A.: CaDiCaL, Lingeling, Plingeling, Treengeling, and YalSAT entering the SAT competition 2017 (2017)
7. Biere, A., Cimatti, A., Clarke, E.M., Zhu, Y.: Symbolic model checking without bdds. In: Tools and Algorithms for Construction and Analysis of Systems (TACAS) (1999)
8. Biere, A., Fazekas, K., Fleury, M., Heisinger, M.: CaDiCaL, Kissat, Paracooba, Plingeling and Treengeling entering the SAT competition 2020 (2020)
9. Biere, A., Fröhlich, A.: Evaluating CDCL variable scoring schemes. In: Theory and Applications of Satisfiability Testing (SAT). LNCS, vol. 9340, pp. 405–422 (2015)
10. Biere, A., Le Berre, D., Lonca, E., Manthey, N.: Detecting cardinality constraints in CNF. In: Theory and Applications of Satisfiability Testing (SAT). LNCS, vol. 8561, pp. 285–301. Springer (2014)
11. Brown, S.T., Buitrago, P., Hanna, E., Sanielevici, S., Scibek, R., Nystrom, N.A.: Bridges-2: A Platform for Rapidly-Evolving and Data Intensive Research, pp. 1–4. Association for Computing Machinery, New York, NY, USA (2021)
12. Bryant, R.E.: Graph-based algorithms for Boolean function manipulation. IEEE Trans. Computers **35**(8), 677–691 (1986)
13. Bryant, R.E., Biere, A., Heule, M.J.H.: Clausal proofs for pseudo-Boolean reasoning. In: Tools and Algorithms for the Construction and Analysis of Systems (TACAS). LNCS, vol. 12651, pp. 76–93 (2022)
14. Bryant, R.E., Biere, A., Heule, M.J.H.: Clausal proofs for pseudo-boolean reasoning. In: Tools and Algorithms for the Construction and Analysis of Systems (TACAS). p. 443–461. Springer (2022)
15. Codel, C.: Verifying SAT Encodings in Lean. Master's thesis, Carnegie Mellon University Pittsburgh, PA (2022)
16. Cook, W., Coullard, C.R., Turán, G.: On the complexity of cutting-plane proofs. Discrete Applied Mathematics **18**(1), 25–38 (1987)
17. Dechter, R.: Bucket elimination: A unifying framework for reasoning. Artificial Intelligence **113**(1–2), 41–85 (1999)
18. Eén, N., Biere, A.: Effective preprocessing in SAT through variable and clause elimination. In: Theory and Applications of Satisfiability Testing (SAT). LNCS, vol. 3569, pp. 61–75. Springer (2005)
19. Eén, N., Sörensson, N.: Temporal induction by incremental SAT solving. Electron. Notes Theor. Comput. Sci. **89**(4), 543–560 (2003)
20. Eén, N., Sörensson, N.: Translating pseudo-Boolean constraints into SAT. Journal on Satisfiability, Boolean Modeling and Computation, **2**(1-4), 1–26 (2006)
21. Elffers, J., Nordström, J.: Divide and conquer: Towards faster pseudo-Boolean solving. In: Lang, J. (ed.) International Joint Conference on Artificial Intelligence (IJCAI). pp. 1291–1299. ijcai.org (2018)

22. Elffers, J., Nordström, J.: A cardinal improvement to pseudo-Boolean solving. In: Conference on Artificial Intelligence (AAAI). pp. 1495–1503. AAAI Press (2020)
23. Freeman, J.W.: Improvements to Propositional Satisfiability Search Algorithms. Ph.D. thesis, University of Pennsylvania, USA (1995)
24. Gent, I.P.: Arc consistency in sat. In: European Conference on Artificial Intelligence (2002)
25. Gocht, S., Martins, R., Nordström, J., Oertel, A.: Certified CNF translations for pseudo-Boolean solving. In: Meel, K.S., Strichman, O. (eds.) Theory and Applications of Satisfiability Testing (SAT). LIPIcs, vol. 236, pp. 16:1–16:25. Schloss Dagstuhl - Leibniz-Zentrum für Informatik (2022)
26. Hooker, J.: Generalized resolution and cutting planes. Annals of Operations Research **12**, 217–239 (1988)
27. Ignatiev, A., Morgado, A., Marques-Silva, J.: PySAT: A Python toolkit for prototyping with SAT oracles. In: Theory and Applications of Satisfiability Testing (SAT). pp. 428–437 (2018)
28. Jabbour, S., Sais, L., Salhi, Y.: A pigeon-hole based encoding of cardinality constraints. Theory and Practice of Logic Programming **13** (2013)
29. Järvisalo, M., Heule, M.J.H., Biere, A.: Inprocessing rules. In: International Joint Conference on Automated Reasoning (IJCAR). LNCS, vol. 7364, pp. 355–370. Springer (2012)
30. Klieber, W., Kwon, G.: Efficient CNF encoding for selecting 1 from n objects. In: Constraints in Formal Verification (CFV). p. 39 (2007)
31. Li, C.M., Xiao, F., Luo, M., Manyà, F., Lü, Z., Li, Y.: Clause vivification by unit propagation in CDCL SAT solvers. Artificial Intelligence **279**(C) (2020)
32. Liang, J., Ganesh, V., Poupart, P., Czarnecki, K.: Learning rate based branching heuristic for SAT solvers. In: Theory and Applications of Satisfiability Testing (SAT). LNCS, vol. 9710, pp. 123–140 (2016)
33. Lotz, K., Goel, A., Dutertre, B., Kiesl-Reiter, B., Kong, S., Majumdar, R., Nowotka, D.: Solving string constraints using sat. In: Enea, C., Lal, A. (eds.) Computer Aided Verification (CAV). pp. 187–208. Springer, Cham (2023)
34. Maglalang, J.C.: Native cardinality constraints: More expressive, more efficient constraints (2019)
35. Manthey, N., Heule, M.J.H., Biere, A.: Automated reencoding of Boolean formulas. In: Haifa Verification Conference (HVC). LNCS, vol. 7857, pp. 102–117 (2013)
36. Marques-Silva, J., Lynce, I., Malik, S.: Conflict-driven clause learning SAT solvers. In: Handbook of Satisfiability, pp. 131–153. IOS Press (2009)
37. Moskewicz, M.W., Madigan, C.F., Zhao, Y., Zhang, L., Malik, S.: Chaff: Engineering an efficient SAT solver. In: Proceedings of the 38th Annual Design Automation Conference, p. 530–535. ACM (2001)
38. Nguyen, V.H., Nguyen, V.Q., Kim, K., Barahona, P.: Empirical study on SAT-encodings of the at-most-one constraint. In: Conference on Smart Media and Applications. p. 470–475. Smart Media and Applications (SMA), ACM, New York, NY, USA (2021)
39. Niemetz, A., Preiner, M.: Bitwuzla. In: Computer Aided Verification (CAV). p. 3–17. Springer (2023)
40. Oh, C.: Between SAT and UNSAT: The fundamental difference in CDCL SAT. In: Theory and Applications of Satisfiability Testing (SAT). pp. 307–323. Springer International Publishing (2015)
41. Pan, G., Vardi, M.Y.: Search vs. symbolic techniques in satisfiability solving. In: Theory and Applications of Satisfiability Testing (SAT). LNCS, vol. 3542, pp. 235–250 (2005)
42. Sinz, C.: Towards an optimal CNF encoding of Boolean cardinality constraints. In: Principles and Practice of Constraint Programming (CP). LNCS, vol. 3709, pp. 827–831 (2005)
43. Soh, T., Le Berre, D., Roussel, S., Banbara, M., Tamura, N.: Incremental SAT-based method with native boolean cardinality handling for the hamiltonian cycle problem. In: European Conference on Logics in Artificial Intelligence. vol. 8761, p. 684-693. Springer (2014)

44. Soos, M., Bryant, R.E.: Combining CDCL, Gauss-Jordan elimination, and proof generation. In: Pragmatics of SAT (2022)
45. Stephan Gocht, Ciaran McCreesh, J.N.: Veripb: The easy way to make your combinatorial search algorithm trustworthy. In: From Constraint Programming to Trustworthy AI (2020)
46. Tan, Y.K., Heule, M.J.H., Myreen, M.O.: cake_lpr: Verified propagation redundancy checking in CakeML. In: Tools and Algorithms for the Construction and Analysis of Systems (TACAS), Part II. LNCS, vol. 12652, pp. 223–241 (2021)
47. Whittemore, J., Kim, J., Sakallah, K.: Satire: A new incremental satisfiability engine. In: Design Automation Conference (DAC). p. 542–545. DAC '01, ACM, New York, NY, USA (2001)
48. Wynn, E.: A comparison of encodings for cardinality constraints in a SAT solver. ArXiv **abs/1810.12975** (2018)

CaDiCaL 2.0

Armin Biere[1,2]($\boxtimes$) 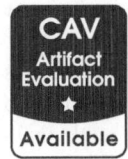, Tobias Faller[1], Katalin Fazekas[3], Mathias Fleury[1,2],
Nils Froleyks[2], and Florian Pollitt[1]

[1] University Freiburg, Freiburg, Germany
[2] Johannes Kepler University Linz, Linz, Austria
biere@cs.uni-freiburg.de
[3] TU Wien, Vienna, Austria

Abstract. The SAT solver CaDiCaL provides a rich feature set with a clean library interface. It has been adopted by many users, is well documented and easy to extend due to its effective testing and debugging infrastructure. In this tool paper we give a high-level introduction into the solver architecture and then go briefly over implemented techniques. We describe basic features and novel advanced usage scenarios. Experiments confirm that CaDiCaL despite this flexibility has state-of-the-art performance both in a stand-alone as well as incremental setting.

1 Introduction

Progress in SAT solving has a large impact on model checking, SMT, theorem proving, software- and hardware-verification, and automated reasoning in general, and, according to "The SAT Museum" [20], SAT solvers get faster and faster, at least on benchmarks consisting of a single formula. For incremental SAT solving it was less clear, particularly as preprocessing [24] and inprocessing [69] heavily contributing to this improvement were considered incompatible with incremental solving (the winners of the SAT competition main track rely on inprocessing since 2009 except in 2011/2012/2016 and since 2005 all on preprocessing).

A simple and elegant solution to this problem is due to the award winning incremental SAT solving approach [39] first implemented in CaDiCaL. It reverts clause removal, i.e., restores clauses removed during pre- and inprocessing, restrictively on a case-by-case basis. It allows incremental solving to make full use of pre- and inprocessing techniques, in contrast to less general solutions [87,89,90,112], without reducing their effectiveness nor burden the user to "freeze" and "melt" variables ("*Don't Touch*" variables in [74]) as necessary with MiniSat [37].

This is the first tool paper on CaDiCaL, while previous, actually well cited, descriptions appeared only as system description in non-peer-reviewed SAT competition proceedings [14–16,18,21,22]. In general, even though "SAT is considered a killer app for the 21st century" (Donald Knuth), there are few tool papers on SAT solvers, with the prominent exception of MiniSat [37], which appeared in 2003 and was awarded the test-of-time award at SAT'22. The descriptions of

© The Author(s) 2024
A. Gurfinkel and V. Ganesh (Eds.): CAV 2024, LNCS 14681, pp. 133–152, 2024.
https://doi.org/10.1007/978-3-031-65627-9_7

CRYPTOMINISAT [106], GLUCOSE [5] and INTELSAT [86] introduce the corresponding SAT solver and can be considered to be tool papers too though.

Development of CADICAL was triggered by discussions at the "Theoretical Foundations of SAT Solving Workshop" in 2016 at the Fields Institute in Toronto, where it became apparent that both theoreticians and practitioners in SAT have a hard time understanding how practical SAT solving evolved, what key components there are in modern SAT solvers and, most importantly, that it was apparently getting harder and harder to modify state-of-the-art solvers for controlled experiments or to try out new ideas. With CADICAL we tried to change this, thus the main objective was to produce a clean solver, with well-documented source code, which is easy to read, understand, modify, test, and debug, without sacrificing performance too much.

The first goals were achieved from the beginning and performance improved over the years. After its introduction in 2017 CADICAL continued to achieve high rankings in yearly SAT competitions, e.g., in 2019 it solved the largest number of instances in the main track, but scored less than the winner. It never won though except for the most recent SAT competition in 2023 where CADICAL was combined with a strong preprocessor employing bounded variable addition [55, 82]. The competition organizers paraphrased this as "CADICAL strikes back".

Moreover, with the show-case of our new incremental approach [39] we invested in increasing the feature set supported by CADICAL culminating for now in supporting "user propagators". This for instance allowed to replace the original but highly modified MINISAT based SAT engine in cvc5 by CADICAL, as described in a recent well-received SAT'23 paper [40].

The users of CADICAL fall into three categories. A first group applies the solver out of the box on benchmarks where CADICAL turns out to have superior performance. As an example consider solving mathematical problems with the help of SAT solving such as [78, 91, 108, 114]. Second, there is an increasing user base, including [6, 11, 23, 39, 40, 65, 92, 95, 101], which relies on the rich application programmable interface (API) provided by CADICAL, particularly its incremental features. Third, there are research prototypes modifying or extending CADICAL to achieve new features, including [7, 17, 43, 55, 64, 71]. Some of these modifications have been integrated [44, 100] but others remain future work [55].

Finally, CADICAL is used as a blue-print for understanding, porting, and integrating state-of-the-art techniques into other solvers. In this regard we are in contact with companies in cloud services, hardware design, and eletronic design automation. It was also consulted in developing IsaSAT [45], the only competitive fully verified SAT solver. Furthermore CADICAL was adopted as template solver for the "hack track" of the yearly SAT competition since 2021 as an "easy to hack" state-of-the-art SAT solver.

Related SAT solvers in the SAT competition often lack documentation, are hard to extend and modify, and, most importantly, do not provide such a rich and clean library interface as CADICAL. For instance our SAT solver KISSAT [18] falls into this category. It has been dominating the SAT competition 2020–2022 (in 2022 all top-ten solvers were descendants of KISSAT), is more compact in memory usage and often faster on individual instances, but is lacking support for even the most basic incremental features such as assumptions.

The majority of the solvers in the SAT competition are restricted in their feature set as they are tuned for stand-alone usage, i.e., running the solver on a single formula stored in a file in DIMACS format [76], even though there is occasionally an incremental track in the SAT competition (last one that really took place was in 2020 as the one announced in 2021 was later cancelled).

Prominent SAT solvers with a richer feature set and particularly supporting incremental solving, beside the rather out-dated MINISAT [37], are newer versions of CRYPTOMINISAT [106], and GLUCOSE [4]. The former is actively developed and in terms of implemented techniques has quite some overlap with CADiCAL. In addition it offers special support for XOR reasoning, solution sampling and model counting [105]. The GLUCOSE solver has been improved for incremental solving [3] but is not comparable in terms of implemented techniques nor features.

Unique and non-common features of CADiCAL include: literal flipping [23], single clause assumption [46], incremental solving without freezing [39], extensive logging support, record & play of API calls, model-based testing, internal proof and solution (model) checking, termination and clause learner interfaces, various preprocessing techniques, an online proof tracing interface, formula extraction (after simplification), support of many external proof formats (DRAT, LRAT, FRAT, VeriPB) [100], and last but not least the user propagator [40].

This paper is structured by describing in the next section the architecture of CADiCAL, which also acts as a summary of integrated techniques and provided features. The rest of the paper consists of highlighting recently added features of the solver or features not presented before, followed by experiments showing that CADiCAL has state-of-the-art performance, before concluding.

2   Architecture

CADiCAL is a modern SAT solver with many features written in C++. It can be used as stand-alone application through the *command-line interface* (CLI) or as library through its *application programming interface* (API) in C++ (or in limited form in C). Figure 1 depicts a structural overview. The central component, called `Internal`, implements CDCL search [83, 103] and formula simplification techniques [24, 69]. On top of it, the `External` facade hides the internals while maintaining the proofs and solutions (aka *models*) of solved problems.

The heart of the solver is the function `cdcl_loop_with_inprocessing` in `Internal` which interleaves the CDCL loop with formula simplification steps (i.e., with inprocessing [69]). During `Search`, CADiCAL supports several techniques, like chronological backtracking [84, 88], rephasing [32], and shrinking [44], which are only some of the important features. See Fig. 1 for more references.

The CDCL loop [83] is scheduled to be preempted in regular intervals to let the solver apply various formula simplification [24] and inprocessing techniques [69]. Each technique is implemented separately (e.g., in file `subsume.cpp`)

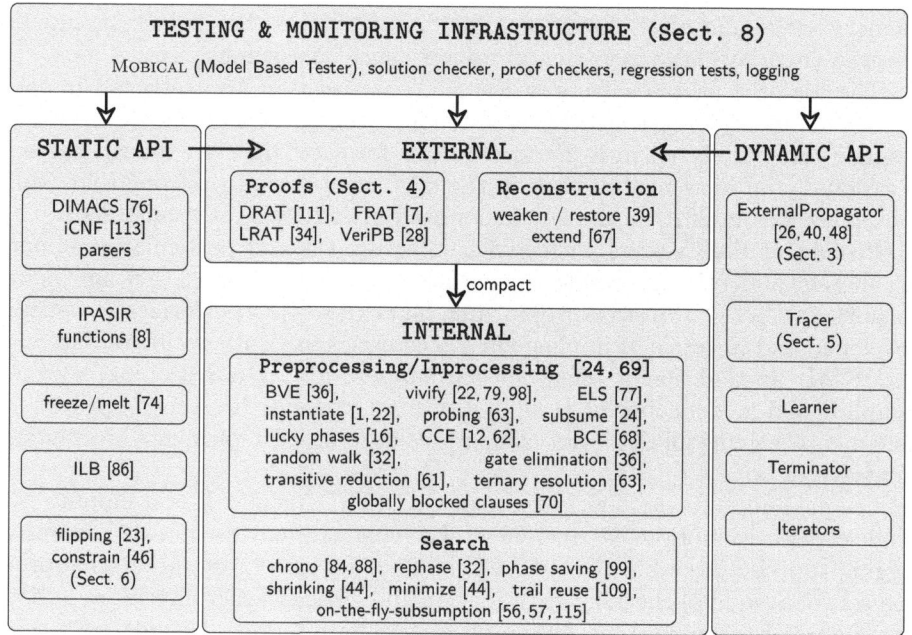

Fig. 1. An overview of the main components of CaDiCaL.

and has (*i*) a corresponding function which determines if the solver should preempt CDCL search and apply the technique (e.g., `subsuming()`) and (*ii*) a function that actually applies the technique (e.g., `subsume()`).

As Fig. 1 shows, CaDiCaL implements a variety of preprocessing/inprocessing techniques, including bounded variable elimination (BVE) [36], arguably the most effective one. As further examples, CaDiCaL also supports vivification [79,98] and instantiation [1]. Combining them [22] won the CaDiCaL "hack track" 2023.

The `External` component communicates with `Internal` by mapping active variables into a consecutive sequence of integers (*compacting*) and extends internal solutions back to complete solution of the input problem with the help of the reconstruction stack [67]. In incremental use cases `External` also keeps the reconstruction stack *clean* [39] by "undoing" previous inprocessing steps. Beyond that, `External` connects internal and external proof generation (see Sect. 4).

We distinguish two types of API usage in CaDiCaL: *static* and *dynamic*. The static API provides access to standard solver functionalities *between* SAT solving calls (like IPASIR [8], parsing DIMACS, or iCNF files). With ILB as proposed by IntelSAT [86], we try to keep the trail unchanged between incremental calls.

The dynamic API interacts and controls the solver *during* `Search`. The solver provides dynamic access to clauses learned during conflict analysis to connected `Learner` instances. The `Terminator` class interface allows users to asynchronously terminate the solving procedure. Through the `Iterator` interface of CaDiCaL, the user can iterate over the irredundant (simplified) clauses of the problem or can iterate through clauses on the reconstruction stack, supporting simplified formula extraction and external model reconstruction.

3   External Propagator

Applications of CaDiCaL, for example within the SMT solver cvc5 [11] (and maybe in the future within other lazy SMT solvers, such as Z3 [85] or Yices [35]), or to support Satisfiability Modulo Symmetries (SMS) [40,116], require more control over the solver than provided by the standard incremental IPASIR interface [8]. To this purpose CaDiCaL supports a more fine-grained and tighter integration into larger systems by allowing an external user propagator [26,48,49] to be connected to it through the IPASIR-UP interface [40].

This abstract interface is defined in the `ExternalPropagator` class which provides corresponding notification and callback functions. Inheriting from this class allows users to implement dedicated external propagators which for instance import and export learned clauses or suggest decisions to the SAT solver. The full description of functionalities supported by the IPASIR-UP interface is available in [40]. Here we focus on CaDiCaL-specific implementation details.

First, CaDiCaL ensures that only external variables appear in the IPASIR-UP interactions, thereby allowing users to ignore the internal (compacted) details. Furthermore, CaDiCaL employs preprocessing and inprocessing even when an external propagator is connected. To avoid the need to restore clauses during the CDCL loop and to ensure that solution reconstruction [67] does not change assignments of *observed variables* (i.e., relevant to the external propagator), every observed variable is automatically frozen. As a side effect, the external propagator can only set *clean* [39] variables as new observed variables during search. As fresh variables are always clean, this is acceptable and mostly sufficient in practice.

Finally, CaDiCaL, by default, considers every external clause as irredundant, exactly as the original input clauses of the problem. Thus, during clause database reduction they are not candidates for removal and so can be deleted only when implied by the rest of the formula. In future work we plan to allow users to specify the redundancy of the external clauses and to support incremental inprocessing [39] even for variables observed by the external propagator.

4   Proofs

Unsatisfiability proof certificates are an integral part of SAT solving [59,60]. Even though clausal proofs were introduced in 2003 [37,52], checking large proofs only became viable with deletion information [58]. The most prominent format today is DRAT [111] which was mandatory in the SAT competition from 2016 [10] to 2022. In 2023 both DRAT [111] and VeriPB [28] were allowed in the competition [9].

```
void add_derived_clause (uint64_t new_id, bool redundant,
                         const vector<int> & literals_of_clause,
                         const vector<uint64_t> & antecedent_ids);
```

Fig. 2. `Tracer` virtual callback function to add a derived clause to the proof.

The proof formats GRAT [75] and LRAT [34] were proposed to allow even faster proof checking, i.e., by trading time for space, but also to facilitate formally verified proof checkers (e.g., CAKE_LPR [110]). They require hints for clause additions in form of antecedent *clause identifiers* (ids). External tools like DRAT-TRIM [111] can add such hints in a post-processing step to DRAT proofs.

The proof formats DRAT [111], FRAT [7], LRAT [34], and VeriPB [28] are supported by CADICAL. It is the first solver to support LRAT natively. Without the need for post-processing this reduces proof checking time [100] substantially.

Recent diversification of proof formats in the SAT competition [9] motivated us to add VeriPB. It is a general proof format for various applications [28,50,51]. The tool-chain for checking SAT solver proofs with the verified VeriPB backend [28] is under development and not fast enough yet. Actually, BREAKID-KISSAT [9], one of the top performers in the SAT competition 2023, lost due to multiple timeouts during proof checking. Similarly to FRAT, CADICAL can provide antecedents in VeriPB proofs. We expect this to speed up VeriPB proof checking considerably.

5   Tracer Interface

The dynamic API allows to extract proof information from CADICAL online without files by connecting user-defined tracers as instances of the virtual C++ class `Tracer`. It provides notifications and callbacks for proof-related events, such as addition and deletion of clauses. Proof writers for all formats (Sect. 4) as well as both internal proof checkers (Sect. 8) go through the `Tracer` class. Furtheremore, there is ongoing work to produce VeriPB proofs for the MaxSAT solver Pacose [97] using the `Tracer` interface in CADICAL.

We support a large set of event types covering a multitude of use cases. Information provided includes antecedent ids and literals of clauses, separation between original, derived, and restored [39] clauses, and information of clause redundancy, as well as weakening [69] and strengthening [28,69]. For example, Fig. 2 shows the callback function for the proof event of adding a derived clause, where "`derived`" means entailed by the formula (i.e., not original input clause). Additional notifications include reserving ids for original clauses, as used for generating file based proof formats, such as VeriPB and LRAT.

For each solve call, a concluding event gives precise information about the result: a model concludes satisfiable instances, whereas for unsatisfiable instances we provide information about the final conflict clause. We have recently started to explore incremental proof tracing as well [41,42].

6   Constraints and Flipping

SAT solvers are used in a wide range of applications in many different ways. For incremental solving, MiniSat has been the predominant choice. However, in recent years, CaDiCaL has begun to replace MiniSat in numerous applications, most prominently cvc5. This can be attributed to its overall better performance and various application-specific features unique to CaDiCaL.

A prime example is the *constraint* feature [46], which allows users to define a temporary clause with the same lifespan as assumptions. It was initially developed to support the SAT based model checking algorithm IC3 [29], which requires often millions of incremental SAT calls during a single run, where each query needs to assume a single clause valid only for that call.

Constraints do not introduce new functionality per se, as temporary clauses can be simulated by activation literals. But they do allow the solver to employ a more efficient implementation, as they particularly avoid to introduce those assumption variables. Beyond IC3, constraints have also proven useful in our backbone extractor CadiBack [23]. The purpose of using *constraint* in backbone extraction is to find maximally diverging models in order to eliminate backbone candidates fast. CadiBack uses constraints to ensure that each new model includes at least one literal not observed in previous models. If this is not possible, all unseen literals are immediately determined to be in the backbone.

Once a model is found, we use another feature called *literal flipping* [19] to eliminate further backbone candidates [23]. A literal is *flippable* if toggling its value also results in a model. This concept was employed to speed-up backbone MiniBones [66] before and also MUS extraction [13]. In these earlier works it was implemented by iterating over all clauses outside the SAT solver, searching for literals that can be flipped in the model provided by the solver. Using clause watching our implementation inside of CaDiCaL is much more efficient.

7   Interpolation

Software-based test generation targeting RISC-V in the Scale4Edge project [38] relied on interpolation-based model checking and MiniCraig to generate interpolants. It uses MiniSat as SAT solver and in this application constitutes a performance bottleneck. Therefore we developed a new more scalable solver CaDiCraig based on CaDiCaL and its proof tracer API (Sect. 5).

The implementation of CaDiCraig is external to CaDiCaL. It uses the same interpolant construction as in MiniCraig but is now seperated from MiniSat. We are not aware of any other modern open-source SAT solver which allows to build interpolants through a generic API without being forced to write the whole proof to a file, trimming and prost-processing it on disk, such as in [53].

The CaDiCraig tracer constructs partial interpolants as usual, e.g., see [73]. Through the proof tracer API the tracer is notified by CaDiCaL about each new clause and its antecedents needed to derive it by resolution. It then builds a partial interpolant for that clause using previously computed partial antecedent interpolants. When the solver concludes deriving an empty clause and thus showing unsatisfiability (Sect. 5) the final interpolant is built from the antecedents of the empty clause. It can then be retrieved by via the CADICRAIG API.

8   Testing and Debugging

Such a sophisticated and complex software as CADICAL necessitates rigorous testing to ensure correctness of interactions between its multitude of features. In this section we discuss our arsenal of essential testing and debugging techniques.

First, we primarily rely on logging for debugging purposes. For instance, when enabled, CADICAL will print every single step from its creation to its deletion. From an implementation perspective, logging features are not compiled in by default to avoid performance overhead in release builds. Furthermore, if enabled at run-time, CADICAL prints verbose information about the inprocessing schedule, useful for debugging performance regressions (e.g., inprocessor scheduling).

Further useful debugging tools are the built-in checkers. The LRAT and DRAT checkers are optional and ensure that every learned clause is properly derived. The new LRAT checker [100] was crucial for achieving LRAT support.

Last but not least we want to mention the API fuzzer MOBICAL, which generates random API calls and minimizes failing runs. Internally, MOBICAL implements a state machine issuing API calls. It also performs option fuzzing by varying available options. This approach is extremely useful to produce short failing API call traces focusing on the actual defect, e.g., like picking a low garbage collection limit to trigger a defect in the garbage collector. Combining checkers with MOBICAL greatly increases its strength. During development it is advisable to build MOBICAL and CADICAL with assertions and checkers enabled.

MOBICAL is similar in spirit to the related model-based tester of LINGELING [2] for SAT and BTORMBT [94] and MURXLA [93] targeting SMT. Note that other SMT fuzzers [27,30,96,102] focus on non-incremental usage or only support incremental "push & pop" [80]. For non-incremental SAT solving, there is also CNFFUZZ fuzzer and the CNFDD delta-debugger [2,31].

Accordingly, we have implemented a MOCKPROPAGATOR class in MOBICAL to test the EXTERNALPROPAGATOR API. It fuzzes the IPASIR-UP implementation in combination with all options and features of the solver. It revealed several corner-cases which we believe would have been very hard to trigger otherwise.

MOBICAL targets only incremental SAT problems and could not help when incorrect interpolants showed up in earlier experiments with MINICRAIG and CADICRAIG. Therefore, we have built an external interpolation fuzzer in Python. It checks interpolants and an accompanying delta-debugger minimizes problems by deleting command line options, clauses, and variables.

9   Experiments

The performance of CADICAL 2.0 was evaluated in three experiments. We first follow the *non-incremental* setup of the main track of the SAT competition, where solvers are run on benchmark files in DIMACS format. The second experiment focuses on *incremental* usage, i.e., following the incremental track of the competition. Finally we show the effectiveness of CaDiCaL in the context of *interpolation* via its Tracer API. All experiments were conducted on our cluster with Intel Xeon E5-2620 v4 CPUs running at 2.10 GHz (turbo-mode disabled).

Non-Incremental. The winner SBVA-CaDiCaL [54] of the main track of the SAT Competition 2023 combined a novel technique for bounded variable addition [82] with CaDiCaL 1.5.3. In their implementation preprocessing was limited to 200 s which yields different preprocessed formulas over multiple runs. Therefore, we ran the preprocessor of SBVA-CaDiCaL separately for 200 s, and then gave the same formulas to CaDiCaL 1.5.3 and our new version CaDiCaL 2.0. Running them for 5000 s as in the competition (ignoring preprocessing time in essence) gave very similar results. We provide more details in the artifact. This confirms that CaDiCaL (also in version 2.0) is state-of-the-art in non-incremental solving.

Incremental. How to assess the incremental performance of a SAT solver is less established. To present an unbiased evaluation, we follow the principles set out by the last incremental track of the SAT competition in 2020 [47]: The solvers are evaluated in six different applications, each featuring 50 benchmarks, with a 2000 s timeout and 24 GB memory limit. Four applications are carried over directly from the 2020 competition: the CEGAR-based QBF solver IJTIHAD, the simple backbone extractor BONES, the longest simple-path search LSP, and the MaxSAT solver MAX. However, we exclude two applications: the essential variable extractor and the classical planner PASAR. Both use features that are not present in all solvers. The former queries ipasir_learned, which is missing from CaDiCaL 1.0, and the latter relies on limiting the number of conflicts. Instead, we include the bounded model checker for bit-level hardware designs CaMiCaL [39] and the sophisticated backbone extractor CaDiBack [23].

The benchmarks from the incremental track from the 2020 SAT Competition remain unchanged. For CaMiCaL, we randomly select 50 Boolean circuits used in HWMCC'17 [25]. Although CaDiBack solves the same problem as BONES, we opt for a distinct set of benchmarks. In 2020 the "smallest and easiest satisfiable" [47] CNF formulas were selected and even though backbone extraction is harder than mere solving, they were rather easy. Conversely, we compile a non-trivial set of benchmarks by randomly selecting satisfiable formulas from past competitions (2004–2022) [23] that take KISSAT 3.0.0 [19] more than 20 s to solve. We use KISSAT as it is not incremental and hence does not compete.

The artifact has a comparison of CRYPTOMINISAT and CaDiCaL on 1798 formulas [23] and indicates that our selection does not impact the outcome. As detailed in Sect. 6, CaDiBack utilizes constraints, which are only available in recent versions of CaDiCaL and are simulated with activation literals otherwise.

Our evaluation includes all solvers that competed in 2020: RISS 7.1.2 [81], CRYPTOMINISAT 5 (CMS) [104,107], and ABCDSAT i20 [33]. The CaDiCaL version from that year is referred to as CaDiCaL 2020. The other two versions are 1.0 from 2019 and our latest release 2.0. We also include MINISAT 2.2 and the latest version of GLUCOSE 4.2.1. Table 1 presents for each SAT solver and application: the PAR2 score, which is the average runtime in seconds with a penalty of 4000 for unsolved instances; and the number of solved instances.

Table 1. Performance comparison of six incremental solvers, with three versions of CADICAL (2000 s timeout). For each solver, we report PAR2 score over 50 benchmarks per application and number of solved instances ("PAR2$_{|\overline{\#solved}}$"). The four applications to the right have been used in the incremental track of the 2020 SAT competition. The best results per application are marked in **bold**. The last row presents the hypothetical *Virtual Best Solver* which always picks the best performing backend for each instance.

		CaDiBack	CaMiCaL	Bones	LSP	Max	Ijtihad	Total
CADICAL	2.0	**3297**$_{|11}$	**2606**$_{|18}$	494$_{|45}$	1898$_{|27}$	**1976**$_{|26}$	**2980**$_{|13}$	**2209**$_{|140}$
	2020	3409$_{|9}$	2677$_{|17}$	622$_{|43}$	1955$_{|26}$	2015$_{|25}$	2986$_{|13}$	2277$_{|133}$
	1.0	3495$_{|7}$	2627$_{|18}$	595$_{|44}$	2011$_{|26}$	2028$_{|25}$	2989$_{|13}$	2291$_{|133}$
	CMS	3491$_{|8}$	2701$_{|17}$	**397**$_{|46}$	**1773**$_{|29}$	2021$_{|25}$	3057$_{|12}$	2240$_{|137}$
	MINISAT	3678$_{|5}$	2807$_{|16}$	687$_{|43}$	1993$_{|26}$	2094$_{|24}$	3123$_{|11}$	2397$_{|125}$
	RISS	3665$_{|6}$	2836$_{|15}$	892$_{|40}$	1835$_{|28}$	2017$_{|25}$	3140$_{|11}$	2398$_{|125}$
	ABCDSAT	3582$_{|7}$	2966$_{|13}$	535$_{|46}$	2493$_{|21}$	2037$_{|26}$	3207$_{|10}$	2470$_{|123}$
	GLUCOSE	3778$_{|4}$	2981$_{|13}$	948$_{|40}$	2078$_{|25}$	2117$_{|24}$	3206$_{|10}$	2518$_{|116}$
	VBS	3127$_{|14}$	2546$_{|19}$	257$_{|48}$	1765$_{|29}$	1856$_{|28}$	2896$_{|14}$	2075$_{|152}$

Our results show that CADICAL 2.0 reaches state-of-the-art performance, demonstrating a distinct improvement over previous versions. Also, differing from the findings in [72], we see a significant advantage of the newer CADICAL and CRYPTOMINISAT, over the older MINISAT, further substantiated below.

Interpolants. To validate CADICRAIG using CADICAL, we converted all 400 benchmarks of the SAT Competition 2023 into interpolation problems split into A and B parts chosen with the goal to assign related clauses to the same part in order to keep the number of global variables limited. The index of the smallest variable of each clause determines the probability of the clause being assigned to A. On our crafted benchmarks (5000 s timeout, 7 GB), CADICRAIG significantly outperforms MINICRAIG, solving 117 benchmarks, compared to only 75.

10   Conclusion

In this very first conference paper on CADICAL we reviewed its most important components and features as well as its testing and debugging infrastructure. We highlighted its use as SAT engine in SMT solving via the user propagator interface and how the tracer API can be used to compute interpolants. Our experiments show that CADICAL remains efficient despite this flexibility.

Producing incremental proofs is ongoing work [41,42]. Further future work consists of producing incremental proofs for all features supported by CADICAL, avoiding to freeze observed variables by the user propagator, and porting into the main branch features provided by other users.

Acknowledgements. This work was supported in part by the Austrian Science Fund (FWF) under project T-1306, W1255-N23, and S11408-N23, the state of Baden-Württemberg through bwHPC, the German Research Foundation (DFG) through grant INST 35/1597-1 FUGG, the German Federal Ministry of Education and Research (BMBF) within the project Scale4Edge under contract 16ME0132, and by a gift from Intel Corporation.

References

1. Andersson, G., Bjesse, P., Cook, B., Hanna, Z.: A proof engine approach to solving combinational design automation problems. In: Proceedings of the 39th Design Automation Conference, DAC 2002, New Orleans, LA, USA, 10–14 June 2002, pp. 725–730. ACM (2002). https://doi.org/10.1145/513918.514101
2. Artho, C., Biere, A., Seidl, M.: Model-based testing for verification back-ends. In: Veanes, M., Viganò, L. (eds.) TAP 2013. LNCS, vol. 7942, pp. 39–55. Springer, Heidelberg (2013). https://doi.org/10.1007/978-3-642-38916-0_3
3. Audemard, G., Lagniez, J.-M., Simon, L.: Improving glucose for incremental SAT solving with assumptions: application to MUS extraction. In: Järvisalo, M., Van Gelder, A. (eds.) SAT 2013. LNCS, vol. 7962, pp. 309–317. Springer, Heidelberg (2013). https://doi.org/10.1007/978-3-642-39071-5_23
4. Audemard, G., Simon, L.: Predicting learnt clauses quality in modern SAT solvers. In: Boutilier, C. (ed.) IJCAI 2009, Proceedings of the 21st International Joint Conference on Artificial Intelligence, Pasadena, California, USA, 11–17 July 2009, pp. 399–404. Morgan Kaufmann Publishers Inc., San Francisco (2009). http://ijcai.org/Proceedings/09/Papers/074.pdf
5. Audemard, G., Simon, L.: On the glucose SAT solver. Int. J. Artif. Intell. Tools **27**(1), 1840001:1–1840001:25 (2018). https://doi.org/10.1142/S0218213018400018
6. Bacchus, F.: MaxHS in the 2022 MaxSat evaluation. In: Bacchus, F., Berg, J., Järvisalo, M., Martins, R. (eds.) Proceedings of MaxSAT Evaluation 2020 – Solver and Benchmark Descriptions. Department of Computer Science Series of Publications B, vol. B-2022-2, p. 17. University of Helsinki (2022)
7. Baek, S., Carneiro, M., Heule, M.J.H.: A flexible proof format for SAT solver-elaborator communication. In: TACAS 2021. LNCS, vol. 12651, pp. 59–75. Springer, Cham (2021). https://doi.org/10.1007/978-3-030-72016-2_4
8. Balyo, T., Biere, A., Iser, M., Sinz, C.: SAT race 2015. Artif. Intell. **241**, 45–65 (2016)
9. Balyo, T., Heule, M.J.H., Iser, M., Järvisalo, M., Suda, M. (eds.): Proceedings of SAT Competition 2023: Solver, Benchmark and Proof Checker Descriptions. Department of Computer Science Series of Publications B, Department of Computer Science, University of Helsinki, Finland (2023)
10. Balyo, T., Heule, M.J.H. (eds.): Proceedings of SAT Competition 2016 – Solver and Benchmark Descriptions. Department of Computer Science Series of Publications B, vol. B-2016-1. University of Helsinki (2016)
11. Barbosa, H., et al.: cvc5: a versatile and industrial-strength SMT solver. In: Fisman, D., Rosu, G. (eds.) TACAS 2022. LNCS, vol. 13243, pp. 415–442. Springer, Cham (2022). https://doi.org/10.1007/978-3-030-99524-9_24

12. Barnett, L.A., Cerna, D., Biere, A.: Covered clauses are not propagation redundant. In: Peltier, N., Sofronie-Stokkermans, V. (eds.) IJCAR 2020. LNCS (LNAI), vol. 12166, pp. 32–47. Springer, Cham (2020). https://doi.org/10.1007/978-3-030-51074-9_3

13. Belov, A., Marques-Silva, J.: Accelerating MUS extraction with recursive model rotation. In: Bjesse, P., Slobodová, A. (eds.) International Conference on Formal Methods in Computer-Aided Design, FMCAD '11, Austin, TX, USA, 30 October–02 November 2011, pp. 37–40. FMCAD Inc. (2011)

14. Biere, A.: CaDiCaL, Lingeling, Plingeling, Treengeling, YalSAT entering the SAT competition 2017. In: Balyo, T., Heule, M.J.H., Järvisalo, M. (eds.) Proceedings of SAT Competition 2017 – Solver and Benchmark Descriptions. Department of Computer Science Series of Publications B, vol. B-2017-1, pp. 14–15. University of Helsinki (2017)

15. Biere, A.: CaDiCaL, Lingeling, Plingeling, Treengeling and YalSAT entering the SAT competition 2018. In: Heule, M.J.H., Järvisalo, M., Suda, M. (eds.) Proceedings of SAT Competition 2018 – Solver and Benchmark Descriptions. Department of Computer Science Series of Publications B, vol. B-2018-1, pp. 13–14. University of Helsinki (2018)

16. Biere, A.: CaDiCaL at the SAT race 2019. In: Heule, M.J.H., Järvisalo, M., Suda, M. (eds.) Proceedings of SAT Race 2019 – Solver and Benchmark Descriptions. Department of Computer Science Series of Publications B, vol. B-2019-1, pp. 8–9. University of Helsinki (2019)

17. Biere, A., Chowdhury, M.S., Heule, M.J.H., Kiesl, B., Whalen, M.W.: Migrating solver state. In: SAT. LIPIcs, vol. 236, pp. 27:1–27:24. Schloss Dagstuhl - Leibniz-Zentrum für Informatik (2022). https://doi.org/10.4230/LIPICS.SAT.2022.27

18. Biere, A., Fazekas, K., Fleury, M., Heisinger, M.: CaDiCaL, Kissat, Paracooba, Plingeling and Treengeling entering the SAT competition 2020. In: Balyo, T., Froleyks, N., Heule, M.J.H., Iser, M., Järvisalo, M., Suda, M. (eds.) Proceedings of SAT Competition 2020 – Solver and Benchmark Descriptions. Department of Computer Science Report Series B, vol. B-2020-1, pp. 51–53. University of Helsinki (2020)

19. Biere, A., Fleury, M.: Gimsatul, IsaSAT and Kissat entering the SAT competition 2022. In: Balyo, T., Heule, M.J.H., Iser, M., Järvisalo, M., Suda, M. (eds.) Proc. of SAT Competition 2022 – Solver and Benchmark Descriptions. Department of Computer Science Series of Publications B, vol. B-2022-1, pp. 10–11. University of Helsinki (2022)

20. Biere, A., Fleury, M., Froleyks, N., Heule, M.J.: The SAT museum. In: Järvisalo, M., Le Berre, D. (eds.) Proceedings of the 14th International Workshop on Pragmatics of SAT Co-located with the 26th International Conference on Theory and Applications of Satisfiability Testing (SAT 2003), Alghero, Italy, 4 July 2023. CEUR Workshop Proceedings, vol. 3545, pp. 72–87. CEUR-WS.org (2023). http://ceur-ws.org/Vol-3545/paper6.pdf

21. Biere, A., Fleury, M., Heisinger, M.: CaDiCaL, Kissat, Paracooba entering the SAT competition 2021. In: Balyo, T., Froleyks, N., Heule, M.J.H., Iser, M., Järvisalo, M., Suda, M. (eds.) Proceedings of SAT Competition 2021 – Solver and Benchmark Descriptions. Department of Computer Science Report Series B, vol. B-2021-1, pp. 10–13. University of Helsinki (2021)

22. Biere, A., Fleury, M., Pollitt, F.: CaDiCaL_vivinst, IsaSAT, Gimsatul, Kissat, and Tabulara SAT entering the SAT competition 2023. In: Balyo, T., Froleyks, N., Heule, M.J.H., Iser, M., Järvisalo, M., Suda, M. (eds.) Proceedings of SAT

Competition 2023 – Solver and Benchmark Descriptions. Department of Computer Science Report Series B, vol. B-2023-1, pp. 14–15. University of Helsinki (2023)

23. Biere, A., Froleyks, N., Wang, W.: CadiBack: extracting backbones with CaDiCaL. In: Mahajan, M., Slivovsky, F. (eds.) 26th International Conference on Theory and Applications of Satisfiability Testing, SAT 2023, Alghero, Italy, 4–8 July 2023. LIPIcs, vol. 271, pp. 3:1–3:12. Schloss Dagstuhl - Leibniz-Zentrum für Informatik (2023). https://doi.org/10.4230/LIPICS.SAT.2023.3

24. Biere, A., Järvisalo, M., Kiesl, B.: Preprocessing in SAT solving. In: Biere, A., Heule, M.J.H., van Maaren, H., Walsh, T. (eds.) Handbook of Satisfiability, Frontiers in Artificial Intelligence and Applications, 2nd edn., vol. 336, pp. 391–435. IOS Press (2021)

25. Biere, A., van Dijk, T., Heljanko, K.: Hardware model checking competition 2017. In: 2017 Formal Methods in Computer Aided Design (FMCAD), pp. 9–9. IEEE (2017)

26. Bjørner, N.S., Eisenhofer, C., Kovács, L.: Satisfiability modulo custom theories in Z3. In: Dragoi, C., Emmi, M., Wang, J. (eds.) VMCAI. LNCS, vol. 13881, pp. 91–105. Springer, Heidelberg (2023). https://doi.org/10.1007/978-3-031-24950-1_5

27. Blotsky, D., Mora, F., Berzish, M., Zheng, Y., Kabir, I., Ganesh, V.: StringFuzz: a fuzzer for string solvers. In: Chockler, H., Weissenbacher, G. (eds.) CAV 2018. LNCS, vol. 10982, pp. 45–51. Springer, Cham (2018). https://doi.org/10.1007/978-3-319-96142-2_6

28. Bogaerts, B., Gocht, S., McCreesh, C., Nordström, J.: Certified symmetry and dominance breaking for combinatorial optimisation. J. Artif. Intell. Res. **77**, 1539–1589 (2023)

29. Bradley, A.R.: SAT-based model checking without unrolling. In: Jhala, R., Schmidt, D. (eds.) VMCAI 2011. LNCS, vol. 6538, pp. 70–87. Springer, Heidelberg (2011). https://doi.org/10.1007/978-3-642-18275-4_7

30. Bringolf, M., Winterer, D., Su, Z.: Finding and understanding incompleteness bugs in SMT solvers. In: ASE, pp. 43:1–43:10. ACM (2022)

31. Brummayer, R., Lonsing, F., Biere, A.: Automated testing and debugging of SAT and QBF solvers. In: Strichman, O., Szeider, S. (eds.) SAT 2010. LNCS, vol. 6175, pp. 44–57. Springer, Heidelberg (2010). https://doi.org/10.1007/978-3-642-14186-7_6

32. Cai, S., Zhang, X., Fleury, M., Biere, A.: Better decision heuristics in CDCL through local search and target phases. J. Artif. Intell. Res. **74**, 1515–1563 (2022). https://doi.org/10.1613/jair.1.13666

33. Chen, J.: optsat, abcdsat and solvers based on simplified data structure and hybrid solving strategies. In: Proceedings of SAT Competition 2020: Solver and Benchmark Descriptions, p. 25 (2020)

34. Cruz-Filipe, L., Heule, M.J.H., Hunt, W.A., Kaufmann, M., Schneider-Kamp, P.: Efficient certified RAT verification. In: de Moura, L. (ed.) CADE 2017. LNCS (LNAI), vol. 10395, pp. 220–236. Springer, Cham (2017). https://doi.org/10.1007/978-3-319-63046-5_14

35. Dutertre, B.: Yices 2.2. In: Biere, A., Bloem, R. (eds.) CAV 2014. LNCS, vol. 8559, pp. 737–744. Springer, Cham (2014). https://doi.org/10.1007/978-3-319-08867-9_49

36. Eén, N., Biere, A.: Effective preprocessing in SAT through variable and clause elimination. In: Bacchus, F., Walsh, T. (eds.) SAT 2005. LNCS, vol. 3569, pp. 61–75. Springer, Heidelberg (2005). https://doi.org/10.1007/11499107_5

37. Eén, N., Sörensson, N.: An extensible SAT-solver. In: Giunchiglia, E., Tacchella, A. (eds.) SAT 2003. LNCS, vol. 2919, pp. 502–518. Springer, Heidelberg (2004). https://doi.org/10.1007/978-3-540-24605-3_37

38. Faller, T., Deligiannis, N.I., Schwörer, M., Reorda, M.S., Becker, B.: Constraint-based automatic SBST generation for RISC-V processor families. In: IEEE European Test Symposium, ETS 2023, Venezia, Italy, 22–26 May 2023, pp. 1–6. IEEE (2023).https://doi.org/10.1109/ETS56758.2023.10174156

39. Fazekas, K., Biere, A., Scholl, C.: Incremental inprocessing in SAT solving. In: Janota, M., Lynce, I. (eds.) SAT 2019. LNCS, vol. 11628, pp. 136–154. Springer, Cham (2019). https://doi.org/10.1007/978-3-030-24258-9_9

40. Fazekas, K., Niemetz, A., Preiner, M., Kirchweger, M., Szeider, S., Biere, A.: IPASIR-UP: user propagators for CDCL. In: Mahajan, M., Slivovsky, F. (eds.) 26th International Conference on Theory and Applications of Satisfiability Testing, SAT 2023, Alghero, Italy. LIPIcs, vol. 271, pp. 8:1–8:13. Schloss Dagstuhl - Leibniz-Zentrum für Informatik (2023). https://doi.org/10.4230/LIPICS.SAT.2023.8

41. Fazekas, K., Pollitt, F., Fleury, M., Biere, A.: Certifying incremental sat solving. In: Bjorner, N., Heule, M., Voronkov, A. (eds.) Logic for Programming, Artificial Intelligence, and Reasoning - 25th International Conference, LPAR-25, Balaclava, Mauritius, 26–31 May 2024. Proceedings (2024)

42. Fazekas, K., Pollitt, F., Fleury, M., Biere, A.: Incremental proofs for bounded model checking. In: Kunz, W., Große, D. (eds.) Workshop on Methods and Description Languages for Modelling and Verification of Circuits and Systems, MBMV 2024, Kaiserslautern, Germany, 14–15 February 2023. ITG Fachberichte, VDE Verlag (2024)

43. Feng, N., Bacchus, F.: Clause size reduction with all-UIP learning. In: Pulina, L., Seidl, M. (eds.) SAT 2020. LNCS, vol. 12178, pp. 28–45. Springer, Cham (2020). https://doi.org/10.1007/978-3-030-51825-7_3

44. Fleury, M., Biere, A.: Efficient All-UIP learned clause minimization. In: Li, C.-M., Manyà, F. (eds.) SAT 2021. LNCS, vol. 12831, pp. 171–187. Springer, Cham (2021). https://doi.org/10.1007/978-3-030-80223-3_12

45. Fleury, M., Lammich, P.: A more pragmatic CDCL for isasat and targetting LLVM (short paper). In: Pientka, B., Tinelli, C. (eds.) Automated Deduction - CADE 29 - 29th International Conference on Automated Deduction, Rome, Italy, 1–4 July 2023, Proceedings. Lecture Notes in Computer Science, vol. 14132, pp. 207–219. Springer, Heidelberg (2023). https://doi.org/10.1007/978-3-031-38499-8_12

46. Froleyks, N., Biere, A.: Single clause assumption without activation literals to speed-up IC3. In: Formal Methods in Computer Aided Design, FMCAD 2021, New Haven, CT, USA, 19–22 October 2021, pp. 72–76. IEEE (2021). https://doi.org/10.34727/2021/ISBN.978-3-85448-046-4_15

47. Froleyks, N., Heule, M., Iser, M., Järvisalo, M., Suda, M.: SAT competition 2020. Artif. Intell. **301**, 103572 (2021). https://doi.org/10.1016/J.ARTINT.2021.103572

48. Ganesh, V., O'Donnell, C.W., Soos, M., Devadas, S., Rinard, M.C., Solar-Lezama, A.: Lynx: a programmatic SAT solver for the RNA-folding problem. In: Cimatti, A., Sebastiani, R. (eds.) SAT 2012. LNCS, vol. 7317, pp. 143–156. Springer, Heidelberg (2012). https://doi.org/10.1007/978-3-642-31612-8_12

49. Gebser, M., Kaminski, R., Kaufmann, B., Ostrowski, M., Schaub, T., Wanko, P.: Theory solving made easy with clingo 5. In: ICLP (Technical Communications). OASIcs, vol. 52, pp. 2:1–2:15. Schloss Dagstuhl - Leibniz-Zentrum für Informatik (2016)

50. Gocht, S.: Certifying Correctness for Combinatorial Algorithms by Using Pseudo-Boolean Reasoning. Ph.D. thesis, Lund University, Lund, Sweden (2022). https://portal.research.lu.se/en/publications/certifying-correctness-for-combinatorial-algorithms-by-using-pseu

51. Gocht, S., Nordström, J.: Certifying parity reasoning efficiently using pseudo-Boolean proofs. In: Proceedings of the 35th AAAI Conference on Artificial Intelligence (AAAI '21), pp. 3768–3777 (2021)

52. Goldberg, E., Novikov, Y.: Verification of proofs of unsatisfiability for cnf formulas. In: 2003 Design, Automation and Test in Europe Conference and Exhibition, pp. 886–891 (2003). https://api.semanticscholar.org/CorpusID:10504432

53. Gurfinkel, A., Vizel, Y.: DRUPing for interpolates. In: Formal Methods in Computer-Aided Design, FMCAD 2014, Lausanne, Switzerland, 21–24 October 2014, pp. 99–106. IEEE (2014). https://doi.org/10.1109/FMCAD.2014.6987601

54. Haberlandt, A., Green, H.: SBVA-CADICAL and SBVA-KISSAT: structured bounded variable addition. In: Balyo, T., Froleyks, N., Heule, M.J.H., Iser, M., Järvisalo, M., Suda, M. (eds.) Proc. of SAT Competition 2023 – Solver and Benchmark Descriptions. Department of Computer Science Report Series B, vol. B-2023-1, p. 18. University of Helsinki (2023)

55. Haberlandt, A., Green, H., Heule, M.J.H.: Effective auxiliary variables via structured reencoding. In: Mahajan, M., Slivovsky, F. (eds.) 26th International Conference on Theory and Applications of Satisfiability Testing, SAT 2023, Alghero, Italy. LIPIcs, 4–8 July 2023, vol. 271, pp. 11:1–11:19. Schloss Dagstuhl - Leibniz-Zentrum für Informatik (2023). https://doi.org/10.4230/LIPICS.SAT.2023.11

56. Hamadi, Y., Jabbour, S., Sais, L.: Learning for dynamic subsumption. In: ICTAI 2009, 21st IEEE International Conference on Tools with Artificial Intelligence, Newark, New Jersey, USA, 2–4 November 2009, pp. 328–335. IEEE Computer Society (2009). https://doi.org/10.1109/ICTAI.2009.22

57. Han, H., Somenzi, F.: On-the-fly clause improvement. In: Kullmann, O. (ed.) SAT 2009. LNCS, vol. 5584, pp. 209–222. Springer, Heidelberg (2009). https://doi.org/10.1007/978-3-642-02777-2_21

58. Heule, M., Jr., W.A.H., Wetzler, N.: Trimming while checking clausal proofs. In: Formal Methods in Computer-Aided Design, FMCAD 2013, Portland, OR, USA, 20–23 October 2013, pp. 181–188. IEEE (2013)

59. Heule, M.J.H.: Proofs of unsatisfiability. In: Biere, A., Heule, M., van Maaren, H., Walsh, T. (eds.) Handbook of Satisfiability - Second Edition, Frontiers in Artificial Intelligence and Applications, vol. 336, pp. 635–668. IOS Press (2021). https://doi.org/10.3233/FAIA200998

60. Heule, M.J.H., Biere, A.: Proofs for satisfiability problems. In: All about Proofs, Proofs for All (APPA), Mathmatical, Logic and Foundations, vol. 55. College Publication (2015)

61. Heule, M., Järvisalo, M., Biere, A.: Clause elimination procedures for CNF formulas. In: Fermüller, C.G., Voronkov, A. (eds.) LPAR 2010. LNCS, vol. 6397, pp. 357–371. Springer, Heidelberg (2010). https://doi.org/10.1007/978-3-642-16242-8_26

62. Heule, M.J.H., Järvisalo, M., Biere, A.: Covered clause elimination. In: Voronkov, A., Sutcliffe, G., Baaz, M., Fermüller, C.G. (eds.) Short papers for 17th International Conference on Logic for Programming, Artificial intelligence, and Reasoning, LPAR-17-short, Yogyakarta, Indonesia, 10–15 October 2010. EPiC Series in Computing, vol. 13, pp. 41–46. EasyChair (2010). https://doi.org/10.29007/CL8S

63. Heule, M.J.H., Järvisalo, M., Biere, A.: Revisiting hyper binary resolution. In: Gomes, C., Sellmann, M. (eds.) CPAIOR 2013. LNCS, vol. 7874, pp. 77–93. Springer, Heidelberg (2013). https://doi.org/10.1007/978-3-642-38171-3_6

64. Hickey, R., Bacchus, F.: Trail saving on backtrack. In: Pulina, L., Seidl, M. (eds.) SAT 2020. LNCS, vol. 12178, pp. 46–61. Springer, Cham (2020). https://doi.org/10.1007/978-3-030-51825-7_4

65. Ignatiev, A., Morgado, A., Marques-Silva, J.: PySAT: a python toolkit for prototyping with SAT oracles. In: Beyersdorff, O., Wintersteiger, C.M. (eds.) SAT 2018. LNCS, vol. 10929, pp. 428–437. Springer, Cham (2018). https://doi.org/10.1007/978-3-319-94144-8_26

66. Janota, M., Lynce, I., Marques-Silva, J.: Algorithms for computing backbones of propositional formulae. AI Commun. 28(2), 161–177 (2015). https://doi.org/10.3233/AIC-140640

67. Järvisalo, M., Biere, A.: Reconstructing solutions after blocked clause elimination. In: Strichman, O., Szeider, S. (eds.) SAT 2010. LNCS, vol. 6175, pp. 340–345. Springer, Heidelberg (2010). https://doi.org/10.1007/978-3-642-14186-7_30

68. Järvisalo, M., Biere, A., Heule, M.: Blocked clause elimination. In: Esparza, J., Majumdar, R. (eds.) TACAS 2010. LNCS, vol. 6015, pp. 129–144. Springer, Heidelberg (2010). https://doi.org/10.1007/978-3-642-12002-2_10

69. Järvisalo, M., Heule, M.J.H., Biere, A.: Inprocessing rules. In: Gramlich, B., Miller, D., Sattler, U. (eds.) IJCAR 2012. LNCS (LNAI), vol. 7364, pp. 355–370. Springer, Heidelberg (2012). https://doi.org/10.1007/978-3-642-31365-3_28

70. Kiesl, B., Heule, M.J.H., Biere, A.: Truth assignments as conditional autarkies. In: Chen, Y.-F., Cheng, C.-H., Esparza, J. (eds.) ATVA 2019. LNCS, vol. 11781, pp. 48–64. Springer, Cham (2019). https://doi.org/10.1007/978-3-030-31784-3_3

71. Kiesl-Reiter, B., Whalen, M.W.: Proofs for incremental SAT with inprocessing. In: Nadel, A., Rozier, K.Y. (eds.) Formal Methods in Computer-Aided Design, FMCAD 2023, Ames, IA, USA, 24–27 October 2023, pp. 132–140. IEEE (2023). https://doi.org/10.34727/2023/ISBN.978-3-85448-060-0_21

72. Kochemazov, S., Ignatiev, A., Marques-Silva, J.: Assessing progress in SAT solvers through the lens of incremental SAT. In: Li, C.-M., Manyà, F. (eds.) SAT 2021. LNCS, vol. 12831, pp. 280–298. Springer, Cham (2021). https://doi.org/10.1007/978-3-030-80223-3_20

73. Kupferschmid, S.: Über Craigsche Interpolation und deren Anwendung in der formalen Modellprüfung. Ph.D. thesis, University of Freiburg (2013)

74. Kupferschmid, S., Lewis, M., Schubert, T., Becker, B.: Incremental preprocessing methods for use in BMC. Formal Methods Syst. Des. 39(2), 185–204 (2011). https://doi.org/10.1007/S10703-011-0122-4

75. Lammich, P.: Efficient verified (UN)SAT certificate checking. J. Autom. Reason. 64(3), 513–532 (2020). https://doi.org/10.1007/s10817-019-09525-z

76. Le Berre, D., Roussel, O., Simon, L.: SAT competition 2009: Benchmark submission guidelines. https://web.archive.org/web/20190325181937/https://www.satcompetition.org/2009/format-benchmarks2009.html. Accessed 15 Jan 2024

77. Li, C.M.: Integrating equivalency reasoning into Davis-Putnam procedure. In: Kautz, H.A., Porter, B.W. (eds.) Proceedings of the Seventeenth National Conference on Artificial Intelligence and Twelfth Conference on on Innovative Applications of Artificial Intelligence, Austin, Texas, USA, 30 July–3 August 2000, pp. 291–296. AAAI Press/The MIT Press (2000), http://www.aaai.org/Library/AAAI/2000/aaai00-045.php

78. Lohn, E., Lambert, C., Heule, M.J.H.: Compact symmetry breaking for tournaments. In: Griggio, A., Rungta, N. (eds.) 22nd Formal Methods in Computer-Aided Design, FMCAD 2022, Trento, Italy, 17–21 October 2022, pp. 179–188. IEEE (2022). https://doi.org/10.34727/2022/ISBN.978-3-85448-053-2_24

79. Luo, M., Li, C., Xiao, F., Manyà, F., Lü, Z.: An effective learnt clause minimization approach for CDCL SAT solvers. In: Sierra, C. (ed.) Proceedings of the Twenty-Sixth International Joint Conference on Artificial Intelligence, IJCAI 2017, Melbourne, Australia, 19–25 August 2017, pp. 703–711. ijcai.org (2017). https://doi.org/10.24963/IJCAI.2017/98

80. Mansur, M.N., Christakis, M., Wüstholz, V., Zhang, F.: Detecting critical bugs in SMT solvers using blackbox mutational fuzzing. In: ESEC/SIGSOFT FSE, pp. 701–712. ACM (2020)

81. Manthey, N.: Riss 7 in proceedings of SAT competition 2020. In: Proceedings of SAT Competition 2020: Solver and benchmark descriptions (2020)

82. Manthey, N., Heule, M.J.H., Biere, A.: Automated reencoding of Boolean formulas. In: Biere, A., Nahir, A., Vos, T. (eds.) HVC 2012. LNCS, vol. 7857, pp. 102–117. Springer, Heidelberg (2013). https://doi.org/10.1007/978-3-642-39611-3_14

83. Marques-Silva, J., Lynce, I., Malik, S.: Conflict-driven clause learning SAT solvers. In: Biere, A., Heule, M., van Maaren, H., Walsh, T. (eds.) Handbook of Satisfiability - Second Edition, Frontiers in Artificial Intelligence and Applications, vol. 336, pp. 133–182. IOS Press (2021). https://doi.org/10.3233/FAIA200987

84. Möhle, S., Biere, A.: Backing backtracking. In: Janota, M., Lynce, I. (eds.) SAT 2019. LNCS, vol. 11628, pp. 250–266. Springer, Cham (2019). https://doi.org/10.1007/978-3-030-24258-9_18

85. de Moura, L., Bjørner, N.: Z3: an efficient SMT solver. In: Ramakrishnan, C.R., Rehof, J. (eds.) TACAS 2008. LNCS, vol. 4963, pp. 337–340. Springer, Heidelberg (2008). https://doi.org/10.1007/978-3-540-78800-3_24

86. Nadel, A.: Introducing Intel(R) SAT Solver. In: Meel, K.S., Strichman, O. (eds.) 25th International Conference on Theory and Applications of Satisfiability Testing (SAT 2022). Leibniz International Proceedings in Informatics (LIPIcs), vol. 236, pp. 8:1–8:23. Schloss Dagstuhl – Leibniz-Zentrum für Informatik, Dagstuhl, Germany (2022). https://doi.org/10.4230/LIPIcs.SAT.2022.8. https://drops.dagstuhl.de/opus/volltexte/2022/16682

87. Nadel, A., Ryvchin, V.: Efficient SAT solving under assumptions. In: Cimatti, A., Sebastiani, R. (eds.) SAT 2012. LNCS, vol. 7317, pp. 242–255. Springer, Heidelberg (2012). https://doi.org/10.1007/978-3-642-31612-8_19

88. Nadel, A., Ryvchin, V.: Chronological backtracking. In: Beyersdorff, O., Wintersteiger, C.M. (eds.) SAT 2018. LNCS, vol. 10929, pp. 111–121. Springer, Cham (2018). https://doi.org/10.1007/978-3-319-94144-8_7

89. Nadel, A., Ryvchin, V., Strichman, O.: Preprocessing in incremental SAT. In: Cimatti, A., Sebastiani, R. (eds.) SAT 2012. LNCS, vol. 7317, pp. 256–269. Springer, Heidelberg (2012). https://doi.org/10.1007/978-3-642-31612-8_20

90. Nadel, A., Ryvchin, V., Strichman, O.: Ultimately incremental SAT. In: Sinz, C., Egly, U. (eds.) SAT 2014. LNCS, vol. 8561, pp. 206–218. Springer, Cham (2014). https://doi.org/10.1007/978-3-319-09284-3_16

91. Neiman, D., Mackey, J., Heule, M.J.H.: Tighter bounds on directed ramsey number R(7). Graphs Comb. **38**(5), 156 (2022). https://doi.org/10.1007/S00373-022-02560-5

92. Niemetz, A., Preiner, M.: Bitwuzla. In: Enea, C., Lal, A. (eds.) Computer Aided Verification - 35th International Conference, CAV 2023, Paris, France, 17–22 July

2023, Proceedings, Part II. Lecture Notes in Computer Science, vol. 13965, pp. 3–17. Springer, Heidelberg (2023). https://doi.org/10.1007/978-3-031-37703-7_1

93. Niemetz, A., Preiner, M., Barrett, C.W.: Murxla: a modular and highly extensible API fuzzer for SMT solvers. In: Shoham, S., Vizel, Y. (eds.) CAV (2). Lecture Notes in Computer Science, vol. 13372, pp. 92–106. Springer, Heidelberg (2022). https://doi.org/10.1007/978-3-031-13188-2_5

94. Niemetz, A., Preiner, M., Biere, A.: Model-based API testing for SMT solvers. In: SMT. CEUR Workshop Proceedings, vol. 1889, pp. 3–14. CEUR-WS.org (2017)

95. Niemetz, A., Preiner, M., Biere, A.: Boolector at the SMT competition 2019. In: Hendrix, J., Sharygina, N. (eds.) Proceedings of the 17th International Workshop on Satisfiability Modulo Theories (SMT 2019), affiliated with the 22nd International Conference on Theory and Applications of Satisfiability Testing (SAT 2019), Lisbon, Portugal, 7–8 July 2019, p. 2 (2019)

96. Park, J., Winterer, D., Zhang, C., Su, Z.: Generative type-aware mutation for testing SMT solvers. Proc. ACM Program. Lang. 5(OOPSLA), 1–19 (2021)

97. Paxian, T., Reimer, S., Becker, B.: Dynamic polynomial watchdog encoding for solving weighted MaxSAT. In: Beyersdorff, O., Wintersteiger, C.M. (eds.) SAT 2018. LNCS, vol. 10929, pp. 37–53. Springer, Cham (2018). https://doi.org/10.1007/978-3-319-94144-8_3

98. Piette, C., Hamadi, Y., Sais, L.: Vivifying propositional clausal formulae. In: Ghallab, M., Spyropoulos, C.D., Fakotakis, N., Avouris, N.M. (eds.) ECAI 2008 - 18th European Conference on Artificial Intelligence, Patras, Greece, 21–25 July 2008, Proceedings. Frontiers in Artificial Intelligence and Applications, vol. 178, pp. 525–529. IOS Press (2008). https://doi.org/10.3233/978-1-58603-891-5-525

99. Pipatsrisawat, K., Darwiche, A.: A lightweight component caching scheme for satisfiability solvers. In: Marques-Silva, J., Sakallah, K.A. (eds.) SAT 2007. LNCS, vol. 4501, pp. 294–299. Springer, Heidelberg (2007). https://doi.org/10.1007/978-3-540-72788-0_28

100. Pollitt, F., Fleury, M., Biere, A.: Faster LRAT checking than solving with CaDiCaL. In: Mahajan, M., Slivovsky, F. (eds.) 26th International Conference on Theory and Applications of Satisfiability Testing (SAT 2023). Leibniz International Proceedings in Informatics (LIPIcs), vol. 271, pp. 21:1–21:12. Schloss Dagstuhl – Leibniz-Zentrum für Informatik, Dagstuhl (2023). https://doi.org/10.4230/LIPIcs.SAT.2023.21

101. Sanders, P., Schreiber, D.: Mallob: scalable SAT solving on demand with decentralized job scheduling. J. Open Source Softw. 7(77), 4591 (2022). https://doi.org/10.21105/JOSS.04591

102. Scott, J., Sudula, T., Rehman, H., Mora, F., Ganesh, V.: BanditFuzz: fuzzing SMT solvers with multi-agent reinforcement learning. In: Huisman, M., Păsăreanu, C., Zhan, N. (eds.) FM 2021. LNCS, vol. 13047, pp. 103–121. Springer, Cham (2021). https://doi.org/10.1007/978-3-030-90870-6_6

103. Silva, J.P.M., Sakallah, K.A.: GRASP - a new search algorithm for satisfiability. In: Rutenbar, R.A., Otten, R.H.J.M. (eds.) Proceedings of the 1996 IEEE/ACM International Conference on Computer-Aided Design, ICCAD 1996, San Jose, CA, USA, 10–14 November 1996, pp. 220–227. IEEE Computer Society/ACM (1996). https://doi.org/10.1109/ICCAD.1996.569607

104. Soos, M., Devriendt, J., Gocht, S., Shaw, A., Meel, K.S.: CryptoMiniSat with ccanr at the SAT competition 2020. In: Proceedings of SAT Competition 2020: Solver and Benchmark Descriptions 2020, vol. 27 (2020)

105. Soos, M., Gocht, S., Meel, K.S.: Tinted, Detached, and Lazy CNF-XOR solving and its applications to counting and sampling. In: Lahiri, S.K., Wang, C. (eds.) CAV 2020. LNCS, vol. 12224, pp. 463–484. Springer, Cham (2020). https://doi.org/10.1007/978-3-030-53288-8_22

106. Soos, M., Nohl, K., Castelluccia, C.: Extending SAT solvers to cryptographic problems. In: Kullmann, O. (ed.) SAT 2009. LNCS, vol. 5584, pp. 244–257. Springer, Heidelberg (2009). https://doi.org/10.1007/978-3-642-02777-2_24

107. Soos, M., Selman, B., Kautz, H., Devriendt, J., Gocht, S.: CryptoMiniSat with WalkSAT at the SAT competition 2020. In: Proceedings of SAT Competition 2020: Solver and Benchmark Descriptions, p. 29 (2020)

108. Subercaseaux, B., Heule, M.J.H.: The packing chromatic number of the infinite square grid is 15. In: Sankaranarayanan, S., Sharygina, N. (eds.) Tools and Algorithms for the Construction and Analysis of Systems - 29th International Conference, TACAS 2023, Held as Part of the European Joint Conferences on Theory and Practice of Software, ETAPS 2022, Paris, France, 22–27 April 2023, Proceedings, Part I. Lecture Notes in Computer Science, vol. 13993, pp. 389–406. Springer, Heidelberg (2023).https://doi.org/10.1007/978-3-031-30823-9_20

109. van der Tak, P., Ramos, A., Heule, M.J.H.: Reusing the assignment trail in CDCL solvers. J. Satisf. Boolean Model. Comput. **7**(4), 133–138 (2011). https://doi.org/10.3233/SAT190082

110. Tan, Y.K., Heule, M.J.H., Myreen, M.O.: `cake_lpr`: verified propagation redundancy checking in CakeML. In: TACAS 2021. LNCS, vol. 12652, pp. 223–241. Springer, Cham (2021). https://doi.org/10.1007/978-3-030-72013-1_12

111. Wetzler, N., Heule, M.J.H., Hunt, W.A.: DRAT-trim: efficient checking and trimming using expressive clausal proofs. In: Sinz, C., Egly, U. (eds.) SAT 2014. LNCS, vol. 8561, pp. 422–429. Springer, Cham (2014). https://doi.org/10.1007/978-3-319-09284-3_31

112. Whittemore, J., Kim, J., Sakallah, K.A.: SATIRE: a new incremental satisfiability engine. In: Proceedings of the 38th Design Automation Conference, DAC 2001, Las Vegas, NV, USA, 18–22 June 2001, pp. 542–545. ACM (2001).https://doi.org/10.1145/378239.379019

113. Wieringa, S., Niemenmaa, M., Heljanko, K.: Tarmo: A framework for parallelized bounded model checking. In: Brim, L., van de Pol, J. (eds.) Proceedings 8th International Workshop on Parallel and Distributed Methods in verifiCation, PDMC 2009, Eindhoven, The Netherlands, 4 November 2009. EPTCS, vol. 14, pp. 62–76 (2009). https://doi.org/10.4204/EPTCS.14.5

114. Yolcu, E., Aaronson, S., Heule, M.J.H.: An automated approach to the collatz conjecture. J. Autom. Reason. **67**(2), 15 (2023). https://doi.org/10.1007/S10817-022-09658-8

115. Zhang, L.: On subsumption removal and on-the-fly CNF simplification. In: Bacchus, F., Walsh, T. (eds.) SAT 2005. LNCS, vol. 3569, pp. 482–489. Springer, Heidelberg (2005). https://doi.org/10.1007/11499107_42

116. Zhang, T., Szeider, S.: Searching for smallest universal graphs and tournaments with SAT. In: Yap, R.H.C. (ed.) 29th International Conference on Principles and Practice of Constraint Programming, CP 2023, Toronto, Canada, 27–31 August 2023. LIPIcs, vol. 280, pp. 39:1–39:20. Schloss Dagstuhl - Leibniz-Zentrum für Informatik (2023). https://doi.org/10.4230/LIPICS.CP.2023.39

Formally Certified Approximate Model Counting

Yong Kiam Tan[1]([✉]) [iD], Jiong Yang[2] [iD], Mate Soos[2] [iD], Magnus O. Myreen[3] [iD],
and Kuldeep S. Meel[4] [iD]

[1] Institute for Infocomm Research (I2R), A*STAR,
Singapore, Singapore
`tanyk1@i2r.a-star.edu.sg`
[2] National University of Singapore, Singapore, Singapore
`jiong@comp.nus.edu.sg`, `soos.mate@gmail.com`
[3] Chalmers University of Technology, Gothenburg, Sweden
`myreen@chalmers.se`
[4] University of Toronto, Toronto, Canada
`meel@cs.toronto.edu`

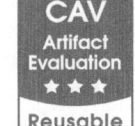

Abstract. Approximate model counting is the task of approximating the number of solutions to an input Boolean formula. The state-of-the-art approximate model counter for formulas in conjunctive normal form (CNF), ApproxMC, provides a scalable means of obtaining model counts with *probably approximately correct* (PAC)-style guarantees. Nevertheless, the validity of ApproxMC's approximation relies on a careful theoretical analysis of its randomized algorithm and the correctness of its highly optimized implementation, especially the latter's stateful interactions with an incremental CNF satisfiability solver capable of natively handling parity (XOR) constraints.

We present the first certification framework for approximate model counting with formally verified guarantees on the quality of its output approximation. Our approach combines: (i) a *static*, once-off, formal proof of the algorithm's PAC guarantee in the Isabelle/HOL proof assistant; and (ii) *dynamic*, per-run, verification of ApproxMC's calls to an external CNF-XOR solver using proof certificates. We detail our general approach to establish a rigorous connection between these two parts of the verification, including our blueprint for turning the formalized, randomized algorithm into a verified proof checker, and our design of proof certificates for both ApproxMC and its internal CNF-XOR solving steps. Experimentally, we show that certificate generation adds little overhead to an approximate counter implementation, and that our certificate checker is able to fully certify 84.7% of instances with generated certificates when given the same time and memory limits as the counter.

Keywords: approximate model counting · randomized algorithms · formal verification · proof certification

---

Y. K. Tan and J. Yang—The first two authors contributed equally.

A. Gurfinkel and V. Ganesh (Eds.): CAV 2024, LNCS 14681, pp. 153–177, 2024.
https://doi.org/10.1007/978-3-031-65627-9_8

1   Introduction

State-of-the-art automated reasoning solvers are critical software systems used throughout formal methods. However, even skilled and trusted developers of such tools can inadvertently introduce errors. Two approaches have evolved to provide assurances that automated reasoning tools behave as intended. The first involves the use of theorem provers to formally verify the correctness of solver implementations [20,30]. This approach guarantees correct outputs for all inputs, but struggles to scale to complex systems such as SAT solvers. The second approach is based on *certifying algorithms* [38], where a solver is required to produce a certificate alongside its output [6,10,24,35,37,53,58]. A *certificate* checker (also called *proof* checker)—which is often formally verified—then checks the correctness of this certificate, ensuring that the system's output adheres to the desired specifications. This latter method has gained significant traction in the SAT solving community, wherein a SAT solver either returns a satisfying assignment that is easy to check through evaluation or a proof of unsatisfiability as a certificate [58]. However, neither of these approaches have been applied to probabilistic systems that rely on *randomized* algorithms. In fact, McConnell et al. [38] argue that randomized algorithms resist deterministic certification.

In this paper, we propose a hybrid approach that harnesses the power of both theorem-proving and certificate-based approaches to certify probabilistic systems. We present our approach on ApproxMC, a probabilistic automated reasoning system which computes approximate model counts for Boolean formulas. Model counting is a fundamental problem in computer science that serves as a key component in a wide range of applications including control improvisation [22], network reliability [14,56], neural network verification [5], probabilistic reasoning [11,18,45,46], and so on. Therefore, it is crucial that the results computed by an approximate model counter, such as ApproxMC, can be trusted.

Two key questions must be tackled by our approach. First, what does it mean to trust a *random* run of ApproxMC? Here, we propose a *verification modulo randomness* approach, i.e., our certification results are modulo a trusted random bit generator. Second, how do we handle the huge volume of (incremental) CNF-XOR satisfiability solver calls which are tightly integrated in ApproxMC [49,50]? Here, we design the certificate format to require only the results of solver calls that are crucial for ApproxMC's correctness. In particular, ApproxMC makes $\mathcal{O}(\varepsilon^{-2} \cdot \log n \cdot \log \delta^{-1})$ many calls to its solver, where n is the number of (projected) variables of the formula, ε is the tolerance parameter, and δ is the confidence parameter (see Sect. 3 for definitions); our crucial insight is that to certify ApproxMC, we only need to check the correctness of $\mathcal{O}(\log \delta^{-1})$ UNSAT calls, which is independent of n. We then observe that existing CNF-XOR UNSAT checkers fail to scale to formulas that are handled by ApproxMC. To this end, we adapt existing solving and verified proof checking pipelines to natively support proof certificates for CNF-XOR unsatisfiability. With this design, our framework is able to independently check certificates generated by a state-of-the-art (but untrusted) implementation of ApproxMC, with *all* of the latter's optimizations enabled. Overall, the key idea is to combine a *static*, once-off, formal proof of

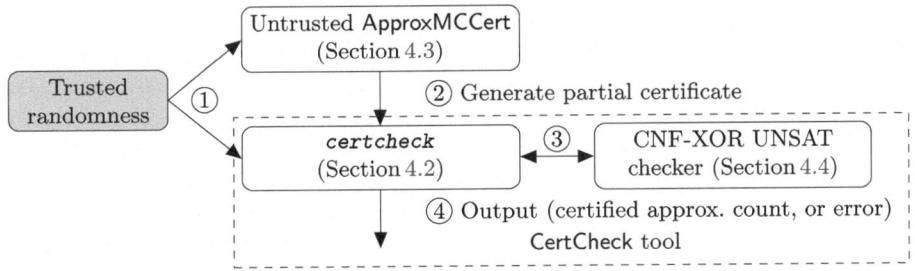

Fig. 1. The certified approximate model counting workflow.

the algorithm's correctness guarantee in Isabelle/HOL [42,43] with *dynamic*, per-run, certification of ApproxMC's calls to an external CNF-XOR solver.

In summary, our contributions are as follows:

1. An abstract specification of ApproxMC and a formal proof of its probably approximately correct (PAC) guarantee in Isabelle/HOL (Sect. 4.1).
2. A refinement of the abstract specification to a concrete certificate format and checker implementation for ApproxMC (Sects. 4.2 and 4.3).
3. Updates to various tools to realize a formally verified proof checking pipeline with native support for CNF-XOR unsatisfiability (Sect. 4.4).
4. Empirical evaluation of the framework on an extensive suite of model counting benchmarks to demonstrate its practical utility (Sect. 5).

Our workflow for certified approximate model counting is shown in Fig. 1. In step ①, it uses a trusted external tool to generate uniform random bits which are handed to an *untrusted* certificate generator ApproxMCCert and to the verified certificate checker CertCheck (extracted from Isabelle/HOL); the random bits are used identically by ApproxMCCert and CertCheck to generate random XOR constraints as part of the counting algorithm. For step ②, ApproxMCCert generates a *partial* certificate which is subsequently checked in step ③ by CertCheck; the certificate is partial because it does not contain CNF-XOR unsatisfiability proofs. Instead, CertCheck calls an external CNF-XOR unsatisfiability checking pipeline (with verified proof checking in CakeML [36,53]). In the final step ④, an approximate model count is returned upon successful certification.

As part of our commitment to reproducibility, all code and proofs have been made available with a permissive open-source license [2,21,54].

Impact. Although our main objective was to enhance end-user trust in answers to their counting queries, undertaking this project led to unexpected benefits that are worth highlighting. While modifying ApproxMC's underlying solver, `CryptoMiniSat` [52], to emit certificates (Sect. 4.4), a bug in `CryptoMiniSat`'s XOR manipulation system was discovered. The bug was introduced during the development of part of the BIRD system [50] that keeps *all* XOR constraints' clausal versions (as well as their compact XOR versions) in-memory at all times.

This allows a substantial level of interaction between XOR and clausal constraints. However, it also led to large overhead in terms of the often hundreds of thousands of clauses needed to encode the XORs in their clausal form. The compromise made by the developers was to detach the clausal representation of XORs from the watchlists. However, that seemed to have led to a level of complexity that both allowed the bug to occur, and more importantly, made it impossible to discover via `CryptoMiniSat`'s standard fuzzing pipeline. Our version of `CryptoMiniSat` fixes this by not keeping around a clausal encoding of all XORs, instead introducing (and deleting) them whenever needed for the proof.

Furthermore, we have also found minor flaws in the theoretical analysis of ApproxMC (see discussion of `events_prob`) and in the implementation, e.g., the sampling of random bits was slightly biased, and an infinite loop could be triggered on certain random seeds. None of these bugs were known to the authors of ApproxMC or were previously reported by users of the tool. All of these issues have been fixed and upstreamed to their tools' respective codebases.

2   Related Work

This discussion is focused on formally verified algorithms and proof checkers. Readers are referred to Chakraborty et al. [13] and references therein for related literature on approximate model counting.

Certified Model Counting. Prior research on certificate-based approaches focuses on deterministic methods in model counting. Prior work on certified *exact* model counting focuses either on the development of proofs, such as MICE [19] and CPOG [10], along with their respective toolchains, or on analyzing the complexity of the proof system [7]. Some efforts have been directed toward certifying deterministic approximate counting algorithms which, however, require access to a Σ_2^P oracle and did not yield practical implementations [40]. Our work develops the first certification framework for randomized approximate model counting.

Formalization of Randomized Algorithms. Various randomized algorithms have been formally analyzed in Isabelle/HOL, including randomized quicksort, random binary tree data structures [15], and approximation of frequency moments in data streams [31–34]. These prior efforts as well as ours, all build upon the foundations for measure and probability theory in Isabelle/HOL [16,28]. Properties of approximate membership query structures (including Bloom filters) have been verified in Coq [26]. Pioneering work on formal verification of randomized algorithms, including the Miller-Rabin primality test, was carried out by Joe Hurd in HOL4 [29]. A common objective of these prior efforts, and that of ours, is to put the guarantees of randomized algorithms on formal foundations.

Verified Proof Checking. Formally verified proof checkers have been developed for several (deterministic) algorithms and theories, such as the CNF unsatisfiability checkers used by the SAT community [27,37,53]. Within Isabelle/HOL, the Pastèque tool [35] checks proofs in the practical algebraic calculus, which can be used to validate algebraic reasoning; the CeTA tool [55] is based on an extensive library of results for certifying properties of rewriting systems; and the LEDA project developed specialized proof checkers for graph algorithms [1]. CoqQFBV [47] is similar in design to our approach in that a higher-level Coq-generated tool for verified bit-blasting is used in concert with a lower-level veri-fied proof checker for CNF formulas.

CNF-XOR Unsatisfiability Checking. Given ApproxMC's reliance on CNF-XOR formulas, certification of CNF-XOR unsatisfiability emerged as a key challenge in our work. To this end, we provide a brief overview of three prior state-of-the-art approaches for certified CNF-XOR reasoning.

1. The first approach uses proof generation and certification of XOR reasoning based on Binary Decision Diagrams (BDDs) [48]. It uses CryptoMiniSat [52], a SAT solver specifically made to work on CNF-XOR instances and TBUDDY [9] to produce FRAT proof certificates [3] for CryptoMiniSat's XOR reasoning; FRAT-rs [3] is used as the elaboration backend and a verified LRAT proof checker [27,53] can be used to check the elaborated proofs.
2. The second approach, due to Gocht and Nordström [24], relies on pseudo-Boolean reasoning and its associated proof system to justify both CNF and parity reasoning. This approach was demonstrated on MiniSat equipped with an XOR reasoning engine, with VeriPB as a proof checker; pseudo-Boolean proofs are also supported by a verified proof checker [23].
3. The third approach is to rely on the standard SAT solvers accompanied with standard CNF proof formats and (verified) checkers [27,37,53].

3 Background

This section gives a brief introduction to ApproxMC (Sect. 3.1) and to theorem-proving in Isabelle/HOL (Sect. 3.2).

3.1 Approximate Model Counting

Given a Boolean formula F, the *model counting* problem is to calculate the num-ber of models (also called *solutions* or *satisfying assignments*) of F. Model count-ing is known to be #P-complete, and therefore has been a target of sustained interest for randomized approximation techniques over the past four decades. The current state-of-the-art approximate approach, ApproxMC [12], is a hashing-based framework that relies on reducing the model counting problem to SAT queries, which are handled by an underlying solver. Importantly, ApproxMC is a *probably approximately correct* (PAC) projected model counter, i.e., it takes in a formula F, a projection set $S \subseteq \mathsf{Vars}(F)$, a tolerance parameter $\varepsilon > 0$, and a confidence parameter $\delta \in (0,1]$, and returns a count c satisfying the PAC guar-antee: $\Pr\left[\frac{|\mathsf{sol}(F)_{\downarrow S}|}{1+\varepsilon} \le c \le (1+\varepsilon)|\mathsf{sol}(F)_{\downarrow S}|\right] \ge 1 - \delta$, where $|\mathsf{sol}(F)_{\downarrow S}|$ denotes the number of the solutions of F projected on S.

Algorithm 1. ApproxMC $(F, S, \varepsilon, \delta)$

1: thresh $\leftarrow 9.84 \left(1 + \frac{\varepsilon}{1+\varepsilon}\right) \left(1 + \frac{1}{\varepsilon}\right)^2$
2: $Y \leftarrow$ BoundedSAT(F, S, thresh)
3: **if** $(|Y| < \text{thresh})$ **then return** $|Y|$
4: $t \leftarrow$ computeIter(δ) ▷ probability amplification using the median method
5: $C \leftarrow$ emptyList, iter $\leftarrow 0$
6: **repeat**
7:     iter $\leftarrow$ iter $+ 1$
8:     nSols $\leftarrow$ ApproxMCCore(F, S, thresh)
9:     AddToList(C, nSols)
10: **until** (iter $\geq t$)
11: **return** FindMedian(C)

Algorithm 2. ApproxMCCore (F, S, thresh)

1: Choose $|S| - 1$ random XOR constraints $X = (X_1, \ldots, X_{|S|-1})$ over S
2: $m \leftarrow$ FindM(F, S, X, thresh) ▷ search for $m \in \{1, \ldots, |S|\}$ using BoundedSAT
3: **if** $(m \geq |S|)$ **then return** $(2^m \times 1)$ ▷ dummy value for failed round
4: $c \leftarrow$ BoundedSAT $(F \wedge X_1 \wedge \cdots \wedge X_m, S, \text{thresh})$;
5: **return** $(2^m \times c)$

An outline of ApproxMC is shown in Algorithms 1 and 2. At a high level, the key idea of ApproxMC is to partition the set of solutions into small cells of roughly equal size by relying on the power of XOR-based hash families [12, 25], then randomly picking one of the cells and enumerating all the solutions in the chosen small cell up to a threshold thresh via calls to BoundedSAT(F, S, thresh). The estimated count is obtained by scaling the number of solutions in the randomly chosen cell by the number of cells, and the success probability of this estimation is amplified to the desired level by taking the median result from several trials.

Syntactically, the solution space partition and random cell selection is accomplished by introducing randomly generated XOR constraints of the form $\left(\bigoplus_{y \in Y} y\right) = b$ for a random subset $Y \subseteq S$ and random bit b. A crucial fact about random XOR constraints exploited by ApproxMC is their 2-universality when viewed as a hash family on assignments—briefly, given any two distinct Boolean assignments over the variable set S, the probability of each one satisfying a randomly chosen XOR constraint is independent and equal to $\frac{1}{2}$.

Accordingly, the BoundedSAT queries made in Algorithms 1 and 2 are conjunctions of the input formula and random XOR constraints, i.e., CNF-XOR formulas. The current implementation of ApproxMC relies on CryptoMiniSat for its ability to handle CNF-XOR formulas efficiently and incrementally [49, 50]. Furthermore, the real-world implementation also relies on three key optimizations. **(1)** The search for the correct value of m in Algorithm 2 (FindM) combines a linear neighborhood search, a galloping search, and a binary search [12]. **(2)** The underlying SAT solver is used as a library, allowing to solve under a set of assumptions, a technique introduced as part of MiniSat [17]. This allows the solver to keep learned lemmas between subsequent calls to `solve()`, significantly improving solving speed, which is especially helpful for proving unsatisfiability. **(3)** To improve the speed of finding satisfying assignments, a solution cache of past solutions is retained [49] which is especially helpful when the optimal number of XORs to add is N, but N+1 have been added and were found to be too much. In these cases, all solutions that are valid for N+1 XORs are also solutions to N XORs and can be reused.

3.2   Formalization in Isabelle/HOL

Notation. All Isabelle/HOL syntax is typeset in `typewriter` font with bold-face Isar **keywords**; $\bigwedge$ and $\implies$ are the universal quantifier and implication of Isabelle's metalogic, respectively. Type variables are written as `'a, 'b`. The type of (total) functions from `'a` to `'b` is written as `'a ⇒ 'b`, and the type of partial functions, which are only defined on some elements of type `'a`, is `'a ⇀ 'b`. For clarity, we often annotate terms with their type using the notation `term :: type`. For types such as reals, integers, or natural numbers, the interval from i to j (inclusive) is written as `{i..j}`; the same interval except endpoint j is `{i..<j}`. More comprehensive introductions can be found in standard references [4, 42].

Locales and Probability. Isabelle/HOL is equipped with *locales* [4], a system of user-declared modules consisting of syntactic parameters, assumptions on those parameters, and module-specific theorems. These modules can be instantiated and inherited, giving users a powerful means of managing mathematical relationships. The following snippet, taken from the Isabelle/HOL standard library, shows an example **locale** declaration for probability spaces followed by an **interpretation** command claiming that the measure space associated with any probability mass function (PMF) `p` is a probability space [28].

```
locale prob_space = finite_measure +
assumes emeasure_space_1: "emeasure M (space M) = 1"
...
interpretation measure_pmf: prob_space "measure_pmf p"
```

Thanks to the locale interpretation, all definitions and theorems associated with probability spaces can be used with PMFs. For example, the probability of an event `A :: 'a set` occurring under `p` is `measure_pmf.prob p A`. The support of PMF `p` is `set_pmf p`, which is `finite` for all PMFs considered in this work.

4   Approximate Model Counting in Isabelle/HOL

This section outlines our formalization of ApproxMC in Isabelle/HOL and its verified certificate checker implementation. The proof follows a refinement-based approach, starting with an abstract mathematical specification of ApproxMC, where its probabilistic approximation guarantees can be formalized without low-level implementation details getting in the way (Sect. 4.1). Then, the abstract specification is progressively concretized to a verified certificate checker which we call CertCheck (Sect. 4.2) and we extend ApproxMC to ApproxMCCert, a certificate-generating counter (Sect. 4.3). As part of CertCheck, we also built a native CNF-XOR unsatisfiability checker, which is external to Isabelle/HOL, but is also based on formally verified proof checking (Sect. 4.4).

4.1 Abstract Specification and Probabilistic Analysis

Throughout this section, the type `'a` abstracts the syntactic representation of variables. For example, in the DIMACS CNF format, variables are represented with positive numbers, while in other settings, it may be more convenient to use strings as variable names. A solution (or model) `w :: 'a ⇒ bool` is a Boolean-valued function on variables and a projection set `S :: 'a set` is a (finite) set of variables. The main result of this section is formalized in a locale with two parameters `sols`, `enc_xor`, and an assumption relating the two:

```
locale ApproxMC =
fixes sols :: "'fml ⇒ ('a ⇒ bool) set"
fixes enc_xor :: "'a set × bool ⇒ 'fml ⇒ 'fml"
assumes "⋀F xor.
  sols (enc_xor xor F) = sols F ∩ {ω. satisfies_xor xor {x. ω x}}"
```

Here, type `'fml` abstracts the syntactic representation of formulas, `sols F` is the set of all solutions of a formula `F`, and `enc_xor xor F` is a formula whose set of solutions satisfies both `F` and the XOR constraint `xor`. An instantiation of the `ApproxMC` locale would need to provide implementations of `sols`, `enc_xor` and prove that they satisfy the latter assumed property.

The PAC theorem for ApproxMC is formalized as follows:

```
theorem approxmc_prob:
assumes "δ > 0" "δ < 1" "ε > 0" "ε ≤ 1" "finite S"
shows "let sz = real (card (proj S (sols F))) in
  measure_pmf.prob (approxmc F S ε δ n)
    {c. c ∈ {sz / (1 + ε) .. (1 + ε) * sz}} ≥ 1 - δ"
```

Here, `sz` is the true count of projected solutions, i.e., the cardinality of the set `proj S (sols F)`, interpreted as a real number. The conclusion says that `approxmc` returns an ε-approximate count c with probability at least $1 - \delta$. The argument `n` is a user-specifiable minimum number of iterations of ApproxMCCore calls inside ApproxMC; in practice, a sufficient number of rounds is automatically determined using the median method. Since the `ApproxMC` locale can be instantiated for *any* Boolean theory in which XOR constraints can be syntactically encoded, this theorem shows that the approximate model counting algorithm of Chakrabory et al. [12] works for any such theory.

The rest of this section gives an overview of our proof of `approxmc_prob`. Technical differences compared to the original proofs are discussed in remarks.

Formalized Analysis of ApproxMCCore. For simplicity, we write $S \Rightarrow bool$ for the type of solutions projected onto set S and $[n] \Rightarrow bool$ for n-dimensional bit-vectors, i.e., the type of Boolean-valued functions on domain $0, 1, \ldots, n-1$. A hash function $h :: (S \Rightarrow bool) \Rightarrow ([n] \Rightarrow bool)$ maps projected solutions into n-dimensional bit-vectors. Let $W :: ('a \Rightarrow bool)$ set be any set of solutions, such as $sols$ F. Abstractly, ApproxMCCore is a way of approximating the cardinality of the projected set $proj$ S W, given an *oracle* that can count up to a specified threshold $thresh$ number of solutions. Without loss of generality, assume $thresh \leq proj$ S W (otherwise, the oracle returns the exact count).

Remark 1. The simple type theory of Isabelle/HOL does not support dependent function types like $S \Rightarrow bool$ and $[n] \Rightarrow bool$. Our formalization represents functions with type $S \Rightarrow bool$ as partial functions $'a \rightharpoonup bool$ along with an assumption that their function domain is equal to S.

For any fixed bit-vector $\alpha :: [card$ S $- 1] \Rightarrow bool$, the sets of hash functions T, L, and U used in the analysis are defined as follows, where $card\_slice$ h i counts the number of entries of $w \in proj$ S W such that the hash value h w agrees with α on their first i entries (also called the i-th slices).

```
definition μ where "μ i = card (proj S W) / 2 ^ i"
definition T where "T i = {h. card_slice h i < thresh}"
definition L where "L i = {h. card_slice h i < μ i / (1+ε)}"
definition U where "U i = {h. card_slice h i ≥ μ i * (1 +
ε/(1+ε))}"
```

For any input hash function h, the following $approxcore$ function (cf. Algorithm 2 Lines 2–5) finds the first index m, if one exists in $[1..<card$ $S]$, where $h \in T$ m. It returns the approximate model count as a multiplier $(2 ^ m)$ and cell size $(card\_slice$ h $m)$. The *failure event* $approxcore\_fail$ is the set of hash functions h such that $approxcore$ returns a non-$(1+ε)$-factor-approximate count.

```
definition approxcore where "
  approxcore h = (
  case List.find (λi. h ∈ T i) [1..<card S] of
    None ⇒ (2 ^ card S, 1)
  | Some m ⇒ (2 ^ m, card_slice h m))"

definition approxcore_fail where "
  approxcore_fail =
  {h. let (cells,sols) = approxcore h ; sz = card (proj S W) in
    cells * sols ∉ {sz / (1 + ε) .. (1 + ε) * sz}}"
```

The key lemma for $approxcore$ (shown with proof sketch below) is that, for hash functions h, which are randomly sampled from an appropriate hash family H, the probability of the aforementioned failure event is bounded above by 0.36 [12]. The lemma uses Isabelle/HOL's formalization of hash families which is *seeded* [31], i.e., p is a PMF on seeds and H is a 2-universal hash family for seeds drawn from p;

`map_pmf` (λs w. H w s) p is a PMF which samples a random seed s and then returns the hash function associated with that seed according to the family H.

```
lemma approxcore_fail_prob:
assumes "(1 + ε / (1 + ε)) * (9.84 * (1 + 1 / ε)^2) ≤ thresh"
assumes "ε ≤ 1" "finite (set_pmf p)"
assumes "prob_space.k_universal (measure_pmf p) 2 H
        {α. dom α = S} {α. dom α = {0..<card S - 1}}"
shows "
  measure_pmf.prob (map_pmf (λs w. H w s) p) approxcore_fail ≤ 0.36"
```

Proof. The proof of `approxcore_fail_prob` proceeds via several sub-lemmas [12], which we discuss inline below. We first show that an index `mstar` exists with the following properties (**obtains** is the Isar keyword for existential claims):

```
lemma mstar_exists:
obtains mstar where
  "μ (mstar - 1) * (1 + ε / (1 + ε)) > thresh"
  "μ mstar * (1 + ε / (1 + ε)) ≤ thresh"
  "mstar ≤ card S - 1"
```

This is proved by noting that there exists m satisfying the first two properties separately in the finite interval 1, 2, ..., card S - 1, so there must be an `mstar` satisfying all three properties in that interval.

Next, the failure event (which is a set of hash functions) is proved to be contained in the union of four separate events involving `mstar` using the properties from `mstar_exists` and unfolding the respective definitions of T, L, and U:

```
lemma failure_subset:
shows "approxcore_fail ⊆
  T (mstar-3) ∪ L (mstar-2) ∪ L (mstar-1) ∪ (L mstar ∪ U mstar)"
```

Finally, we bound the probability for each of the four events separately.

```
lemma events_prob:
assumes "(1 + ε / (1 + ε)) * (9.84 * (1 + 1 / ε)^2) ≤ thresh"
assumes "finite (set_pmf p)"
assumes "prob_space.k_universal (measure_pmf p) 2 H
        {α. dom α = S} {α. dom α = {0..<card S - 1}}"
shows "let Hp = map_pmf (λs w. H w s) p in
  (ε ≤ 1 ⟶ measure_pmf.prob Hp (T (mstar-3)) ≤ 1 / 62.5) ∧
  measure_pmf.prob Hp (L (mstar-2)) ≤ 1 / 20.68 ∧
  measure_pmf.prob Hp (L (mstar-1)) ≤ 1 / 10.84 ∧
  measure_pmf.prob Hp (L mstar ∪ U mstar) ≤ 1 / 4.92"
```

Lemma `approxcore_fail_prob` follows from `failure_subset`, `events_prob`, and the union bound on probabilities.   □

Remark 2. Our implicit construction of `mstar` in `mstar_exists` avoids an explicit calculation from `F`, `S` and ε [12], which is more intricate to analyze. Additionally, in `events_prob`, the first bound for `T (mstar-3)` works only when $\varepsilon \leq 1$, an omitted condition from the pen-and-paper proof [12, Lemma 2]; we also verified a looser bound of `1 / 10.84` without this condition, but this leads to a weaker overall guarantee for ApproxMCCore (which we do not use subsequently).

Formalized Analysis of ApproxMC. Random XORs and XOR-based hash families are defined as follows:

```
definition random_xor where "
  random_xor V = pair_pmf (pmf_of_set (Pow V)) (bernoulli_pmf (1/2))"
definition random_xors where "
  random_xors V n = prod_pmf {..<n} (λ_. map_pmf Some (random_xor
V))"
definition xor_hash where "
  xor_hash w xors =
  (map_option (λxor. satisfies_xor xor {x. w x = Some True}) ∘
xors)"
```

Here, `random_xor V` is the PMF which samples a pair of a uniformly randomly chosen subset of the (projection) variables `V` and the outcome of a fair coin flip; `random_xors V n` is the PMF that samples n independent XORs according to `random_xor V`. Given `card S - 1` randomly chosen seed `xors`, the associated `xor_hash` hash function takes a projected solution `w` to the bit-vector whose bit `i` indicates whether the `i`-th XOR is satisfied by `w`.

The following definition of `approxmccore` (cf. Algorithm 2) randomly samples `card S - 1` XOR constraints over the variables `S` and runs `approxcore_xors` (`approxcore` instantiated with XOR-based hash families using `xor_hash`). The top-level function `approxmc` (cf. Algorithm 1) selects appropriate values for `thresh` and the number of rounds `t` for amplification using the median method.

```
definition approxmccore :: "'fml ⇒ 'a set ⇒ nat ⇒ nat pmf"
where "approxmccore F S thresh =
  map_pmf (approxcore_xors F S thresh) (random_xors S (card S - 1))"

definition approxmc::"'fml ⇒ 'a set ⇒ real ⇒ real ⇒ nat ⇒ nat
pmf"
where "approxmc F S ε δ n = (
  let thresh = compute_thresh ε in
  if card (proj S (sols F)) < thresh
  then return_pmf (card (proj S (sols F)))
  else
    let t = compute_t δ n in
    map_pmf (median t)
      (prod_pmf {0..<t::nat} (λi. approxmccore F S thresh)))"
```

The main result `approxmc_prob` follows from 2-universality of XOR-based hash families and the facts that `compute_thresh` returns a correct value of `thresh` and `compute_t` chooses a sufficient number of rounds for the median method.

Library Contributions. We added reusable results to Isabelle/HOL's probability libraries, such as the Paley-Zigmund inequality (a concentration inequality used in the analysis of ApproxMCCore) and a slightly modified (tighter) analysis of the median method based on the prior formalization by Karayel [31,33]; the latter modification does not change the asymptotic analysis of the method but it is needed as ApproxMC implementations use the tighter calculation to reduce the number of rounds for success probability amplification.

We also formalized the 3-universality of XOR-based hash families [25], which implies its 2-universality, as needed by ApproxMC. The proof is sketched in the online extended version of this paper. Our (new) proof is of independent interest as it is purely combinatorial, using a highly symmetric case analysis which helps to reduce formalization effort because many cases can be proved using without-loss-of-generality-style reasoning in Isabelle/HOL.

4.2   Concretization to a Certificate Checker

The specification from Sect. 4.1 leaves several details abstract. For example, `card_slice` refers to set cardinalities and `approxmc` uses a bounded solution counter as an oracle, neither of which are *a priori* computable terms. This section gives a concrete implementation strategy where the abstract details are obtained from certificates generated by an untrusted external implementation, and checked using verified code. The main result is formalized in a locale `CertCheck` with two key extensions compared to `ApproxMC` from Sect. 4.1: (i) the `ApproxMCL` locale, switching from set-based to computable list-based representations for the projection set and XORs; (ii) the additional locale parameters `check_sol` determining whether a formula is satisfied by a specified assignment, and `ban_sol` that syntactically blocks a solution from further consideration.

```
locale CertCheck = ApproxMCL sols enc_xor
for sols :: "'fml ⇒ ('a ⇒ bool) set"
and enc_xor :: "'a list × bool ⇒ 'fml ⇒ 'fml" +
fixes check_sol :: "'fml ⇒ ('a ⇒ bool) ⇒ bool"
fixes ban_sol :: "'a sol ⇒ 'fml ⇒ 'fml"
assumes "⋀F w. check_sol F w ⟷ w ∈ sols F"
assumes "⋀F vs. sols (ban_sol vs F) =
  sols F ∩ {ω. map ω (map fst vs) ≠ map snd vs}"
```

The correctness of the `certcheck` checker (shown below) has two conjuncts in its conclusion. In both conjuncts, `f` models an external (untrusted) implementation returning a certificate and `r` is a random seed passed to both `f` and `certcheck`. The checker either returns an error string (`isl`) or a certified count. The *soundness* guarantee (left conjunct) says that the probability of the checker returning an incorrect count (without error) is bounded above by δ. Note that for a buggy counter f that always returns an invalid certificate, `certcheck` returns an error for all random seeds, i.e., it returns a count (whether correct or not) with probability 0. Thus, the *promise-completeness* guarantee (right conjunct) says that *if* the function f is promised to return valid certificates for all seeds r, then the checker returns a correct count with probability $1 - \delta$.

```
theorem certcheck_prob:
assumes "(⋀F. check_unsat F ⟹ sols F = {})"
assumes "δ > 0" "δ < 1" "ε > 0" "distinct S"
shows "
  let sz = real (card (proj (set S) (sols F))) in
  let seeds = random_seed_xors (find_t δ) (length S) in
  let pr = measure_pmf.prob
    (map_pmf (λr. certcheck check_unsat F S ε δ (f r) r) seeds) in
  pr {c. ¬isl c ∧ projr c ∉ {sz / (1 + ε) .. (1 + ε) * sz}} ≤ δ ∧
  ( (∀r ∈ set_pmf seeds.
      ¬isl (certcheck check_unsat F S ε δ (f r) r)) ⟶
    pr {c. projr c ∈ {sz / (1 + ε) .. (1 + ε) * sz}} ≥ 1 - δ)"
```

Additional differences in `certcheck_prob` compared to `approxmc_prob` are: (iii) the oracle function `check_unsat`, which is assumed to be an interface to an external unsatisfiability checker; (iv) the additional certificate arguments $m0$ and ms; and (v) the eager sampling of XORs using random bits (`random_seed_xors`), compared to `approxmc` which samples lazily.

Remark 3. Note that `ban_sol` and `check_sol` are locale parameters with assumptions that must be *proven* when `CertCheck` is instantiated to a Boolean theory; in contrast, `check_unsat` appears as an *assumption*. The pragmatic reason for this difference is that `ban_sol` and `check_sol` can be readily implemented in Isabelle/HOL with decent performance. In contrast, developing efficient verified *unsatisfiability* proof checkers and formats, e.g., for CNFs, is still an active area of research [3,27,37,53]. Leaving `check_unsat` outside the scope of Isabelle/HOL allows us to rely on these orthogonal verification efforts (as we do in Sect. 4.4).

From `approxmc` to `certcheck`. We briefly list the steps in transporting the PAC guarantee from `approxmc` to `certcheck`, with reference to the differences labeled (i)–(v) above. The proof follows a sequence of small refinement steps which are individually straightforward as they do not involve significant probabilistic reasoning. First, cf. (v), a variant of `approxmc` is formalized where all XORs are eagerly sampled upfront, as opposed to lazily at each call to `approxmccore`. Without loss of generality, it suffices to sample $t \times (card\ S - 1)$ XORs. Next, cf. (i), the representations are swapped to executable ones, e.g., the projection set is represented as a list S of distinct elements. Accordingly, the left-hand side of each XOR is represented as a list of `length S` bits, where the i-th bit indicates whether the i-th entry of S is included in the XOR. Note that it suffices to sample $t \times (card\ S - 1) \times (card\ S + 1)$ bits for ApproxMC. Finally, cf. (iv),

Input formula   `certcheck` partial certificate file

```
p cnf 10 7
1 2 3 4 5 0
6 7 8 9 10 0
-1 -6 0
-2 -7 0
-3 -8 0
-4 -9 0
-5 -10 0
```

```
0     // initial m0
73    // number and list of solutions
-1 2 -3 -4 -5 6 -7 -8 -9 -10 0
...
1 -2 -3 4 5 -6 7 -8 -9 -10 0
2     // round 1 value of m
73    // number and list of solutions
... //    after adding m - 1 XORs
51    // number and list of solutions
... //    after adding m XORs
      //    *UNSAT after excluding 51 solutions
      //    checked by external pipeline
2     // round 2 value of m
      // ... repeat for t rounds ...
```

Approximate count

```
...
s mc 184
```

Fig. 2. An example pigeon-hole formula (2 pigeons, 5 holes, 180 solutions) in DIMACS format and a valid certificate for the checker at $\varepsilon = 0.8$ and $\delta = 0.2$ (`thresh` $= 73, t =$ 9). The certificate is shown with colored comments and with redundant spaces added for clarity. In clauses, the negative (resp. positive) integers are negated (resp. positive) literals, with a 0 terminator; solutions are lists of literals assigned to true. Part of the certificate (marked with ∗) is checked with an external UNSAT proof checking pipeline.

partial certificates are introduced. The key observation is that the final value of `m` in `approxcore` from Sect. 4.1 can be readily *certified* because it is the first entry where adding `m` XORs causes the solution count to fall below `thresh`—the solution count is monotonically decreasing as more XORs are added. Thus, for a claimed value of `m` it suffices to check, cf. (ii) and (iii) that the following three conditions hold. (**1**) Firstly, `1` $\leq$ `m` $\leq$ `card S - 1`. (**2**) Secondly, the solution count after adding `m - 1` XORs reaches or exceeds `thresh`, which can be certified (`check_sol`) by a list of solutions of length at least `thresh`, which are distinct after projection on `S`. (**3**) Thirdly, if `m < card S - 1`, then the solution count after adding `m` XORs is below `thresh`, which can be certified (`check_sol`) by a list of solutions of length below `thresh`, which are distinct after projection, and where the formula after excluding all those projected solutions (`ban_sol`) is unsatisfiable (`check_unsat`).

An example partial certificate is shown in Fig. 2. Note that we call these *partial* certificates because of the reliance on an external pipeline for checking unsatisfiability, as illustrated in the example.

Code Extraction for CertCheck. To obtain an executable implementation of `certcheck`, we instantiated the Isabelle/HOL formalization with a concrete syntax and semantics for CNF-XOR formulas, and extracted source code using Isabelle/HOL's Standard ML extraction mechanism. The extracted implementation is compiled together with user interface code, e.g., file I/O, parsing, and interfacing with a trusted random bit generator and CNF-XOR unsatisfiability checking, as shown in Fig. 1. The resulting tool is called CertCheck.

4.3   Extending ApproxMC to ApproxMCCert

To demonstrate the feasibility of building a (partial) certificate generation tool, we modified the mainline implementation of ApproxMC to accept and use an externally generated source of random bits. We also modified it to write its internally calculated values of m and a log of the respective models reported by its internal solver to a file. The resulting tool is called ApproxMCCert. An implementation of ApproxMC (and thus ApproxMCCert) requires logarithmically many solver calls to *find* the correct value of m and it can employ many search strategies [12]. The partial certificate format is agnostic to how m is found, requiring certification only for the final value of m in each round.

Remark 4. It is worth remarking that CertCheck requires checking the validity of $\mathcal{O}(\varepsilon^{-2} \cdot \log \delta^{-1})$ solutions (each of size n, the number of variables), and unsatisfiability for $\mathcal{O}(\log \delta^{-1})$ formulas, while ApproxMC requires $\mathcal{O}(\varepsilon^{-2} \cdot \log n \cdot \log \delta^{-1})$ calls to its underlying solver. In the next section, we instantiate `check_unsat` with a CNF-XOR unsatisfiability checking pipeline that generates proofs which are checkable by a verified checker in polynomial time (in the size of the proofs).

4.4   CNF-XOR Unsatisfiability Checking

A crucial aspect of CertCheck is its reliance on an external checker for unsatisfiability of CNF-XOR formulas. As mentioned in Sect. 2, there are several prior approaches for certified CNF-XOR reasoning that can be plugged into CertCheck.

We opted to build our own *native* extension of FRAT [3] because none of the previous options scaled to the level of efficient XOR proof checking needed for certifying ApproxMC (as evidenced later in Sect. 5). For brevity, the new input and proof format(s) are illustrated with inline comments in Fig. 3. We defer a format specification to the tool repository.

In a nutshell, when given an input CNF-XOR formula, CryptoMiniSat has been improved to emit an unsatisfiability proof in our extended FRAT-XOR format. Then, our FRAT-xor tool elaborates the proof into XLRUP, our extension of Reverse Unit Propagation (RUP) proofs [27] with XOR reasoning. The latter format can be checked using cake_xlrup, our formally verified proof checker. Such an extension to FRAT was suggested as a possibility by Baek et al. [3] and we bear their claim out in practice.

Extending FRAT-rs to FRAT-xor. Our FRAT-xor tool adds XOR support to FRAT-rs [3], an existing tool for checking and elaborating FRAT proofs. This extension is designed to be *lightweight*—FRAT-xor does not track XORs nor check the correctness of any XOR-related steps; instead, it defers the job to an underlying verified proof checker. Our main changes were: (i) adding parsing support for XORs; (ii) ensuring that clauses implied from XORs can be properly

Input CNF-XOR formula

```
p cnf 3 4
1 2 0
-1 -2 0
x 1 2 -3 0
-3 0
```

XLRUP proof file

```
// Add at XOR ID 1, XOR x 1 2 -3 0,
// from the input formula
o x 1 1 2 -3 0
// Add at XOR ID 2, XOR x 1 2 0,
// implied by clauses 1 and 2
i x 2 1 2 0 1 2 0
// Add at XOR ID 3, XOR x 3 0,
// implied by XORs 1 and 2
x 3 3 0 1 2 0
// Add at clause ID 4, Clause 3 0,
// implied by XOR 3
i 4 3 0 3 0
// Derive empty clause by RUP,
// hints generated by FRAT-xor
5 0 3 4 0
```

FRAT-XOR proof file

```
...
o x 1 1 2 -3 0
i x 2 1 2 0 1 1 2 0
a x 3 3 0 1 1 2 0
i 4 3 0 1 3 0
a 5 0
...
```

Fig. 3. (top left) A sample input CNF-XOR formula where XOR lines start with x and indicate the literals that XOR to 1, e.g., the line x 1 2 -3 represents the XOR constraint $x_1 \oplus x_2 \oplus \bar{x}_3 = 1$; (bottom left) a FRAT-XOR proof; (right) an XLRUP proof. The steps in **bold** indicate newly added XOR reasoning. Note that the XOR steps are (mostly) syntactically and semantically unchanged going from FRAT-XOR to XLRUP, so we focus on the latter here. The meaning of each XLRUP step (analogously for FRAT-XOR) is annotated in color-coded comments above the respective line.

used for further clausal steps, including automatic elaboration of RUP [3]; and (iii) ensuring the clauses used to imply XORs are trimmed from the proof at proper points, i.e., after the last usage by either a clausal or XOR step.

Extending cake_lpr to cake_xlrup. We also modified cake_lpr [53], a verified proof checker for CNF unsatisfiability, to support reasoning over XOR constraints. The new tool supports: (i) clause-to-clause reasoning via RUP steps; (ii) deriving new XORs by adding together XORs; (iii) XOR-to-clause and clause-to-XOR implications. The main challenge here was to represent XORs efficiently using byte-level representations to take advantage of native machine instructions in XOR addition steps. The final verified correctness theorem for cake_xlrup is similar to that of cake_lpr [53] (omitted here).

Modifications to CryptoMiniSat. A refactoring of CryptoMiniSat was performed in response to the bug described in Sect. 1 and in order to add FRAT-XOR proof logging. As part of this rewrite, a new XOR constraint propagation engine has been added that had been removed as part of BIRD [50]—that system did not need it, as it kept all XOR constraints also in a blasted form. Furthermore, XOR constraints have been given IDs instead of a pointer to a TBUDDY BDD previously used, and all XOR manipulations such as XOR-ing

together XOR constraints, constant folding [57], satisfied XOR constraint deletion, etc., had to be documented in the emitted FRAT-XOR proof log. Further,
CryptoMiniSat had to be modified to track which clause IDs were responsible
for recovered XOR constraints. To make sure our changes were correct, we modified CryptoMiniSat's fuzzing pipeline to include XOR constraint-generating
problems and to check the generated proofs using our certification tools.

5   Experimental Evaluation

To evaluate the practicality of partial certificate generation (ApproxMCCert) and
certificate checking (CertCheck), we conducted an extensive evaluation over a
publicly available benchmark set [41] of 1896 problem instances that were used
in previous evaluations of ApproxMC [49,51]. The benchmark set consists of
(projected) model counting problems arising from applications such as probabilistic reasoning, plan recognition, DQMR networks, ISCAS89 combinatorial
circuits, quantified information flow, program synthesis, functional synthesis,
and logistics. Most instances are satisfiable with large model counts and only
approximately 6% are unsatisfiable for testing corner cases.

To demonstrate the effectiveness of our new CNF-XOR unsatisfiability checking pipeline, we also compared it to the three prior state-of-the-art approaches
discussed in Sect. 2. The approaches are labeled as follows:

CMS+frat-xor. Our new (default) pipeline based on FRAT-XOR (Sect. 4.4); here,
    CMS is short for CryptoMiniSat.
CMS+tbuddy. The pipeline consisting of CryptoMiniSat with TBUDDY, FRAT-rs,
    and a verified CNF proof checker (Sect. 2, item 1).
MiniSatXOR+pbp. The pipeline consisting of MiniSat with XOR engine, VeriPB,
    and its verified proof checker (Sect. 2, item 2)
CaDiCaL+lrat. A state-of-the-art SAT solver CaDiCaL [8,44] which generates
    proofs checkable by a verified CNF proof checker (Sect. 2, item 3).

We experimented with each of these approaches as the CNF-XOR unsatisfiability checking pipeline for CertCheck, checking the same suite of certificates
produced by ApproxMCCert.

The empirical evaluation was conducted on a high-performance computer
cluster where every node consists of an AMD EPYC-Milan processor featuring
2×64 real cores and 512 GB of RAM. For each instance and tool (ApproxMC,
ApproxMCCert, or CertCheck), we set a timeout of 5000 s, memory limit of 16GB,
and we used the default values of $\delta = 0.2$ and $\varepsilon = 0.8$ for all tools following
previous experimental conventions [49]. For each given tool, we report the PAR-
2 score which is commonly used in the SAT competition. It is calculated as the
average of all runtimes for solved/certified instances out of the relevant instances
for that tool, with unsolved/uncertified instances counting for double the time
limit (i.e., 10000 s).

Our empirical evaluation sought to answer the following questions:

RQ1 How does the performance of ApproxMCCert and CertCheck compare to that of ApproxMC?

RQ2 How does the performance of CMS+frat-xor compare to prior state-of-the-art approaches for CNF-XOR UNSAT checking for use in CertCheck?

RQ1 Feasibility of Certificate Generation and Checking. We present the results for ApproxMC, ApproxMCCert, and CertCheck in Table 1. For certificate generation, our main observation is that ApproxMCCert is able to solve and generate certificates for 99.3% (i.e., 1202 out of 1211) instances that ApproxMC can solve alone, and their PAR-2 scores (out of 1896 instances) are similar. Indeed, in the per-instance scatter plot of ApproxMC and ApproxMCCert runtimes in Fig. 4, we see that for almost all instances, the overhead of certificate generation in ApproxMCCert is fairly small. This is compelling evidence for the practicality of adopting *certificate generation* for approximate counters with our approach.

Table 1. Performance comparison of ApproxMC, ApproxMCCert, and CertCheck. The PAR-2 score is calculated out of 1896 instances for ApproxMC and ApproxMCCert, and out of the 1202 instances with certificates for CertCheck.

	ApproxMC	ApproxMCCert	CertCheck
Counted Instances	1211	1202	1018
PAR-2 Score	3769	3815	1743

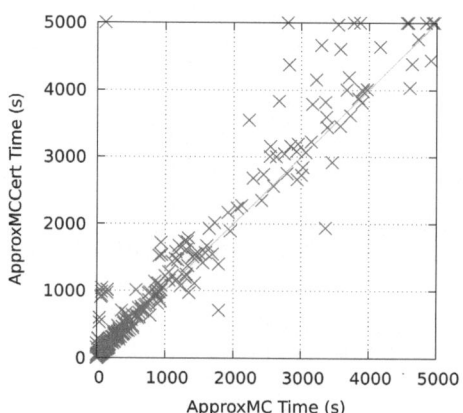

Fig. 4. Per instance runtime (s) comparison for ApproxMCCert and ApproxMC.

Turning to the feasibility of certificate checking, we observe in Table 1 that CertCheck is able to fully certify 84.7% of the instances (i.e., 1018 out of 1202) with certificates. Of the remaining instances, CertCheck timed out for 46 and ran out of memory for 138 instances (no certificate errors were reported in our latest

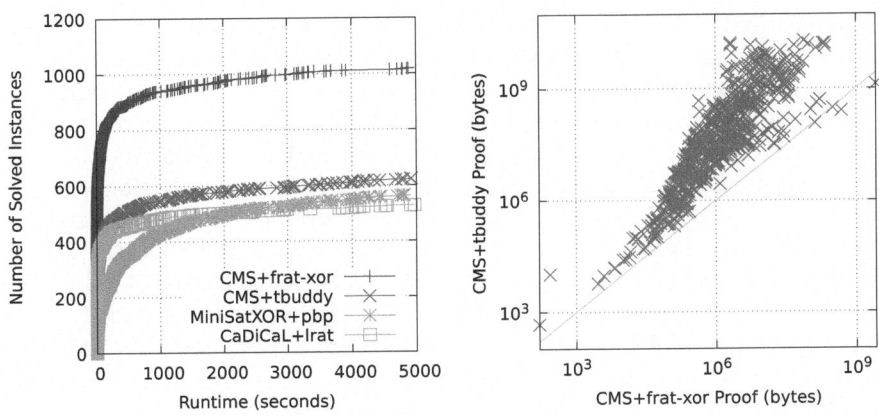

Fig. 5. (left) Runtime performance comparison between CNF-XOR unsatisfiability checkers. (right) Per instance CNF-XOR unsatisfiability proof size (bytes) comparison for CMS+frat-xor and CMS+tbuddy.

versions of the tools). On average, CertCheck requires 4.6 times the runtime of ApproxMCCert across all certified instances. Note that each instance of CertCheck requires nine separate calls to the CNF-XOR unsatisfiability checking pipeline (because $\delta = 0.2$). It is worth emphasizing that in other certificate checking setups, such as the SAT competitions, one would typically provide an order of magnitude more time and memory to the checkers compared to solvers. Thus, CertCheck performs well even though our time and memory limits are stringent. Furthermore, we believe that CertCheck's ability to achieve a fairly low PAR-2 score (computed out of 1202 instances) is compelling evidence for the practicality of certificate checking in approximate counting. Future work could explore *parallelized* certificate checking since each round used in CertCheck can be checked independently of each other.

RQ2 Comparison of CNF-XOR Unsatisfiability Checkers. We present results using various alternative unsatisfiability checking pipelines as part of CertCheck in Table 2. Here, we observe that the use of CMS+frat-xor allows CertCheck to fully certify significantly more instances than can be certified by prior approaches, and with a much lower PAR-2 score.

Table 2. Performance comparison of CNF-XOR unsatisfiability checkers in CertCheck. The PAR-2 score is calculated out of the 1202 instances with certificates for all checkers.

Total	CaDiCaL+lrat	MiniSatXOR+pbp	CMS+tbuddy	CMS+frat-xor
Counted Instances	527	563	623	**1018**
PAR-2 Score	5742	5659	5027	**1743**

Figure 5 (left) visualizes the performance gap between CMS+frat-xor and the prior methods using a CDF (cumulative distribution function) plot; a point (x, y) indicates that the corresponding tool certifies y number of instances when given a timeout of x seconds for each instance. This plot provides strong justification for our claim of the need to develop CMS+frat-xor for native CNF-XOR unsatisfiability proof checking in Sect. 4.4. The ability to log XOR proof steps compactly in our new CNF-XOR unsatisfiability proof format is also significant. This is illustrated in Fig. 5 (right) which gives a scatter plot comparing FRAT (resp. FRAT-XOR) proof sizes generated by CMS+tbuddy (resp. CMS+frat-xor) within 600 s on instances that were successfully certified by CMS+tbuddy. Recall that the solver in CMS+tbuddy supports XOR reasoning and uses TBUDDY to emit its proof log in terms of a clausal proof system, i.e., without native XOR proof steps. Overall, our new proof format achieves an average 30-fold reduction in proof size, with the maximum reduction reaching up to 8,251 times.

6   Conclusion and Future Work

This work shows that it is feasible to use proof assistants to formalize practical randomized automated reasoning algorithms. Such formalizations are valuable—our end-to-end certification approach for ApproxMCCert has led to bug-fixes for both ApproxMC and its underlying CryptoMiniSat solver.

An interesting line of future work would be to support recently proposed techniques such as *sparse hashing* [39] or *rounding* [60] in the context of ApproxMC. Furthermore, this work leaves preprocessing techniques, such as independent support identification, out of scope. It is worth noting that efficient identification of the independent support set, in conjunction with a new rounding-based algorithm [60], significantly boosts the counting performance of ApproxMC; in the experimental setting of Table 1, this combination solves 1787 instances with a PAR-2 score of 625. Thus, certifying these extensions is a tantalizing avenue for future research. Another potential line of future work involves developing extensions for theories other than CNF-XOR model counting [59].

Acknowledgement. This work has been financially supported by the Swedish Research Council grant 2021-05165, National Research Foundation Singapore under its NRF Fellowship Programme [NRF-NRFFAI1-2019-0004], Ministry of Education Singapore Tier 2 Grant [MOE-T2EP20121-0011], Ministry of Education Singapore Tier 1 Grant [R-252-000-B59-114], and by A*STAR, Singapore. The computational experiments were performed on resources of the National Supercomputing Centre, Singapore https://www.nscc.sg. Part of this work was carried out while some of the authors participated in the Spring 2023 *Extended Reunion: Satisfiability* program at the Simons Institute for the Theory of Computing and at Dagstuhl workshop 22411 *Theory and Practice of SAT and Combinatorial Solving*.

References

1. Abdulaziz, M., Mehlhorn, K., Nipkow, T.: Trustworthy graph algorithms (invited talk). In: Rossmanith, P., Heggernes, P., Katoen, J. (eds.) MFCS. LIPIcs, vol. 138, pp. 1:1–1:22. Schloss Dagstuhl - Leibniz-Zentrum für Informatik (2019). https://doi.org/10.4230/LIPICS.MFCS.2019.1
2. ApproxMCCert and CertCheck tool repository. https://github.com/meelgroup/approxmc-cert
3. Baek, S., Carneiro, M., Heule, M.J.H.: A flexible proof format for SAT solver-elaborator communication. Log. Methods Comput. Sci. **18**(2) (2022). https://doi.org/10.46298/LMCS-18(2:3)2022
4. Ballarin, C.: Locales: a module system for mathematical theories. J. Autom. Reason. **52**(2), 123–153 (2014). https://doi.org/10.1007/s10817-013-9284-7
5. Baluta, T., Shen, S., Shinde, S., Meel, K.S., Saxena, P.: Quantitative verification of neural networks and its security applications. In: Cavallaro, L., Kinder, J., Wang, X., Katz, J. (eds.) CCS, pp. 1249–1264. ACM (2019). https://doi.org/10.1145/3319535.3354245
6. Barbosa, H., Blanchette, J.C., Fleury, M., Fontaine, P.: Scalable fine-grained proofs for formula processing. J. Autom. Reason. **64**(3), 485–510 (2020). https://doi.org/10.1007/s10817-018-09502-y
7. Beyersdorff, O., Hoffmann, T., Spachmann, L.N.: Proof complexity of propositional model counting. In: Mahajan, M., Slivovsky, F. (eds.) SAT. LIPIcs, vol. 271, pp. 2:1–2:18. Schloss Dagstuhl - Leibniz-Zentrum für Informatik (2023). https://doi.org/10.4230/LIPICS.SAT.2023.2
8. Biere, A., Fazekas, K., Fleury, M., Heisinger, M.: CaDiCaL, Kissat, Paracooba, Plingeling and Treengeling entering the SAT competition 2020. In: Balyo, T., Froleyks, N., Heule, M., Iser, M., Järvisalo, M., Suda, M. (eds.) Proceedings of SAT Competition 2020 – Solver and Benchmark Descriptions. Department of Computer Science Report Series B, vol. B-2020-1, pp. 51–53. University of Helsinki (2020)
9. Bryant, R.E.: TBUDDY: a proof-generating BDD package. In: Griggio, A., Rungta, N. (eds.) FMCAD, pp. 49–58. TU Wien Academic Press (2022).https://doi.org/10.34727/2022/ISBN.978-3-85448-053-2_10
10. Bryant, R.E., Nawrocki, W., Avigad, J., Heule, M.J.H.: Certified knowledge compilation with application to verified model counting. In: Mahajan, M., Slivovsky, F. (eds.) SAT. LIPIcs, vol. 271, pp. 6:1–6:20. Schloss Dagstuhl - Leibniz-Zentrum für Informatik (2023). https://doi.org/10.4230/LIPIcs.SAT.2023.6
11. Chakraborty, S., Fremont, D.J., Meel, K.S., Seshia, S.A., Vardi, M.Y.: Distribution-aware sampling and weighted model counting for SAT. In: Brodley, C.E., Stone, P. (eds.) AAAI, pp. 1722–1730. AAAI Press (2014). https://doi.org/10.1609/AAAI.V28I1.8990
12. Chakraborty, S., Meel, K.S., Vardi, M.Y.: Algorithmic improvements in approximate counting for probabilistic inference: from linear to logarithmic SAT calls. In: Kambhampati, S. (ed.) IJCAI, pp. 3569–3576. IJCAI/AAAI Press (2016). http://www.ijcai.org/Abstract/16/503
13. Chakraborty, S., Meel, K.S., Vardi, M.Y.: Approximate model counting. In: Biere, A., Heule, M., van Maaren, H., Walsh, T. (eds.) Handbook of Satisfiability - Second Edition, Frontiers in Artificial Intelligence and Applications, vol. 336, pp. 1015–1045. IOS Press (2021). https://doi.org/10.3233/FAIA201010
14. Dueñas-Osorio, L., Meel, K.S., Paredes, R., Vardi, M.Y.: Counting-based reliability estimation for power-transmission grids. In: Singh, S., Markovitch, S. (eds.) AAAI, pp. 4488–4494. AAAI Press (2017). https://doi.org/10.1609/AAAI.V31I1.11178

15. Eberl, M., Haslbeck, M.W., Nipkow, T.: Verified analysis of random binary tree structures. J. Autom. Reason. **64**(5), 879–910 (2020). https://doi.org/10.1007/s10817-020-09545-0

16. Eberl, M., Hölzl, J., Nipkow, T.: A verified compiler for probability density functions. In: Vitek, J. (ed.) ESOP 2015. LNCS, vol. 9032, pp. 80–104. Springer, Heidelberg (2015). https://doi.org/10.1007/978-3-662-46669-8_4

17. Eén, N., Sörensson, N.: An extensible SAT-solver. In: Giunchiglia, E., Tacchella, A. (eds.) SAT 2003. LNCS, vol. 2919, pp. 502–518. Springer, Heidelberg (2004). https://doi.org/10.1007/978-3-540-24605-3_37

18. Ermon, S., Gomes, C.P., Sabharwal, A., Selman, B.: Taming the curse of dimensionality: discrete integration by hashing and optimization. In: ICML. PMLR, vol. 28, pp. 334–342. PMLR (2013). http://proceedings.mlr.press/v28/ermon13.html

19. Fichte, J.K., Hecher, M., Roland, V.: Proofs for propositional model counting. In: Meel, K.S., Strichman, O. (eds.) SAT. LIPIcs, vol. 236, pp. 30:1–30:24. Schloss Dagstuhl - Leibniz-Zentrum für Informatik (2022). https://doi.org/10.4230/LIPICS.SAT.2022.30

20. Fleury, M.: Optimizing a verified SAT solver. In: Badger, J.M., Rozier, K.Y. (eds.) NFM 2019. LNCS, vol. 11460, pp. 148–165. Springer, Cham (2019). https://doi.org/10.1007/978-3-030-20652-9_10

21. FRATxor and cakexlrup tool repository. https://github.com/meelgroup/frat-xor

22. Gittis, A., Vin, E., Fremont, D.J.: Randomized synthesis for diversity and cost constraints with control improvisation. In: Shoham, S., Vizel, Y. (eds.) CAV. LNCS, vol. 13372, pp. 526–546. Springer, Heidelberg (2022). https://doi.org/10.1007/978-3-031-13188-2_26

23. Gocht, S., McCreesh, C., Myreen, M.O., Nordström, J., Oertel, A., Tan, Y.K.: End-to-end verification for subgraph solving. In: Wooldridge, M.J., Dy, J.G., Natarajan, S. (eds.) AAAI, pp. 8038–8047. AAAI Press (2024). https://doi.org/10.1609/AAAI.V38I8.28642

24. Gocht, S., Nordström, J.: Certifying parity reasoning efficiently using pseudo-Boolean proofs. In: AAAI, pp. 3768–3777. AAAI Press (2021). https://doi.org/10.1609/AAAI.V35I5.16494

25. Gomes, C.P., Sabharwal, A., Selman, B.: Near-uniform sampling of combinatorial spaces using XOR constraints. In: Schölkopf, B., Platt, J.C., Hofmann, T. (eds.) NIPS, pp. 481–488. MIT Press (2006)

26. Gopinathan, K., Sergey, I.: Certifying certainty and uncertainty in approximate membership query structures. In: Lahiri, S.K., Wang, C. (eds.) CAV 2020. LNCS, vol. 12225, pp. 279–303. Springer, Cham (2020). https://doi.org/10.1007/978-3-030-53291-8_16

27. Heule, M., Hunt, W., Kaufmann, M., Wetzler, N.: Efficient, verified checking of propositional proofs. In: Ayala-Rincón, M., Muñoz, C.A. (eds.) ITP 2017. LNCS, vol. 10499, pp. 269–284. Springer, Cham (2017). https://doi.org/10.1007/978-3-319-66107-0_18

28. Hölzl, J., Lochbihler, A., Traytel, D.: A formalized hierarchy of probabilistic system types. In: Urban, C., Zhang, X. (eds.) ITP 2015. LNCS, vol. 9236, pp. 203–220. Springer, Cham (2015). https://doi.org/10.1007/978-3-319-22102-1_13

29. Hurd, J.: Formal verification of probabilistic algorithms. Technical Report. UCAM-CL-TR-566, University of Cambridge, Computer Laboratory (2003). https://doi.org/10.48456/tr-566

30. Kan, S., Lin, A.W., Rümmer, P., Schrader, M.: CertiStr: a certified string solver. In: Popescu, A., Zdancewic, S. (eds.) CPP, pp. 210–224. ACM (2022) https://doi.org/10.1145/3497775.3503691

31. Karayel, E.: Formalization of randomized approximation algorithms for frequency moments. In: Andronick, J., de Moura, L. (eds.) ITP. LIPIcs, vol. 237, pp. 21:1–21:21. Schloss Dagstuhl - Leibniz-Zentrum für Informatik (2022). https://doi.org/10.4230/LIPIcs.ITP.2022.21

32. Karayel, E.: Formalization of randomized approximation algorithms for frequency moments. Archive of Formal Proofs (2022). https://isa-afp.org/entries/Frequency_Moments.html, Formal proof development

33. Karayel, E.: Median method. Archive of Formal Proofs (2022). https://isa-afp.org/entries/Median_Method.html, Formal proof development

34. Karayel, E.: Universal hash families. Archive of Formal Proofs (2022). https://isa-afp.org/entries/Universal_Hash_Families.html, Formal proof development

35. Kaufmann, D., Fleury, M., Biere, A.: The proof checkers Pacheck and Pastèque for the practical algebraic calculus. In: FMCAD, pp. 264–269. TU Wien Academic Press (2020).https://doi.org/10.34727/2020/isbn.978-3-85448-042-6_34

36. Kumar, R., Myreen, M.O., Norrish, M., Owens, S.: CakeML: a verified implementation of ML. In: Jagannathan, S., Sewell, P. (eds.) POPL, pp. 179–192. ACM (2014). https://doi.org/10.1145/2535838.2535841

37. Lammich, P.: Efficient verified (UN)SAT certificate checking. J. Autom. Reason. **64**(3), 513–532 (2020). https://doi.org/10.1007/s10817-019-09525-z

38. McConnell, R.M., Mehlhorn, K., Näher, S., Schweitzer, P.: Certifying algorithms. Comput. Sci. Rev. **5**(2), 119–161 (2011). https://doi.org/10.1016/J.COSREV.2010.09.009

39. Meel, K.S., Akshay, S.: Sparse hashing for scalable approximate model counting: theory and practice. In: Hermanns, H., Zhang, L., Kobayashi, N., Miller, D. (eds.) LICS, pp. 728–741. ACM (2020). https://doi.org/10.1145/3373718.3394809

40. Meel, K.S., Chakraborty, S., Akshay, S.: Auditable algorithms for approximate model counting. In: Wooldridge, M.J., Dy, J.G., Natarajan, S. (eds.) AAAI, pp. 10654–10661. AAAI Press (2024). https://doi.org/10.1609/AAAI.V38I9.28936

41. Meel, K.S., Soos, M.: Model counting and uniform sampling instances (2020). https://doi.org/10.5281/zenodo.3793090

42. Nipkow, T., Wenzel, M., Paulson, L.C. (eds.): Isabelle/HOL. LNCS, vol. 2283. Springer, Heidelberg (2002). https://doi.org/10.1007/3-540-45949-9

43. Paulson, L.C.: The foundation of a generic theorem prover. J. Autom. Reasoning **5**(3), 363–397 (1989). https://doi.org/10.1007/BF00248324

44. Pollitt, F., Fleury, M., Biere, A.: Faster LRAT checking than solving with CaDiCaL. In: Mahajan, M., Slivovsky, F. (eds.) SAT. LIPIcs, vol. 271, pp. 21:1–21:12. Schloss Dagstuhl - Leibniz-Zentrum für Informatik (2023). https://doi.org/10.4230/LIPICS.SAT.2023.21

45. Roth, D.: On the hardness of approximate reasoning. Artif. Intell. **82**(1–2), 273–302 (1996). https://doi.org/10.1016/0004-3702(94)00092-1

46. Sang, T., Beame, P., Kautz, H.A.: Performing Bayesian inference by weighted model counting. In: Veloso, M.M., Kambhampati, S. (eds.) AAAI, pp. 475–482. AAAI Press/The MIT Press (2005). http://www.aaai.org/Library/AAAI/2005/aaai05-075.php

47. Shi, X., Fu, Y.-F., Liu, J., Tsai, M.-H., Wang, B.-Y., Yang, B.-Y.: CoqQFBV: a scalable certified SMT quantifier-free bit-vector solver. In: Silva, A., Leino, K.R.M. (eds.) CAV 2021. LNCS, vol. 12760, pp. 149–171. Springer, Cham (2021). https://doi.org/10.1007/978-3-030-81688-9_7

48. Soos, M., Bryant, R.E.: Proof generation for CDCL solvers using Gauss-Jordan elimination. CoRR arxiv:2304.04292 (2023). https://doi.org/10.48550/ARXIV.2304.04292

49. Soos, M., Gocht, S., Meel, K.S.: Tinted, detached, and lazy CNF-XOR solving and its applications to counting and sampling. In: Lahiri, S.K., Wang, C. (eds.) CAV 2020. LNCS, vol. 12224, pp. 463–484. Springer, Cham (2020). https://doi.org/10.1007/978-3-030-53288-8_22

50. Soos, M., Meel, K.S.: BIRD: engineering an efficient CNF-XOR SAT solver and its applications to approximate model counting. In: AAAI, pp. 1592–1599. AAAI Press (2019). https://doi.org/10.1609/AAAI.V33I01.33011592

51. Soos, M., Meel, K.S.: Arjun: An efficient independent support computation technique and its applications to counting and sampling. In: Mitra, T., Young, E.F.Y., Xiong, J. (eds.) ICCAD, pp. 71:1–71:9. ACM (2022). https://doi.org/10.1145/3508352.3549406

52. Soos, M., Nohl, K., Castelluccia, C.: Extending SAT solvers to cryptographic problems. In: Kullmann, O. (ed.) SAT 2009. LNCS, vol. 5584, pp. 244–257. Springer, Heidelberg (2009). https://doi.org/10.1007/978-3-642-02777-2_24

53. Tan, Y.K., Heule, M.J.H., Myreen, M.O.: Verified propagation redundancy and compositional UNSAT checking in CakeML. Int. J. Softw. Tools Technol. Transf. **25**(2), 167–184 (2023). https://doi.org/10.1007/s10009-022-00690-y

54. Tan, Y.K., Yang, J.: Approximate model counting. Archive of Formal Proofs (2024). https://isa-afp.org/entries/Approximate_Model_Counting.html, Formal proof development

55. Thiemann, R., Sternagel, C.: Certification of termination proofs using CeTA. In: Berghofer, S., Nipkow, T., Urban, C., Wenzel, M. (eds.) TPHOLs 2009. LNCS, vol. 5674, pp. 452–468. Springer, Heidelberg (2009). https://doi.org/10.1007/978-3-642-03359-9_31

56. Valiant, L.G.: The complexity of enumeration and reliability problems. SIAM J. Comput. **8**(3), 410–421 (1979). https://doi.org/10.1137/0208032

57. Wegman, M.N., Zadeck, F.K.: Constant propagation with conditional branches. ACM Trans. Program. Lang. Syst. **13**(2), 181–210 (1991). https://doi.org/10.1145/103135.103136

58. Wetzler, N., Heule, M.J.H., Hunt, W.A.: DRAT-trim: efficient checking and trimming using expressive clausal proofs. In: Sinz, C., Egly, U. (eds.) SAT 2014. LNCS, vol. 8561, pp. 422–429. Springer, Cham (2014). https://doi.org/10.1007/978-3-319-09284-3_31

59. Yang, J., Meel, K.S.: Engineering an efficient PB-XOR solver. In: Michel, L.D. (ed.) CP. LIPIcs, vol. 210, pp. 58:1–58:20. Schloss Dagstuhl - Leibniz-Zentrum für Informatik (2021https://doi.org/10.4230/LIPIcs.CP.2021.58

60. Yang, J., Meel, K.S.: Rounding meets approximate model counting. In: Enea, C., Lal, A. (eds.) CAV. LNCS, vol. 13965, pp. 132–162. Springer, Heidelberg (2023). https://doi.org/10.1007/978-3-031-37703-7_7

Scalable Bit-Blasting with Abstractions

Aina Niemetz[1]([✉]) [iD], Mathias Preiner[1] [iD], and Yoni Zohar[2] [iD]

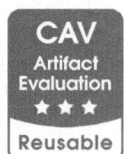

[1] Stanford University, Stanford, USA
niemetz@cs.stanford.edu
[2] Bar-Ilan University, Ramat Gan, Israel

Abstract. The dominant state-of-the-art approach for solving bit-vector formulas in Satisfiability Modulo Theories (SMT) is bit-blasting, an eager reduction to propositional logic. Bit-blasting is surprisingly efficient in practice but does not generally scale well with increasing bit-widths, especially when bit-vector arithmetic is present. In this paper, we present a novel CEGAR-style abstraction-refinement procedure for the theory of fixed-size bit-vectors that significantly improves the scalability of bit-blasting. We provide lemma schemes for various arithmetic bit-vector operators and an abduction-based framework for synthesizing refinement lemmas. We extended the state-of-the-art SMT solver Bitwuzla with our abstraction-refinement approach and show that it significantly improves solver performance on a variety of benchmark sets, including industrial benchmarks that arise from smart contract verification.

1 Introduction

Bit-precise reasoning as provided by Satisfiability Modulo Theories (SMT) for the theory of fixed-size bit-vectors is a key requirement for many applications in computer-aided verification. The dominant, state-of-the-art approach for solving bit-vector formulas is a technique called *bit-blasting* [24], an eager reduction of bit-vector constraints to a propositional satisfiability problem (SAT). Bit-blasting is usually combined with aggressive simplifications of the input constraints prior to the actual reduction step. Even though this eager reduction may come at the cost of significantly increasing the formula size, it is surprisingly efficient in practice—mainly due to the fact that state-of-the-art SAT solvers are usually able to efficiently deal with complex formulas over millions of variables. This size increase, however, is a potential bottleneck and the main reason why bit-blasting does not generally scale well for large bit-widths. This is especially true in the presence of arithmetic operators, which translate to large and complex Boolean circuits on the bit-level. In practice, this scaling issue can already

This work was supported in part by the Stanford Center for Automated Reasoning, the Stanford Center for Blockchain Research, ISF grant number 619/21, and a gift from Amazon Web Services.

A. Gurfinkel and V. Ganesh (Eds.): CAV 2024, LNCS 14681, pp. 178–200, 2024.
https://doi.org/10.1007/978-3-031-65627-9_9

occur with bit-widths as low as 32 bits, and it is especially severe for applications that reason over considerably larger bit-widths due to the nature of their domain, e.g., 256 bits in the context of smart contract verification [15].

In this paper, we propose a novel abstraction-refinement framework for the theory of fixed-size bit-vectors that significantly improves the scalability of bit-blasting on increasing bit-widths. Rather than providing an alternative to bit-blasting, our approach is explicitly aimed at improving its performance via an abstraction-refinement scheme based on the counterexample-guided abstraction refinement (CEGAR) paradigm [16]. Constructs and operators that are potentially expensive when translated to the bit-level are abstracted with fresh uninterpreted functions (UF), which corresponds to over-approximating the original problem and translates to significantly smaller circuits on the bit-level. When an abstraction is unsatisfiable, so is the original problem. However, when it is satisfiable and inconsistent with the true semantics of the abstracted operators, it must be refined with lemmas to rule out spurious counterexamples. We iteratively repeat the abstraction-refinement process until all abstractions are consistent, and only fall back to bit-blasting an abstracted term when it cannot be further refined, as a last resort. Thus, the main challenge is finding lemmas for abstraction refinement that, ideally, allow to avoid bit-blasting of abstracted terms, entirely. To this extent, this paper makes the following *contributions*:

- We present a modular and configurable CEGAR-style abstraction-refinement framework for the theory of fixed-size bit-vectors, based on bit-blasting.
- We provide a set of refinement lemmas for a restricted but sufficient set of arithmetic bit-vector operators (bvmul, bvudiv, bvurem). This set of lemmas consists of a set of basic, *hand-crafted* lemmas (encoding core properties of abstracted operators) and a set of lemmas synthesized via *abduction*.
- We provide a lemma scoring scheme and an abduction-based framework for synthesizing lemmas, utilizing the syntax-restricted abduction reasoning capabilities of the SMT solver cvc5 [7].
- We extend the open-source SMT solver Bitwuzla [29] with our approach and show that it significantly improves performance on a wide range of benchmarks, including industrial benchmarks from smart contract verification.

Related Work. Developing scalable approaches for solving bit-vector formulas with large bit-widths is a long-standing challenge. Previous efforts to tackle this challenge can be mainly divided into two categories: alternative approaches to bit-blasting that primarily rely on word-level reasoning, and techniques based on bit-blasting that try to reduce the size of the original problem on the bit-level.

Alternative approaches to bit-blasting include: translations to linear integer arithmetic [11] and non-linear integer arithmetic (in combination with CEGAR-style handling of bit-wise operators) [36]; layered CDCL(T)-style approaches that rely on encoding fragments of the input problem into other theories before resorting to bit-blasting [13,21]; instances of the model-constructing satisfiability (mcSAT) calculus [20,35], a generalization of propositional conflict-driven clause learning (CDCL) to SMT; and incomplete techniques such as local search [19,

28,30], which are only able to determine satisfiability. All of these approaches are generally not competitive with bit-blasting.

Techniques based on bit-blasting that aim at mitigating the impact of increasing bit-widths on the bit-level are mainly based on some form of under-approximation. Bryant et al. [14] proposed a combination of under-approximation via restricting the value range of input variables with over-approximation of the unsat core of the under-approximated problem. This over-approximation consists of two strategies: eliminating if-then-else (*ite*) operations, and abstracting bit-vector multiplication $x \cdot y$ with a partially interpreted function of the form $\lambda x.\lambda y.ite(x \approx 0 \lor y \approx 0, 0, ite(x = 1, y, ite(y \approx 1, x, f(x, y))))$ where $f(x, y)$ is a fresh uninterpreted function. An early version of Boolector [12] implemented a refined version of the above under-approximation strategy in [14]. More recently, in the context of quantified bit-vector reasoning, Jonáš et al. proposed an abstraction-based approach that reduces the size of the input problem via interpreting bits as don't care bits [22], and an under-approximation-based framework based on bit-width reduction [23] similar to [14].

2   Preliminaries

We assume and briefly review the usual notions and terminology of many-sorted first-order logic with equality (see, e.g., [18,25]). Let S be a set of *sort symbols*, and let Σ be a *signature* containing a set $\Sigma^s \subseteq S$ of sort symbols and a set Σ^f of function symbols $f^{\sigma_1 \cdots \sigma_n \sigma}$ with arity $n \geq 0$ and $\sigma_1, ..., \sigma_n, \sigma \in \Sigma^s$. We usually omit the superscript from function symbols and refer to 0-arity function symbols as *constants*. We assume that Σ includes a designated sort Bool, values $\top$ (true) and $\bot$ (false) of sort Bool, Boolean connectives $\{\land, \neg\}$ defined as usual, equality and disequality symbols $\{\approx, \not\approx\}$ of sort $\sigma \times \sigma \to$ Bool for every $\sigma \in \Sigma^s$, and an if-then-else operator *ite* of sort Bool $\times \sigma \times \sigma \to \sigma$ for every $\sigma \in \Sigma^s$.

Let $\mathcal{I}$ be a Σ-*interpretation* that maps each $\sigma \in \Sigma^s$ to a non-empty set $\sigma^{\mathcal{I}}$ (the *domain* of $\mathcal{I}$), with Bool$^{\mathcal{I}} = \{\top, \bot\}$; and each $f^{\sigma_1 \cdots \sigma_n \sigma} \in \Sigma^f$ to a total function $f^{\mathcal{I}} : \sigma_1^{\mathcal{I}} \times ... \times \sigma_n^{\mathcal{I}} \to \sigma^{\mathcal{I}}$ if $n > 0$, and to an element in $\sigma^{\mathcal{I}}$ if $n = 0$. The interpretation of Boolean connectives, Boolean values, equality symbols and *ite* symbols is fixed and standard. We use the usual inductive definition of the satisfiability relation $\models$ between Σ-interpretations and Σ-formulas. We write $\varphi[x_1, \ldots, x_n]$ to denote a Σ-formula φ defined over (a subset of) symbols $\{x_1, \ldots, x_n\}$. We further use $\varphi[x_1 \mapsto a_1, \ldots, x_n \mapsto a_n]$ for the formula obtained from φ by simultaneously replacing each occurrence of x_i with a_i.

A *theory* is a pair (Σ, I) where Σ is some signature, and I is a class of Σ-interpretations. A Σ-formula is T-*satisfiable* (resp. T-*unsatisfiable*) if it is satisfied by some (resp. no) interpretation in I; it is T-*valid* if it is satisfied by all interpretations in I. We assume the usual definition of well-sorted terms, literals, and formulas, and call Σ-formulas T-formulas and Σ-literals T-literals.

We focus on the theory of fixed-size bit-vectors T_{BV} as defined by the SMT-LIB 2 standard [8]. The theory of fixed-size bit-vectors T_{BV} is defined as the pair (Σ_{BV}, I_{BV}). Signature Σ_{BV} includes a unique sort $\sigma_{[w]}$ for each bit-width w, function symbols overloaded for every $\sigma_{[w]}$, and all *bit-vector values* of sort $\sigma_{[w]}$ for each w. The non-empty class of Σ_{BV}-interpretations I_{BV} (the *models* of T_{BV}) interpret sort and function symbols as specified in SMT-LIB 2.

Without loss of generality, we consider Σ_{BV} to contain a restricted, arbitrary set of bit-vector operators as listed in Table 1. This set is complete in the sense that it suffices to express all bit-vector operators defined in SMT-LIB 2. We further use logical connectives $\{\vee, \Rightarrow, \Leftrightarrow\}$ and bit-vector operator $-$ for subtraction and negation as shorthand when convenient. In the context of this paper it is important to note that both bit-vector subtraction and negation are expressed in terms of bit-vector addition.

We denote a Σ_{BV}-term (or *bit-vector term*) x of width w as $x_{[w]}$ when we want to specify its bit-width explicitly, and will omit w from the notation when it is clear from the context. The width of a bit-vector term is given by function κ, e.g., $\kappa(x_{[w]}) = w$. We refer to the bit at index i of $x_{[w]}$ as $x[i]$ and represent a bit-vector value $v_{[w]}$ as a bit-string of 0 s and 1 s, with the most significant bit (MSB) as the left-most bit $v[msb]$ at index $msb = w - 1$, and the least significant bit (LSB) as the right-most bit $v[lsb]$ at index $lsb = 0$. To simplify the notation, we will sometimes represent a value $v_{[w]}$ as a natural number in $\{0, \ldots, 2^{w-1}\}$.

Table 1. Set of considered bit-vector operators.

Symbol	SMT-LIB Syntax	Sort
$<_u, \leq_u, >_u, \geq_u$	bvult, bvule, bvugt, bvuge	$\sigma_{[w]} \times \sigma_{[w]} \rightarrow$ Bool
$\sim$	bvnot	$\sigma_{[w]} \rightarrow \sigma_{[w]}$
$\&, \mid, \oplus, \ll, \gg$	bvand, bvor, bvxor, bvshl, bvlshr	$\sigma_{[w]} \times \sigma_{[w]} \rightarrow \sigma_{[w]}$
$+, \cdot, \mathrm{mod}, \div$	bvadd, bvmul, bvurem, bvudiv	$\sigma_{[w]} \times \sigma_{[w]} \rightarrow \sigma_{[w]}$
$\circ$	concat	$\sigma_{[w]} \times \sigma_{[m]} \rightarrow \sigma_{[w+m]}$
$[u : l]$	extract ($l \leq u < w$)	$\sigma_{[w]} \rightarrow \sigma_{[u-l+1]}$

3   Abstraction-Refinement Framework

Our abstraction-refinement framework is integrated into an SMT solver as a CEGAR procedure that combines an abstraction module with the theory solver that is responsible for reasoning about T_{BV}-formulas (the *bit-vector solver*). Since our main goal is to improve the scalability of *bit-blasting*, we assume that the bit-vector solver implements bit-blasting as its main strategy. For simplicity, we further assume that bit-blasting is its only strategy. However, this is not a requirement. Our abstraction-refinement technique can be combined with any complete technique for determining the satisfiability of T_{BV}-formulas that produces models for satisfiable formulas.

Algorithm 1 shows the main abstraction-refinement procedure of our approach. Given a set of bit-vector constraints $\mathcal{A}$, the abstraction module (AM)

Algorithm 1. Abstraction-refinement loop around the T_{BV}-solver.

---

 1   **function** ABSTRACTSOLVEBV($\mathcal{A}$)
 2   result $\leftarrow$ *unknown*, $\mathcal{L} \leftarrow \emptyset$
 3        $\mathcal{A}' \leftarrow$ AM::ABSTRACT($\mathcal{A}$)   ▷ generate abstraction
 4   **repeat**
 5            $\mathcal{A}' \leftarrow \mathcal{A}' \cup \mathcal{L}$ ▷ refine abstraction
 6   result, $\mathcal{M} \leftarrow T_{BV}$::SOLVE($\mathcal{A}'$)   ▷ query bit-vector solver
 7   **if** result $=$ *unsat* **then** break
 8            $\mathcal{L} \leftarrow$ AM::CHECK($\mathcal{M}$)   ▷ check consistency
 9   **until** $\mathcal{L} = \emptyset$
10   **return** result
11   **end function**

---

first generates an abstraction $\mathcal{A}'$ of $\mathcal{A}$ (AM::ABSTRACT) by replacing abstracted terms with fresh constants. This abstraction is then iteratively refined with lemmas $\mathcal{L}$, starting from an empty set. First, the bit-vector solver is queried for a satisfiability result of the current abstraction $\mathcal{A}'$ and a model $\mathcal{M}$ of $\mathcal{A}'$ if it is satisfiable (T_{BV}::SOLVE). If $\mathcal{A}'$ is unsatisfiable, the procedure concludes with *unsat*. If $\mathcal{A}'$ is satisfiable, the abstraction module checks the consistency of $\mathcal{M}$ for all abstracted terms with respect to their true semantics (AM::CHECK) as follows. Starting from an empty set of refinement lemmas $\mathcal{L}$, for each abstracted term, function AM::CHECK determines if the model value of its abstraction is consistent. If it is inconsistent, we add a refinement lemma to $\mathcal{L}$ that rules out the inconsistency. When the model values of all abstracted terms have been checked for consistency, AM::CHECK returns the set of refinement lemmas $\mathcal{L}$, which extends abstraction $\mathcal{A}'$ in the next iteration. If model $\mathcal{M}$ is consistent for all abstracted terms (i.e., $\mathcal{L} = \emptyset$), the procedure concludes with *sat*.

Note that conceptually, our term abstractions are uninterpreted functions that map bit-vector arguments to a term of bit-vector sort, e.g., $mul_{32}(x, s)$ of sort $\sigma_{[32]} \times \sigma_{[32]} \rightarrow \sigma_{[32]}$ as abstraction of a bit-vector multiplication $x_{[32]} \cdot s_{[32]}$. When combining bit-vector theory reasoning with UF theory reasoning, from the point of view of the bit-vector solver, these UF are seen as fresh bit-vector constants. However, by construction, our procedure ensures that term abstractions are refined until consistency. Thus, when the UF theory solver is invoked after the bit-vector theory solver, additional UF theory reasoning is not required. Hence, introducing uninterpreted functions is redundant—it is sufficient to introduce a fresh constant of the same bit-vector sort as the abstracted term, e.g., $mul_{[32]}^{x,s}$ for $x_{[32]} \cdot s_{[32]}$. This allows the integration of our approach into any SMT solver that supports bit-vector reasoning, even when UF reasoning is not supported. Preliminary experiments showed that in the context of integrating our techniques in the SMT solver Bitwuzla, using UF as abstractions and scheduling the UF theory solver prior to our abstraction-refinement loop introduced redundant overhead and negatively impacted performance. Our approach, however, allows to freely choose between introducing UF vs. fresh bit-vector constants, depending on what is more beneficial for a specific solver architecture.

One of the main tasks of the *abstraction module* is consistency checking of satisfying assignments of the current abstraction, and refining the abstraction in case of inconsistency. This refinement is driven by a pre-defined *refinement scheme* for each abstracted operator. A refinement scheme is a four-tiered set of lemmas that is checked tier-wise, in ascending order, during consistency checking. We describe the refinement scheme for each operator and their tiers in more detail in Sect. 4.

4   Refinement Schemes

We define four-tiered refinement schemes for bit-vector operators $\diamond \in \{\cdot, \div, \mathrm{mod}\}$, with tiers 1–2 as the main and predefined sets of refinement lemmas that describe properties of the abstracted operators in the usual bit-vector semantics (notably, with respect to overflow semantics). The *first* tier consists of *hand-crafted* lemmas that mostly encode basic properties (described in more detail in Sect. 4.1), while the *second* tier is entirely comprised of lemmas that were *synthesized* via our abduction-based lemma synthesis framework (see Sect. 4.3).

The *third* tier is not pre-defined but encodes so-called *value instantiation lemmas* to rule out the current inconsistent model value as a limited fallback strategy before we have to, as the *fourth* and final tier, resort to *bit-blasting*. For example, for $x_{[32]} \cdot s_{[32]}$ with $\mathcal{M} = \{x = 3, s = 6, mul^{x,s}_{[32]} = 1\}$, we add $(x = 3 \land s = 6) \Rightarrow mul^{x,s}_{[32]} = 18$ as value instantiation lemma. Value instantiation lemmas are only added if none of the lemmas in previous tiers were violated. We further limit the number of value instantiation lemmas that are added for an abstracted term since they each only rule out a single spurious model value of the term abstraction (see Sect. 5). Lemmas in tiers 1–2 do not necessarily fully capture all properties of an abstracted operator, and thus, inconsistent assignments may remain uncovered. When this is the case and the number of value instantiation lemmas to add is exhausted, we add a so-called *bit-blasting lemma*, e.g., $mul^{x,s}_{[32]} \approx x \cdot s$, which enforces bit-blasting of the abstracted term.

Note that of the considered arithmetic operators, addition is the only one we do not abstract. Even though addition is more expensive when bit-blasting compared to bit-wise operators, it is considerably cheaper than the operators we abstract. Preliminary experiments showed that the trade-off between abstracting the addition operator (which also occurs in our lemmas) versus bit-blasting addition terms suggests that it is more beneficial to not abstract addition.

Table 2 lists all lemmas of tiers 1–2 for all three operators, with hand-crafted lemmas marked with an asterisk. We use x for the left-hand operand, s for the right-hand operand, and t for the constant introduced to abstract $x \diamond s$. We further indicate with a subscript on the lemma ID if there is a restriction on the bit-widths for which the lemma is correct (see Sect. 4.4). Note that while our abstraction approach does not generally restrict the bit-width of operators to abstract, lemmas that are incorrect for certain bit-widths must be removed from the lemma sets when terms of that size are abstracted. In practice, we only abstract terms of bit-width 32 and above (see Sect. 5) and thus these restrictions are not applicable. Further, note that in practice we consider both commutative cases (when applicable) while Table 2 only gives one. In the following, we describe our set of hand-crafted lemmas, our lemma scoring scheme and how we derive lemmas via abduction reasoning in more detail.

4.1   Hand-Crafted Lemmas

For each refinement scheme, our set of hand-crafted lemmas mostly contains lemmas that cover basic properties of the abstracted operators (e.g., when one of its operands is a special value). We also include lemmas that describe more elaborate properties based on invertibility conditions [31], i.e., conditions that exactly describe when operand x of operator $\diamond$ has a solution in literal $x \diamond s \approx y$. More formally, an invertibility condition IC for a literal $\varphi[x, s, y]$ is a formula defined over s and y such that $\exists x. \varphi \Leftrightarrow IC$. In the following, we summarize the properties encoded by each hand-crafted lemma.

Multiplication. Lemmas 1–2 capture the fact that multiplication by a power of 2 (and its arithmetic negation) can be described as a left shift operation. Lemma 3 states that the result of the multiplication must have at least as many trailing zeros in its binary representation as one of its arguments and is derived from the invertibility condition $(-s \mid s)$ & $y \approx y$ for $x \cdot s \approx y$. The left-to-right direction of $\exists x. \varphi \Leftrightarrow IC$ gives us (after Skolemization) the implication $x \cdot s \approx y \Rightarrow (-s \mid s)$ & $y \approx y$, of which lemma 3 is the right-hand side. Lemma 4 is a parity lemma that states that the result of a multiplication $x \cdot s$ must be odd if both x and s are odd, and even otherwise. Note that properties related to multiplication by special values 1, −1 and 0 are subsumed by lemmas 1, 2 and 3, respectively. Further note that [31] also provides invertibility conditions for literals defined over disequality and inequalities. We only consider invertibility conditions for literals $x \diamond s \approx y$ as this allows to instantiate y in the corresponding lemma with term abstraction t. For literals over predicates other than equality, e.g., $x \diamond s <_u y$, a good strategy for instantiating y in the resulting lemma is not obvious and left to future work.

Division. Lemma 1 states that unsigned division by a power of 2 can be described as a logical right shift operation. Lemmas 2–3 cover special cases: division by itself and division by 0 (the latter is a defined case in SMT-LIB). Lemma 4 states that zero divided by a non-zero value is zero. Lemma 5 captures a natural property of division by a non-zero value: its result is always less than its left-hand argument. Lemma 6 describes the property that division by ~ 0 (the maximum unsigned value) yields zero if the dividend is less than ~ 0. Note that for division, we do not utilize the corresponding invertibility conditions from [31] since they introduce new division terms that may not yet appear in the input constraints, which may lead to non-termination of the abstraction procedure.

Table 2. Lemmas for terms $x_{[w]} \diamond s_{[w]}$ with $\diamond \in \{\cdot, \div, \bmod\}$. We use t for the constant introduced to abstract $x \diamond s$, hand-crafted lemmas are marked with $*$, and $i \in [0, w-1]$. Lemma ID subscripts indicate bit-width restrictions for correctness.

bvmul

1^*	$s \approx 2^i \Rightarrow t \approx x \ll i$	$11_{>1}$	$t \not\approx (1 \mid \sim(x \oplus s))$
2^*	$s \approx -2^i \Rightarrow t \approx -x \ll i$	$12_{>1}$	$t \not\approx (\sim 1 \mid (x \oplus s))$
3^*	$((-s \mid s) \,\&\, t) \approx t$	13	$x \not\approx ((x \ll (s+t)) - 1)$
4^*	$t[0] \approx (x[0] \,\&\, s[0])$	14	$x \not\approx (1 - (x \ll (s-t)))$
$5_{>1}$	$s \not\approx \sim(t \mid (1 \,\&\, (x \mid s)))$	15	$s \not\approx (1 + (s \ll (t-x)))$
$6_{>1}$	$(x \,\&\, t) \not\approx (s \mid \sim t)$	16	$s \not\approx (1 - (s \ll (t-x)))$
$7_{>1}$	$t \not\approx ((s \mid 1) \ll (t \ll x))$	17	$s \not\approx (1 + (s \ll (x-t)))$
8	$s \approx (s \ll (x \,\&\, (1 \gg t)))$	$18_{>1}$	$t \not\approx (1 \mid (x+s))$
$9_{\neq 2}$	$t \geq_u (1 \,\&\, ((x \,\&\, s) \gg 1))$	19	$x \not\approx \sim(x \ll (s+t))$
10	$x \not\approx (1 \oplus (x \ll (s \oplus t)))$		

bvudiv

1^*	$s \approx 2^i \Rightarrow t \approx x \gg i$	19	$(x \gg t) \not\approx (s \mid t)$
2^*	$(s \approx x \wedge s \not\approx 0) \Rightarrow t \approx 1$	20	$s \not\approx \sim(s \gg (t \gg 1))$
3^*	$s \approx 0 \Rightarrow t \approx \sim 0$	$21_{>1}$	$x \not\approx \sim(x \,\&\, (t \ll 1))$
4^*	$(x \approx 0 \wedge s \not\approx 0) \Rightarrow t \approx 0$	22	$t \geq_u ((x \ll 1) \gg s)$
5^*	$s \not\approx 0 \Rightarrow t \leq_u x$	23	$x \geq_u (s \ll \sim(x \mid t))$
6^*	$(s \approx \sim 0 \wedge x \not\approx \sim 0) \Rightarrow t \approx 0$	24	$x \geq_u (t \ll \sim(x \mid s))$
7	$x \geq_u -(-s \,\&\, -t)$	25	$x \geq_u (t \oplus (t \gg (s \gg 1)))$
8	$-(s \mid 1) \geq_u t$	26	$x \geq_u (s \oplus (s \gg (t \gg 1)))$
9	$t \not\approx -(s \,\&\, \sim x)$	27	$x \geq_u (s \ll \sim(x \oplus t))$
10	$(s \mid t) \not\approx (x \,\&\, \sim 1)$	28	$x \geq_u (t \ll \sim(x \oplus s))$
11	$(s \mid 1) \not\approx (x \,\&\, \sim t)$	29	$x \not\approx (t + (s \mid (x+s)))$
12	$(x \,\&\, -t) \geq_u (s \,\&\, t)$	$30_{>2}$	$x \not\approx (t + (1 + (1 \ll x)))$
13	$s \geq_u (x \gg t)$	31	$s \geq_u ((x+t) \gg t)$
14	$x \geq_u ((s \gg (s \ll t)) \ll 1)$	$32_{>1}$	$x \not\approx (t + (t + (x \mid s)))$
15	$x \geq_u ((t \ll 1) \gg (t \ll s))$	33	$(s \oplus (x \mid t)) \geq_u (t \oplus 1)$
16	$t \geq_u ((x \gg s) \ll 1)$	34	$t \geq_u (x \gg (s-1))$
17	$x \geq_u ((x \mid t) \,\&\, (s \ll 1))$	35	$(s-1) \geq_u (x \gg t)$
18	$x \geq_u ((x \mid s) \,\&\, (t \ll 1))$	$36_{\neq 2}$	$x \not\approx (1 - (x \ll (x-t)))$

bvurem

1^*	$s \approx 2^i \Rightarrow t \approx (0_{[\kappa(x)-i]} \circ x[i-1:0])$	9	$x \geq_u (t \mid (x \,\&\, s))$
2^*	$s \not\approx 0 \Rightarrow t \leq_u s$	10	$1 \not\approx (t \,\&\, \sim(x \mid s))$
3^*	$x \approx 0 \Rightarrow t \approx 0$	11	$t \not\approx (\sim x \mid -s)$
4^*	$s \approx 0 \Rightarrow t \approx x$	12	$(t \,\&\, (x \mid s)) \geq_u (t \,\&\, 1)$
5^*	$s \approx x \Rightarrow t \approx 0$	$13_{>2}$	$x \not\approx (-x \mid -\sim t)$
6^*	$x <_u s \Rightarrow t \approx x$	14	$(x + -s) \geq_u t$
7^*	$\sim -s \geq_u t$	15	$(-s \oplus (x \mid s)) \geq_u t$
8	$x \approx (x \,\&\, (s \mid (t \mid -s)))$		

Remainder. Lemma 1 exploits the fact that unsigned division by a power of 2 can be described as a logical right shift operation: the resulting remainder corresponds to the value of the bits that are shifted out. Lemma 2 states that a division by a non-zero divisor yields a remainder that cannot be greater than the divisor. Lemmas 3–5 cover special cases: when one of the operands is zero, and division by itself. Lemma 6 captures the fact that a division with a dividend that is less than the divisor yields the dividend as the remainder. Lemma 7 is derived from invertibility condition $\sim - s \geq_u y$ for $x \bmod s \approx y$ from [31] in a similar manner as the lemma derived from the invertibility condition for multiplication.

Powers of Two Lemmas. The powers of two lemmas for multiplication (lemmas 1–2), division (lemma 1), and remainder (lemma 1) use 2^i to denote a specific power of two. They do not symbolically encode whether a term s represents a power of two since this would require counting the number of trailing zero bits i. Instead, if the current model value of s is a power of two, we instantiate the corresponding lemma with this value. In the worst case, this will add $\kappa(s)$ instantiations of the lemma if all powers of two for bit-width $\kappa(s)$ are enumerated. However, this is rarely the case and the lemmas are cheap in terms of bit-blasting.

4.2   Lemma Scoring Scheme

Compiling a set of lemmas to describe properties of an abstracted operator $\diamond$ requires careful consideration of several key aspects: (*i*) lemmas for $\diamond$ should not introduce new terms that will be abstracted (introducing new terms with $\diamond$ may lead to non-termination of the abstraction procedure and introducing terms with abstracted operators other than $\diamond$ may yield potentially expensive abstractions in case they have to be bit-blasted); (*ii*) lemmas should minimize introducing new terms with potentially expensive operators that are not abstracted (e.g., bit-vector addition); and (*iii*) possible candidate lemmas should be *filtered* based on their *quality* to avoid adding redundant (subsumed) lemmas and to ensure that included lemmas maximize the number of spurious models to rule out.

The former two impose syntax restrictions (see Sect. 4.3), and for the purpose of addressing (*iii*), we define a scoring scheme that measures the quality of a candidate lemma for operator $\diamond$ as follows.

Definition 1 (Lemma Score). *Let $x \diamond s$ be the term to abstract, and let t be the constant abstracting $x \diamond s$ such that $x \diamond s \approx t$. Given a lemma $\ell[x, s, t]$ defined over $\{x, s, t\}$ such that $x \diamond s \approx t \Rightarrow \ell$. We define $\text{SCORE}(\ell, w)$, the score of ℓ for a given bit-width w, as the number of triplets (v^x, v^s, v^t) of bit-vector values of bit-width w where $\ell[x \mapsto v^x, s \mapsto v^s, t \mapsto v^t]$ evaluates to $\top$.*

For a term $x_{[4]} \diamond s_{[4]}$, the worst possible lemma score is the number of all possible combinations of triplets ($2^4 \times 2^4 \times 2^4 = 4096$), and the best possible score is the number of possible combinations of x and s ($2^4 \times 2^4 = 256$). Thus, the difference between the worst and best possible lemma score for any $x \diamond s$ is the number of *incorrect* triplets, i.e., triplets for which $v^x \diamond v^s \not\approx v^t$. Since lemmas over-approximate literals $x \diamond s \approx t$, their score is a measure for the *degree of over-approximation*: a lower score indicates higher quality of a lemma as a higher number of incorrect triplets is ruled out.

For our hand-crafted lemmas for multiplication from Sect. 4.1, for bit-width 4 we compute as scores: {1: 2416, 2: 2791, 3: 1961, 4: 2048}. This indicates that they, individually, rule out 34–55% of incorrect triplets. Further, lemma 3, the lemma derived via the invertibility condition for multiplication over equality, is the strongest lemma of the four. Similarly, our hand-crafted lemmas for division and remainder rule out 6–50% of incorrect triplets for bit-width 4, with lemma 5 the strongest lemma for division, and lemma 7, the lemma derived from an invertibility condition, the strongest for remainder.

Individual lemma scores are a valuable measure of quality for a single lemma. However, triplet coverage for individual lemmas may intersect. Thus, when considered as a set, in a refinement scheme, it is necessary to define a measure for the quality of sets of lemmas to determine if extending the set with additional lemmas improves the number of incorrect triplets that are ruled out.

Definition 2 (Score of Lemma Set). *Given a set of lemmas $\mathcal{L}$ such that for each $\ell[x, s, t] \in \mathcal{L}$, $x \diamond s \approx t \Rightarrow \ell$. We define the score of $\mathcal{L}$ for a given bit-width w SCORE$(\mathcal{L}, w)$ as the number of triplets (v^x, v^s, v^t) of bit-vector values of bit-width w where $\bigwedge_{l \in \mathcal{L}} \ell[x \mapsto v^x, s \mapsto v^s, t \mapsto v^t] = \top$.*

For example, for $x_{[4]} \cdot s_{[4]}$, the score of the set of hand-crafted lemmas is 704, which indicates that it already rules out 88% of the incorrect triplets. Similarly, for division and remainder, for bit-width 4 the sets of hand-crafted lemmas rule out 71% and 91% of incorrect triplets. Note that extending a set of lemmas $\mathcal{L}$ with a lemma $\ell \notin \mathcal{L}$ can improve but not worsen its score. If ℓ is subsumed by $\mathcal{L}$, SCORE$(\mathcal{L}, w)$ remains unchanged. While our sets of hand-crafted lemmas from Sect. 4.1 already rule out a large number of incorrect triplets, their score also indicates that a considerable number of incorrect triplets is still not covered. We thus, in the following, propose an automated framework for synthesizing lemmas with respect to our sets of hand-crafted lemmas via abductive reasoning.

4.3   Synthesizing Lemmas via Abduction

The lemmas from Sect. 4.1 describe basic properties of the abstracted operators and are hand-crafted but strong, as indicated by their score. However, a considerable number of incorrect triplets is still uncovered for each set. Further, manually crafting lemmas that are effective with respect to an already existing set is challenging for arithmetic bit-vector operators, mainly due to overflow semantics. In this section, we propose an *automated* way to synthesize lemmas with respect to our sets of hand-crafted lemmas via *syntax-restricted abductive* reasoning [34] and focus on synthesizing lemmas for bit-vector operators $\{\cdot, \div, \mathrm{mod}\}$. Our approach, however, can easily be generalized to other operators and theories.

Since we are over-approximating literals $x \diamond s \approx t$, we are trying to find lemmas $\ell[x, s, t]$ such that $(x \diamond s) \approx t \Rightarrow \ell$. Further, as mentioned in Sect. 4.2, we require that ℓ does not contain specific operators (the set of abstracted operators, including $\diamond$ itself) and that the number of occurrences of more expensive operators (such as bit-vector addition) is limited. The best possible over-approximation of operator $\diamond$ would exactly describe the semantics of $\diamond$ without including $\diamond$, which seems unattainable under the given constraints. The worst possible over-approximation, on the other hand, is the formula $\top$. We are thus looking for simple but *non-trivial* lemmas that improve the scores of our initial, hand-crafted lemma sets. We formulate this problem as an instance of the general *abduction* problem, which is defined as follows.

Definition 3 (T_{BV}-Abduct). *Given two quantifier-free T_{BV}-formulas A and B, a T_{BV}-abduct is a quantifier-free formula C such that $A \wedge C \Rightarrow B$ is T_{BV}-valid, and $A \wedge C$ is T_{BV}-satisfiable.*

Definition 4 (Non-trivial Lemma). *Given a T_{BV}-literal φ as $x \diamond s \approx t$, a φ-lemma $\ell[x, s, t]$ is a quantifier-free T-formula defined over $\{x, s, t\}$ such that $\varphi \Rightarrow \ell$ is T_{BV}-valid. Lemma ℓ is non-trivial if it is not T_{BV}-valid.*

Finding a non-trivial lemma ℓ for a given literal φ amounts to finding an abduct $\neg\ell$ of the formulas $\top$ and $\neg\varphi$.

Lemma 1. *Let φ be a T_{BV}-literal as above. T_{BV}-formula ℓ is a non-trivial φ-lemma if and only if $\neg\ell$ is a T_{BV}-abduct of the formulas $\top$ and $\neg\varphi$.*

Proof. Suppose $\neg\ell$ is a T_{BV}-abduct of $\top$ and $\neg\varphi$. In particular, $\top \wedge \neg\ell \Rightarrow \neg\varphi$, and therefore $\varphi \Rightarrow \ell$, and thus ℓ is a φ-lemma. And since, by Definition 3, $\top \wedge \neg\ell$ is T_{BV}-satisfiable, we get that ℓ is not T_{BV}-valid. For the converse, suppose ℓ is a non-trivial φ-lemma. Then, $\varphi \Rightarrow \ell$ is T_{BV}-valid. In particular, $\top \wedge \neg\ell \Rightarrow \neg\varphi$ is T_{BV}-valid. Further, since ℓ is not T_{BV}-valid, $\top \wedge \neg\ell$ is T_{BV}-satisfiable.   □

Since we require certain syntactic restrictions for φ-lemmas, we base our lemma synthesis framework on the syntax-restricted abductive reasoning framework of [34] as implemented in the SMT solver cvc5 [7]. This abduction framework is based on Syntax-Guided Synthesis (SyGuS) [6] and thus guided by a user-defined grammar. Note that, alternatively, our lemma synthesis problem could be directly expressed as a SyGuS problem. However, non-triviality of lemmas requires the introduction of quantifiers in the specification of the formula to synthesize, whereas this quantification is implicit in the abduction formulation.

Our goal is to automatically extend a set of φ-lemmas $\mathcal{L}$ (may be empty) for a given literal φ (as defined above) with a set of lemmas Γ such that each lemma $\ell \in \Gamma$ improves the score of $\mathcal{L}$. Algorithm 2 shows the main procedure of our abduction-based lemma synthesis approach. Function SYNTHLEM takes as input a literal φ, the bit-width w for which φ is defined, a set of initial lemmas $\mathcal{I}$, a set $\mathcal{G}$ of grammars that define syntax restrictions for lemma construction, and a limit n of number of lemmas to synthesize for each grammar. The procedure constructs and returns a set of φ-lemmas $\mathcal{L}$ such that $\mathcal{I} \subseteq \mathcal{L}$ and

Algorithm 2. Synthesizing lemmas. Function SYNTHLEM assumes the availability of an abduction reasoner GETABDUCT. Function SCORE computes the score of a set of lemmas w.r.t. a given bit-width w as in Definition 2.

```
 1   function SYNTHLEM(φ, w, I, G, n)
 2       L ← I                                       ▷ Populate with initial lemmas
 3       for γ in G do
 4           Γ ← ∅
 5           for i in [1, n] do                      ▷ Synthesize lemmas via abduction
 6               a ← GETABDUCT(⊤, ¬φ, γ)
 7               if a = ⊥ then break
 8               Γ ← Γ ∪ {¬a}
 9           end for
10           repeat                                  ▷ Merge synthesized lemma with L
11               ℓ_min ← some ℓ ∈ Γ that minimizes SCORE(L ∪ {ℓ}, w)
12               L ← L ∪ {ℓ_min}, Γ ← Γ \ {ℓ_min}
13           until ℓ_min = ⊤ ∨ Γ = ∅
14       end for
15       return L
16   end function
```

$I \subset L \Rightarrow \text{SCORE}(L, w) < \text{SCORE}(I, w)$ as follows. The resulting set of lemmas L is initialized with the given set of initial lemmas I (in our case our hand-crafted lemmas). Then, for each grammar $\gamma \in G$, in lines 5–9, first a set of at most n lemmas Γ is generated via abductive reasoning (GETABDUCT). From this set, in lines 10–13, L is extended only with those lemmas ℓ that improve the score of L. Lemmas are synthesized via an incremental abduction engine GETABDUCT (in our case cvc5) by iteratively asking for n new T_{BV}-abducts of formulas $\top$ and $\neg\varphi$, constructed from the operators in grammar γ. Function GETABDUCT returns $\bot$ if no more abducts are found (line 7), either because the search terminated or a resource limit was reached. Note that we used $n = 100$ and a time limit of $100\,\text{s}$ per call to GETABDUCT. Both limits were found to be a good middle ground between generating sufficiently many lemmas while not overwhelming the solver with too many abduction queries.

In the context of synthesizing lemmas for T_{BV} operators, the search for lemmas via abduction is limited to formulas where the bit-width of T_{BV}-terms is explicitly given. Consequently, the T_{BV}-abducts determined via GETABDUCT (and thus the resulting lemmas) are only guaranteed to be correct for this specific bit-width. Further, abductive reasoning for theory T_{BV} as in [34] is based on a T_{BV}-solver with the same limitations our abstraction-based approach aims to address: it relies on bit-blasting and thus does not scale well for increasing bit-widths. We thus chose a bit-width of 4 for x, s and t as a reasonable compromise to not overwhelm the abduction engine while avoiding the generation of lemmas that are specific to very small bit-widths. To minimize the risk of including bit-width specific lemmas in the set of synthesized lemmas L, in function SYNTHLEM, before adding lemma ℓ to L, we introduce an additional step where we verify the correctness of ℓ for bit-widths 4–10. And finally, before incorporating synthesized lemmas in our refinement schemes, we verify each lemma up to a certain, large bit-width (see Sect. 4.4). Note that while the additional verification step during synthesis encountered lemmas that were only valid for bit-width 4, no lemmas that passed this verification step failed verification for larger bit-widths. Further note that bit-vector multiplication is commutative. As an optimization we thus add the corresponding symmetric cases of hand-crafted lemmas to the set of initial lemmas $\mathcal{I}$ when applicable.

Our abduction-based lemma synthesis procedure requires the definition of a set of grammars $\mathcal{G}$ to describe syntax restrictions for constructing lemmas. Since the search space for SyGuS-based abduction heavily depends on such an input grammar, we opted for diversification via a set of grammars rather than a single, larger grammar. Set $\mathcal{G}$ consists of the of grammars γ_0 to γ_6 defined via a common grammar $\gamma_c = \{x, s, t, \approx, \not\approx, <_u, \leq_u, 0, 1\}$ as follows:

$$\gamma_0 = \gamma_c \cup \{\sim, \&, |, \oplus\} \qquad \gamma_4 = \gamma_3 \cup \{\oplus\}$$
$$\gamma_1 = \gamma_c \cup \{-, \sim, \&, |\} \qquad \gamma_5 = \gamma_4 \cup \{+\}$$
$$\gamma_2 = \gamma_1 \cup \{\oplus\} \qquad \gamma_6 = \gamma_c \cup \{-, +, -_+, \ll, \gg\}$$
$$\gamma_3 = \gamma_1 \cup \{\ll, \gg\}$$

Note that in grammars γ_0 to γ_6 above, we use symbol '$-$' for negation and '$-_+$' for subtraction to ensure that they are distinguishable. Further note that we include bit-vector addition (and operators such as subtraction and negation that can be rewritten as addition) even though it is an arithmetic operation and thus one of the more expensive operators when bit-blasting. Preliminary experiments showed that including addition, negation and subtraction in some of the grammars is beneficial for finding useful lemmas.

Extending our set of hand-crafted lemmas from Sect. 4.1 with the lemmas synthesized via abduction as given in Table 2 improves the score for multiplication from 704 to 490, which corresponds to ruling out 94% of incorrect triplets for our final set of tier 1 and tier 2 lemmas. Similarly, the score for division improves from 1366 to 394 (96% coverage of incorrect triplets), and the score for remainder improves from 616 to 400 (96% coverage of incorrect triplets).

Finally, it is important to note that we synthesized lemmas via abduction in an offline manner, as opposed to during the solving process. That is, after automatically generating the lemmas, they were incorporated into the solver together with the hand-crafted lemmas. Thus, the set of incorporated tier 1 and tier 2 lemmas is fixed and independent from the input problem.

4.4   Lemma Verification

We verified the correctness of lemmas ℓ from Table 2 for bit-widths from 1–256 by checking for literal $x \diamond s \approx t$ if formula $x \diamond s \approx t \wedge \neg\ell$ is T-unsatisfiable. Given that the lemmas based on powers of two are well-known and universally valid properties of the corresponding bit-vector operators, we omit the additional

131,584 benchmarks required to check each instance of these lemmas up to bit-width 256. For the remaining lemmas, we generated 16,896 benchmarks and used the SMT solvers Bitwuzla [29], cvc5 [7], Yices [17], and Z3 [27] for verification. We ran these verification tasks on a cluster of 22 machines with Intel(R) Xeon(R) Gold 6348 CPUs. For each solver and benchmark pair, we used a CPU time limit of 8 h and a memory limit of 8GB. For a given bit-width, we consider a lemma to be correct if at least one solver determined *unsat*, and as incorrect if at least one solver determined *sat*. Overall, all solver-benchmark pairs required 1,112 d of CPU time. We did not encounter any disagreements between solvers and were able to complete all verification tasks, with Yices individually solving 96.49%, Bitwuzla 96.47%, cvc5 96.29%, and Z3 95.05% of all tasks.

We were able to verify the correctness of all hand-crafted lemmas for bit-widths 1–256, and of all synthesized lemmas for bit-widths 3–256. Synthesized lemmas are correct by construction for bit-width 4, which is confirmed by this experiment. However, some of the synthesized lemmas do not hold for very small bit-widths, as indicated by the bit-width restrictions given in Table 2. As mentioned above, if terms of such a restricted size are abstracted, these lemmas must not be considered for refinement. However, in the context of integrating our abstraction approach into Bitwuzla, all lemmas are applicable since we only abstract terms of size 32 and above (see Sect. 5).

Verification of the correctness of our lemmas up to bit-width 256 establishes sufficient confidence of their correctness for bit-widths larger than 256. We leave the task of formally proving their correctness for all bit-widths to future work. A recent technique for reasoning over bit-vectors with parametric bit-width based on a reduction to the quantified combination of the theories of uninterpreted functions and non-linear arithmetic was proposed in [32]. However, preliminary experiments showed that except for a small number of lemmas, verification of our lemmas using this technique is not feasible.

5   Integration

We extended the state-of-the-art SMT solver Bitwuzla [29] with our proposed framework. Bitwuzla supports quantified and quantifier-free bit-vector reasoning in combination with arrays, floating-point arithmetic and uninterpreted functions and was the best performing solver across supported logics in the SMT competition in 2023 [5]. Further, Bitwuzla reduces floating-point arithmetic to the theory of bit-vectors, which allows us to also apply our approach to floating-point arithmetic problems that do not involve bit-vector constraints.

Bitwuzla implements a lazy, CEGAR-based SMT paradigm called *lemmas on demand* [10,26], but with a bit-vector abstraction (and thus a T_{BV}-solver) instead of a propositional abstraction at its core. In this bit-vector abstraction, non-T_{BV}-atoms are abstracted as Boolean constants and non-T_{BV}-terms are abstracted as bit-vector constants. These abstracted terms are then handled by the corresponding theory solvers. This architecture allows an easy and seamless integration of our abstraction module. The interaction between the T_{BV}-solver of

Algorithm 3. The lemmas on demand loop of Bitwuzla with multiple theory solvers, extended with our abstraction module AM (highlighted in blue).

```
1   function SOLVE(A)
2       r ← UNKNOWN, L ← ∅
3       repeat
4           A ← AM::ABSTRACT(A ∪ L)
5           r, M ← T_BV::SOLVE(A)                    ▷ Solve Bit-Vector Abstraction of A
6           if r = UNSAT then break end if
7           if (L ← T_FP::CHECK(M)) ≠ ∅ then continue end if        ▷ FP Solver
8           if (L ← AM::CHECK(M)) ≠ ∅ then continue end if
9           if (L ← T_A::CHECK(M)) ≠ ∅ then continue end if        ▷ Arrays Solver
10          if (L ← T_UF::CHECK(M)) ≠ ∅ then continue end if        ▷ UF Solver
11          L ← T_Q::CHECK(M)                                       ▷ Quantifiers Solver
12      until L = ∅
13      return r
14  end function
```

Bitwuzla and our abstraction module AM is implemented as shown in Algorithm 3. Prior to sending assertions to the T_{BV}-solver, the abstraction module processes each assertion and introduces abstractions for all relevant bit-vector terms. After the T_{BV}-solver determines that the set of abstracted assertions is satisfiable, the abstraction module checks if all abstracted bit-vector terms are consistent and adds refinement lemmas when needed.

Note that the order in which the theory solvers and the abstraction module are called is not arbitrary. The T_{FP}-solver word-blasts floating-point constraints to T_{BV} and, thus, introduces new bit-vector terms. Hence, the abstraction module is called after the T_{FP}-solver to ensure that for pure T_{FP}-formulas, the T_{FP}-solver first generates word-blasting lemmas so that the abstraction module has bit-vector terms to abstract. For the arrays (T_A) and UF (T_{UF}) theory solvers and the quantifiers module (T_Q), on the other hand, we have to ensure that the bit-vector abstraction is consistent before checking the theory axioms based on the current bit-vector abstraction model M. In preliminary experiments, the abstraction module was called after the T_A- and T_{UF}-solvers, which resulted in a degraded performance for problems involving these theories. This was a consequence of the T_A- and T_{UF}-solvers generating substantially more lemmas due to an inconsistent bit-vector abstraction. Similarly, when quantifiers are involved, the quantifiers module is called last to ensure that the bit-vector abstraction of all ground terms and formulas is consistent.

As an additional extension, we also implemented a more coarse-grained abstraction approach that *abstracts assertions* as fresh Boolean constants. This is not a novel technique and has been proposed in earlier literature [24]. However, it can be easily implemented in our proposed abstraction framework with a simple refinement scheme for assertions. The goal of this refinement scheme is to incrementally add assertions as refinements that evaluate to ⊥ under the current model of the bit-vector abstraction. This is combined with our main approach of term abstraction in an interleaved manner by limiting the number of assertion refinements added per refinement iteration. When adding assertions as refinement, the abstraction module abstracts all relevant bit-vector terms occurring in these assertions, and before new assertions are added, it ensures that the current set of term abstractions is consistent. Only when all currently abstracted terms are consistent, more assertions may be added as refinement. The termination criteria are the same as with term abstraction only. If all of the remaining assertions evaluate to $\top$ under the current model, we conclude with *sat*. If a subset of the added assertions is already *unsatisfiable*, we found an *unsat core* and conclude with *unsat*.

Configuration. The number of assertion refinements per iteration is configurable and set to 100 refinements per iteration. Similarly, the minimum bit-width of terms defined over $\{\cdot, \div, \text{mod}\}$ that we abstract is configurable and limited to terms of size 32 and above. Further, since value instantiation lemmas only rule out one spurious model, our implementation limits the number of value instantiations per abstraction t based on its bit-width to $\kappa(t)/8$ instantiations. For example, for an abstracted term t of bit-width 32, we add at most four value instantiations before we add a bit-blasting lemma as final refinement for t.

6   Evaluation

We evaluate the performance of our bit-vector abstraction approach as integrated in Bitwuzla on five different benchmark sets: *certora* (1,988 benchmarks), *ethereum* (3,173 benchmarks), *syrew* (15,000 benchmarks), *ff* (1,224 benchmarks), and *smtlib* (155,269 benchmarks). Benchmark sets *certora* and *ethereum* are industrial benchmarks that arise from smart contract verification applications [15], provided by Certora [1] and the Ethereum Foundation [3]. The *certora* set consists of SMT queries generated by the Certora Prover [2] and is split into sets *certora₁* and *certora₂*. The *ethereum* set contains benchmarks generated by hevm [4], a symbolic execution engine for the Ethereum virtual machine. Benchmarks in these sets are specifically encoded over bit-vectors of size 256, in combination with arrays, uninterpreted functions, and quantifiers.

Benchmark set *syrew* serves as a more controlled and balanced set to specifically evaluate the effectiveness of our abstraction approach for each abstracted operator. We generated three sets of equivalence checks, each only involving one of the abstracted operators. For that purpose, we enumerated T_{BV}-terms and T_{BV}-formulas that are equivalent for bit-width 4 with the SyGuS-solver of cvc5. For each set, we enumerated 500 equivalence checks using as SyGuS grammar $\{0, 1, x, s, t, \approx, \not\approx, <_u, \leq_u, \sim, \&, \ll, \gg\}$, extended with only one of $\{\cdot, \div, \text{mod}\}$. The resulting 1,500 benchmarks were then instantiated for bit-widths 2^i with $i \in [4, 13]$ yielding 15,000 benchmarks in total, the majority unsatisfiable.

The *ff* benchmark set originates from [33] and consists of translation validation problems of zero-knowledge proof compilers in two sets: an encoding in the theory of finite fields T_{FF} and a translation to T_{BV} that exclusively uses arithmetic bit-vector operators $\{+, \cdot, \bmod\}$ over bit-vectors of size 510.

Benchmark set *smtlib* contains all non-incremental benchmarks of all logics in the SMT-LIB [9] benchmark library supported by Bitwuzla. This includes all quantified and quantifier-free logics involving the theories of bit-vectors, arrays, floating-point arithmetic and uninterpreted functions (24 in total). Note that this also includes floating-point arithmetic logics that do not involve the theory of bit-vectors since Bitwuzla word-blasts floating-point terms to bit-vector terms.

We implemented our novel *term abstraction* technique in our main configuration ABSTR-T. We additionally distinguish two configurations that enable *assertion abstraction* as described in Sect. 5: configuration ABSTR-A, which enables *assertion abstraction* only, and configuration ABSTR-TA, which enables *both* term and assertion abstraction. We evaluate these configurations against Bitwuzla version 0.3.2, cvc5 version 1.1.0, and Z3 version 4.12.4 (in their default configuration, using bit-blasting for T_{BV}). Both cvc5 and Z3 are industrial-strength SMT solvers that support a wide range of theories, including the theories supported by Bitwuzla. We further compare against cvc5-ib, a configuration of cvc5 that reduces bit-vector problems to non-linear integer arithmetic problems via *int-blasting* [36]. Note that on the *ff* benchmark set, we evaluate these configurations only on the T_{BV} subset, and additionally compare against a dedicated T_{FF}-solver implementation of cvc5 (cvc5-ff) on the T_{FF} subset.

We ran all experiments on a cluster of 25 machines with Intel(R) Xeon E5-2620 v4 CPUs. For each solver and benchmark pair, we allocated one CPU core and 8GB of memory with a time limit of 1200 s. In case that a solver terminated with an error or ran into the memory limit on a specific benchmark, we counted its runtime on that benchmark as 1200 s as a penalty.

Table 3 summarizes the results for each solver grouped by benchmark set and ordered by number of solved benchmarks. Overall, ABSTR-T significantly outperforms all other bit-blasting solvers and the int-blasting solver cvc5-ib on all benchmark sets. Our abstraction approach considerably reduces the memory usage across all sets, solving more benchmarks with a lower number of memory outs. Only on the *certora* sets, cvc5-ib has a smaller memory footprint, which is due to the more memory-efficient translation of bit-vector to integer arithmetic.

The *certora* set is divided into the *certora₁* and *certora₂* subsets, which correspond to the use of two different encodings arising from the same application. Both sets rely on 256-bit bit-vectors and uninterpreted functions and make heavy use of arithmetic operators. Set *certora₁* is a proprietary and more diverse set of benchmarks and is sampled from a different (and more diverse) set of smart contracts than *certora₂*. It uses an older, less optimized encoding that involves quantifiers and overflow predicates, while *certora₂* does not rely on quantifiers and was successfully optimized for existing bit-blasting solvers, which struggled on the older encoding. This can be seen in Table 3, where the best non-abstraction-based bit-blasting configuration (Bitwuzla) solves only 13% of *certora₁* but 74% of *certora₂*. Benchmarks in the *certora₁* set usually contain a large number of assertions (15k on average, up to 100k) and are thus

Table 3. Number of solved benchmarks (Solved), timeouts (TO), memory outs (MO), penalized runtime (T), memory usage of all benchmarks (M), and runtime T_c on commonly solved benchmarks, grouped by benchmark set and solvers. Note that the number (x/y) for each benchmark set indicates the number of commonly solved instances x and the total number of benchmarks y in the set.

Benchmarks	Solver	Solved	TO	MO	T [s]	M [GB]	T_c [s]
certora$_1$ (10/850)	Abstr-ta	573	231	46	$448k$	2,492	234
	Abstr-a	386	140	324	$681k$	5,201	963
	Abstr-t	258	155	437	$760k$	4,807	83
	cvc5-ib	147	674	0	$879k$	667	52
	Bitwuzla	111	86	653	$915k$	6,182	192
	cvc5	90	113	610	$923k$	6,064	341
	Z3	30	447	373	$989k$	4,944	484
certora$_2$ (227/1,138)	Abstr-ta	866	264	8	$370k$	1,024	$11k$
	Abstr-t	866	263	9	$384k$	1,402	$17k$
	Abstr-a	844	269	25	$433k$	2,661	$19k$
	Bitwuzla	843	266	29	$439k$	2,944	$23k$
	cvc5	705	223	210	$603k$	4,027	$22k$
	cvc5-ib	666	472	0	$643k$	106	$15k$
	Z3	612	492	34	$679k$	1,866	$24k$
ethereum (3,138/3,173)	Abstr-t	3,173	0	0	407	11	102
	Bitwuzla	3,173	0	0	720	29	228
	Z3	3,169	4	0	$6k$	107	679
	cvc5	3,158	0	1	$18k$	36	377
	cvc5-ib	3,141	20	0	$39k$	21	128
syrew (5,528/15,000)	Abstr-t	14,142	583	276	$1,225k$	4,409	$2k$
	Bitwuzla	11,961	744	2,296	$3,955k$	23,483	$24k$
	Z3	9,992	833	4,175	$6,198k$	39,506	$78k$
	cvc5	9,003	797	5,200	$7,498k$	48,421	$109k$
	cvc5-ib	7,974	5,137	1,632	$8,836k$	19,850	$180k$
ff (12/1,224)	cvc5-ff	973	129	122	$313k$	1,364	0
	Abstr-t	480	729	15	$913k$	2,762	0
	cvc5-ib	304	822	98	$1,104k$	1,074	0
	Bitwuzla	223	71	930	$1,211k$	8,360	277
	Z3	145	56	1,023	$1,299k$	8,893	3
	cvc5	40	0	1,184	$1,422k$	9,523	589
smtlib (125,037/155,269)	Abstr-t	148,554	1,944	152	$8,770k$	8,566	$64k$
	Bitwuzla	148,492	1,966	193	$8,748k$	8,953	$64k$
	Z3	145,121	4,846	565	$13,528k$	18,278	$693k$
	cvc5	144,829	3,775	285	$13,513k$	11,029	$213k$
	cvc5-ib	127,144	24,479	194	$39,647k$	15,233	$5,666k$

good candidates for evaluating assertion abstraction in combination with term abstraction. Benchmarks in the *certora$_2$* set, on the other hand, usually contain a significantly smaller number of assertions (less than 1k per benchmark). Hence, on the *certora* benchmark sets, in addition to configuration ABSTR-T, we also evaluate the two configurations ABSTR-A and ABSTR-TA that enable assertion abstraction. On both sets, ABSTR-T considerably improves over bit-blasting. On the *certora$_1$* set, ABSTR-A outperforms ABSTR-T, and combining assertion and term abstraction (ABSTR-TA) significantly outperforms either, both in terms of solved benchmarks and memory usage. We observed that in the majority of cases where ABSTR-TA improves over ABSTR-T, the benchmark is unsatisfiable and the size of the unsatisfiable core is only a small fraction of the overall number of assertions. On the *certora$_2$* set, however, ABSTR-A is less effective since these benchmarks contain a significantly smaller number of assertions. Configuration ABSTR-TA still improves over ABSTR-T in terms of overall memory usage.

Note that for the benchmark sets *ethereum*, *ff* and *syrew*, enabling assertion abstraction was not applicable for a majority of the benchmarks due to the low number of assertions (less than 100 per benchmark). On benchmark set *smtlib*, the effects of assertion abstraction were overall inconclusive. Thus, due to space constraints, for the remaining sets, we exclude configurations ABSTR-A and ABSTR-TA from the evaluation.

On the *ethereum* set, both ABSTR-T and Bitwuzla solve all benchmarks. However, ABSTR-T is more than 40% faster and requires 60% less memory. On the commonly 3,138 solved benchmarks, ABSTR-T is the fastest solver, closely followed by cvc5-ib. Both outperform the other bit-blasting solvers. Note that on this benchmark set, cvc5 and cvc5-ib returned with errors due to unsupported cases of equality over constant arrays on 14 and 12 benchmarks, respectively.

On the *syrew* set, ABSTR-T significantly outperforms all other solvers and is more than 3× faster with a 5× lower memory usage compared to the second best solver Bitwuzla. On the commonly solved 5,528 benchmarks, ABSTR-T is 12–90× faster than the competition. The int-blasting configuration cvc5-ib comes in last, mainly due to the occurrence of *bit-wise* operations. Bit-wise operators do not have a direct translation to integers and require cvc5-ib to resort to abstraction schemes, which is more expensive than the direct translation via bit-blasting.

On the *ff* benchmark set, as expected, the native finite field solver cvc5-ff solves the most benchmarks overall. However, ABSTR-T significantly improves over bit-blasting (Bitwuzla) and int-blasting (cvc5-ib) with the least number of memory outs overall. Surprisingly, ABSTR-T is able to solve 36 benchmarks that cvc5-ff cannot. None of the other solvers solves benchmarks that cvc5-ff cannot.

On the *smtlib* set, ABSTR-T improves over Bitwuzla in 10 out of the 24 logics in terms of number of solved benchmarks, with 6 of them being floating-point arithmetic logics. Most notably, ABSTR-T was able to improve the number of solved instances X and runtime in percent Y on commonly solved instances (X, Y%) over Bitwuzla in logics FP (+5, −16%), BVFP (0, −45%), QF_ABVFP (+1, −33%), QF_ABVFPLRA (0, −23%), QF_BVFP (+1, −45%), QF_BVFPLRA (+9, −46%), QF_FP (+23, −13%), and QF_FPLRA (+1, -7%).

The only significant loss of -13 benchmarks is in the QF_BV logic, which is also the only logic where ABSTR-T is significantly slower (33%) on commonly solved instances compared to Bitwuzla. This slowdown can be primarily attributed to the two benchmark families *Sage2* and *uclid*. On these two families, on the commonly solved instances, ABSTR-T is slower by 40% and 4,100%, respectively. This slowdown is unexpected and needs further investigation. Nevertheless, in logic QF_BV, ABSTR-T is able to solve more unsatisfiable benchmarks with less memory outs compared to Bitwuzla and outperforms cvc5, cvc5-ib and Z3 by a significant margin (more than 1,400 solved benchmarks).

Table 4. Number of overall abstracted terms and abstraction refinements on solved benchmarks grouped by abstracted operator and refinement tier (1: hand-crafted, 2: abduction, 3: value instantiation, 4: bit-blasting).

Terms		Refinement Tier				
Operator	*Abstracted*	*1*	*2*	*3*	*4*	*Total*
·	367,101	579,369	67,221	650,086	134,525	1,431,201
÷	55,461	126,223	109,137	73,019	7,024	315,403
mod	62,328	161,270	5,614	30,350	1,326	198,560

We further performed an analysis of term abstractions and abstraction refinements for all benchmarks solved by ABSTR-T in all benchmark sets. Table 4 summarizes our findings, grouped by refinement tier and abstracted operator. Overall, ABSTR-T abstracted 367,101 multiplication terms, 55,461 unsigned division terms, and 62,328 unsigned remainder terms. Out of these, only 134,525 (37%) multiplications, 7,024 (13%) divisions, and 1,326 (2%) remainders were bit-blasted as last resort via adding tier-4 lemmas. For the remaining 63%/87%/98% of multiplication/division/remainder terms, refinement with tier 1–3 lemmas only was sufficient to solve the benchmarks. Out of the solved benchmarks where ABSTR-T abstracted any bit-vector terms, 80% were solved without bit-blasting any of the abstracted terms. For the remaining 20% of solved benchmarks, 78% of abstracted terms were bit-blasted.

For the benchmarks solved with abstraction, ABSTR-T required on average 37 refinement iterations (median 4). Further, all lemmas except bvudiv lemma 21 and bvurem lemma 11 from Table 2 were used for solving these instances. Tier-1/2/3/4 lemmas were used in 76%/27%/30%/20% of solved instances.

We further evaluated the usefulness of the abduction-based lemmas (tier 2) by disabling these lemmas on the *syrew* benchmark set. Without these lemmas, ABSTR-T solves 336 less benchmarks, has 2× more memory outs, and is 23% slower on commonly solved instances while consuming 61% more memory. Without tier-3 lemmas the number of solved instances for benchmark sets $certora_1$/$certora_2$/$syrew$/ff/$smtlib$ change by $-12\%/-1\%/-1\%/-6\%/+0.01\%$. The artifact of this paper is archived and available in the Zenodo open-access repository at https://zenodo.org/record/10913320.

7 Conclusion

We have presented a novel abstraction-refinement approach to improve the scalability of bit-blasting arithmetic terms with large bit-widths. We have introduced a lemma scoring scheme and an abduction-based framework for synthesizing refinement lemmas, which we include in our four-tiered refinement schemes. We have extended the state-of-the-art SMT solver Bitwuzla with our techniques and showed that this significantly improves solver performance on a diverse set of benchmarks coming from a variety of applications, including smart contract verification and zero-knowledge proofs. Incorporating existing under-approximation techniques with our approach is an interesting direction for future work.

References

1. Certora (2024). https://www.certora.com/
2. Certora prover white paper (2024). https://docs.certora.com/en/latest/docs/whitepaper/index.html
3. Ethereum foundation (2024). https://ethereum.foundation/
4. hevm symbolic execution engine smt queries (2024). https://github.com/msooseth/eth-bench-smt-queries
5. SMT competition 2023 (2024). https://github.com/smt-comp/2023
6. Alur, R., et al.: Syntax-guided synthesis. In: Formal Methods in Computer-Aided Design, FMCAD 2013, Portland, OR, USA, October 20-23, 2013, pp. 1–8. IEEE (2013). https://ieeexplore.ieee.org/document/6679385/
7. Barbosa, H., et al.: cvc5: a versatile and industrial-strength SMT solver. In: TACAS 2022. LNCS, vol. 13243, pp. 415–442. Springer, Cham (2022). https://doi.org/10.1007/978-3-030-99524-9_24
8. Barrett, C., Fontaine, P., Tinelli, C.: The SMT-LIB Standard: Version 2.6. Tech. rep., Department of Computer Science, The University of Iowa (2017). http://smt-lib.org
9. Barrett, C., Stump, A., Tinelli, C.: The Satisfiability Modulo Theories Library (SMT-LIB). www.SMT-LIB.org (2023)
10. Barrett, C.W., Dill, D.L., Stump, A.: Checking satisfiability of first-order formulas by incremental translation to SAT. In: Brinksma, E., Larsen, K.G. (eds.) Computer Aided Verification, pp. 236–249. Springer Berlin Heidelberg, Berlin, Heidelberg (2002). https://doi.org/10.1007/3-540-45657-0_18
11. Bozzano, M., et al.: Encoding RTL constructs for MathSAT: a preliminary report. Electron. Notes Theor. Comput. Sci. **144**(2), 3–14 (2006)
12. Brummayer, R.: Efficient SMT Solving for Bit-Vectors and the Extensional Theory of Arrays. Ph.D. thesis, Informatik, Johannes Kepler University Linz (2009)
13. Bruttomesso, R., et al.: A lazy and layered SMT($\mathcal{BV}$) solver for hard industrial verification problems. In: Damm, W., Hermanns, H. (eds.) Computer Aided Verification, pp. 547–560. Springer Berlin Heidelberg, Berlin, Heidelberg (2007). https://doi.org/10.1007/978-3-540-73368-3_54
14. Bryant, R.E., Kroening, D., Ouaknine, J., Seshia, S.A., Strichman, O., Brady, B.A.: An abstraction-based decision procedure for bit-vector arithmetic. Int. J. Softw. Tools Technol. Transf. **11**(2), 95–104 (2009). https://doi.org/10.1007/S10009-009-0101-X

15. Buterin, V.: Ethereum whitepaper (2023). https://ethereum.org/en/whitepaper/
16. Clarke, E., Grumberg, O., Jha, S., Lu, Y., Veith, H.: Counterexample-guided abstraction refinement. In: Emerson, E.A., Sistla, A.P. (eds.) Computer Aided Verification, pp. 154–169. Springer Berlin Heidelberg, Berlin, Heidelberg (2000). https://doi.org/10.1007/10722167_15
17. Dutertre, B.: Yices 2.2. In: Biere, A., Bloem, R. (eds.) Computer Aided Verification, pp. 737–744. Springer International Publishing, Cham (2014). https://doi.org/10.1007/978-3-319-08867-9_49
18. Enderton, H.B.: A mathematical introduction to logic. Academic Press (1972)
19. Fröhlich, A., Biere, A., Wintersteiger, C., Hamadi, Y.: Stochastic local search for satisfiability modulo theories. Proc. AAAI Conf. Artif. Intell. **29**(1) (2015). https://doi.org/10.1609/aaai.v29i1.9372
20. Graham-Lengrand, S., Jovanović, D., Dutertre, B.: Solving Bitvectors with MCSAT: explanations from bits and pieces. In: Peltier, N., Sofronie-Stokkermans, V. (eds.) Automated Reasoning: 10th International Joint Conference, IJCAR 2020, Paris, France, July 1–4, 2020, Proceedings, Part I, pp. 103–121. Springer International Publishing, Cham (2020). https://doi.org/10.1007/978-3-030-51074-9_7
21. Hadarean, L., Bansal, K., Jovanović, D., Barrett, C., Tinelli, C.: A tale of two solvers: eager and lazy approaches to bit-vectors. In: Biere, A., Bloem, R. (eds.) Computer Aided Verification, pp. 680–695. Springer International Publishing, Cham (2014). https://doi.org/10.1007/978-3-319-08867-9_45
22. Jonáš, M., Strejček, J.: Abstraction of bit-vector operations for BDD-based SMT solvers. In: Fischer, B., Uustalu, T. (eds.) Theoretical Aspects of Computing – ICTAC 2018: 15th International Colloquium, Stellenbosch, South Africa, October 16–19, 2018, Proceedings, pp. 273–291. Springer International Publishing, Cham (2018). https://doi.org/10.1007/978-3-030-02508-3_15
23. Jonáš, M., Strejček, J.: Speeding up quantified bit-vector SMT Solvers by Bit-Width Reductions and Extensions. In: Pulina, L., Seidl, M. (eds.) Theory and Applications of Satisfiability Testing – SAT 2020: 23rd International Conference, Alghero, Italy, July 3–10, 2020, Proceedings, pp. 378–393. Springer International Publishing, Cham (2020). https://doi.org/10.1007/978-3-030-51825-7_27
24. Kroening, D., Strichman, O.: Decision Procedures. Springer Berlin Heidelberg, Berlin, Heidelberg (2016)
25. Manzano, M.: Introduction to many-sorted logic. In: Many-sorted logic and its applications, pp. 3–86. John Wiley & Sons, Inc., New York, NY, USA (1993)
26. Moura, L.D., Rueß, H.: Lemmas on demand for satisfiability solvers. In: The 5th International Symposium on the Theory and Applications of Satisfiability Testing, SAT 2002, Cincinnati, USA, May 15, 2002 (2002)
27. de Moura, L., Bjørner, N.: Z3: an efficient SMT solver. In: Ramakrishnan, C.R., Rehof, J. (eds.) Tools and Algorithms for the Construction and Analysis of Systems, pp. 337–340. Springer Berlin Heidelberg, Berlin, Heidelberg (2008). https://doi.org/10.1007/978-3-540-78800-3_24
28. Niemetz, A., Preiner, M.: Ternary propagation-based local search for more bit-precise reasoning. In: 2020 Formal Methods in Computer Aided Design, FMCAD 2020, Haifa, Israel, September 21-24, 2020, pp. 214–224. IEEE (2020). https://doi.org/10.34727/2020/ISBN.978-3-85448-042-6_29, https://doi.org/10.34727/2020/isbn.978-3-85448-042-6_29
29. Niemetz, A., Preiner, M.: Bitwuzla. In: Enea, C., Lal, A. (eds.) Computer Aided Verification: 35th International Conference, CAV 2023, Paris, France, July 17–22, 2023, Proceedings, Part II, pp. 3–17. Springer Nature Switzerland, Cham (2023). https://doi.org/10.1007/978-3-031-37703-7_1

30. Niemetz, A., Preiner, M., Biere, A.: Propagation based local search for bit-precise reasoning. Formal Methods Syst. Des. **51**(3), 608–636 (2017). https://doi.org/10.1007/S10703-017-0295-6, https://doi.org/10.1007/s10703-017-0295-6

31. Niemetz, A., Preiner, M., Reynolds, A., Barrett, C.W., Tinelli, C.: On solving quantified bit-vector constraints using invertibility conditions. Formal Methods Syst. Des. **57**(1), 87–115 (2021)

32. Niemetz, A., Preiner, M., Reynolds, A., Zohar, Y., Barrett, C.W., Tinelli, C.: Towards satisfiability modulo parametric bit-vectors. J. Autom. Reason. **65**(7), 1001–1025 (2021). https://doi.org/10.1007/S10817-021-09598-9

33. Ozdemir, A., Kremer, G., Tinelli, C., Barrett, C.: Satisfiability modulo finite fields. In: Enea, C., Lal, A. (eds.) Computer Aided Verification: 35th International Conference, CAV 2023, Paris, France, July 17–22, 2023, Proceedings, Part II, pp. 163–186. Springer Nature Switzerland, Cham (2023). https://doi.org/10.1007/978-3-031-37703-7_8

34. Reynolds, A., Barbosa, H., Larraz, D., Tinelli, C.: Scalable algorithms for abduction via enumerative syntax-guided synthesis. In: Peltier, N., Sofronie-Stokkermans, V. (eds.) Automated Reasoning: 10th International Joint Conference, IJCAR 2020, Paris, France, July 1–4, 2020, Proceedings, Part I, pp. 141–160. Springer International Publishing, Cham (2020). https://doi.org/10.1007/978-3-030-51074-9_9

35. Zeljić, A., Wintersteiger, C.M., Rümmer, P.: Deciding bit-vector formulas with mcSAT. In: Creignou, N., Le Berre, D. (eds.) Theory and Applications of Satisfiability Testing – SAT 2016, pp. 249–266. Springer International Publishing, Cham (2016). https://doi.org/10.1007/978-3-319-40970-2_16

36. Zohar, Y.: Bit-precise reasoning via int-blasting. In: Finkbeiner, B., Wies, T. (eds.) Verification, Model Checking, and Abstract Interpretation: 23rd International Conference, VMCAI 2022, Philadelphia, PA, USA, January 16–18, 2022, Proceedings, pp. 496–518. Springer International Publishing, Cham (2022). https://doi.org/10.1007/978-3-030-94583-1_24

Hardware Model Checking

The MoXI Model Exchange Tool Suite

Chris Johannsen[1]([✉]), Karthik Nukala[2], Rohit Dureja[3], Ahmed Irfan[2],
Natarajan Shankar[2], Cesare Tinelli[4], Moshe Y. Vardi[5],
and Kristin Yvonne Rozier[1]

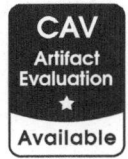

[1] Iowa State University, Ames, USA
{cgjohann,kyrozier}@iastate.edu
[2] SRI International, Menlo Park, USA
{karthik.nukala,ahmed.irfan,
natarajan.shankar}@sri.com
[3] Advanced Micro Devices, Inc., Santa Clara, USA
rohit.dureja@amd.com
[4] The University of Iowa, Iowa City, USA
cesare-tinelli@uiowa.edu
[5] Rice University, Houston, USA
vardi@cs.rice.edu

Abstract. We release the first tool suite implementing MoXI (Model eXchange Interlingua), an intermediate language for symbolic model checking designed to be an international research-community standard and developed by a widespread collaboration under a National Science Foundation (NSF) CISE Community Research Infrastructure initiative. Although we focus here on hardware verification, the MoXI language is useful for software model checking and verification of infinite-state systems in general. MoXI builds on elements of SMT-LIB 2; it is easy to add new theories and operators. Our contributions include: (1) introducing the first tool suite of automated translators into and out of the new model-checking intermediate language; (2) composing an initial example benchmark set enabling the model-checking research community to build future translations; (3) compiling details for utilizing, extending, and improving upon our tool suite, including usage characteristics and initial performance data. Experimental evaluations demonstrate that compiling SMV-language models through MoXI to perform symbolic model checking with the tools from the last Hardware Model Checking Competition performs competitively with model checking directly via NUXMV.

1 Overview

As model checking becomes more integrated into the standard design and verification process for safety-critical systems, the platforms for model-checking research have become more limited (e.g., for the SMV language [47], neither CadenceSMV [46] nor NuSMV [24] are actively maintained; only closed source NUXMV [15] remains). Continuing advances in the field require utilizing

This work was funded by NSF: CCRI Awards #2016592, #2016597, and #2016656.

A. Gurfinkel and V. Ganesh (Eds.): CAV 2024, LNCS 14681, pp. 203–218, 2024.
https://doi.org/10.1007/978-3-031-65627-9_10

higher-level languages that offer sufficient expressive power to describe modern, complex systems and enable validation by industrial system designers. At the same time, contributing advances to back-end model-checking algorithms requires the ability to compare across the full range of state-of-the-art algorithms without regard for which open- or closed-source model checkers implement them or what input languages those tools accept. Comparing new advances in model-checking algorithms to state-of-the-art algorithms requires re-implementing entire model checkers, e.g., [30]. We need a sustainable tool flow that can model the system in the most domain-appropriate high-level modeling language, analyze it with the full range of state-of-the-art model-checking algorithms, and return counterexamples or certificates in the original modeling language.

Our tool suite represents an initial step in unifying model-checking research platforms. We seed an extensible framework designed around a model-checking intermediate language, MoXI (Model eXchange Interlingua). MoXI aims to serve as a common language for the international research community that can connect popular front-end modeling languages with the state of the art in back-end model-checking algorithms. Our vision is that MoXI will enable researchers to model-check a new or extended modeling language simply by writing translators to and from MoXI. Similarly, developing a new backend model-checking algorithm will only require writing a translator to and from MoXI to enable comparisons with existing algorithms and evaluations on every benchmark model, regardless of its original modeling language.

Our initial tool suite accepts models in the higher-level language SMV [47] and efficiently interfaces with the back-end model checkers that competed in the last Hardware Model Checking Competition (HWMCC) [13]. We choose SMV because it is a popular, expressive modeling language successfully used in a wide range of industrial verification efforts [14, 17, 23, 29, 30, 33, 34, 36, 42, 45, 48, 49, 54, 61, 63–65]. SMV is important because, uniquely from other model-checking input languages, it includes high-level constructs critically required for modeling and validating safety-critical systems, such as many aerospace operational systems from Boeing's Wheel Braking System [14] to NASA's Automated Airspace Concept [34, 45, 64, 65] to a variety of Unmanned Aerial Systems [55, 59]. SMV has been used extensively by the hardware model-checking community as well (e.g., at FMCAD [38]) and has appealing qualities that could further the integration of formal methods with the embedded-systems community. Two freely available model checkers, CadenceSMV [46] and NuSMV [24] (which is integrated into today's nuXmv [52]), previously provided viable research platforms. However, today, CadenceSMV's 32-bit pre-compiled binary and nuXmv's closed-source releases are no longer suitable for research, e.g., into improved model-checking algorithms. We provide accessibility to continue the progression of high-level language model checking in SMV via an open-source research platform that allows the use of new algorithms under the hood.

Pushing the state of the art are several open-source, award-winning model-checking tools, including AVR [35], Pono [44], BtorMC [51], and ABC [18].

These tools support a hardware-oriented bit-level input language like AIGER or a bit-precise, word-level format like BTOR2. Unfortunately, such languages do not enable the direct modeling of modern complex systems as SMV does, hindering validation efforts. For instance, it is challenging to convince industrial system designers that AIGER models correctly capture their higher-level systems. Perhaps driven by HWMCC, most systems for translating from high-level models to AIGER currently focus on hardware designs, without providing a natural way to describe other computational systems, e.g., embedded systems. Also, the problem of translating counterexamples produced by low-level model-checking algorithms back into meaningful counterexamples for a non-hardware-centric higher-level language model, such as one in SMV, remains a challenge.

Section 2 provides a basic introduction to MoXI, sufficient to enable understanding of the tool suite functionality; a description of the full language and its semantics appears in [57,58]. Section 3 details the extensible research and verification suite of tools, including translators between the languages SMV, MoXI (in concrete and JSON dialects), and BTOR2; utilities for validation; and a full model-checking implementation. Here, we provide a detailed example of behaviorally equivalent models in SMV, MoXI, and BTOR2. Our efforts to validate their correctness appear in Sect. 4. Section 5 demonstrates the efficiency of model checking SMV-language models with a tool portfolio including NUXMV and via translation through MoXI, which performs better than checking with NUXMV alone. The tool[1] and all of the benchmarks[2] used in this experiment are available online for others to utilize in building additional translators to extend our tool suite and the use of MoXI as an intermediate language for symbolic model checking. Section 6 concludes with a discussion of future work.

2   Intermediate Language

MoXI (detailed in [57]) is an intermediate language designed to serve as a common input and output standard for model checkers for finite- and infinite-state systems. It is general enough to encode high-level modeling languages like SMV yet simple enough to enable efficient model checking, including through low-level languages such as BTOR2 or SAT/SMT-based engines. Key features include a simple and easily parsable syntax, a rich set of data types, minimal syntactic sugar (at least for now), well-understood formal semantics, and a small but comprehensive set of commands.

MoXI maximizes machine-readability. Therefore, it does not support several human-interface features found in high-level languages such as SMV, TLA+ [43], PROMELA [37], Simulink [27], SCADE [28], and Lustre [19]; nor does it directly support the full features of hardware modeling languages such as VHDL [40], or Verilog [39]. However, many models and queries expressed in these languages can be reduced to MoXI representations. MoXI development was directly informed by previous intermediate formats for formal verification, their successful

---

[1] https://github.com/ModelChecker/moxi-mc-flow.
[2] https://modelchecker.github.io/benchmarks.

applications, and their limitations. The eventual form of MoXI stems from a combination of previous work as well as direct conversations with model checking and SMT researchers, including the developers of AIGER [2–4], BTOR2 [51], Kind 2 [22], NuSMV [21], nuXmv [16,20], SAL/SALLY [9,32,50], VMT [26,41], and SMT-LIB (the standard I/O language for SMT solvers) [6,7]. MoXI also benefited from the feedback from a technical advisor board of prominent researchers and practitioners in academia and industry [58].

MoXI's base logic is the same as that of SMT-LIB Version 2: many-sorted first-order logic with equality, quantifiers, *let* binders, and algebraic datatypes. MoXI extends this logic to (first-order) temporal logic while adopting a discrete and linear notion of time with standard finite and infinite trace-based semantics. MoXI also extends the SMT-LIB language with new commands for defining and verifying multi-component reactive systems. For the latter, it focuses on the specification and checking of reachability conditions (or, indirectly, state and transition invariants) and deadlocks, possibly under fairness conditions on system inputs. Each system definition command defines a transition system by specifying an initial state condition, a transition relation, and system invariants. These are provided as SMT formulas, with minimal syntactic restrictions, for flexibility and future extensibility. Each defined system is parameterized by a state signature, provided as a sequence of typed variables, and can be expressed as the synchronous composition of other systems.[3] The signature partitions state variables into input, output, and local variables. Each system verification command expresses one or more reachability queries over a previously defined system. The queries can be conditional on environmental assumptions on the system's inputs and fairness conditions on its executions. Together with the ability to write observer systems, this allows the expression of arbitrary LTL specifications via standard encodings [56]. Responses to a system verification command can contain (finite or lasso) witness traces for reachable properties or proof certificates for unreachable ones.

Figure 1 contains an example (adapted from [5]) of a three-bit counter and its modular definition in MoXI, together with a *reachability* query and a sample response to the query. Figure 2 contains an extension of that model with an observer system and a query for checking the observational equivalence of the three-bit counter with a bit-vector counter of matching width. The various components of each system definition or check command are provided as attribute-value pairs, following the syntax of SMT-LIB annotations. Transition predicates use primed variables to denote next-state values.

3   Tool Suite

We provide a suite of tools for translating into and out of MoXI and validating MoXI scripts. The tools are implemented in type-annotated Python with a focus on finite-state systems (for now). Figure 3 illustrates the end-to-end toolchain for model checking using MoXI, including relationships between the various tools.

---

[3] We plan to include asynchronous composition in a later release.

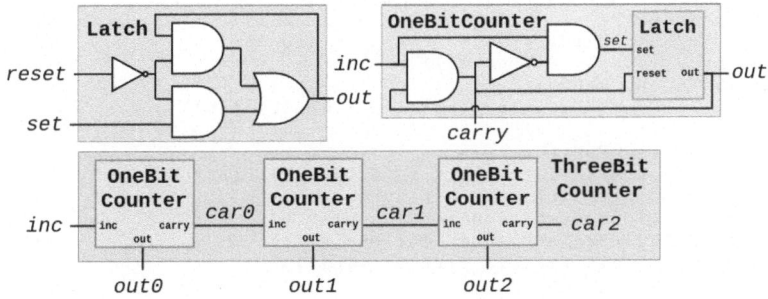

```
1  (define-system Latch :input ((set Bool) (reset Bool))
2    :output ((out Bool))
3    :init (not out)
4    :trans ((= out' (or (and set (not reset))
5                        (and (not reset) out))))
6  )
7  (define-system OneBitCounter :input ((inc Bool))
8    :output ((out Bool) (carry Bool)) :local ((set Bool))
9    :subsys (L (Latch set carry out))
10   :inv (and (= set (and inc (not carry)))
11             (= carry (and inc out)))
12 )
13 (define-system ThreeBitCounter :input ((inc Bool))
14   :output ((out0 Bool) (out1 Bool) (out2 Bool))
15   :local ((car0 Bool) (car1 Bool) (car2 Bool))
16   :init (and (not out0) (not out1) (not out2))
17   :subsys (C1 (OneBitCounter inc out0 car0))
18   :subsys (C2 (OneBitCounter car0 out1 car1))
19   :subsys (C3 (OneBitCounter car1 out2 car2))
20 )
21 (check-system ThreeBitCounter :input ((inc Bool))
22   :output ((out0 Bool) (out1 Bool) (out2 Bool))
23   :local ((car0 Bool) (car1 Bool) (car2 Bool))
24   :reachable (r (and (not out0) out1 (not out2)))
25   :query (query1 (r))
26 )
```

```
1  (check-system-response ThreeBitCounter
2    :query (query1 :result sat :trace query1_trace)
3    :trace (query1_trace :prefix query1_trail)
4    :trail (query1_trail
5      (0 (out0 0) (out1 0) (out2 0) (inc 1) (car0 0) (car1 0) (car2 0))
6      (1 (out0 1) (out1 0) (out2 0) (inc 1) (car0 1) (car1 0) (car2 0))
7      (2 (out0 0) (out1 1) (out2 0) (inc 1) (car0 0) (car1 0) (car2 0))
8  ))
```

Fig. 1. (Top) The three-bit counter circuit composes three one-bit counters together, where each counter uses a latch to store that counter's current value. (Middle) A MoXI implementation of the circuit uses **define-system** (lines 1–20) to describe and compose each counter component. It then queries (lines 21–26) whether the counter can output 2. (Bottom) A possible query response provides a trace showing that the counter outputs 2 within 3 execution steps. We write **Bool** values as integers here for compactness.

```
27  (set-logic QF_BV)
28  (define-system BitVecCounter :input ((inc Bool))
29    :output ((out (_ BitVec 3)))
30    :init (= out #b000)
31    :trans (= out' (ite inc (bvadd out #b001) out))
32  )
33  (define-system Monitor
34    :local ((inc Bool) (out_bit (_ BitVec 3)) (out_bv (_ BitVec 3))
35      (bit0 Bool) (bit1 Bool) (bit2 Bool))
36    :subsys (C1 (ThreeBitCounter inc bit0 bit1 bit2 ))
37    :subsys (C2 (BitVecCounter inc out_bv ))
38    :inv (= out_bit (to_bv3 bit0 bit1 bit2))
39  )
40  (check-system Monitor
41    :local ((inc Bool) (out_bit (_ BitVec 3)) (out_bv (_ BitVec 3))
42      (bit0 Bool) (bit1 Bool) (bit2 Bool))
43    :reachable (reach1 (distinct out_bit out_bv))
44    :query (query1 (reach1))
45  )
```

```
1  (check-system-response Monitor
2    :query (query1 :result unsat)
3  )
```

Fig. 2. (Top) Extending the MoXI model shown in Fig. 1, a `Monitor` (lines 33–40) computes the output for a `ThreeBitCounter` and a bit-vector-based counter (lines 28–32). The function `to_bv3` (definition is omitted for space constraints) converts bit values to the corresponding bit-vector value. The `check-system` command (lines 40–45) queries whether their outputs can possibly differ. (Bottom) The `check-system-response` reports an unsatisfiable query, proving the two counters equivalent.

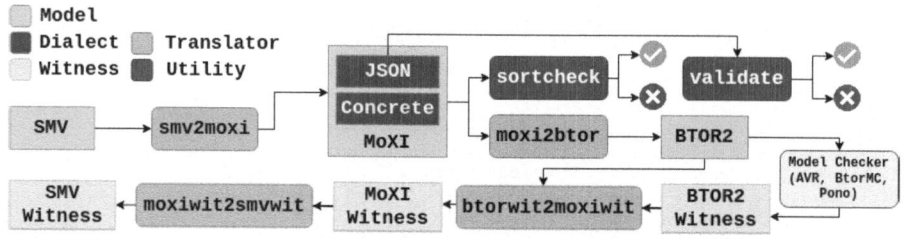

Fig. 3. Starting with a NUXMV model, `smv2moxi` generates a behaviorally equivalent MoXI model in either the MoXI concrete syntax or a JSON dialect syntax. `moxi2btor` translates this MoXI model to a set of BTOR2 models, one for each query, which an off-the-shelf model checker (e.g., AVR [35], PONO [44], BTORMC [51]) solves. Then, `btorwit2moxiwit` creates a MoXI witness from the BTOR2 witness using the BTOR2 model to map variable names properly, and similarly for `moxiwit2smvwit`. The sort checker validates MoXI input against any of the SMT-LIB logics listed in Sect. 3.2. The validator checks JSON dialect input against our provided schema.

3.1   Translators

The tool suite provides four translators that take as input a model, query, or witness specified in a source language and output a *behaviorally equivalent* model, query, or witness in the configured target language.

(1) smv2moxi translates specifications written in (a common subset of) the SMV language into MoXI. Broadly, this tool supports Finite State Machine (FSM) definitions (NuXMV manual, Sect. 2.3 [16]). It currently supports only statically typed expressions; for example, all module instantiations of the same defined module must share the same signature. (For a module M with parameters p1 and p2, the types of p1, p2 must be the same across all instantiations of M.) Fig. 4 shows that the translation preserves the hierarchy between the SMV modules and submodule instantiations.

The MoXI encoding captures SMV macro and function declarations (DEFINE, FUN), variable declarations (VAR, IVAR, FROZENVAR), state machine declarations (INIT, TRANS, INVAR, ASSIGN), invariant specifications (AG [property], INVARSPEC) and fairness constraints (FAIRNESS, JUSTICE, COMPASSION). To support LTL specifications (LTLSPEC), smv2moxi runs PANDA [56], an open-source tool offering a portfolio of LTL-to-symbolic automaton translations in SMV format.

The smv2moxi tool consists of (1) preprocessing that renames identifiers deviating from the SMV grammar (discussed in Sect. 4); (2) running the C preprocessor (SMV supports C-style macros) and PANDA [56] (for LTL specifications); (3) parsing via a SLY-generated [8] parser; (4) running an SMV type checker; (5) translating to MoXI. We emphasize that tool guarantees apply to *well-formed* SMV models as determined by NuXMV.

(2) moxi2btor translates MoXI to BTOR2 by creating a BTOR2 file for each :query attribute in each check-system command. Some crucial differences between MoXI and BTOR2 present non-trivial challenges. Firstly, BTOR2 does not support hierarchical models. moxi2btor flattens the system hierarchy in its translation as a result. Secondly, MoXI allows for declarative-style initial, transition, and invariant conditions while BTOR2 allows only assignment-style. Figure 4 shows how moxi2btor encodes each system's conditions using three variants of each variable. Thirdly, a MoXI query with multiple reachability properties asks for a trace that eventually satisfies each property. In BTOR2, multiple **bad** properties in a file ask for a trace that eventually satisfies at least one such property. Figure 4 again shows how the translation resolves this difference. The moxi2btor tool's workflow consists of (1) parsing via a SLY-generated parser [8]; (2) running sortcheck (Sect. 3.2); (3) translating to a set of BTOR2 files, each behaviorally equivalent to its corresponding :query.

(3) btorwit2moxiwit translates BTOR2 witnesses to MoXI witnesses using the check-system-response syntax. It assumes moxi2btor created the BTOR2 input files used to generate the witness and uses information that moxi2btor encodes in the comments of each BTOR2 file, e.g., to map bit vectors to enumeration values for variables of such sorts.

(4) moxiwit2smvwit translates MoXI witnesses to SMV-language witnesses.

SMV	MoXI	BTOR2

```
SMV                      MoXI                           BTOR2

                         (set-logic QF_BV)              1   sort bitvec 8
MODULE Delay(i,o)        (define-system Delay           2   sort bitvec 1
INIT                       :input ((i (_ BitVec 8))     3   state 1 D.o.init
  (o = 0ud8_0);                    (o (_ BitVec 8)))    4   state 1 D.o.cur
TRANS                      :init (= o #x00)             5   state 1 D.o.next
  (next(o) = i);           :trans (= o' i)             6   state 1 D.i.cur
                         )                              7   state 1 o.cur
MODULE main              (define-system main           8   state 1 i.cur
IVAR                       :input ((i (_ BitVec 8)))   9   init 1 4 3
i: unsigned                :output ((o (_ BitVec 8)))  10  next 1 4 5
   word[8];                :local ((D.i (_ BitVec 8)) 11  constd 1 0
VAR                                (D.o (_ BitVec 8))) 12  eq 2 3 11
o: unsigned                :inv (and                   13  constraint 12
   word[8];                  (= D.i i) (= D.o o))      14  eq 2 5 6
D: Delay(i,o);             :subsys                      15  constraint 14
                             (D (Delay D.i D.o))        16  constd 2 1
                         )                              17  constraint 16
INVARSPEC                (check-system main            18  eq 2 4 7
! (o = 0ud8_2);            :input ((i (_ BitVec 8)))   19  eq 2 6 8
                           :output ((o (_ BitVec 8)))  20  and 2 19 18
                           :local ((D.i (_ BitVec 8)) 21  constraint 20
                                   (D.o (_ BitVec 8))) 22  constd 2 0
                           :reachable (rch             23  constd 1 2
                             (not (not (= o #x02))))   24  eq 2 7 23
                           :query (qry_rch (rch))      25  not 2 24
                         )                              26  not 2 25
                                                        27  state 2 F_rch
                                                        28  init 2 27 22
                                                        29  ite 2 27 16 26
                                                        30  next 2 27 29
                                                        31  bad 27
```

Fig. 4. The toolchain translates the SMV model for a delay circuit on the left to the MoXI model in the center by creating a **define-system** command for each **MODULE**. It then generates the BTOR2 model on the right, introducing three variants of each **check-system** variable (.init, .cur, .next) and setting constraints such as the :init and :next of **Delay** on lines 13 and 15 respectively. The BTOR2 "flag" variable F_rch (line 27) encodes if formula rch has been true at least once during the execution; the presence of multiple BTOR2 bad properties asks for a trace where at least one such property is eventually true, we conjunct the *flag* variables to ask for a trace where every property is eventually true.

3.2   Utilities

sortcheck We provide a sort-checker for MoXI that supports the following SMT-LIB logics: QF_BV, QF_ABV, QF_LIA, QF_NIA, QF_LRA, and QF_NRA.

validate We define a JSON Schema for MoXI and support a JSON dialect for MoXI in our tools. Given the evolving nature of new languages and their standards, tool writers often pay an unnecessary overhead keeping front-end tools up to date. By supporting the representation of MoXI constructs in the JSON dialect, we expect to facilitate tool development, improve tool interoperability, and ensure conformance to the language standard. Tool writers can use off-the-shelf JSON parsers (e.g., simdjson, RapidJSON) to obtain industrial-strength MoXI parsers in the language they choose "for free." We plan to include a JSON schema for each MoXI release, enabling seamless front-end compatibility with the latest MoXI standard along with language/platform independence. The `validate` utility invokes a JSON validator from Python's `jsonschema` package to validate a MoXI script (in the JSON dialect) against the MoXI JSON schema.

4 Tool Suite Validation

We validate our tools using a combination of manual inspection, sort checking of translated output, and comparing witnesses between those generated by NUXMV and our end-to-end tool suite. We use CATBTOR [51] for sort checking and BTORMC, AVR, and PONO for bounded model checking (BMC) of BTOR2 files. For benchmark generation, we use the set of NUXMV input files provided in the most recent release of NUXMV (Fig. 5).

SMV	MoXI	BTOR2
| ``` 
Trace Description:
  nuxmv2btor
  counterexample
Trace Type:
  Counterexample
-> State: 1.1 <-
  D.i = 0ud8_2
  D.o = 0ud8_0
  o = 0ud8_0
-> Input: 1.2 <-
  i = 0ud8_0
-> State: 1.2 <-
  D.i = 0ud8_0
  D.o = 0ud8_2
  o = 0ud8_2
``` | ``` 
(check-system-response main
  :query (qry_rch
    :result sat
    :trace qry_rch_trace
  )
  :trace (qry_rch_trace
    :prefix qry_rch_trail
  )
  :trail (qry_rch_trail
    (0 (D.i #b00000010)
       (D.o #b00000000)
       (o #b00000000)
       (i #b00000010))
    (1 (D.i #b00000000)
       (D.o #b00000010)
       (o #b00000010)
       (i #b00000000))
))
``` | ``` 
sat ___ b0 ___ #0
0 00000000 D.o.init
1 00000000 D.o.cur
2 00000010 D.o.next
3 00000010 D.i.cur
4 00000000 o.cur
5 00000010 i.cur
6 0 F_rch
#1
1 00000010 D.o.cur
2 00000000 D.o.next
3 00000000 D.i.cur
4 00000010 o.cur
5 00000000 i.cur
#2
1 00000000 D.o.cur
4 00000000 o.cur
6 1 F_rch
``` |

Fig. 5. The witness translation after model checking the BTOR2 file in Fig. 4 works right to left: it maps each BTOR2 `.cur` variable to its MoXI counterpart and discards the last frame of the witness due to the delay caused by using *flag* variables. Similarly, it maps each MoXI variable to its SMV counterpart.

Manual Inspection. We provide an initial set of hand-written MoXI benchmarks to perform manual validation. Each benchmark is well-sorted according to `sortcheck`, generates well-sorted BTOR2 via `moxi2btor` according to CATBTOR, and generates correct, manually-inspected witnesses via BTORMC and `btorwit2moxiwit`.[4]

Sort Checked Translations. Using the benchmarks distributed with NUXMV as input, we check that the output of `smv2moxi` and `moxi2btor` are well-sorted according to `sortcheck` and CATBTOR. We discovered discrepancies in benchmarks distributed with NUXMV while developing these utilities, where the benchmarks did not conform to the grammar defined in Chap. 2 of the NUXMV User

---

[4] Many thanks to Daniel Larraz for writing many of the MoXI examples.
```

Manual [16] but were accepted by NUXMV nonetheless, particularly concerning identifiers. The preprocessor of smv2moxi transforms these identifiers into valid ones. There were also numerous ill-typed benchmarks that smv2moxi's type checker correctly rejects.

Output Comparison. Using the NUXMV benchmarks again as input, we run NUXMV and our tool suite to generate witnesses for each specification. Both NUXMV and our tool suite agree on the result of every model-checking query. Section 5 describes how our toolchain (using BTORMC, AVR, or PONO as its back end) shows a similar number of timeouts compared with NUXMV when the latter is set to use BMC or k-induction.

5   Benchmarks

We provide an initial set of MOXI benchmarks for the model-checking community generated from the set of SMV input files provided in the most recent release of NUXMV. Noting that many of the SMV benchmarks are results of a BTOR2 to NUXMV translation themselves, we stress that this set of benchmarks is intended to be an *initial* set. We expect to achieve greater benchmark diversity with continued toolchain development and increased adoption of MOXI by other researchers.

Experimental Evaluation. We compare the end-to-end performance of model-checking SMV-language models with a portfolio comprising NUXMV and BTOR2 model checkers: AVR, PONO, and BTORMC, on a set of 960 QF_ABV-compatible SMV benchmarks, i.e., SMV models with boolean, word or array types. We use the HWMCC 2020 versions of AVR and PONO, the version of BTORMC from the latest version of Boolector [51], and the latest public release of NUXMV (version 2.0.0). Each checker is configured with a 1-h time limit and 8GB memory limit and runs BMC [12] and k-induction [60] with a max bound of 1000. (We do not run BTORMC with k-induction due to a bug in its implementation.)

Figure 6 shows our evaluation, with portfolio performance depicted as *virtualbest (vb)*. While we consider this a proof-of-concept evaluation, we observe that SMV-language model checking using BTOR2 model checkers, enabled via a translation through MOXI, delivers superior performance on unsafe queries compared to model checking with NUXMV alone: vb-bmc solves 57% more benchmarks than NUXMV-bmc while ensuring all BTOR2 witnesses are correctly translated to SMV traces. We measure competitive performance with vb-kind solving 6% more benchmarks than NUXMV-kind for safe queries. The vb performance gains are due to its ability to use a variety of model checkers with different SMT solver backends of varying strengths, e.g., NUXMV uses MathSAT [25], AVR uses Yices [31], and PONO uses Boolector [51], while ensuring correct model and witness translation through MOXI. Section 4 of Rozier et al. [57] includes experimental data using each tool's IC3-based algorithms.

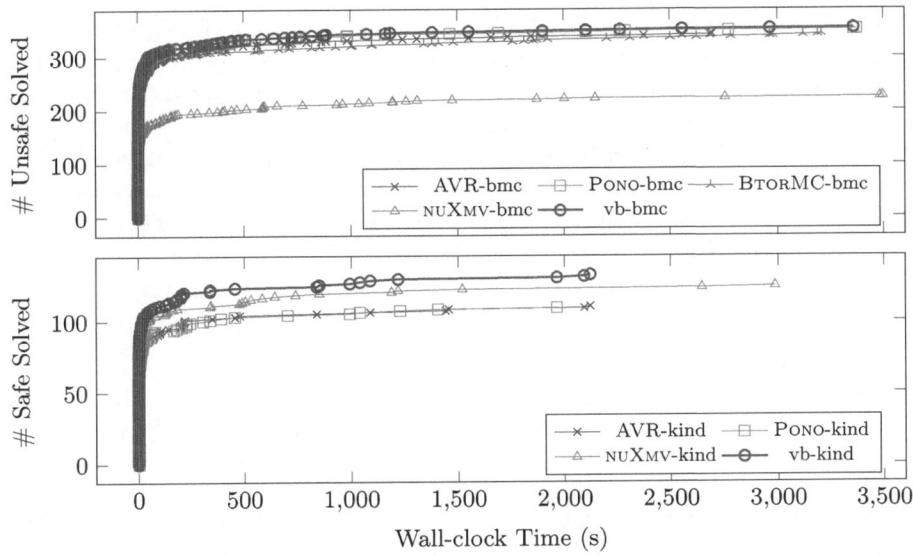

Fig. 6. Performance comparison on unsafe and safe queries with BMC and k-induction across different model checkers. vb-* represents the virtual best solver. Wall-clock time for the non-NUXMV plots includes translation time.

6   Conclusion and Future Work

The presented tool suite provides the foundational step in developing an open-source, state-of-the-art symbolic model-checking framework for the research community. It constitutes the first tool support for the new intermediate language MoXI, the first experimental evidence of the potential for efficient translation through MoXI, and a basis upon which the hardware and software model-checking communities can build. Adding support for checking models in a high-level modeling language is now as easy as adding a translator between that language and MoXI to this tool suite. Similarly, experimenting with a novel back-end model-checking algorithm to check all supported input modeling languages only requires writing a new MoXI translator interfacing with that algorithm. Benchmarking against other model-checking algorithms no longer require re-implementing existing tools to achieve an apples-to-apples comparison.

Connecting this toolchain to existing tools enables the immediate application of verification techniques for BTOR2 to MoXI beyond just hardware model checkers. For example, a software model checker can verify a MoXI model via BTOR2C [11], making at least 59 other backend verifiers for MoXI available [10].

This release enables future instantiations of HWMCC [13] to add competition tracks centered around MoXI, with extensions from the model-checking research community. Specifying, proving correct, and extracting efficient C code for our translation using a theorem prover such as PVS [53] would provide an additional trusted translation between languages beyond the validation techniques in Sect. 4.

We are writing a back end to Yosys [62], the open-source RTL synthesis framework, to generate files directly from Verilog designs and facilitate a more extensive set of realistic benchmarks to add to the initial set in Sect. 5. Additionally, once MoXI certificates are fully defined, we can translate BTOR2-CERT [1] certificates back to MoXI from BTOR2-CERT-supported verifiers. Finally, we expect developers of model checkers for higher-level modeling languages than a language like BTOR2 may choose to support MoXI directly. We have work in this direction underway for the Kind 2 checker [22].

References

1. Ádám, Z., Beyer, D., Chien, P.C., Lee, N.Z., Sirrenberg, N.: Btor2-Cert: a certifying hardware-verification framework using software analyzers. In: Finkbeiner, B., Kovács, L. (eds.) TACAS 2024. LNCS, vol. 14572, pp. 129–149. Springer, Cham (2024). https://doi.org/10.1007/978-3-031-57256-2_7
2. The AIGER and-inverter graph (AIG) format version 20071012. http://fmv.jku.at/aiger/FORMAT. Accessed 25 July 2016
3. AIGER 1.9 and beyond. http://fmv.jku.at/hwmcc11/beyond1.pdf. Accessed 25 July 2016
4. AIGER website. http://fmv.jku.at/aiger/. Accessed 25 July 2016
5. Alur, R.: Principles of Cyber-physical Systems. MIT Press, Cambridge (2015)
6. Barrett, C., Fontaine, P., Tinelli, C.: The Satisfiability Modulo Theories Library (SMT-LIB). https://smt-lib.org
7. Barrett, C., Stump, A., Tinelli, C.: The SMT-LIB standard: version 2.0. In: Gupta, A., Kroening, D. (eds.) Proceedings of the 8th International Workshop on Satisfiability Modulo Theories (Edinburgh, UK) (2010)
8. Beazley, D.: SLY (sly lex yacc) (2018). https://sly.readthedocs.io/en/latest/
9. Bensalem, S., et al.: An overview of SAL. In: Holloway, C.M. (ed.) LFM 2000: Fifth NASA Langley Formal Methods Workshop, pp. 187–196. NASA Langley Research Center, Hampton, June 2000. http://www.csl.sri.com/papers/lfm2000/
10. Beyer, D.: State of the art in software verification and witness validation: SV-COMP 2024. In: Finkbeiner, B., Kovács, L. (eds) TACAS 2024. LNCS, vol. 14572, pp. 299–329. Springer, Cham (2024). https://doi.org/10.1007/978-3-031-57256-2_15
11. Beyer, D., Chien, P.C., Lee, N.Z.: Bridging hardware and software analysis with BTOR2C: a word-level-circuit-to-C translator. In: Sankaranarayanan, S., Sharygina, N. (eds.) TACAS 2023. LNCS, vol. 13994, pp. 152–172. Springer, Cham (2023). https://doi.org/10.1007/978-3-031-30820-8_12
12. Biere, A., Cimatti, A., Clarke, E., Zhu, Y.: Symbolic model checking without BDDs. In: Cleaveland, W.R. (ed.) TACAS 1999. LNCS, vol. 1579, pp. 193–207. Springer, Heidelberg (1999). https://doi.org/10.1007/3-540-49059-0_14
13. Biere, A., Froleyks, N., Preiner, M.: Hardware Model Checking Competition (HWMCC) (2020). https://fmv.jku.at/hwmcc20/index.html
14. Bozzano, M., et al.: Formal design and safety analysis of AIR6110 wheel brake system. In: Kroening, D., Păsăreanu, C.S. (eds.) CAV 2015. LNCS, vol. 9206, pp. 518–535. Springer, Cham (2015). https://doi.org/10.1007/978-3-319-21690-4_36
15. Bozzano, M., et al.: nuXmv 1.0 User Manual. Technical report, FBK - Via Sommarive 18, 38055 Povo (Trento) - Italy (2014)

16. Bozzano, M., et al.: nuXmv 2.0. 0 user manual. Fondazione Bruno Kessler, Technical report, Trento, Italy (2019)
17. Bozzano, M., Cimatti, A., Katoen, J.-P., Nguyen, V.Y., Noll, T., Roveri, M.: The COMPASS approach: correctness, modelling and performability of aerospace systems. In: Buth, B., Rabe, G., Seyfarth, T. (eds.) SAFECOMP 2009. LNCS, vol. 5775, pp. 173–186. Springer, Heidelberg (2009). https://doi.org/10.1007/978-3-642-04468-7_15
18. Brayton, R., Mishchenko, A.: ABC: an academic industrial-strength verification tool. In: Touili, T., Cook, B., Jackson, P. (eds.) CAV 2010. LNCS, vol. 6174, pp. 24–40. Springer, Heidelberg (2010). https://doi.org/10.1007/978-3-642-14295-6_5
19. Caspi, P., Pilaud, D., Halbwachs, N., Plaice, J.: LUSTRE: a declarative language for programming synchronous systems. In: Proceedings of the 14th Annual ACM Symposium on Principles of Programming Languages, pp. 178–188 (1987)
20. Cavada, R., et al.: The NUXMV symbolic model checker. In: Biere, A., Bloem, R. (eds.) CAV 2014. LNCS, vol. 8559, pp. 334–342. Springer, Cham (2014). https://doi.org/10.1007/978-3-319-08867-9_22
21. Cavada, R., et al.: NuSMV 2.6 user manual (2016)
22. Champion, A., Mebsout, A., Sticksel, C., Tinelli, C.: The KIND 2 model checker. In: Chaudhuri, S., Farzan, A. (eds.) CAV 2016. LNCS, vol. 9780, pp. 510–517. Springer, Cham (2016). https://doi.org/10.1007/978-3-319-41540-6_29
23. Choi, Y., Heimdahl, M.: Model checking software requirement specifications using domain reduction abstraction. In: IEEE ASE, pp. 314–317 (2003)
24. Cimatti, A., et al.: NuSMV 2: an opensource tool for symbolic model checking. In: Brinksma, E., Larsen, K.G. (eds.) CAV 2002. LNCS, vol. 2404, pp. 359–364. Springer, Heidelberg (2002). https://doi.org/10.1007/3-540-45657-0_29
25. Cimatti, A., Griggio, A., Schaafsma, B.J., Sebastiani, R.: The MathSAT5 SMT solver. In: Piterman, N., Smolka, S.A. (eds.) TACAS 2013. LNCS, vol. 7795, pp. 93–107. Springer, Heidelberg (2013). https://doi.org/10.1007/978-3-642-36742-7_7
26. Cimatti, A., Griggio, A., Tonetta, S., et al.: The VMT-LIB language and tools. In: Proceedings of the 20th Internal Workshop on Satisfiability ModuloTheories co-located with the 11th International Joint Conference on Automated Reasoning {(IJCAR} 2022) part of the 8th Federated Logic Conference (FLoC 2022), Haifa, Israel, 11–12 August 2022, vol. 3185, pp. 80–89. CEUR-WS. org (2022)
27. Documentation, S.: Simulation and model-based design (2020). https://www.mathworks.com/products/simulink.html
28. Documentation, SCADE: Ansys SCADE Suite (2023). https://www.ansys.com/products/embedded-software/ansys-scade-suite
29. Dureja, R., Rozier, E.W.D., Rozier, K.Y.: A case study in safety, security, and availability of wireless-enabled aircraft communication networks. In: Proceedings of the 17th AIAA Aviation Technology, Integration, and Operations Conference (AVIATION). American Institute of Aeronautics and Astronautics, June 2017. https://doi.org/10.2514/6.2017-3112
30. Dureja, R., Rozier, K.Y.: FuseIC3: an algorithm for checking large design spaces. In: Proceedings of Formal Methods in Computer-Aided Design (FMCAD), Vienna, Austria. IEEE/ACM, October 2017
31. Dutertre, B.: Yices 2.2. In: Biere, A., Bloem, R. (eds.) CAV 2014. LNCS, vol. 8559, pp. 737–744. Springer, Cham (2014). https://doi.org/10.1007/978-3-319-08867-9_49
32. Dutertre, B., Jovanović, D., Navas, J.A.: Verification of fault-tolerant protocols with sally. In: Dutle, A., Muñoz, C., Narkawicz, A. (eds.) NFM 2018. LNCS, vol.

10811, pp. 113–120. Springer, Cham (2018). https://doi.org/10.1007/978-3-319-77935-5_8

33. Gan, X., Dubrovin, J., Heljanko, K.: A symbolic model checking approach to verifying satellite onboard software. Sci. Comput. Programm. (2013). http://dx.doi.org/10.1016/j.scico.2013.03.005

34. Gario, M., Cimatti, A., Mattarei, C., Tonetta, S., Rozier, K.Y.: Model checking at scale: automated air traffic control design space exploration. In: Chaudhuri, S., Farzan, A. (eds.) CAV 2016. LNCS, vol. 9780, pp. 3–22. Springer, Cham (2016). https://doi.org/10.1007/978-3-319-41540-6_1

35. Goel, A., Sakallah, K.: AVR: abstractly verifying reachability. In: TACAS 2020. LNCS, vol. 12078, pp. 413–422. Springer, Cham (2020). https://doi.org/10.1007/978-3-030-45190-5_23

36. Gribaudo, M., Horváth, A., Bobbio, A., Tronci, E., Ciancamerla, E., Minichino, M.: Model-checking based on fluid petri nets for the temperature control system of the ICARO co-generative plant. In: Anderson, S., Felici, M., Bologna, S. (eds.) SAFECOMP 2002. LNCS, vol. 2434, pp. 273–283. Springer, Heidelberg (2002). https://doi.org/10.1007/3-540-45732-1_27

37. Holzmann, G.: Design and Validation of Computer Protocols. Prentice-Hall Int, Editions (1991)

38. Hunt, W.: FMCAD organization home page. http://www.cs.utexas.edu/users/hunt/FMCAD/

39. IEEE: IEEE standard for Verilog hardware description language (2005)

40. IEEE: IEEE standard for VHDL language reference manual (2019)

41. Kessler, F.B.: Verification modulo theories. https://vmt-lib.fbk.eu/. Accessed 30 Sept 2017

42. Lahtinen, J., Valkonen, J., Björkman, K., Frits, J., Niemelä, I., Heljanko, K.: Model checking of safety-critical software in the nuclear engineering domain. Reliab. Eng. Syst. Safety **105**(0), 104–113 (2012). http://www.sciencedirect.com/science/article/pii/S0951832012000555

43. Lamport, L.: Specifying Systems: The TLA+ Language and Tools for Hardware and Software Engineers. Addison-Wesley, Reading (2002)

44. Mann, M., et al.: Pono: a flexible and extensible SMT-based model checker. In: Silva, A., Leino, K.R.M. (eds.) CAV 2021, Part II. LNCS, vol. 12760, pp. 461–474. Springer, Cham (2021). https://doi.org/10.1007/978-3-030-81688-9_22

45. Mattarei, C., Cimatti, A., Gario, M., Tonetta, S., Rozier, K.Y.: Comparing different functional allocations in automated air traffic control design. In: Proceedings of Formal Methods in Computer-Aided Design (FMCAD 2015). IEEE/ACM, Austin, Texas, U.S.A, September 2015

46. McMillan, K.: The SMV language. Technical report, Cadence Berkeley Lab (1999)

47. McMillan, K.L.: Symbolic Model Checking, chap. The SMV System, pp. 61–85. Springer, Boston (1993). https://doi.org/10.1007/978-1-4615-3190-6_4

48. Miller, S.P.: Will this be formal? In: Mohamed, O.A., Muñoz, C., Tahar, S. (eds.) TPHOLs 2008. LNCS, vol. 5170, pp. 6–11. Springer, Heidelberg (2008). https://doi.org/10.1007/978-3-540-71067-7_2

49. Miller, S.P., Tribble, A.C., Whalen, M.W., Per, M., Heimdahl, E.: Proving the shalls. STTT **8**(4–5), 303–319 (2006)

50. de Moura, L., Owre, S., Shankar, N.: The SAL language manual. CSL Technical report SRI-CSL-01-02 (Rev. 2), SRI Int'l, 333 Ravenswood Ave., Menlo Park, CA 94025, August 2003

51. Niemetz, A., Preiner, M., Wolf, C., Biere, A.: BTOR2 , BtorMC and Boolector 3.0. In: Chockler, H., Weissenbacher, G. (eds.) CAV 2018. LNCS, vol. 10981, pp. 587–595. Springer, Cham (2018). https://doi.org/10.1007/978-3-319-96145-3_32
52. The nuXmv model checker (2015). https://nuxmv.fbk.eu/
53. Owre, S., Rushby, J.M., Shankar, N.: PVS: a prototype verification system. In: Kapur, D. (ed.) CADE 1992. LNCS, vol. 607, pp. 748–752. Springer, Heidelberg (1992). https://doi.org/10.1007/3-540-55602-8_217
54. Lomuscio, A., Łasica, T., Penczek, W.: Bounded model checking for interpreted systems: preliminary experimental results. In: Hinchey, M.G., Rash, J.L., Truszkowski, W.F., Rouff, C., Gordon-Spears, D. (eds.) FAABS 2002. LNCS (LNAI), vol. 2699, pp. 115–125. Springer, Heidelberg (2003). https://doi.org/10.1007/978-3-540-45133-4_10
55. Reinbacher, T., Rozier, K.Y., Schumann, J.: Temporal-logic based runtime observer pairs for system health management of real-time systems. In: Ábrahám, E., Havelund, K. (eds.) TACAS 2014. LNCS, vol. 8413, pp. 357–372. Springer, Heidelberg (2014). https://doi.org/10.1007/978-3-642-54862-8_24
56. Rozier, K.Y., Vardi, M.Y.: A multi-encoding approach for LTL symbolic satisfiability checking. In: Butler, M., Schulte, W. (eds.) FM 2011. LNCS, vol. 6664, pp. 417–431. Springer, Heidelberg (2011). https://doi.org/10.1007/978-3-642-21437-0_31
57. Rozier, K.Y., et al.: MoXI: an intermediate language for symbolic model checking. In: Proceedings of the 30th International Symposium on Model Checking Software (SPIN). LNCS, Springer (2024)
58. Rozier, K.Y., Shankar, N., Tinelli, C., Vardi, M.Y.: Developing an open-source, state-of-the-art symbolic model-checking framework for the model-checking research community (2019). https://modelchecker.github.io
59. Schumann, J., Rozier, K.Y., Reinbacher, T., Mengshoel, O.J., Mbaya, T., Ippolito, C.: Towards real-time, on-board, hardware-supported sensor and software health management for unmanned aerial systems. In: Proceedings of the 2013 Annual Conference of the Prognostics and Health Management Society (PHM2013), pp. 381–401, October 2013
60. Sheeran, M., Singh, S., Stålmarck, G.: Checking safety properties using induction and a SAT-solver. In: Hunt, W.A., Johnson, S.D. (eds.) FMCAD 2000. LNCS, vol. 1954, pp. 127–144. Springer, Heidelberg (2000). https://doi.org/10.1007/3-540-40922-X_8
61. Tribble, A., Miller, S.: Software safety analysis of a flight management system vertical navigation function-a status report. In: DASC, pp. 1.B.1–1.1–9 v1 (2003)
62. Wolf, C.: Yosys open synthesis suite (2016)
63. Yoo, J., Jee, E., Cha, S.: Formal modeling and verification of safety-critical software. Softw. IEEE 26(3), 42–49 (2009)
64. Zhao, Y., Rozier, K.Y.: Formal specification and verification of a coordination protocol for an automated air traffic control system. In: Proceedings of the 12th International Workshop on Automated Verification of Critical Systems (AVoCS 2012). Electronic Communications of the EASST, vol. 53, pp. 337–353. European Association of Software Science and Technology (2012)
65. Zhao, Y., Rozier, K.Y.: Formal specification and verification of a coordination protocol for an automated air traffic control system. Sci. Comput. Programm. J. 96(3), 337–353 (2014)

SMLP: Symbolic Machine Learning Prover

Franz Brauße[1]([✉]) [ID], Zurab Khasidashvili[2] [ID], and Konstantin Korovin[1] [ID]

[1] The University of Manchester, Manchester, UK
franz.brausse@manchester.ac.uk
[2] Intel, Haifa, Israel

Abstract. *Symbolic Machine Learning Prover (SMLP)* is a tool and a library for system exploration based on data samples obtained by simulating or executing the system on a number of input vectors. SMLP aims at exploring the system based on this data by taking a grey-box approach: SMLP uses symbolic reasoning for ML model exploration and optimization under verification and stability constraints, based on SMT, constraint, and neural network solvers. In addition, the model exploration is guided by probabilistic and statistical methods in a closed feedback loop with the system's response. SMLP has been applied in industrial setting at Intel for analyzing and optimizing hardware designs at the analog level. SMLP is a general purpose tool and can be applied to any system that can be sampled and modeled by machine learning models.

1 Introduction

Verification of assertions on machine learning (ML) models has received a wide attention from formal methods community in recent years, and multiple approaches have been developed for formal analysis of ML models, mostly focused on neural networks [9]. In this work we introduce the SMLP tool – *Symbolic Machine Learning Prover* – aiming at going beyond this mainstream in several ways: SMLP helps to approach the system's design, optimization and verification as one process by offering multiple capabilities for system's *design space exploration*. These capabilities include methods for selecting which parameters to use in modeling design for configuration optimization and verification; ensuring that the design is robust against environmental effects and manufacturing variations that are impossible to control, as well as ensuring robustness against malicious attacks from an adversary aiming at altering the intended configuration or mode of operation. Environmental affects like temperature fluctuation, electromagnetic interference, manufacturing variation, and product aging effects are especially more critical for correct and optimal operation of devices with analog components, which is our current focus.

To address these challenges, SMLP offers multiple modes of design space exploration, which are based on symbolic reasoning using SMT solvers guided by statistical and probabilistic methods. These modes will be described in detail

---

This research was supported by a grant from Intel Corporation.

A. Gurfinkel and V. Ganesh (Eds.): CAV 2024, LNCS 14681, pp. 219–233, 2024.
https://doi.org/10.1007/978-3-031-65627-9_11

in Sect. 6. The definition of these modes refers to the concept of *stability* of an assignment to system's parameters that satisfies all model constraints (which include the constraints defining the model itself and any constraint on model's interface). We will refer to such a parameter assignment satisfying the model constraints as a *(stable) solution*. Informally, stability of a solution means that any eligible assignment in the specified region around the solution also satisfy the required constraints. This notion is sometimes referred to as robustness. We work with parameterized systems, where parameters (also called *knobs*) can be tuned to optimize the system's performance under all legitimate inputs. For example, in the circuit board design setting, topological layout of circuits, distances, wire thickness, properties of dielectric layers, etc. can be such parameters, and the exploration goal would be to optimize the system performance under the system's requirements [19]. The difference between knobs and inputs is that knob values are selected during design phase, before the system goes into operation; on the other hand, inputs remain free and get values from the environment during the operation of the system. Knobs and inputs correspond to existentially quantified and universally quantified variables in the formal definition of model exploration tasks. Thus in the usual meaning of verification, optimization and synthesis, respectively, all variables are inputs, all variables are knobs, and some of the variables are knobs and the rest are inputs.

In this work by a *model* we refer to an ML model that models the system under exploration. The main capabilities of SMLP for system exploration include:

assertion verification: Verifying assertions on the model's interface.

parameter synthesis: Finding model parameter values such that design constraints are valid.

parameter optimization: Optimizing the model parameters under constraints.

stable optimized synthesis: Combining model parameter synthesis and optimization into one algorithm, enhanced by stability guarantees, to achieve safe, stable and optimal configurations.

root cause analysis: Generating root-causing hints in terms of subset of parameters and their ranges that explain the failure.

model refinement: Targeted refinement of the model based on stability regions found by model exploration and on feedback from system in these stability regions.

The *model exploration cube* in Fig. 1 provides a high level and intuitive idea on how the model exploration modes supported in SMLP are related. The three dimensions in this cube represent synthesis ($\searsow$-axis), optimization ($\rightarrow$-axis) and stability ($\uparrow$-axis). On the bottom plane of the cube, the edges represent the synthesis and optimization problems in the following sense: synthesis with constraints configures the knob values in a way that guarantees that assertions are valid, but unlike optimization, does not guarantee optimally with respect to optimization objectives. On the other hand, optimization by itself is not aware of assertions on inputs of the system and only guarantees optimality with respect

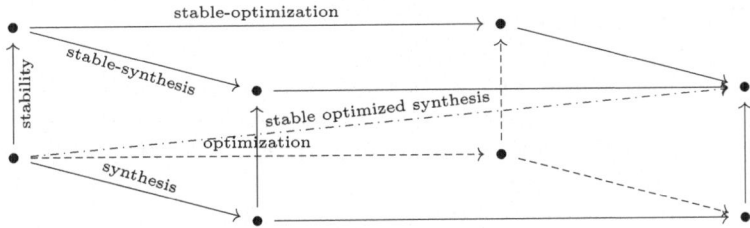

Fig. 1. Exploration Cube

to knobs, and not the validity of assertions in the configured system. We refer to the procedure that combines synthesis with optimization and results in an optimal design that satisfies assertions as *optimized synthesis*. The upper plane of the cube represents introducing stability requirements into synthesis (and as a special case, into verification), optimization, and optimized synthesis. The formulas that make definition of stable verification, optimization, synthesis and optimized synthesis precise are discussed in Sect. 4.

Compared to digital design, it is fair to say that formal methods have had a limited success in the analog domain. A practical approach to this challenge is to use models as a way of abstraction that can be refined based on model analysis and feedback from the real system to narrow the gap between the model and the system to levels tolerable by stability requirements of the design. SMLP applies formal analysis to systems represented by ML models, and assists designers in product development, in particular, helps to refine the design to make it safe and optimized, see Sect. 8.

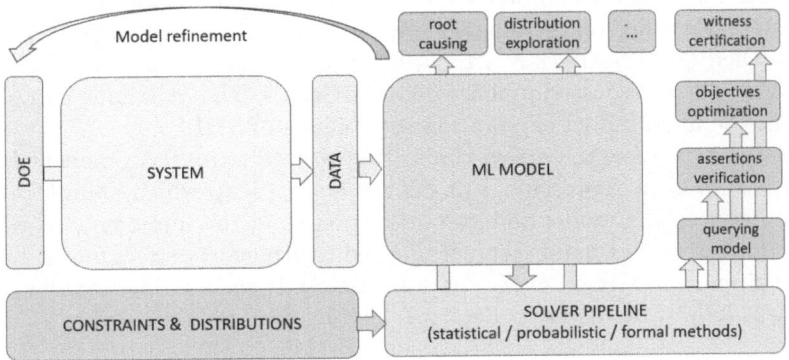

Fig. 2. SMLP Tool Architecture

2   SMLP Architecture

SMLP tool architecture is depicted in Fig. 2. It consists of the following components: 1) Design of experiments (DOE), 2) System that can be sampled based on DOE, 3) ML model trained on the sampled data, 4) SMLP solver that handles different system exploration modes on a symbolic representation of the ML model, 5) Targeted model refinement loop.

SMLP supports multiple ways to generate training data known under the name of *Design Of Experiments*. These methods include: full-factorial, fractional-factorial, Plackett-Burman, Box-Behnken, Box-Wilson, Sukharev-grid, Latin-hypercube, among other methods, which try to achieve a smart sampling of the entire input space with a relatively small number of data samples. In Fig. 2, the leftmost box-shaped component called DOE represents SMLP capabilities to generate test vectors to feed into the system and generate training data; the latter two components are represented with boxes called SYSTEM and DATA, respectively.

In a simplified setting, SMLP can be directly applied to the training data representing the input output behaviour of the system, skipping the DOE step.

The component called ML MODEL represents SMLP capabilities to train models; currently neural network, polynomial and tree-based regression models are supported. Modeling analog devices using polynomial models was proposed in the seminal work on *Response Surface Methodology (RSM)* [3], and since then has been widely adopted by the industry. Neural networks and tree-based models are used increasingly due to their wider adoption, and their exceptional accuracy and simplicity, respectively.

The component called SOLVER PIPELINE represents model exploration engines of SMLP (e.g., connection to SMT solvers), which besides a symbolic representation of the model takes as input several types of constraints and input sampling distributions specified on the model's interface; these are represented by the component called CONSTRAINTS & DISTRIBUTIONS located at the low-left corner of Fig. 2, and will be discussed in more detail in Sect. 4. The remaining components represent the main model exploration capabilities of SMLP.

Last but not least, the arrow connecting the ML MODEL component back to the DOE component represents a *model refinement* loop which allows to reduce the gap between the model and system responses in the input regions where it matters for the task at hand (there is no need to achieve a perfect match between the model and the system everywhere in the input space). The targeted model refinement loop is discussed in Sect. 6.7.

3   Symbolic Representation of Models and Constraints

We assume that system interface consists of free inputs, knobs, and outputs. The set of inputs and/or knobs, can be empty. For the sake of ML-based analysis, we build an ML model, represent it symbolically, and the aim is to analyze the system through exploring the model instead.

A *domain* $\mathcal{D}$ is a Cartesian product of reals, integers and finite non-empty sets. A *parameterized system* can be represented as a function $f : \mathcal{D}_{par} \times \mathcal{D}_{in} \rightarrow \mathcal{D}_{out}$, where $\mathcal{D}_{par}, \mathcal{D}_{in}, \mathcal{D}_{out}$ are domains of parameters (knobs), inputs and outputs, respectively. For simplicity of the presentation we assume all domains are products of sets of reals but methods and implementation are applicable also for domains over integers and arbitrary finite sets. We consider formulas over $\langle \mathbb{R}, 0, 1, \mathcal{F}, P \rangle$, where P contains the usual predicates $<, \leq, =$, etc. and $\mathcal{F}$ contains addition, multiplication with rational constants and can also contain non-linear functions supported by SMT solvers including polynomials, transcendental functions and more generally computable functions [6,7,10,11,15].

We extend functions $\mathcal{F}$ by functions *definable* by formulas: $\mathcal{F}_D$, i.e., we assume $f \in \mathcal{F}_D$ is represented by a formula $F(x_1, \ldots, x_n, y)$ over variables $x_1, \ldots, x_n$ corresponding to the n inputs and y corresponding to the output $f(x_1, \ldots, x_n)$. We assume that satisfiability of quantifier free formulas over this language is decidable or more generally δ-decidable [7,15]. Let us note that even when basic functions $\mathcal{F}$ contain just linear functions, $\mathcal{F}_D$ will contain, e.g., functions represented by neural networks with ReLU activation functions as well as decision trees and random forests. When representing parameterized systems using ML models we assume that parameters are treated as designated inputs to the ML model.

Throughout, p, x, y denote respectively knob, input and output variables (or variable vectors) in formulas while r, z range over reals. Whenever we use a norm $\| \cdot \|$, we refer to a norm representable in our language, such as the Chebyshev norm $(x_1, \ldots, x_n) \mapsto \max\{|x_1|, \ldots, |x_n|\}$.

4   Symbolic Representation of the ML Model Exploration

The main system exploration tasks handled by SMLP can be defined using $\exists^* \forall^*$ formulas in the GEAR-fragment [4]:

$$\exists p \; [\eta(p) \wedge \forall p' \; \forall xy \; [\theta(p, p') \rightarrow (\varphi_M(p', x, y) \rightarrow \varphi_{cond}(p', x, y))]] \qquad (1)$$

where x ranges over inputs, y ranges over outputs, and p, p' range over knobs, $\eta(p)$ are constraints on the knob configuration p, $\varphi_M(p', x, y)$ defines the machine learning model, $\theta(p, p')$ defines stability region for the configuration p, and $\varphi_{cond}(p', x, y)$ defines conditions that should hold in the stability region. An assignment to variables p that makes formula (1) true is called a *θ-stable solution* to (1).

In our formalization θ, η and φ_{cond} are quantifier free formulas in the language. These constraints and how they are implemented in SMLP are described below.

$\eta(p)$ Constraints on values of knobs; this formula need not be a conjunction of constraints on individual knobs, can define more complex relations between allowed knob values of individual knobs. $\eta(p)$ can be specified through the SMLP specification file (see Sect. 5).

```
{
  "version": "1.2",
  "variables": [
    {"label":"y1", "interface":"output", "type":"real"},
    {"label":"y2", "interface":"output", "type":"real"},
    {"label":"x1", "interface":"input", "type":"real", "range":[0,10]},
    {"label":"x2", "interface":"input", "type":"int", "range":[-1,1]},
    {"label":"p1", "interface":"knob", "type":"real", "range":[0,10], "rad-rel":0.1, "grid":[2,4,7]},
    {"label":"p2", "interface":"knob", "type":"int", "range":[3,7], "rad-abs":0.2}
  ],
  "alpha": "p2<5 and x1==10 and x2<12",
  "beta": "y1>=4 and y2==8",
  "eta": "p1==4 or (p1==8 and p2 > 3)",
  "assertions": {
    "assert1": "(y2**3+p2)/2>6",
    "assert2": "y1>=0",
    "assert3": "y2>0"
  },
  "objectives": {
    "objective1": "(y1+y2)/2",
    "objective2": "y1"
  }
}
```

Fig. 3. Example of SMLP's format specifying the problem conditions for the displayed model of the system.

$\theta(p, p')$ Stability constraints that define a region around a candidate solution. This can be specified using either absolute or relative radius r in the specification file. This region corresponds to a ball (or box) around p: $\theta(p, p') = \|p - p'\| \leq r$. In general, our methods do not impose any restrictions on θ apart from reflexivity.

$\varphi_M(p, x, y)$ Constraints that define the function represented by the ML model M, thus $\varphi_M(p, x, y) = (M(p, x) = y)$. In the ML model, knobs are represented as designated inputs (and can be treated in the same way as system inputs, or the machine model architecture can reflect the difference between inputs and knobs). $\varphi_M(p, x, y)$ is computed by SMLP internally, based on the ML model specification.

$\varphi_{cond}(p, x, y)$ Conditions that should hold in the θ-region of the solution. These conditions depend on the exploration mode and could be: (1) verification conditions, (2) model querying conditions, (3) parameter optimization conditions, or (4) parameter synthesis conditions. The exploration modes are described in Sect. 6.

SMLP solver is based on specialized procedures GearSAT$_\delta$ [4] and GearSAT$_\delta$-BO [5] for solving formulas in the GEAR fragment using quantifier-free SMT solvers. The GearSAT$_\delta$ procedure interleaves search for candidate solutions using SMT solvers with exclusion of θ-regions around counter-examples. GearSAT$_\delta$-BO combines GearSAT$_\delta$ search with Bayesian optimization guidance. These procedures find solutions to GEAR formulas with user-defined accuracy ε (defined in Sect. 6.4) and they have been proven to be sound, (δ)-complete and terminating.

5   Problem Specification in SMLP

The specification file defines the problem conditions in a JSON compatible format, whereas SMLP exploration modes can be specified via command line options. Figure 3 depicts a toy system with two inputs, two knobs, and two outputs and a matching specification file for model exploration modes in SMLP. For each variable it specifies its *label* (the name), its *interface* function ("input", "knob", or "output"), its *type* ("real", "int", or "set", for categorical features), *ranges* for variables of real and int types, and optionally, a *grid* of values for knobs that they are allowed to take on within the respective declared ranges, independently from each other (unless there are constraints further restricting the multi-dimensional grid). Both integer and real typed knobs can be restricted to grids (but do not need to). Additional fields *alpha, beta, eta, assertions* and *objectives* can optionally be specified, as shown in the example. These correspond to the predicates α, β, η, 'assert' and objective function o described in Sect. 6.

The details about the concrete format are described in the manual [8], also distributed with SMLP.

6 SMLP Exploration Modes of ML Models

In this section we describe ML model exploration modes supported by SMLP, which are based on Formula (1).[1]

6.1 Stable Parameter Synthesis

The goal of *stable synthesis* is to find values of the system parameters such that required conditions hold in the θ-region of the parameters for all inputs. For this, SMLP solves Formula (1), where

$$\varphi_{cond}(p, x, y) = \alpha(p, x) \rightarrow \beta(p, x, y).$$

Here, $\alpha(p, x)$ restricts points in the region around the solutions to points of interest and $\beta(p, x, y)$ is the requirement that these points should satisfy. The α constraints define the domain of inputs and knobs and constraints on them which play the role of assumptions in the assume-guarantee paradigm, while β constraints can be viewed as guarantees; they can express some external/additional requirements from system not covered by assertions. In case of synthesis and optimization, β constraints can be used to express constraints that should be satisfied by synthesized, respectively, optimized system. For example consider $\alpha(p, x) = (x_1 > x_2 + x_3)$, $\beta(p, x, y) = y_1 > 2 \cdot x_1$ and $\theta = \|p - p'\| \leq 0.5$. In this mode SMLP will find values of parameters of the system such that for all parameters in the 0.5 region and all inputs such that $x_1 > x_2 + x_3$ the output value y_1 is greater than $2 \cdot x_1$.

---

[1] A comprehensive description of the exploration modes can be found in the SMLP manual [8].

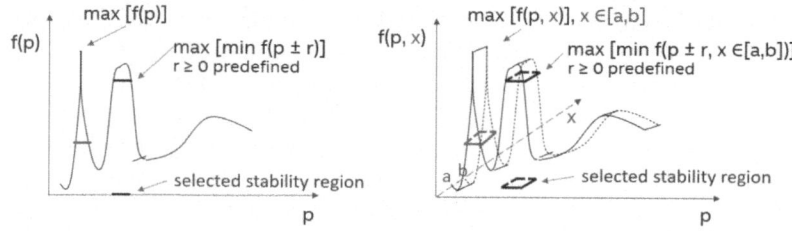

Fig. 4. SMLP max-min optimization. On both plots, p denote the knobs. On the right plot we also consider inputs x (which are universally quantified) as part of f.

6.2 Verifying Assertions on a Model

For verifying an assertion $\text{assert}(p, x, y)$ on a model M under given parameters p we can simplify Formula (1) to:

$$\eta(p) \wedge \forall p' \, \forall xy \, [\theta(p, p') \rightarrow (\varphi_M(p', x, y) \rightarrow \text{assert}(p', x, y))].$$

Since p is fixed, $\eta(p)$ can be eliminated by evaluation. Further, if one is not concerned with stability, then θ can be replaced with the identity and the problem can be reduced to a standard verification problem.

$$\forall xy \, (\varphi_M(p, x, y) \rightarrow \text{assert}(p, x, y)).$$

In the case of neural networks, there is a large range of verification tools to solve this problem such as Marabou [16], α, β-CROWN [20,22]. Most of these tools rely on floating point computations, which can quickly accumulate errors. SMLP supports SMT solvers with arbitrary precision which can produce exact results, at the expense of the computational cost. Nevertheless, dedicated ML solvers are very useful as they scale to much larger problems [9]. We are currently working on supporting dedicated ML solvers in SMLP and let user decide which traded-off to choose. SMLP also supports other ML models such as decision trees, random forests and polynomial models.

6.3 Querying Conditions on the Model

The task of querying ML model for a stable witness to $\text{query}(p, x, y)$ consists in finding value assignments p^*, x^* for knobs p and inputs x that represent a solution for Eq. (2):

$$\exists p, x \, [\eta(p) \wedge \forall p' \, \forall y \, [\theta(p, p') \rightarrow (\varphi_M(p', x, y) \rightarrow \varphi_{cond}(p', x, y))]] \qquad (2)$$

where

$$\varphi_{cond}(p, x, y) = \alpha(p, x) \rightarrow \text{query}(p, x, y).$$

Queries can be used to explore the model, e.g., to explore regions around failures where query corresponds to negation of the assertion, or to explore near optimal regions in the optimization tasks, or other conditions of interest.

6.4   Stable Optimized Synthesis

In this subsection we consider the optimization problem for a real-valued function f (in our case, an ML model), extended in two ways: (1) we consider a θ-stable maximum to ensure that the objective function does not drop drastically in a close neighborhood of the configuration where its maximum is achieved, and (2) we assume that the objective function besides knobs depends also on inputs, and the function is maximized in the stability θ-region of knobs, for any values of inputs in their respective legal ranges. We explain these extensions using two plots in Fig. 4.

The left plot represents optimization problem for $f(p, x)$ when f depends on knobs only (thus x is an empty vector), while the right plot represents the general setting where x is not empty (which is usually not considered in optimization research). In each plot, the blue threshold (in the form of a horizontal bar or a rectangle) denotes the stable maximum around the point where f reaches its (regular) maximum, and the red threshold denotes the stable maximum, which is approximated by our optimization algorithms. In both plots, the regular maximum of f is not stable due to a sharp drop of f's value in the stability region.

Let us first consider optimization without stability or inputs, i.e., far low corner in the exploration cube Fig. 1. Given a formula φ_M encoding the model, and an objective function $o : \mathcal{D}_{par} \times \mathcal{D}_{out} \to \mathbb{R}$, the standard optimization problem solved by SMLP is stated by Formula (3).

$$\llbracket \varphi_M \rrbracket_o = \max_p \{ z \mid \forall y \ (\varphi_M(p, y) \to o(p, y) \geq z) \} \tag{3}$$

A solution to this optimization problem is the pair $(p^*, \llbracket \varphi_M \rrbracket_o)$, where $p^* \in \mathcal{D}_{par}$ is a value of parameters p on which the maximum $\llbracket \varphi_M \rrbracket_o \in \mathbb{R}$ of the objective function o is achieved for the output y of the model on p^*. In most cases it is not feasible to exactly compute the maximum. To deal with this, SMLP computes maximum with a specified accuracy. Consider $\varepsilon > 0$. We refer to values $(\tilde{p}, \tilde{z})$ as a solution to the optimization problem with *accuracy* ε, or ε-*solution*, if $\tilde{z} \leq \llbracket \varphi_M \rrbracket_o < \tilde{z} + \varepsilon$ holds and $\tilde{z}$ is a lower bound on the objective, i.e., $\forall y [\varphi_M(p, y) \to o(p, y) \geq \tilde{z}]$ holds.

Now, we consider *stable optimized synthesis*, i.e., the top right corner of the exploration cube. The problem can be formulated as the following Formula (4), expressing maximization of a lower bound on the objective function o over parameter values under stable synthesis constraints.

$$\llbracket \varphi_M \rrbracket_{o,\theta} = \max_p \{ z \mid \eta(p) \wedge \forall p' \ \forall xy \ [\theta(p, p') \to (\varphi_M(p', x, y) \to \varphi_{cond}^{\geq}(p', x, y, z))] \} \tag{4}$$

where

$$\varphi_{cond}^{\geq}(p', x, y, z) = \alpha(p', x) \to (\beta(p', x, y) \wedge o(p', x, y) \geq z).$$

The stable synthesis constraints are part of a GEAR formula and include usual η, α, β constraints together with the stability constraints θ. Equivalently, stable optimized synthesis can be stated as the *max-min* optimization problem,

Formula (5)

$$\llbracket \varphi_M \rrbracket_{o,\theta} = \max_p \min_{x,p'} \{z \mid \eta(p) \land \forall y \, [\theta(p,p') \to (\varphi_M(p',x,y) \to \varphi_{cond}^{\leq}(p',x,y,z))]\}$$

$$(5)$$

where

$$\varphi_{cond}^{\leq}(p',x,y,z) = \alpha(p',x) \to (\beta(p',x,y) \land o(p',x,y) \leq z).$$

In Formula (5) the minimization predicate in the stability region corresponds to the universally quantified x and p' ranging over this region in (4). An advantage of this formulation is that this formula can be adapted to define other aggregation functions over the objective's values on stability region. For example, that way one can represent the *max-mean* optimization problem, where one wants to maximize the mean value of the function in the stability region rather one the min value (which is maximizing the worst-case value of f in stability region). Likewise, Formula (5) can be adapted to other interesting statistical properties of distribution of values of f in the stability region.

We can explicitly incorporate assertions in stable optimized synthesis by defining $\beta(p',x,y) = \beta'(p',x,y) \land \text{assert}(p',x,y)$, where $\text{assert}(p',x,y)$ are assertions required to be valid in the entire stability region around the selected configuration of knobs p. The notion of ε-solutions for these problems carries over from the one given above for Formula (3).

SMLP implements stable optimized synthesis based on the GearOPT$_\delta$ and GearOPT$_\delta$-BO algorithms [4,5], which are shown to be complete and terminating for this problem under mild conditions. These algorithms were further extended in SMLP to Pareto point computations to handle multiple objectives simultaneously.

6.5 Design of Experiments

Most DOE methods are based on understanding multivariate distribution of legal value combinations of inputs and knobs in order to sample the system. When the number of system inputs and/or knobs is large (say hundreds or more), the DOE may not generate a high-quality coverage of the system's behavior to enable training models with high accuracy. Model training process itself becomes less manageable when number of input variables grows, and models are not explainable and thus cannot be trusted. One way to curb this problem is to select a subset of input features for DOE and for model training. The problem of combining feature selection with DOE generation and model training is an important research topic of practical interest, and SMLP supports multiple practically proven ways to select subsets of features and feature combinations as inputs to DOE and training, including the *MRMR* feature selection algorithm [13], and a *Subgroup Discovery (SD)* algorithm [1,18,21]. The MRMR algorithm selects a subset of features according to the principle of *maximum relevance and minimum redundancy*. It is widely used for the purpose of selecting a subset of features for building accurate models, and is therefore useful for selecting a subset of features to be used in DOE; it is a default choice in SMLP for that usage. The

SD algorithm selects regions in the input space relevant to the response, using heuristic statistical methods, and such regions can be prioritized for sampling in DOE algorithms.

6.6   Root Cause Analysis

We view the problem of root cause analysis as dual to the stable optimized synthesis problem: while during optimization with stability we are searching for regions in the input space (or in other words, characterizing those regions) where the system response is good or excellent, the task of root-causing can be seen as searching for regions in the input space where the system response is not good (is unacceptable). Thus simply by swapping the definition of excellent vs unacceptable, we can apply SMLP to explore weaknesses and failing behaviors of the system.

Even if a number of counter-examples to an assertion are available, they represent discrete points in the input space and it is not immediately clear which value assignments to which variables in these counter-examples are critical to explain the failures. Root causing capability in SMLP is currently supported through two independent approaches: a *Subgroup Discovery (SD)* algorithm that searches through the data for the input regions where there is a higher ratio (thus, higher probability) of failure; to be precise, SD algorithms support a variety of *quality functions* which play the role of optimization objectives in the context of optimization. To find input regions with high probability of failure, SMLP searches for stable witnesses to failures. These capabilities, together with feature selection algorithms supported in SMLP, enable researchers to develop new root causing capabilities that combine formal methods with statistical methods for root cause analysis.

6.7   Model Refinement Loop

Support in SMLP for selecting DOE vectors to sample the system and generate a training set was discussed in Subsect. 6.5. Initially, when selecting sampling points for the system, it is unknown which regions in the input space are really relevant for the exploration task at hand. Therefore some DOE algorithms also incorporate sampling based on previous experience and familiarity with the design, such as sampling nominal cases and corner cases, when these are known. For model exploration tasks supported by SMLP, it is not required to train a model that will be an accurate match to the system everywhere in the legal search space of inputs and knobs. We require to train a model that is an *adequate* representation of the system for the task at hand, meaning that the exploration task solved on the model solves this task for the system as well. Therefore SMLP supports a *targeted model refinement* loop to enable solving the system exploration tasks by solving these tasks on the model instead. The idea is as follows: when a stable solution to model exploration task is found, it is usually the case that there are not many training data points close to the stability region of that solution. This implies that there is a high likelihood that the model does not accurately represent the system in the stability region of the solution. Therefore the system is sampled in the stability region of the solution, and these data samples are added to the initial training data to retrain the model and make it more adequate in the stability region of interest.

7   Implementation

SMLP code is open-source and publicly available[2]. Its frontend is implemented in Python, and its backend is implemented in C++ , while the interface between the two is realized using the Boost library. For training tree-based and polynomial models we use the scikit-learnand pycaretpackages, and for training neural networks we use the Keras package with TensorFlow. Our focus is on analyzing regression models arising from systems with analog pins and analog output, but classification models are also covered as they can be reduced to binary classification with output values 0 and 1, or by treating the binary classification problem as a regression problem of predicting the probability of the output to be 1 (the latter is usually preferable for more finer analysis). For generating training data from a system, SMLP supports DOE approaches available in package pyDOE. The MRMR algorithm for feature selection is integrated in SMLP using the mrmr package, and the Subgroup Discovery algorithm is integrated using package pysubgroup.

SMLP can use any external SMT solver which supports SMT-LIB2 format, as a back end of the GearSAT/OPT algorithms (via command line options), and also natively integrates Z3 via the Python interface. We successfully experimented with Z3 [11], Yices [14], CVC5 [2], MathSAT [10] and ksmt [6].

8   Industrial Case Studies

Previous publications [4,5] on SMLP report detailed experimental results on 10 real-life training datasets originating from Electrical Validation and Signal Integrity domains. The output is a measurement of the quality of an analog signal between a transmitter and a receiver of a channel to a peripheral device. The datasets are freely available[3]: 5 transmitter (TX) datasets and 5 receiver (RX) counterparts. The count of inputs and knobs together in these experiments, as well as in current usage of the SMLP tool at Intel, is around 5 to 20 variables. In [4] the experimental evaluation is performed using GEARSAT_δ algorithm, and experimental results using the GEAROPT_δ-BO algorithm that combines SMT-based optimization procedure with Bayesian optimization are reported in [5]. While these datasets are relatively small in terms of parameter counts, they are representative of modeling I/O devices at Intel, and SMLP has been useful in suggesting safe and optimized configurations for a number of real-life I/O devices in recent years.

---

[2] https://github.com/fbrausse/smlp
[3] https://fbrausse.github.io/smlp/benchmarks-intel/

Some of the challenges of design space exploration at Intel in the design stage of product developed are described in [17]. This work focuses on design challenges for 112 Gb SerDes I/O serialization systems. This work uses Feature Range Analysis [17] as ML analysis engine which has initial support in SMLP in the subgroups mode. The parameters relevant to the system exploration include those characterizing topological layout of circuits, physical characteristics, requirements for manufacturability, and more, such as relative locations of vias, distances between parallel wires, wire thickness, wire lengths, properties of dielectric layers. The exploration goal is to optimize the system performance under the system's requirements, to find one safe and optimal configuration that supports multiple modes of operations – in particular, to improve the timing and voltage margins, co-optimized with power and area requirements. SMLP is currently being applied for analysis and optimization of such I/O systems, through analyzing NN, tree and polynomial models trained on design and lab data.

9   Future Work

Currently we are extending SMLP to support ONNX format used by VNN-LIB [12] so more specialized solvers for ML can also be used alongside SMT solvers. We are working on combining different solving strategies into a user-definable solver pipeline of ML and SMT solvers within the SMLP framework. We recently released a new set of benchmarks and intend to release more real-life industrial datasets in the future (See Footnote 3).

Acknowledgments. We would like to thank Shai Amara, Alex Manukovsky, Joshua N. Fontaine, and Yunhui Chu for providing us with data and ML models that helped us in developing and tuning SMLP on real-life problem instances.

References

1. Atzmueller, M.: Subgroup discovery. WIREs Data Mining Knowl. Discov. **5**(1), 35–49 (2015)
2. Barbosa, H.: cvc5: a versatile and industrial-strength SMT solver. In: TACAS 2022. LNCS, vol. 13243, pp. 415–442. Springer, Cham (2022). https://doi.org/10.1007/978-3-030-99524-9_24
3. Box, G.E.P., Wilson, K.B.: On the experimental attainment of optimum conditions. J. Royal Stat. Soc. Ser. B (Methodological) **13**(1), 1–45 (1951)
4. Brauße, F., Khasidashvili, Z., Korovin., K.: Selecting stable safe configurations for systems modelled by neural networks with ReLU activation. In: 2020 Formal Methods in Computer Aided Design, FMCAD 2020, Haifa, Israel, 21–24 September 2020, pp. 119–127. IEEE (2020)
5. Brauße, F., Khasidashvili, Z., Korovin, K.: Combining constraint solving and bayesian techniques for system optimization. In: De Raedt, L. (ed.) Proceedings of the Thirty-First International Joint Conference on Artificial Intelligence, IJCAI 2022, Vienna, Austria, 23–29 July 2022, pp. 1788–1794. ijcai.org (2022)

6. Brauße, F., Korovin, K., Korovina, M., Müller, N.: A CDCL-style calculus for solving non-linear constraints. In: Herzig, A., Popescu, A. (eds.) FroCoS 2019. LNCS (LNAI), vol. 11715, pp. 131–148. Springer, Cham (2019). https://doi.org/10.1007/978-3-030-29007-8_8

7. Brauße, F., Korovin, K., Korovina, M.V., Müller, N.T.: The KSMT calculus is a δ-complete decision procedure for non-linear constraints. Theor. Comput. Sci. **975**, 114125 (2023)

8. Brauße, F., Khasidashvili, Z., Korovin, K.: SMLP: symbolic machine learning prover (user manual). *CoRR*, abs/2405.10215 (2024)

9. Brix, C., Müller, M.N., Bak, S., Johnson, T.T., Liu, C.: First three years of the international verification of neural networks competition (VNN-COMP). Int. J. Softw. Tools Technol. Transf. **25**(3), 329–339 (2023)

10. Cimatti, A., Griggio, A., Schaafsma, B.J., Sebastiani, R.: The MathSAT5 SMT solver. In: Piterman, N., Smolka, S.A. (eds.) TACAS 2013. LNCS, vol. 7795, pp. 93–107. Springer, Heidelberg (2013). https://doi.org/10.1007/978-3-642-36742-7_7

11. de Moura, L., Bjørner, N.: Z3: an efficient SMT solver. In: Ramakrishnan, C.R., Rehof, J. (eds.) TACAS 2008. LNCS, vol. 4963, pp. 337–340. Springer, Heidelberg (2008). https://doi.org/10.1007/978-3-540-78800-3_24

12. Demarchi, S., Guidotti, D., Pulina, L., Tacchella, A.: Supporting standardization of neural networks verification with VNN-LIB and CoCoNet. In: Proceedings of the 6th Workshop on Formal Methods for ML-Enabled Autonomous Systems, vol. 16, pp. 47–58 (2023)

13. Ding, C.H.Q., Peng, H.: Minimum redundancy feature selection from microarray gene expression data. J. Bioinform. Comput. Biol. **3**(2), 185–206 (2005)

14. Dutertre, B.: Yices 2.2. In: Biere, A., Bloem, R. (eds.) CAV 2014. LNCS, vol. 8559, pp. 737–744. Springer, Cham (2014). https://doi.org/10.1007/978-3-319-08867-9_49

15. Gao, S., Avigad, J., Clarke, E.M.: δ-complete decision procedures for satisfiability over the reals. In: Gramlich, B., Miller, D., Sattler, U. (eds.) IJCAR 2012. LNCS (LNAI), vol. 7364, pp. 286–300. Springer, Heidelberg (2012). https://doi.org/10.1007/978-3-642-31365-3_23

16. Katz, G., et al.: The Marabou framework for verification and analysis of deep neural networks. In: Dillig, I., Tasiran, S. (eds.) CAV 2019, Part I. LNCS, vol. 11561, pp. 443–452. Springer, Cham (2019). https://doi.org/10.1007/978-3-030-25540-4_26

17. Khasidashvili, Z., Norman, A.J.: Feature range analysis. Int. J. Data Sci. Anal. **11**(3), 195–219 (2021)

18. Klösgen, W.: Explora: a multipattern and multistrategy discovery assistant. In: Fayyad, U.M., Piatetsky-Shapiro, G., Smyth, P., Uthurusamy, R. (eds.) Advances in Knowledge Discovery and Data Mining, pp. 249–271. AAAI/MIT Press (1996)

19. Manukovsky, A., Shlepnev, Y., Khasidashvili, Z.: Machine learning based design space exploration and applications to signal integrity analysis of 112Gb SerDes systems. In: 2021 IEEE 71st Electronic Components and Technology Conference (ECTC), pp. 1234–1245 (2021)

20. Wang, S., et al.: Beta-CROWN: efficient bound propagation with per-neuron split constraints for complete and incomplete neural network verification. Adv. Neural Inf. Process. Syst. **34** (2021)

21. Wrobel, S.: An algorithm for multi-relational discovery of subgroups. In: Komorowski, J., Zytkow, J. (eds.) PKDD 1997. LNCS, vol. 1263, pp. 78–87. Springer, Heidelberg (1997). https://doi.org/10.1007/3-540-63223-9_108

22. Xu, K., et al.: Fast and Complete: enabling complete neural network verification with rapid and massively parallel incomplete verifiers. In: International Conference on Learning Representations (2021)

Avoiding the Shoals - A New Approach
to Liveness Checking

Yechuan Xia[1], Alessandro Cimatti[2], Alberto Griggio[2], and Jianwen Li[1(✉)]

[1] East China Normal University, Shanghai, China
jwli@sei.ecnu.edu.cn
[2] Fondazione Bruno Kessler, Trento, Italy
{cimatti,griggio}@fbk.eu

Abstract. We present rlive, a new SAT-based model-checking algorithm
for the verification of liveness properties of finite-state symbolic transition systems. Like other recent approaches, rlive works by reducing
liveness checking to a sequence of safety checks. Similarly to FAIR, it
incrementally strengthens the input system using constraints obtained
by refuting candidate counterexamples to the input liveness property,
assumed (w.l.o.g.) to be of the form FGq. Differently from FAIR (and
crucially), however, instead of directly searching for lasso-shaped counterexamples visiting $\neg q$ infinitely-often, rlive searches for counterexamples incrementally, via a recursive chain of safety checks, each of which
tries to determine whether it is possible to reach a $\neg q$-state from a given
$\neg q$-state (which was previously determined to be reachable), in a manner similar to k-Liveness. When the current candidate counterexample is
refuted, rlive exploits the inductive invariants generated by the (recursive) safety checks to restrict the search space, until either no more reachable $\neg q$-states remain, or a real lasso-shaped counterexample is found.

In this paper, we describe rlive in detail, prove its soundness and completeness, and compare it against the state of the art both theoretically
and empirically. Our experimental results show that our implementation
of rlive outperforms state-of-the-art implementations of FAIR, k-Liveness
and other SAT-based liveness checking algorithms on a wide range of
benchmarks from the literature.

1 Introduction

The design of efficient algorithms for model checking has been a major research
challenge for over three decades. Following the SAT breakthrough in the late
90 s [22, 25], many novel SAT-based techniques have been proposed, which have
tremendously increased the efficiency and scalability of (symbolic) model checking and its applicability to real-world systems (e.g., [6, 8, 15, 17, 18, 20, 21, 24, 27]).
Although the vast majority of such approaches have focused on safety properties, their benefits have extended also to liveness model checking, thanks to the
development of liveness verification algorithms that work by exploiting efficient
safety checkers, either via a monolithic reduction from liveness to safety [4],

© The Author(s) 2024
A. Gurfinkel and V. Ganesh (Eds.): CAV 2024, LNCS 14681, pp. 234–254, 2024.
https://doi.org/10.1007/978-3-031-65627-9_12

or via more sophisticated strategies that use safety checkers incrementally [13], exploiting also the inductive invariants generated when the verification is successful [9,16].

In this paper, we present a novel SAT-based liveness checking algorithm, which we call rlive, that also takes advantage of efficient safety model checkers and their capability of producing inductive invariants for verified properties. Like all other SAT-based approaches to liveness checking, rlive works on properties of the form FGq, stating that q has to eventually stabilize to true in all traces of the system, relying on standard procedures (e.g., [12,14]) for transforming a model checking problem for an arbitrary LTL property into this form.

Similar to the FAIR algorithm of [9], rlive then proceeds by refuting candidate counterexamples to the property, i.e. traces in which $\neg q$ holds infinitely often, using a sequence of calls to a safety checker, and exploiting the inductive invariants generated by such safety checks to prune the set of reachable $\neg q$-states, until either a real (lasso-shaped) counterexample for FGq is found, or no $\neg q$-states are reachable, implying that the property holds. However, in contrast to FAIR, which directly searches for lasso-shaped traces where $\neg q$ holds in at least one state of the loop, rlive searches for counterexamples incrementally, via a recursive chain of safety checks, each of which tries to determine whether it is possible to reach a $\neg q$-state starting from the successors of a previously-reached $\neg q$-state, in a manner conceptually similar to k-Liveness [13]. If a $\neg q$-state is found for the second time during this recursive chain, a (lasso-shaped) counterexample witnessing the violation of FGq is constructed, and the algorithm terminates. Otherwise, eventually one of the recursive safety checks will generate an inductive invariant C proving that no other $\neg q$-state can be reached from (the successors of) a given $\neg q$-state s. rlive then uses C to derive constraints that exclude s from the reachable states of the system, forcing it to (recursively) consider a different $\neg q$-state to continue the current candidate counterexample trace. Specifically, C is used to strengthen the target states to reach, by asking the safety checker to ignore $\neg q$-states whose successors are all contained in C (since all such states in C cannot visit $\neg q$ infinitely-often); furthermore, C can be used also to strengthen the transition relation of the input system, since no state in C can be part of a counterexample. To give this intuition, we refer to states in C as *shoals*, as they represent regions of the state space that must be avoided in order to not "get stuck" in the search for a counterexample. Eventually, the shoals (recursively) produced will either exclude all $\neg q$-states, thus proving that the input property holds, or compel rlive to find a lasso-shaped counterexample for it.

Intuitively, rlive effectively identifies counterexamples by searching, in a depth-first manner, for traces that contain as many $\neg q$-states as possible. Performing the search incrementally, by a sequence of simple reachability checks, turns out to be computationally cheaper than searching directly for loops in practice. Moreover, whenever the current candidate counterexample trace cannot be completed, the shoals obtained from the safety checks can be used globally to strengthen the transition system and reduce the search space that needs to be explored, thus accelerating the convergence of the algorithm.

We have implemented rlive on top of the nuXmv model checker [10] which has a mature, state-of-the-art IC3 implementation, and compared it against state-of-the-art implementations of other SAT-based liveness checking algorithms, including FAIR, k-Liveness, and their recent combination called k-FAIR [16]. Our experimental results, conducted on a wide range of benchmarks taken from recent hardware model checking competitions [1,2], demonstrate the strengths of our algorithm: rlive solves more benchmarks than any other competitor in the given resource bounds, and very often with significantly shorter time.

Paper Structure. The rest of the paper is structured as follows. After the introduction of the necessary background in Sect. 2, we describe rlive in Sect. 3 and prove its soundness and correctness. We compare rlive with related work in Sect. 4, and experimentally evaluate its performance in Sect. 5. Finally, we conclude in Sect. 6 outlining also directions for future work.

2   Preliminaries

2.1   Boolean Satisfiability

A *literal* is a Boolean variable or its negation. If l is a literal, we denote its corresponding variable with $var(l)$. A *cube* (resp. *clause*) is a conjunction (resp. disjunction) of literals. The negation of a clause is a cube and vice versa. A formula in *Conjunctive Normal Form* (CNF) is a conjunction of clauses. For simplicity, we also treat a CNF formula ϕ as a set of clauses and make no difference between the formula and its set representation. Similarly, a cube or a clause c can be treated as a set of literals or a Boolean formula, depending on the context.

We say a CNF formula ϕ is satisfiable if there exists an assignment of its Boolean variables, called a *model*, that makes ϕ true; otherwise, ϕ is unsatisfiable. A SAT solver is a tool that can decide the satisfiability of a CNF formula ϕ. In addition to providing a yes/no answer, modern SAT solvers can also produce *models* for satisfiable formulas, and *unsatisfiable cores* (UC), i.e. a reason for unsatisfiability, for unsatisfiable ones. More precisely, in the following we shall assume to have a SAT solver that supports the following API (which is standard in state-of-the-art SAT solvers based on the CDCL algorithm [19]):

- IS-SAT$(\phi, \mathcal{A})$ checks the satisfiability of ϕ under the given assumptions $\mathcal{A}$, which is a list of literals. This is logically equivalent to checking the satisfiability of $\phi \wedge \bigwedge \mathcal{A}$, but is typically more efficient;
- GET-UC() retrieves an UC of the assumption literals of the previous SAT call when the formula $\phi \wedge \bigwedge \mathcal{A}$ is unsatisfiable. That is, the result is a set $uc \subseteq \mathcal{A}$ such that $\phi \wedge \bigwedge uc$ is unsatisfiable;
- GET-MODEL() retrieves the model of the formula $\phi \wedge \bigwedge \mathcal{A}$ of the previous SAT call, if the formula is satisfiable.

2.2   Boolean Transition Systems

A Boolean transition system Sys is a tuple $\langle X, I, T \rangle$, where X is a set of variables, and I and T are formulae. The state space of Sys is the set of possible assignments to X. $I(X)$ is a Boolean formula corresponding to the set of initial states, and $T(X, X')$ is a Boolean formula representing the transition relation, where $X' = \{x' \mid x \in X\}$ represent the next state variables. In the following, we extend the prime notation to states and formulae in the natural way. The state s_2 is a successor of a state s_1 iff $s_1 \wedge s_2' \models T$, which is also denoted by $(s_1, s_2) \in T$. A *finite* path of length k is a finite state sequence $s_1, s_2, \ldots, s_k$, where $(s_i, s_{i+1}) \in T$ holds for $(1 \leq i \leq k-1)$. An *infinite* path is an infinite state sequence $s_1, s_2, \ldots$, where $(s_i, s_{i+1}) \in T$ holds for $i \geq 1$. The number of states is finite for any (Boolean) transition system. An infinite path is *lasso-shaped* if it can be presented as $\alpha \cdot \beta^\omega$, where α is the finite prefix, e.g. $s_1, s_2, \ldots, s_{l-1}$, and β is an infinitely-repeating suffix, e.g. $s_l, s_{l+1}, \ldots, s_k$. A state t is reachable from s in k steps if there is a path of length k from s to t. Let S be a set of states in Sys. We overload T and denote the set of successors of states in S as $T(S) = \{t \mid (s, t) \in T, s \in S\}$. Conversely, we define the set of predecessors of states in S as $T^{-1}(S) = \{s \mid (s, t) \in T, t \in S\}$. Recursively, we define $T^0(S) = S$ and $T^{i+1}(S) = T(T^i(S))$ where $i \geq 0$; the notation $T^{-i}(S)$ is defined analogously. In short, $T^i(S)$ denotes the states that are reachable from S in i steps, and $T^{-i}(S)$ denotes the states that can reach S in i steps.

2.3   Invariant Checking

Let a Boolean transition system $Sys = \langle X, I, T \rangle$ be given. A Boolean formula P over X is an invariant iff it holds in all the reachable states of Sys. An invariant checker either proves that P holds for any state reachable from an initial state in I, or disproves P by producing a *counterexample*. In the former case, we say that the property is *proven* in the system, while in the latter case, the property is *disproved*. A *counterexample* is a finite path from an initial state s to a state t violating P, i.e., $t \in \neg P$; such a state is also called a *bad* state.

   Invariant checking, also referred to as safety checking, is reduced to symbolic reachability analysis. Reachability analysis can be performed in a forward or backward search. Forward search starts from initial states I and searches for bad states by computing $T^i(I)$ with increasing values of i, while backward search begins with states in $\neg P$ and searches for initial states by computing $T^{-i}(\neg P)$ with increasing values of i.

   State-of-the-art safety checking algorithms utilize SAT techniques to explore the state space so as to improve the overall performance dramatically. Representative approaches include IC3/PDR [8,15], interpolation-based model checking [20], combinations of IC3 with interpolation [27] or k-induction [17], and (forward and backward) CAR [18]. In the following, we abstract from specific invariant checking algorithms, and assume that they implement the following API:

- CHECK-REACHABLE($I, T, \neg P$) denotes a generic procedure for safety checking. It takes as input a set of initial states I, the transition relation T, and the negation of the candidate invariant P. CHECK-REACHABLE returns *unsafe* if P is not an invariant. Otherwise, it returns *safe*.
- GET-INVARIANT() retrieves an inductive invariant proving that the bad states are unreachable, i.e. a set ι of states closed under T, containing the states reachable from I, and not intersecting $\neg P$. More formally, ι is such that $I \models \iota$, $\iota \wedge T \models \iota'$, and $\iota \models P$.
- GET-CEX-TRACE() retrieves, if the property is violated, the counterexample found by the safety checker, i.e. a finite path from I to $\neg P$.

2.4   Liveness Checking

We now consider the general model checking problem, denoted $Sys \models \phi$, where ϕ is a formula in Linear Temporal Logic (LTL) [23]. Following the standard automata-theoretic approach [26], the problem can be reduced to checking $Sys \times \mathcal{A}_{\neg\phi} \models FGq$, where $\neg q$ can be seen as the Büchi acceptance condition of $\mathcal{A}_{\neg\phi}$. (Symbolic techniques such as [12,14] can be used in practice to encode such reduction.) FGq intuitively means that, in any satisfying trace, q eventually holds in all the future states, so that the acceptance condition $\neg q$ can only be visited a finite number of times. Dually, a counterexample is an infinite path where $\neg q$ is visited an infinite number of times, i.e. a trace satisfying $GF\neg q$.

In the following, we focus on the (simplified) $Sys \models FGq$ problem, referred to as *liveness checking*. If the property is violated, there always exists a lasso-shaped counterexample[1], i.e., an infinite path $\alpha \cdot \beta^\omega$ where (i) the prefix α is a finite trace of Sys whose last state t violates q, i.e., $t \in \neg q$, and (ii) the infinitely-repeating suffix β is a path in Sys from a successor of t to t. We refer to a state $t \in \neg q$ as a $\neg q$-state.

The algorithms for liveness checking are more complicated than those for invariant checking. In order to show that a candidate invariant does not hold, it is sufficient to find a finite path. Liveness checking, on the other hand, requires finding an infinite (lasso-shaped) counter-example (or proving that none exists). The most effective solutions to liveness checking are based on invariant checking. The most relevant to our work are the following.

- The L2S [4] (Liveness-to-Safety) construction introduces a copy of the state variables in Sys, to record the first state of the loop, and a fresh variable $inLoop$, to record that the loop has started. The state vector copy is non-deterministically assigned a state violating q, i.e. the start of the loop, and can never change after that. The search tries to reach a state where each state variable has the same value as its copy and $inLoop = true$, which implies that a violating lasso is detected. This translation is sound and complete.

---

[1] Note that this fact only holds in the finite-state case; for infinite-state systems, the existence of a lasso-shaped counterexample is not guaranteed in case of violation.

Algorithm 1. k-FAIR = k-Liveness + FAIR

1: **Liveness Property:** FGq
2: **procedure** K-FAIR(I, T, q)
3:     $k := 0$, $C := \varnothing$, $W := \varnothing$ *// C: states not in loop, W: wall*
4:     **while** *true* **do**
5:         **if** not IS-SAT($\neg q_k \wedge \neg C$) **then**   *// FAIR*
6:             **return safe**
7:         **if** CHECK-REACHABLE(I, T, $\neg q_k \wedge \neg C$) is **safe then**
8:             **return safe**
9:         s is the last state from GET-CEX-TRACE()   *// FAIR*
10:         **if** CHECK-REACHABLE($T(s)$, $T \wedge (W \leftrightarrow W')$, s) is **unsafe then**
11:             **return unsafe**
12:         **else**
13:             $D :=$ GET-INVARIANT()
14:             $W := W \cup D$
15:             $g :=$ GENERALIZING-NOLOOP(s, D)
16:             $C := C \cup g$
17:         $(I, T, \neg q_k) :=$ INCREASECOUNTER($\neg q_k$)   *// k++*
18:
19: **function** GENERALIZING-NOLOOP(s, D)
20:     **assert**($s \in \neg D$ and $T(s) \subseteq D$)
21:     **assert(not** IS-SAT($T \wedge \neg D'$, s))   *// $s \wedge T \rightarrow D'$*
22:     $g_1 :=$ GET-UC()
23:     **assert(not** IS-SAT(D, s))   *// $s \rightarrow \neg D$*
24:     $g_2 :=$ GET-UC()
25:     **return** $g_1 \wedge g_2$

- FAIR [9] tries to construct a lasso-shaped counterexample as follows: first, it searches for a candidate prefix (α); then, starting from the last (bad) state t of α, it searches for a suffix (β) that ends with t. Both steps are based on invariant checking. If the loop cannot be found, this bad state will be pruned. Fundamental optimizations include state generalization and, more importantly, extraction of *walls* (where, intuitively, states in a loop can only exist on one side of the wall). Then, FAIR iterates trying to find another candidate prefix for the lasso. The procedure terminates as soon as no prefix can be detected, in which case the property is proved.
- k-Liveness [13] tries to prove FGq based on the following intuition: if FGq holds, then there is a (finite) maximum number of times in which q can be violated in any path. The k-Liveness construction introduces a counter of the number of times q is violated and calls a safety checker to prove that the counter cannot exceed the given limit k. In case of failure, the limit is increased. k-Liveness proves the property if a k is found such that no path visits $\neg q$ more than k times. In general, k-Liveness is considered effective in *proving* the property. Notice, however, that k-Liveness – as described above – is incomplete, and will diverge if the property does not hold. On the other hand, it is possible to find counterexamples by checking the existence of repeated

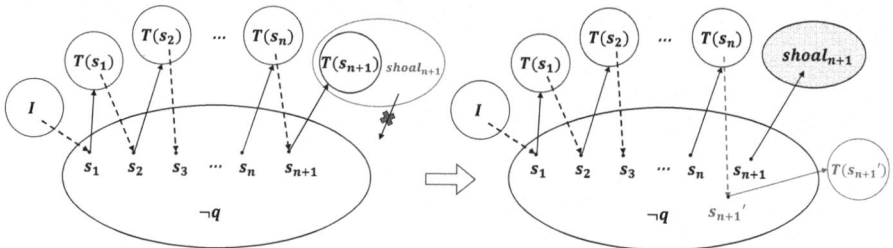

Fig. 1. Forward expansion and shoal construction (left); Rollback (right).

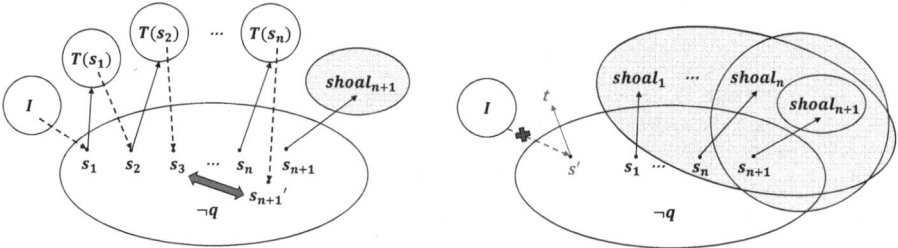

Fig. 2. Terminating conditions: counterexample found, unsafe (left); $\neg q$ no longer reachable from I, safe (right).

bad states from the path returned by the safety-checking call. As already suggested in [13], k-Liveness can be run in parallel to bounded model checking [6], that is complete in the case of violation.

– k-FAIR [16] is a more recent approach, designed to inherit advantages from FAIR and k-Liveness. k-FAIR utilizes k-Liveness for proving correctness while leveraging FAIR for finding counterexamples. The k-FAIR algorithm is shown in Algorithm 1. We see that FAIR and k-Liveness can both be considered a special case of k-FAIR. If line 17 is removed, the algorithm becomes FAIR. If line 5 and lines 9–16 are removed, it becomes k-Liveness.

3 Liveness Checking with rlive

In this section we informally describe rlive, then present the pseudo code and some optimizations, and finally characterize its formal properties.

3.1 Overview

rlive is a new algorithm for liveness checking ($Sys \models FGq$). At a high level, rlive can be seen as a depth-first search with chronological backtracking and learning. rlive incrementally tries to build a counterexample to FGq, progressively extending it with more states in $\neg q$. In the *forward expansion* phase, rlive first looks for a finite path π_1 from I to $\neg q$, with s_1 being the last state of π_1. Then, rlive looks for another path π_2 from $T(s_1)$ to $\neg q$, and so on. See Fig. 1, left. The forward expansion proceeds until one of two conditions holds.

1. if s_n is equal to s_i, with $i < n$, then a lasso-shaped counterexample exists, and the search terminates with *unsafe* (Fig. 2, left). The counterexample can be constructed by concatenating the previously found π_i.
2. if s_{n+1} cannot reach $\neg q$, then a *shoal* is built, i.e. a set of states closed under T and containing $T(s_{n+1})$, that can reach no target state ($shoal_{n+1}$ in Fig. 1, left). Clearly, no state in a shoal can belong to the counterexample; hence, shoals are learned and used to block the subsequent forward expansions.

In the second case, the algorithm *rolls back* to the previous level, and restarts the forward search, looking for a new way to enter $\neg q$. However, to avoid entering the shoals again, the target $\neg q$-state must have successors outside the shoals. (e.g. s'_{n+1} in Fig. 1, right). The algorithm terminates with *safe* whenever it rolls back to level 0, and finds no way to reach, from the initial states, the remaining subset of $\neg q$ while avoiding the shoal constraints (Fig. 2, right).

We remark that, upon backtracking, the forward search space is restricted to avoid the shoal constraints as well as the states in $\neg q$ that do not belong to the counterexample. Hence, the navigation toward the target is increasingly restricted because of the discovered shoal constraints and also because the target is progressively shrunk.

The algorithm described above is naturally implemented with primitives provided by the safety checker, such as deciding reachability and constructing the counterexamples and the invariants. A further practical optimization called *deadstate pruning*, trades off calls to the safety checker with calls to the SAT solver, enlarging the shoals with a cheap form of look ahead to further prune the target set.

3.2   Algorithm

Algorithm 2 describes how rlive is implemented using a generic invariant-checking engine implementing the API introduced in Sect. 2.3. To prove or falsify the liveness property FGq, rlive will maintain a global state set C at line 2, representing the shoals (i.e. states from which $\neg q$ can be reached only a finite number of times) discovered so far.

The algorithm starts from line 4, checking whether $\neg q$ is reachable from the initial states, using CHECK-REACHABLE. If it is not reachable, Gq is proved, and so FGq is verified. Otherwise, from the counterexample trace returned by CHECK-REACHABLE, we get a reachable $\neg q$-state s. Then the SEARCH-CEX function is called to search for the next $\neg q$-state from s.

When C is not empty, we block the states in C from the transition system by adding the constraint $\neg C \wedge \neg C'$ to T (lines 5 and 17). At the same time, the states to be searched become $\neg q \cap T^{-1}(\neg C)$, which ensures that the searched $\neg q$-states have $\neg C$ successors, to exclude the $\neg q$-states that are proved not to be part of a counterexample.

Algorithm 2. Implementation of rlive

1: **Liveness Property:** FGq
2: $C := \varnothing$ // *shoals:* $\neg q$ *can only be reached finitely-many times from states in* C
3:
4: **procedure** rlive(I, T, q)
5:     **while** CHECK-REACHABLE(I, $T \wedge (\neg C \wedge \neg C')$, $\neg q \cap T^{-1}(\neg C)$) is **unsafe do**
6:         s is the reached $\neg q$-state from GET-CEX-TRACE()
7:         **if** SEARCH-CEX(s, $\varnothing$) **then**
8:             **return unsafe**
9:     **return safe**
10:
11: **function** SEARCH-CEX(s, B)
12:     **if** $s \in B$ **then**   // B: *reachable* $\neg q$-*states from initial states*
13:         **return True**
14:     **while True do**
15:         **if** PRUNE-DEAD(s) **then**
16:             **return False**
17:         **if** CHECK-REACHABLE($T(s)$, $T \wedge (\neg C \wedge \neg C')$, $\neg q \cap T^{-1}(\neg C)$) is **unsafe then**
18:             t is the reached $\neg q$-state from GET-CEX-TRACE()
19:             **if** SEARCH-CEX(t, $B \cup \{s\}$) **then**
20:                 **return True**
21:         **else**
22:             $D :=$ GET-INVARIANT()
23:             $C := C \cup D$ // $\neg q \cap T^{-1}(\neg C)$ *cannot be reached from states in* D
24:             **return False**
25:
26: **function** PRUNE-DEAD(s)
27:     **while** IS-SAT($s \wedge T \wedge \neg C'$) **do**
28:         $\mu :=$ GET-MODEL()
29:         $d := \{l \mid l' \in \mu\}$
30:         **if not** IS-SAT($T \wedge \neg C'$, d) **then**
31:             $D :=$ GET-UC( )   // *unsatisfiable core returned by the* SAT *solver*
32:             $C := C \cup D$ // *states in* D *have no successor not in* C
33:         **else**
34:             **return False**
35:     **return True**

In the SEARCH-CEX(s, B) function of line 11, the parameter s serves as a new reached $\neg q$-state, and the parameter B contains the $\neg q$-states that have been previously reached along the current trace. Therefore, in lines 12–13, when s has appeared in B, a lasso-shape counterexample has been found, so the function returns True (a counterexample has been detected). Line 15 is the implementation of an important heuristic called *dead-pruning*, which we describe in detail in the next subsection. A new call to CHECK-REACHABLE is performed to find the next $\neg q \cap T^{-1}(\neg C)$-state starting from the successor of s on line 17. The reason for searching from the $T(s)$-states is that s itself is a state that meets $\neg q \cap T^{-1}(\neg C)$. However, calculating the exact set $T(s)$ might be quite expensive, so we use an overapproximation of $T(s)$, which we describe below in Sect. 3.3. If a state t can be reached, then the function is called recursively, t is used as the new starting state, and the s state is added to B. Otherwise, CHECK-REACHABLE would return an inductive invariant D on line 22.[2] This invariant is an overapproximation of the reachable states starting from $T(s)$, and none of these states can reach $\neg q \cap T^{-1}(\neg C)$. Therefore, states in D are shoals, so they can be added to C, and then the function returns False.

3.3   Optimizations

Avoiding the Explicit Computation of $T^{-1}(\neg C)$. When asking for the next $\neg q \cap T^{-1}(\neg C)$-state in the current trace, we can avoid the explicit computation of $T^{-1}(\neg C)$ by exploiting some additional knowledge about how the reachability engine CHECK-REACHABLE works. For example, if CHECK-REACHABLE is based on IC3 [8], we can simply add a constraint $T \wedge \neg C'$ to the SAT solver when asking for a $\neg q$-state.

Efficiently Over-Approximating $T(s)$. Using IC3 as an implementation of CHECK-REACHABLE allows us also to efficiently overapproximate the states $T(s)$ in the (recursive) searches for the next $\neg q$-states in the current trace (line 17). To do so, we slightly modify IC3,[3] and in particular the query that checks whether a given predecessor b of a bad ($\neg q$-)state intersects the initial states of the system. Rather than checking whether $T(s) \wedge b$ is satisfiable, we check the satisfiability of $s \wedge T$ under the assumption of b'. If the formula is unsat, we add the cube $c \subseteq b$ corresponding to the unsat core produced by the SAT solver (i.e. such that $c' = \text{GET-UC}()$) to the 0-th frame of IC3. In this way, the 0-th frame of IC3 will effectively be our desired over-approximation of $T(s)$.

Dead States Pruning. During rlive, lots of *dead states*, i.e. states that do not have any successors, are formed due to the strengthening of T and $\neg q$ using the discovered shoals. To prove that $\neg q$ cannot be reached from such a dead state, CHECK-REACHABLE needs to search for the predecessor states of $\neg q$ and describe the overapproximation of the reachable set from the dead state with the literals in the predecessors, which might require a large number of SAT queries.

Dead-pruning optimization is a simple and effective optimization (but probably not the only one) used to detect and quickly block the *dead states*. The optimization is used before calling CHECK-REACHABLE, to check whether a successor of the starting bad state is a dead state. If it is, then it can be excluded from the search and used to strengthen the shoals C.

---

[2] When the recursive call returns to the previous level, due to the incremental nature of the IC3, it can reuse the lemmas previously calculated in this level. However, we empirically found that such reuse doesn't result in an obvious boost in performance.

[3] Note that the same optimization can be applied also to other engines that use an "IC3-like" search, such as CAR.

Line 26 in Algorithm 2 is the implementation of the *dead-pruning* heuristic. A successor d of s is computed on lines 27–29. If d is determined to be a dead state (line 30), then it can be added to C (after being generalized using the unsat core produced by the SAT solver). The function returns False once it finds a successor of s with successors outside of C. If all the successors of s are blocked as dead states, the function returns True.

3.4   Correctness Proof

This section presents the proofs for the correctness of rlive (Algorithm 2). We first show the following lemmas which are crucial for the proof.

Lemma 1. *Every state $t \in C$ can only reach a $\neg q$-state a finite number of times.*

Proof. According to Algorithm 2, C can be updated in either the SEARCH-CEX or PRUNE-DEAD procedure. Since the latter one is optional (it is an optimization), we first consider the proof without the PRUNE-DEAD procedure.

In the SEARCH-CEX procedure, C is the state set that is updated by the union of different inductive invariants returned by CHECK-REACHABLE (line 23), whose initial states are an over-approximation of successors of some $\neg q$-state s. From the correctness of CHECK-REACHABLE, every state t in the inductive invariant satisfies: (1) it may be reachable from the initial states (and $\neg q$-state s) due to over-approximation, thus may be reachable from s, and (2) it cannot reach the states in $\neg q \cap T^{-1}(\neg C)$ (line 17). By construction, assume $C = C_1 \cup C_2 \cup \ldots \cup C_n$ where C_k $(1 \leq k \leq n)$ is the k-th inductive invariant added into C. We prove the lemma by induction over n. Obviously, every state $t \in C_1$ cannot reach states in $\neg q$ (and $C_1 \cap \neg q = \emptyset$). So the lemma holds in the base case. For the inductive step (when $k > 1$), since every state $t \in C_k$ cannot reach $\neg q \cap T^{-1}(\neg(\bigcup_{1 \leq i \leq k-1} C_i))$, we consider a state $\tilde{s} \in \neg q$ in two different sets. If $\tilde{s} \in T^{-1}(\neg(\bigcup_{1 \leq i \leq k-1} C_i))$, t cannot reach $\tilde{s}$; otherwise, $\tilde{s} \notin T^{-1}(\neg(\bigcup_{1 \leq i \leq k-1} C_i))$ implies that $T(\tilde{s}) \subseteq (\bigcup_{1 \leq i \leq k-1} C_i)$, i.e., every successor of $\tilde{s}$ is in $(\bigcup_{1 \leq i \leq k-1} C_i)$. From the inductive hypothesis, every state in $(\bigcup_{1 \leq i \leq k-1} C_i)$ can only reach a $\neg q$-state a finite number of times. Therefore, we have that t can only reach a $\neg q$-state finitely-many times as well.

Taking the PRUNE-DEAD procedure into consideration, only those states whose successors are all in C are added into C (line 32). From the hypothesis assumption, every state in C can only visit a $\neg q$-state a finite number of times, so as the predecessors, those states can only visit a $\neg q$-state finitely-many times as well.   □

Lemma 2. *Given $s \models \neg C$, when the PRUNE-DEAD (s) procedure returns, it returns True if and only if every successor of s, if existing, is in C.*

Proof. ($\Rightarrow$) The procedure returns True implies that either the SAT call at line 27 returns *unsat*, which indicates that every successor of s is in C, or there is some successor d of s that is not in C. However, since the procedure returns True, the SAT call at line 30 must return *unsat*, which indicates that every successor of d, if existing, is in C. Then d will be added into C according to lines 31-32. So $d \in C$ becomes true. The above process will repeat inside the *while* loop at line 27 until every successor of s is in C.

($\Leftarrow$) If every successor of s is in C, the SAT call at line 27 will return *unsat*. Therefore, the *while* loop directly stops and the procedure returns True at line 35.   □

Lemma 3. *1.* SEARCH-CEX(s, B) *returns True if and only if there is a lasso starting from s and its loop part contains a $\neg q$-state.*
2. SEARCH-CEX(s, B) *always terminates.*

Proof. 1. ($\Rightarrow$) The procedure is recursively implemented and it returns True as soon as a $\neg q$-state t (which can be the same as s) is already in B, indicating that a loop is detected. Moreover, t is reachable from the input state s, since t is detected from the successors of s by CHECK-REACHABLE. Therefore, a lasso starting from s and looping with t is found when the procedure returns True.

($\Leftarrow$) Assume the lasso is $s, \ldots, t_1, \ldots, (t_i, \ldots, t_j)$ in which $t_j = t_i$ $(1 \le j \le i)$ and every t_k $(1 \le k \le j)$ is a $\neg q$-state. First of all, we can prove that for each t_k, it is true that $t_k \in T^{-1}(\neg C)$, i.e., there is some successor of t_k that is not in C; otherwise, from t_k there cannot be a lasso looping with a $\neg q$-state, as based on Lemma 1, all successors of t_k being in C implies they can only visit a $\neg q$-state a finite number of times. Therefore, t_k can be found by the CHECK-REACHABLE call at line 17 and PRUNE-DEAD(t_k) cannot return True according to Lemma 2, implying that SEARCH-CEX(s, B) will not return False at line 16. As a result, SEARCH-CEX(s, B) will finally return True at line 13 once it finds t_j for the second time.

2. We prove that the *while* loop of line 17 of SEARCH-CEX(s, B) is terminating. The point is that the size of the state set $\neg q \cap T^{-1}(\neg C)$ keeps shrinking after each iteration of the loop, because the $\neg q$-state t at line 18 will be removed from $\neg q \cap T^{-1}(\neg C)$. The reason is that when the recursive SEARCH-CEX$(s, \emptyset)$ procedure returns False at line 19, the proof of Item 1 above guarantees that there is no lasso starting from t and looping with a $\neg q$-state. So C will be updated either by the inductive invariant (line 23) or the unsat core in the PRUNE-DEAD procedure (line 32) such that $t \notin T^{-1}(\neg C)$ is true, according to Lemmas 1 and 2. Therefore, t is successfully removed from $\neg q \cap T^{-1}(\neg C)$. In the worst case, the state set will become empty and CHECK-REACHABLE can terminate with *safe* as no bad state can be found at line 5.   □

Lemma 4. *1.* rlive(I, T, q) *always terminates.*
2. rlive(I, T, q) *returns safe if and only if the system (I, T) satisfies the property FGq.*

Proof. 1. The proof is analogous to that of Item 2 of Lemma 3, so it is omitted.
2. ($\Rightarrow$) Assume by contradiction that rlive returns safe, but the property doesn't hold. Therefore, there exists a lasso-shaped trace π of the form $s, \ldots, t_1,$

$\ldots,(t_i,\ldots,t_j)$ in which $t_j = t_i$ $(1 \leq j \leq i)$ and every $t_k(1 \leq k \leq j)$ is a $\neg q$-state. By Lemma 1, none of the states in π is in C, and moreover $t_i \in \neg q \cap T^{-1}(\neg C)$. Therefore, $s,\ldots,t_1$ is a trace reaching the bad state $\neg q \cap T^{-1}(\neg C)$ in the system $\langle X, I, T \wedge (\neg C \wedge \neg C') \rangle$, which is found by the CHECK-REACHABLE call at line 5. But then, SEARCH-CEX$(t_1, \varnothing)$ at line 7 returns False by Lemma 3, and so rlive returns unsafe, which is a contradiction. ($\Leftarrow$) The system satisfies the property implies that every $\neg q$-state that is reachable from the initial states, if existing, can only be visited finitely-many times. Assume the number of such reachable $\neg q$-states is k $(k < +\infty)$. If $k = 0$, the CHECK-REACHABLE procedure in the while loop of rlive (line 5) will directly return *safe* and thus rlive returns safe. When $k > 0$, assume the reachable $\neg q$-states are $s_1,\ldots,s_k$. So there are at most k iterations of the while loop, since each s_i $(1 \leq i \leq k)$ can be found at most once by the CHECK-REACHABLE call on line 5 (the argument is similar to the one used in the proof of Item 2 of Lemma 3). However, SEARCH-CEX$(s_i, \emptyset)$ will return False, because s_i can be visited only a finite number of times and thus no lasso can be detected. As a result, rlive cannot return unsafe inside the loop. And finally, rlive can only return safe in the worst case that every s_i is found and blocked in the while loop.

$\square$

Theorem 1 (Correctness). rlive *can always terminate and terminate with the correct result.*

Proof. Directly from Lemma 4. $\square$

4   Related Work

We have already introduced the main SAT-based liveness checking algorithms in Sect. 2.4. Here, we discuss their relation with rlive, highlighting both similarities and differences with our approach.

rlive *vs* L2S [4]. The original liveness-to-safety transformation is conceptually very simple, and it can be applied with any off-the-shelf safety model checking algorithm, not necessarily based on SAT. The eager L2S transformation can however be inefficient, as it requires a duplication of the state variables, which might lead to significant performance penalties. In contrast, rlive follows a lazier approach, using an incremental reduction to safety, designed to exploit the invariant generation capability of modern SAT-based safety checking engines, which does not require duplicating the state variables and can be more efficient in practice.

rlive *vs* FAIR [9]. At a high level, rlive and FAIR follow the same principle of incremental strengthening the input problem by exploiting the inductive invariants generated when refuting candidate counterexamples with a safety model checker. The main difference is in how the candidate counterexamples are identified and blocked: while FAIR does that by checking directly for looping paths that start from a given reachable $\neg q$-state, rlive follows a more incremental approach, in which repeated (and recursive) safety checks are used to build a bad loop incrementally. As our experimental results show (see Sect. 5), this difference turns out to be crucial for performance in practice. A second difference regards the nature of the information extracted from the inductive invariants produced by the safety checker: in general, the walls of FAIR are regions that *cannot be crossed* to find a counterexample (i.e., all states of a counterexample to FGq are on one side of the wall), whereas shoals are regions that *must be avoided* completely (i.e., no state in a counterexample can part of a shoal).

rlive *vs* k-Liveness [13]. The incremental approach used by rlive for constructing counterexamples is inspired by the k-Liveness algorithm; in some sense, rlive can in fact be seen as a depth-first (DFS) variant of k-Liveness, which performs instead a breadth-first (BFS) search (relative to the number k of times in which $\neg q$ can occur in the traces of the system). Thanks to its DFS approach, rlive doesn't need to maintain a global k value, but uses a different k for each trace; as such, it can sometims reach values of k which are beyond the capabilities of k-Liveness (see our results in Sect. 5).[4] Another difference between the two approaches is in the capability of finding counterexamples: although in principle complete, k-Liveness is more effective at proving properties than at disproving them, and already in the original paper [13] the authors recommend complementing it with BMC for finding counterexamples; on the other hand, rlive is effective both for safe and unsafe properties.

rlive *vs* k-FAIR [16]. k-FAIR is a parametric combination of FAIR and k-Liveness, in which each candidate counterexample to FGq either is analyzed using FAIR, or causes an increase in the k counter of k-Liveness (see Algorithm 1). As such, the comparisons made above between rlive and FAIR or k-Liveness apply also to k-FAIR. Like k-FAIR, rlive can also be seen as trying to combine the strengths of the two techniques in a single algorithm; however, the two approaches differ significantly in how such integration is performed.

5   Evaluation

We have implemented rlive inside the nuXmv model checker [10]. Our implementation can use three different safety-checking engines, namely IC3, fCAR (Forward CAR), and bCAR (Backward CAR), relying on the latest version of CaDiCaL [7] as backend SAT solver. In this section, we experimentally evaluate rlive by comparing it with different state-of-the-art SAT-based liveness checking algorithms.

5.1   Experimental Setup

We include in our evaluation nuXmv [10] and IIMC [3], two state-of-the-art tools implementing SAT-based liveness-checking algorithms which are among the best-performing ones in the most recent liveness-checking tracks of the Hardware

---

[4] Note that here by k we mean the maximum recursion depth reached by rlive for a given candidate counterexample trace, as there is no explicit k counter in rlive.

Table 1. Tools and algorithms evaluated in the experiments.

Tools	Algorithms	Engines
nuXmv	rlive [-d] k-Liveness FAIR k-FAIR L2S	IC3, fCAR, bCAR
	k-Liveness + BMC	IC3, BMC
IIMC	k-Liveness FAIR	IC3

Model Checking Competition (HWMCC) [1,2]. nuXmv implements L2S and k-Liveness, using a configuration that runs k-Liveness in lockstep with BMC as suggested in [13] for the latter (which we refer to as k-Liveness + BMC below). In addition to rlive, we also implemented other three liveness-checking algorithms on top of nuXmv, namely k-Liveness, FAIR, and k-FAIR. FAIR and k-FAIR are implemented according to Algorithm 1, and k-Liveness is added with the ability to find counterexamples by checking for repeated $\neg q$-states in the violated traces (before increasing the value of k). IIMC implements FAIR and "plain" k-Liveness instead (without BMC). Table 1 summarizes the tested tools, algorithms, and their engines. Regarding rlive, the '-d' flag is used to enable the dead-pruning optimization, otherwise rlive ignores lines 15–16 of Algorithm 2.

We evaluate all the configurations on 223 benchmarks, in *aiger* [5] format, of the liveness property track of HWMCC 2015 and 2017 [1,2].[5] We ran the experiments on a cluster, which consists of Gold 6132 2.6GHz CPUs in 240 nodes running RedHat 4.8.5 with a total of 96GB RAM. For each test, we set the memory limit to 8GB and the time limit to 1 h. During the experiments, each model-checking run has exclusive access to a dedicated node. For correctness checking, we compared the results from different solvers and found no discrepancies.

5.2 Experimental Results

Overview. The main results of the experiment are summarized in Table 2, in which the different tools/configurations are ordered by the total number of successfully solved instances within the given resource budget. From the table, we can see that rlive is the algorithm with the overall best performance in terms of the number of solved cases. More explicitly, rlive with the dead-pruning optimization and using IC3 as the backend solves the largest number of instances (159), and it is also the configuration that verifies the most cases (66). rlive is also the algorithm that finds the largest number of counterexamples, and this is

---

[5] Note that HWMCC editions after 2017 did not include a liveness track.

Table 2. Summary of overall results among different tools/configurations.

Configuration	#Solved	#Verified	#Violated
nuXmv -rlive -d	<u>159</u>	<u>66</u>	93
nuXmv -rlive -d (fCAR)	158	62	96
nuXmv -k-Liveness + BMC	146	61	85
nuXmv -rlive	145	54	91
nuXmv -rlive -d (bCAR)	142	45	<u>97</u>
nuXmv -L2S	139	65	74
nuXmv -k-Liveness	138	63	75
nuXmv -k-FAIR	124	54	70
IIMC -FAIR	82	47	35
nuXmv -FAIR	66	29	37
IIMC -k-Liveness	50	50	0

true for all configurations that we tested (with 'rlive -d' using bCAR being the best one).

Regarding other tools/algorithms, the best performing one is the k-Liveness + BMC implementation in nuXmv, solving a total number of 146 cases, which is 11% less than the best configuration of rlive (i.e., 'rlive -d'). All the other configurations solve significantly fewer instances than rlive.

The results in Table 2 also show that using different engines to run the rlive algorithm preserves good performance.[6] Under the same implementation platform, their overall performance is better than k-Liveness using IC3: 'rlive -d (fCAR)/ (bCAR)' solves 158/142 instances in total, while k-Liveness only solves 124. Using fCAR results in a much better performance than bCAR on verifying properties (62 vs. 45). However, applying the bCAR engine seems to be an advantage in finding counterexamples, although the gap with other engines is modest (and rlive in general performs very well on finding counterexamples).

Finally, the results show also the importance of the dead-pruning optimization. Before the dead-pruning optimization is enabled, the performance of rlive is similar to k-Liveness + BMC from nuXmv (145 vs. 146). Dead-pruning improves rlive (using IC3) by verifying 12 more instances and finding 2 additional violations.

Runtime Efficiency. In order to evaluate the runtime efficiency of rlive, we show in Fig. 3 a plot on the number of solved instances (y-axis) in the given time limit (x-axis) for a subset of the tested configurations (all using IC3 as a backend). From the plot, it is evident that 'rlive -d' is significantly more efficient than the other competitors, always solving the largest number of instances within the timeout ranging from 600 s to 3600 s.

---

[6] It should be mentioned that we also tried k-Liveness, FAIR and k-FAIR with the fCAR and bCAR engines in our tool as well, but they do not have better performance than using IC3. For page limit, we do not list the relevant data in the paper.

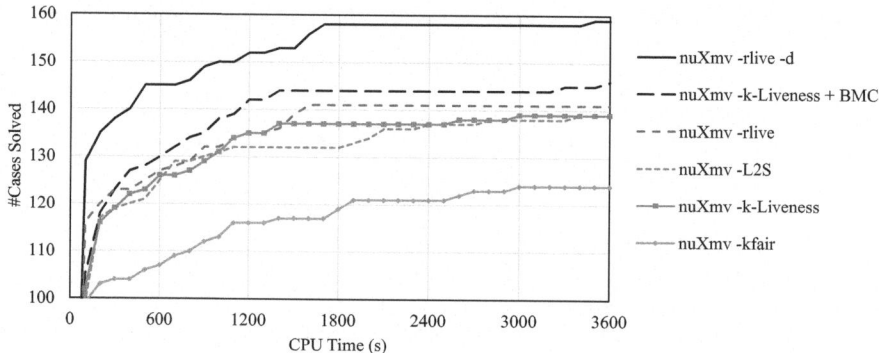

Fig. 3. Comparisons among the implementations under different configurations. (Note that for better readability the y-axis starts from a value of 100.)

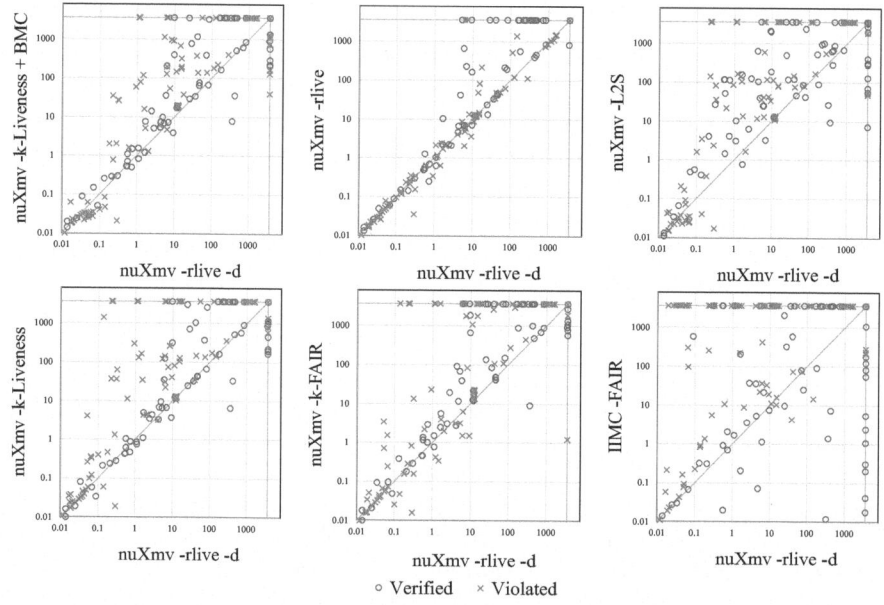

Fig. 4. Time comparison between rlive (with dead-pruning) and other implementations/configurations. rlive is always on the x-axis. Points above the diagonal indicate better performance of rlive. Points on the borders indicate timeouts (3600 s).

A more detailed comparison between rlive and other algorithms is shown in Fig. 4. From the plots, we can see that rlive outperforms other algorithms in a large number of cases, especially in the case of violated properties. An interesting exception is IIMC-FAIR, which shows strengths that are complementary to those of rlive, particularly for verified properties.

Portfolio Configurations. We analyze the behaviour of rlive in "portfolio" configurations, which is a technique often used in practice to improve performance when multiple CPU cores are available. For this, we performed two (virtual) experiments. In the first experiment, we consider a (virtual) portfolio consisting of the algorithms using IC3 as the backend, [7] and compare it with (virtual) portfolios obtained by excluding a single algorithm at a time, in order to analyze the contribution of the excluded algorithm to the virtual best. The results are shown in Table 3. From the table, we can see that rlive contributes significantly to the performance of the virtual best, particularly for violated properties. Moreover, when multiple engines solve the same property, rlive is the fastest in the vast majority of cases (81 over 183 verified by the virtual best, with the 2nd best performing being the fastest only in 26 cases).

Table 3. Virtual Best results among implementations by IC3 engine. **VBS \ (Algorithm** a**)** refers to the removal of a from the portfolio, so the reduction in the number of solutions represents the contribution of a to the portfolio. **#Fastest Solution** represents the number of times algorithm a solves a case fastest in the full VBS portfolio.

Configuration	#Verified	#Violated	#Contribute	#Fastest Solution
VBS	82	101	–	–
VBS \ (nuXmv -rlive -d)	82	85	17	81
VBS \ (IIMC -FAIR)	78	101	4	20
VBS \ (nuXmv -k-Liveness + BMC)	82	97	4	14
VBS \ (nuXmv -L2S)	82	101	0	26
VBS \ (nuXmv -k-FAIR)	82	101	0	18
VBS \ (nuXmv -FAIR)	82	101	0	15
VBS \ (nuXmv -k-Liveness)	82	101	0	10

In the second experiment, we compose (virtual) portfolios in a "bottom up" way, by considering only configurations running two different algorithms in parallel. Also, in this case, the results in Table 4 clearly show the impact of rlive.

Table 4. Top 10 combinations of 2 algorithms implementation into one portfolio.

Configurations	#Solved	#Verified	#Violated
nuXmv -rlive -d & IIMC -FAIR	174	78	96
nuXmv -rlive -d & nuXmv -k-Liveness + BMC	172	71	101
nuXmv -rlive -d & nuXmv -L2S	172	76	96
nuXmv -rlive -d & nuXmv-k-Liveness	170	74	96
nuXmv -rlive -d & nuXmv-k-FAIR	166	71	95
nuXmv -rlive -d & nuXmv-FAIR	161	66	95
nuXmv -k-Liveness + BMC & nuXmv -L2S	161	76	85
nuXmv -k-Liveness + BMC & IIMC -FAIR	159	74	85
nuXmv -L2S & nuXmv -k-FAIR	152	76	76
nuXmv -L2S & nuXmv -k-Liveness	151	76	75

---

[7] We exclude 'nuXmv -rlive' because it is subsumed by 'nuXmv -rlive -d'.

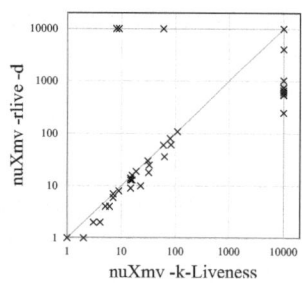

nuXmv -k-Liveness

Fig. 5. Comparison of the k values (maximum recursion depths reached) at termination on property verified cases between k-Liveness and rlive. Points on the borders indicate timeouts.

Analysis of rlive Behaviour. We explore the reasons for the excellent performance of rlive through Fig. 5, which compares the k value of k-Liveness to the corresponding maximum recursion depth in rlive on verified properties. They both represent that the algorithm can find a path containing at most k $\neg q$-states before terminating with safe. When both algorithms terminate within the time limit, the k value of rlive is always less (or equal) than the value of k-Liveness. Since k-Liveness performs a breadth-first search (in terms of k), it always needs to find the path that contains the most $\neg q$-states before it can terminate. On the other hand, the shoals generated by rlive during the search process help in blocking other $\neg q$-states, allowing rlive to converge at a smaller depth. In addition, rlive is better at solving cases where there is a path containing a large number of $\neg q$-states in the system, where k-Liveness needs to reach a very large k value to converge. These cases are located on the right border of Fig. 5. The recursion depths of rlive on these cases reach far over 100, with the deepest one reaching 4095. However, the maximum k value of k-Liveness is only around 100. Figure 5 shows also some cases (located in the upper border of the plot) which could be solved by k-Liveness but not by rlive. We investigated them and found that dead states caused the rollback steps of rlive to be slower. The current dead-pruning optimization, which only performs a one-step lookahead to discover dead states, is not effective for such instances (though in most cases this simple strategy works), suggesting future directions for improvement.

6   Conclusions

We presented rlive, a novel algorithm for the liveness checking problem FGq. The idea is to search for a lasso-shaped counterexample by repeatedly calling a safety checker to re-enter the $\neg q$ states set. The search proceeds in depth-first, backtracking when a state in $\neg q$ can be excluded by proving that $\neg q$ can only be reached finitely-many times from its successors, and cannot be part of a counterexample. The invariants returned by the underlying safety checker restrict the search progressively. We called such invariants shoals, as intuitively they represent states that must be avoided when searching for a counterexample. A thorough experimental evaluation clearly demonstrates that rlive is superior to the other liveness checkers, both in terms of benchmarks solved and run time.

Regarding future research, we plan to extend this work in several directions. First, we will investigate heuristics to control the exploration order of bad states and the counterexamples produced by the safety checker. Second, we will consider the extraction of proofs from rlive. Third, we will consider extensions of rlive to the infinite-state case, in combination with algorithms for finding non-lasso-shaped counterexamples such as [11].

Acknowledgment. We thank anonymous reviewers for their helpful comments. Yechuan Xia and Jianwen Li are supported by the National Natural Science Foundation of China (Grant #62372178 and #U21B2015), "Digital Silk Road" Shanghai International Joint Lab of Trustworthy Intelligent Software under Grant 22510750100, and Shanghai Collaborative Innovation Center of Trusted Industry Internet Software. A. Cimatti and A. Griggio acknowledge the support of the PNRR project FAIR - Future AI Research (PE00000013), under the NRRP MUR program funded by the NextGenerationEU, and of the PNRR MUR project VITALITY (ECS00000041), Spoke 2 ASTRA - Advanced Space Technologies and Research Alliance.

References

1. HWMCC 2015. http://fmv.jku.at/hwmcc15/
2. HWMCC 2017. http://fmv.jku.at/hwmcc17/
3. IIMC. https://github.com/mgudemann/iimc
4. Biere, A., Artho, C., Schuppan, V.: Liveness checking as safety checking. In: Proceedings of the 7th International Workshop on Formal Methods for Industrial Critical Systems. Electronic Notes in Theoretical Computer Science, vol. 66:2 (2002)
5. Biere, A.: AIGER Format. http://fmv.jku.at/aiger/FORMAT
6. Biere, A., Cimatti, A., Clarke, E., Zhu, Y.: Symbolic model checking without BDDs. In: Cleaveland, W.R. (ed.) TACAS 1999. LNCS, vol. 1579, pp. 193–207. Springer, Heidelberg (1999). https://doi.org/10.1007/3-540-49059-0_14
7. Biere, A., Fazekas, K., Fleury, M., Heisinger, M.: CaDiCaL, Kissat, Paracooba, Plingeling and Treengeling entering the SAT Competition 2020. In: Balyo, T., Froleyks, N., Heule, M., Iser, M., Järvisalo, M., Suda, M. (eds.) Proc. of SAT Competition 2020 – Solver and Benchmark Descriptions. Department of Computer Science Report Series B, vol. B-2020-1, pp. 51–53. University of Helsinki (2020)
8. Bradley, A.R.: SAT-based model checking without unrolling. In: Jhala, R., Schmidt, D. (eds.) VMCAI 2011. LNCS, vol. 6538, pp. 70–87. Springer, Heidelberg (2011). https://doi.org/10.1007/978-3-642-18275-4_7
9. Bradley, A.R., Somenzi, F., Hassan, Z., Zhang, Y.: An incremental approach to model checking progress properties. In: FMCAD, pp. 144–153. FMCAD Inc. (2011)
10. Cavada, R., et al.: The NuXmv symbolic model checker. In: Biere, A., Bloem, R. (eds.) CAV 2014. LNCS, vol. 8559, pp. 334–342. Springer, Cham (2014). https://doi.org/10.1007/978-3-319-08867-9_22
11. Cimatti, A., Griggio, A., Magnago, E.: LTL falsification in infinite-state systems. Inf. Comput. **289**(Part), 104977 (2022)
12. Claessen, K., Eén, N., Sterin, B.: A circuit approach to LTL model checking. In: FMCAD, pp. 53–60. IEEE (2013)
13. Claessen, K., Sörensson, N.: A liveness checking algorithm that counts. In: FMCAD, pp. 52–59. IEEE (2012)
14. Clarke, E.M., Grumberg, O., Hamaguchi, K.: Another look at LTL model checking. Formal Methods Syst. Des. **10**(1), 47–71 (1997)
15. Een, N., Mishchenko, A., Brayton, R.: Efficient implementation of property directed reachability. In: Proceedings of the International Conference on Formal Methods in Computer-Aided Design, pp. 125–134. FMCAD '11, FMCAD Inc, Austin, Texas (2011)

16. Ivrii, A., Nevo, Z., Baumgartner, J.: k-fair = k-liveness + FAIR revisiting sat-based liveness algorithms. In: FMCAD, pp. 1–5. IEEE (2018)
17. Jovanovic, D., Dutertre, B.: Property-directed k-induction. In: Formal Methods in Computer-Aided Design, pp. 86–92 (2016)
18. Li, J., Zhu, S., Zhang, Y., Pu, G., Vardi, M.Y.: Safety model checking with complementary approximations. In: Proceedings of the 36th International Conference on Computer-Aided Design, pp. 95–100. ICCAD '17, IEEE Press (2017)
19. Marques-Silva, J., Lynce, I., Malik, S.: Conflict-driven clause learning sat solvers. In: Handbook of Satisfiability, vol. 185 (2009)
20. McMillan, K.L.: Interpolation and SAT-based model checking. In: Hunt, W.A., Somenzi, F. (eds.) CAV 2003. LNCS, vol. 2725, pp. 1–13. Springer, Heidelberg (2003). https://doi.org/10.1007/978-3-540-45069-6_1
21. McMillan, K.L.: Applying SAT methods in unbounded symbolic model checking. In: Brinksma, E., Larsen, K.G. (eds.) CAV 2002. LNCS, vol. 2404, pp. 250–264. Springer, Heidelberg (2002). https://doi.org/10.1007/3-540-45657-0_19
22. Moskewicz, M.W., Madigan, C.F., Zhao, Y., Zhang, L., Malik, S.: Chaff: engineering an efficient SAT solver. In: DAC, pp. 530–535. ACM (2001)
23. Pnueli, A.: The temporal logic of programs. In: 18th Annual Symposium on Foundations of Computer Science (sfcs 1977), pp. 46–57 (Oct 1977)
24. Sheeran, M., Singh, S., Stålmarck, G.: Checking safety properties using induction and a SAT-solver. In: Hunt, W.A., Johnson, S.D. (eds.) FMCAD 2000. LNCS, vol. 1954, pp. 127–144. Springer, Heidelberg (2000). https://doi.org/10.1007/3-540-40922-X_8
25. Silva, J.P.M., Sakallah, K.A.: GRASP: a search algorithm for propositional satisfiability. IEEE Trans. Comput. 48(5), 506–521 (1999)
26. Vardi, M.Y.: An automata-theoretic approach to linear temporal logic. In: Moller, F., Birtwistle, G. (eds.) Logics for Concurrency. LNCS, vol. 1043, pp. 238–266. Springer, Heidelberg (1996). https://doi.org/10.1007/3-540-60915-6_6
27. Vizel, Y., Gurfinkel, A.: Interpolating property directed reachability. In: Biere, A., Bloem, R. (eds.) CAV 2014. LNCS, vol. 8559, pp. 260–276. Springer, Cham (2014). https://doi.org/10.1007/978-3-319-08867-9_17

Toward Liveness Proofs at Scale

Kenneth L. McMillan(✉)

University of Texas at Austin, Austin, USA
kenmcmil@gmail.com

Abstract. While the problem of mechanized proof of liveness of reactive programs has been studied for decades, there is currently no method of proving liveness that is conceptually simple to apply in practice to realistic problems, can be scaled to large problems without modular decomposition, and does not fail unpredictably due to the use of fragile heuristics. We introduce a method of liveness proof by relational rankings, implement it, and show that it meets these criteria in a realistic industrial case study involving a model of the memory subsystem in a CPU.

1 Introduction

The problem of mechanized proof of liveness of reactive programs has been studied for decades. Yet proving liveness of practical systems remains a challenge that is typically beyond the capability or time constraints of practicing engineers. This is not to say that we lack the conceptual framework or the tools needed to prove liveness properties. Rather, the difficulty lies in applying the tools and methods at the scale and complexity of systems encountered in industry. Here, we study the source of these difficulties with the goal of developing an approach that allows engineers with a reasonable degree of sophistication in formal methods to prove liveness of real systems.

The inspiration to study this problem comes from an effort to prove liveness of models of memory systems that have been developed by hardware engineers at Apple, Inc. The engineers use a tool and language called Ivy [18] to prove safety properties of memory subsystem models. These properties guarantee the consistency of memory operations from the point of view of the processor cores. Liveness of these models is considered important, in part to ensure the liveness of the underlying hardware implementation, but also to guarantee that the consistency proofs are not vacuous, owing to oversights in the models that might result in deadlock. Unfortunately, proving liveness using an existing approach implemented in Ivy was found by the engineers to be excessively difficult.

To understand why this is this is case, we must consider first the safety proofs. These are accomplished using a large number of hand-written inductive invariants of the models that were verified using a decision procedure (the SMT solver Z3 [5]). It is significant that it was possible to construct these proofs and maintain them through model changes on the time scale of industrial processor design.

One important factor in this success is that the models and proofs are constructed in a way that allows automated verification using only *effectively propositional reasoning*, or EPR [22], in which category we include extended logical fragments implemented

© The Author(s) 2024
A. Gurfinkel and V. Ganesh (Eds.): CAV 2024, LNCS 14681, pp. 255–276, 2024.
https://doi.org/10.1007/978-3-031-65627-9_13

in modern SMT solvers, such as FAU [9]. This means that the verifier is a decision procedure and hence can provide both proofs and counterexamples. Empirically, automated verification within EPR is far more efficient, stable and reliable than verification in the richer logics that SMT solvers provide [21,23]. This makes it possible to rapidly iterate while crafting a proof by invariant, while rarely having to debug failures of the verifier. Using EPR also makes it practical to verify a large model representing the entire memory system without resorting to compositional methods (*i.e.*, without using assume/guarantee specifications of the system components). The ability to carry out proof without modular decomposition significantly reduces the conceptual complexity of the proof task for engineers.

Unfortunately, these advantages of EPR do not currently carry over to liveness proofs. Known methods for liveness proof either *(1)* do not produce verification conditions in EPR, *(2)* cannot be applied at the necessary scale or *(3)* are too conceptually complex to be applied in industry. We will enumerate here the primary approaches to liveness proof the and difficulty of applying them in industrial applications.

Model Checking. Because the models are complex and not finite-state it is a significant challenge to apply model checking to them. Model checkers for infinite-state systems generally do not support liveness proofs and do not, in any event, scale to the needed size and complexity even for safety. This rules out model checking approaches such as [8,10,11,13,17] as well as Invisible Ranking [6]. Proofs combining model checking with compositional refinement and abstraction methods are possible [16] but have high conceptual complexity.

Deductive Approaches. In addition to inductive invariants, the common deductive approaches to liveness require the user to provide a *ranking* that maps the system state into a well-founded pre-order [14,15]. This is conceptually simple, but reasoning about well-founded orders generally takes us outside of EPR. We will consider why this is the case in more detail shortly, and how undecidable reasoning makes the problem of constructing large proofs substantially more difficult.

Liveness-to-Safety Translations. In this approach, we prove liveness by proving safety of a transformed program [2]. Although the approach has primarily been applied to finite-state systems, a recent method due to Padon *et al.* can be applied to infinite-state systems and produces verification conditions in EPR [19,20]. Unfortunately, it requires a user to provide an inductive invariant for the transformed program. The conceptual complexity of this task is high due to the subtlety and complexity of the transformation. This is the approach that the Apple engineers found difficult to apply.

Motivated by the practical experience at Apple, the goal of the proposed work is to create a liveness proof methodology with the following characteristics:

1. It is conceptually simple and easy to apply in common cases,
2. It supports a rich class of systems and temporal specifications,
3. It requires users to reason only about their own system, not about automatically constructed state machines,

4. It is as automated as is practical, relying only on decidable automated reasoning, and
5. It can be scaled to large models without modular decomposition.

To achieve these goals, we propose to apply the novel concept of a *relational rank-ing*. Using a relational ranking, we hypothesize that we can retain the relative simplicity of proof by well-founded ranking, allowing us to express rankings of height up to ω^n while avoiding any automated reasoning about well-founded orders, thus keeping the proof obligations within EPR. This allows us to reason automatically about the entire model, without modular decompositions, and thus without the need to write complete interface specifications for the system components (a task which is difficult for engineers). In place of this, we can re-use the inductive invariants needed to prove safety to supply almost all of the liveness proof. In fact, our experience with a generic memory system model provided by Apple bears out these expectations.

The primary contributions of this work are, first *a novel deductive proof approach for liveness*, based on relational rankings, and second, a *case study of industrial interest*, applying the method and motivating the features of the proof approach.

2   Background and Related Work

The classical approach to proving liveness properties deductively is to apply a *ranking*. A ranking is a function of the system state that ranges over a well-founded pre-order (often the natural numbers). This approach is well known for proving termination of sequential programs and was adapted to the proof temporal logic properties of con-current, reactive programs by Manna and Pnueli [15]. To apply their ranking rule, the user must supply inductive invariants and a ranking that are expressed over the system state. The proof is then reduced to non-temporal *verification conditions* that in principle can be discharged automatically. Approaches to proving liveness or termination using rankings include [4, 12, 24], some of which can synthesize rankings in limited cases.

2.1   Liveness-to-Safety with Rankings

We will use linear temporal logic (LTL) to define temporal properties, with $\Box$ for 'always' and $\Diamond$ for 'eventually'. Following Manna and Pnueli, $\rightarrow$ stands for implication, while $\Rightarrow$ stands for temporal entailment. That is, $p \Rightarrow q$ is a shorthand for $\Box(p \rightarrow q)$. We prove properties of standard first-order symbolic transition systems. As usual, we assume a vocabulary Σ of function and relation symbols representing the program state and a corresponding vocabulary of primed symbols Σ' representing the next state. A transition system is a pair $\langle \mathcal{I}, \mathcal{T} \rangle$, where $\mathcal{I}$ is a first-order formula over Σ representing the initial states and $\mathcal{T}$ is a first-order formula over Σ and Σ' representing the set of system transitions. We take $\mathcal{I} \wedge \Box\mathcal{T}$ as an axiom. That is, $\mathcal{I}$ holds initially, and $\mathcal{T}$ for every successive pair of states.

Manna and Pnueli gave a basic rule for proving properties of the form:

$$(\Box\Diamond r) \rightarrow (p \Rightarrow \Diamond q). \tag{1}$$

The condition r is assumed to occur infinitely often. We will call this a *justice con-straint*, and the formula r a *justice condition*. If justice condition r holds infinitely

init:	**action** send(x):	**action** poll:
pend := λx. false;	**requires** $x >$ last;	**if** $\exists t.$ pend(t):
last := 0;	last := x;	x := $\min_y$(pend(y));
	pend(x) := true;	**emit** recv(x);
		pend(x) := false;

Fig. 1. Simple timestamped queue example in a notional synchronous language.

often, then whenever p holds, q must hold in the future. For now, we will assume that p, r and q are non-temporal. To prove such a formula, we show that p establishes an invariant ϕ that holds until q is true. Moreover, while ϕ holds, a ranking δ never increases, and whenever r holds, δ decreases. We require that δ be a function from the program state into some well-founded set.

In our notation, the rule for proving formulas of form (1) is as follows:

$$
\begin{array}{l}
\text{B1. } p \Rightarrow (q \vee \phi) \\
\text{B2. } \phi \Rightarrow (q' \vee (\phi' \wedge (\delta' \leq \delta))) \\
\underline{\text{B3. } \phi \wedge r \Rightarrow (q' \vee (\delta' < \delta))} \\
(\square \lozenge r) \rightarrow (p \Rightarrow \lozenge q)
\end{array}
\tag{2}
$$

Notice that premises B1–B3 are temporal entailments. Normally, these are proved using the safety rule, stated below:

$$
\begin{array}{l}
\text{I1. } \mathcal{I} \rightarrow \rho \\
\text{I2. } \mathcal{T} \wedge \rho \rightarrow \rho' \\
\underline{\text{I3. } \mathcal{T} \wedge \rho \rightarrow p} \\
\square\, p
\end{array}
\tag{3}
$$

Thus, we can think of (2) as a liveness-to-safety rule. We will call the invariant ρ used in the safety rule the 'safety invariant' to distinguish it from the invariant ϕ in the liveness rule.

A Simple Example. As an example, Fig. 1 shows a simple transition system representing a message queue, inspired by the Apple generic memory model. The actions represent atomic system transitions, which we assume are proved terminating (for example, because they are loop-free, as here). A sender enters messages in the queue with logical time stamps, drawn from the natural numbers. We assume the time stamps of messages entering the queue are increasing, but there may be gaps in the time stamp sequence. A receiver polls the queue for messages. When there is a message, the message with minimum time stamp is removed and a signal 'recv' is emitted. The state predicate 'pend' represents the time stamps that are currently present in the queue.

We would like to prove the following property for all t:

$$
(\square\lozenge\text{poll}) \rightarrow (\text{send}(t) \Rightarrow \lozenge\text{recv}(t)).
\tag{4}
$$

where send(t) is true when sender enters a message with time stamp t, recv(t) is true when the receiver removes a message with time stamp t, and poll is true when the receiver polls the queue. In other words, if the receiver polls the queue infinitely often, then every sent message is eventually received. Note that t is a temporal constant.

An obvious ranking function for this proof counts the number of time stamps $\leq t$ that are pending in the queue, that is, $\delta = |\{\tau \mid \tau \leq t \wedge \text{pend}(\tau)\}|$. While timestamp t is pending, δ will decrease each time the queue is polled, since the removed time stamp, being minimal, must be $\leq t$. We can define δ in first-order logic using a simple recursion over the natural numbers. That is, $\text{cnt}(\tau)$, the number of pending timestamps $\leq \tau$, is defined recursively as:

$$\text{cnt}(\tau) \triangleq \text{ite}(\tau = 0, 0, \text{cnt}(\tau - 1)) + \text{ite}(\text{pend}(\tau), 1, 0)$$

We then have $\delta = \text{cnt}(t)$. For the liveness invariant ϕ in the proof rule, we can use just $\text{pend}(t)$. Our justice condition r is that the queue is polled, *i.e.*, $r = \text{poll}$.

In principle, we can now discharge the premises of Rule (2) using the safety rule, with safety invariant $\rho = \forall x.\ \text{pend}(x) \rightarrow x \leq \text{last}$. Notice this invariant is also need to prove the safety property that timestamps are dequeued in increasing order. Since all of the premises of the safety rule are (quantified) first-order formulas over the theory of linear arithmetic, we should be able to discharge them automatically using Z3, a powerful automated theorem prover that supports this theory. When we attempt this, however, we obtain a disappointing result. When trying to discharge premise B3 (stating that δ decreases when the queue is polled) Z3 runs for a few minutes and then returns an inconclusive result – neither a proof nor a counterexample. The solvers CVC4 and CVC5 also fail.

The problem is that the formula we want to prove is outside Z3's decidable fragment. To show that removing a timestamp $\leq t$ reduces $\text{cnt}(t)$ requires induction over t. Z3 is unable to do this. The needed inductive generalization may seem trivial in this small example, so one might easily imagine that a heuristic approach could solve the problem. In a large proof, however, such heuristics are fragile and fail in opaque ways. This failure puts a heavy burden on the user to debug the prover heuristics or discover the necessary instance of the induction axiom by hand. One may imagine alternative ranking schemes, for example using list or finite set datatypes to represent the ranking. This does not escape the fundamental problem, however, that reasoning about well-founded sets requires instantiating an induction schema.

To see how these issues play out in a typical ranking approach, consider the ranking-based liveness proof method of [24]. This method synthesizes a ranking as a polynomial over the integer variables in the program as well as the cardinalities of certain predicates appearing in the program. This heuristic is fragile, however. In our simple example, the predicate whose cardinality we require is $\lambda \tau.\ \text{pend}(\tau) \wedge \tau \leq t$. This predicate appears nowhere in the program or the property, and so the ranking synthesis must fail (we cannot build a ranking from just the 'pend' predicate). Moreover, if we use the cardinality of this predicate in the ranking, the method will be unsound, since this cardinality is not verified to be finite. Even given the predicate and a proof of its finiteness, the approach must infer 'deltas' which are upper and lower bounds on the changes in the integer variables for each action. This is done by an approximate analysis. Unfortunately, the method cannot infer an upper bound of -1 for the delta of our predicate for the 'poll' action, because the inference is based on pattern matching and requires updates to the predicate to occur in the program. Thus the method cannot infer that the ranking is eventually reduced. Even if this were somehow fixed, verifying the resulting safety properties could still fail because the mixing of quantifiers, uninterpreted predicates and non-linear integer arithmetic makes the verification conditions undecidable. The same issues would be faced using other methods based on linear ranking functions over integers (*e.g.*, [4]). The fundamental problem is that unreliable heuristics must be used to skirt undecidability, leading to methods that fail even on very simple problems. The Ironfleet approach [12] is substantially more manual, but still relies on undecidable reasoning about well-founded orders. Users must therefore diagnose opaque and unpredictable failures of the prover and provide manual guidance. By contrast, Invisible Ranking [6,7] produces decidable verification conditions, but cannot express rankings of height above ω.

2.2 Dynamic Liveness-to-Safety Construction

An alternative to well-founded rankings for infinite-state systems is the dynamic liveness-to-safety method (DL2S) proposed by Padon *et al.* [19]. It works by translating a program P and a liveness property ϕ into a *different* program P' and *safety* property ϕ', such that $P' \models \phi'$ implies $P \models \phi$. Space prohibits a detailed description of the method here. At a high level, it is similar to the method of Biere for finite-state systems [2] in that it detects bad cycles by storing a shadow copy of the system state and testing whether the system can return to the shadow state after certain fairness constraints have been satisfied. The DL2S method is similar to the finite-state method, except that it stores in the shadow state only a finite amount of information about the system state that is dynamically chosen. Restricting the shadow state to a finite projection of the system state guarantees that every infinite behavior must visit some shadow state infinitely often.

The DL2S approach is quite flexible, and has the advantage that in common cases, it yields safety verification conditions in EPR. Thus, the automated part of the proof tends to be reliable and we do not obtain inconclusive results as we did above, using a well-founded ranking. Unfortunately, the safety proof requires us to construct an inductive invariant over the transformed program P'. This greatly increases the conceptual complexity of proof development task for the user. Quoting Padon *et* al. [20] "Because our approach relies on an inductive invariant supplied by the user, it requires the user to understand the liveness-to-safety transformation and it requires both cleverness and a deep understanding of the protocol." To illustrate this, Fig. 2 shows an invariant obtained manually for the simple queue example of Fig. 1, after many failed attempts and counterexamples. The symbols D, A, O and W, 'frz' and 'svd' (some with subscripts) represent auxiliary state variables that are introduced by the DL2S construction. The user must understand the semantics of these variables as well as the safety property to be proved. Compare this in complexity to the proof by ranking that required the user only to introduce a function that counts the pending time stamps, and needed no auxiliary invariants apart from the simple one needed for safety. Unlike the ranking proof, the DL2S proof can be completed rapidly and automatically by Z3. Unfortunately, we have relieved the burden of undecidability on the automated prover at the cost of a substantial burden of complexity on the user. Our goal here is to eliminate this invidious trade-off.

$$\forall x.\ \text{pend}(x) \rightarrow x \leq \text{last}$$

$$\forall \tau.\text{pend}(\tau) \rightarrow D(\tau)$$

$$\forall \tau.\text{frz} \wedge (\text{pend}(\tau) \vee O_{\text{pend}}(\tau)) \rightarrow A(\tau)$$

$$\text{svd} \wedge \neg W_{\text{poll}} \rightarrow \exists \tau.\ (\tau \leq t \wedge O_{\text{pend}}(\tau) \wedge \neg \text{pend}(\tau))$$

$$(\text{frz} \vee \neg W_{\neg \text{rsp}}) \rightarrow \text{pend}(t) \wedge \Box \neg \text{recv}(t)$$

$$(\neg \text{frz} \wedge W_{\neg \text{rsp}}) \rightarrow \neg \Box \text{rsp}$$

$$\Box \Diamond \text{poll}$$

$$\forall \tau.\ \text{svd} \wedge \tau \leq t \wedge \text{pend}(\tau) \rightarrow O_{\text{pend}}(\tau)$$

$$\text{where rsp} \triangleq \text{send}(t) \rightarrow \Diamond \text{recv}(t)$$

Fig. 2. Invariants for DL2S proof of simple queue example.

3 Relational Rankings

A key point that we failed to notice in the proof of our simple example by well-founded ranking is that the liveness of the time stamped queue does not actually depend on the well-foundedness of the time stamp order. In fact, we could use real numbers for the time stamps, and the queue would still be live. The need for induction over the natural numbers was an artifact of our proof rule, which requires a well-founded ranking. This also explains why the proof by DL2S can be accomplished in EPR – the time stamps are treated as a simple total order, which can be axiomatized within EPR.

This observation suggests a middle path that maintains the conceptual simplicity of the proof by ranking, but eliminates reasoning about well-founded orders other than time. To achieve this, we propose to express rankings as relations over infinite sets, ordered by implication. While this order is not well-founded, we establish finiteness of the ranking relations outside of the logic. This gives us the best of both worlds: we remove the burden of undecidability on the automated prover without the extra burden of complexity imposed on the user by DL2S.

To guarantee that relational rankings are sound for infinite-state systems, we adapt a key idea from the DL2S method to prove that a relation is always finite (that is, its extension as a set of tuples is always finite). To do this, we guarantee that all tuples in the relational ranking are constructed from values that have been produced in a finite computation. This ensures that the ranking relations are finite and therefore that they cannot be infinitely reduced in the implication order.

Our proof approach uses a generic proof rule that is parameterized by a few user-provided relations over the user's program state. The rule avoids exposing the user to the state of a machine-constructed program and still keeps the verification conditions within EPR. For the sake of simple exposition, we will consider a succession of increasingly general rules, culminating in a rule that supports many justice conditions and lexicographic rankings.

3.1   The Relational Reactivity Rule

We begin with a simple proof rule that simulates the Manna and Pnueli reactivity Rule (2). We first consider the problem of proving that some relation R, a function of the program state, is always finite. This can be accomplished by the following proof rule:

$$\frac{\begin{aligned} &\text{F1. } \forall x. \ \neg R(x) \\ &\text{F2. } \Box \ \forall x. \ R'(x) \rightarrow (R(x) \lor x = e_1 \lor \cdots \lor x = e_n) \end{aligned}}{\Box \ R \text{ is finite}} \qquad (5)$$

In this rule, $e_1 \ldots e_2$ are expressions that depend on the program state. Typically, they represent the values computed during a single atomic step of the program. This set is necessarily finite. Premise F1 says that the relation R is initially empty. Premise F2 says that at most the elements $e_1 \ldots e_n$ can be added to relation R in each transition. In practice, $e_1 \ldots e_n$ can be just the ground terms occurring in the transition condition. Since a finite number of elements is added to R at each time step, R must be finite at every finite time. Notice we did not state that R is finite in the logic, since this is not expressible in first-order logic.

Now we replace our well-founded ranking δ by a relation, using two shorthands:

$$\text{conserves } \delta \ \triangleq \ \forall x. \ \delta'(x) \rightarrow \delta(x)$$
$$\text{reduces } \delta \ \triangleq \ \exists x. \ \delta(x) \land \neg \delta'(x)$$

That is, a transition 'conserves' the ranking if it does not add any elements, and it 'reduces' the ranking if it removes at least one element. We can now prove formulas of form (1) using the following rule:

$$\frac{\begin{aligned} &\text{C0. } \Box \ R \text{ is finite} \\ &\text{C1. } p \Rightarrow (q \lor \phi \land (\forall x. \delta(x) \rightarrow R(x))) \\ &\text{C2. } \phi \Rightarrow (q' \lor (\phi' \land (\text{conserves } \delta))) \\ &\text{C3. } \phi \land r \Rightarrow (q' \lor (\text{reduces } \delta)) \end{aligned}}{(\Box \Diamond r) \rightarrow (p \Rightarrow \Diamond q)} \qquad (6)$$

Premises C1-3 correspond closely to the premises of Rule (2). The key difference is that, in premise C1, we establish that the ranking relation δ is finite at the moment when condition p holds. This is done by establishing that δ is contained in the finite relation R. Using just first-order connectives, we can also express that the ranking is conserved unless q holds (right-hand side of C2) and that the ranking is reduced when r holds (right-hand side of C3). Since δ must be finite while the invariant ϕ holds, it follows that q eventually holds. The advantage of this formulation is that it allows us to express the verification conditions in pure first-order logic, without additional theories. If we take care in the use of quantifier alternations, this allows us to keep the verification conditions within EPR [23].

Now consider proving liveness, of our simple time stamped queue. To prove property (4) using rule (6), we use the following definitions of the predicates in the rule:

$$\delta(\tau) \ \triangleq \ \text{pend}(\tau) \land \tau \leq t$$
$$\phi \ \triangleq \ \text{pend}(t)$$

Notice that the ranking δ is very similar to the one we used above, but it represents simply the set of pending time stamps $\leq t$ and not the cardinality of this set. The invariant ϕ is the same. We can let $R = \delta$, since the program adds only one element to δ at each step, thus finiteness of δ can be proved automatically using Rule (5). This proof has essentially the same conceptual complexity as the proof using well-founded ranking (in fact, slightly less, since we need not define the counting function). However, unlike that proof, it can be checked efficiently and reliably in EPR using Z3, whereas Z3 fails to find a proof for the well-founded ranking. If we make a mistake in the proof, Z3 can produce a true counterexample, guiding us to correct the proof.

3.2 Chaining Liveness Lemmas

Consider proving liveness of a cascade of two queues of the type described above. That is, when we poll $queue_1$, if a time stamp is received, we enter it into $queue_2$. We would like to show an end-to-end response property, that is, assuming $\Box\Diamond poll_i$ for $i = 1, 2$, we have $send_1(t) \Rightarrow \Diamond recv_2(t)$. One way to do this is to prove response properties for the two queues, that is, $send_i(t) \Rightarrow \Diamond recv_i(t)$ for $i = 1, 2$ and then use these properties to prove end-to-end response.

Unfortunately, we do not yet have a proof rule that would allow us to prove a response property assuming two response properties. To remedy this, we will relax Rule (6) slightly. First, we first observe that the condition r need not hold true infinitely. It suffices that it hold in the future *until* q is true. Second, we can relax q and q' in the rule's premises to the weaker $\Diamond q$. This gives us the following rule:

$$
\begin{array}{l}
\text{C0. } \Box R \text{ is finite} \\
\text{D1. } p \Rightarrow ((\Diamond q) \vee \phi \wedge (\forall x . \delta(x) \rightarrow R(x))) \\
\text{D2. } \phi \Rightarrow ((\Diamond q) \vee (\phi' \wedge (\text{conserves } \delta))) \\
\text{D3. } \phi \wedge r \Rightarrow ((\Diamond q) \vee (\text{reduces } \delta)) \\
\text{D4. } \phi \Rightarrow ((\Diamond q) \vee (\Diamond r)) \\
\hline
p \Rightarrow \Diamond q
\end{array}
\tag{7}
$$

Notice that we have moved the assumption about r into the premises of the rule, making r effectively a parameter of the rule. Also, observe that the premises now have temporal operators in them (other than the prime symbol, representing 'at the next time'). This may seem to defeat the purpose of a program logic rule, since it does not reduce the proof to ordinary logic. However, we will see that, by appropriate abstractions, we can reduce the temporal verification conditions to decidable propositions.

In our two-queue example, to prove $send_1(t) \Rightarrow \Diamond recv_2(t)$, we can use the following values of the rule parameters:

$$R \triangleq \text{true}$$
$$\delta \triangleq \text{true}$$
$$\phi \triangleq \Diamond \text{recv}_1(t)$$
$$r \triangleq \text{recv}_1(t)$$
$$R(\tau) \triangleq \text{pend}_1(\tau) \vee \text{pend}_2(\tau)$$
$$\phi \triangleq \text{pend}_1(t) \vee \text{pend}_2(t)$$

$$\delta_1(\tau) \triangleq \text{pend}_1(\tau) \wedge \tau \leq t \qquad \delta_2(\tau) \triangleq (\text{pend}_1(\tau) \vee \text{pend}_2(\tau)) \wedge \tau \leq t$$
$$r_1 \triangleq \text{poll}_1 \qquad\qquad\qquad r_2 \triangleq \text{poll}_2$$
$$\psi_1 \triangleq \text{pend}_1(t) \qquad\qquad\quad \psi_2 \triangleq \text{pend}_2(t)$$

Fig. 3. Rule parameters for liveness of the cascaded queues.

We then have to prove the following simplified premises:

D1. $\text{send}_1(t) \Rightarrow ((\Diamond \text{recv}_2) \vee \phi)$
D2. $\phi \Rightarrow ((\Diamond \text{recv}_2) \vee \phi')$
D3. $\phi \wedge \text{recv}_1 \Rightarrow (\Diamond \text{recv}_2))$
D4. $\phi \Rightarrow \Diamond \text{recv}_1$

We can prove D1 using our lemma that $\text{send}_1(t) \Rightarrow \Diamond \text{recv}_1(t)$. This proof is propositional, in the sense that it does not depend on the semantics of the propositions $\Diamond \text{recv}_1$ or $\Diamond \text{recv}_2$. For D2 and D3, we need our lemma $\text{send}_2(t) \Rightarrow \Diamond \text{recv}_2(t)$. That is, if $\text{send}_2(t)$ then $\text{recv}_2(t)$ by the lemma, otherwise $\text{recv}_1(t)$ is false, thus $\Diamond \text{recv}_1(t)$ remains true. The proof for D3 is again purely propositional: the transition relation guarantees that recv_1 implies $\text{send}_2(t)$ which in turn guarantees $\Diamond \text{recv}_2(t)$ by the lemma. We needed one tautology of temporal logic to prove D2, that is, $\Diamond \text{recv}_1 \Rightarrow (\text{recv}_1 \vee (\Diamond \text{recv}_1)')$. This is one of the facts about the $\Diamond$ operator that form the symbolic tableau constraints [3], the other being $\text{recv}_1 \Rightarrow \Diamond \text{recv}_1$. The tableau axioms can be generated automatically from the verification conditions allowing Z3 to discharge the premises. Though this approach is not complete, it allows us to avoid adding further inference rules, for example, to prove single-step eventualities, or to use response properties as assumptions.

Notice that we don't need a ranking for this proof, but we require that receiving on queue$_1$ and sending on queue$_2$ occur in the same transition, so that D3 is provable from the tableau axioms. Otherwise we would need a third lemma stating $\text{recv}_1(t) \Rightarrow \Diamond \text{send}_2(t)$. We also need a safety invariant, implying that time stamps in queue$_1$ are always greater than time stamps in queue$_2$:

$$\text{last}_2 \leq \text{last}_1 \wedge \forall x. \, \text{pend}_1(x) \rightarrow x \geq \text{last}_2$$

This invariant is also needed to prove the safety property that timestamps are entered into queue$_2$ in order. Often, invariants needed to prove safety properties are also sufficient for liveness.

3.3   Stable Schedulers

Reducing the proof to many small lemmas, each with its own relational ranking, is an effective approach, but each lemma adds complexity to the proof and opportunities for errors that are time-consuming to correct. Since we require a ranking for each lemma, it would seem more parsimonious, if possible, to combine these rankings into a single ranking and dispense with the statements of the lemmas.

With multiple rankings come multiple justice conditions. In a given state, only one of these must cause the ranking to decrease. We call this justice condition *helpful* in the given state [6]. To establish a justice condition that must eventually reduce the ranking in a given state, we introduce a function called a *stable scheduler*.

As a simple example, consider proving liveness of the cascaded queues above without proving liveness lemmas for the individual queues. It is not difficult to define a ranking over the combined state of the two queues. Let us say that δ_i is the number of time stamps $\tau \le t$ that are pending in $queue_i$, for $i = 1, 2$. A suitable numeric ranking δ is $2\delta_1 + \delta_2$.

We have two justice conditions to consider, that is, we assume that both queues are polled infinitely often. Unfortunately, neither of these conditions *always* reduces the ranking, since there may be no time stamps $\tau \le t$ in one or the other of the two queues. One solution to this would be to define a combined justice condition $r \triangleq \text{poll}_1$ if $\delta_1 > 0$ else poll_2. This condition would indeed imply that the ranking decreases, but we would have to prove a lemma that it is true infinitely often.

As an alternative, for each justice condition r_i, we provide a *scheduler predicate* ψ_i that determines when r_i is helpful, in the sense of reducing the ranking δ_i, when it eventually holds. We require the scheduler predicates to be *stable*, in the sense that ψ_i, when true, remains true until r_i holds.

A proof rule for response properties with multiple justice conditions and a stable scheduler can be stated as follows:

$$
\begin{aligned}
&\text{S1. } p \wedge \neg(\Diamond q) \Rightarrow \phi \\
&\text{S2. } \bigwedge_{i=1}^{n} \phi \wedge \neg(\Diamond q) \Rightarrow \\
&\qquad \phi' \wedge \\
&\qquad (\text{conserves } \delta_i) \wedge \\
&\qquad (\psi_i \wedge r_i \to (\text{reduces } \delta_i)) \wedge \\
&\qquad (\psi_i \wedge \neg r_i \to \psi_i') \\
&\text{S3. } \bigwedge_{i=1}^{n} \phi \wedge \neg(\Diamond q) \wedge \psi_i \Rightarrow \Diamond r_i \\
&\text{S4. } \phi \wedge \neg(\Diamond q) \Rightarrow \bigvee_{i=1}^{n} \psi_i \\
&\text{S5. } \bigwedge_{i=1}^{n} \phi \Rightarrow (\forall x.\delta_i(x) \to R(x)) \\
&\text{S6. } \Box R \text{ is finite} \\
&\overline{p \Rightarrow \Diamond q}
\end{aligned}
\tag{8}
$$

Premise S1 of the rule says that the invariant ϕ is established whenever p is true but the desired eventuality $\Diamond q$ is false. Premise S2 gives several conditions that system transitions must satisfy, in the case invariant ϕ holds, but the eventuality does not. First, the invariant ϕ must be preserved. Second, the each ranking component δ_i must be conserved. Third, if scheduler predicate ψ_i is true and justice condition r_i is true, then the ranking δ_i must be reduced. Fourth, if scheduler predicate ψ_i is true and justice condition r_i is *false*, then ψ_i must remain true. The last is the stability condition for the scheduler. Premise S3 ensures that every scheduled justice condition eventually occurs. Premise S4 guarantees that at least one justice condition is always scheduled when the invariant holds. Finally, S5 and S6 guarantee that the ranking is always finite while the invariant holds. A proof of soundness of this rule can be found in Appendix A.

For the cascaded queues, we can use the rule parameters shown in Fig. 3. Notice that $\delta_2(\tau)$ is true when time stamp τ appears in either queue, so that moving a time stamp from queue_1 to queue_2 does not cause δ_2 to increase. Also, notice that δ_2 is reduced when r_2 occurs and ψ_2 holds, because $\text{pend}_1(\tau)$ and $\text{pend}_2(\tau)$ cannot both be true. This is implied by the safety invariant used above.

Now suppose we change the system so that the queues can hold a bounded number of time stamps. This means that if queue_2 is full, we cannot move a time stamp from queue_1 to queue_2 (in other words, the action that polls queue_1 must block). We can prove this system live by a small change to ψ_1 and ψ_2, that is:

$$\psi_1 \triangleq \neg \exists \tau.\ \text{pend}_2(\tau) \wedge \tau \le t$$
$$\psi_2 \triangleq \exists \tau.\ \text{pend}_2(\tau) \wedge \tau \le t$$

If there is a time stamp $\tau \le t$ to send in queue_2, then δ_2 must be reduced on polling queue_2. Otherwise, by the safety invariant above, queue_2 must be empty. Therefore it cannot block, and polling queue_1 must reduce δ_1. That is, we design the scheduler to prioritize actions that unblock other actions. To handle a longer cascade of queues, we would prioritize the queues later in the cascade.

3.4 Lexicographic Rankings

Consider now a cascade of queues in which messages can be *reordered*. For example, suppose we have two classes of messages, A and B. We have two corresponding polling actions for queue_1: poll_{1A} and poll_{1B}. Each action moves the message of its given class with the least time stamp from queue_1 to queue_2. Thus, messages of different classes can bypass each other in transit. We will assume that queue_2 delivers messages in FIFO order, that is, in order of their time of arrival. We will denote the time of arrival of a message with time stamp t at queue_2 by a natural number $t_a(t)$.

Reordering of messages presents us with a difficulty in establishing a ranking. That is, at the time a message of class A is sent, we do not have an upper bound on the number of future messages of class B that will bypass it before it reaches queue_2. Thus, we cannot establish a finite ranking. One solution to this problem is to take a lemma, such as $\forall \tau.\ \text{send}_1(\tau) \Rightarrow \Diamond \text{pend}_2(\tau)$. At that point when message t reaches queue_2, the number of messages in queue_2 is known, so we can establish a ranking to prove that message t is eventually received. Alternatively, we could use temporal prophecy to achieve the same effect [20]. However, in both cases we are adding complexity to the proof by asking the user to provide the necessary cut formulas, as well as the rankings. This is unnecessary, however, if we use a lexicographic ranking.

To do this, we introduce a proof rule that combines multiple rankings lexicographically. That is, we introduce a hierarchy of rankings $\delta_1 \ldots \delta_n$, where δ_1 is the high-order component and δ_n is the low-order component. This induces a lexicographic ranking δ such that $\delta(s_1) < \delta(s_2)$ when $\delta_i(s_1)$ is finite for all $i = 1 \ldots n$, and

$$\vee_{i=1}^n \left(\delta_i(s_1) < \delta_i(s_2) \wedge (\wedge_{j=1}^{n-1} \delta_j(s_1) = \delta_j(s_2)) \right). \tag{9}$$

We will not, however, explicitly represent δ. Instead, we will establish verification conditions guaranteeing that the δ_i are always finite and that δ is conserved and eventually reduced. For this, a lower-order ranking must be conserved only when no high-order ranking is reduced. Given a scheduler ψ for the rankings, we will say that ranking δ_i is *preempted* if, for some $j < i$, δ_j is scheduled. A preempted ranking need not be reduced, and in fact is allowed to increase, as long as it remains finite. We say that a ranking is *required* if it is scheduled and not preempted. A required ranking must eventually be reduced. This allows us to relax the condition of stability of the schedulers as well, since only the schedulers of required rankings need be stable. We will introduce two shorthands:

$$\mathrm{pre}_i(\psi) = \vee_{j=1}^{i-1} \psi_j$$
$$\mathrm{req}_i(\psi) = \psi_i \wedge \neg\mathrm{pre}_i(\psi)$$

The predicate $\mathrm{pre}_n(\psi)$ indicates that the ranking component δ_i is preempted under scheduler ψ and $\mathrm{req}_n(\psi)$ indicates that δ_i is required.

Using these notations, a suitable rule for establishing liveness with lexicographic relational rankings with stable schedulers is as follows:

$$
\begin{array}{l}
\text{S1. } p \wedge \neg(\Diamond q) \Rightarrow \phi \\
\text{L2. } \bigwedge_{i=1}^n \phi \wedge \neg(\Diamond q) \Rightarrow \\
\qquad \phi' \wedge \\
\qquad (\neg\mathrm{pre}_i(\psi) \rightarrow (\text{conserves } \delta_i)) \wedge \\
\qquad (\mathrm{req}_i(\psi) \wedge r_i \rightarrow (\text{reduces } \delta_i)) \wedge \\
\qquad (\mathrm{req}_i(\psi) \wedge \neg r_i \rightarrow \psi_i') \\
\text{S3. } \bigwedge_{i=1}^n \phi \wedge \neg(\Diamond q) \wedge \psi_i \Rightarrow \Diamond r_i \\
\text{S4. } \phi \wedge \neg(\Diamond q) \Rightarrow \bigvee_{i=1}^n \psi_i \\
\text{S5. } \bigwedge_{i=1}^n \phi \Rightarrow (\forall x. \delta_i(x) \rightarrow R(x))) \\
\text{S6. } \Box R \text{ is finite} \\
\hline
p \Rightarrow \Diamond q
\end{array}
\tag{10}
$$

As before, premise S1 establishes the liveness invariant ϕ. Premise L2 differs from S2 in the previous rule in that transitions must conserve a ranking δ_i *only* if it is not preempted, must reduce the ranking when the justice condition occurs *only* if it is required, and must keep the scheduler stable *only* if the ranking is required. The remainder of the premises are the same as in the previous rule. A proof of soundness of this rule can be found in Appendix A.

Now consider again our problem of cascaded queues with reordering, and suppose we want to prove that messages of class A are always eventually received, that is, $\mathrm{send}_1(t) \wedge A(t) \Rightarrow \Diamond\mathrm{recv}_2(t)$, under the assumption the actions poll_{1A} and poll_2 are called infinitely often. This is done with the lexicographic ranking defined in Fig. 4.

Notice that, as long as ψ_1 remains true, executing action poll_{1A} must reduce ranking δ_1, since the earliest class A message must have time stamp $\leq t$. While this is true,

$$R(\tau) \triangleq \text{pend}_1(\tau) \vee \text{pend}_2(\tau)$$
$$\phi \triangleq (\text{pend}_1(t) \vee \text{pend}_2(t)) \wedge A(t)$$

$$\delta_1(\tau) \triangleq \text{pend}_1(\tau) \wedge \tau \leq t \qquad\qquad \delta_2(\tau) \triangleq \text{pend}_2(\tau) \wedge t_a(\tau) \leq t_a(t)$$
$$r_1 \triangleq \text{poll}_{1A} \qquad\qquad\qquad\qquad r_2 \triangleq \text{poll}_2$$
$$\psi_1 \triangleq \text{pend}_1(t) \qquad\qquad\qquad\qquad \psi_2 \triangleq \text{pend}_2(t)$$

Fig. 4. Rule parameters for liveness of the cascaded queues with reordering.

the ranking δ_2 is allowed to increase arbitrarily, so long as it remains contained in R. This allows any number of B messages to be added to queue$_1$, bypassing message t. However, when message t is removed from queue$_1$, δ_2 becomes scheduled and must be conserved. This is true because no new messages in queue$_2$ can have arrival times less than $t_a(t)$. The ranking must decrease every time poll$_2$ occurs, since the least arrival time in queue$_2$ must be $\leq t_a(t)$ as long as t remains in the queue. All of the premises of the proof rule are in EPR and can easily be checked automatically.

Parameterized Systems. The are practical situations in which we have an infinite or unbounded number of justice conditions. For example, we may have an infinite or unbounded number of concurrent processes (or to be more precise, process id's may be drawn from an infinite set, if we have dynamic process creation). We wish to assume that every process is scheduled to run infinitely often. In the Apple generic model, this situation arises in various ways, due to fairness assumptions involving unbounded numbers of processors, controllers, addresses and so on. It is straightforward to generalize Rule 10 to parameterized justice conditions. We can do this by simply replacing conjunction and disjunction over finite sets with universal and existential quantification over infinite sets:

$$
\begin{array}{l}
\text{S1. } p \wedge \neg(\Diamond q) \Rightarrow \phi \\
\text{P2. } \forall x. \ \bigwedge_{i=1}^{n} \phi \wedge \neg(\Diamond q) \Rightarrow \\
\qquad \phi' \wedge \\
\qquad (\neg\text{pre}_i(\psi)(x) \rightarrow (\text{conserves } \delta_i)) \wedge \\
\qquad (\text{req}_i(\psi_i)(x) \wedge r_i(x) \rightarrow (\text{reduces } \delta_i)) \wedge \\
\qquad (\text{req}_i(\psi)(x) \wedge \neg r_i(x) \rightarrow \psi'_i(x)) \\
\text{P3. } \forall x. \ \bigwedge_{i=1}^{n} \phi \wedge \psi_i(x) \Rightarrow \Diamond r_i(x) \\
\text{P4. } \phi \Rightarrow \exists x. \ \bigvee_{i=1}^{n} \psi_i(x) \\
\text{S5. } \bigwedge_{i=1}^{n} \phi \Rightarrow (\forall x.\delta_i(x) \rightarrow R(x))) \\
\text{S6. } \Box R \text{ is finite} \\
\hline
p \Rightarrow \Diamond q
\end{array}
\tag{11}
$$

Notice here that premises P2, P3 and P4 are similar to L2, S3 and S4 in Rule (10), except that the predicates ψ_i and r_i have a parameter x that is quantified. Also, notice that n is the number of rankings, not the number of processes, which is conceptually infinite. We can also easily extend the rule to rankings that are n-ary relations rather then unary relations, which is useful in some cases.

Relative Completeness. A temporal proof system is *relatively complete* if it reduces the validity of all temporal propositions to the validity of a finite collection of formulas of arithmetic. We are explicitly *not* concerned with relative completeness here, since our goal is to reduce the proof to *decidable* propositions in EPR *in practice*. Having said this, there are two obvious ways in which the relative incompleteness of our system manifests. First, Rule 5 is not complete for proving finiteness of the ranking in cases where the system can non-deterministically choose an unbounded natural number or set in a single transition, as opposed to computing these values. Second, due to the finiteness requirement, our lexicographic ranking (9) has ordinal height at most ω^n. However, we can describe systems whose reachability relations have greater ordinal height than this. For example, a program that chooses an arbitrary natural number n and descends lexically over the tuples in $\mathbb{N}^n$ has ordinal height ω^ω and hence cannot be proved in our system. This incompleteness has not proved to be an issue, however, our case study.

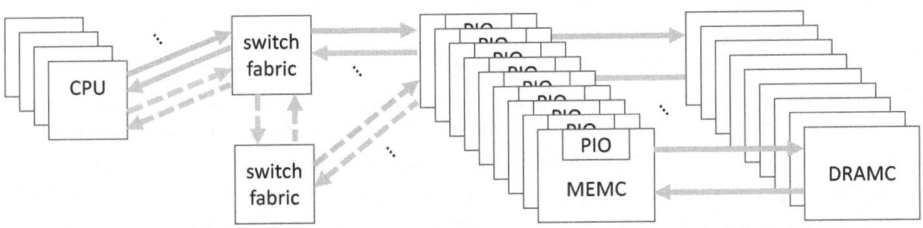

Fig. 5. Apple generic memory model architecture. The flow of memory operations (reads and writes) is depicted by the solid arrows in the diagram, and the flow of I/O operations by dashed arrows. Requests are depicted in light blue, with responses in gray. (Color figure online)

4   Case Study: The Apple Generic Memory Subsystem Model

We now consider applying the relational ranking approach to the Apple generic memory model mentioned in the introduction. Apple provided a generic abstract memory system model that was designed to capture the essential difficulties in proving memory system consistency and liveness without revealing intellectual property. This model has been contributed to the open-source the Ivy project, as have our proofs [1].

The high-level structure of the Apple generic model is sketched in Fig. 5. The system connects a collection of processor cores with a collection of memory and I/O modules, via switch fabrics and controllers. The number of processor cores and controllers is unbounded in the model. At each stage, memory operations (reads and writes) are queued and may be reordered. The order of transmission depends on a set of ordering rules specific to the given stage. In some cases, operations may be blocked by operations that are present in later stages. Whether one operation can bypass another may depend on various attributes of the operations, including the initiating processor, the address, the operation type, and the destination memory controller. While operations may be completed by the memory units out-of-order, they are ultimately retired in-order at the processor cores, by means of a reorder buffer. The Apple engineers developed a safety proof, using hand-written inductive invariants, that the ordering rules provide a consistent view of memory to the processor cores, according to the desired memory consistency model. The generic model consists of approximately 1200 SLOC in the Ivy language. The safety proof consists of 78 invariants, comprising approximately 500 SLOC.

It was also considered important to prove a liveness property of this model, that is, that every operation issued by a core is eventually retired. This property depends upon a large number of fairness assumptions that constrain the behavior of different units. There are two compelling reasons to verify this specification. First, from a system point of view, we need to know that the ordering rules do not cause any operation to be blocked indefinitely. Second, from a modeling point of view, we need to be certain that the guarantee of memory consistency is not rendered vacuous by a modeling error that prevents certain operations from being retired. However, the DL2S method was found to be too difficult and counterintuitive to be applied in practice for this.

4.1 Liveness Proof with Lemmas

We initially implemented a liveness proof rule in the Ivy tool similar to Rule (8) that allows parameterized justice conditions, without lexicographic ranking. The earliest version of this rule lacked the ability for the user to specify the stable scheduler. Instead, it used a default priority-based scheduler (*i.e.*, the first non-empty ranking is scheduled). Using this implementation, we constructed a liveness proof for the Apple model. The lack of lexicographic ranking made it necessary to break the proof into many lemmas. The proof consists of 26 lemmas expressed in first-order temporal logic, chained together in the style of Sect. 3.2. The basic lemmas are liveness properties relating to the liveness of specific channels in specific modules. Most of these state that an operation reaching one module is eventually transferred to the next module on the appropriate flow path. Additional non-blocking properties are used to state that space eventually becomes available for an operation of a given type in a given module. These basic liveness properties were chained to prove end-to-end liveness.

Most of the lemmas in the proof are universally quantified, typically over module identifiers (*i.e.*, processors or memory controllers) or operation time stamps. When proving the properties, these quantifiers were Herbrandized, that is, replaced by fresh constants. This replacement of variables with constants played a significant role in the construction of rankings, just as the use of a time stamp constant t allowed us to construct a ranking in our simple examples. Moreover, replacing quantified variables with constants also helps in keeping verification conditions within EPR, and thus allowing Ivy to automatically discharge them and produce counterexamples in a reliable way using the Z3 theorem prover.

As an example, the DRAM controllers block incoming operations that have the same address as operations that are already queued. To prove that operations are not indefinitely blocked, we first prove that operation t eventually leaves the DRAM controller, using a ranking. Universally generalizing t, we can then show that all operations in the memory controller eventually reach the DRAM controller, since the blocking operation must eventually depart. Similarly, we first show that the completion of operation timestamped t eventually reaches the reorder buffer at the CPU. Generalizing

t universally, we can then show that every operation u eventually leaves the reorder buffer, since every predecessor of u, for which it waits, must eventually arrive.

We found that it was straightforward to prove all the lemmas save two using the basic relational ranking approach. In all of these cases, Z3 was able to discharge the relevant proof obligations quickly and reliably, without timeouts or divergences. This was critical as each lemma required a few counterexamples to help correct errors in the rule application. Without these counterexamples, developing the proof would have been extremely challenging.

The two lemmas we were unable to prove were instructive. One case involved a queue containing two kinds of operations. We needed to show that if both kinds of operations are removed infinitely often, then every element is eventually removed. The other case was proving that, if completions of all operations eventually reach the reorder buffer (out of order) then all operations are eventually retired (in order). We discharged the two lemmas by model checking a small abstract model (using the eager abstraction method [17]) and then used refinement maps to transfer liveness properties of the small models to the larger model. This method, while effective, was conceptually complex and time-consuming. This experience motivated us to consider the more general proof approach using stable schedulers.

The overall liveness proof consumed approximately 90 person-hours of effort and resulted in fixing several issues in the Apple generic model. The overall textual size of the proof was approximately 1000 SLOC, and all of the proof obligations were checked by Ivy in approximately 115 min on a laptop computer.

4.2   Lemma-Free Proof of Liveness

After adding stable schedulers to the Ivy proof rule, we found that it was straightforward to prove the two lemmas that were previous proved using model checking and refinement relations. However, the complexity of the proof remained high due to the large number of lemmas. Eliminating the lemmas from the proof proved difficult for two reasons. First, as in our simple reordering queue example, the presence of reordering of operations at various places in the system prevented us from expressing the overall ranking as a sum of simple relational rankings. Second, without taking lemmas and Herbrandizing them, we faced the problem of quantifier alternations in the verification conditions that took them outside EPR.

To handle the first problem, we extended the liveness proof rule with lexicographic rankings. This made it possible to express a ranking for the entire end-to-end liveness property without taking lemmas, instead using only a single application of the liveness proof rule. This proof relied on 14 justice assumptions, and for each justice assumption introduced one component in the lexicographic relation ranking.

Checking this proof with Z3 was not possible, however. We found that Z3 produced unpredictable timeouts and was unable to produce the counterexamples needed to debug the proof. The root cause of the problem was quantifier alternations occurring in certain invariants of the system that were needed to prove liveness, but not to prove safety. As a simple example of this phenomenon, consider a mutual exclusion protocol based on ticket numbers, as in [19]. To prove liveness, we must show that every unserved tick number is held by some process that is waiting to enter its critical section.

Otherwise the protocol deadlocks. Deadlock does not affect safety but, of course, does rule out liveness. The invariant we need says that for all ticket numbers t, if t is waiting be served, then some process p holds ticket t. This quantifier alternation introduces a Skolem function from tickets to processes, which forms a function cycle with the map in the system state from processes to ticket numbers. This breaks stratification of the verification conditions, which are thus not in EPR.

Similar situations occur in the Apple generic model. For example, we must show that in every memory module, some time stamp occurs in the first queue position, assuming the queue is not empty. In the proof with lemmas, the quantifier alternations were avoided by simply Herbrandizing the quantifier over memory modules, reducing it to a constant. In the lemma-free proof, however, this was not possible. We found it impractical to carry out the proof with Z3 using non-stratified invariants, because of frequent and unpredictable timeouts.

As an alternative, auxiliary variables were added to the system to provide sufficient witnesses for the offending existential quantifiers, as needed to prove liveness. For example, one auxiliary variable represents the least time stamp present in *any* memory module, and another the identifier of the memory controller module holding this time stamp. The defining properties of these auxiliary variables must be stated as invariants. In some cases, this also entailed more complex ranking definitions.

The textual size of the proof without lemmas is greatly reduced from the proof with lemmas, at about 280 SLOC, of which about 120 represent the auxiliary variables and their invariants, and the checking time is reduced to 15 min (11 for liveness only). The human effort required for the proof was also substantially less, at about 20 h. This figure should be taken with a grain of salt, however, since the second proof effort benefited from the understanding of the system gained in the first.

It is interesting to note that, in the liveness proofs, only one new safety invariant was needed, consisting of a disequality between two variables. The remaining invariants came from the safety proof, or were invariants over the auxiliary variables. The ability to re-use the safety proof greatly reduced the overall effort in proving liveness.

5   Conclusions and Future Work

We have endeavored in this work to develop a method of proving liveness that is is conceptually simple to apply in practice to realistic problems, can be scaled to large problems without modular decomposition, and does not fail unpredictably due to the use of fragile heuristics. No existing method meets these conditions. In a realistic case study, we have seen that relational rankings do. The case study is an of an order of magnitude greater complexity than problems that have been solved by comparable existing methods.

We have also observed that there is a trade-off between the use of lemmas in the proof and the use of lexicographic rankings. The latter approach yielded a proof of lesser textual complexity, but required more sophisticated reasoning to construct the proof, in order to keep the verification conditions within decidable bounds. Handling quantifier alternations in lexicographic proofs is an issue that requires further exploration.

There are several possible directions for further work. One is the problem of assigning root causes to liveness proof failures. One approach would be use state space exploration on the concrete model. For example, we could use model checking to test whether in fact a scheduled justice condition always reduces one of the rankings. If so, the fault likely likes in the safety invariant. Or if the scheduled justice condition implies that the ranking is eventually but not immediately reduced, then an additional ranking may be needed. It is not clear, however, how to effectively explore the state space of complex, infinite-state models to obtain this information.

A related question is automated synthesis of relational rankings. A natural approach is to use a syntax-guided or template-based definition of the search space and to perform the search in a counterexample-guided manner (that is, using CEGIS, or counterexample-guided inductive synthesis). To use CEGIS effectively, we require an effective counterexample diagnosis approach that allows us to rule out large spaces of incorrect proofs. To be useful in practice, such a technique would have to fail transparently, in a way allows effective user guidance.

Another interesting question is whether there are useful classes of distributed systems for which the method is complete, that is, for which there always exist relational rankings that can be verified within EPR.

Finally, while a single realistic case study is useful for motivating and guiding research, it does not allow us to draw conclusions about the general utility of any given method. For this we need a large, representative class of benchmark problems to use in evaluation. Such a benchmark does not currently exist. Developing it would be a significant step toward liveness proof methods that are effective at scale.

A   Soundness proofs

In this section, we prove that Rules (8) and (10) are sound. We start by defining the necessary background notions. We use standard multi-sorted first order logic. If s is a multi-sorted first-order structure, we write $\sigma[s]$ for the universe of sort σ in structure s, and $\phi[s]$ for the interpretation of formula ϕ in structure s. For the sake of notational simplicity, we restrict our attention in the sequel to unary relations, but the extension to n-ary relations is straightforward. A (unary) relation over sort σ is a formula ψ of the form $\lambda x.\ p(x)$, where p is a first-order formula whose only free variable is x and x is of sort σ. We write $\psi[s]$ for the function that takes x to $p(x)[s]$. We adopt the standard semantics of first-order linear temporal logic with the prime operator, so that t' indicates the value of t at the next time. Moreover, we take the axiom $\mathcal{I} \wedge \Box \mathcal{T}$ (where $\langle \mathcal{I}, \mathcal{T} \rangle$ is intended to represent a transition system with initial condition $\mathcal{I}$ and transition condition $\mathcal{T}$).

Definition 1. *A* lexicographic relational ranking *is an indexed set (possibly empty) of unary predicates, $\delta = \{\delta_{i=1...n}\}$, where each predicate may be over a different sort. We say δ is* finite *in structure s if $\delta_i[s]$ is finite for all $i = 1 \ldots n$. The ranking on structures induced by δ is the pre-order $<_\delta$ such that, for any two structures $s_{1,2}$ over the same universe, $s_1 <_\delta s_2$ iff:*

– δ is finite in s_1, and

– *for some $i \in 1 \ldots n$, $\delta_i[s_1] \subset \delta_i[s_2]$ and for all $1 \leq j < i$, $\delta_j[s_1] = \delta_j[s_2]$.*

Theorem 1. *For any lexicographic relational ranking $\delta = \{\delta_{i=1\ldots n}\}$, the pre-order $<_\delta$ is well-founded.*

Proof. By induction on n. In the base case, $n = 0$, the order is well-founded because it is empty. In the induction step, we show that if there is an infinite downward chain in the order $<_\delta$, there is an infinite downward chain in the order $<_\epsilon$ where ϵ is the ranking $\{\epsilon_{i=1\ldots n-1}\}$ such that $\epsilon_i = \delta_{i+1}$. This is a contradiction, since by inductive hypothesis, ϵ is well-founded. To see this, suppose we have an infinite descending chain $t_0 >_\delta t_1 >_\delta \cdots$. By definition, δ must be finite in t_1. Moreover, for all $i = 1 \ldots$, we must have $\delta_1[t_i] \supseteq \delta_1[t_{i+1}]$. Since $\delta_1[t_1]$ is finite, in cannot infinitely decrease, therefore there exists an i such that $\delta_1[t_j] = \delta_1[t_{j+1}]$ for all $j \geq i$. It follows that the sequence $t_j, t_{j+1}, \ldots$ is an infinite descending chain of ϵ. □

Theorem 2. *Rule (10) is sound.*

Proof. Suppose toward a contradiction that there exists a sequence of structures $s = s_0, s_1, \ldots$ satisfying $\mathcal{I} \wedge \Box \mathcal{T}$, such that $p[s_i]$ is true for some i, but $q[s_j]$ is false for all $j \geq i$, and all the premises of the rule hold in s. From premise S1 we have $\phi[s_i]$ and from L2, by induction on time, that $\phi[s_j]$ for all $j \geq i$. By S5 and S6, we know that delta is finite in s_j for all $j \geq i$. Now we show that for all $j \geq i$, there exists a $k > j$ such that $s_j >_\delta s_k$. By S4, we know that there exists an $l \in 1 \ldots n$ such that $\psi_i[s_j]$. Therefore, let l be the *least* number in $1 \ldots n$ such that, for *some* $m \geq j$, we have $\psi_l[s_m]$. We have $\neg\mathrm{pre}_l(\psi)[s_k]$ for all $k \geq j$ and therefore by L2 and induction, $\delta_l(s_j) \supseteq \delta_l(s_k)$. From S3, it follows that there exists $k \geq j$ such that $r_i[s_k]$. Moreover, by L2 and induction on time, we have, for all $j \leq m \leq k$, $\mathrm{req}_l(\psi)[s_m]$ and $\psi_l[s_m]$. Thus, by L2 we have $\delta_l[s_k] \supset \delta_l[s_{k+1}]$, hence $\delta_l[s_j] \supset \delta_l[s_{k+1}]$. We have proved that for all $j \geq i$, there exists a $k > j$ such that $s_j >_\delta s_k$. It follows that there exists an infinite descending chain in $<_\delta$, which contradicts Theorem 1. □

Theorem 3. *Rule (8) is sound.*

Proof. Since premise S2 of Rule (8) implies premise L2 of Rule (10), and the remaining premises of the two rules are identical, it follows by Theorem 3 that Rule (8) is sound.

References

1. Apple, Inc. Apple Generic Memory Model. https://github.com/kenmcmil/ivy/tree/master/doc/examples/apple
2. Biere, A., Artho, C., Schuppan, V.: Liveness checking as safety checking. Electr. Notes Theor. Comput. Sci. **66**(2), 160–177 (2002)
3. Burch, J.R., Clarke, E.M., McMillan, K.L., Dill, D.L., Hwang, L.J.: Symbolic model checking: 10^{20} states and beyond. In: LICS, pp. 428–439. IEEE Computer Society (1990)
4. Cook, B., Podelski, A., Rybalchenko, A.: Abstraction refinement for termination. In: Hankin, C., Siveroni, I. (eds.) SAS 2005. LNCS, vol. 3672, pp. 87–101. Springer, Heidelberg (2005). https://doi.org/10.1007/11547662_8
5. de Moura, L.M., Bjørner, N.: Z3: An efficient SMT solver. In: TACAS, pp. 337–340 (2008)

6. Fang, Y., Piterman, N., Pnueli, A., Zuck, L.: Liveness with invisible ranking. In: Steffen, B., Levi, G. (eds.) VMCAI 2004. LNCS, vol. 2937, pp. 223–238. Springer, Heidelberg (2004). https://doi.org/10.1007/978-3-540-24622-0_19

7. Fang, Y., Piterman, N., Pnueli, A., Zuck, L.: Liveness with incomprehensible ranking. In: Jensen, K., Podelski, A. (eds.) TACAS 2004. LNCS, vol. 2988, pp. 482–496. Springer, Heidelberg (2004). https://doi.org/10.1007/978-3-540-24730-2_36

8. Fedyukovich, G., Prabhu, S., Madhukar, K., Gupta, A.: Quantified invariants via syntax-guided synthesis. In: Dillig, I., Tasiran, S. (eds.) CAV 2019. LNCS, vol. 11561, pp. 259–277. Springer, Cham (2019). https://doi.org/10.1007/978-3-030-25540-4_14

9. Ge, Y., de Moura, L.: Complete instantiation for quantified formulas in Satisfiabiliby modulo theories. In: Bouajjani, A., Maler, O. (eds.) CAV 2009. LNCS, vol. 5643, pp. 306–320. Springer, Heidelberg (2009). https://doi.org/10.1007/978-3-642-02658-4_25

10. Ghilardi, S., Ranise, S.: MCMT: a model checker modulo theories. In: Giesl, J., Hähnle, R. (eds.) IJCAR 2010. LNCS (LNAI), vol. 6173, pp. 22–29. Springer, Heidelberg (2010). https://doi.org/10.1007/978-3-642-14203-1_3

11. Gurfinkel, A., Shoham, S., Vizel, Y.: Quantifiers on demand (2021). CoRR, abs/2106.00664

12. Hawblitzel, C., et al.: IronFleet: proving safety and liveness of practical distributed systems. Commun. ACM, **60**(7), 83–92 (2017)

13. Komuravelli, A., Gurfinkel, A., Chaki, S.: SMT-based model checking for recursive programs (2014)

14. Lamport, L.: The temporal logic of actions. ACM Trans. Program. Lang. Syst. **16**(3), 872–923 (1994)

15. Manna, Z., Pnueli, A.: Completing the temporal picture. Theor. Comput. Sci. **83**(1), 91–130 (1991)

16. McMillan, K.L.: Circular compositional reasoning about liveness. In: Correct Hardware Design and Verification Methods, 10th IFIP WG 10.5 Advanced Research Working Conference, CHARME '99, Bad Herrenalb, Germany, September 27-29, 1999, Proceedings, pp. 342–345 (1999)

17. McMillan, K.L.: Eager abstraction for symbolic model checking. In: Chockler, H., Weissenbacher, G. (eds.) CAV 2018. LNCS, vol. 10981, pp. 191–208. Springer, Cham (2018). https://doi.org/10.1007/978-3-319-96145-3_11

18. McMillan, K.L., Padon, O.: Ivy: a multi-modal verification tool for distributed algorithms. In: Lahiri, S.K., Wang, C. (eds.) CAV 2020. LNCS, vol. 12225, pp. 190–202. Springer, Cham (2020). https://doi.org/10.1007/978-3-030-53291-8_12

19. Padon, O., Hoenicke, J., Losa, G., Podelski, A., Sagiv, M., Shoham, S.: Reducing liveness to safety in first-order logic. Proc. ACM Program. Lang. **2**(POPL), 26:1–26:33 (2018)

20. Padon, O., Hoenicke, J., McMillan, K.L., Podelski, A., Sagiv, M., Shoham, S.: Temporal prophecy for proving temporal properties of infinite-state systems. In: FMCAD, pp. 1–11. IEEE (2018)

21. Padon, O., Losa, G., Sagiv, M., Shoham, S.: Paxos made EPR: decidable reasoning about distributed protocols. Proc. ACM Program. Lang. **1**(OOPSLA), 108:1–108:31 (2017)

22. Ramsey, F.: On a problem in formal logic. Proc. London Math. Soc. (1930)

23. Marcelo Taube, et al.: Modularity for decidability of deductive verification with applications to distributed systems. In: Foster, J.S., Grossman, D. (eds.) Proceedings of the 39th ACM SIGPLAN Conference on Programming Language Design and Implementation, PLDI 2018, Philadelphia, PA, USA, June 18-22, 2018, pp. 662–677. ACM (2018)

24. Yao, J., Tao, R., Gu, R., Nieh, J.: Mostly automated verification of liveness properties for distributed protocols with ranking functions. In: POPL (2024). To appear

Software Verification

Strided Difference Bound Matrices

Arjun Pitchanathan[1]([email]) [ID], Albert Cohen[2] [ID], Oleksandr Zinenko[2] [ID], and Tobias Grosser[3] [ID]

[1] University of Edinburgh, Edinburgh, UK
arjun.pitchanathan@ed.ac.uk
[2] Google DeepMind, Paris, France
[3] University of Cambridge, Cambridge, UK
tobias.grosser@cst.cam.ac.uk

Abstract. A wide range of symbolic analysis and optimization problems can be formalized using polyhedra. Sub-classes of polyhedra, also known as sub-polyhedral domains, are sought for their lower space and time complexity. We introduce the Strided Difference Bound Matrix (SDBM) domain, which represents a sweet spot in the context of optimizing compilers. Its expressiveness and efficient algorithms are particularly well suited to the construction of machine learning compilers. We present decision algorithms, abstract domain operators and computational complexity proofs for SDBM. We also conduct an empirical study with the MLIR compiler framework to validate the domain's practical applicability. We characterize a sub-class of SDBMs that frequently occurs in practice, and demonstrate even faster algorithms on this sub-class.

1 Introduction and Motivation

The analysis and verification of computing systems involves a variety of abstractions of the system semantics. Among these, numerical abstractions capture arithmetic properties of system variables, supporting mathematical models of systems such as timed and hybrid automata [2,3,25] and the static analysis of inductive definitions in loops and recursive programs [18]. Many of these abstractions implement special cases of Presburger arithmetic [50] where typical decision problems are NP-hard. The simplest special cases are non-relational, such as interval bounds $\pm x \leq c$ where x is a variable and c is a numeric constant. More expressive, relational cases include systems of inequalities of the form $\pm x \pm y \leq c$ known as Unit Two Variable Per Inequality (UTVPI) systems. They form the *octagon abstract domain* [38]. While being much cheaper to operate upon than convex polyhedra [4,18], UTVPI are sufficiently expressive to represent a wide range of multi-variable problems [39].

UTVPI algorithms rely on a Difference Bound Matrix (DBM) representation [7], with inequalities of the form $x - y \leq c$ or $\pm x \leq c$. DBMs are ubiquitous in formal verification [6] and static analysis [8]. Other abstractions such as congruences over linear combinations of integral variables [24] capture only the lattice

© The Author(s) 2024
A. Gurfinkel and V. Ganesh (Eds.): CAV 2024, LNCS 14681, pp. 279–302, 2024.
https://doi.org/10.1007/978-3-031-65627-9_14

structure of Presburger sets but not the inequalities. The special case of congruence equalities $x \equiv r \mod d$ where r, d are integral constants and $0 \leq r < d$ has low complexity [23] and is often used to enhance other abstract domains [14].

It has remained an open problem whether there are efficient algorithms for the conjunction of UTVPI and congruence constraints. Such a domain would have numerous applications in the analysis and optimization of machine learning (ML) models. Indeed, modern ML compilers [11,33,48,53] often use a form of Presburger representation for ML compute graphs and operations, e.g. to capture the data layout in memory or conversions such as reshaping and padding.

Affine expressions also arise in program transformations to leverage modern hardware, such as vectorization, fusion and thread-level parallelization. Most of these expressions represent hyper-rectangular shapes, with occasional cases of symmetric and triangular ones (Cholesky factorization and sequence models [12,35]), all of which can be expressed as UTVPI [49]. On the other hand, strides and block sizes resulting from (dilated) convolutions, pooling and normalization operations as well as the results of the tiling (block-wise decomposition) transformation require congruence constraints. While some of the most advanced compiler optimizations justify the efforts to implement full-fledged Presburger arithmetic packages such as isl [50] and FPL [44], the majority of simpler cases call for a definition of a relational abstract domain combining UTVPI and congruences with a low-degree polynomial complexity. We also expect such a domain to be applicable to verification efforts [5,13,46] that currently rely on Presburger arithmetic libraries and SMT solvers; we present early results in Sect. 6.3.

This paper considers the conjunction of inequalities represented as a DBM with single-variable congruences, a novel abstract domain we call *Strided Difference Bound Matrices* (SDBM). We also study a sub-case of these, *Harmonic SDBM* (HSDBM), where such congruences form a harmonic sorted chain, which is common in congruences produced by loop tiling in high-performance code.

Although the SDBM satisfiability problem turns out to be NP-hard, we are able to provide and algorithm that runs in $\mathcal{O}(nmD_{\mathrm{lcm}})$ time, where n is the number of variables, m is the number of constraints and D_{lcm} is the least common multiple of all congruence divisors. This time complexity, which is pseudo-linear in D_{lcm}, is practical for program analysis applications. We also present an $\mathcal{O}(n^4)$ complexity algorithm for HSDBM satisfiability.

Finally, we define a normal form for SDBM constraint systems that is computable in at most $3m + m\log(nD_{\mathrm{lcm}}) + nD_{\mathrm{lcm}}$ satisfiability checks in the general case, and $3m + m\log(nD_{\mathrm{lcm}}) + n$ checks in the harmonic case. Given two systems in normal form, we show that it only takes linear time to perform the join operation, producing a constraint set admitting a union of solutions, common in abstract interpretation. Moreover, we can perform an equality check based on direct comparison of normal forms.

2 DBMs, SDBMs, and HSDBMs

We consider sets over the integers only, i.e., subsets of $\mathbb{Z}^n$ for some $n \in \mathbb{N}$. We first define some notation. For $m, n \in \mathbb{N}$, $[n]$ denotes the set $\{1, \ldots n\}$, $n\mathbb{Z}$ denotes the set of integer multiples of n, and $m \mid n$ denotes that m divides n. If G is a weighted graph with no negative cycles and u and v are vertices in it, then $\delta_G(u,v)$ is the distance from u to v in G. $\lfloor x \rfloor_y$ refers to x rounded down to the nearest multiple of y smaller than or equal to x. If x, y are vectors and t a scalar, $x + t$ refers to element-wise addition.

Let us first formally recall the definition of Difference Bound Matrices (DBM) over integers and their properties [20, 37] before presenting SDBM.

Definition 1. *A* Difference Bound Matrix (DBM) *is a constraint system over variables* $x_1, \ldots x_n \in \mathbb{Z}$ *of the form*

$$-x_i + x_j \le c_{ij} \qquad \ell_i \le x_i \le u_i \qquad (i, j, c_{ij}) \in E \text{ and } l_i, l_j \in \mathbb{Z}$$

where $E \subseteq [n] \times [n] \times \mathbb{Z}$ *denotes the set of difference bound constraints. We will use* $m = |E|$ *to denote the number of such constraints.*

Not all upper and lower variable bounds ℓ_i, u_i *may be present. When no such variable bounds are present we call the system* variable-bound-free (VBF); *otherwise we say that the system has variable bounds.*

It is known that the satisfiability of DBM constraints can be determined in $\mathcal{O}(n^3)$ time and $\mathcal{O}(n^2)$ space [7, 39]. We now define two special cases of Presburger sets derived from DBMs by introducing additional congruence constraints.

Lemma 2 (DBM Shifting Lemma). *If* x *is a solution to a VBF DBM, then so is* $x+t$ *for* $t \in \mathbb{Z}$, *i.e., adding a constant to all variables preserves satisfiability.*

Proof. All constraints are bounds on differences of variables, and the differences don't change when adding a constant to all variables.   □

Corollary 3. *If* $S_{i,t}$ *is the set of solutions to a VBF DBM such that* $x_i = t$, *then* $S_{i,t} = \{x + t \mid x \in S_{i,0}\}$.

Given a DBM with variable bounds, we can construct a new VBF system by adding a new variable x_0 and converting all variable bounds $\ell_i \le x_i \le u_i$ to difference bound constraints $\ell_i \le x_i - x_0 \le u_i$. Clearly $(x_1, \ldots x_n)$ is a solution to the original system iff $(0, x_1, \ldots x_n)$ is a solution to the new system. By the above lemma, the new system has a solution with $x_0 = 0$ iff it has any solution. Thus the original DBM with variable bounds is satisfiable iff the new VBF DBM is. VBF DBMs are best understood by analyzing their *potential graphs*.

Definition 4. *The* potential graph of a DBM *is a weighted directed graph over vertex set* $[n]$ *with an edge from* i *to* j *of weight* c_{ij} *for each* $(i, j, c_{ij}) \in E$. *The weights may be negative and the graph may contain negative cycles.*

Lemma 5. *Let* $G = ([n], E)$ *be the potential graph of a DBM. If* G *has a path from vertex* u *to* v *of total weight* W, *then* $-x_u + x_v \le W$ *for every solution* x *to the DBM.*

Corollary 6. *If the graph has negative cycles, then no solution x exists.*

If the graph has no negative cycles, then for all $u, v \in [n]$, it holds that $-x_u + x_v \leq \delta_G(u, v)$. This is useful to define a normal form of the DBM.

Definition 7. *A* Strided DBM (SDBM) *is one that is satisfiable and, for all u, v such that there exists a path from u to v in the potential graph G, the bound on $-x_u + x_v$ exists and is equal to $\delta_G(u, v)$.*

Clearly, any DBM can be brought to path-closed form by computing the distances in the potential graph, and by Corollary 6, doing so does not change the solution set. Moreover, the path-closed form has the following useful property.

Lemma 8 (DBM Projection Lemma). *If a DBM is path-closed, then the projection of its solution set onto a subset of variables is equal to the solution set of the constraints involving only those variables.*

It follows that the path-closed form is the tightest constraint system with the same solution set as the original system, i.e., in a path-closed DBM there exist solutions on the surface of every inequality, so no inequality can be further tightened without changing the solution set. Moreover, if there is no constraint on some $-x_i + x_j$ then adding any upper bound on this changes the solution set. Finally, the following is useful to compute a complete explicit solution.

Lemma 9. *For any vertex u in the potential graph from which all other vertices are reachable, the assignment $x_v = \delta_G(u, v)$ satisfies the DBM.*

Note that in this solution, $x_u = 0$. We now define the new abstract domains.

Definition 10. *A* Strided DBM (SDBM) *is a DBM with additional constraints*

$$x_i \equiv r_i \mod d_i \qquad\qquad i \in [n]$$

where all d_i, r_i are in $\mathbb{Z}$. When referring to such a system, D_{lcm} will denote $\mathrm{lcm}(d_1, \ldots d_n)$. Given an SDBM, we define the underlying DBM *as the constraint system without these congruence constraints.*

Note that one may encode the lack of a congruence constraint as $x_i \equiv 0 \mod 1$.

Definition 11. *A* Harmonic SDBM (HSDBM) *constraint system is an SDBM where the congruence divisors are sorted and each one divides the next, i.e., $d_1 \mid d_2 \mid \cdots \mid d_n$.*

3 Satisfiability

We start by reducing the SDBM satisfiability problem to a simpler form. Firstly, let $y_i = x_i - r_i$. Then we can see that $x_i \equiv r_i \mod d_i$ iff $y_i \equiv 0 \mod d_i$. Furthermore, $-x_i + x_j \leq c_{ij}$ iff $-y_i + y_j \leq c_{ij} + r_i - r_j$. Thus the original SDBM

$$x_i \equiv r_i \mod d_i \qquad -x_i + x_j \leq c_{ij} \qquad \ell_i \leq x_i \leq u_i$$

is satisfiable iff the following system is:

$$y_i \equiv 0 \mod d_i \qquad -y_i + y_j \leq c_{ij} + r_i - r_j \qquad \ell_i - r_i \leq y_i \leq u_i - r_i.$$

Thus we reduce satisfiability of any SDBM to the satisfiability of another SDBM where all congruence constraints have remainder zero. We can further reduce satisfiability of SDBMs with variable bounds to satisfiability of VBF SDBMs. To do this, we generalize the DBM shifting lemma to SDBMs.

Lemma 12 (SDBM Shifting Lemma). *If x is a solution to a VBF SDBM, then so is $x + tD_{lcm}$ for $t \in \mathbb{Z}$.*

Proof. By the DBM shifting lemma (Lemma 2), the inequality constraints continue to be satisfied. Since the scalar being added is a multiple of all the congruence divisors, the congruence constraints also continue to be satisfied.   □

Corollary 13. *For a given VBF SDBM with the congruence constraint on x_n being $x_n \equiv 0 \mod D_{lcm}$, let S_t be the set of solutions such that $x_n = t$. Then $S_t = \{x + t \mid x \in S_0\}$ for $t \in D_{lcm}\mathbb{Z}$. (Of course, $S_t = \varnothing$ for non-congruent t).*

We convert SDBMs to VBF form similarly to the procedure for DBMs. Let C be an SDBM with variable bounds and all remainders zero. Now create a VBF SDBM C' by adding a variable x_0 and replacing the constant bounds $\ell_i \leq x_i \leq u_i$ of C with inequalities $\ell_i \leq x_i - x_0 \leq u_i$. Then the set of solutions of C is equal to the set of solutions of C' such that $x_0 = 0$. Now by the above corollary, if we add the constraint that $x_0 \equiv 0 \mod D_{lcm}$, then C' is satisfiable iff C is satisfiable. Thus satisfiability of SDBMs with variable bounds can be efficiently reduced to satisfiability of the following simpler class of SDBMs.

Definition 14. *A constraint system of the form*

$$x_i \in d_i\mathbb{Z} \qquad -x_i + x_j \leq c_{ij} \qquad (i, j, c_{ij}) \in E$$

is called a simple SDBM. *We sometimes refer to d_i as the* stride *of the variable x_i. When the system satisfies $d_1 \mid \cdots \mid d_n$, we call it a* simple HSDBM.

3.1   GCD-Tightening Constraints

If a DBM is unsatisfiable, repeatedly applying the following inference rule will produce a contradiction eventually.

$$-x_i + x_j \leq c_{ij} \wedge -x_j + x_k \leq c_{jk} \Rightarrow -x_i + x_k \leq c_{ij} + c_{jk} \qquad \text{(path inference rule)}$$

This is because if the DBM is unsatisfiable then a negative cycle exists, and in that case, repeatedly applying the above leads to an inequality of the form $0 \leq c$ for some negative c. In an SDBM, if the underlying DBM is unsatisfiable then the above is true. However, it is possible for an unsatisfiable SDBM to have its underlying DBM be satisfiable. Consider the following example:

$$x, y \in 2\mathbb{Z} \qquad\qquad 1 \leq x - y \leq 1$$

The inequalities on their own are clearly satisfiable over the integers. However, because both x and y are even, $x - y$ cannot be 1 as required by the above system. Due to the congruence constraints, $x - y \leq 1$ implies $x - y \leq 0$ and similarly $1 \leq x - y$ implies $2 \leq x - y$, so the system is unsatisfiable. In general, by Bézout's lemma, when $x \in a\mathbb{Z}$, $y \in b\mathbb{Z}$, then $x - y \in \gcd(a, b)\mathbb{Z}$. Thus we can always tighten bounds to a multiple of the GCD, leading to a new inference rule:

$$-x_i + x_j \leq c_{ij} \implies -x_i + x_j \leq \lfloor c_{ij} \rfloor_{\gcd(d_i, d_j)} \qquad \text{(GCD-tightening rule)}$$

We use the above to define a GCD-tight SDBM.

Definition 15. *A GCD-tight SDBM is one where, for all $i, j \in [n]$, we have $c_{ij} \mid \gcd(d_i, d_j)$.*

These two rules are still not sufficient to determine if an SDBM is satisfiable. The following system is GCD-tight, path-closed, and the inequalities are satisfiable over integers, but the system as a whole is unsatisfiable.

$$
\begin{aligned}
x &\equiv 0 \quad \mod 4 \cdot 5 & 0 &\leq y - x \leq 5 \\
y &\equiv 0 \quad \mod 5 \cdot 7 & 20 &\leq x - z \leq 24 \qquad (1) \\
z &\equiv 0 \quad \mod 4 \cdot 7 & 21 &\leq y - z \leq 28
\end{aligned}
$$

To see that it is unsatisfiable, reparameterize the solution as $(c + a, c + b, c)$; this vector is a solution to the congruences iff

$$c \equiv a \quad \mod 4 \cdot 5 \qquad c \equiv b \quad \mod 5 \cdot 7 \qquad c \equiv 0 \quad \mod 4 \cdot 7$$

which by the general Chinese remainder theorem [42] has solutions iff

$$a \equiv b \quad \mod 5 \qquad a \equiv 0 \quad \mod 4 \qquad b \equiv 0 \quad \mod 7.$$

Since the solution is of the form $(a, b, 0) + c$, it satisfies the inequalities iff $(a, b, 0)$ does, by Lemma 2. Thus the inequalities hold iff

$$0 \leq b - a \leq 5 \qquad 20 \leq a \leq 24 \qquad 21 \leq b \leq 28.$$

Due to the congruence constraints we have $a \in \{20, 24\}$, $b \in \{21, 28\}$, and $b - a \in \{0, 5\}$, which cannot be satisfied simultaneously, so the SDBM is unsatisfiable. For the case of HSDBMs however, path-closure and GCD-tightening suffice.

3.2   Satisfiability for HSDBMs in $O(n^4)$ Time

By the earlier discussion, we can assume that the given HSDBM is simple. In this case, path-closure and GCD-tightening are sufficient to determine satisfiability. To show this, we prove a projection lemma for HSDBMs; while the general projection lemma for DBMs (Lemma 8) does not apply to HSDBMs, it does hold when the subset of variables chosen forms a suffix. We will call an HSDBM path-closed when its underlying DBM is path-closed.

Lemma 16. *Let H be a path-closed, GCD-tight VBF HSDBM. If $S_{k:n}$ is the projection of the solution set of H onto $x_k, \ldots x_n$, then $S_{k:n}$ is equal to the set of solutions to the inequalities and congruence constraints involving only $x_k, \ldots x_n$.*

Proof. Suppose $(p_{k+1}, \ldots p_n) \in S_{k+1:n}$. We show that there exists a p_k such that $(p_k, \ldots p_n) \in S_{k:n}$. By substituting $p_{k+1}, \ldots p_n$ into the system, we obtain bounds of the form $p_i - c_{ki} \leq x_k \leq p_i + c_{ik}$ for $k < i \leq n$ on x_k when the corresponding inequalities exist. If none of the lower bounds exist or none of the upper bounds exist, then we can definitely find a multiple of d_k satisfying these bounds to assign to x_k.

Otherwise, if at least one upper bound and one lower bound is produced, then the set of x_k satisfying the inequalities is $[\max_i(p_i - c_{ki}), \min_i(p_i + c_{ik})]$, which is of the form $[p_i - c_{ki}, p_j + c_{jk}]$ for some $i, j \in \{k+1, \ldots n\}$. This interval is non-empty by the DBM projection lemma (Lemma 8).

Now note that $p_i \in d_i \mathbb{Z} \subseteq d_k \mathbb{Z}$ by the harmonic property and similarly $p_j \in d_k \mathbb{Z}$. Also, $c_{ki} \in \gcd(d_k, d_i)\mathbb{Z} = d_k \mathbb{Z}$ by path-closure and the harmonic property; similarly, $c_{jk} \in d_k \mathbb{Z}$. So both the endpoints lie in $d_k \mathbb{Z}$ and therefore it certainly contains a multiple of d_k. Repeating this, we can extend any point in $S_{k:n}$ into a point in $S_{1:n}$, a full solution to the whole system. $\square$

Corollary 17. *A path-closed GCD-tight HSDBM is satisfiable.*

Proof. $S_{n:n} = d_n \mathbb{Z} \neq \varnothing$ is the projection of the solution set onto x_n. $\square$

This forms the basis of the SOLVEHSDBM algorithm in Fig. 1 to decide the satisfiability of HSDBMs: first, obtain the path-closure of the inequalities by running the Floyd-Warshall algorithm [16] on the potential graph, then GCD-tighten all inequalities, and repeat these two steps until a fixpoint or contradiction is reached, at which point we know whether the system is satisfiable.

```
1: function SOLVEHSDBM(E, d)              1: function SOLVESDBM(E, d)
2:     Path-close inequalities E          2:     if no integral solution to E then
3:     while (E, d) not a fixpoint do     3:         return ⊥
4:         Set every c_ij in E to         4:     p ← an integral solution to E
5:                   ⌊c_ij⌋_gcd(d_i,d_j)  5:     D_lcm ← lcm(d_1, ... d_n)
6:     if negative cycles in E then       6:     ℓ ← p − nD_lcm
7:         return ⊥                       7:     u ← p + nD_lcm
8:     Compute all pairs of distances     8:     for i ∈ [n] do u_i ← ⌊u_i⌋_d_i
9:     Set every c_uv to δ_E(u, v)        9:     while fixpoint not reached do
10:    return SAT                         10:        for (i, j, c_ij) ∈ E do
                                          11:            if u_j < ⌊u_i + c_ij⌋_d_j then
                                          12:                u_j ← ⌊u_i + c_ij⌋_d_j
                                          13:                if u_j < ℓ_j then return ⊥
                                          14:    return u
```

Fig. 1. HSDBM and SDBM satisfiability.

Lemma 18. *Let $G = (V, E)$ be a transitively closed graph with no negative cycles, i.e. whenever there is a path from u to v, there is an edge from u to v of weight $\delta_G(u, v)$. Let $U \subseteq V$. Now let F be a copy of E in which we have decreased the weights of some edges that go from one vertex in U to another in U. Finally, let $H = (V, F)$.*

Suppose that H has no negative cycles. Then for any vertices u and v in U with a path from u to v, there is a shortest path from u to v that never leaves U.

Proof. Let $p = (p_1, \ldots p_k)$ be the vertices of a path starting and ending in U and with all the intermediate vertices lying outside U. Let W be the weight of p in H and let c be the weight of the edge from p_1 to p_k in H. Then $W \geq \delta_G(p_1, p_k)$ because only edges that stay within U decreased, and $\delta_G(p_1, p_k) \geq c$ because the edge in G had weight equal to $\delta_G(p_1, p_k)$ and it can only have decreased or stayed the same in H. Thus the path p cannot have weight less than the weight of the direct edge in H.

For a general path that goes in and out of U repeatedly, we can always replace all sections of the path that go outside and come back in with the direct edges that stay in U, to obtain a path within U whose weight is at most that of the original path. Thus for any start and end point in U, the shortest path that stays in U has weight equal to the shortest path in the entire graph H. ☐

Theorem 19. SOLVEHSDBM *in Fig. 1 terminates in* $O(n^4)$ *time.*

Proof. We will view the algorithm as operating on the potential graph; all modifications to c_{ij} then become modifications to the edge weights. We will show that at most $n-1$ repetitions are needed for fixpoint. We prove that after the ith application of GCD tightening, all edges between vertices in $\{v_i, \ldots v_n\}$ will stay multiples of d_i for the rest of the algorithm. We prove this by induction. The base case for $i = 1$ is true since when all edges are multiples of d_1, path-closure cannot change this divisibility, and GCD-tightening will not change this either.

Now assume it to be true for i; we will show it for $i + 1$. The $i + 1$-th application of GCD tightening only decreases edge weights between vertices in $U = \{v_{i+1}, \ldots v_n\}$, by the induction hypothesis. Now we want to analyze how path closure affects the edge weights in the subgraph induced by U. After tightening, all edges in the subgraph are multiples of d_{i+1}, so distances between nodes in the subgraph are also multiples of d_{i+1} by Lemma 18. Thus path closure does not affect divisibility at this step. Therefore, subsequent GCD-tightening does not affect it either. Repeated applications of these preserve the property.

Thus the nth application of GCD tightening does nothing since there are no edges in the graph induced on the single vertex v_n for $i = n$. Therefore, neither does the subsequent application of path-closure. Thus, fixpoint is achieved after $n - 1$ runs of GCD-tightening and path-closure. ☐

3.3   Satisfiability for SDBMs in $O(nmD_{\text{lcm}})$ Time

Extending work by Lagarias [32], it can be shown that the SDBM satisfiability problem is NP-hard (see the appendix of the extended paper [43]) so no polynomial-time algorithm is likely to exist. In program analysis applications, the inequality coefficients can be large, so we would like an algorithm that runs in polynomial time in the representation size of these coefficients. On the other hand, in these applications, the congruence divisors are typically small, so we are willing to let the algorithm be polynomial in the *values* of these, i.e., pseudo-polynomial in these. In fact, these divisors typically share many common factors, so that their LCM is not much bigger than the divisors. We present an algorithm that is pseudo-linear in the LCM.

The intuition for the algorithm comes from the following extensions of our inference rules to upper bounds $x_i \le u_i$ on the variables.

$$x_i \le u_i \implies x_i \le \lfloor u_i \rfloor_{d_i}$$
$$x_i \le u_i \wedge -x_i + x_j \le c_{ij} \implies x_j \le u_i + c_{ij}$$

Suppose we have an SDBM with all variables bounds present and we keep applying these rules. Then we either obtain a contradiction $u_i < \ell_i$, or a fixpoint. At the fixpoint it holds that $u_i \in d_i\mathbb{Z}$ and moreover $u_j \le u_i + c_{ij}$. So in fact, u becomes a solution to the SDBM. Each successful application of an inference rule reduces the gap $u_i - \ell_i$ between some upper bound and lower bound. If this difference becomes negative, a contradiction is obtained and the algorithm halts.

So the worst-case runtime of this method depends on the sum of the gaps $u_i - \ell_i$ between the upper bounds and the lower bounds, which could naively be exponential in the representation size of the constraint system. To avoid this worst-case scenario, we reduce the satisfiability of SDBMs to the satisfiability of SDBMs with variable bounds where the gap between the upper and lower bound is at most $2nD_{\mathrm{lcm}}$ for each variable.

For a matrix A, let $\mathrm{MASD}(A)$ be the maximum absolute determinant among all square submatrices of A. A standard fact [15] in the theory of integer programming is that if $P \subseteq \mathbb{R}^n$ is a polyhedron, $P \cap \mathbb{Z}^n$ is non-empty, and x is in P, then there exists a point y in $P \cap \mathbb{Z}^n$ such that $\|x - y\| \le n\,\mathrm{MASD}(A)$. We slightly generalize this to obtain the following lemma.

Lemma 20. *Let $S = \{x \in \mathbb{R}^n \mid Ax \le b\}$ be a non-empty polyhedron. Let L be the set of solutions to some single-variable congruence constraints such that $S \cap L \ne \varnothing$, and let D_{lcm} be the LCM of the congruence divisors of L. Let $y \in S$. Then there exists a solution $x \in S \cap L$ such that $\|x - y\|_\infty \le nD_{lcm}\,\mathrm{MASD}(A)$.*

Moreover, we show that $\mathrm{MASD}(A) = 1$ for DBMs, making the bound nD_{lcm}.

Lemma 21. *Let A be an $m \times n$ matrix where each row has exactly one $+1$ and one -1. Then $\mathrm{MASD}(A) = 1$.*

We defer the proofs to the appendix of the paper's extended version [43]. These lemmas allow to solve an SDBM by first finding any integral solution p to the inequalities and adding constant bounds on the variables to lie within a box of side length $2nD_{\mathrm{lcm}}$ centered at p, then applying the above inference rules until reaching a contradiction or fixpoint.

In SOLVESDBM in Fig. 1, we first GCD-tighten all the upper bounds and then look for opportunities to apply the path-closure inference rule to the upper bounds, by checking each difference bound. Whenever an upper bound decreases due to path-closure, we immediately apply the GCD-tightening rule to it. It takes $O(m)$ time to look over all edges. Since each variable's upper and lower bounds differ by $2nD_{\text{lcm}}$, there can be at most $2n^2D_{\text{lcm}}$ steps of such tightening, for an overall runtime of $\mathcal{O}(n^2mD_{\text{lcm}})$.

We have to process the edge (i, j, c_{ij}) once in the beginning. After that, we only have to process it again when the RHS of the if-condition on line 11 changes, i.e., only when u_i decreases. So we can replace lines 9–13 with the following.

```
1: dirty ← [n]
2: while dirty ≠ ∅ do
3:     Pick i ∈ dirty
4:     Remove i from dirty
5:     for (i, j, c_ij) ∈ E do
6:         if u_j < ⌊u_i + c_ij⌋_d_j then u_j ← ⌊u_i + c_ij⌋_d_j
7:             if u_j < ℓ_j then return ⊥
8:             Add j to dirty
```

Here u_i can decrease at most $2nD_{\text{lcm}}$ times since after that it will go below the lower bound ℓ_i and produce a contradiction. Each time u_i decreases, we check all edges that go out from i, as these are the edges that might use the reduced value of u_i. Thus if o_i is the number of edges leaving i, then the time complexity of this more careful implementation is $\sum_i \mathcal{O}(nD_{\text{lcm}}o_i) = \mathcal{O}(nD_{\text{lcm}}m)$ since $\sum_i o_i = m$.

4   HSDBM Normalization

We consider normalization for satisfiable systems; if a system is unsatisfiable we normalize it by setting it to some canonical unsatisfiable system. We first normalize the inequalities and then the congruence constraints.

Definition 22. *An* inequality-normalized (H)SDBM *is one where for any bound* $-x_i + x_j \leq c$, *if it holds in the solution set that* $-x_i + x_j \leq d$, *then* $c \leq d$, *i.e. the bound in the system is the tightest valid bound.*

Note that any two SDBMs with the same solution sets will have the same normalized inequalities, since this depends only on the solution set and not on the form of the initial constraint system. The above definition is equivalent to saying that every bound $-x_i + x_j \leq c$ has a solution that makes it tight, and whenever a bound does not exist that expression can take arbitrarily large values in the solution set. Also, an inequality-normalized system is always path-closed and GCD-tight since no such tightening inference rules can decrease any bound.

We previously showed that path-closure and GCD-tightening are not sufficient to check satisfiability of SDBMs. Thus, we do not expect these to be sufficient for inequality normalization either. One might hope that it is enough for HSDBMs, but in fact it is not the case either. Consider the following example.

$$-1 \leq x - y \leq 1 \qquad -1 \leq x - w \leq 0 \qquad 0 \leq x - z \leq 1 \qquad x, y \in \mathbb{Z}$$
$$0 \leq w - z \leq 2 \qquad -1 \leq y - w \leq 0 \qquad 0 \leq y - z \leq 1 \qquad z, w \in 2\mathbb{Z}$$

It is obviously GCD-tight and path-closed. But all constraints are not as tight as possible. Note that w is either z or $z+2$. If $w = z$ then $x - z = x - w = 0$, and similarly $y - z = 0$, implying $x - y = 0$. Otherwise $w = z+2$, then $x - w = x - z = 1$ and $y - z = 1$, so $x - y = 0$ again, yielding tighter inequalities $0 \leq x - y \leq 0$. Therefore, we need to do more for inequality normalization.

First, let us consider variable-bound-free systems. Suppose the system has an inequality $-x_i + x_j \leq c$ and we want to check if replacing it by $-x_i + x_j \leq b$ for $b < c$ excludes any solutions. This is equivalent to asking if there are any solutions with $b+1 \leq -x_i + x_j \leq c$, which is a single satisfiability check. We can thus binary search over the values of b to find the minimum valid one, to obtain the tightest form of the inequality. We now establish a bound on the range of such b values over which we have to search.

By the projection lemma (Lemma 8), path-closing the underlying DBM brings it to normal form. Therefore every difference bound $-x_i + x_j \leq c_{ij}$ has an integral point y satisfying all the inequalities and such that $-y_i + y_j = c_{ij}$. By Lemma 20, there exists a solution z to the whole system with $z_j \geq c_{ij} - nD_{\mathrm{lcm}}$ and $z_i \leq c_{ij} + nD_{\mathrm{lcm}}$, so that $-z_i + z_j \geq c_{ij} - 2nD_{\mathrm{lcm}}$. Therefore, the tightest version of the inequality has a bound that is tighter by at most $2nD_{\mathrm{lcm}}$. The binary search then takes at most $3 + \log(nD_{\mathrm{lcm}})$ steps. Inequality normalization thus takes at most $m(3 + \log(nD_{\mathrm{lcm}}))$ emptiness checks.

Now consider systems with variable bounds, still with remainder zero congruence constraints. Path-closure and GCD-tightening are sufficient to normalize these, by converting them to VBF form and applying the following lemma.

Lemma 23. *If an HSDBM is path-closed and GCD-tight then all inequalities involving x_n are tight. If a bound on $-x_i + x_n$ is missing then $-x_i + x_n$ is unbounded in that direction, and similarly for bounds on $-x_n + x_i$.*

Proof. First, we show it for bounds of the form $-x_n + x_i \leq c_{ni}$. Suppose all such bounds exist. Then the point with $x_n = 0$ and $x_i = c_{ni}$ for $i < n$ is a solution. By GCD-tightening and the harmonic property, it satisfies the congruences. By path-closure, we have $c_{nj} \leq c_{ni} + c_{ij}$, so it satisfies the inequalities.

Now consider the case where all bounds do not exist. Let R be the set of variables that have a bound on $-x_n + x_i$ and let $\overline{R}$ be its complement. Set $x_i = c_{ni}$ as before, for variables in R, except x_n which we set to zero. Now we find a way to fill in the values of x_j in $\overline{R}$. Note that there can be no bound of the form $-x_i + x_j \leq c_{ij}$ for $x_i \in R, x_j \in \overline{R}$ because then by path-closure we would have a bound $-x_n + x_j \leq c_{ni} + c_{ij}$ which contradicts $x_j \in \overline{R}$.

Thus, assigning values to variables in R can impose lower bounds on variables in $\overline{R}$, but not upper bounds. Since the whole HSDBM is non-empty we can find a solution y to the subsystem of constraints that only involve variables in $\overline{R}$. Moreover, $t + y$ is a solution for any real $t \in D_{\overline{R}}\mathbb{Z}$ where $D_{\overline{R}}$ is the LCM of the congruence divisors of variables in $\overline{R}$. By making t sufficiently large, $t + y$

satisfies the lower bounds imposed by substituting values for R variables. Thus we have a solution making all the bounds c_{ni} tight. Also, by increasing t we can make the variables in $\overline{R}$ arbitrarily large so these are unbounded above.

To prove the case of bounds on $-x_i + x_n$, negate all the variables so that bounds on $-x_n + x_i$ become bounds on $-x_i + x_n$ and vice versa. Now we can apply the same proof as above. □

Therefore, to normalize a satisfiable HSDBM with variable bounds, we:

1. Convert the system into VBF form,
2. Bring the converted system into path-closed and GCD-tightened form,
3. Convert the system back to a form with variable bounds, and
4. Binary search on the remaining inequalities to normalize them.

If the system was not satisfiable, we would find out at step 2, at which point we can normalize the system by setting it to some canonical unsatisfiable HSDBM.

Let us now consider how to congruence-normalize simple HSDBMs; in this setting we require that the normal form's congruence constraints have remainder zero.

Definition 24. *A* congruence-normalized VBF HSDBM *where the congruence constraint system implies all other valid congruence constraint systems for that solution set, i.e., an HSDBM with congruence divisors $d_1^*, \ldots d_n^*$ is congruence-normalized if for all HSDBMs with the same solution set having congruence divisors say $d_1, \ldots d_n$, it holds that each $d_i \mid d_i^*$.*

Note that the above definition depends only on the solution set of a system, and so the normalized congruence system of any two systems having the same solution set will be the same. In a simple HSDBM, x_n can always take all values in $d_n\mathbb{Z}$ by the shifting lemma (Lemma 12), so any system with the same solution set will have the same congruence d_n for x_n. Therefore, $d_n^* = d_n$. We now normalize the remaining congruences iteratively, starting from x_{n-1} and going downwards. Suppose that we already computed $d_{i+1}^*, \ldots d_n^*$ and we want to compute d_i^*.

Note that for any valid congruence system it holds that $d_i \mid d_{i+1} \mid d_{i+1}^*$ by the harmonic property and congruence normalization. Thus d_i^* is the maximum of all $d_i \mid d_{i+1}^*$ such that $x_i \in d_i\mathbb{Z}$ holds in the solution set. By the projection lemma (Lemma 16), we can reduce this to finding the largest possible divisor for x_1 in a given constraint system with divisors $d_1, \ldots d_n$. As shown above we only need to consider divisors $m \mid d_2$. For it to be a valid divisor, it also needs to not be so dense as to allow additional solutions; we ensure this by mandating that $d_1 \mid m$. Note that the greatest divisor cannot be a non-multiple of d_1 anyway, since if m is a valid congruence for x_1 then so is $\mathrm{lcm}(d_1, m)$.

Theorem 25. *Let H be an inequality-normalized simple HSDBM. Let L be the set of $m \in \mathbb{N}$ such that $d_1 \mid m \mid d_2$ and for any solution x of H, it holds that $x_1 \in m\mathbb{Z}$. We are interested in the sparsest possible congruence divisor, $\max L$. Let g be the GCD of all c_{i1} and c_{1i}, and let $q = \gcd(g, d_2)$.*

Then $\max L$ *is either* d_1 *or* q. *Moreover, it is* q *iff a specific other HSDBM* H' *is unsatisfiable, where the constraint system* H' *can be computed in linear time from the system* H.

Proof. We first show that for any $r \in L$, $r \mid g$. Suppose not, then without loss of generality, r does not divide some c_{i1}. Since the system is inequality normalized, it has some solution satisfying $x_1 = x_i + c_{i1}$. But since $x_i \in d_i \mathbb{Z} \subseteq r\mathbb{Z}$ and $c_{1i} \notin r\mathbb{Z}$, we have $x_1 \notin r\mathbb{Z}$, so $r \notin L$ which is a contradiction. So this case is impossible and we have $r \mid g$. Since $r \mid d_2$, we have $r \mid \gcd(g, d_2) = q$. Thus, $\max L \mid q$. If $q = d_1$, we are done and $\max L = d_1$.

Otherwise, let $q \neq d_1$. We now show that either $q \mid \max L$, implying $\max L = q$, or $\max L = d_1$. Let $S_{2:n}$ be the projection of the solution set onto $x_2, \ldots x_n$. For now, assume that all constraints in the system exist. Then every assignment $(p_2, \ldots p_n) \in S_{2:n}$ implies constraints of the form $p_i - c_{1i} \leq x_1 \leq p_i + c_{i1}$. So the set of possible x_1 values for this assignment is $\bigcap_{i=2}^{n} [p_i - c_{1i}, p_i + c_{i1}] \cap d_1\mathbb{Z}$. This set is non-empty by the definition of $S_{2:n}$. Since $q \mid d_2 \mid p_i$ for all $i \geq 2$ and q divides all the coefficients c_{1i} and c_{i1}, all interval endpoints are multiples of q. Therefore the endpoints of the intersection are also multiples of q. Since $d_1 \mid q$, if the intersection contains more than one element then it definitely contains two adjacent multiples of d_1, implying $\max L = d_1$. Otherwise, if the intersection contains exactly one element, that element is surely a multiple of q.

Thus, $q \mid \max L$ if for all points in $S_{2:n}$, the intersection of the intervals is a singleton. Otherwise, $\max L = d_1$. The intersection of some intervals is a singleton iff the right endpoint of some interval equals the left endpoint of some interval, possibly the same one. So we have to check whether, for every valid assignment in $S_{2:n}$, some two intervals $[x_i - c_{1i}, x_i + c_{i1}]$ and $[x_j - c_{1j}, x_j + c_{j1}]$ intersect only at their endpoints, i.e., there always exist some $i, j \in \{2, \ldots n\}$ such that $x_i + c_{i1} = x_j - c_{1j}$, i.e., $-x_j + x_i = c_{i1} + c_{1j}$. Note that by path closure, if $x_2, \ldots x_n \in S_{2:n}$, then it already holds that $-x_j + x_i \leq c_{ji} \leq c_{j1} + c_{1i}$. So it is only left to check whether $\forall x_2, \ldots x_n \in S_{2:n}$, $\exists i, j \in \{2, \ldots n\}$, $-x_j + x_i \geq c_{j1} + c_{1i}$. This is equivalent to $\nexists x_2, \ldots x_n \in S_{2:n}$, $\forall i, j \in \{2, \ldots n\}$, $-x_j + x_i < c_{j1} + c_{1i}$, by logically negating twice. The strict inequality is equivalent to the constraint that $-x_j + x_i \leq c_{j1} + c_{1i} - 1$ since all variables are integers. By the HSDBM projection lemma (Lemma 16), a vector belongs to $S_{2:n}$ iff it satisfies the constraints on those variables in the HSDBM. Thus the condition above can be checked using a single HSDBM satisfiability check.

If some of the c_{1i} or c_{i1} bounds did not exist then the corresponding intervals in the intersection would have ranged till infinity on that side. Still, the same conclusion holds: $\max L \neq d_1$ iff the intersection is a singleton, meaning that some two finite endpoints have to coincide, and the rest of the proof proceeds the same way. Whenever some c_{1i} or c_{i1} does not exist we simply do not add any of the bounds in the constructed system that depend on that bound.   □

Generalizing to HSDBMs with Variable Bounds. When variable bounds exist, it is possible for a variable to take only a single value, in which case any congruence divisor is valid and the sparsest congruence constraint is not well-defined. In this case, in inequality-normalized form, the variable will have upper and lower bounds equal, so we can immediately detect this case by looking at the variable bounds. When this happens, we first eliminate these variables by substituting in the single value that they can take. We then compute the congruence normalization of the resulting system, then add back the eliminated variables and give them some canonical congruence constraint that preserves the harmonic property. For example, use $x_1 \equiv 0 \mod 1$ if it is the first variable and use the divisor of the previous variable otherwise.

We now consider congruence normalization of systems with variable bounds where every variable takes at least two values.

Lemma 26. *Let C be an SDBM with variable bounds, where each variable takes at least two values. Let C' be the system converted into VBF form with the added variable x_{n+1} having divisor D, with $D_{lcm} \mid D$. Let $e_1, \ldots e_n$ be the normalized congruence divisors of the converted system, and let $d_1^*, \ldots d_n^*$ be the sparsest congruences for the original system. Then $\forall i, e_i = \gcd(D, d_i^*)$.*

Proof. Let S be the set of values x_i takes in C and let T be the set of values it takes in C'. Then $T = \{x + tD \mid x \in S, t \in \mathbb{Z}\}$ by the shifting lemma (Lemma 12). The sparsest congruence divisor for S is the GCD of all elements in S, which we call g. Similarly, the sparsest congruence divisor for T is the GCD of all elements in T, which is equal to $\gcd(g, D)$ since for any a, $\gcd_{t \in \mathbb{Z}}(a + tD) = \gcd(a, D)$. □

Lemma 27. *In an HSDBM with variable bounds where x_n takes at least two possible values, the sparsest possible congruence divisor for x_n is d_n.*

Proof. Convert the system to VBF form. Let x_{n+1} be the variable added for the conversion. By the projection lemma (Lemma 16), the set of valid values of these two variables is the set of constraints involving only them. The set of valid values of x_n in the original system is the set of values of x_n in the converted system with $x_{n+1} = 0$, and is therefore the set of multiples of d_n within the variable bounds of x_n. Thus the sparsest congruence divisor for x_n is still d_n. □

We now show how to compute the sparsest congruence constraints.

Theorem 28. *Given an HSDBM with variable bounds where every variable takes at least two values, the sparsest congruence constraints are equal to sparsest constraints for the system after converting to VBF form.*

Proof. We convert the system to VBF form by adding a variable x_{n+1} with congruence divisor $d_{n+1} := d_n$. We then compute its congruence normalization to obtain divisors $e_1 \mid \cdots \mid e_n \mid e_{n+1}$. Let $d_1^* \mid \cdots \mid d_n^*$ be the true sparsest congruences for the input system. Then $e_i = \gcd(d_{n+1}, d_i^*)$ by Lemma 26 and $d_{n+1} = d_n = d_n^*$ by Lemma 27. Hence $e_i = \gcd(d_n^*, d_i^*) = d_i^*$ since $d_i^* \mid d_n^*$. □

Generalizing to Arbitrary Congruence Constraints. For HSDBMs with arbitrary congruence constraints, we can find any solution and shift the system so that the origin becomes a solution. Then all valid congruence constraints have remainder zero since there is a solution at the origin. Computing the sparsest possible congruence for this system and performing the inverse shift therefore gives us the sparsest possible congruence for the original system.

5 Operations for Abstract Interpretation

We introduce intersection, equality, inclusion, and join operations for (H)SDBMs, completing the set of operations typically required for abstract interpretation.

Intersection. To intersect, we just take the tighter of the bounds on each $-x_i + x_j$ and of the variable bounds.

Equality. We check if two HSDBMs have equal solution sets by checking if their normal forms are equal. For simple SDBMs, we first check if their normalized inequalities are equal, then compare congruences: given an SDBM C, $D \in \mathbb{N}$ such that all $d_i \mid D$, and $r \in \{1, \ldots D - 1\}$, there exists a solution with $x_i \equiv r$ mod D iff there exists one with $x_i = r$, by the shifting lemma (Lemma 12).

Now given two VBF SDBMs, let D be the LCM of their congruence divisors. Checking which values modulo D each variable can take in each system takes $2nD$ satisfiability checks. If both are equal and the normalized inequalities are also equal then both systems have equal solution sets. Otherwise, they do not.

Now given two SDBMs with variable bounds, we again set D to be the LCM of the congruence divisors and inequality normalize both, then convert them to VBF form using the same congruence divisor D for the added variable. The two original systems are equivalent iff the converted systems are, and we know how to check equality of solution sets for VBF SDBMs.

Inclusion. We can check for inclusion using intersection and equality checks since for sets A and B, we have $A \subseteq B$ iff $A \cap B = A$.

Join. Given two SDBMs in normal form, the system with the smallest solution set that encompasses both the inputs' solution sets is the system that takes the looser of the two bounds on each $-x_i + x_j$. When one of the systems has no bound, the result should have no bound either. This follows from Definition 22.

For the congruences of the joined system, we compute the congruence normalization of both the input systems and for each variable, take the sparsest congruence constraints that encompass both. Say the two constraints are $x \equiv r_1$ mod q_1 and $x \equiv r_2$ mod q_2. Let p be any solution to these two constraints, then the two constraints are equivalent to $x - p \equiv 0$ mod q_1 and $x - p \equiv 0$ mod q_2 respectively. The sparsest constraint that holds for $x - p$ satisfying either one of these constraints is $x - p \equiv 0$ mod $\gcd(q_1, q_2)$, i.e., $x \equiv p$ mod $\gcd(q_1, q_2)$.

Finding an Equivalent Simple Representation of an SDBM. It may sometimes be useful to find a simple representation of an SDBM, if one exists. A satisfiable SDBM C with variable bounds can never have the same solution set as a VBF SDBM C', because by the shifting lemma (Lemma 12), for any solution x of C', there exists a constant D such that $x + kD$ is also a solution for any integer k. Hence the solution set of C' does not satisfy any variable bounds and so is different from that of C.

A VBF SDBM C with non-zero remainders admits a simple SDBM representation if there is a way to replace its congruence constraints with zero-remainder constraints while preserving the same solution set. This can be determined by computing the possible remainders of all variables modulo D_{lcm}. By the shifting lemma, a remainder $x_i \equiv r_i \mod D_{\text{lcm}}$ is possible iff there is a solution with $x_i = r_i$, which amounts to a satisfiability check.

Let g_i be the GCD of all possible remainders obtained above and D_{lcm}. By the shifting lemma, g_i is the GCD of all valid values of x_i. To ensure that our new congruence constraint for x_i does not invalidate any solutions of the original system, it is necessary and sufficient that the new divisor be a divisor of g_i.

To disallow any extraneous solutions, we make the congruence constraint as sparse as possible. Consider the system C' with congruence constraints $x_i \equiv 0 \mod g_i$ and the inequality constraints of C. C can be represented by a simple SDBM with the same solution set iff C and C' have the same solution set, which we can check as described above.

6   Empirical Study

The goal of this study is to demonstrate the *suitability* of SDBM for program representation and analysis. To this end, we instrumented several optimizing compilers that use polyhedral domains internally and analyzed those domains. Evaluating the compilation time or the run time of the compiled program is beyond the scope of the study as it requires additional engineering to compete with highly-optimized Presburger arithmetic libraries [44,50].

6.1   Methodology

We instrumented the following compilation and analysis projects.

- The MLIR compiler infrastructure [33], widely used in production to support domains ranging from machine learning compilers to hardware synthesis. We used MLIR version `llvmorg-18-init-16246-g4daea501c4fc` (Jan 5, 2024) and compiled the test suite provided with the project using `ninja check-mlir`. We collected statistics from 2176 compiler invocations. Some tests feature multiple invocations.
- The Polygeist CUDA-to-OpenMP cross-compiler [40] based on the archived artifact [41]. We compiled 17 benchmarks from the CUDA subset of the Rodinia suite [10] accepted by Polygeist with the same 7 configurations as [41].

– The PPCG polyhedral compiler [51] version `0.09.1` (Apr 2, 2023, most recent release). We compiled 30 benchmarks from the Polybench/C benchmark suite version `4.2.1` [45] using `ppcg -target=c -openmp -tile` to enable autoscheduling, parallelization and tiling.

MLIR and MLIR-based Polygeist were instrumented to intercept the creation of affine expressions and sets bounded by such expressions as well as (integer) emptiness checks of these sets. For each expression and set, we verified whether it can be expressed as a (H)SDBM. We say that an expression can be In MLIR, unique expressions are reused so that the collected statistics reflect unique SDBM objects that existed throughout the execution of the test. PPCG, and its underlying isl library [50], were instrumented to check if the following objects fit (H)SDBM: affine constraints, convex sets, unions thereof and unions of non-convex sets in multiple vector spaces. We collected all such objects at several moments in the compilation process: after constructing the initial representation, after performing dependence analysis, before and after scheduling, and just before final code generation.

6.2   Prevalence of SDBMs

MLIR. Out of 2176 test cases, 1264 (58.1%) construct affine expressions throughout their lifetime. The following analysis focuses only on those. Overall, 96.3% of affine expressions and 95.6% of integer sets (we consider MLIR multi-dimensional affine maps as such) can be represented using SDBM. 714 (56.5%) of the cases use only SDBM expressions. In the remaining cases, $90.3\% \pm 15.9$[1] of expressions and $88.2\% \pm 17.5$ sets can be represented using SDBM.

45 of the test cases perform a total of 7695 emptiness checks. 6262 (81.4%) of these are performed on HSDBM integer sets, and none on more general SDBMs. 22 (48.9%) test cases perform emptiness checks only on HSDBM. In the remaining cases, $73.5\% \pm 37.7$ of the checks are performed on HSDBM sets.

These results suggest that SDBM is sufficient to represent a large fraction of affine constructs appearing in a compiler infrastructure supporting polyhedral compilation [31], machine learning compilers [34], high-level synthesis [54] and other hardware design [21]. It is worth noting that the test suite covers rare representational edge cases, so practical applications may have better coverage. For example, many non-SDBM expressions are found in Affine dialect tests, which exercise the full expressive power of (quasi-)affine expressions, including divisions by parameters, huge coefficients, or expressions with hundreds of terms.

Some of the 17 compiled benchmarks consist of multiple translation units processed separately, for a total of 39. Each one was compiled with 7 different configurations, leading to the total of 273 test cases. Out of these, 266 (97.4%) construct affine expressions and 50 (18.3%) perform emptiness checks.

---

[1] The $\mu \pm \sigma$ notation indicates the mean and standard deviation.

Polygeist. 96.3% of the affine expressions and 95.6% of the integer sets fit the SDBM domain. 185 (69.5%) cases use only SDBM constructs. The remaining cases have $95\% \pm 5.1$ and $93.8\% \pm 6.4$ SDBM expressions and sets, respectively.

These test cases perform a total of 540 emptiness checks all of which can be expressed using HSDBM. In Polygeist, emptiness checks are performed during dependence analysis. Since the benchmarks are originally written in CUDA, they use only simple single-variable subscript expressions, leading to compatible $i - j$ expressions in dependence relations.

These results indicate that SDBM is suitable for end-to-end compilation, even if a more expressive representation may be occasionally required. Note also the higher ratio compared to the MLIR test suite.

PPCG. While none of the benchmarks can be completely processed using exclusively SDBM, most steps of the compilation process are largely compatible. Specifically, the initial representation of the program uses only SDBM for 25 (83.3%) programs, and the result of dependence analysis is representable for 26 (86.7%) programs. ILP-based affine scheduling does not match SDBM requirements for any of the programs since it extensively uses multi-variable expressions through its use of the Farkas lemma [49]. On the other hand, the resulting schedule can be expressed as a union of SDBM integer sets for 21 (70%) programs. Using the hierarchical form of the schedule [52] instead of a flat union brings this number up to 24 (80%). When applying loop tiling on a hierarchical schedule, 23 (76.7%) programs still use only SDBM with divisibility constraints associated with tile sizes. Finally, code generation is expressible only for the one program, `durbin.c`, as it produces linearized expressions of the form $C \cdot i + ii$ to recombine loop indexes after tiling (such linearization was previously avoided in the hierarchical schedule); `durbin.c` does not contain a tileable loop nest and only accesses single-dimensional arrays with subscripts of the form `i` and `i - j - C`, which are SDBM. We could also confirm our intuition that *all SDBM expressions are also HSDBM*. This is due to congruences being introduced by tiling, which uses the fixed factor of 32 by default. We verified this by disabling tiling, which brought the number of supported test cases for flat schedule and code generation to 21 (70%). Tile factors are typically chosen as powers of two or fractions of the problem sizes, so they are likely to remain divisible.

Overall, across all stages and benchmarks, $85.6\% \pm 21.6$ of affine constraints and $78.1\% \pm 37$ sets are SDBM. This number ranges from $41.5\% \pm 14.3$ constraints for the ILP set to $99.8\% \pm 0.5$ for dependency analysis, and from $10.8\% \pm 24.2$ sets for code generation to $99.6\% \pm 1.1$ for dependency analysis. These results suggest that SDBM combined with structured affine representations such as schedule trees may power a large part of a polyhedral compiler, for all stages except ILP-based affine scheduling.

6.3   Applications to Translation Validation

We additionally used our instrumented version of MLIR[2] to process three end-to-end machine learning models as described in [5]. Specifically, we took the following models (fetched on January 19, 2024).

- `text_classification_v2` obtained from https://www.tensorflow.org/lite/examples/text_classification/overview.
- MobileNet v3, variation "large-075-224-classification" obtained from https://www.kaggle.com/models/google/mobilenet-v3/frameworks/tfLite.
- SqueezeNet: https://www.kaggle.com/models/tensorflow/squeezenet.

We further converted these models from the original TFLite format into the MLIR TOSA dialect using the TensorFlow tool `flatbuffer_translate -tflite-flatbuffer-to-mlir` to yield a TFLite MLIR representation, as well as `tf-opt -tfl-to-tosa-pipeline` to obtain TOSA.[3] We do not run the models but (partially) compile them along the lines of [5] using the command:[4]

```
mlir-opt --pass-pipeline='builtin.module(func.func(tosa-optional-decompositions),
   canonicalize, func.func(tosa-infer-shapes, tosa-make-broadcastable, tosa-to-linalg-named),
   canonicalize, func.func(tosa-layerwise-constant-fold, tosa-make-broadcastable),
   tosa-validate, func.func(tosa-to-linalg, tosa-to-arith, tosa-to-tensor),
   linalg-fuse-elementwise-ops, one-shot-bufferize)'
```

We collected SDBM-related statistics from all three cases in Table 1. None of the models required an emptiness check.

Table 1. SDBM is sufficient to represent most affine sets and expressions during the partial compilation pipeline from TOSA to the bufferized Linalg dialect in MLIR.

Model	Sets			Expressions		
	Total	SDBM		Total	SDBM	
Text Classification	4099	4099	(100%)	9148	9148	(100%)
MobileNet	58876	52596	(89.3%)	208840	202110	(96.8%)
SqueezeNet	28131	27806	(98.8%)	96140	95490	(99.3%)

---

[2] `llvmorg-18-init-16246-g4daea501c4fc`(Jan 5,2024), same for MLIR test suite.

[3] Both were compiled from source: https://github.com/tensorflow/tensorflow version `ae7eb0931d2973095`, which depends on a different version of MLIR, but the textual representation of TOSA in both is compatible.

[4] We noticed the existing flag `tosa-to-linalg-pipeline` does not produce any code, so we reconstructed the MLIR pass pipeline from its source code in `mlir/lib/Conversion/TosaToLinalg/TosaToLinalgPass.cpp`. Notable differences with the previously reported pipeline include additional TOSA normalization passes and the decomposition of the Standard MLIR dialect into the Arith and Tensor dialects, as well as the recomposition of bufferization passes into a single one.

7   Related Work

The relevance of weakly relational domains for loop parallelization and optimization is well established [1]. More recently, UTVPI approximations enabling complex affine transformations (such as those enabled by PPCG in the empirical evaluation) have also been identified [49]. But these techniques remain unaware of congruence properties, missing optimization opportunities as a result [49].

There is a rich literature on sub-polyhedral domains [22]. APRON[5] [30] provides a reference implementation for many of these. See also ELINA[6] [47] for advanced algorithms and optimizations. Combinations of abstract domains are popular in static analysis [14,17]. These aim at increasing precision by "cross-fertilization" of analyses without the need for new abstract domains. Yet actual intersections of sub-polyhedral domains received much less attention. Bygde surveys some of these [9], the most closely related being the trapezoidal domain [36] which combines lattices with intervals, forming a non-relational domain.

Considering SDBM algorithms themselves, our iterative approach to the satisfiability problem is reminiscent of the dynamic all-pairs shortest paths [19] and incremental closure algorithms [29]. Complexity results in this space relate to the cubic upper bound of the Floyd-Warshall algorithm and do not contribute to improving the complexity of the GCD tightening iterations.

The weak NP-completeness of TVPI has been established by Hochbaum and Naor [26–28], together with a (pseudo-polynomial) integer linear programming algorithm that is quadratic in the largest bound of the inequalities. Our SDBM algorithm has lower complexity and also makes it pseudo-polynomial in the congruence divisors instead. In compilation problems of interest, congruences correspond to tile and vector sizes dictated by hardware parameters; they are much smaller than bounds of the iteration spaces and arrays.

8   Conclusion

We introduced the Strided Difference Bound Matrix (SDBM) abstraction combining two-variable inequalities with congruence constraints. We demonstrated the prevalence of these across the compiler test suites of MLIR, Polygeist and PPCG. We showed that the satisfiability of SDBM is NP-hard but also admits an algorithm pseudo-linear in the LCM of the congruence divisors. We identified the Harmonic SDBM (HSDBM) sub-case that commonly arises in compilation problems for deep learning and other areas. HSDBM satisfiability has a worst-case complexity of $\mathcal{O}(n^4)$, which is practical for uses in compilers and has the potential to accelerate verification tools based on more general Presburger arithmetic. We gave an $\mathcal{O}(mn^4 \log(nD_{\text{lcm}}))$ algorithm for HSDBM normalization. Finally, given a pair of normalized HSDBM, we showed linear-time algorithms to check for equality and to perform the join operation. The design of a widening operator, also necessary for abstract interpretation, is left for future work.

---

[5] https://antoinemine.github.io/Apron/doc/api/c.
[6] https://elina.ethz.ch.

Disclosure of Interests.. The authors have no competing interests to declare that are relevant to the content of this article.

References

1. Allen, R., Kennedy, K.: Optimizing Compilers for Modern Architectures: A Dependence-Based Approach. Morgan Kaufmann, San Francisco (2001)
2. Alur, R.: Timed automata. In: Halbwachs, N., Peled, D. (eds.) CAV 1999. LNCS, vol. 1633, pp. 8–22. Springer, Heidelberg (1999). https://doi.org/10.1007/3-540-48683-6_3
3. Alur, R., Dill, D.L.: A theory of timed automata. Theoret. Comput. Sci. **126**(2), 183–235 (1994)
4. Bagnara, R., Hill, P.M., Ricci, E., Zaffanella, E.: Precise widening operators for convex polyhedra. Sci. Comput. Program. **58**(1–2), 28–56 (2005). https://doi.org/10.1016/j.scico.2005.02.003
5. Bang, S., Nam, S., Chun, I., Jhoo, H.Y., Lee, J.: SMT-based translation validation for machine learning compiler. In: Shoham, S., Vizel, Y. (eds.) CAV 2022. LNCS, vol. 13372, pp. 386–407. Springer, Cham (2022). https://doi.org/10.1007/978-3-031-13188-2_19
6. Bengtsson, J., Larsen, K., Larsson, F., Pettersson, P., Yi, W.: UPPAAL — a tool suite for automatic verification of real-time systems. In: Alur, R., Henzinger, T.A., Sontag, E.D. (eds.) HS 1995. LNCS, vol. 1066, pp. 232–243. Springer, Heidelberg (1996). https://doi.org/10.1007/BFb0020949
7. Berthomieu, B., Menasche, M.: An enumerative approach for analyzing time petri nets. In: Mason, R.E.A. (ed.) Information Processing 83, Proceedings of the IFIP 9th World Computer Congress, Paris, France, 19–23 September, 1983, pp. 41–46. North-Holland/IFIP (1983)
8. Blanchet, B., et al.: A static analyzer for large safety-critical software. In: Proceedings of the ACM SIGPLAN 2003 Conference on Programming Language Design and Implementation, pp. 196–207 (2003)
9. Bygde, S.: Abstract Interpretation and Abstract Domains. Master's thesis, Mälardalen University (2006). http://www.es.mdu.se/publications/948-
10. Che, S., et al.: Rodinia: a benchmark suite for heterogeneous computing. In: 2009 IEEE International Symposium on Workload Characterization (IISWC), pp. 44–54 (2009). https://doi.org/10.1109/IISWC.2009.5306797
11. Chen, T., et al.: TVM: an automated End-to-End optimizing compiler for deep learning. In: 13th USENIX Symposium on Operating Systems Design and Implementation (OSDI 18), Carlsbad, CA, pp. 578–594. USENIX Association (2018). https://www.usenix.org/conference/osdi18/presentation/chen
12. Child, R., Gray, S., Radford, A., Sutskever, I.: Generating long sequences with sparse transformers. CoRR **abs/1904.10509** (2019). http://arxiv.org/abs/1904.10509
13. Clément, B., Cohen, A.: End-to-end translation validation for the halide language. Proc. ACM Program. Lang. **6**(OOPSLA1) (2022). https://doi.org/10.1145/3527328
14. Codish, M., Mulkers, A., Bruynooghe, M., de la Banda, M.G., Hermenegildo, M.: Improving abstract interpretations by combining domains. In: Proceedings of the 1993 ACM SIGPLAN Symposium on Partial Evaluation and Semantics-Based Program Manipulation. PEPM '93, New York, NY, USA, pp. 194–205. Association for Computing Machinery (1993). https://doi.org/10.1145/154630.154650

15. Cook, W., Gerards, A.M.H., Schrijver, A., Tardos, É.: Sensitivity theorems in integer linear programming. Math. Program. **34**(3), 251–264 (1986)
16. Cormen, T.H., Leiserson, C.E., Rivest, R.L., Stein, C.: Introduction to Algorithms, 3rd edn. The MIT Press, Cambridge (2009)
17. Cousot, P., Cousot, R., Mauborgne, L.: The reduced product of abstract domains and the combination of decision procedures. In: Hofmann, M. (ed.) FoSSaCS 2011. LNCS, vol. 6604, pp. 456–472. Springer, Heidelberg (2011). https://doi.org/10.1007/978-3-642-19805-2_31
18. Cousot, P., Halbwachs, N.: Automatic discovery of linear restraints among variables of a program. In: Proceedings of the 5th ACM SIGACT-SIGPLAN Symposium on Principles of Programming Languages. POPL '78, New York, NY, USA, pp. 84–96, Association for Computing Machinery (1978).https://doi.org/10.1145/512760.512770
19. Demetrescu, C., Italiano, G.F.: A new approach to dynamic all pairs shortest paths. In: Proceedings of the Thirty-Fifth Annual ACM Symposium on Theory of Computing, pp. 159–166. STOC '03, New York, NY, USA. Association for Computing Machinery (2003). https://doi.org/10.1145/780542.780567
20. Dill, D.L.: Timing assumptions and verification of finite-state concurrent systems. In: Sifakis, J. (ed.) CAV 1989. LNCS, vol. 407, pp. 197–212. Springer, Heidelberg (1990). https://doi.org/10.1007/3-540-52148-8_17
21. Eldridge, S., et al.: MLIR as hardware compiler infrastructure. In: Workshop on Open-Source EDA Technology (WOSET) (2021)
22. Gange, G., Ma, Z., Navas, J.A., Schachte, P., Søndergaard, H., Stuckey, P.J.: A fresh look at zones and octagons. ACM Trans. Program. Lang. Syst. **43**(3) (2021). https://doi.org/10.1145/3457885
23. Granger, P.: Static analysis of arithmetical congruences. Int. J. Comput. Math. **30**(3–4), 165–190 (1989). https://doi.org/10.1080/00207168908803778
24. Granger, P.: Static analysis of linear congruence equalities among variables of a program. In: Abramsky, S., Maibaum, T.S.E. (eds.) CAAP 1991. LNCS, vol. 493, pp. 169–192. Springer, Heidelberg (1991). https://doi.org/10.1007/3-540-53982-4_10
25. Henzinger, T.: The theory of hybrid automata. In: Proceedings 11th Annual IEEE Symposium on Logic in Computer Science, pp. 278–292 (1996).https://doi.org/10.1109/LICS.1996.561342
26. Hochbaum, D.S.: Monotonizing linear programs with up to two nonzeroes per column. Oper. Res. Lett. **32**(1), 49–58 (2004). https://doi.org/10.1016/S0167-6377(03)00074-9
27. Hochbaum, D.S.: Applications and efficient algorithms for integer programming problems on monotone constraints. Networks **77**(1), 21–49 (2021)
28. Hochbaum, D.S., Naor, J.S.: Simple and fast algorithms for linear and integer programs with two variables per inequality. SIAM J. Comput. **23**(6), 1179–1192 (1994). https://doi.org/10.1137/S0097539793251876
29. Howe, J.M., King, A., Simon, A.: Incremental closure for systems of two variables per inequality. Theoret. Comput. Sci. **768**, 1–42 (2019)
30. Jeannet, B., Miné, A.: APRON: a library of numerical abstract domains for static analysis. In: Bouajjani, A., Maler, O. (eds.) CAV 2009. LNCS, vol. 5643, pp. 661–667. Springer, Heidelberg (2009). https://doi.org/10.1007/978-3-642-02658-4_52
31. Katel, N., Khandelwal, V., Bondhugula, U.: MLIR-based code generation for gpu tensor cores. In: Proceedings of the 31st ACM SIGPLAN International Conference

on Compiler Construction. CC 2022, New York, NY, USA, pp. 117–128. Association for Computing Machinery (2022). https://doi.org/10.1145/3497776.3517770, https://doi.org/10.1145/3497776.3517770

32. Lagarias, J.C.: The computational complexity of simultaneous diophantine approximation problems. SIAM J. Comput. **14**(1), 196–209 (1985)

33. Lattner, C., et al.: MLIR: scaling compiler infrastructure for domain specific computation. In: 2021 IEEE/ACM International Symposium on Code Generation and Optimization (CGO), pp. 2–14 (2021). https://doi.org/10.1109/CGO51591.2021.9370308

34. Liu, H.I.C., Brehler, M., Ravishankar, M., Vasilache, N., Vanik, B., Laurenzo, S.: TINYIREE: an ml execution environment for embedded systems from compilation to deployment. IEEE Micro **42**(5), 9–16 (2022). https://doi.org/10.1109/MM.2022.3178068

35. Martens, J., Grosse, R.: Optimizing neural networks with kronecker-factored approximate curvature. In: Proceedings of the 32nd International Conference on International Conference on Machine Learning - Volume 37. ICML'15, pp. 2408-2417. JMLR.org (2015)

36. Masdupuy, F.: Array abstractions using semantic analysis of trapezoid congruences. In: Kennedy, K., Polychronopoulos, C.D. (eds.) Proceedings of the 6th International Conference on Supercomputing, ICS 1992, Washington, DC, USA, July 19-24, 1992, pp. 226–235. ACM (1992).https://doi.org/10.1145/143369.143414

37. Miné, A.: A new numerical abstract domain based on difference-bound matrices. In: Danvy, O., Filinski, A. (eds.) PADO 2001. LNCS, vol. 2053, pp. 155–172. Springer, Heidelberg (2001). https://doi.org/10.1007/3-540-44978-7_10

38. Miné, A.: The octagon abstract domain. In: Proceedings of the Eighth Working Conference on Reverse Engineering (WCRE'01). WCRE '01, USA, p. 310. IEEE Computer Society (2001)

39. Miné, A.: The octagon abstract domain. CoRR **abs/cs/0703084** (2007). http://arxiv.org/abs/cs/0703084

40. Moses, W.S., Chelini, L., Zhao, R., Zinenko, O.: Polygeist: raising c to polyhedral MLIR. In: 2021 30th International Conference on Parallel Architectures and Compilation Techniques (PACT), pp. 45–59 (2021).https://doi.org/10.1109/PACT52795.2021.00011

41. Moses, W.S., Ivanov, I.R., Domke, J., Endo, T., Doerfert, J., Zinenko, O.: High-performance GPU-to-CPU transpilation and optimization via high-level parallel constructs. In: PPoPP '23, New York, NY, USA, pp. 119–134. Association for Computing Machinery (2023). https://doi.org/10.1145/3572848.3577475

42. Ore, O.: The general Chinese remainder theorem. Am. Math. Mon. **59**(6), 365–370 (1952)

43. Pitchanathan, A., Cohen, A., Zinenko, O., Grosser, T.: Strided difference bound matrices. CoRR abs/2405.11244 (2024) .https://doi.org/10.48550/ARXIV.2405.11244

44. Pitchanathan, A., Ulmann, C., Weber, M., Hoefler, T., Grosser, T.: FPL: fast presburger arithmetic through transprecision. Proc. ACM Program. Lang. **5**(OOPSLA) (2021). https://doi.org/10.1145/3485539

45. Pouchet, L.N., Yuki, T.: Polybench/c 4.2.1. https://sourceforge.net/projects/polybench/

46. Reinking, A., Bernstein, G.L., Ragan-Kelley, J.: Formal semantics for the halide language. CoRR abs/2210.15740 (2022). https://doi.org/10.48550/ARXIV.2210.15740

47. Singh, G., Püschel, M., Vechev, M.: Fast polyhedra abstract domain. In: Proceedings of the 44th ACM SIGPLAN Symposium on Principles of Programming Languages. POPL '17, New York, NY, USA, pp. 46–59. Association for Computing Machinery (2017). https://doi.org/10.1145/3009837.3009885

48. Tillet, P., Kung, H.T., Cox, D.: Triton: an intermediate language and compiler for tiled neural network computations. In: Proceedings of the 3rd ACM SIGPLAN International Workshop on Machine Learning and Programming Languages. MAPL 2019, pp. 10–19, New York, NY, USA. Association for Computing Machinery (2019). https://doi.org/10.1145/3315508.3329973

49. Upadrasta, R., Cohen, A.: Sub-polyhedral scheduling using (unit-)two-variable-per-inequality polyhedra. In: Proceedings of the 40th Annual ACM SIGPLAN-SIGACT Symposium on Principles of Programming Languages. POPL '13, New York, NY, pp. 483–496. USA. Association for Computing Machinery (2013). https://doi.org/10.1145/2429069.2429127

50. Verdoolaege, S.: *isl*: an integer set library for the polyhedral model. In: Fukuda, K., Hoeven, J., Joswig, M., Takayama, N. (eds.) ICMS 2010. LNCS, vol. 6327, pp. 299–302. Springer, Heidelberg (2010). https://doi.org/10.1007/978-3-642-15582-6_49

51. Verdoolaege, S., Carlos Juega, J., Cohen, A., Ignacio Gómez, J., Tenllado, C., Catthoor, F.: Polyhedral parallel code generation for CUDA. ACM Trans. Archit. Code Optim. **9**(4) (2013). https://doi.org/10.1145/2400682.2400713

52. Verdoolaege, S., Guelton, S., Grosser, T., Cohen, A.: Schedule trees. In: International Workshop on Polyhedral Compilation Techniques, Date: 2014/01/20-2014/01/20, Location: Vienna, Austria (2014)

53. XLA: Accelerated linear algebra. https://www.tensorflow.org/xla and https://github.com/openxla/xla

54. Zhao, R., Cheng, J.: PHISM: polyhedral high-level synthesis in MLIR. CoRR **abs/2103.15103** (2021). https://arxiv.org/abs/2103.15103

The Top-Down Solver Verified: Building Confidence in Static Analyzers

Yannick Stade[1] , Sarah Tilscher[1,2(✉)] , and Helmut Seidl[1]

[1] TUM School of Computation, Information and Technology,
Technical University of Munich, Munich, Germany
{yannick.stade,sarah.tilscher,helmut.seidl}@tum.de
[2] Department of Computer Science,
Ludwig-Maximilians-Universität Munich, Munich, Germany

Abstract. The top-down solver (TD) is a local fixpoint algorithm for arbitrary equation systems. It considers the right-hand sides as black boxes and detects dependencies between unknowns on the fly—features that significantly increase both its usability and practical efficiency. At the same time, the recursive evaluation strategy of the TD, combined with the non-local destabilization mechanism, obfuscates the correctness of the computed solution. To strengthen the confidence in tools relying on the TD as their fixpoint engine, we provide a first machine-checked proof of the partial correctness of the TD. Our proof builds on the observation that the TD can be obtained from a considerably simpler recursive fixpoint algorithm, the plain TD, by applying an optimization that neither affects the termination behavior nor the computed result. Accordingly, we break down the proof into a partial correctness proof of the plain TD, which is only then extended to include the optimization. The backbone of our proof is a mutual induction following the solver's computation trace. We establish sufficient invariants about the solver state to conclude the correctness of its optimization, i.e., the plain TD terminates if and only if the TD terminates, and they return the identical result. The proof is written using Isabelle/HOL and is available in the archive of formal proofs.

Keywords: fixpoint algorithm · correctness proof · static analysis

1 Introduction

Fixpoint engines are at the heart of static program analyzers based on abstract interpretation [9]. An analysis introduces a set of *unknowns* and a domain of *abstract values*, which encode the properties of interest. Consider, e. g., the analysis of uninitialized variables as used by JAVA [13] or KOTLIN [1]. Here, the

---

Y. Stade and S. Tilscher—Contributed equally to this research and are ordered alphabetically.

A. Gurfinkel and V. Ganesh (Eds.): CAV 2024, LNCS 14681, pp. 303–324, 2024.
https://doi.org/10.1007/978-3-031-65627-9_15

unknowns are program points, while the abstract values are sets of local variables that have been initialized. The abstract value of an unknown may depend on the abstract values of preceding program points. These dependencies are formalized as an equation $x = f_x$. The right-hand side f_x is the intersection of all sets of definitely initialized variables arriving at x via incoming edges. Such an incoming edge may be an assignment like a = 5, which adds the variable a to the set of initialized unknowns. Accordingly, the analysis of the program compiles it into a system of equations, cf. Example 1. A solution to this system approximates the concrete set of initialized variables when reaching a program point.

Solutions of equation systems can be computed using fixpoint iteration. Popular fixpoint algorithms are round-robin [14] and worklist iteration [20]. Both algorithms, though, have limitations. Round-robin iteration requires a fixed finite equation system; also, its running time depends on the evaluation order of unknowns. Worklist iteration is generally more efficient but, at least in the base setting, also suffers from the restriction that the dependencies between unknowns must be known beforehand. The latter short-coming is overcome by Vergauwen et al. [29], de Vilhena et al. [30] where the evaluation of right-hand side functions is enhanced with *self-observation* to dynamically detect the dependencies. More enhanced solvers recursively descend into queried unknowns to obtain their best values before the evaluation of a right-hand side proceeds. One instance of the latter is the recursive local descent solver (RLD) [16]. The unknowns, affected by an updated value, are collected in a *local* worklist for immediate re-evaluation.

This is in contrast to the top-down solver (TD) [21,22,28]. Like RLD, it relies on a recursive descent into queried unknowns combined with dynamic detection of dependencies. However, when an unknown changes its value, the influenced unknowns are *not* immediately scheduled for re-evaluation. Instead, all transitively influenced unknowns are marked as *unstable* so that, when queried again, their re-evaluation is triggered. The destabilization mechanism, combined with the delayed re-evaluation, potentially further increases the efficiency of the iteration but also obfuscates the correctness of the TD. Still, due to its conceptual simplicity, the TD opens possibilities for extensions, e.g., with *widening* and *narrowing* [4,9,10,28] or *side-effects* [26], which otherwise are not so easy to incorporate [3]. This is one of the reasons why tools like the Ciao system [15] or GOBLINT [31] rely on variants of the TD as fixpoint engines. To strengthen the confidence in these tools, we formalize the TD with the interactive theorem prover Isabelle [24,25] and prove it to be partially correct. Here, partial correctness means that assuming the TD terminates, it returns a partial solution of the equation system.

To accomplish the proof, we build on the observation [28] that the original TD, which we will also call TD for short, can be obtained from a significantly simpler fixpoint algorithm that we call the *plain* TD. The plain TD still uses a recursive descent into queried unknowns while using a set *called* to avoid infinite descent due to unknowns with cyclic dependencies. However, it neither keeps track of dependencies between unknowns nor maintains a set of *stable* unknowns whose value has already been computed. Adding these features to obtain the TD thus can be seen as an optimization of the plain TD. Accordingly, the proof is structured into two steps: In the first step, we show the partial correctness of the plain TD. As this algorithm consists of several mutually recursive functions, the proof consists of a mutual induction. To make the proof more comprehensible, we utilize the concept of a *computation trace* to explain its structure and to highlight important invariants. In the second step, the invariants of the plain TD are extended to obtain invariants for the TD. The extensions cover the correctness and modifications of the additional data structures that collect the already computed stable unknowns and the dependencies between unknowns. Additional effort is required to capture the effect of the non-local destabilization mechanism on those two data structures. Altogether, we prove that the TD and the plain TD are equivalent, i.e., the TD terminates if and only if the plain TD terminates and returns the same result whenever they terminate.

For our formalization, we use the function package with domain predicates and mutual recursion to define the solver algorithms in Isabelle. This allows for a clean proof structure. The combination of features is, however, not supported by the code generation framework provided by Isabelle. To obtain executable solver programs from our formalization we, therefore, refine the programs and use equivalent versions of the solver algorithms based on partial functions with options for the code generation. We extract executable code for both solvers and demonstrate their application on a small example. The formalization in Isabelle/HOL is publicly available in the archive of formal proofs [27].

2   Preliminaries

We first introduce some notation used throughout the paper. The powerset of a set M is denoted by $\mathcal{P}(M)$, and the set difference of two sets A and B is written as $A - B$. Given a mapping $f : X \to Y$, the updated mapping $f \oplus \{x \mapsto y\} : X \to Y$ is defined by $(f \oplus \{x \mapsto y\})\, x = y$ and $(f \oplus \{x \mapsto y\})\, x' = f\, x'$ for all $x' \neq x$. For a mapping $f : X \to \mathcal{P}(X)$, the transitive closure is the mapping $f^+ : X \to \mathcal{P}(X)$ where $f^+ x$ is the minimal set such that $f\, x \subseteq f^+ x$ and $f\, y \subseteq f^+ x$ for all $y \in f^+ x$. Moreover, the reflexive and transitive closure is the mapping $f^* : X \to \mathcal{P}(X)$ where $f^* x$ is defined as $f^* x := \{x\} \cup f^+ x$.

For the remainder of this article, we consider some (possibly infinite) set $\mathcal{U}$ of unknowns[1] and a domain[2] $\mathbb{D}$ of abstract values. The set $\mathbb{D}$ contains one special element $\bot$ (bottom), used as the initial value for the fixpoint iteration. Elements from $\mathbb{D}$ need to be comparable for equality, but there is no need to require a partial order or existence of least upper bounds. The equation system associates each unknown x (the left-hand side) with a right-hand side function f_x, specifying other unknowns' contribution to the left-hand side x. Following

---

[1] We use the term *unknown* instead of *variable* because, in the context of program analysis, variables usually denote program variables, not unknowns in the equation system.

[2] In program analysis this is often a complete lattice of abstract values describing concrete program states.

Fecht and Seidl [11], the right-hand side function f_x is considered as a *black box* functional. The only requirement is that the right-hand side is *pure* [17], i.e., parametric in the solver state. That limitation has slightly been relaxed by de Vilhena et al. [30] to *apparent purity*, which allows functions to have internal side effects, e.g., logging important events or spawning a new thread—as long as two identical calls of a function return the same result. Here, we stick to the original notion of purity. For pure functionals in that sense, Hofmann et al. [17] prove that they can be represented as *strategy trees*. A strategy tree is composed of `Answer` nodes, the leaves of the tree, containing an element of $\mathbb{D}$, and `Query` nodes that contain an unknown y to be queried together with a function g. Based on the value d_y of the queried unknown y, the call $g\, d_y$ returns the subtree to continue the evaluation of the right-hand side. In this work, we assume the depth of strategy trees to be finite, i.e., only finitely many unknowns may be queried in a right-hand side. As a shorthand, we write t σ when evaluating the strategy treet t using the mapping σ.

---

type $(\mathcal{U}, \mathbb{D})$ strategy-tree $=$ `Answer` $\mathbb{D}$ | `Query` $\mathcal{U}$ $(\mathbb{D} \rightarrow (\mathcal{U}, \mathbb{D})$ strategy-tree$)$

Note that the strategy trees can describe right-hand sides with varying dependencies, which the TD can cope with. Further, their tree representation lends itself to a structural induction on the right-hand sides. A system of equations $\mathcal{T}$ is then formally the function

$$\mathcal{T} : \mathcal{U} \rightarrow (\mathcal{U}, \mathbb{D}) \text{ strategy-tree} \tag{1}$$

that maps every unknown in $\mathcal{U}$ to a strategy tree.

Example 1. Consider the following code snippet and the corresponding control-flow graph, where a and b are local program variables.

The domain for the variable initialization analysis is $\mathbb{D} = \mathcal{P}(\{a, b\})$, with $\bot$ being the complete set $\{a, b\}$ and $\top$ the empty set. A variable is added to the set of initialized variables whenever it occurs on the left-hand side of an assignment. Accordingly, we retrieve the following equation system and show its strategy tree representation in Fig. 1:

$$\mathcal{T} : \begin{aligned} w &= \emptyset \\ z &= (y \cup \{a\}) \cap (w \cup \{a\}) \\ y &= z \cup \{b\} \\ x &= y \cap z \end{aligned} \tag{2}$$

For the remaining part, we fix some system of equations $\mathcal{T}$ and assume that it is globally available. A *total solution* of such a system of equations is a mapping

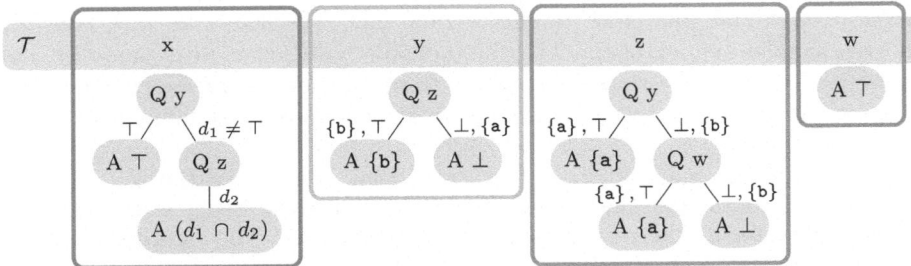

Fig. 1. The figure shows the value table of $\mathcal{T}$ from Example 1. Each unknown maps to a strategy tree with query nodes (Q) and answer nodes (A). The trees are defined over the domain $\mathcal{P}\left(\{a,b\}\right)$ where $\bot$ represents the full set $\{a,b\}$ and $\top$ the empty set.

$\sigma : \mathcal{U} \to \mathbb{D}$ from unknowns to values such that for all unknowns $x \in \mathcal{U}$

$$\mathcal{T} \, x \, \sigma = \sigma \, x \, . \tag{3}$$

However, we are often not interested in a solution for the entire (potentially infinite) equation system, but rather in a *partial solution*. For an unknown $x \in \mathcal{U}$ and a mapping $\sigma : \mathcal{U} \to \mathbb{D}$, let the function $\mathsf{dep}\, x \, \sigma$ return the set of all unknowns occurring in $\mathcal{T} \, x$ when traversed with σ, the so-called (direct) dependencies of x. Then, the mapping $\sigma : \mathcal{U} \to \mathbb{D}$ is a partial solution for a set $s \subseteq \mathcal{U}$ if[3]

$$\forall x \in s. \; \mathsf{dep}^* \, x \, \sigma \subseteq s \wedge \mathcal{T} \, x \, \sigma = \sigma \, x. \tag{4}$$

If x is in $\mathsf{dep}^+ x \, \sigma$ for some σ, i.e., the unknown x depends transitively on itself, we call the associated system of equations $\mathcal{T}$ *recursive* (with respect to σ). In the proof, we argue about the subset of dep^* composed of all unknowns visited when solving some unknown x. Such unknowns are reachable from x via the depends-relation without passing through (but including) unknowns of a set X, where the recursive descent stops. Hence, we define the set R_X inductively for a given mapping $\sigma : \mathcal{U} \to \mathbb{D}$ and an unknown x to contain all unknowns in $\mathsf{dep}\, \sigma \, x$ if $x \notin X$, and all unknowns in $\mathsf{dep}\, \sigma \, y$ if $y \in R_X - X$. We denote R_X by

$$\mathsf{dep}\big|_{\mathcal{U}-X}^{*} \, \sigma \, x \, .$$

Note that $\mathsf{dep}^* \, \sigma \, x = \mathsf{dep}\big|_{\mathcal{U}-\emptyset}^{*} \, \sigma \, x$ holds. We extend the definitions of dep and $\mathsf{dep}\big|_{\mathcal{U}-X}^{*}$ to strategy trees and use the same symbol for simplicity. This allows to compute both sets also for partial right-hand sides.

3   The Plain Top-Down Solver

The TD can be obtained from a considerably simpler fixpoint algorithm [28], which we call the plain TD. First, we prove the plain TD to be partially correct;

---

[3] Recall, dep^* denotes the reflexive and transitive closure of dep.

second, we extend this proof to the original TD. Tilscher et al. [28], consider an even simpler version of the TD, the monadic base solver. It is, however, not as powerful as the TD since it does not track the set of *called* unknowns and thus cannot solve recursive equation systems. Therefore we excluded it from our layered approach.

The plain TD maintains a solver state that consists of the set of called unknowns c containing the unknowns that are already being evaluated, and a mapping σ storing the current value of every unknown. The algorithm consists of three mutually recursive functions: $\text{iterate}_{\text{plain}}$, $\text{eval}_{\text{plain}}$, and $\text{query}_{\text{plain}}$. The function $\text{iterate}_{\text{plain}}$ iterates one unknown x until a fixpoint is reached for it, i. e., the newly computed value and the value from the previous iteration coincide. When the iteration continues because the value has changed, the mapping σ of unknowns to values is updated.

```
iterate_plain x c σ =
  let (d, σ) = eval_plain x (T x) c σ in
  if d = σ x then (d, σ)
  else iterate_plain x c (σ ⊕ {x ↦ d})
```

For the evaluation of x's right-hand side, the function $\text{eval}_{\text{plain}}$ is invoked. The function $\text{eval}_{\text{plain}}$ receives a right-hand side in the form of a strategy tree and traverses it top-down until reaching an answer node, whose value it returns.

```
eval_plain x t c σ = case t of
    Answer d ⇒ (d, σ)
  | Query y g ⇒ let (d, σ) = query_plain x y c σ in eval_plain x (g d) c σ
```

The function $\text{query}_{\text{plain}}$ is called to determine the current value for y and thereby the subtree g d in which to descend next, when $\text{eval}_{\text{plain}}$ is called for some query node Query y g. A call to $\text{query}_{\text{plain}}$ checks whether a call to $\text{query}_{\text{plain}}$ for the same unknown y already occurred in the current call stack. If this is the case, i. e., the unknown is contained in the set c of called unknowns, the current value of y is looked up in the mapping σ. Otherwise, $\text{query}_{\text{plain}}$ invokes the function $\text{iterate}_{\text{plain}}$ with y added to c to start the fixpoint iteration for y.

```
query_plain x y c σ =
  if y ∈ c then (σ y, σ)
  else iterate_plain y (c ∪ {y}) σ
```

Finally, we have a function $\text{solve}_{\text{plain}}$ that wraps the initial call to $\text{iterate}_{\text{plain}}$ and provides it with the initial arguments, the singleton set $\{x\}$ as called unknowns, and the empty mapping σ_0 that implicitly maps every unknown to $\bot$.

```
solve_plain x = let (_, σ) = iterate_plain x {x} σ_0 in σ
```

A *computation trace* captures the execution of a solver's run. It is a tree that contains a node for each function call, along with essential parameters and result values. The $\text{solve}_{\text{plain}}$ node constitutes its root node. Nested calls to other

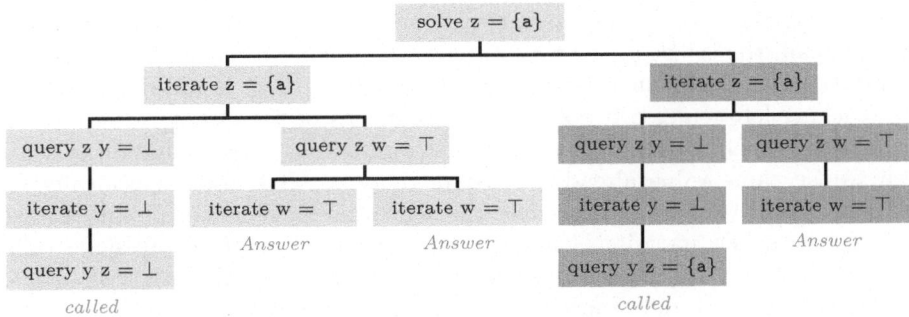

Fig. 2. The figure shows the computation trace of the plain TD for solving the unknown z from the equation system from Example 1. In dark, we highlight the function calls corresponding to unknowns in $\mathsf{dep}^* x\sigma$ where σ is the final result. (Color figure online)

functions are added as children, while recursive calls (to the same function) are appended to the right as siblings.[4] In Figs. 2 and 4, we omit $\mathsf{eval}_{\text{plain}}$ nodes for clarity since they essentially only add an intermediate node between $\mathsf{iterate}_{\text{plain}}$ and $\mathsf{query}_{\text{plain}}$ nodes. The backbone of the partial correctness proof is an induction over this computation trace, which can be conveniently implemented with the induction rules generated by Isabelle for the mutually recursive functions. The concept of a computation trace is illustrated in the following example.

Example 2. Consider the equation system from Example 1. We observe the execution of the TD when solving the unknown z and illustrate the occurring mutually recursive function calls as computation trace in Fig. 2.

The initial call $\mathsf{solve}_{\text{plain}}$ z invokes the function $\mathsf{iterate}_{\text{plain}}$ to iterate on the queried unknown z. In z's first iteration, the call to $\mathsf{eval}_{\text{plain}}$ queries the unknowns y and w to fully traverse the right-hand side of z. The querying of y entails a call to $\mathsf{iterate}_{\text{plain}}$ for its iteration which takes only one turn to stabilize. The evaluation of y's right-hand side only depends on the unknown z, for which the call to $\mathsf{query}_{\text{plain}}$ immediately returns since z is already being evaluated. The iteration of w entails no further queries because the strategy tree representing its right-hand side is an answer node.

The computation trace reveals the information available during the solver's computations. When the algorithm reaches a node v in the computation trace, (computations of) all nodes on the path to the root are in progress, and nodes in subtrees on the left of this path are already completed; we call this history the reaching left-context of v. The solver's state, i.e., the internal data structures maintained by the solver, can be seen as an abstraction of the (concrete) left-context. Since the algorithm always refers to the latest abstraction of the solver state, it could also be implemented as a reference to a mutable data structure.

---

[4] For the TD, the order of function calls during execution corresponds to the preorder traversal of the computation trace, because all recursive calls are tail calls.

For a subtree t of the computation trace and σ' returned by the corresponding function call, the set $\mathsf{dep}|_{\mathcal{U}-c}^{*}\,t\,\sigma'$ matches the unknowns occurring in the last iterations of t. Based on this, we introduce a set s that is an abstraction of the reaching left-context: it collects the unknowns of the last iterations in the reaching left-context, and unknowns under evaluation. A re-evaluation of $x \in s$ returns the same value already stored in σ for x. This holds specifically for unknowns in c, a subset of s, because the algorithm looks up their value instead of initiating a new iteration. Unknowns in $s - c$ re-evaluate to the same value because they only depend on unknowns in s; hence, we call them *truly stable*. Accordingly, the two milestones for proving the correctness of the plain TD are:

(i) defining the set $\mathsf{dep}|_{\mathcal{U}-c}^{*}$ to describe the set of unknowns queried in the last iterations for a subtree of the computation trace, and

(ii) introducing the set s to collect unknowns that, when re-evaluated, evaluate to the same value.

Milestone *(ii)* is essential to ensure that the plain TD computes the same value for recurring occurrences of an unknown in a right-hand side.

For unknowns in s we show that σ is a partial solution after updating the value for the current unknown in $\mathtt{iterate_{plain}}$.

Lemma 1. *Assume σ is a partial solution for all $x \in s - c$, the set s is closed under* dep *except for elements that are in c, i.e., $\forall y \in s - c,\ \mathsf{dep}\,\sigma\,y \subseteq s$, and σ and σ' are identical on s, i.e., $\forall x \in s.\,\sigma\,x = \sigma'\,x$. Then, σ' is also a partial solution for all $x \in s - c$.*

Recall that σ is a partial solution of all unknowns in the set s. Within the $\mathtt{iterate_{plain}}$ function, when the newly computed value for an unknown x and its old value stored in σ differ, we can conclude that x was not a member of s because the old σ would not have been a partial solution.

Lemma 2. *Assume $\mathcal{T}\,x\,\sigma \neq \sigma\,x$ and σ is a partial solution of all unknowns in a set s. Then, x is not a member of s.*

The following definition summarizes the properties used as invariant for the partial correctness proof in one predicate.

Definition 1 (Plain TD Invariant). *For $c, s \subseteq \mathcal{U}$ and the mapping $\sigma : \mathcal{U} \to \mathbb{D}$ the predicate* $\mathsf{valid_{plain}}\,c\,s\,\sigma$ *is satisfied if*

(i) $\forall x \in s - c.\,\mathsf{dep}\,\sigma\,x \subseteq s$, *i.e., the set s is closed under* dep *except for unknowns that are also in c, and*

(ii) $\forall x \in s - c.\,\mathcal{T}\,x\,\sigma = \sigma\,x$, *i.e., σ fulfills the equations for truly stable unknowns.*

For $c = \emptyset$, which holds after a call to $\mathtt{solve_{plain}}$ terminated, the predicate implies that σ is a partial solution for s. Using the predicate, we formulate the partial correctness theorem.

Theorem 1 (Partial Correctness of the plain TD). *The theorem shows three mutual statements:*

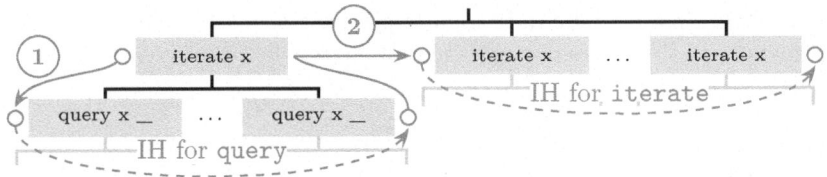

Fig. 3. The figure illustrates exemplary for the *Continue* subcase in the *Iterate* case an induction step. First, the induction hypothesis (IH) for the nested query$_{\text{plain}}$ is instantiated, such that its premises are fulfilled. Its application then provides facts to reason that the premises of the IH for the recursive iterate$_{\text{plain}}$ call are satisfied.

- *Assume* query$_{\text{plain}}$ x y $c\,\sigma = (d_y, \sigma')$ *is defined and* valid$_{\text{plain}}$ $c\,s\,\sigma$ *holds. Then, we show (i)* valid$_{\text{plain}}$ $c\,s'\,\sigma'$, *and (ii)* $\forall u \in s.\ \sigma\,u = \sigma'\,u$ *where* $s' := s \cup \mathsf{dep}\big|_{\mathcal{U}-c}^{\;*}\,\sigma'\,y$.
- *Let* $c' = c - \{x\}$. *Assume* iterate$_{\text{plain}}$ x $c\,\sigma = (d_x, \sigma')$ *is defined,* $x \in c$, *and* valid$_{\text{plain}}$ $c'\,s\,\sigma$ *holds. Then, we show (i)* valid$_{\text{plain}}$ $c'\,s'\,\sigma'$, *and (ii)* $\forall u \in s.\,\sigma\,u = \sigma'\,u$ *where* $s' := s \cup \mathsf{dep}\big|_{\mathcal{U}-c'}^{\;*}\,\sigma'\,x$.
- *Assume* eval$_{\text{plain}}$ x t $c\,\sigma = (d_x, \sigma')$ *is defined, and* valid$_{\text{plain}}$ $c\,s\,\sigma$ *holds. Then, we show (i)* valid$_{\text{plain}}$ $c\,s'\,\sigma'$, *(ii)* $\forall u \in s.\,\sigma\,u = \sigma'\,u$, *and (iii)* $t\,\sigma' = d_x$ *where* $s' := s \cup \mathsf{dep}\big|_{\mathcal{U}-c}^{\;*}\,\sigma'\,t$.

Proof. This proof is more of a sketch to convey the proof idea; for a rigorous proof, see the Isabelle formalization [27]. We prove the statement by mutual induction. The induction rule derived from the three mutually recursive functions leads to three cases. Figure 3 illustrates an induction step in the computation trace exemplary for the iterate case.

Case 1 (Query). The first case reasons about a call to the query$_{\text{plain}}$ function. Let $x, y \in \mathcal{U}, c \subseteq \mathcal{U}, \sigma, \sigma' : \mathcal{U} \to \mathbb{D}$, and $d_y \in \mathbb{D}$ such that query$_{\text{plain}}$ x y $c\,\sigma = (d_y, \sigma')$ is defined. We distinguish two subcases: the queried unknown can either be called or not, the former leading to a lookup and the latter to an iteration.

Subcase 1.1 (Lookup). This case is a base case since there are no further mutual recursive calls. In the computation trace, it corresponds to a query node as leaf. The proof goal follows directly from the premises since σ is not changed.

Subcase 1.2 (Iterate). In this case, the function iterate$_{\text{plain}}$ is called, and its result directly returned by the enclosing query$_{\text{plain}}$ function. Thus, iterate$_{\text{plain}}$ y $(c \cup \{y\})\,\sigma = (d_y, \sigma')$ and the induction hypothesis for the iterate$_{\text{plain}}$ call can be applied. The proof goal follows immediately because the result of the call to iterate$_{\text{plain}}$ is returned without modifications.

Case 2 (Iterate). Let $c \subseteq \mathcal{U}, x \in c, \sigma, \sigma' : \mathcal{U} \to \mathbb{D}$, and $d_x \in \mathbb{D}$ such that iterate$_{\text{plain}}$ x $c\,\sigma = (d_x, \sigma')$ is defined. We distinguish two subcases: either a fixpoint is reached or not. In either case, the function eval$_{\text{plain}}$ is invoked first, and the subcase depends on its result. Both subcases constitute two different induction steps, and both cases use the induction hypothesis for eval$_{\text{plain}}$.

Subcase 2.1 (Fixpoint). The induction hypothesis of $\texttt{eval}_{\texttt{plain}}$ provides all necessary facts, and since σ is not updated anymore, the proof goal follows.

Subcase 2.2 (Continue). Obtain $d'_{\text{x}} \in \mathbb{D}$ and $\sigma_1 : \mathcal{U} \to \mathbb{D}$ such that the call $\texttt{eval}_{\texttt{plain}}\, \text{x}\, (\mathcal{T}\, \text{x})\, c\sigma = (d'_{\text{x}}, \sigma_1)$ is defined. The induction hypothesis for $\texttt{eval}_{\texttt{plain}}$ states *(i)* $\texttt{valid}_{\texttt{plain}}\, s'\, c\, \sigma_1$, *(ii)* $\forall \text{y} \in s \cup \{\text{x}\}.\, \sigma\, \text{y} = \sigma_1\, \text{y}$, and *(iii)* $\mathcal{T}\, \text{x}\, \sigma_1 = d'_{\text{x}}$ where $s' := s \cup \{\text{x}\} \cup \texttt{dep}|_{\mathcal{U}-c}^{*}\, \sigma_1\, c\, \text{x}$. Since we are in the *Continue* case, we know that $\sigma_1\, \text{x} \neq d'_{\text{x}}$. From Lemma 2 it follows $\text{x} \notin s$. This allows us to show together with Lemma 1 that also $\texttt{valid}_{\texttt{plain}}\, s\, (c - \{\text{x}\})\, (\sigma_1 \oplus \{\text{x} \mapsto d'_{\text{x}}\})$ holds. This is required to instantiate the induction hypothesis for the successive call to $\texttt{iterate}_{\texttt{plain}}$, which concludes the case.

Case 3 (Eval). The strategy tree passed to $\texttt{eval}_{\texttt{plain}}$ can either be a single answer node or a non-trivial strategy tree with a query node as a root.

Subcase 3.1 (Answer). This case is the second induction base of the entire induction and follows trivially.

Subcase 3.2 (Query). The proof follows from the facts retrieved from the induction hypotheses for both recursive calls to $\texttt{query}_{\texttt{plain}}$ and $\texttt{eval}_{\texttt{plain}}$ using the fact that σ remains unchanged for unknowns in s. $\qquad\Box$

The corollary below summarizes the results from this section. It follows directly from Theorem 1.

Corollary 1 (Partial Correctness of the plain TD). *Assume the equality* $\texttt{solve}_{\texttt{plain}}\, \text{x} = \sigma$ *is defined. Then,* σ *is a partial solution for* $\texttt{dep}^{*}\, \text{x}\, \sigma$.

4   The Top-Down Solver

So far, we have proven partial correctness only for the plain TD. In the following, we extend the correctness statement to the original TD by showing that both fixpoint algorithms are equivalent. The TD improves the plain TD through more extensive self-observation. While the plain TD solely maintains a set of called unknowns to prevent non-termination in the case of recursive equation systems, the TD introduces two additional data structures for self-observation:

- A set $\texttt{stable}$ collecting all unknowns that do not need to be re-evaluated, because they only depend on other stable unknowns whose value has not changed since their last evaluation.
- An $\texttt{infl}$ map that dynamically records for each unknown x a set of unknowns influenced by x. It, therefore, records the inverse of the $\texttt{dep}$ relationship.

The set $\texttt{stable}$ is similar to set s used in the proof of the plain TD; and indeed, s is in every step a subset of $\texttt{stable}$. However, $\texttt{stable}$ additionally collects unknowns that have been fully evaluated in earlier iterations but are not affected by any unknowns whose value changed in the meantime. Its additional maintenance allows skipping unnecessary re-evaluations of already stable unknowns.

Three modifications are necessary to integrate the new data structures and to keep them consistent. In the following code snippets, we highlight those changes. The function eval is only adapted marginally to facilitate the passing of the additional parameters (not highlighted).

```
eval x t c infl stable σ = case t of
    Answer d ⇒ (d, infl, stable, σ)
  | Query y g ⇒ let (d, infl, stable, σ) = query x y c infl stable σ in
                eval x (g d) c infl stable σ
```

At the end of a call to query, the dependency is recorded in the map infl, i. e., the parent unknown is inserted into the set of unknowns influenced by the queried unknown.

```
query y x c infl stable σ =
  let (d, infl, stable, σ) =
      if x ∈ c then (σ x, infl, stable, σ)
      else iterate x (c ∪ {x}) infl stable σ
  in (d, infl ⊕ {x ↦ infl x ∪ {y}}, stable, σ)
```

The improvement to skip re-evaluations of unknowns in stable is implemented in the function iterate. If iterate is invoked for an unknown that is already in stable, its right-hand side is not evaluated; instead, its value is simply looked up in σ. In case the current unknown is not yet stable, it is optimistically added to the set stable when starting the evaluation of its right-hand side.

```
iterate x c infl stable σ =
  if x ∉ stable then
    let (d, infl, stable, σ) = eval x (T x) c infl (stable ∪ {x}) σ in
    if d = σ x then (d, infl, stable, σ)
    else
      let (infl, stable) = destab x infl stable in
      iterate x c infl stable (σ ⊕ {x ↦ d})
  else (σ x, infl, stable, σ)
```

After the evaluation of the right-hand side of x, iterate x updates the value of x in σ. If the value has changed, the values of unknowns that are (indirectly) influenced by x need to be recomputed. Instead of recomputing them immediately, all affected unknowns are removed from stable. This will trigger their re-evaluation in case they are queried again. To remove all indirectly influenced unknowns the additional function destab is provided. A call destab x first removes all unknowns directly influenced by x from stable and resets the set of influenced unknowns of x in infl to the empty set, and then continues recursively to destabilize indirectly influenced unknowns of x. Note that destab x only removes x itself from the set stable if x (transitively) depends on itself. If x does not depend on itself, x remains in stable, and the fixpoint iteration terminates after one iteration.[5]

---

[5] Recall that x is inserted optimistically into stable before its iteration.

```
destab x infl stable =
  let f y (infl, stable) = destab y infl (stable − {y}) in
  fold f (infl ⊕ {x ↦ ∅}, stable) (infl x)
```

With those changes, the `solve` function of the TD is defined as follows, where $infl_0$ represents the empty mapping, i. e., where every unknown in $\mathcal{U}$ maps to the empty set.

```
solve x = let (_, _, stabl, σ) = iterate x {x} infl₀ ∅ σ₀ in (stabl, σ)
```

Calling `solve` for the unknown x and the equation system from Example 1 results in the computation trace shown in Fig. 4. The figure illustrates the effect of skipping superfluous computations. Nodes that belong to additional computations the plain TD would perform but which are skipped by the TD are indicated with small grey nodes. In this example, the TD saves more than half of the computations.

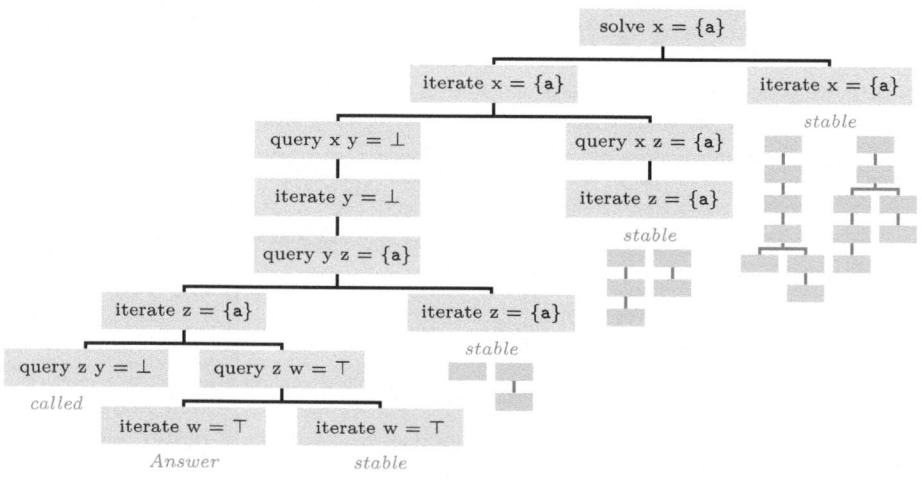

Fig. 4. The figure shows the computation trace corresponding to the TD when solving the equation system from Example 1 for unknown x. Some computation paths terminate because the queried unknown is called, others because the iterated unknown is already stable. The grey nodes below stable leaves indicate the additional computation steps that the plain TD would execute.

A crucial part of showing the correctness of the optimizations in the TD, is verifying that the destabilization preserves the essential properties of the solver's state. This includes proving that destabilization is thorough enough to remove all unknowns possibly affected by a changed value from `stable`, such that no evaluation builds on possibly outdated values of stable unknowns. On the other hand, it also requires showing that destabilization is specific enough to not remove from `stable` any unknown that was already stable before the iteration started. This ensures that the set of called unknowns remains a subset of `stable` and thus invariants for `stable` unknowns also hold for called unknowns where values are simply looked up without further descending. To guarantee these bounds of destabilization, we have found two invariants to be essential milestones:

(i) An invariant that the data structure `infl` is complete, i.e., records all relevant dependencies, and
(ii) An invariant stating that, when evaluating an unknown x, only influences to previously unstable unknowns or x itself, are recorded.

Similarly to Definition 1 for the plain TD, we define a predicate to describe valid input solver states.

Definition 2 (TD Invariant). *For* c, stable $\subseteq \mathcal{U}, \sigma : \mathcal{U} \to \mathbb{D}$ *and* infl $: \mathcal{U} \to \mathcal{P}(\mathcal{U})$ *the predicate* valid $c\,\sigma$ infl stable *is satisfied if:*

(i) $c \subseteq$ stable
(ii) $\forall x \in$ stable $- c.\, \mathcal{T}\,x\,\sigma = \sigma x$, *i.e., the mapping* σ *fulfills the equations for all truly stable unknowns,*
(iii) $\{x \in \mathcal{U} \mid$ infl $x \neq \emptyset\} \subseteq$ stable, *i.e., keys mapping to non-trivial values in* infl *are members of* stable, *and*
(iv) $\forall y \in$ stable $- c.\, \forall x \in$ dep σ y. y $\in$ infl x, *i.e.,* infl *stores the mapping "x influences y" for all unknowns x on which any truly stable unknown y depends on.*

Item *(i)* allows to conclude that x is not only in c but also in `stable` when the unknown x is looked up in the `query` function. We remark that for the plain TD this can be implicitly concluded, for s respectively, from the fact that $\text{dep}|_{\mathcal{U}-c}^{*} \sigma x \subseteq s$ for the currently evaluated unknown x. Item *(iv)* corresponds to milestone *(i)* and relates the map of influences to the dependencies of the equation system. It helps to show that `stable` remains closed under `dep` also after the application of `destab`. With Item *(ii)* and *(iii)* the predicate valid extends valid$_{\text{plain}}$ from Definition 1.

Lemma 3. *Let* infl $: \mathcal{U} \to \mathcal{P}(\mathcal{U})$, *and* c, stable $\subseteq \mathcal{U}$. *Assume*

- $\{u \in \mathcal{U} \mid$ infl $u \neq \emptyset\} \subseteq$ stable *and*
- $\forall u \in$ stable $- c.\, \forall v \in$ dep σ u. u $\in$ infl v.

Then $\forall u \in$ stable $- c.$ dep σ u. $\subseteq$ stable. *This immediately implies*

$$\text{valid } c\,\sigma \text{ infl stable} \implies \text{valid}_{\text{plain}}\, c \text{ stable } \sigma \,.$$

Besides the predicate for valid solver states, we define a predicate relating the output solver state to the corresponding input state.

Definition 3. (Update relation). *For* x $\in \mathcal{U}$, stable, stable$'$ $\subseteq \mathcal{U}$, *and* infl, infl$'$ $: \mathcal{U} \to \mathcal{P}(\mathcal{U})$ *the predicate* update x infl stable infl$'$ stable$'$ *is satisfied if* *(i)* $\text{stable} \subseteq \text{stable}'$, *i. e., the stable set is increasing,*

(ii) $\forall u.\ (\text{infl}'\,u - \text{infl}\,u) \cap (\text{stable} - \{x\}) = \emptyset$, *i. e., only unknowns that were not previously stable (or x) are inserted into* infl, *and*

(iii) $\forall u \in \text{stable}.\ \text{infl}\,u \subseteq \text{infl}'\,u$, *i. e., the set of influenced unknowns increases for all stable unknowns.*

Item *(i)* is used to show that Definition 2 *(i)* still holds after destabilization (cf. Lemma 4). It also aids in deriving the appropriate variants of Item *(ii)* and Item *(iii)* in the induction steps. Definition 3 *(ii)* formalizes the earlier described milestone *(ii)* and allows to show that Item *(i)* still holds after destabilization. Item *(iii)* expresses that a dependency, recorded due to an unknown occurring in some right-hand side, persists till the end of this right-hand side's evaluation. This is required to establish Definition 2 *(iv)*.

Both defined predicates enable the formalization of the preservation of invariants by the destabilization mechanism.

Lemma 4. *For* $x \in \mathcal{U}$, $\text{infl} : \mathcal{U} \to \mathcal{P}(\mathcal{U})$, *and* $\text{stable} \subseteq \mathcal{U}$, *let* $\text{infl}' : \mathcal{U} \to \mathcal{P}(\mathcal{U})$, *and* $\text{stable}' \subseteq \mathcal{U}$ *such that* $\text{destab}\ x\,\text{infl}\,\text{stable} = (\text{infl}', \text{stable}')$ *holds. Let* $c' := c - \{x\}$ *and* $\sigma' := \sigma \oplus \{x \mapsto d_x\}$.

(i) *Assume* $c \subseteq \text{stable}$ *and* $\text{stable} \subseteq \text{stable}'$. *Then* $c \subseteq \text{stable}'$ *holds.*

(ii) *Assume*
  - $\forall x \in \text{stable} - c.\ \mathcal{T}\,x\,\sigma = \sigma\,x$,
  - $\mathcal{T}\,x\,\sigma = d_x$, *and*
  - $\forall u \in \text{stable} - c'.\forall v \in \text{dep}\,\sigma\,u.\ u \in \text{infl}\,v$.

  Then $\forall x \in \text{stable}' - c'.\ \mathcal{T}\,x\,\sigma' = \sigma'\,x$ *holds.*

(iii) *Assume* $\{u \in \mathcal{U} \mid \text{infl}\,u \neq \emptyset\} \subseteq \text{stable}$.

  Then $\{u \in \mathcal{U} \mid \text{infl}'\,u \neq \emptyset\} \subseteq \text{stable}'$ *holds.*

(iv) *Assume* $\forall u \in \text{stable} - c'.\ \forall v \in \text{dep}\,\sigma\,u.\ u \in \text{infl}\,v$.

  Then $\forall u \in \text{stable}' - c'.\ \forall v \in \text{dep}\,\sigma'\,u.\ u \in \text{infl}'\,v$.

The TD skips re-evaluation of stable unknowns because it would yield the same value. The following lemma supports this and shows that the plain TD will return the same value as already computed if an unknown is stable.

Lemma 5. *This lemma shows:*

- *Assume* $\text{query}_{\text{plain}}\,x\,y\,c\,\sigma = (d_y, \sigma')$ *is defined,* $\text{valid}_{\text{plain}}\,c\,s\,\sigma$ *is satisfied, and* $y \in s$. *Then* σ *and* σ' *are equal.*
- *Assume* $\text{iterate}_{\text{plain}}\,x\,c\,\sigma = (d_x, \sigma')$ *is defined,* $x \in c$, $\text{valid}_{\text{plain}}\,(c - \{x\})\,s\,\sigma$ *is satisfied, and* $x \in s$. *Then* σ *and* σ' *are equal.*
- *Assume* $\text{eval}_{\text{plain}}\,x\,t\,c\,\sigma = (d_x, \sigma')$ *is defined,* $\text{valid}_{\text{plain}}\,c\,s\,\sigma$ *is satisfied, and* $\text{dep}\,t\,\sigma \subseteq s$. *Then* $t\,\sigma' = d_x$ *and* $\sigma = \sigma'$.

Following the auto-generated induction rules for the plain TD and the TD, we split the equivalence proof of both fixpoint algorithms into two directions. The first assumes the termination of the plain TD and shows that the TD terminates, yielding the same value, cf. Theorem 2. The second proves that the plain TD returns the same value as the TD under the assumption that the TD terminates, cf. Theorem 3. Both results are combined afterward in Corollary 2, and Corollary 3 concludes the correctness of the TD.

Theorem 2 (Equivalence I). *The theorem shows:*

- *Assume* query$_\mathrm{plain}$ x y $c\,\sigma = (d_y, \sigma')$ *is defined, and* valid $c\,\sigma$ infl stable *holds. Then there exist* infl$'$: $\mathcal{U} \to \mathcal{P}(\mathcal{U})$ *and a set* stable$' \subseteq \mathcal{U}$ *such that*
  (i) query x y c infl stable $\sigma = (d_y, \mathrm{infl}', \mathrm{stable}', \sigma')$ *is defined and*
  (ii) valid $c\,\sigma'$ infl$'$ stable$'$ *holds.*
  Furthermore, (iii) the statements update x infl stable infl$'$ stable$'$, *and*
  (iv) x $\in$ infl$'$ y *hold.*
- *Assume* iterate$_\mathrm{plain}$ x $c\,\sigma = (d_x, \sigma')$ *is defined,* valid $c'\,\sigma$ infl stable *holds for* $c' := c - \{x\}$, *and* x $\in c$. *Then there exist* infl$'$: $\mathcal{U} \to \mathcal{P}(\mathcal{U})$ *and* stable$' \subseteq \mathcal{U}$ *such that*
  (i) iterate x c infl stable $\sigma = (d_x, \mathrm{infl}', \mathrm{stable}', \sigma')$ *is defined and*
  (ii) valid $c'\,\sigma'$ infl$'$ stable$'$ *holds.*
  Furthermore, (iii) the statements update x infl stable infl$'$ stable$'$, *and*
  (iv) x $\in$ stable$'$ *hold.*
- *Assume* eval$_\mathrm{plain}$ x t $c\,\sigma = (d_x, \sigma')$ *is defined,* valid $c\,\sigma$ infl stable *holds, and* x $\in$ stable. *Then there exist* infl$'$: $\mathcal{U} \to \mathcal{P}(\mathcal{U})$ *and* stable$' \subseteq \mathcal{U}$ *such that*
  (i) eval x t c infl stable $\sigma = (d_x, \mathrm{infl}', \mathrm{stable}', \sigma')$ *is defined,*
  (ii) valid $c\,\sigma'$ infl$'$ stable$'$ *holds.*
  Furthermore, (iii) the statements update x infl stable infl$'$ stable$'$, *(iv)*
  t $\sigma' = d_x$, *and (v)* $\forall u \in$ dep σ' t. x $\in$ infl$'$u *hold.*

Proof. The complete proof is extensive, thus we only highlight pivotal steps and direct the reader to the formalization in Isabelle [27] for a detailed proof. The proof uses the same induction rules and covers the same cases as in Theorem 1.

Case 1 (Query). Let $x, y \in \mathcal{U}, c \subseteq \mathcal{U}, \sigma, \sigma' : \mathcal{U} \to \mathbb{D}, d_y \in \mathbb{D}$ such that the call query$_\mathrm{plain}$ x y $c\,\sigma = (d_y, \sigma')$ is defined. And let infl : $\mathcal{U} \to \mathcal{P}(\mathcal{U})$, stable $\subseteq \mathcal{U}$ such that valid $c\,\sigma$ infl stable holds.

Subcase 1.1 (Lookup). This case follows directly from the premises.

Subcase 1.2 (Iterate). Using the induction hypothesis, we obtain infl$_1$ and stable$_1$ such that iterate y c infl stable $\sigma = (d_y, \mathrm{infl}_1, \mathrm{stable}_1, \sigma')$ is defined. The induction hypothesis for the iterate call provides the fact $(\mathrm{infl}_1 \, u - \mathrm{infl}\, u) \cap (\mathrm{stable} - \{x\}) = \emptyset$. Using the definition of iterate, we can conclude that the subtraction of $\{x\}$ can be omitted, which aids in proving the subgoal.

Case 2 (Iterate). First, assume that x $\in$ stable. Lemma 5 implies that the plain TD returns σ unchanged, and the same holds for the TD since it skips computation altogether. Thus, the proof goals are trivially satisfied. Now, assume that x $\notin$ stable. Let $x \in \mathcal{U}, c \subseteq c, \sigma, \sigma' : \mathcal{U} \to \mathbb{D}, d_x \in \mathbb{D}$ such that iterate$_\mathrm{plain}$ x $c\,\sigma = (d_x, \sigma')$ is defined, and let infl : $\mathcal{U} \to \mathcal{P}(\mathcal{U})$, stable $\subseteq \mathcal{U}$ such that valid $c\,\sigma$ infl stable holds.

Subcase 2.1 (Fixpoint). The premises directly imply the subgoal.

Subcase 2.2 (Continue). Let $d'_x \in \mathbb{D}, \sigma_1 : \mathcal{U} \rightarrow \mathbb{D}$ such that $\text{eval}_{\text{plain}} \, x \, (\mathcal{T} \, x) \, c \, \sigma = (d'_x, \sigma_1)$ is defined. According to the induction hypothesis for eval, there exists $\text{infl}_1 : \mathcal{U} \rightarrow \mathcal{P}(\mathcal{U})$, $\text{stable}_1 \subseteq \mathcal{U}$ such that

$$\text{eval} \, x \, (\mathcal{T} \, x) \, c \, \text{infl} \, (\{x\} \cup \text{stable}) \, \sigma = (d'_x, \text{infl}_1, \text{stable}_1, \sigma_1)$$

is defined. Let furthermore $\text{infl}_2 : \mathcal{U} \rightarrow \mathcal{P}(\mathcal{U})$, $\text{stable}_2 \subseteq \mathcal{U}$ such that

$$\text{destab} \, x \, \text{infl}_1 \, \text{stable}_1 = (\text{infl}_2, \text{stable}_2) \ .$$

Lemma 4 states that the predicate valid is preserved for infl_2 and stable_2. This is key to applying the induction hypothesis for the tail call to $\text{iterate}_{\text{plain}}$. After that, one must show that

(i) $\forall u \in \text{stable}. \, \text{infl} \, u \subseteq \text{infl}' \, u$ and
(ii) $\forall u. \, (\text{infl}' \, u - \text{infl} \, u) \cap (\text{stable} - \{x\}) = \emptyset.$

For the first, we exploit the fact that we have previously shown that $\text{stable} \subseteq \text{stable}_2$ and that destab only removes key-value mappings with keys that are not in stable. For the second, we show similar to the Iterate subcase in the Query case above, that $(\text{infl}' \, u - \text{infl}_2 \, u) \cap (\text{stable} - \{x\}) = \emptyset$ and $(\text{infl}_1 \, u - \text{infl} \, u) \cap (\text{stable} - \{x\}) = \emptyset$. Together with the fact that $\text{infl}_2 \, u \subseteq \text{infl}_1 \, u$ for all u, the statement follows.

Case 3 (Eval). Let $x \in \mathcal{U}, c \subseteq \mathcal{U}, \sigma, \sigma' : \mathcal{U} \rightarrow \mathbb{D}, d_y \in \mathbb{D}$ and t a strategy tree such that $\text{eval}_{\text{plain}} \, x \, t \, c \, \sigma = (d_x, \sigma')$ is defined. Furthermore, let $\text{infl} : \mathcal{U} \rightarrow \mathcal{P}(\mathcal{U})$, $\text{stable} \subseteq \mathcal{U}$ such that $\text{valid} \, c \, \sigma \, \text{infl} \, \text{stable}$ holds.

Subcase 3.1 (Answer). This case follows directly from the premises.

Subcase 3.2 (Query). The main step here is to show, as in Theorem 1, that once a value for an unknown has been calculated, this value is preserved during the evaluation of the remaining right-hand side. To accomplish this, we use Lemma 3 to derive $\text{valid}_{\text{plain}} \, c \, \text{stable} \, \sigma$ and then use the value preserving property Theorem 1 *(ii)* of the plain TD.   □

A crucial part for the proof in the other direction is to show that when the TD reaches the *Stable* case, i. e., stops further descent because the iterated unknown is in stable, the plain TD terminates for the same parameters and returns the same value. Since the *Stable* case constitutes a base case of the induction using the rules for the TD, no induction hypotheses are available to conclude this fact. Hence, we add the obvious but vital premise that the set stable is finite.

Lemma 6. *Assume* $x \in c$, $x \in \text{stable}$, $\text{valid}_{\text{plain}} \, (c - \{x\}) \, \text{stable} \, \sigma$ *holds, and the set* stable *is finite. Then there exists* $d_x \in \mathbb{D}$ *such that* $\text{iterate}_{\text{plain}} \, x \, c \, \sigma = (d_x, \sigma)$ *is defined and* $d_x = \sigma \, x$.

This lemma holds since the resulting computation trace has finite width and height. The fixpoint iterations at any level terminate after one iteration since the input is already a solution. Also, the number of query nodes in a right-hand side is bounded, because we restrict strategy trees to be of finite height. Finally, its height is finite because one unknown is added to c at every second level and it is always a subset of s. Formally, this lemma is proven by structural induction over s. With the help of the lemma we can show the remaining direction of the equivalence:

Theorem 3 (Equivalence II). *The theorem shows:*

- *Assume* query x y c infl stable $\sigma = (d_y, \text{infl}', \text{stable}', \sigma')$ *is defined,* x $\in$ stable, stable *is finite, and* valid $c\,\sigma$ infl stable *holds. Then*
    (i) query$_{\text{plain}}$ x y c $\sigma = (d_y, \sigma')$ *is defined and*
    (ii) valid $c\,\sigma'$ infl' stable' *holds.*
  Furthermore, in this case (iii) update x infl stable infl' stable' *holds, (iv)* stable' *is finite, and (v)* x $\in$ infl'y.
- *Assume* iterate x c infl stable $\sigma = (d_x, \text{infl}', \text{stable}', \sigma')$ *is defined,* x $\in$ c, stable *is finite, and* valid $c'\,\sigma$ infl stable *holds. Let* $c' := c - \{x\}$. *Then*
    (i) iterate$_{\text{plain}}$ x c $\sigma = (d_x, \sigma')$ *is defined and*
    (ii) valid $c'\,\sigma'$ infl' stable' *holds.*
  Furthermore, in this case (iii) update x infl stable infl' stable' *holds, (iv) the set* stable' *is finite, and (v)* x $\in$ stable'.
- *Assume* eval x t c infl stable $\sigma = (d_x, \text{infl}', \text{stable}', \sigma')$ *is defined,* x $\in$ stable, stable *is finite, and* valid $c\,\sigma$ infl stable *holds. Then*
    (i) eval$_{\text{plain}}$ x t c $\sigma = (d_x, \sigma')$ *is defined and*
    (ii) valid $c\,\sigma'$ infl' stable' *holds.*
  Furthermore, in this case (iii) update x infl stable infl' stable' *holds, (iv)* stable' *is finite, (v)* t $\sigma' = d_x$, *and (vi)* $\forall$u $\in$ dep σ' t. x $\in$ infl'u.

Proof. This proof uses the induction rules for the TD; which results in an additional subcase *Stabl* in the *Iterate* case. This is the only case that differs significantly from the previous proof; it is proven using Lemma 6.   □

Both theorems combined establish the equivalence of the plain TD and the TD, which is expressed in the following corollary.

Corollary 2 (Equivalence of the TDs). *The equation* solve$_{\text{plain}}$ x $= \sigma$ *is defined for some* $\sigma \in \{f : \mathcal{U} \to \mathbb{D}\}$ *whenever* solve x $= (\text{stable}, \sigma')$ *is defined for some* stable $\subseteq \mathcal{U}$ *and* $\sigma' : \mathcal{U} \to \mathbb{D}$. *In this case,* σ *and* σ' *are equal.*

The following corollary reads identically to Corollary 1 but refers to the implementation of the TD. It is a straightforward consequence of Theorem 3.

Corollary 3 (Partial Correctness of the TD). *Assume that the equation* solve x = (stable, σ) *is defined. Then the corollary shows that σ is a partial solution for* stable *and* $x \in$ stable.

5   Related Work

In the scope of verifying dataflow analyses, round-robin iteration [6] and variations of Kildall's algorithm [5,8,23] have been verified. The latter maintain a global worklist for a chaotic iteration over the control-flow graph. Others formalize syntax-directed fixpoint iterators as part of their work on formalizing abstract interpreters [7,12,18]. Instead of iterating over the control-flow graph of a program, their abstract interpreters are guided by the program's syntax. These dedicated solvers, however, are not generically applicable to all equation systems. Instead of dynamically detecting dependencies, the dependencies are derived directly from the program's control flow.

The partial correctness of the local generic fixpoint solver RLD has been proven by Hofmann et al. [16]. This algorithm records dependencies dynamically to deal with changing dependencies between unknowns. In contrast to the TD, it locally destabilizes directly influenced unknowns when the value of the current unknown has been updated, and immediately triggers their re-evaluation through a local worklist. This may lead to different values being computed by the solver for repeated queries of the same unknown within a right-hand side. Extra mechanisms are required to avoid this undesired behavior [19]. In contrast, the TD relies on non-local destabilization to remove all unknowns from the set of stable unknowns that transitively depend on an updated unknown. The local worklist iteration of RLD is avoided and the same value is computed if the same unknown is queried multiple times within one right-hand side. In fact, the latter property constitutes an essential proof step in our formalization. Furthermore, the RLD solver always combines the old value for an unknown with its new value. This implies that the domain of values should provide some *join* operator, whereas our algorithm is fully generic by making no assumptions on the domain of values—except providing an element $\bot$, and an equality operator.

De Vilhena et al. [30] use Iris to formalize a local generic solver and prove its partial correctness. Like the RLD, their solver detects dependencies between unknowns on the fly and can deal with a possibly infinite equation system. It does, however, not rely on recursive descent into encountered unknowns. Instead, it uses a worklist to iterate over the unknowns, which are either new or whose current values are possibly outdated. Similarly to the RLD, this does not require a non-local destabilization. In comparison, recursive descent into unknowns, as done by the TD, is likely to be more efficient than plain worklist iteration. Due to recursive descent, the evaluation of right-hand sides always uses the currently best values for encountered unknowns and thus may avoid useless computation. To prove that the results computed by their solver are part of an optimal least fixpoint, Vilhena et al. [30] assume that the domain of values is partially ordered and right-hand sides are monotonic. In practical applications such as interprocedural analysis, or the analysis of concurrent systems, though, monotonicity cannot always be assumed. This is why our solver is proven partially correct independent of any assumptions on ordering or monotonicity.

6   Conclusion

This work provides a formal proof of the partial correctness of the TD. We first proved the plain TD to be partially correct and then proved that the TD is equivalent to the plain TD. For complete lattices and monotonic right-hand sides, the computed partial solution agrees with the *least* solution of the equation system on all stable unknowns. A proof of this fact can be obtained by extending the given proof with further invariants. When the complete lattice additionally satisfies the ascending chain condition and the set of unknowns is finite, the TD is guaranteed to terminate. In this case, partial correctness turns into *total* correctness.

Another task for future work is to incorporate widening and narrowing [3, 28] into the solver and prove correctness. Widening and narrowing cannot be considered another semantics-preserving optimization. Even for complete lattices, the computed result is generally no longer the least solution. In case that narrowing is intertwined with widening as proposed by Seidl and Vogler [26] and right-hand sides are non-monotonic, the result need not be a (post-)solution. Further future work is to support side-effecting equation systems [2], where right-hand sides may not only contribute to the left-hand side but also contribute to other unknowns.

Acknowledgements. This work was supported by the German Research Foundation (DFG) - 378803395/2428 ConVeY and by Shota Rustaveli National Science Foundation of Georgia under the project FR-21-7973.

References

1. Akhin, M., Belyaev, M.: Variable initialization analysis (2020). https://kotlinlang. org/spec/control--and-data-flow-analysis.html#variable-initialization-analysis
2. Apinis, K., Seidl, H., Vojdani, V.: Side-effecting constraint systems: a Swiss army knife for program analysis. In: Jhala, R., Igarashi, A. (eds.) Programming Languages and Systems - 10th Asian Symposium, APLAS 2012, Kyoto, Japan, 11–13 December 2012. Proceedings. LNCS, vol. 7705, pp. 157–172. Springer, Cham (2012). https://doi.org/10.1007/978-3-642-35182-2_12
3. Apinis, K., Seidl, H., Vojdani, V.: How to combine widening and narrowing for non-monotonic systems of equations. In: Boehm, H., Flanagan, C. (eds.) ACM SIG-PLAN Conference on Programming Language Design and Implementation, PLDI 2013, Seattle, WA, USA, 16–19 June 2013, pp. 377–386. ACM (2013). https://doi. org/10.1145/2491956.2462190
4. Apinis, K., Seidl, H., Vojdani, V.: Enhancing top-down solving with widening and narrowing. In: Probst, C.W., Hankin, C., Hansen, R.R. (eds.) Semantics, Logics, and Calculi - Essays Dedicated to Hanne Riis Nielson and Flemming Nielson on the Occasion of Their 60th Birthdays. LNCS, vol. 9560, pp. 272–288. Springer, Cham (2016). https://doi.org/10.1007/978-3-319-27810-0_14

5. Bertot, Y., Grégoire, B., Leroy, X.: A structured approach to proving compiler optimizations based on dataflow analysis. In: Filliâtre, J., Paulin-Mohring, C., Werner, B. (eds.) Types for Proofs and Programs, International Workshop, TYPES 2004, Jouy-en-Josas, France, 15–18 December 2004, Revised Selected Papers. LNCS, vol. 3839, pp. 66–81. Springer, Cham (2004). https://doi.org/10.1007/11617990_5
6. Cachera, D., Jensen, T.P., Pichardie, D., Rusu, V.: Extracting a data flow analyser in constructive logic. In: Schmidt, D.A. (ed.) Programming Languages and Systems, 13th European Symposium on Programming, ESOP 2004, Held as Part of the Joint European Conferences on Theory and Practice of Software, ETAPS 2004, Barcelona, Spain, 29 March–2 April 2004, Proceedings. LNCS, vol. 2986, pp. 385–400. Springer, Cham (2004). https://doi.org/10.1007/978-3-540-24725-8_27
7. Cachera, D., Pichardie, D.: A certified denotational abstract interpreter. In: Kaufmann, M., Paulson, L.C. (eds.) Interactive Theorem Proving, First International Conference, ITP 2010, Edinburgh, UK, 11–14 July 2010, Proceedings. LNCS, vol. 6172, pp. 9–24. Springer, Cham (2010). https://doi.org/10.1007/978-3-642-14052-5_3
8. Coupet-Grimal, S., Delobel, W.: A uniform and certified approach for two static analyses. In: Filliâtre, J., Paulin-Mohring, C., Werner, B. (eds.) Types for Proofs and Programs, International Workshop, TYPES 2004, Jouy-en-Josas, France, 15–18 December 2004, Revised Selected Papers. LNCS, vol. 3839, pp. 115–137. Springer, Cham (2004). https://doi.org/10.1007/11617990_8
9. Cousot, P., Cousot, R.: Abstract interpretation: a unified lattice model for static analysis of programs by construction or approximation of fixpoints. In: Graham, R.M., Harrison, M.A., Sethi, R. (eds.) Conference Record of the Fourth ACM Symposium on Principles of Programming Languages, Los Angeles, California, USA, January 1977, pp. 238–252. ACM (1977). https://doi.org/10.1145/512950.512973
10. Cousot, P., Cousot, R.: Abstract interpretation frameworks. J. Log. Comput. **2**(4), 511–547 (1992). https://doi.org/10.1093/LOGCOM/2.4.511
11. Fecht, C., Seidl, H.: A faster solver for general systems of equations. Sci. Comput. Program. **35**(2), 137–161 (1999). https://doi.org/10.1016/S0167-6423(99)00009-X
12. Franceschino, L., Pichardie, D., Talpin, J.: Verified functional programming of an abstract interpreter. In: Dragoi, C., Mukherjee, S., Namjoshi, K.S. (eds.) Static Analysis - 28th International Symposium, SAS 2021, Chicago, IL, USA, 17–19 October 2021, Proceedings. LNCS, vol. 12913, pp. 124–143. Springer, Cham (2021). https://doi.org/10.1007/978-3-030-88806-0_6
13. Gosling, J., et al.: Chapter 16. Definite Assignment, September 2023. https://docs.oracle.com/javase/specs/jls/se21/html/jls-16.html
14. Hecht, M.S., Ullman, J.D.: Analysis of a simple algorithm for global data flow problems. In: Proceedings of the 1st Annual ACM SIGACT-SIGPLAN Symposium on Principles of Programming Languages, pp. 207–217, POPL 1973. Association for Computing Machinery, New York, NY, USA (1973). https://doi.org/10.1145/512927.512946

15. Hermenegildo, M.V., et al.: An overview of the Ciao system. In: Bassiliades, N., Governatori, G., Paschke, A. (eds.) Rule-Based Reasoning, Programming, and Applications - 5th International Symposium, RuleML 2011 - Europe, Barcelona, Spain, 19–21 July 2011. Proceedings. LNCS, vol. 6826, p. 2. Springer, Cham (2011). https://doi.org/10.1007/978-3-642-22546-8_2

16. Hofmann, M., Karbyshev, A., Seidl, H.: Verifying a local generic solver in Coq. In: Cousot, R., Martel, M. (eds.) Static Analysis - 17th International Symposium, SAS 2010, Perpignan, France, 14–16 September, 2010. Proceedings. LNCS, vol. 6337, pp. 340–355. Springer, Cham (2010). https://doi.org/10.1007/978-3-642-15769-1_21

17. Hofmann, M., Karbyshev, A., Seidl, H.: What is a pure functional? In: Abramsky, S., Gavoille, C., Kirchner, C., auf der Heide, F.M., Spirakis, P.G. (eds.) Automata, Languages and Programming, 37th International Colloquium, ICALP 2010, Bordeaux, France, 6–10 July 2010, Proceedings, Part II. LNCS, vol. 6199, pp. 199–210. Springer, Cham (2010). https://doi.org/10.1007/978-3-642-14162-1_17

18. Jourdan, J.: Verasco: a formally verified C static analyzer. (Verasco: un analyseur statique pour C formellement vérifié). Ph.D. thesis, Paris Diderot University, France (2016). https://tel.archives-ouvertes.fr/tel-01327023

19. Karbyshev, A.: Monadic parametricity of second-order functionals. Ph.D. thesis, Technische Universität München (2013). https://mediatum.ub.tum.de/1144371

20. Kildall, G.A.: A unified approach to global program optimization. In: Fischer, P.C., Ullman, J.D. (eds.) Conference Record of the ACM Symposium on Principles of Programming Languages, Boston, Massachusetts, USA, October 1973, pp. 194–206. ACM Press (1973). https://doi.org/10.1145/512927.512945

21. Le Charlier, B., Van Hentenryck, P.: A universal top-down fixpoint algorithm. Technical report CS-92-25, University of Namur and Brown University, May 1992

22. Muthukumar, K., Hermenegildo, M.V.: Compile-time derivation of variable dependency using abstract interpretation. J. Log. Program. **13**(2&3), 315–347 (1992). https://doi.org/10.1016/0743-1066(92)90035-2

23. Nipkow, T.: Verified bytecode verifiers. In: Honsell, F., Miculan, M. (eds.) Foundations of Software Science and Computation Structures, 4th International Conference, FOSSACS 2001 Held as Part of the Joint European Conferences on Theory and Practice of Software, ETAPS 2001 Genova, Italy, 2–6 April 2001, Proceedings. LNCS, vol. 2030, pp. 347–363. Springer, Cham (2001). https://doi.org/10.1007/3-540-45315-6_23

24. Nipkow, T., Klein, G.: Concrete Semantics - With Isabelle/HOL. Springer, Cham (2014). ISBN 978-3-319-10541, https://doi.org/10.1007/978-3-319-10542-0

25. Nipkow, T., Paulson, L.C., Wenzel, M.: Isabelle/HOL - A Proof Assistant for Higher-Order Logic. LNCS, vol. 2283. Springer, Cham (2002). ISBN 3-540-43376, https://doi.org/10.1007/3-540-45949-9

26. Seidl, H., Vogler, R.: Three improvements to the top-down solver. Math. Struct. Comput. Sci. **31**(9), 1090–1134 (2021). https://doi.org/10.1017/S0960129521000499

27. Stade, Y., Tilscher, S., Seidl, H.: Partial correctness of the top-down solver. Archive of Formal Proofs, May 2024. ISSN 2150-914x. https://isa-afp.org/entries/Top_Down_Solver.html. Formal proof development

28. Tilscher, S., Stade, Y., Schwarz, M., Vogler, R., Seidl, H.: The top-down solver—an exercise in A^2I. In: Arceri, V., Cortesi, A., Ferrara, P., Olliaro, M. (eds.) Challenges of Software Verification, vol. 238, pp. 157–179. Springer, Singapore (2023). https://doi.org/10.1007/978-981-19-9601-6_9

29. Vergauwen, B., Wauman, J., Lewi, J.: Efficient fixpoint computation. In: Charlier, B.L. (ed.) Static Analysis, First International Static Analysis Symposium, SAS 1994, Namur, Belgium, 28–30 September 1994, Proceedings. LNCS, vol. 864, pp. 314–328. Springer, Cham (1994). https://doi.org/10.1007/3-540-58485-4_49

30. de Vilhena, P.E., Pottier, F., Jourdan, J.: Spy game: verifying a local generic solver in Iris. Proc. ACM Program. Lang. **4**(POPL), 33:1–33:28 (2020). https://doi.org/10.1145/3371101

31. Vojdani, V., Apinis, K., Rõtov, V., Seidl, H., Vene, V., Vogler, R.: Static race detection for device drivers: the Goblint approach. In: Lo, D., Apel, S., Khurshid, S. (eds.) Proceedings of the 31st IEEE/ACM International Conference on Automated Software Engineering, ASE 2016, Singapore, 3–7 September 2016, pp. 391–402. ACM (2016). https://doi.org/10.1145/2970276.2970337

End-to-End Mechanized Proof of a JIT-Accelerated eBPF Virtual Machine for IoT

Shenghao Yuan[1,3]($\boxtimes$) , Frédéric Besson[2], and Jean-Pierre Talpin[1]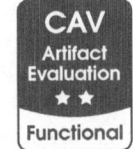

[1] Inria, Irisa, Rennes, France
{shenghao.Yuan,jean-Pierre.talpin}@inria.fr,
shenghaoyuan0928@163.com
[2] Univ Rennes, CNRS, Rennes, France
[3] State Key Laboratory of Blockchain and Data Security,
Zhejiang University, Hangzhou, China

Abstract. Modern operating systems have adopted Berkeley Packet Filters (BPF) as a mechanism to extend kernel functionalities dynamically, *e.g.*, Linux's eBPF or RIOT's rBPF. The just-in-time (JIT) compilation of eBPF introduced in Linux eBPF for performance has however led to numerous critical issues. Instead, RIOT's rBPF uses a slower but memory-isolating interpreter (a virtual machine) which implements a defensive semantics of BPF; and therefore trades performance for security. To increase performance without sacrificing security, this paper presents a fully verified JIT implementation for RIOT's rBPF, consisting of: i/ an end-to-end refinement workflow to both proving the JIT correct from an abstract specification and by deriving a verified concrete C implementation; ii/ a symbolic CompCert interpreter for executing jited binary code; iii/ a verified JIT compiler for rBPF; iv/ a verified hybrid rBPF virtual machine. Our core contribution is, to the best of our knowledge, the first and fully verified rBPF JIT compiler with correctness guarantees from high-level specification to low-level implementation. Benchmarks on microcontrollers hosting the RIOT operating system demonstrate significant performance improvements over the existing implementations of rBPF, even in worst-case application scenarios.

Keywords: mechanized proof · virtual machines · JIT compiler · eBPF

1 Introduction

Kernel extensibility is the capability of an operating system to extend its core functionalities with privileged services at runtime. It is an essential operating system feature for mainframes, PCs, phones but also smaller devices of the Internet of Things (IoT). Berkeley Packet Filters (BPF) was originally introduced [22,23] to provide such extensions for Unix-BSD systems (e.g. network packets filtering, cryptographic protocols, tools such as tcpdump, etc.). BPF is an assembly language that defines a virtual RISC-like instruction set architecture (ISA). BPF scripts are executed in kernel to parameterize or extend

© The Author(s) 2024
A. Gurfinkel and V. Ganesh (Eds.): CAV 2024, LNCS 14681, pp. 325–347, 2024.
https://doi.org/10.1007/978-3-031-65627-9_16

privileged network stacks. For devices like PCs, servers and routers, the Linux community adopted the concept of BPF and extended it to provide ways to run custom in-kernel virtualized code, hooked as "plugins" to various services, and for many other purposes beyond packet filtering [9]. The ISA of Linux's extended BPF (eBPF) is derived from the 64-bit RISC-V instruction set. It features a sophisticated verifier [27], to statically analyze eBPF binary instructions, and an interpreter/just-in-time (JIT) compiler, to execute eBPF binaries on varieties of 64/32-bit architectures, *e.g.,* x86, ARM and RISC-V.

The correctness of the eBPF VM and/or JIT is critical for the integrity of the Linux kernel. Bugs in their implementations have led to security vulnerabilities, *e.g.,* allowing execution of arbitrary code within the kernel context [16]. For high-assurance of correctness, researchers have successfully applied verification methods to eBPF JITs *e.g.,* [28,34,35], to find and fix previously unknown bugs. The eBPF instruction set is also used at the lowest end of the spectrum of the IoT, on low-power and resource-constrained devices using micro-controller units (MCUs) such as ARM Cortex-M, running smaller and resource-frugal operating systems, such as the RIOT operating system [2]. Recent work has extended the RIOT micro-kernel runtime with rBPF [38], a 64-bit register-based VM, using fixed-size 64-bit instructions and a reduced ISA derived from eBPF. This extension provides so-called femto-containers [39]: the capability for RIOT to run privileged services, compiled as BPF binaries, each run in a sandboxed VM.

However, low-power IoT devices that run RIOT rarely support hardware memory protections and they cannot afford the resource demands of an online verifier to detect possibly faulty scripts. Instead, MCU-class femto-containers implement a defensive semantics which checks dynamically the preconditions of each instruction before executing it. This ensures the safety and isolation of the eBPF script. Previous works [37,39] have tackled the challenges of implementing a fully-verified and memory isolating VM for RIOT.

While previous works focused on trust (verified fault-isolation) and frugality (minimal footprint), the challenge addressed in this paper is to boost performance while maintaining the highest degree of reliability, security, and frugality. For that purpose, we extend the existing fault-isolating VM, namely CertrBPF [37], with a JIT compiler that comes with mechanized correctness proofs. Our goal is to improve efficiency while providing certified security guarantees *i.e.,* the integrity of the host device, even in the presence of malicious code. In this aim, we present a *hybridly* accelerated virtual machine (HAVM), the first rBPF virtual machine that locally Just-In-Time compiles and executes sequences of safe instructions (either exempt from, or subject to benign, runtime checks), while behaving as a virtual machine for the most sensitive memory transactions which, if `jited`, would require multiple runtime checks ruining any performance or resources benefit. JIT acceleration highly improves the efficiency of rBPF femto-containers, but may potentially introduce subtle errors due to the sheer complexity of designing a JIT compiler. We exhaustively waive such risks by a correctness theorem mechanically verified using the Coq proof assistant [5].

1.1   Challenges

Typically, a JIT compiler manipulates three different programming or interme-diate languages: it translates bytecode (the *source language*) to specific machine code (the *target languages*), and it is usually implemented in a low-level system language such as C (the *host language*) for space efficiency and performance. Developing a JIT compiler of high-assurance hence poses major challenges.

JIT Design is Error-Prone. JIT compilers are more complex than ahead of time compilers. The translations of instructions and protocols they perform are error-prone: 1/ they perform transformations of architecture-dependent informa-tion at binary level, different instruction encoding formats and specific calling conventions and 2/ the host C language of the compiler eases low-level mem-ory management mistakes, *e.g., array-out-of-bound.* Unsurprisingly, many eBPF *JIT-related* vulnerabilities have been reported to the Linux community, regard-ing kernel execution of arbitrary code [12] or confidentiality [14].

Formalizing a JIT Compiler is Challenging. Ahead-of-Time compilers usually output assembly code by relying on separate assembler and linker to produce machine code (plus runtime libraries in, e.g., Rust, OCaml). JIT compilers pro-duce machine code directly, exposing vital semantics-level gaps: the host (C) language, source, and target (ARM) binary have different semantics along with specific calling convention. Existing compiler verification works, *e.g.,* CompCert, provide semantics from C to assembly languages but not to binary level currently. One cannot directly reuse a CompCert backend assembly semantics to formalize the target binary semantics of a JIT compiler as it does not conforms its calling convention.

End-to-End Verification Gap. Our JIT compiler is intended to run within the RIOT operating system kernel on resource-limited micro-controller devices. In that context, the provision of a formally verified JIT model with a high-level specification is not enough: there is still a verification gap to produce a veri-fied low-level C implementation from that abstract specification. The CompCert verification workflow is not suitable to that aim as it extracts OCaml code and depends on unverified OCaml runtime libraries, assembler and linker. Other JIT verification approaches, such as Jitterbug [28], suffer from this very same verifi-cation gap: the high-level specification is verified, not its extracted compiler.

1.2   Contributions

In this paper, we address these challenges by presenting the first end-to-end refinement workflow for application to the verified extraction of equivalent C implementations of a hybrid virtual machine embedding a JIT compiler. Specif-ically, we make the following contributions:

End-to-End Refinement Methodology. We propose an end-to-end refinement methodology that i/ *Horizontally, from source to target*, formally verifies a JIT compiler's correctness in Coq using the standard CompCert simulation framework, and ii/ *Vertically, from Gallina model to C code*, formally extracts an equivalent, optimized and executable C implementation from its own JIT specification in Gallina (the functional language embedded in Coq). A strength of our proof methodology lies in the capacity of extracting a verified C model from the standard compiler verification workflow in Coq, from specification to executable (end-to-end).

Symbolic CompCert ARM Interpreter. We extend the standard CompCert ARM backend with symbolic execution, for the purpose of reusing the existing CompCert calling convention to support binary code execution. This extension allows our new CompCert ARM interpreter to correctly interpret (jited) binary code while ensuring the preservation of the ARM calling convention.

A Verified JIT Compiler for rBPF. We design a JIT compiler translating rBPF Arithmetic and Logic (ALU) instructions into binary code. To implement our end-to-end approach, we prove a semantics preservation theorem between the source transition system (rBPF) and the target transitive semantics (rBPF with jited code), and extract a verified C implementation of the JIT compiler.

A Verified Hybrid Virtual Machine for rBPF. We introduce HAVM, a Hybridly jit-Accelerated VM. HAVM can switch between (*verified*) interpreted, runtime-costly, defensive memory bound checks (for load-store operations) and fully *verified* JIT-compiled code (for arithmetic operations). The verified C model of HAVM is derived from its abstract semantics by our end-to-end workflow.

Plan. The rest of the paper is organized as follows: Sect. 2 provides background on CompCert. Section 3 outlines our end-to-end refinement workflow and introduces the application to produce both a verified JIT compiler and VM in C. Section 4 defines our symbolic CompCert ARM interpreter. Section 5 introduces our JIT design and applies our workflow to produce a verified C implementation of the JIT with semantics preservation. Section 6 presents the complete HAVM mixing with a hardware ARM interpreter, a rBPF interpreter, and an interface function allowing them to interleave execution. Section 7 case-studies the performance of our generated VM implementation in comparison to all existing VMs. Section 8 reports our lessons learned, Sect. 9 discusses related works and Sect. 10 concludes.

2   Preliminaries

CompCert [17] is a C compiler that is both programmed and proven correct using the Coq proof assistant. It compiles C programs into assembly code *e.g.,* ARM. The compiler is structured into passes using several intermediate languages. Each intermediate language is equipped with an operational semantics defined by a labelled transition system denoted as $E \vdash st \xrightarrow{t} st'$. It represents one execution step from machine state st to machine state st' in some environment E. The trace t denotes the observable events generated by the execution step.

Each pass is proven to preserve observational equivalence of programs using a *simulation* relation. CompCert employs two types of simulations: forward simulation (*i.e.*, every behaviour of the source program is also a behaviour of the compiled program) and backward simulation. CompCert proves most of its passes using forward simulation because it is easier to reason with. It uses a *forward to backward* lemma to construct a backward simulation from a forward one. The composition of all the simulation lemmas for the individual compiler passes forms the semantic preservation theorem:

Theorem 1 (Semantic Preservation). *Suppose that $tp \in T$ is the result of the successful compilation of the program $p \in S$. If bh is a behaviour of tp ($bh \in [\![tp]\!]^T$) then there exists a behaviour bh' such that bh' is a behaviour of p ($bh' \in [\![p]\!]^S$) and bh' improves bh, i.e.:*

$$\forall\, p\, tp\, bh,\ compcert\ p = \lfloor tp \rfloor \rightarrow bh \in [\![tp]\!]^T \rightarrow \exists\, bh', bh' \in [\![p]\!]^S \wedge bh' \subseteq bh$$

$bh' \subseteq bh$ if either, bh' is equal to bh, or bh' is an undefined behaviour replaced by a defined behaviour in bh. CompCert returns an option-typed object: $\lfloor tp \rfloor$ denotes success with result tp, and $\emptyset$ denotes failure.

The memory model and data structures (representation of values) are shared across all the intermediate languages of CompCert [18,19]. CompCert defines machine integers with different sizes, *e.g.*, *int* for 32-bit words and *int64* for 64-bits long integers. A value $v \in val$ can either be a 32-bit Vint(i_{32}) or 64-bit Vlong(i_{64}) machine integer, a pointer Vptr(b, o) to a block b and offset o, a floating-point number, or the undefined value *Vundef*. A CompCert memory m consists of a collection of partitioned arrays. Each array has a fixed size and is identified by an uninterpreted block $b \in block$.

In addition to CompCert, our project employs the same Gallina-to-C transpiler ∂x as the verified virtual machine presented in [37]. ∂x is an unverified translator that was developed to design the verified PIP proto-kernel [13] in Coq. It transpiles a monadic (imperative) Gallina source definition to CompCert C code of identical structure and terms. We chose to reuse ∂x for its practicality (traceability) and to reuse the same translation validation methodology as [37].

3   A Workflow for End-to-End Refinement

This section presents an overview of our methodology to prove the correctness of a virtual machine which dynamically compiles, at load time, a subset of the instructions. Informally, the end-to-end correctness guarantee of the virtual machine can be phrased as follows. Suppose that a source code s executes according to the small-step operational semantics and returns a value v. The virtual machine just-in-time compiles a subset of the source instructions of s

into binary code and, therefore, generates a *compound* program t composed of original instructions augmented with calls to binary code. The virtual machine then executes the program t and returns the exact same value v.

In the following, we explain the high-level structure of the proof and how to get a rigorously end-to-end formal guarantee for a virtual machine written in the C language using the Coq proof assistant and the CompCert compiler.

3.1   Methodology

At high-level, the methodology can be explained using T-diagrams [6]. The T-diagram of Fig. 1a depicts a compiler which given as input a source program $s \in S$, generates a target program $t \in T$ and is implemented using the implementation language I. We will also make use of the diagram of Fig. 1b which depicts an interpreter for the language T implemented in the language I. As our methodology is formally grounded each diagram comes with a soundness proof. In particular, each language is equipped with a formal semantics and a compiler diagram comes with a semantic preservation theorem similar to Theorem 1.

(a) T-diagram for a compiler.   (b) Diagram for an interpreter.

Fig. 1. T-diagrams.

JIT Compiler Structure. The JIT compiler and its proof follow the structure of the diagram of Fig. 2a. To begin with, we write a compiler for the source language S to the target language T using the Gallina language, written G, of the Coq proof assistant. We also prove a semantics preservation theorem guaranteeing the correctness of the compiler. To get an executable compiler outside

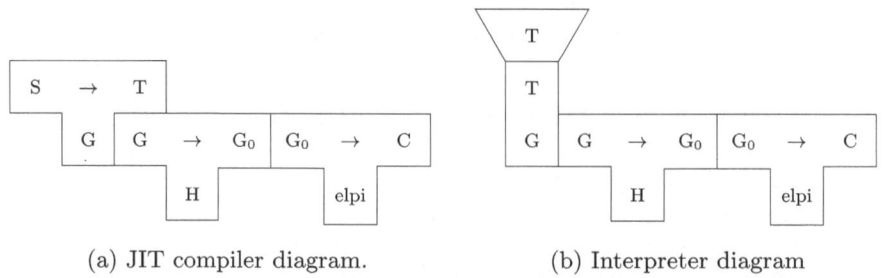

(a) JIT compiler diagram.   (b) Interpreter diagram

Fig. 2. Virtual machine diagrams.

the proof assistant, the usual approach is to perform program extraction [20,32] to a functional language. However, functional languages require a sophisticated runtime *e.g.* a garbage collector, that is not compatible with our constrained resources. Instead, we perform a rewrite of the compiler to a tiny subset of Gallina (G_0). Though the transformation is systematic, it is manual as indicated in Fig. 2a by the implementation language H which stands for *Human*. In that case, that associated correctness is that both compilers compute the exact same output program. However, the compiler using the language G (Gallina without restriction) is designed as a composition of passes. This simplifies the semantic preservation proof but constructs intermediate functional data-structures. The compiler restricted to G_0 is using more imperative data-structures (using an explicit state-monad) and is using a more direct generation of binary code avoiding intermediate data-structures thus using resources that are compatible with our resource constrained environment. The last step consists in using the ∂x Coq plugin, written in elpi [8], which converts the language G_0 into C. As ∂x is not proof generating, we perform a manual but systematic translation validation step with respect to the formal semantics of CompCert showing that both the G_0 program and the generated C code compute the same result.

Execution of JIT Compiled Code. The proofs of the JIT compiler are performed over the small-step operation semantics of the target language which is the combination of source semantics for the non-JIT compiled instruction and the semantics of the binary code. The diagram of Fig. 2b shows how to derive an executable C Virtual Machine for this language. To execute a program $\boxed{T}$ in language T, we program in Gallina (G) an interpreter for the language T. As we explain in Sect. 4, the interpreter is equipped with a sub-interpreter for executing binary code. Here, the proof is that if the interpreter terminates without exhausting its allocated execution steps, it computes the same result as the small-step semantics. To get an executable C code, we follow a similar methodology: express the interpreter in restricted Gallina G_0 and run the ∂x tool to get a C program. What may be puzzling is how the Gallina semantics of binary code may be compiled into C code. This indeed requires some substantial work. What we do is to augment the semantics of all the intermediate language of CompCert with a so-called `builtin` which embeds the semantics of our Gallina interpreter for executing binary code. Eventually, we show that this semantics coincide with the existing semantics of CompCert assembly augmented to fetch and decode instructions from memory.

Terminology. In the following, we call *horizontal* refinement a proof related to a Gallina program $p \in G$ and *vertical* refinement a proof related to lower-level programs $p \in G_0$ or $p \in C$.

3.2   Application to a rBPF Virtual Machine

We instantiate our approach to derive a verified C implementation of a VM for rBPF enhanced with a JIT compiler. As we target a 32-bit ARM architecture,

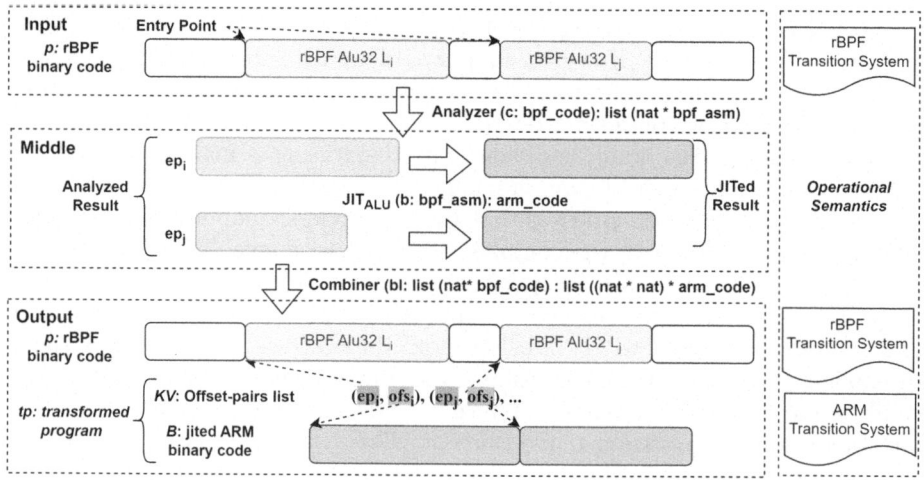

Fig. 3. *JITCompiler* Structure (left) and related Semantics (right).

we consider the rBPF variant operating on 32 bit registers. The JIT compiler is invoked at load time and translates to ARM code straight-line sequence of arithmetic and logic (ALU) instructions. The rationale is that these are the part of the code for which we can expect a substantial speedup as the rBPF registers can be mapped to ARM registers and an ALU instructions is mapped to a short sequence of ALU ARM instructions. For memory operations, rBPF implements a costly dynamic defensive semantics which consists in iterating over a list of allowed memory regions and checking that the memory address is correctly aligned and respect the access rights. Yet, a partial JIT compiler does not simplify the verification task as the VM needs to ensure the inter-operability between streams of rBPF and ARM instructions while reasoning at high-level using formal models.

JIT Compiler Structure. The structure of the JIT compiler is illustrated in Fig. 3. As hinted in the previous Section, the JIT compiler is not monolithic but made of three passes. The *Analyzer* pass identifies sequences of rBPF ALU instructions and disassemble them. The core of the JIT compiler is JIT_{ALU} (see Sect. 5) which translates a list of rBPF instructions into the correponding ARM code. Eventually, *Combiner* collects all the binary instructions into a single array B and generates another array KV such that $KV[i] = ofs$ if i is the entry point of a sequence of rBPF ALU instructions si and $B[ofs]$ is the start of the binary ARM code corresponding to si.

Horizontal Refinement: JIT Correctness. The proof of our JIT compiler follows the structure of a standard CompCert compiler proof, with the difference that the target language is made of both rBPF instructions and binary ARM code.

This multi-language semantics requires the calling-conventions of ARM to ensure the interoperability of the rBPF semantics and ARM semantics.

Vertical Refinement: Verified JIT and HAVM. The goal of vertical refinement is to extract a verified C $JITCompiler_C$ from its Gallina model $JITCompiler$ and generate a VM $HAVM_C$. One challenge is to ensure that the C program is a valid refinement of the Gallina program. It appears, however, that calling some in-memory ARM code from a C program has no defined semantics in CompCert. To tackle the issue, we augment the semantics of CompCert with a defensive symbolic ARM semantics.

4   Symbolic CompCert ARM Interpreter

The current standard CompCert backend defines various assembly languages, *e.g.*, ARM, along with their formal semantics. Unfortunately, it cannot be reused for our JIT compiler because *JITCompiler* requires the binary-level semantics of ARM. Additionally, the calling convention of the `jited` code exceeds the capability of the existing CompCert ARM semantics.

To address this issue, we firstly define an ARM decoding function to link the ARM semantics from binary-level to CompCert assembly-level. Subsequently, we introduce a symbolic CompCert ARM semantics that lifts the ARM instruction semantics and the calling convention into a symbolic form. This new CompCert backend employs symbolic execution to interpret binary ARM instructions, and symbolic values allow to i/ initialise ARM registers when switching from C to binary; ii/ define an executable semantics of ARM capable of simulating (and verifying) the calling conventions. Yet, during the assembly code generation pass of CompCert, the symbolic ARM semantics is switched to the concrete CompCert ARM semantics.

ARM Decode. We implement a decoding function in Gallina that translates binary ARM instructions to standard CompCert assembly ARM instructions. We also define an encode function embedded in the JIT process, and prove that this 'decode-encode' pair is consistent.

Lemma 1 (Decode-Encode Consistency). $\forall\, i,\ decode\,(encode\,i) = \lfloor i \rfloor$

ARM Calling Convention. When interpreting ('calling') a list of `jited` binary code, the ARM calling conventions need to be preserved: i/ the caller must save the value of argument registers $(r_0 - r_3)$, and ii/ the callee must save the value of $(r_4 - r_{11})$. For efficiency purposes, we stipulate that:

- callee-saved registers must be dynamically preserved by the `jited` binary code, as it may not modify all registers during one procedure call.
- all caller-saved registers are statically preserved by our ARM backend.

We also allocate a stack frame to implement the calling convention before binary execution, and verify that all ARM callee-saved registers in the final register state have been reset to their initial values, relying on a symbolic execution technique.

Symbolic Execution. The register map SReg is symbolic: each register sr is either an abstract value or a concrete value bound to an actual ARM register r.

$$\text{SReg} \ni sr ::= \text{abstract}(r) \mid \text{concrete}(v)$$

All initial registers $init\_rs$ have abstract values, *e.g.,* $SReg[r_0] = \text{abstract}(r_0)$. The concrete values of registers are inserted by running the jited code.

CompCert ARM Interpreter. We design a symbolic variant of the CompCert ARM interpreter that utilizes the existing CompCert ARM transition function to execute user-specific ARM binary code. We first introduce the initial and final states of the interpreter, then explain how the interpreter works.

We define a function init_state to create a new ARM environment for interpreting binary code. It first copies values from the arguments list $args$ to caller-saved registers of the symbolic register map $init\_rs$, according to the function's signature sig. Then, init_state allocates a new memory block stk in CompCert memory with a fixed stack size sz. It stores the previous stack pointer sp at position pos in stk and updates the stack pointer with the start address of this block. Finally, it stores the return address, *i.e.,* the next address of the old pc, to r_{14}. Since the first argument always points to the location of the jited binary code to be executed, init_state also assigns the program counter pc with the first argument value r_0.

init_state(sig, $args$, sz, pos, m) =
  match alloc_arguments(sig, $args$, $init\_rs$) **with**
  $\mid \emptyset \Rightarrow \emptyset$
  $\mid \lfloor rs \rfloor \Rightarrow$ **match** alloc_frame(sz, pos, rs, m) **with**
    $\mid \emptyset \Rightarrow \emptyset$
    $\mid \lfloor (rs', m') \rfloor \Rightarrow \lfloor (rs'\{r_{14} \leftarrow \text{abstract}(pc) + 1,\ pc \leftarrow rs'[r_0]\},\ m') \rfloor$

We then define a Boolean predicate *is_final_state* to describe a well-formed final state of the jited code.

$$is\_final\_state(rs : SReg) : bool = rs[pc] == \text{abstract}(r_{14})\ \&\&$$
$$rs[sp] == \text{abstract}(sp)\ \&\&\ (\forall i.\ 4 \le i \le 11 \to rs[r_i] == \text{abstract}(r_i))$$

The predicate *is_final_state* stipulates that 1/ pc should hold the return address stored in r_{14}; 2/ The stack pointer is restored; 3/ All callee-saved registers should have their initial values.

The symbolic CompCert ARM interpreter is defined as follows:

bin_exec($fuel$, sig, $args$, sz, pos, m) =
  match init_state(sig, $args$, sz, pos, m) **with**
  $\mid \emptyset \Rightarrow \emptyset$
  $\mid \lfloor (rs', m') \rfloor \Rightarrow$ bin_interp($fuel$, rs', m')

where the parameters include: 1/ *fuel*, ensuring the termination of its recursive call to bin_interp. 2/ *sig*, the signature of the arguments used by the input ARM binary code. 3/ *args*, the arguments list. 4/ *sz*, the size of the allocated stack frame. 5/ *pos*, the position of the old stack pointer in the new stack frame. 6/ *m*, the CompCert memory.

First, bin_exec uses init_state to create a proper ARM environment, including the initialized ARM register map rs' and the new memory m'. It then calls bin_interp recursively to interpret ARM binary code until it reaches the final state. It either returns r_0's value or exhausts *fuel*. Each iteration of find_instr fetches the instruction at the program counter *pc* and decodes it. If its binary instruction decodes successfully, bin_interp then calls the symbolic ARM transition function symbolic_transf to execute it and proceeds to the next instruction, if no errors occur.

$$\text{bin\_interp}(fuel, rs, m) =$$
$$\textbf{if } \text{is\_final\_state}(rs) \textbf{ then } \lfloor (rs[r_0], m) \rfloor \textbf{else if } fuel == 0 \textbf{ then } \emptyset$$
$$\textbf{else match } \text{find\_instr}(rs[pc], m) \textbf{ with}$$
$$| \emptyset \Rightarrow \emptyset$$
$$| \lfloor ins \rfloor \Rightarrow \textbf{match } \text{symbolic\_transf}(ins, rs, m) \textbf{ with}$$
$$| \emptyset \Rightarrow \emptyset$$
$$| \lfloor (rs', m') \rfloor \Rightarrow \text{bin\_interp}(fuel - 1, rs', m')$$

We have integrated this symbolic ARM backend into the CompCert environment and proven that it is compatible with the standard CompCert ARM semantics. This interpreter also provides an equivalent built-in C function '*bin_exec*': the CompCert "builtins" mechanism ensures that the semantics preservation theorem still holds between the Gallina function bin_exec and its built-in '*bin_exec*'.

5 A Verified Just-In-Time Compiler for rBPF

Our JIT compiler is exclusively designed to translate rBPF Alu instructions into target binary code. The compiler structure is shown in Fig. 3. This section highlights the JIT$_{\text{ALU}}$ translation as the other two are straightforward. We then detail the end-to-end refinement verification process introduced to prove this JIT compiler correct.

5.1 JIT Design

High-Level Intuition. JIT$_{\text{ALU}}$ translates a list of rBPF Alu instructions into a list of ARM binary code. As depicted in Fig. 4, the target jited binary list has a specific linear structure: i/ The Head part copies r_1's to r_{12} as the following stages may override r_1; ii/ The dotted part is made of the following stages: *Spilling* copies ARM registers on the stack, *Load* transfers register values from rBPF to ARM, and *Core* performs the arithmetic computation operating on

ARM registers that is equivalent to the behaviour of the source rBPF `Alu` list; iii/ The subsequent part *Store* updates registers from ARM to rBPF, and *Reloading* pulls stack values into ARM registers; iv/ The *Tail* part frees the current stack frame and branches to the return address.

Fig. 4. Structure of `jited` code.

The *Load and Store* stages perform interactions between ARM registers and rBPF registers for consistency after executing the `jited` code, while the *Spilling and Reloading* stages guarantee the ARM calling convention. As the ARM binary can only 'see' ARM registers and memory blocks, the rBPF register map is stored in the special block *st_blk* and its start location ($\mathtt{Vptr}(st\_blk, o)$) is stored in r_1 with the argument passed by the *jit_call* function. In the layout of *st_blk*, cells $[4 * i, 4 * i + 4)$ have the value of R_i ($0 \leq i \leq 10$), and $[44, 48)$ have the rBPF PC's value.

Core Mapping. The rBPF `Alu` instructions include common arithmetic operations where the destination operator is a general rBPF register ($R_0 - R_9$) and the source could be a rBPF register ($R_0 - R_{10}$) or an 32-bit immediate number.

$$op \ ::= ADD \mid SUB \mid MUL \mid DIV \mid OR \mid AND \mid XOR \mid MOV \text{ general}$$
$$\mid LSH \mid RSH \mid ARSH \qquad\qquad\qquad\qquad\quad \text{shift}$$
$$ins \ ::= \mathtt{Alu} \ op \ dst \ src \mid \dots \qquad\qquad\qquad\qquad \text{instruction}$$

The core mapping of $\mathtt{JIT_{ALU}}$ includes two general rules and one specific rule.

- *G1*: maps a register-based rBPF operation (source is a register) into its corresponding ARM instruction operating the related ARM registers, *e.g.*, `Alu` $ADD \ R_d \ R_s$ is translated into *add $r_d \ r_d \ r_s$*.
- *G2*: maps an immediate rBPF operation according to the provided range i.
  - *G2.1*: If the immediate constant i is in the range $[0, 255]$, each instruction is directly mapped to an 8-bit-immediate ARM instruction.
  - *G2.2*: If i is within the range $[256, 65535]$, it is first copied into ARM register r_{11} using *movw*, and then mapped to an ARM instruction with r_{11} as the second operand. *movw* writes an immediate value to the low 16 bits of the destination register.
  - *G2.3*: Otherwise, i is loaded into r_{11} using *movt* and *movw* before performing the operation. *movt* modifies the high 16 bits.
- *S1*: For the rBPF division and shift instructions, the immediate operation is mapped if the constant i is valid, *i.e.*, $i \neq 0$ for division and ($0 \leq i \leq 31$) for shifts. For completion, $\mathtt{JIT_{ALU}}$ returns failure if it encounters an invalid i. Note that validity is however a pre-condition guaranteed by the host virtual machine [37], which analyzes script prior to execution and, among other things, checks the validity of immediate instructions.

Interaction. In the Core stage, source instructions operate over rBPF registers, while the `jited` ARM code operates on ARM registers. Hence, a consistent interaction between rBPF and ARM registers is mandatory. JIT_{ALU} generates extra binary code performing the interaction in the *Load* and *Store* stages, which relies on two special sets LD (rBPF registers that have been loaded into ARM registers) and ST (rBPF registers that should be updated in the *Store* stage). For each rBPF `Alu` instruction, JIT_{ALU} adopts two rules to produce memory instructions and update the register sets before it performs the core mapping.

- *I1*: if the rBPF destination register R_d isn't in the LD, i/ if r_d is an ARM callee-saved register, generate '*str* r_d [*sp*, #($d * 4$)]' for spilling; ii/ generate '*ldr* r_d [r_{12}, #($d * 4$)]' for the *Load* stage; iii/ add R_d into LD and ST.
- *I2*: if the rBPF source is a register R_s that isn't in the LD, generate the same code as *I1* but only add R_s into LD.

After all rBPF `Alu` instructions are `jited`, JIT_{ALU} updates the rBPF register map by generating '*str* r_i [r_{12}, #($i * 4$)]' for all $r_i \in ST$. Then, to preserve the ARM calling convention, JIT_{ALU} resets all modified ARM callee-saved registers r_i from the stack frame by '*ldr* r_i [*sp*, #($i * 4$)]'.

Example. Figure 5 illustrates the entire JIT_{ALU} process. Consider a source rBPF `Alu` snippet composed of n instructions: '[*ADD* R_0 R_1; *MOV* R_5 R_0; *MUL* R_6 *0xf*;...]'. The *Head* is always '*mov* r_{12} r_1'. Then, the *Spilling* stage saves r_{11} in the stack frame because it will be modified later. For the first rBPF instruction, the `jited` code copies R_0 and R_1 into r_0 and r_1, and then performs the ARM addition. The initial LD and ST are $\emptyset$, the updated state is $LD = \{R_0, R_1\}$ and $ST = \{R_0\}$. For the second rBPF instruction, the `jited` code requires a *Spilling* stage to save r_5 first, then performs the move and updates LD and ST with R_5. After the n-th rBPF instruction, there are two instructions to update the rBPF's PC with the length of the input list. The *Store* stage updates all modified rBPF registers in ST and PC, and the *Reloading* stage resets all used call-save registers to their previous values stored in the stack frame during the *Spilling* stage. The last stage is *Tail*.

5.2 JIT Correctness

We employ the standard CompCert framework to prove the JIT compiler correct. The proof initially refines the source rBPF semantics into an intermediate model (after analysis), and subsequently refines into the target HAVM semantics.

Machine State. The rBPF state is a pair $state ::= (R, M)$, consisting of a CompCert memory model M and the register map R, which associates (32-bit) values with the rBPF registers ($R_0 - R_{10}$ and PC).

Transition Semantics of rBPF. The core of rBPF's semantics is a transition function $T(ins, st) = \lfloor st' \rfloor$ that determines the new state st' after executing

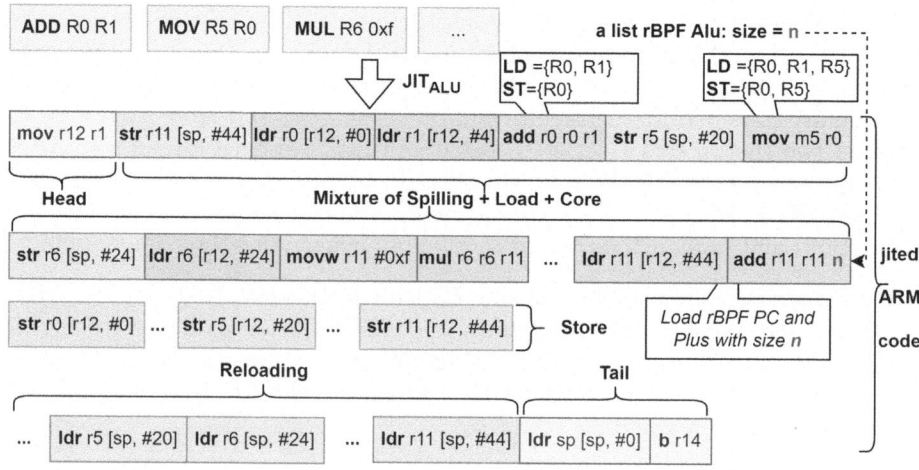

Fig. 5. JIT_ALU example.

instruction *ins* in the initial state *st*. In particular, the program counter PC is incremented. For simplification, we only present the transition rule of arithmetic instructions in one execution step $step_{rBPF}$. The first two premises model the actions of reading and decoding the *n*-th instruction *ins*, which is pointed to by the program counter *PC*, from the list *C*. Then, the rule executes *ins* and returns a new state.

$$\frac{R[PC] = \texttt{Vint}(n) \quad C[n] = \lfloor ins \rfloor \quad ins = \texttt{Alu } op \; dst \; src \quad T(ins,(R,\,M)) = \lfloor (R',\,M') \rfloor}{C \vdash (R,\,M) \xrightarrow{\epsilon} (R',\,M')}$$

Transition Semantics of the Analyzer. The first module of *JITCompiler* is an analyzer that generates a list of analysis results *BL*, a pair of entry point and a list of (decoded) rBPF Alu instructions, from the input rBPF binary *C*. The refined semantics only replaces the previous arithmetic rule with the following one. When *PC* is an entry point and its related rBPF Alu list is in *BL*, a refined transition function T^L is used to sequentially execute all instructions in *l*.

$$\frac{R[PC] = \texttt{Vint}(n) \quad (n,l) \in BL \quad T^L(l,(R,\,M)) = \lfloor (R',\,M') \rfloor}{C,\,BL \vdash (R,\,M) \xrightarrow{\epsilon} (R',\,M')}$$

We prove that, for one step '$step_A$' of this refined machine, TS_A has a backward simulation relation with respect to several steps '$step_{rBPF}^*$' of the source machine TS_{rBPF}.

Lemma 2 (TS_A simulates TS_{rBPF} in one step). $\forall C \; BL \; t \; st \; st'$,

$$Analyzer \; C = \lfloor BL \rfloor \wedge (step_A \; C \; BL) \; st \; t \; st' \rightarrow (step_{rBPF}^* \; C) \; st \; t \; st'$$

Transition Semantics of HAVM. The *Combiner* module calls JIT_{ALU} to generate all binary code lists from the analyzing results and combines all `jited` code into one list. The target semantics only changes the arithmetic rule compared to the source semantics. Where PC is an entry point and its related `jited` list located in bl starting from offset ofs, the transition function T^{ARM} calls the symbolic ARM interpreter `bin_exec` to execute the `jited` code.

$$\frac{R[PC] = \texttt{Vint}(n) \quad ((n, ofs), bl) \in TP \quad T^{ARM}(ofs, bl, (R,\ M)) = \lfloor (R',\ M') \rfloor}{C,\ TP \vdash (R,\ M) \xrightarrow{\epsilon} (R',\ M')}$$

Lemma 3 proves that one step '$step_A$' of TS_A has a forward simulation relation with one step '$step_{HAVM}$' of the target machine TS_{HAVM}. Since the semantics of TS_{HAVM} encompasses rBPF and ARM, this proof features some interesting inter-operations: i/ Both machines start from the same rBPF state; ii/ When TS_{HAVM} executes its ALU rule using T^{ARM}, we prove a simulation between the rBPF state of TS_A and the ARM state of TS_{HAVM}; iii/ After completing the ALU rule, we prove that the `jited` code respects the ARM calling convention, and both machines achieve the same final rBPF state.

Lemma 3 (*TS_A simulates TS_{HAVM} in one step*). $\forall\ C\ BL\ TP\ t\ st\ st'$,

$Combiner\ BL = \lfloor TP \rfloor \wedge (step_A\ C\ BL)\ st\ t\ st' \rightarrow (step_{HAVM}\ C\ TP)\ st\ t\ st'$

From Lemma 2 and Lemma 3, we can prove that *JITCompiler* is correctness because the forward simulation in Lemma 3 can be reconstructed into a backward proof, and composed to a complete simulation proof from target to source.

5.3   JIT Vertical Refinement

The goal of this section is to design a verified and optimized *JITCompiler* C implementation. The refinement process is step-wise.

Removing Intermediate Representation. *JITCompiler* adopts a modular design for proof simplification. Expectedly, *JITCompiler* is memory-consuming and of low efficiency, as it takes additional memory to save analysis results (Figrue 3, middle). *JITCompiler$_{opt}$* instead operates as "find a rBPF `Alu`, *jit* immediately, and check the next one", with minimal resources and better performances.

Refining Data Structure. *JITCompiler$_{opt}$* refines data structures for optimization and synthesis requirements. For example, LD and ST are implemented as sorted ListSets, which cannot be directly mapped to a C type. We refine ListSet as a Coq Record type *regSet* that states which rBPF registers are modified (*e.g.*, flagged *true*). Then '$LD : regSet$' can be extracted as '$\_Bool\ LD[11]$' in C.

Record $regSet := \{\ f\_R0 : \textbf{bool}; \dots; f\_R10 : \textbf{bool}\ \}$

∂x *Refinement.* $JITCompiler_{\partial x}$ adopts an option-state monad to model effectful behaviours. For example, reading rBPF input binary p and writing the jited code into the pre-allocated list tp_bin with a proper offset in jit_state.

Record $jit\_state := \{ \ldots; p : list\ int64; \ldots; tp\_kv : \ldots; tp\_bin : list\ int \}$

We use ∂x to extract an executable C code $JITCompiler_C$ from $JITCompiler_{\partial x}$ using a global state where Coq lists are mapped to C pointers.

struct $jit\_state \{ \ldots; uint64\_t * p; \ldots; \ldots tp\_kv; uint32\_t * tp\_bin \}$

The end-to-end proof of the JIT compiler refinement proceeds in two steps: i/ from $JITCompiler$ to $JITCompiler_{\partial x}$, we prove that the refinement is correct (see Lemma 4) and, ii/ from $JITCompiler_{\partial x}$ to $JITCompiler_C$, we reuse the ∂x end-to-end verification workflow.

Lemma 4 (∂x-Refinement Correctness). *Suppose that $Compiler_{\partial x}$ is the refinement of $Compiler$. $Compiler$ and $Compiler_{\partial x}$ must generate the same result tp when they accept the same input program p.*

$$\forall\ p\ tp\ st_1,\ Compiler\ p = \lfloor tp \rfloor \wedge\ p\ \in\ st_1\ \wedge\ Allocate(tp)\ \in\ st_1\ \rightarrow$$
$$\exists\ st_2, Compiler_{\partial x}\ st_1 = \lfloor (unit, st_2) \rfloor \wedge\ p\ \in\ st_2\ \wedge\ tp\ \in\ st_2$$

where $x \in st$ if x is a field of state st and $Allocate(x)$ creates an empty list of the same size as x.

6   HAVM: A Hybrid Interpreter for rBPF

This section introduces the first (and fully-verified) hybrid rBPF interpreter HAVM, which interprets the composition of a rBPF binary script with jited ARM binary code.

HAVM Design. HAVM is formalized as a monadic function in Gallina. First, we highlight several fields in the monadic state of HAVM: 1/ $R.pc$ is the PC of rBPF register map R; 2/ tp_kv is the offset-pairs list; 3/ M is the CompCert memory including a special memory block jit_blk storing the jited code list.

Then, we extend the standard rBPF interpreter of [39] to implement HAVM. Its step function $hybrid\_step$ interprets different rBPF instructions. For rBPF Alu instructions, it directly calls jit_call, which is a monadic instantiation of our transition function T^{ARM}. For rBPF memory instructions, $hybrid\_step$ inherits the defensive semantics from the vanilla rBPF VM: the $check\_mem$ function guarantees the (verified) safety of all memory operations.

hybrid_step(hst) =
　　match $hst.p[hst.R.pc]$ **with** $\ |\ ../..$
　　$|\ Alu\ op\ dst\ src \Rightarrow$ jit_call($hst.tp\_kv[hst.R.pc]$, hst)
　　$|\ Mem\ dst\ src\ \ldots \Rightarrow$ **if** $check\_mem(\ldots)$ **then** $safe\_mem\_op$ **else** $\ldots$

Refinement Proof. The vertical refinement proof focuses on the proof from TS_{HAVM} to the monadic model $HAVM$ (see Lemma 5) where the simulation relation $st \sim hst$ is defined as $st.R = hst.R \wedge st.M = hst.M$.

Lemma 5 (Interpreter Refinement). $\forall\ st_1\ st_2\ t\ hst_1,\ st_1 \sim hst_1 \wedge$

$$step_{havm}\ st_1\ t\ st_2 \rightarrow \exists\ hst_2, hybrid\_step\ hst_1 = \lfloor (unit,\ hst_2) \rfloor \wedge st_2 \sim hst_2$$

C Implementation. We use ∂x to extract a verified C implementation $HAVM_C$. The C version jit_call_C is implemented by the verified '*bin_exec*' built-in function. This allows us to prove that the refinement from $HAVM_{\partial x}$ to $HAVM_C$: jit_call is equivalent to jit_call_C due to the verified CompCert built-in mechanism. The Non-Alu cases reuse most of the refinement proofs of [37].

7   Evaluation: Case Study of RIOT's Femto-Containers

We integrated our JIT compiler and the HAVM into the RIOT-OS to provide the same functionalities as the previous vanilla-rBPF module.

Implementation. The whole project, available on [36], consists of more than 70k lines of Coq code: The CompCert variant is completed by 6k lines and the rBPF-related transitive systems are approx. 1k lines long. The specification of the JIT compiler 1k lines large and our main proof effort, the JIT correctness theorem, demanded 45k proof code. The vertical refinement to monadic form contains the JIT part (about 4k lines) and the HAVM part (about 3k lines). From the monadic models to the final C implementation, about 10k lines proof code, we rely on the existing end-to-end verification workflow of [37].

Experiment. Our experiments are performed on a *nrf52840dk* development board which uses an Arm Cortex-M4 micro-controller, a popular 32-bit architecture (arm-v7m). The experimental benchmark code is compiled using the Arm GNU toolchain version 12.2. The compilation is using level 2 optimization enabled and the GCC option `-foptimize-sibling-calls` to optimize all tail-recursive calls and in turn, bound the stack usage. We also enable `-falign-functions=16` to reduce the performance variation caused by the instruction cache on the device. Lastly, we compare the HAVM implementation against both CertrBPF and Vanilla-rBPF using real-world benchmarks shown in Table 1.

The first four benchmarks test purely computational tasks, mainly consisting of rBPF `Alu` operations. Then, two special benchmarks comprise more memory operations but fewer `Alu` operations (worst cases for HAVM): the classical BPF socket buffer read/write and memory copy functions. Finally, we benchmark the performance of actual IoT data processing algorithms such as the Fletcher32 hash function or a bubble sort. We observed that, for all real-world benchmarks, HAVM improves performance because of the numerical acceleration JIT-feature.

Table 1. Execution time of real-world benchmarks

Interpreter	incr	square	bitswap	fib	sock_buf	memcpy	fletcher32	bsort
vanilla-rBPF	8.44 μs	8.50 μs	42.25 μs	94.38 μs	325 μs	887 μs	2283 μs	11722 μs
CertrBPF	5.13 μs	5.50 μs	34.75 μs	92.38 μs	300 μs	822 μs	1980 μs	10697 μs
HAVM	4.38 μs	4.37 μs	15.63 μs	51.75 μs	185 μs	588 μs	1196 μs	7120 μs

8   Lessons Learned

In this section, we clarify the prospects and limitations of the methodology proposed in the paper and its application to the rBPF JIT compiler.

Our Goal and Limitations. The methodology aims at proving the high-level specification of the JIT compiler correct and at extracting a verified C implementation directly from this specification, using refinement. As mentioned in Sect. 7, our methodology requires a lot of manual proof effort.

Regarding its application to rBPF JIT compilation, our JIT compiler is, more precisely, a hardware accelerator for numerical operations: it only translates a subset of rBPF ISA, the ALU instructions, into ARM binary. We made this choice as the other memory operations of rBPF must be given a defensive semantics to meet the requirement of (memory) fault isolation. This defensive code is large and, if jitted, would significantly increase the binary code size for a limited performance gain.

Adaptability: Move to Other Targets. Should we consider instantiating our methodology and proofs to another target architecture, say RISC-V, then most of the current JIT design and proof techniques could be reused. The only modification would regard platform-dependent elements: the semantics model would need to be based on CompCert/RISC-V, and the JIT's spilling and reloading stages would have to be modified to match RISC-V's calling conventions.

Adaptability: Turn to Linux eBPF. However, our ARM-ALU JIT compiler may not directly be extended to a full-fledged Linux eBPF JIT compiler, as eBPF doesn't have a defensive semantics for memory operations. Instead, Linux' eBPF uses a sophisticated verifier to validate memory operations, which would not fit the memory resources onboard IoT devices, as it is larger than 20k lines of C code, and be an end-to-end verification project in its own rights.

Finally, this paper does not discuss JIT optimizations, unlike modern JIT compilers, which have sophisticated optimization strategies. Proving their correctness in Coq would also be a non-trivial verification task.

However, we believe that these two last limitations could be relaxed once we complete a fully verified "JIT-all" compiler for rBPF. Essentially, the last mile of our journey toward a complete JIT compiler would be one capable of calling a verified ARM binary implementation of the (verified) defensive "*check_mem*" function and to embed it in the JITed code block. This would essentially amount to verifying an adhoc linker between the JITed code and the embedded *check_mem*'s binary code.

9   Related Works

Verified Compilers, OS kernels, and VMs. There is a rich literature on verified software design. Verified compilers include CompCert [17] (from C to assembly) and CakeML [26] (from ML to binary), etc. Verified OS kernels comprise for instance SeL4 [15] (L4 microkernel) and CertiKOS [11] (multi-cores). Verified virtual machines have been developed for richer scripting languages, such as Java VM [21], JavaScript VM [7], and Ethereum [40].

Our work build upon CertrBPF [37], the first verified eBPF VM for RIOT providing a service of so-called femto-containers [39]. CertrBPF provides an end-to-end verification workflow from monadic Gallina models to executable C implementation. However, it has no JIT compiler. The main novelty presented in this paper is the first and fully verified JIT compiler for RIOT rBPF, reusing and enriching the CompCert and CertrBPF projects.

Verified JITs. Barriere et al. [3,4] extend the CompCert backend to support general-purpose JIT compilation. They adopt an additional memory model for defining the behaviours of `jited` code and require unverified C glue code to obtain a runnable JIT compiler. Wang et al. [35] extend CompCert to extract a verified JIT compiler *Jitk* from classic BPF (not eBPF) to assembly code in OCaml. All aforementioned extensions rely on unverified TCB consisting of the OCaml runtime, an assembler, and a linker, which are not suitable for a security-critical and resources-limited OS kernel like RIOT. Myreen [25] proves a JIT compiler from a simple stack-based bytecode language to x86 in the HOL4 proof assistant. Van Geffen et al. [10] present an optimized JIT compiler for Linux eBPF, embedded with automated static analysis. Nelson et al. [28,34] develop the domain-specific language *Jitterbug* to write JITs and prove them correct.

All the above approaches only verify the JIT correctness in a high-level abstract model, but do not produce a verified C implementation which is vital for, e.g., field deployment on networks of micro-controllers (IoT) or embedded devices. This paper fills this verification gap: the JIT correctness proof is conducted over an abstract specification in Coq and then propagated down to a concrete C implementation of the JIT compiler.

End-to-End Verification. There are various solutions for extracting executable C code from high-level programs, but most of them are not compatible with our goal: *i.e.,* a verified JIT C implementation running the real-time OS kernel deployed on IoT devices. Some of them are unverified, *e.g.,* KaRaMeL [30] (from F* to C) and Codegen [33] (from Gallina to C). Some require a garbage collector, *e.g.,* CertiCoq [1] and Œuf [24] (from Gallina to C) or CakeML (from Standard ML to binary). The Cogent framework [31] (from Cogent to Isabelle/HOL and C) is verified but depends on calls to foreign C functions to perform loops, and Rupicola [29] (from Gallina to bedrock2, a C-like language) has only been tested for small algorithms. The end-to-end refinement method proposed in the paper instead reuses the existing verification workflow and proof efforts of CertrBPF and CompCert to provide the first, fully verified and resource-efficient, hybrid virtual machine, HAVM.

10   Conclusion

As use-cases for eBPF virtual machines multiply, their applicability encompasses not only PCs and servers but also low-power devices based on microcontrollers. In this context, we presented an end-to-end design, proof, and synthesis methodology to bring the first BPF Just-in-Time compiler tailored to the hardware and resources constraints of popular low-power microcontroller architectures, proven correct end-to-end using the proof assistant Coq. We combined our proven JIT implementation with the BPF interpreter provided in the RIOT operating system to create a hybrid virtual machine, HAVM: a defensive, kernel-privileged service capable of accelerating numerical tasks at runtime using partial JIT compilation. Benchmarking HAVM in practice on Cortex-M microcontrollers show that HAVM achieves significant execution speed improvements compared to prior works.

We are carrying on designing a fully verified JIT-all compiler for RIOT that translates all rBPF instructions into binary. One of the most challenging aspect of this project is to link and embed tailor-optimized *check_mem* algorithms into jited code (using loop unrolling, partial evaluation).

References

1. Anand, A., et al.: CertiCoq : a verified compiler for Coq. In: CoqPL (2017)
2. Baccelli, E., et al.: RIOT: an open source operating system for low-end embedded devices in the IoT. IoT-J **5**(6), 4428–4440 (2018)
3. Barrière, A., Blazy, S., Flückiger, O., Pichardie, D., Vitek, J.: Formally verified speculation and deoptimization in a JIT compiler. Proc. ACM Program. Lang. **5**(POPL), 26 (2021). https://doi.org/10.1145/3434327
4. Barrière, A., Blazy, S., Pichardie, D.: Formally verified native code generation in an effectful JIT: Turning the CompCert backend into a formally verified JIT compiler. Proc. ACM Program. Lang. **7**(POPL), 249–277 (2023). https://doi.org/10.1145/3571202
5. Bertot, Y., Castéran, P.: Interactive theorem proving and program development: Coq'Art: the calculus of inductive constructions. Springer (2013)
6. Bratman, H.: A alternate form of the "uncol diagram". Commun. ACM **4**(3), 142 (1961). https://doi.org/10.1145/366199.366249
7. Desharnais, M., Brunthaler, S.: Towards efficient and verified virtual machines for dynamic languages. In: CPP, pp. 61–75. ACM (2021)
8. Dunchev, C., Guidi, F., Sacerdoti Coen, C., Tassi, E.: ELPI: fast, embeddable, λprolog interpreter. In: Davis, M., Fehnker, A., McIver, A., Voronkov, A. (eds.) LPAR 2015. LNCS, vol. 9450, pp. 460–468. Springer, Heidelberg (2015). https://doi.org/10.1007/978-3-662-48899-7_32
9. Fleming, M.: A Thorough Introduction to eBPF. Linux Weekly News (2017)

10. Van Geffen, J., Nelson, L., Dillig, I., Wang, X., Torlak, E.: Synthesizing JIT compilers for in-kernel DSLs. In: Lahiri, S.K., Wang, C. (eds.) CAV 2020. LNCS, vol. 12225, pp. 564–586. Springer, Cham (2020). https://doi.org/10.1007/978-3-030-53291-8_29

11. Gu, R., et al.: CertiKOS: an extensible architecture for building certified concurrent OS kernels. In: OSDI, pp. 653–669. USENIX (2016)

12. Hutchings, B.: Executing arbitrary code within the kernel (2021). https://cve.mitre.org/cgi-bin/cvename.cgi?name=CVE-2021-29154

13. Jomaa, N., Torrini, P., Nowak, D., Grimaud, G., Hym, S.: Proof-oriented design of a separation kernel with minimal trusted computing base. In: AVOCS. vol. 76. Electronic Communications of the EASST (2018)

14. Keshri, R.: confidentiality problem (2021). https://cve.mitre.org/cgi-bin/cvename.cgi?name=CVE-2021-20320

15. Klein, G., et al.: seL4: formal verification of an OS kernel. In: SOSP, pp. 207. ACM Press (2009)

16. Krysiuk, P.: Linux kernel vulnerability in NetApp products (2021). https://cve.mitre.org/cgi-bin/cvename.cgi?name=CVE-2021-38300

17. Leroy, X.: Formal verification of a realistic compiler. Commun. ACM **52**(7), 107–115 (2009)

18. Leroy, X., Appel, A.W., Blazy, S., Stewart, G.: The CompCert Memory Model, Version 2. Research Report RR-7987, INRIA (2012)

19. Leroy, X., Blazy, S.: Formal verification of a C-like memory model and its uses for verifying program transformations. JAR **41**(1), 1–31 (2008)

20. Letouzey, P.: A new extraction for Coq. In: Geuvers, H., Wiedijk, F. (eds.) TYPES 2002. LNCS, vol. 2646, pp. 200–219. Springer, Heidelberg (2003). https://doi.org/10.1007/3-540-39185-1_12

21. Lochbihler, A.: A Machine-Checked, Type-Safe Model of Java Concurrency: Language, Virtual Machine, Memory Model, and Verified Compiler. Ph.D. thesis, Karlsruhe Institute of Technology (2012)

22. McCanne, S., Jacobson, V.: The BSD Packet Filter: A New Architecture for User-level Packet Capture. In: Usenix Winter Conference. vol. 46, pp. 259–270. USENIX (1993)

23. Mogul, J., Rashid, R., Accetta, M.: The packer filter: an efficient mechanism for user-level network code. In: SOSP, pp. 39–51. ACM (1987)

24. Mullen, E., Pernsteiner, S., Wilcox, J.R., Tatlock, Z., Grossman, D.: Œuf: minimizing the Coq extraction TCB. In: CPP, pp. 172–185. ACM (2018)

25. Myreen, M.O.: Verified just-in-time compiler on x86. In: POPL, pp. 107–118. ACM (2010)

26. Myreen, M.O., Owens, S.: Proof-producing synthesis of ml from higher-order logic. In: Proceedings of the 17th ACM SIGPLAN International Conference on Functional Programming, pp. 115–126. ICFP '12, Association for Computing Machinery, New York, NY, USA (2012). https://doi.org/10.1145/2364527.2364545

27. Nelson, L., Geffen, J.V., Torlak, E., Wang, X.: Specification and verification in the field: applying formal methods to BPF just-in-time compilers in the Linux kernel. In: OSDI, pp. 41–61. USENIX (2020)

28. Nelson, L., Geffen, J.V., Torlak, E., Wang, X.: Specification and verification in the field: Applying formal methods to BPF just-in-time compilers in the Linux kernel. In: 14th USENIX Symposium on Operating Systems Design and Implementation (OSDI 20), pp. 41–61. USENIX Association, USA (2020)

29. Pit-Claudel, C., Philipoom, J., Jamner, D., Erbsen, A., Chlipala, A.: Relational compilation for performance-critical applications. In: PLDI. ACM (2022)

30. Protzenko, J., et al.: Verified low-level programming embedded in F*. PACMPL **1**(ICFP), 17:1–17:29 (2017). https://doi.org/10.1145/3110261
31. Rizkallah, C., et al.: A framework for the automatic formal verification of refinement from COGENT to C. In: Blanchette, J.C., Merz, S. (eds.) ITP 2016. LNCS, vol. 9807, pp. 323–340. Springer, Cham (2016). https://doi.org/10.1007/978-3-319-43144-4_20
32. Sozeau, M., Boulier, S., Forster, Y., Tabareau, N., Winterhalter, T.: Coq coq correct! verification of type checking and erasure for coq, in Coq. Proc. ACM Program. Lang. **4**(POPL), 8:1–8:28 (2020). https://doi.org/10.1145/3371076
33. Tanaka, A.: Coq to C translation with partial evaluation. In: PEPM@POPL, pp. 14–31. ACM (2021)
34. Van Geffen, J., Nelson, L., Dillig, I., Wang, X., Torlak, E.: Synthesizing JIT compilers for in-kernel DSLs. In: Lahiri, S.K., Wang, C. (eds.) CAV 2020. LNCS, vol. 12225, pp. 564–586. Springer, Cham (2020). https://doi.org/10.1007/978-3-030-53291-8_29
35. Wang, X., Lazar, D., Zeldovich, N., Chlipala, A., Tatlock, Z.: Jitk: a trustworthy In-Kernel interpreter infrastructure. In: 11th USENIX Symposium on Operating Systems Design and Implementation (OSDI 14), pp. 33–47. USENIX Association, Broomfield, CO (2014)
36. YUAN, S.: CertrBPF-JIT: A verified JIT for RIOT-OS rBPF (2024). https://gitlab.inria.fr/x-SYuan/certrbpf-jit/-/tree/CAV24-AE
37. Yuan, S., Besson, F., Talpin, J.P., Hym, S., Zandberg, K., Baccelli, E.: End-to-end mechanized proof of an eBPF virtual machine for micro-controllers. In: Shoham, S., Vizel, Y. (eds.) Computer Aided Verification, pp. 293–316. Springer International Publishing, Cham (2022). https://doi.org/10.1007/978-3-031-13188-2_15
38. Zandberg, K., Baccelli, E.: Minimal virtual machines on IoT microcontrollers: the case of Berkeley Packet Filters with rBPF. In: PEMWN, pp. 1–6. IEEE (2020)
39. Zandberg, K., Baccelli, E., Yuan, S., Besson, F., Talpin, J.P.: Femto-containers: lightweight virtualization and fault isolation for small software functions on low-power IoT microcontrollers. In: Proceedings of the 23rd ACM/IFIP International Middleware Conference, pp. 161–173. Middleware '22, Association for Computing Machinery, New York, NY, USA (2022). https://doi.org/10.1145/3528535.3565242
40. Zhang, X., Li, Y., Sun, M.: Towards a formally verified EVM in production environment. In: Bliudze, S., Bocchi, L. (eds.) COORDINATION 2020. LNCS, vol. 12134, pp. 341–349. Springer, Cham (2020). https://doi.org/10.1007/978-3-030-50029-0_21

A Framework for Debugging Automated Program Verification Proofs via Proof Actions

Chanhee Cho$^{(\boxtimes)}$, Yi Zhou, Jay Bosamiya, and Bryan Parno

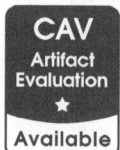

Carnegie Mellon University, Pittsburgh, PA, USA
{chanheec,yeet,jaybosamiya,parno}@cmu.edu

Abstract. Many program verification tools provide automation via SMT solvers, allowing them to automatically discharge many proofs. However, when a proof fails, it can be hard to understand why it failed or how to fix it. The main feedback the developer receives is simply the verification result (i.e., success or failure), with no visibility into the solver's internal state. To assist developers using such tools, we introduce ProofPlumber, a novel and extensible *proof-action* framework for understanding and debugging proof failures. Proof actions act on the developer's *source-level proofs* (e.g., assertions and lemmas) to determine why they failed and potentially suggest remedies. We evaluate ProofPlumber by writing a collection of proof actions that capture common proof debugging practices. We produce 17 proof actions, each only 29–177 lines of code.

1 Introduction

Software verification tools typically fall into two camps. The first camp relies on interactive proof assistants, such as Coq [1] or Lean [2]. These proof assistants show the developer the current *proof state*; i.e., the proof goal and all hypotheses in scope. Developers then complete a proof by invoking tactics (user-developed programs, e.g., in Ltac [3], that manipulate the proof state), viewing the effects of the tactics in sophisticated IDEs. By default, these tools typically provide less automation and generally require the developer to manipulate the proof at a low-level. Some tactics (e.g., `sledgehammer` [4–6] or `crush` [7]) provide considerably more automation, but as a result, their strengths and weaknesses tend to match those of tools in the second camp.

In the second camp are languages and tools designed specifically for automated program verification, e.g., Spec# [8], ESC/Java [9], VCC [10], Dafny [11], F* [12], Viper-based languages [13–16], and Verus [17]. With these tools, developers add specifications to their programs, and the tool attempts to automatically prove (potentially with help from developer-provided *source-level* assertions/lemmas) that the spec holds. Typically this is done by reducing the problem to a logical formula (e.g., via a weakest precondition calculus [18]) that can be checked by an SMT solver [19–23]. Because SMT solvers can discharge many proofs fully automatically, they enable developers to take large, logical steps.

© The Author(s) 2024
A. Gurfinkel and V. Ganesh (Eds.): CAV 2024, LNCS 14681, pp. 348–361, 2024.
https://doi.org/10.1007/978-3-031-65627-9_17

However, when a proof fails, it can be hard to understand why it failed or how to fix it. The main feedback the developer receives is simply the verification result (i.e., success or failure), with no visibility into the solver's internal state. Exposing such internal state in a useful manner is challenging, since an SMT solver might generate millions of terms during its proof search. Hence, unlike in interactive proof assistants, it can be difficult to answer questions like "What propositions has the solver proven at this program point?" or "What additional facts are needed for the solver to complete the proof?". Indeed, because verification is generally undecidable, the developer does not even know initially if the proof failed because it is invalid, or because the tool's automation is incomplete. As a result, when developing verified code in automated program verification languages, significant time goes into trying to figure out why the code is failing to verify and what needs to be done to address the failure.

To assist developers using automated program verification techniques, we introduce ProofPlumber, a novel *proof-action* framework for understanding and debugging proof failures. Unlike tactics, which are primarily used to manipulate (low-level) *proof state*, proof actions act on the developer's *source-level proofs* (e.g., assertions and lemmas) to determine why they have failed and potentially suggest remedies. ProofPlumber comes prepackaged with a set of proof actions that automate a wide variety of standard proof debugging techniques, and it is also fully extensible, so that as developers devise new or project-specific techniques, those can be automated as well. Ultimately, we hope that ProofPlumber-style proof actions will reduce tedium for experienced developers and help bootstrap developers just starting to write verified programs.

We implement ProofPlumber[1] in the context of Verus [17], a verification-oriented language for Rust [24,25]. ProofPlumber offers three categories of APIs (with a total of 36 API calls) for manipulating source-level Verus proofs. In Sect. 4, we demonstrate ProofPlumber's expressivity and extensibility by implementing a collection of 17 proof actions, each of which requires only 29–177 lines of code. We also show that ProofPlumber reduces Verus' trusted computing base (TCB).

2 Proof Debugging Considered Painful

2.1 Background on Automated Program Verification in Verus

ProofPlumber is implemented for Verus [17], an SMT-based verification language for formally verifying Rust programs. The basic syntax of Verus, shown in Fig. 1, is similar to that used in most languages for automated program verification. The **requires** clause on line 8 describes the function's precondition, and the **ensures** clause on line 9 describes its postcondition. The **assert** statement on line 20 is a static check performed by an SMT solver; when a proof fails, proof engineers add assertions to a program to extract information from the solver.

---

[1] ProofPlumber's code and proof actions are available as open source at https://github.com/verus-lang/verus-analyzer.

2.2 Examples of Proof Debugging

Today, developers typically debug their failed proofs by manually adding source-level assertions to their program. Such an assertion has no effect on the executable code; instead, it breaks the proof into smaller steps, and it indirectly queries the solver's internal state, extracting two pieces of information: (1) Is the code's precondition sufficient to prove the new assertion? (determined by whether the assertion verifies); and (2) Is the assertion sufficient to prove the code's postcondition? (determined by whether the postcondition now verifies).

Effective assertion choice and placement is a key part of the proof engineering process. Choosing the wrong assertion or inserting it in the wrong place sheds little light on the cause of the proof failure. Further, a single assertion is seldom sufficient; instead, multiple iterations are required to further break down the proof goal, until either the proof succeeds, or the developer determines the key missing facts the prover needs (or finds a bug in the code).

Unfortunately, assertion-based debugging is an arcane art. Beginners find it hard to understand what assertions to add, where to add them, and how to use them to break down the proof goal. We frequently see beginners become stuck randomly adding assertions that do not improve their understanding of the proof failure. Even for experts, assertion-based debugging is tedious and error prone.

We illustrate the challenges with two simplified examples. In real verification projects, the properties involved are much larger and more complex, making the manual manipulation of source-level assertions a remarkably laborious, error-prone process. While our examples are based on Verus, manipulating source-level proofs is the standard debugging technique in automated program verification; see, for example, Dafny's manual assertion guide [26], F*'s guide [27], and various proof debugging examples on StackOverflow [28, 29].

The left side of Fig. 1 presents a failing proof for `fibo_is_monotonic`; the postcondition does not hold. An experienced proof engineer typically starts by

```
 1  spec fn fibo(n: nat) -> nat {
 2    if n == 0 { 0 } else if n == 1 { 1 }      22  // second attempt
 3    else { fibo(n - 2) + fibo(n - 1) }        23  proof fn fibo_is_monotonic(i: nat, j: nat)
 4  }                                           24    requires i <= j,
 5                                              25    ensures fibo(i) <= fibo(j),
 6  // first attempt                            26  {
 7  proof fn fibo_is_monotonic(i: nat, j: nat)  27    if i < 2 && j < 2 {
 8    requires i <= j,                          28      assert(fibo(i) <= fibo(j)); // succeeds
 9    ensures fibo(i) <= fibo(j), // fails      29    } else if i == j {
10  {                                           30      assert(fibo(i) <= fibo(j)); // succeeds
11    if i < 2 && j < 2 {}                      31    } else if i == j - 1 {
12    else if i == j {}                         32      fibo_is_monotonic(i, j - 1);
13    else if i == j - 1 {                      33      assert(fibo(i) <= fibo(j)); // fails
14      fibo_is_monotonic(i, j - 1);            34    } else {
15    } else {                                  35      fibo_is_monotonic(i, j - 1);
16      fibo_is_monotonic(i, j - 1);            36      fibo_is_monotonic(i, j - 2);
17      fibo_is_monotonic(i, j - 2);            37      assert(fibo(i) <= fibo(j)); // succeeds
18    }                                         38    }
19    // Debug by copying the failing ensures   39    assert(fibo(i) <= fibo(j)); // fails
20    assert(fibo(i) <= fibo(j)); // fails      40  }
21  }
```

Fig. 1. "Stepping up" an assertion to identify the failing case.

copying the failing postcondition to the end of the function, so that they can manipulate it for further debugging. When that assertion fails (as expected), the proof engineer still does not know which of the four branches is causing the proof failure, so she then copies the same assertion into each branch, as shown on the right side of the figure. When she calls the verifier again, she observes that the assertion in the third branch fails and can start fixing it.

```
1  // easy proof for unbounded integers          18  // second attempt for bounded integers
2  proof fn mul_inequality(x:int, y:int, z:int)   19  proof fn mul_inequality_bounded(
3    requires x <= y && 0 < z                     20    x: int, xbound: int, y: int, ybound: int)
4    ensures x * z <= y * z                       21    requires x < xbound && y < ybound
5  {...}                                          22            && 0 <= x && 0 <= y
6                                                 23    ensures x * y <= (xbound - 1) * (ybound - 1)
7  // first attempt for bounded integers          24  {
8  proof fn mul_inequality_bounded(               25    // Step #2: split the assertion into pieces
9    x: int, xbound: int, y: int, ybound: int)    26    assert(x <= xbound - 1); // succeeds
10   requires x < xbound && y < ybound            27    assert(0 < y);           // fails
11           && 0 <= x && 0 <= y                  28    // Step #1: inline precondition for first call
12   ensures x * y <= (xbound - 1) * (ybound - 1) 29    assert(x <= xbound -1 && 0 < y); // fails
13 {                                              30    mul_inequality(x, xbound-1, y);
14   // precondition fails for both calls         31    mul_inequality(y, ybound-1, xbound-1);
15   mul_inequality(x, xbound-1, y);              32  }
16   mul_inequality(y, ybound-1, xbound-1);
17 }
```

Fig. 2. Inlining a precondition.

Figure 2 illustrates how proof engineers start debugging when the verifier tells them that a function's precondition fails to hold. In this example, after proving `mul_inequality` for unbounded integers, the proof engineer tries to prove a similar property (`mul_inequality_bounded`) for bounded integers. After drafting the proof on the left side, she learns that the precondition on line 3 fails at both callsites (lines 15 and 16). She then copies over the failing precondition, and replaces the lemma's formal arguments with the concrete values at the call site, as in line 29. When she runs the verifier again, the added assertion fails as expected. To learn which part of the conjunction fails, she splits the assertion into two separate assertions (lines 26 and 27). After running the verifier yet again, the proof engineer identifies the cause of the proof failure: 0 < z does not hold.

2.3   Automated Proof Debugging with Proof Actions

We observe that much of the effort of proof debugging is consumed by steps that can clearly be automated. We therefore propose *proof actions*,[2] which can automatically transform a program and its proof. With proof actions, we can capture in an automated manner the existing proof-debugging practices used by experts. This reduces their tedium and transcription errors, and it enables the "wisdom" that these practices represent to be easily handed to new developers.

---

[2] Inspired by the code actions supported by the Language Server Protocol (LSP) [30].

For example, the Sect. 2.2 examples can be automated with these proof actions:

Weakest Precondition Step. This proof action moves an assertion above the statement that precedes it: in the case of a branch statement, it moves the assertion to the end of each of the branch statements. More generally, the proof action implements the rules of the weakest precondition calculus.

Insert Failing Preconditions. When preconditions cannot be established at a call site, this proof action inlines the precondition in the caller's context.

2.4   Challenges with Automatic Code Transformation

Automating proof debugging through proof actions is achievable but challenging, since it is hard to write programs that automatically and correctly transform programs [31–33]. Such transformations require information about the program's control flow, the types of expressions, and the definitions of variables, functions, and types. To act on this knowledge, we need easy and intuitive ways to manipulate source-level proofs. Finally, to understand proof failures, we need to interact with the verifier in an automated way. Existing program verifiers lack support for one or more of these features.

Furthermore, providing a fixed set of proof actions is insufficient. Since program verification is still rapidly evolving, proof engineers will need to add new proof actions. Moreover, different verification projects come with different proof styles, and hence each project may benefit from project-specific proof actions.

3   ProofPlumber: An Extensible Proof Action Framework

We start with the design of ProofPlumber's API, which provides the functionality for developing proof actions. We then discuss the API's implementation.

At a high level, ProofPlumber provides APIs that allow a proof action to **(1)** lookup context information (e.g., types and definitions), **(2)** manipulate the source-level program and proof, and **(3)** interact with the verifier. Proof actions can be exposed to proof engineers in various ways; our current implementation does so via the engineer's editor (e.g., Visual Studio Code), where she can, say, click on a failing assertion to invoke an appropriate proof action.

Figure 3 illustrates the workflow of a proof action built using ProofPlumber. Once the program text from the editor is parsed, it is lifted to a simplified form, and type-checked. The lifted and type-checked version of the program text is available to proof actions. After a proof action manipulates the proof using ProofPlumber's APIs, it is then pretty printed into the proof engineer's editor.

3.1   ProofPlumber's API Design

Fundamentally, a proof action is a procedure that edits the user's source program based on results from type checking and verification. The corresponding data structures in ProofPlumber are: **(a)** Transformation-Oriented Syntax

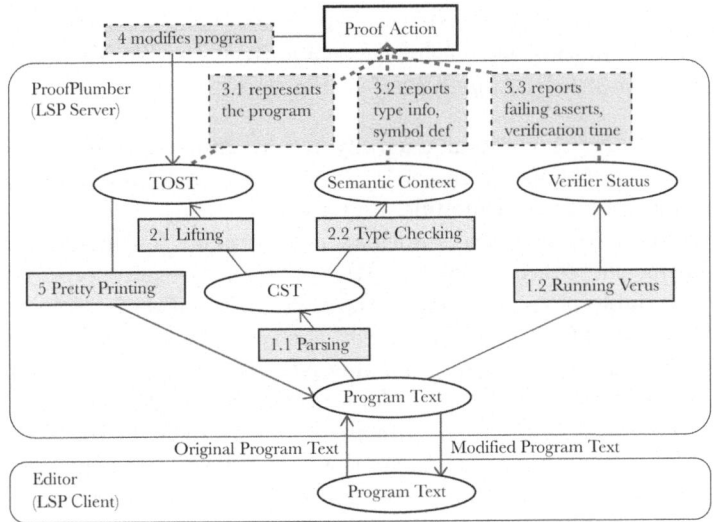

Fig. 3. Overview of ProofPlumber.

Tree (TOST) nodes representing the user's source code; **(b)** the Context, which contains additional source-level information such as types and definitions; and **(c)** the Verus verifier, which contains information about failing assertions.

The TOST is the core data structure that represents the source program. It is an abstract syntax tree, with each language construct represented as an **enum** (e.g., **assertExpr, blockExpr**). Since the TOST is not a concrete syntax tree (CST), it omits semantically irrelevant syntactic details. The TOST thus allows easy manipulation of the user's source code, ignoring trivialities like whitespace. The TOST offers the following APIs (corresponding to *3.1 represents the program, 4. modifies program,* and *5. Pretty printing* in Fig. 3).

- *Traverse/Edit.* A TOST node allows direct access to its children. For example, **assertExpr** has a field **expr** that contains the asserted expression, which can be accessed and modified directly. Additionally, ProofPlumber offers a visitor pattern for recursively filtering or transforming TOST nodes.
- *Create.* When developing proof actions, it is often necessary to create new TOST nodes. While this can be done through each node's constructor, it can be tedious for large expressions; e.g., consider the expression "x + y * 4", which needs five constructor calls. To simplify this process, ProofPlumber provides an option to parse user-provided text into a TOST node.
- *Concretize.* When the proof action is done modifying the TOST, it needs to apply the changes to the program. Since the TOST is abstract, ProofPlumber provides an API to convert it back to a CST, hiding the details of the conversion.

Context is another core data structure for writing a proof action. It contains the following information not easily accessible from the TOST (corresponding to *3.2 reports type info and symbol def* in Fig. 3):

- *Node in Scope.* A proof action generally acts within a specific scope indicated by the user; e.g., the user's cursor location may identify an expression that is inside a function, a file, a module, and a crate.
- *Type.* Needless to say, type information is crucial for understanding and manipulating the source program. Rust does not require type annotations for every variable or expression, so the type information is often unavailable at the source (or TOST) level. However, the type of every expression has been computed by the type checker, and this API provides that information.
- *Definition.* It is often necessary to look up the full definition for an identifier. For example, when case matching on an enum variable `c:Color`, it is necessary to look up the variants of `Color`. At the TOST level, the definition of `Color` may be in a different module or even a different crate than the occurrence of c. This API provides the definition of an identifier, which can be a name for a struct, an enum, a function, etc.

The Verifier (Verus driver) is the last core data structure. It allows the proof action to interact with the verifier. A proof action does not have to finish all of its rewriting in one pass; instead, it can make a change, invoke the verifier, and then continue rewriting based on the verifier's response. Corresponding to *3.3 reports failing asserts and verification time* in Fig. 3, this structure provides:

- *Errors.* The list of failing assertions, preconditions, and postconditions.
- *Time.* It often helps to know how long verification takes, since proofs with shorter verification time are often more robust [34]. If a proof takes too long, the proof action may choose a more efficient one.

3.2   ProofPlumber's Implementation

As Verus [17] is based on Rust, ProofPlumber extends rust-analyzer [35], the official language server for Rust, to understand Verus. As with rust-analyzer, ProofPlumber adheres to the Language Server Protocol (LSP) [30]. In turn, proof actions developed with ProofPlumber are compatible with editors that implement the client-side of the LSP. We construct our *Context* APIs by extending rust-analyzer's type checking implementation (*2.2 Type Checking* in Fig. 3).

In our implementation, we have extended rust-analyzer's grammar and parser to obtain the Verus CST (*1.1 Parsing* in Fig. 3). We then lift the CST to a TOST, eliminating details like whitespace (*2.1 Lifting* in Figrue 3). After a proof action manipulates a TOST node using ProofPlumber's APIs, our pretty printer restores the TOST to a concrete program (*5 Pretty Printing* in Figrue 3).

4 Evaluation

We evaluate ProofPlumber with the following three research questions.

- **RQ1**: Are proof actions expressive enough for real proof debugging tasks?
- **RQ2**: Does ProofPlumber make it easy to write proof actions?
- **RQ3**: Can proof actions reduce the TCB of automated program verifiers?

4.1 RQ1: Are proof actions expressive enough?

We demonstrate ProofPlumber's expressivity by writing 17 proof actions, divided into two groups: **(1)** proof actions inspired by Dafny's reference for verification debugging [26], which suggests a set of manual rewrites to perform while debugging proofs, and **(2)** proof actions distilled from the experiences of Verus developers. While these groups were developed independently, they overlap, as Dafny and Verus share proof styles common to automated program verification tools.

Figure 4 presents the list of proof actions and the ProofPlumber features used by each. As analyzed in detail below, we observe that ProofPlumber's APIs are expressive enough to implement all of the suggested rewrites from Dafny, excluding the ones that are not applicable to Verus or that are inherently

	Proof Actions	Group	#lines	Verif. Errors	Verif. Time	TOST R/W	TOST Conc.	TOST Create	Lookup Node	Lookup Type	Lookup Defn.
1	Split Implication in Ensures	Dafny	48			✓	✓		✓		
2	Split Smaller or Equal to	Dafny	70			✓	✓		✓		
3	Convert Implication into If	Dafny	40			✓	✓		✓		
4	Introduce Assert Forall	Dafny	42			✓	✓		✓		
5	Introduce Assert Forall Implies	Dafny	57			✓	✓		✓		
6	Introduce Assume False	Dafny	30			✓	✓	✓	✓		
7	Reveal Opaque Function above	Dafny	45			✓	✓		✓		✓
8	Reveal Opaque Function in block	Dafny	45			✓	✓		✓		✓
9	Add Seq "in-bounds" predicate	Dafny	54			✓	✓		✓	✓	✓
10	Insert Assert-By Block	Dafny	29			✓	✓		✓		
11	Weakest Precondition Step	Verus/Dafny(5)	177			✓	✓		✓	✓	✓
12	Decompose Failing Assertion	Verus/Dafny(1)	88	✓		✓	✓		✓	✓	✓
13	Insert Failing Postconditions	Verus	64	✓		✓	✓		✓		
14	Insert Failing Preconditions	Verus	45	✓		✓	✓		✓	✓	✓
15	Introduce Matching Assertions	Verus	84	✓		✓	✓	✓	✓	✓	✓
16	Remove Redundant Assertions	Verus	74	✓	✓	✓	✓		✓		
17	Apply Induction	Verus	133	✓	✓	✓	✓	✓	✓	✓	✓

Fig. 4. For each proof action, we report the source lines of code to implement it, and the ProofPlumber features it uses. For proof actions that overlap in both groups, the number of corresponding Dafny rewrite suggestions is in parentheses; e.g., five of Dafny's rewrite suggestions are special cases of the *Weakest Precondition Step*. *Weakest Precondition Step* and *Decompose Failing Assertion* generalize their Dafny counterparts.

manual (see Sect. 5 for details). Furthermore, ProofPlumber provides enough expressivity to implement eight distinct proof actions that automate the routine efforts of Verus developers. Figure 4 also demonstrates that all of ProofPlumber's features are utilized to implement these proof actions.

Proof Actions Inspired by Dafny. Dafny provides 29 suggested rewrites for manual proof debugging [26], of which we have implemented 16 as proof actions. We exclude the other 13 rewrites, as 9 of them are not applicable to Verus, and 4 are inherently manual (Sect. 5). Of the 16 suggested Dafny rewrites we implemented, 12 are purely syntactic. Among the remaining 4, the first (9 in Fig. 4) automatically adds an "in-bounds" predicate for a sequence's index; it uses the Lookup Type API to decide if an assertion contains a sequence. The second rewrite (one of the five in *Weakest Precondition Step* – rewrite 11 in Fig. 4) adds the precondition and postcondition of a function at the callsite. The last two (7 and 8 in Figrue 4) are related to reveal, which is used to control the visibility of a function to the verifier. These automatic rewrites lookup the function's definition and the function's "proof visibility".

Proof Actions for Verus. We implemented 7 additional proof actions to automate routine proof engineering tasks in Verus. We discuss *Weakest Precondition Step* and *Insert Failing Preconditions* in Sect. 2.3, and the rest below.

Decompose Failing Assertion. When a complex assertion fails to verify, it is not always obvious which portion of the failing expression is responsible. This proof action automates the process of decomposing and isolating the failing sub-formulas. We discuss it in more detail in Sect. 4.2.

Insert Failing Postconditions. A common proof failure is that a procedure's postconditions cannot be established. Since there can be multiple postconditions and multiple exit points (e.g., due to an early return), developers often employ a tedious manual process to pinpoint the failing conditions at each exit point. This proof action automatically adds the failing postcondition(s) at each exit.

Introduce Match Case Assertions. A special case of assertion decomposition is when the assertion is about an enum. Today, the developer tediously writes a match statement for the enum and then adds assertions to each case to identify where the problem lies. This proof action emits a boilerplate match statement for the enum, but only presents the failing variants.

Remove Redundant Assertions. During proof debugging, to understand the solver's state, proof engineers typically introduce multiple assertions, most of which are redundant (i.e., they help the human, not the verification). Hence, after debugging a proof, to maintain source code readability, developers manually remove these redundant assertions. This proof action mechanizes the process.

Apply Induction. If the selected variable is a natural number or an abstract datatype, this proof action generates the boilerplate code for an inductive proof, including the base and inductive cases. When the selected variable is an enum, it introduces a match statement with an empty proof block for each variant, generating the recursive call to the lemma when the variant is defined recursively.

4.2 RQ2: Does ProofPlumber make it easy to write proof actions?

Figrue 4 shows that each proof action from Sect. 4.1 needs only 29–177 lines of code. To qualitatively illustrate how ProofPlumber's API enables the easy creation of a proof action, Figrue 5 presents a snippet from `Decompose Failing Assertion` from Sect. 4.1. This proof action uses all three of ProofPlumber's APIs to analyze a failing assertion with a conjunction of clauses and present the specific clauses that fail. Specifically, the proof action retrieves the surrounding function using the `Context` API (line 6). Inside the function, the original assertion is replaced (using the `TOST` API) with an assertion of one conjunct (line 11). The proof action then uses the `Verifier` API to invoke the verifier on this modified function (line 12) and check if the new assertion fails. If so, it is added to the source code.

```
1  fn decompose_failing_assertion(
2      api: &AssistContext<'_>, // handle for API calls
3      assertion: AssertExpr,    // TOST Node to modify
4  ) -> Option<BlockExpr> {    // ''None'' indicates the proof action is not applicable
5      let split_exprs = split_expr(&assertion.expr)?; // split into logical conjuncts
6      let this_fn = api.tost_node_in_scope::<Fn>()?; // Find assertion's enclosing ''Fn''
7      let mut stmts: StmtList = StmtList::new();
8      for e in split_exprs {
9          // make each logical conjunct into an assertion of its own
10         let split_assert = AssertExpr::new(e);
11         let modified_fn = api.replace_statement(&this_fn, assertion, split_assert)?;
12         if api.run_verus(&modified_fn)?.is_failing(&split_assert) {
13             stmts.statements.push(split_assert.into());
14         }
15     }
16     stmts.statements.push(assertion.into()); // restore the original assertion
17     Some(BlockExpr::new(stmts))
18 }
```

Fig. 5. Main routine for the `Decompose Failing Assertion` proof action.

While ProofPlumber primarily focuses on automating proof debugging, we observe that ProofPlumber's extensibility also supports the broader proof engineering process. In Sect. 4.1, we described *Remove Redundant Assertions* which helps with proof refactoring, and *Apply Induction* which helps with proof development.

4.3 RQ3: Can proof actions reduce the verifier's TCB?

ProofPlumber can reduce a verification tool's TCB by replacing baked-in debugging support. For example, Verus provides a command line option called

--`expand-errors`, which tries to localize the cause of a proof failure. The code implementing this functionality is intertwined with the process of verification condition generation (VCG). However, this functionality is essentially a combination of *Decompose Failing Assertion*, *Insert Failing Postconditions*, and *Insert Failing Preconditions*. Similarly, Dafny's VCG includes custom code similar to our *Apply Induction*. In both cases, we can replace functionality inside the trusted VCG with external, untrusted proof actions. Given the importance of the VCG for sound verification results, this enhances the trustworthiness of those results.

5   Limitations

While ProofPlumber provides automation for most of the existing proof debugging practices for automated program verification, some debugging practices are still not automatable. To illustrate this, we elaborate on Dafny's four rewrite suggestions that we considered inherently manual in Sect. 4.1.

The first two are related to quantifiers (`exists` and `forall`). If a failing assertion contains a `forall`, the Dafny manual suggests that the proof engineer should replace the `forall` binding with a "guessed" concrete value that is likely to fail. Similarly, if a failing assertion contains an `exists`, the manual suggests that the proof engineer should replace the `exists` binding with a "guessed" concrete value for which the updated assertion is likely to hold. The "guessing" part is inherently manual as SMT solvers often do not produce a useful concrete model (which could be used to build the source-level counterexample) when they return an "unknown" result, which is the common case when a Verus or Dafny proof fails.

The other two rewrite suggestions are about controlling "proof visibility" when proof engineers encounter a very slow and/or unstable proof [34]. In Dafny, a function's body is available to the solver by default. If an engineer suspects a function definition is contributing to the proof's problematic performance, the Dafny manual first suggests making the function's body invisible to the solver. This change can cause the proof to fail in several locations that previously relied on information about the function's body. Therefore, it then suggests making the function's definition locally available to the solver "only when it is necessary". Deciding if the definition is necessary for the proof to succeed often involves the proof engineers' judgment regarding the proof context, potentially relevant lemmas (that might complete the proof without revealing the function's definition), and their tolerance for proof instability.

6   Related Work and Conclusion

Frameworks such as Meta-F* [36] for F* [12] and Tacny [37] for Dafny [11] focus on developing tactics to help write proofs, whereas ProofPlumber's primary focus is on proof debugging. Another line of work [38–40] attempts to reconstruct a source-level counterexample from an SMT solver's model [41]. However, when the solver returns 'unknown', the common case in program verification queries, the model is typically only partial and may be inconsistent with in-scope quantifiers, due to the incomplete heuristics used to for quantifier instantiation. Such inconsistency can be quite confusing for developers.

In everyday software engineering, a counterexample is critical in debugging, as a software engineer can inspect the program's concrete state, and hence localize the error. In contrast, a verification failure can happen for various reasons, including incorrect executable code, incorrect proofs, or even the SMT solver's incompleteness. Therefore, proof engineers still need debugging support to understand the failure.

Conclusion We have presented ProofPlumber, a framework for understanding and debugging proof failures in automated program verification proofs. ProofPlumber supports custom proof actions, which act on the developer's *source-level proofs* to determine why they have failed and potentially suggest remedies. Our evaluation shows that ProofPlumber can automate today's manual debugging practices and provides the extensibility needed for a rapidly evolving area.

Acknowledgments. The authors thank the CAV reviewers and the Verus team for feedback and support. This work was also supported by an Amazon Research Award (Fall 2022 CFP), a gift from VMware, the Future Enterprise Security initiative at Carnegie Mellon CyLab (FutureEnterprise@CyLab), NSF grant CCF 2318953, and funding from AFRL and DARPA under Agreement FA8750-24-9-1000. Chanhee Cho is additionally supported by the Kwanjeong Educational Foundation.

References

1. Coq Development Team. The Coq Proof Assistant. https://coq.inria.fr/
2. d. Moura, L., Ullrich, S.: The Lean 4 theorem prover and programming language. In: International Conference on Automated Deduction (2021)
3. Delahaye, D.: A tactic language for the system Coq. In: Proceedings of the 7th International Conference on Logic for Programming and Automated Reasoning (2000)
4. Blanchette, J.C., Böhme, S., Paulson, L.C.: Extending sledgehammer with SMT solvers. In: International Conference on Automated Deduction (2011)
5. Meng, J., Paulson, L.C.: Translating higher-order clauses to first-order clauses. J. Autom. Reasoning **40**(1), 35–60 (2008). https://doi.org/10.1007/s10817-007-9085-y
6. Paulson, L.C., Susanto, K.W.: Source-level proof reconstruction for interactive theorem proving. In: Proceedings of the 20th International Conference on Theorem Proving in Higher Order Logics (2007)
7. Chlipala, A.: Certified Programming with Dependent Types: A Pragmatic Introduction to the Coq Proof Assistant. MIT Press, Cambridge (2022)
8. Barnett, M., Leino, K.R.M., Schulte, W.: The Spec# programming system: an overview. In: Proceedings of the 2004 International Conference on Construction and Analysis of Safe, Secure, and Interoperable Smart Devices (2004). https://doi.org/10.1007/978-3-540-30569-9_3

9. Chalin, P., Kiniry, J.R., Leavens, G.T., Poll, E.: Beyond assertions: advanced specification and verification with JML and ESC/Java2. In: Proceedings of the 4th International Conference on Formal Methods for Components and Objects (2005). https://doi.org/10.1007/11804192_16

10. Dahlweid, M., Moskal, M., Santen, T., Tobies, S., Schulte, W.: VCC: contract-based modular verification of concurrent C. In: 31st International Conference on Software Engineering - Companion Volume (2009)

11. Leino, K.R.M.: Dafny: an automatic program verifier for functional correctness. In: Logic for Programming, Artificial Intelligence, and Reasoning (2010)

12. Swamy, N., et al.: Dependent types and multi-monadic effects in F*. In: Proceedings of the ACM Symposium on Principles of Programming Languages (POPL) (2016)

13. Müller, P., Schwerhoff, M., Summers, A.J.: Viper: a verification infrastructure for permission-based reasoning. In: Proceedings of the 17th International Conference on Verification, Model Checking, and Abstract Interpretation (2016). https://doi.org/10.1007/978-3-662-49122-5_2

14. Wolf, F.A., Arquint, L., Clochard, M., Oortwijn, W., Pereira, J.C., Müller, P.: Gobra: modular specification and verification of Go programs. In: Computer Aided Verification (CAV) (2021)

15. Eilers, M., Müller, P.: Nagini: a static verifier for Python. In: Computer Aided Verification (2018)

16. Astrauskas, V., Müller, P., Poli, F., Summers, A.J.: Leveraging Rust types for modular specification and verification. In: Object-Oriented Programming Systems, Languages, and Applications (OOPSLA) (2019). https://doi.org/10.1145/3360573

17. Lattuada, A., et al.: Verus: verifying Rust programs using linear ghost types. In: Proceedings of the ACM Conference on Object-Oriented Programming Systems, Languages, and Applications (OOPSLA) (2023)

18. Dijkstra, E.W.: A Discipline of Programming. Prentice-Hall, Hoboken (1976)

19. De Moura, L., Bjørner, N.: Z3: An Efficient SMT Solver. In: Tools & Algorithms for the Construction and Analysis of Systems (TACAS) (2008)

20. Barbosa, H., et al.: cvc5: a versatile and industrial-strength SMT solver. In: Tools and Algorithms for the Construction and Analysis of Systems (TACAS) (2022)

21. Dutertre, B.: Yices 2.2. In: Computer Aided Verification (CAV) (2014)

22. Niemetz, A., Preiner, M.: Bitwuzla. In: Computer Aided Verification (CAV) (2023). https://doi.org/10.1007/978-3-031-37703-7_1

23. Niemetz, A., Preiner, M., Wolf, C., Biere, A.: BTOR2, BtorMC and Boolector 3.0. In: Computer Aided Verification (CAV) (2018)

24. Matsakis, N.D., Klock, F.S.: The Rust Language. ACM SIGAda Ada Lett. **34**(3), 103–104 (2014). https://doi.org/10.1145/2692956.2663188

25. Klabnik, S., Nichols, C.: The Rust Programming Language. No Starch Press, San Francisco (2018)

26. Verification Debugging When Verification Fails. https://dafny.org/dafny/DafnyRef/DafnyRef#sec-verification-debugging

27. Sliding Admit Verification Style. https://github.com/FStarLang/FStar/wiki/Sliding-admit-verification-style

28. StackOverflow Question: With Dafny, Verify Function to Count Integer Set Elements less than a Threshold. https://stackoverflow.com/questions/76924944/with-dafny-verify-function-to-count-integer-set-elements-less-than-a-threshold/76925258#76925258

29. StackOverflow Question: Hint on FStar Proof Dead End. https://stackoverflow.com/questions/61938833/hint-on-fstar-proof-dead-end

30. Language Server Protocol. https://microsoft.github.io/language-server-protocol/specifications/lsp/3.17/specification/#textDocument_codeAction
31. van Tonder, R., Le Goues, C.: Lightweight multi-language syntax transformation with parser parser combinators. In: Proceedings of the 40th ACM SIGPLAN Conference on Programming Language Design and Implementation (2019). https://doi.org/10.1145/3314221.3314589
32. Maletic, J.I., Collard, M.L.: Exploration, analysis, and manipulation of source code using SrcML. In: Proceedings of the 37th International Conference on Software Engineering (2015)
33. Klint, P., van der Storm, T., Vinju, J.: RASCAL: a domain specific language for source code analysis and manipulation. In: 2009 Ninth IEEE International Working Conference on Source Code Analysis and Manipulation (2009)
34. Zhou, Y., Bosamiya, J., Takashima, Y., Li, J., Heule, M., Parno, B.: Mariposa: measuring SMT instability in automated program verification. In: Proceedings of the Formal Methods in Computer-Aided Design (FMCAD) Conference (2023)
35. Rust Analyzer. https://github.com/rust-lang/rust-analyzer
36. Martínez, G., et al.: Meta-F*: proof automation with SMT, tactics, and metaprograms. In: European Symposium on Programming (2019)
37. Grov, G., Tumas, V.: Tactics for the Dafny program verifier. In: Tools and Algorithms for the Construction and Analysis of Systems (2016)
38. Christakis, M., Leino, K.R.M., Müller, P., Wüstholz, V.: Integrated environment for diagnosing verification errors. In: Tools and Algorithms for the Construction and Analysis of Systems (2016)
39. Chakarov, A., Fedchin, A., Rakamarić, Z., Rungta, N.: Better counterexamples for Dafny. In: Tools and Algorithms for the Construction and Analysis of Systems (2022)
40. Le Goues, C., Leino, K.R.M., Moskal, M.: The Boogie verification debugger. In: Software Engineering and Formal Methods (2011)
41. Barrett, C., Fontaine, P., Tinelli, C.: The satisfiability modulo theories library (SMT-LIB) (2016). www.SMT-LIB.org

Verification Algorithms for Automated Separation Logic Verifiers

Marco Eilers$^{(\boxtimes)}$ ⓘ, Malte Schwerhoff ⓘ, and Peter Müller ⓘ

Department of Computer Science, ETH Zurich, Zurich, Switzerland
{marco.eilers,malte.schwerhoff,peter.mueller}@inf.ethz.ch

Abstract. Most automated program verifiers for separation logic use either symbolic execution or verification condition generation to extract proof obligations, which are then handed over to an SMT solver. Existing verification algorithms are designed to be sound, but differ in performance and completeness. These characteristics may also depend on the programs and properties to be verified. Consequently, developers and users of program verifiers have to select a verification algorithm carefully for their application domain. Taking an informed decision requires a systematic comparison of the performance and completeness characteristics of the verification algorithms used by modern separation logic verifiers, but such a comparison does not exist.

This paper describes five verification algorithms for separation logic, three that are used in existing tools and two novel algorithms that combine characteristics of existing symbolic execution and verification condition generation algorithms. A detailed evaluation of implementations of these five algorithms in the Viper infrastructure assesses their performance and completeness for different classes of input programs. Based on the experimental results, we identify candidate portfolios of algorithms that maximize completeness and performance.

Keywords: Symbolic execution · verification condition generation · separation logic · heap representation · SMT solver · portfolio

1 Introduction

Given a program and a specification, automated deductive program verifiers such as Boogie [36], Corral [35], Dafny [37], and Why3 [27] compute *proof obligations* whose validity implies the correctness of the input program. These proof obligations are typically checked using SMT solvers, such as CVC5 [5] or Z3 [41].

For program verifiers based on separation logic [50] or related permission logics [59], proof obligations are computed using two prevalent verification algorithms: symbolic execution (SE) and verification condition generation (VCG). For instance, Caper [17], Gillian [40], JaVerT [56], SecC [26], Smallfoot [8], and VeriFast [32] are separation logic verifiers based on symbolic execution, whereas Chalice [39] and GrassHopper [48] use verification condition generation. Viper [44] provides two backend-verifiers, one based on SE and one on VCG.

ⓒ The Author(s) 2024
A. Gurfinkel and V. Ganesh (Eds.): CAV 2024, LNCS 14681, pp. 362–386, 2024.
https://doi.org/10.1007/978-3-031-65627-9_18

Even though these tools differ in many aspects of the supported programming language, separation logic, and proof automation, they employ fairly uniform SE and VCG algorithms. Their SE algorithms use a symbolic heap representation based on separation logic's *partial-heap semantics* [46]: a symbolic heap maps those separation logic resources (in particular, heap locations) to symbolic values that are owned in a given program state. Each owned resource is represented by one or more *heap chunks*, which map resources to ownership and value information. In contrast, the VCG algorithms implemented in separation logic verifiers use a *total-heap representation*, in which the heap is a total map from memory locations to values, and the currently-owned resources are tracked in a separate data structure. These two different ways of *internally* modeling the heap both implement the same *source-level* language semantics.

These verification algorithms, and their variations implemented in various tools, are all designed to be sound, but strike different trade-offs between performance and completeness. For instance, SE verifies each path through a method separately, whereas VCG typically generates one proof obligation for the entire method. Therefore, VCG produces fewer, but larger proof obligations, which may affect the effectiveness and performance of the underlying SMT solver.

Consequently, developers of program verifiers need to choose the verification algorithm carefully, depending on the intended application area of their tools. For verifiers that support several algorithms, such as the verifiers built on top of the Viper infrastructure [9,22,65], this choice needs to be made by users. Taking an informed decision requires a systematic comparison of the performance and completeness characteristics of the verification algorithms used by modern separation logic verifiers. Such a comparison necessitates implementations of all relevant algorithms for the same programming language, verification logic, and tool because comparisons across different settings would not yield meaningful results. To the best of our knowledge, such implementations and, consequently, a comprehensive comparison do not exist.

This Work. This paper describes the following five verification algorithms and performs a detailed comparison.

1. **SE-PS:** An SE algorithm that looks up information in the *partial* symbolic heap by trying to identify a *single* heap chunk to provide the required information. This algorithm is used in JaVerT, SecC, VeriFast, and Viper's SE-backend.
2. **SE-PC:** An SE *partial* heap algorithm that performs look-ups by *combining* the information available in all heap chunks. Combining different heap chunks may provide additional information, for instance, by summing up fractional permissions [12] or by using disjunctive properties.
3. **SE-TR:** An SE algorithm that uses a *total* heap representation per individual *resource*, akin to VCG-TR below.
4. **VCG-TR:** A VCG *total* heap algorithm that uses a separate map per *resource*. This representation is used by GrassHopper.

5. **VCG-TA:** A VCG *total* heap algorithm that stores the information for *all* resources in a single map. This representation is used in Chalice and Viper's VCG-backend.

SE-PC and SE-TR are novel algorithms, which introduce characteristics of existing VCG algorithms into SE, namely simultaneous reasoning about multiple chunks of the (partial) heap, and a total heap representation, respectively. Thereby, they offer different trade-offs than existing algorithms.

To enable a fair comparison, we implemented all five algorithms for Viper. We evaluated them on a diverse benchmark suite that includes existing Viper examples and code produced by different Viper frontends, which allows us to draw conclusions for different kinds of input programs.

Our comparison identifies SE-PS as the best algorithm overall, but shows that the different verification algorithms have complementary strengths. Based on our findings, we identify and discuss several *portfolios* of algorithms, which maximize completeness across the benchmark suite. In deductive verification, portfolio approaches have been used successfully for the underlying SMT solver [27,42], but, to our knowledge, not for the equally-important verification algorithms.

Contributions and Outline. We make the following contributions:

- We survey the SE and VCG algorithms used in existing separation logic verifiers and propose two new algorithms, which combine characteristics of existing SE and VCG algorithms (Sect. 2).
- We provide the first systematic comparison of verification algorithms for separation logic. A diverse set of benchmarks provides insights into the performance and completeness for different classes of input programs (Sect. 3).
- We identify candidate portfolios of verification algorithms to maximize performance and completeness, several of which include SE-TR, one of the novel algorithms we propose (Sect. 4).

The implementations of the five algorithms, the example benchmarks, as well as the data from our experiments, are available as an artifact [24].

2   Verification Algorithms

In this section, after providing necessary background on the Viper language, we discuss the two main design dimensions for verification algorithms for separation logic (SE vs. VCG, and total vs. partial heap representations), give an overview of the considered algorithms, and discuss various design trade-offs.

2.1   Viper Verification Language

The Viper language [44] is a simple object-based imperative language with specification features like pre- and postconditions and loop invariants. Viper is based on implicit dynamic frames [59], a variant of separation logic, and supports advanced separation logic features such as *fractional permissions* [12], *predicates* [45], *magic wands*, and *quantified resources* [43] (also called iterated separating conjunctions). Verification algorithms for Viper have to support all of these features, which makes Viper an interesting target for a comparison.

A Viper state consists of local variables and a built-in heap that maps locations (consisting of a reference and a field) to values. Control flow is expressed via conditionals, loops, method calls, and gotos. Whereas statements may have side effects, expressions are always side-effect free and include calls to (partial) functions, which may inspect the heap.

Following the implicit dynamic frames approach, Viper assertions express resource ownership separately from value information. For example, the assertion `acc(x.f) * x.f = 1` (corresponding to separation logic's points-to predicate `x.f` $\mapsto$ 1) includes an *accessibility predicate* `acc(x.f)`, expressing exclusive ownership of the heap location, and a *heap-dependent expression* to constrain its value. The general shape of accessibility predicates is `acc(R, p)` , where R denotes a *resource* and p a fractional permission. Resources can be heap locations, predicate instances, and magic wands; all resources can be universally quantified over. Predicates abstract over (possibly unbounded) heap data structures, whereas magic wands are used to express partial data structure, which occur, for instance, during iterative traversals.

2.2   Design Dimensions

Verification algorithms for separation logic can be classified according to the technique they use to compute proof obligations (SE or VCG) and according to their heap representation (total or partial). In the following, we survey these dimensions and their main trade-offs.

SE vs VCG. Verification in separation logic is modular, that is, each method is verified independently, using method specifications to reason about calls. SE and VCG differ in how they compute the proof obligations for each method.

SE uses a symbolic state, typically a triple of symbolic store, heap, and path conditions. It explores each path through a method body separately (using loop invariants to represent a statically-unknown number of loop iterations). Statements on the path may update the symbolic state; in particular, the conditions of if-statements and loops are recorded in the path conditions. Expressions and assertions are evaluated in the symbolic state. Proof obligations, for instance, to show that an assertion holds, are expressed over the current symbolic state and discharged on the fly via an SMT query. Consequently, SE typically generates many SMT queries for each method body.

In contrast, VCG uses a predicate transformer, usually weakest preconditions, to produce (typically) a single proof obligation (and, thus, SMT query) per method body. This predicate transformer is based on a state model that, in the context of separation logic, must encode heap and ownership information (e.g., via a map axiomatization, see below).

There are two fundamental differences between SE and VCG. First, SE generates many, but comparably small and simple SMT queries, whereas VCG produces a single, more complicated query. This difference may affect verification times. Moreover, the complexity of the SMT queries can affect the SMT solver's ability to discharge (valid) queries. Second, for a rich verification logic such as Viper's, an SE algorithm is complex and performs substantial work for maintaining the symbolic state, whereas VCG delegates most of the heavy lifting to the SMT solver. This makes SE more difficult to implement, but also offers the potential for many optimizations (possibly with the use of additional SMT queries), whereas it is more difficult to direct the proof search of an SMT solver. Our evaluation in the next section explores these trade-offs and others.

Partial vs Total Heaps. Both SE and VCG need to represent heap and ownership information. Existing SE algorithms do that by maintaining an *internal* map data structure, typically a *collection of heap chunks* (also called *heaplets*). A heap chunk is typically a tuple (x, f, v, p), denoting p permission to memory location $x.f$ at which value v is stored. Resources that are not owned in a state have no corresponding heap chunk (or a chunk with permission amount $p = 0$). Consequently, these internal map data structures represent *partial heaps*, which represent value and ownership information simultaneously.

In contrast, VCG algorithms use an *external* representation that tracks heap information only as part of the SMT queries. Since maps in SMT are total, value and ownership need to be encoded separately as two total maps H and M. The *heap $H : Resource \mapsto Value$* maps resources to their values, whereas the *permission mask $M : Resource \mapsto Permission$* tracks ownership by mapping each resource to the permission amount currently held (1 for exclusive ownership, and 0 if the resource is not owned in the current state). Suitable proof obligations ensure that H is accessed only at resources for which M contains the necessary permission. That is, the mask effectively represents the domain of a partial heap. We call this representation *total heaps*.

We highlight three key differences between partial and total heaps here. First, total heaps generally lead to more complex SMT queries. In particular, each change of the heap (or mask) leads to an SMT term that relates the new heap to the previous one, leading to increasingly large formulas, whereas the data structure for partial heaps can be updated destructively. Moreover, encoding the heap information in an SMT query typically uses many universal quantifiers for total heaps, whereas partial heaps are finite collections whose content can be described in quantifier-free formulas.

Second, partial heaps generally require more complex algorithms to perform heap look-ups and modifications, possibly involving SMT queries. In contrast, total heaps delegate much of the heavy lifting to the SMT solver. This difference is especially prominent for resources that represent an unbounded number of heap locations, such as recursive predicates and iterated separating conjunction. These require dedicated data structures and operations in partial heaps [43], but fairly trivial encodings with total heaps.

Third, total heaps greatly simplify the encoding of heap-dependent functions to SMT, as uninterpreted functions of the total heap and corresponding axioms [31]. In contrast, partial heaps require non-trivial algorithms to extract the information needed to determine a function's value [57].

2.3   Algorithms

In this subsection, we sketch five verification algorithms that occupy different spots in the design space described above and, thus, have different performance and completeness characteristics. Note that these algorithms do not directly correspond to the four combinations of heap representation and technique used to compute proof obligations explained before: First, there is no algorithm combining VCG and partial heaps, since VCG algorithms necessarily require an external heap representation. Second, we discuss two different algorithms that combine SE with partial heaps. Three of the algorithms are used in existing tools, whereas two are novel SE algorithms, including the first SE algorithm that uses total heaps. We will see later in Sect. 4 that these new algorithms complement existing ones, which makes them especially useful for portfolio approaches.

We focus the following presentation on two core operations: evaluating an expression, as well as consuming an assertion, which includes checking that it holds and removing its resources from the current state.

SE-PS. This algorithm combines symbolic execution with the partial heap model and is used by the existing SE tools for separation logic. Evaluating a source-level heap read $x.f$ is performed by trying to find a chunk (y, f, v, p) in the symbolic heap such that $x = y$ and $0 < p$. If such a chunk can be found, the result of the symbolic evaluation is v. Otherwise, verification fails. Analogously, consuming q permissions to a heap location $x.f$ is implemented by finding a chunk (y, f, v, p) such that $x = y$ and $q \leq p$. If found, the chunk is replaced by $(y, f, v, p - q)$; otherwise, verification fails. Finding matching chunks in general requires SMT queries to account for aliasing; in practice, however, syntactical checks often suffice, and can significantly reduce the number of SMT queries.

Note that both operations are performed on a single heap chunk, which may lead to incomplete heap information and, thus, spurious errors. For instance, when the permission to a heap location is split over several chunks, this algorithm will use only one of them (rather than computing the total sum of permission amounts) and might, thus, report a verification error if the permission amount in that one chunk is not sufficient to perform an operation. To reduce the number of such spurious errors, the algorithm performs various *state consolidation* steps at heuristically determined points (e.g., triggered by an imminent verification failure). For instance, it may merge two heap chunks (i.e., add their permission amounts) if the SMT solver can prove that they refer to the same resource. State consolidation may also introduce non-aliasing constraints, i.e., assume for any pair of chunks (x_1, f, v_1, p_1) and (x_2, f, v_2, p_2) that $x_1 \neq x_2$ if $p_1 + p_2 > 1$.

State consolidation eliminates some spurious errors, but performing operations on a single heap chunk remains incomplete, for instance, in situations with *disjunctive aliasing.* In a state where $x = y \lor x = z$ and where permissions to both $y.f$ and $z.f$ are available, consuming permission to a location $x.f$ fails because the algorithm cannot find a *single* chunk that definitely provides the necessary permission. To work around this issue, users can force the SE to branch on the disjunction (e.g., by inserting if-statements), such that a single chunk can be found on each branch.

SE-PC. To address the shortcomings of SE-PS, we designed a novel variation that also uses ̲partial heaps, but consults and ̲combines information from all chunks. Evaluating a source-level heap read $x.f$ summarizes facts scattered across all relevant heap chunks $(y_1, f, v_1, p_1), \ldots, (y_n, f, v_n, p_n)$: The effective value of $x.f$ is denoted by a fresh symbol v that is defined by the new path condition $(x = y_1 \Rightarrow v = v_1) \land \ldots \land (x = y_n \Rightarrow v = v_n)$. Analogously, the effective permission to $x.f$ is denoted by a fresh symbol p that is defined by the symbolic expression $p = (x = y_1 \mathbin{?} p_1 : 0) + \ldots + (x = y_n \mathbin{?} p_n : 0)$. Consuming q permission to a heap location $x.f$ similarly may remove fractions of q from different heap chunks.

Compared to SE-PS, SE-PC effectively shifts work from the SE algorithm to the SMT solver: it reduces the number of state consolidation steps (but does not entirely eliminate them), at the price of more complex path conditions and SMT queries. The next algorithm pushes this trade-off even further.

SE-TR. Even though all existing SE algorithms for separation logic use partial heaps, SE is also compatible with ̲total heaps, as this novel algorithm shows. It uses a heap/mask pair (H_R, M_R) for each kind of ̲resource (i.e., field or predicate) R. Evaluating a source-level heap read $x.f$ simply asserts $0 < M_f[x]$ and produces the symbolic look-up expression $H_f[x]$, where H_f and M_f are the current heap and mask component of the symbolic state. Consuming q permission checks $q \leq M_f[x]$ and then replaces the symbolic state's mask M_f with an updated version $M'_f = M_f[x \mapsto M_f[x] - q]$. The necessary map update axioms are part of the heap's background axiomatization that is given to the SMT solver. To prevent the verifier from unsoundly framing information about heap locations for which no permission is held and which may thus be modified by whoever has obtained the permission, they are assigned non-deterministic values.

Using a total heap eliminates the need for state consolidation because all information about a resources is represented by a single heap/mask pair, rather than multiple chunks. Non-aliasing can be assumed using a global axiom stating that for all masks M_R and receivers x, $M_R[x] \leq 1$. Nevertheless, the algorithm retains some of the key benefits of SE, such as cheap syntactical comparisons, which are sufficient in many cases. However, compared to partial heap algorithms, it complicates SMT queries, which now require a theory for maps or a suitable axiomatization.

VCG-TR. VCG algorithms do not have an internal representation of the heap and, therefore, they necessarily use ̲total heaps, which can be encoded in SMT. One option, implemented in GrassHopper, is to use a heap/mask pair per resource, like in the previous algorithm. Evaluating source-level heap reads, or consuming permissions, are incorporated into the verification condition as described for the previous algorithm. Doing that in a VCG algorithm leads to the advantages and disadvantages outlined in Sect. 2.2.

VCG-TA. A variation of VCG-TR that uses a single heap/mask pair across all resources. It is used, for instance, in VeriCool [59] and Viper's VCG-backend. Heap reads and mask updates are encoded as described for SE-TR, with the only change that the field becomes another index into the single heap or mask.

Using a single heap simplifies, for example, the encoding of predicates (see Sect. 2.1) but, on the other hand, complicates framing for heap-dependent functions, since updating *any* resource changes the (only) heap and, thus, requires proof steps to show that other resources are not affected.

The discussion of these five algorithms illustrates various design choices, which may affect performance, for instance, by shifting work between the verification algorithm and the SMT solver. These choices also affect completeness. Most prominently, algorithms using total heaps make heavy use of universal quantifiers, making the SMT queries undecidable. In practice, verification tools use the SMT solver's E-matching [16], which allows them to guide quantifier instantiations by specifying matching patterns (also called triggers). However, making those too strict can prevent necessary instantiations (causing spurious errors), whereas making them too permissive may cause too many unnecessary instantiations (and, thus, bad performance). It is thus crucial to assess performance *and* completeness of verification algorithms empirically, as we do next.

3   Evaluation

This section presents our empirical evaluation. We first discuss relevant implementation details of the algorithms, introduce the benchmarks, and describe our set-up. We then present and interpret our evaluation results, in terms of completeness and performance of the different algorithms. Finally, we conclude by discussing potential threats to the validity of our results.

3.1   Implementations

Viper's two existing backends implement SE-PS and VCG-TA, respectively. We have extended Viper to implement the remaining three algorithms (for the full Viper language as of version 23.07), reusing parts of the existing implementations where possible: We based SE-PC on Viper's SE-PS backend, which allowed us to reuse the entire SE engine and the state representation, but required re-implementing all heap-related parts of the algorithm. We also based SE-TR on Viper's SE-PS backend. Here, we could still re-use the SE engine, but had to re-implement the heap representation, all heap-manipulating operations, and code for axiomatizing heap-dependent functions. Lastly, we based VCG-TR on Viper's

VCG-TA backend, which encodes a Viper program into a Boogie [6] program; Boogie then computes a verification condition and interacts with Z3. We reused this entire mechanism and the general encoding of statements and expressions, but had to adapt all heap-handling code. All SE algorithms implement various optimizations: they perform syntactic equality checks (e.g., in SE-PS to find a matching heap chunk) to avoid SMT queries, they simplify terms on the fly (e.g., SE-TR, to keep mask terms simple, simplifies a mask M_R to which the same permission has been added and later removed to be just M_R again), they cache values (e.g., the term resulting from reading a field in SE-PC), they actively query the SMT solver to check if paths can be pruned, and they optimize their communication with the SMT solver to avoid repeating large terms. Some of these optimizations are crucial for scaling the algorithms to large examples, while others are only relevant for corner cases. In the VCG algorithms, most of these optimizations are not possible; thus, they mainly rely on Boogie to generate efficient verification conditions [7].

3.2   Benchmark Selection

For our comparison, we selected a total of 537 example programs to be verified. About 80% of these were generated by one of several Viper frontends from programs written in different source languages, the other programs were manually written in Viper. Each example represents a meaningful verification task (e.g., from a publication's case study or verification competition): in particular, we excluded programs that represent regression tests or that test specific features in isolation. The majority of the examples (388) is expected to verify; for the remainder, the expected result is some set of verification failures.

The examples vary along several dimensions: source level language (e.g., Rust, Java, Python), frontend verifier (e.g., we obtained Viper programs from different Rust verifiers), application area and complexity (ranging from individual functions to large case studies, e.g., to verify cryptographic security of network protocols), verified properties (e.g., memory safety, complex functional specifications, or hyperproperties such as secure information flow), Viper features used to encode source languages and properties, and code size (ranging from 15 to 99,110 lines of Viper code, with a mean/median of 2400/495 LOC).

To observe the effect that these variations have on the completeness or performance of different verification algorithms, we partitioned the examples into different groups, listed below. We first grouped by frontend verifiers, which we then further refined: e.g., by application area or typical usage patterns of Viper features. This resulted in the following groups:

- Ru_1 represents Rust programs verified using Prusti [4], which heavily use predicates and magic wands but no quantified resources.
- Ru_2 and Ru_3 contain unsafe Rust code encoded by prototype versions of two different Viper frontends [3,49]; the former heavily mutates the heap, whereas the latter does not use Viper's heap at all.

- *Go* contains smaller Go programs encoded by Gobra [65]. *Go$_C$* contains larger examples from two case studies that prove correctness and security of real-world implementations of security protocols [2,47].
- *RSL* contains weak-memory programs generated by a frontend [61] for Relaxed Separation Logic [64].
- *SC* and *SC$_R$* contain smart contracts encoded to Viper by 2vyper [13]; the former group does not use Viper's heap at all, whereas the latter uses quantified resources, and additionally generates a lot of branches.
- *PP* contains a product program encoding [23] that is used to prove a 3-safety hyperproperty. The generated programs lightly use the heap and heavily utilize branching.
- *Py* contains Python programs encoded by Nagini [20,22], including two case studies [28,60] that prove complex functional properties. *Py$_P$* contains Nagini-generated programs that additionally use a product program encoding to prove information flow security of the original Python programs [21].
- *Rea* proves reachability properties about graph-manipulating programs [63]; it heavily relies on heap-dependent functions and quantified resources.
- *Vi* contains various programs directly written in Viper, including examples from publications on quantified resources [43] and magic wands [58], and from the VerifyThis verification challenge [18].
- *Ve$_C$* contains examples encoded by VerCors [9] that stem from larger case studies that verify properties of Java [1] and CUDA [53] programs as well as examples written in VerCors's custom (Java-like) PVL language [52]. *Ve$_V$* contains VerCors-encoded examples from VerifyThis.
- *Da$_V$* and *Da$_G$* contain Viper [29] and Gobra versions [19], respectively, of examples from a verification textbook [37,38].
- *Vo* contains examples that heavily manipulate the heap, generated by Voila [66], a frontend automating the fine-grained concurrency logic TaDA [51].

In all groups, the examples combine several Viper features to encode the desired language semantics and properties; some groups use certain features very prominently, while others are more heterogeneous. Overall, we believe that our examples and groups form a good representation of the many different usages of Viper, and that our results can be transferred to other separation logic verifiers.

3.3 Experimental Setup

We evaluated completeness and performance of the different algorithms for each of the examples. Our test system uses an AMD Ryzen 5900X with 32GB of RAM running Ubuntu 23.10. For the VCG algorithms, we use Boogie 2.15.9. Our SMT solver is Z3 4.8.7[1]. All algorithms run with the same Z3 options and the same axiomatization for background theories other than the heap (e.g., sequences).

We ran each algorithm five times on each example on a warmed-up JVM, each time with a timeout of ten minutes. We let each algorithm report all errors for

---

[1] While this is an older version of Z3, it is the default version used with Viper 23.07.

Table 1. Incompletenesses per algorithm per example group. Σ is the total across all groups. For each algorithm, we show first the percentage of examples where it was incomplete for any reason, and then the percentage of examples where it was incomplete due to timeouts and inconsistent results.

	Σ	SE-PS		SE-PC		SE-TR		VCG-TR		VCG-TA	
All	537	5.4	3.7	5.4	3.7	7.4	3.7	8.8	3.7	13.8	7.8
Ru_1	156	0.0	0.0	0.6	0.6	3.8	0.0	9.0	0.6	18.6	5.1
Ru_2	11	0.0	0.0	0.0	0.0	45.5	45.5	54.5	54.5	63.6	63.6
Go	11	18.2	9.1	0.0	0.0	18.2	0.0	0.0	0.0	0.0	0.0
Go_C	17	5.9	0.0	0.0	0.0	17.6	17.6	29.4	11.8	35.3	29.4
RSL	21	19.0	14.3	19.0	14.3	0.0	0.0	38.1	28.6	33.3	28.6
SC	8	0.0	0.0	0.0	0.0	0.0	0.0	0.0	0.0	0.0	0.0
SC_R	13	0.0	0.0	0.0	0.0	0.0	0.0	0.0	0.0	0.0	0.0
PP	38	0.0	0.0	0.0	0.0	0.0	0.0	0.0	0.0	0.0	0.0
Py	23	8.7	8.7	13.0	4.3	4.3	4.3	13.0	0.0	21.7	8.7
Py_P	18	16.7	11.1	11.1	5.6	11.1	0.0	5.6	5.6	5.6	5.6
Rea	16	93.8	62.5	93.8	62.5	37.5	37.5	12.5	0.0	18.8	6.3
Vi	46	2.2	2.2	2.2	2.2	4.3	0.0	4.3	4.3	8.7	6.5
Ve_C	19	0.0	0.0	10.5	10.5	42.1	5.3	10.5	5.3	10.5	10.5
Ve_V	5	0.0	0.0	0.0	0.0	20.0	0.0	20.0	0.0	0.0	0.0
Da_G	8	0.0	0.0	0.0	0.0	0.0	0.0	25.0	12.5	25.0	12.5
Da_V	41	0.0	0.0	0.0	0.0	0.0	0.0	0.0	0.0	0.0	0.0
Vo	34	2.9	2.9	2.9	2.9	11.8	11.8	0.0	0.0	20.6	17.6
Ru_3	52	0.0	0.0	0.0	0.0	0.0	0.0	1.9	0.0	1.9	0.0

every example (i.e., we did not stop after some number of errors were found). To ensure that we measure the total workload, we disabled all parallelization along the tool chains. To account for the heuristics-driven nature of SMT solvers, we consistently varied Z3's random seeds: we picked five fixed seeds and always used the ith seed for the ith run of every algorithm-example combination. Lastly, we measured the verification time of each algorithm on an empty Viper program to obtain their fixed startup overhead (e.g., from starting Boogie), and subtracted, from all times of a given algorithm, the difference between its own overhead and the overall lowest overhead. In practice, this difference was at most 320 ms.

3.4   Completeness Results

Table 1 shows the number of incompletenesses per algorithm and example group, i.e., the number of examples for which the algorithm reported unexpected errors, timed out, or reported inconsistent results over the five runs. The latter is typically caused by differences in the SMT solver's proof search, e.g., due to different random seeds.

Overall Results. Every algorithm is able to report the desired result for over 86% of the examples. However, there is a clear distinction: VCG-TA has the most incompletenesses with 13.8% (and the most timeouts by far), followed by VCG-TR with 8.8% and SE-TR with 7.4%. The two partial heap algorithms perform the best with 5.4% each.

Thus, our first, perhaps surprising observation is that for our test set, (sufficiently optimized) **partial heap algorithms are more complete than total heap algorithms**. That is, performing heap reasoning in the verification algorithm is more effective than leaving it entirely to the SMT solver. This conclusion is supported by further observations: (1) SE algorithms, with their greater potential for optimizations, generally outperform the VCG algorithms; (2) SE-PS, despite its conceptual incompleteness, performs identically to SE-PC overall, which produces more complex SMT queries by summarizing heap chunks; (3) VCG-TA, with its single heap, has a much higher number of timeouts than VCG-TR with its separate heaps per resource.

Impact of Optimizations. To evaluate how much SE-PS's completeness depends on optimizations, we re-ran all examples with a version of SE-PS with the majority of its optimizations disabled. The resulting algorithm performs notably worse, with 59 (instead of 29) incompletenesses. We thus conclude that **the good performance of SE-PS is due to significant optimization efforts**.

Complementarity. A pairwise comparison shows that, for each algorithm, there are a number of examples that this algorithm is incomplete on, but another algorithm is not. For example, while SE-PC and SE-PS perform identically in overall numbers, SE-PC is complete on three examples where SE-PS is not and vice versa. Other pairs differ more strongly, with SE-PS and VCG-TA forming the extreme pair: there are in total 75 examples for which only one of the two algorithms is complete. We thus conclude that **being able to use more than one algorithm is advantageous in practice**, and we explore this further in Sect. 4.

Differences Between Groups. While comparisons of the different algorithms for our overall test set can give us an indication of their overall performance, their results may be skewed due to over- or underrepresentation of different patterns in our test set. Thus, a more important observation is that the number of incompletenesses per algorithm differs significantly between example groups. The two algorithms using partial heaps (SE-PS, SE-PC) are both incomplete on 15 out of 16 examples in the *Rea* group, making them essentially unusable for this group. This indicates that the **heavy use of heap-dependent functions framed by quantified resources** is problematic for partial heap algorithms. All total heap algorithms perform better: SE-TR is incomplete on 6 out of 16 examples, the VCG algorithms on 2 and 3.

The opposite is the case for group Ru_2, where all total heap algorithms time out for at least 5 out of 11 examples, while both partial heap algorithms are complete for all examples. Other groups that also heavily manipulate the heap are Ru_1 and Vo; both exhibit the similar tendencies, and likewise for Go_C with its large and complex case studies. These observations suggest that **total heap algorithms can struggle with a large number of heap updates**. Correspondingly, the heap representation does *not* affect completeness for the two groups that do not use the heap at all (Ru_3 and SC).

Conclusions. Given the previous observations and interpretations, we can draw three final conclusions regarding completeness: First, **the heap representation has a bigger impact on completeness than the verification mechanism** (SE or VCG), since all groups that have large differences in completeness numbers have the largest difference between the partial heap and the total heap algorithms. Second, **certain example groups effectively require specific combinations** (e.g., VCG + total for Rea, SE + partial for Ru_2). Third, a general-purpose separation logic verifier should **implement at least two algorithms to be reasonably complete**.

3.5   Performance Results

To compare the performance of different verification algorithms, we measured the run time of each of the five algorithms on each of the examples five times, as explained in Sect. 3.3. We discarded the shortest and longest run times and computed the mean of the remaining three, leading to one data point for each algorithm-example combination.

Comparison Method. Comparing algorithms on an example is sensible only if each algorithm reports the same verification result (otherwise, an algorithm that always immediately fails would be the fastest). Therefore, we compare *pairs* of algorithms on examples for which both report the same result; using pairs instead of all five algorithms minimizes the number of examples to discard.

For each pair of algorithms and example, we compute the *relative percentage difference* (RPD) of the two mean run times t_1 and t_2, defined as $(t_2 - t_1)/(0.5 \cdot (t_2 + t_1)) \cdot 100$, which relates the run time *difference* to the *average* run time of the example. Consequently, RPDs are independent of the absolute run times, which allows us to compare algorithms across examples with vastly different run times. An RPD of 0 means equal performance, a positive value means that the first algorithm was faster, with higher values indicating bigger differences: e.g., +66.6 indicates that the first algorithm took half the time of the second. The maximum RPD is +200, obtained when the first algorithm is essentially instant compared to the second. Conversely, negative values mean that the second algorithm was faster.

Overview. Figure 1 shows box plots of the RPDs of the two extreme points in the design space, SE-PS vs. VCG-TA. Figure 2 shows the RDPs of the closely

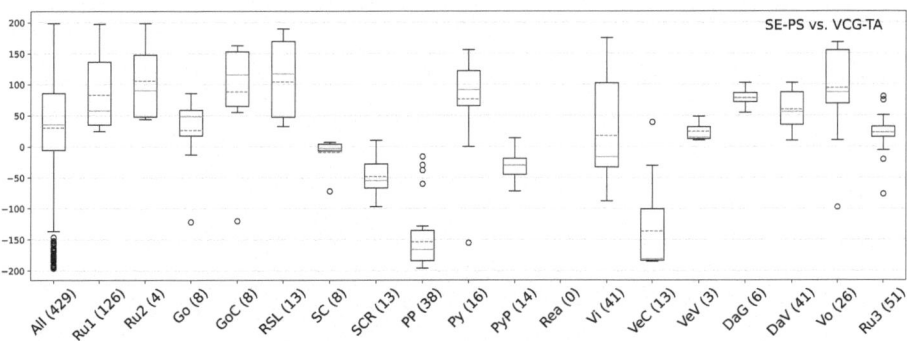

Fig. 1. Box plot of relative percentage difference (RPD) of mean performance per group for the two extreme points in the design space, SE-PS vs. VCG-TA. Values greater than zero indicate that the first algorithm in the pair is faster, values less than zero that the second is faster; the orange line denotes the median and the dashed green line the mean. (Color figure online)

related pairs (a) SE-PS vs. SE-PC, (b) SE-PS vs. SE-TR, (c) SE-TR vs. VCG-TR, and (d) VCG-TR vs. VCG-TA. The orange line indicates the median, the dashed green line the mean. The lower and upper ends of the box signify the first and third quartiles (Q_1 and Q_3), respectively. The whiskers show the 1.5 interquartile range (IQR) values, i.e., the lowest point in the range between $Q_1 - 1.5 \times IQR$ and Q_1 and the highest point between Q_3 and $Q_3 + 1.5 \times IQR$, where $IQR = Q_3 - Q_1$.

Extreme Designs. We first compare the two extreme points, SE-PS and VCG-TA, which show significant performance differences across many groups (see Fig. 1): SE-PS performs better for most groups, in particular for Ru_1, Ru_2, RSL, Py, Da_G, Da_V, and Vo, while VCG-TA performs significantly better for PP, and to a lesser extent for Py_P, SC_R, and Ve_C. Only SC shows essentially the same performance for both algorithms, and Vi contains examples that favor each of the two algorithms. For PP and SC_R, VCG-TA's advantage is likely due to a high amount of branching: they have an average of 133 and 7.5 branches per method, respectively, whereas all other groups have an average of 2 branches per method. Py_P also results from product program constructions; the verification work again stems mostly from branching, even if the average is only 2.5 branches per method. For Ve_C, VCG-TA's advantage cannot be explained with branching, and we will revisit this group further below. Thus, we conclude that **SE-PS usually outperforms VCG-TA**, but **VCG-TA performs much better on branch-heavy programs**.

Related Designs. To asses the impact of individual design decisions, we compare each algorithm to the most similar alternative(s); all comparisons can be found in Fig. 2.

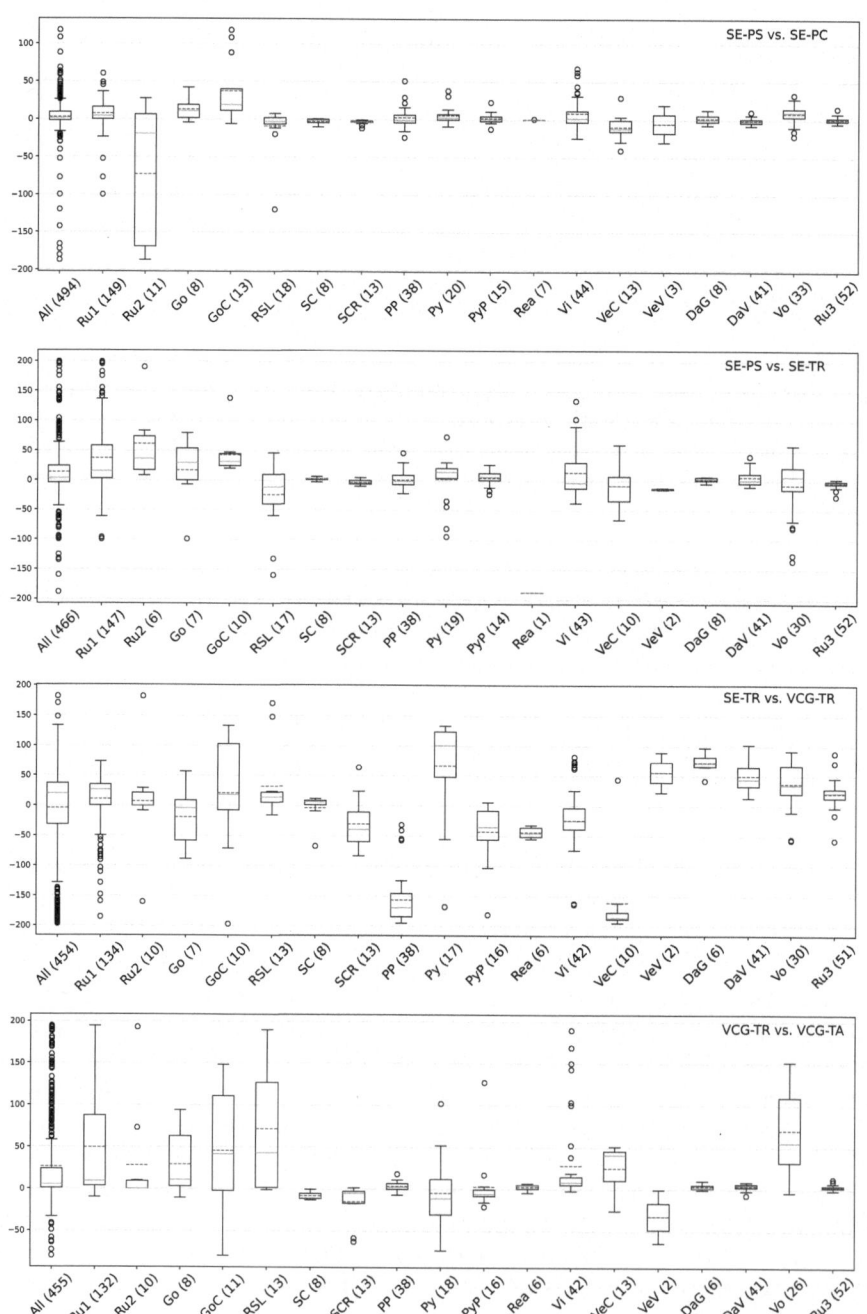

Fig. 2. Box plots of relative percentage difference (RPD) of mean performance per group. From top to bottom: (a) SE-PS vs. SE-PC, (b) SE-PS vs. SE-TR, (c) SE-TR vs. VCG-TR, (d) VCG-TR vs. VCG-TA. As before, values greater than zero indicate that the first algorithm in the pair is faster, values less than zero that the second is faster. The orange line denotes the median, the dashed green line the mean. (Color figure online)

Comparing SE-PS vs. SE-PC, we observe that the two algorithms exhibit very similar performance, with some small advantages for SE-PS, and a few outliers where SE-PC is significantly faster, in particular from Ru_2. This is in line with our completeness evaluation, where the two partial heap algorithms were also the most similar pair. Analogous to completeness, the existence of outliers again allows concluding that **being able to use more than one algorithm can result in performance advantages for individual examples**, even if the alternatives perform similar on average.

Moving from a partial heap algorithm (SE-PS) to a total heap algorithm (SE-TR), we observe the following: both SE algorithms exhibit similar performance for most groups; but SE-PS performs minimally better on Ru_1, Ru_2, and Go_C, while SE-TR has an advantage on RSL and Ve_V. This leads to the surprising conclusion that the choice of **heap representation has a comparably small impact on the average performance** of an SE verifier, whereas it had a large impact on completeness. Exceptions exist, however, and they exhibit a pattern: when SE-TR outperforms SE-PS, it is almost exclusively on examples that heavily use quantified resources. Conversely, when SE-PS is much faster, it tends to be on Ru_1 examples, which do not use quantified resources but whose heap access patterns are amenable to SE-PS's optimizations.

Comparing SE-TR and VCG-TR shows that **the biggest difference in average performance is caused by the switch from SE to VCG** (while keeping the same heap model). As for the two extremes (SE-PS vs. VCG-TA), the branch-heavy groups (PP, Py_P, and SC_R), as well as Rea (and the aforementioned Ve_C[2]), show a significant advantage for VCG-TR, whereas Py, Go_C, Da_G, Da_V and Vo are faster with SE-TR (which also slightly outperforms VCG-TR on most of the other groups).

Finally, comparing VCG-TR (heap per resource) to VCG-TA (single heap) shows very similar performance for many groups, with some exceptions (Go, Go_C, RSL, Ru_1 and Vo) that show a significant advantage for VCG-TR and no significant advantages for VCG-TA. From that, we conclude that **one total heap per resource generally performs better than a single total heap**.

3.6   Recommendation

The overall winner of our comparison in terms of both completeness and performance is SE-PS, which makes SE-PS a good default algorithm, followed closely by SE-PC. However, for both metrics, we have also found that (1) on individual examples, any of the other algorithms may outperform SE-PS, (2) some amount

---

[2] We investigated this group in more detail, and observed that the run time in SE algorithms is dominated by certain SMT queries that involve heap-dependent functions and mathematical sequences, and that non-deterministically take a long time to be answered. It is ultimately unclear to us why VCG should pose a conceptual advantage here, but it is plausible that for example slightly different function axiomatizations accidentally influence how the SMT solver instances the sequence axioms, which are known to be challenging for performance.

of optimization is required to achieve this performance and a less-optimized version of SE-PS would perform worse, and, most importantly, (3) there are entire categories of examples where SE-PS is substantially less complete than a total-heap algorithm (*Rea*), or where SE-PS is substantially slower than a VCG algorithm (*PP*). We thus recommend to either choose the algorithm based on the expected examples (e.g., for domain-specific applications), or to combine SE-PS with other algorithms, as discussed in Sect. 4.

Our novel SE-TR algorithm, combining total heaps and SE, has shown that it provides a different and useful trade-off compared to existing algorithms. Its completeness is comparable to (and often slightly better than) existing total-heap algorithms (which use VCG), while its performance is comparable to (albeit in general slightly slower than) existing SE algorithms (which use partial heaps).

Our SE-PC algorithm performs very similarly to SE-PS, i.e., very well, with some exceptions in both directions. SE-PC is thus also a good default algorithm, in particular, if SE-PS's disjunctive aliasing incompleteness is not acceptable.

VCG-TA is almost universally worse than VCG-TR and we thus recommend VCG-TR when developing a VCG verifier.

3.7 Threats to Validity

Benchmark Selection. Our evaluation covers a wide range of use cases and feature combinations, but cannot be representative of all existing (and future) examples. Our recommendation to use multiple algorithms (see also Sect. 4) increases the robustness of a verifier against unexpected examples.

We focused on verifying complex examples (often with quantifier-heavy specifications), whose verification time is between tenths of seconds and several minutes. As demonstrated by other tools (e.g., VeriFast), simpler settings (e.g., without fractional permissions and quantified resources) can lead to substantially shorter verification times, in which case the differences between the algorithms might be much less pronounced. Our Ru_1 group (comparably few quantifiers, no quantified resources) comes closest to such a setting, so our results for this group should be transferable: here, the clear result is that SE-PS performs the best in terms of both completeness and performance.

Verification examples are typically developed while getting feedback from the verification tool. In our case, the algorithms used by this tool were (earlier versions of) SE-PS, SE-PC, or VCG-TA, since SE-TR and VCG-TR were not yet implemented when any of the examples used in our evaluation were developed. This may skew the results in favor of these algorithms, because developers might have chosen designs that are handled well in the used algorithm.

Impact of Optimizations and Implementation Maturity. The completeness and performance of the different implementations can be influenced both by optimizations they perform and by bugs they may contain. Of the algorithms we used, the implementations of SE-PS and VCG-TA are the most mature (in terms of development time); since these are the two best and worst performing implementations in terms of completeness, we conclude that our results are not a consequence of implementation maturity but of the algorithms themselves. It is, however, possible that the remaining three algorithms with less mature implementations could be further improved with more development time. The fact that SE-PS and SE-PA perform the largest amount of explicit optimization is mostly because, as said before, partial-state SE-algorithms offer more potential for optimization, not because of implementation maturity; the VCG algorithms (and to a lesser degree SE-TR) leave much more work to the SMT solver, and as a result, almost no optimization beyond tuning quantifier heuristics and generating efficient VCs are possible. We have done the former for all algorithms, and Boogie is well-optimized to do the latter.

SMT Solver. We have performed our evaluation using Z3 4.8.7, Viper's default solver. Different SMT solvers have different performance characteristics, but experiments with other SMT solvers determined that Z3 offers the best completeness (and performance) for our examples, and thus, was the best current choice for performing the evaluation. Future improvements in SMT solvers may disproportionately affect the evaluation results of certain algorithms: e.g., improvements in quantifier reasoning may be particularly beneficial for total-heap algorithms, while improvements to incremental subsolvers may be particularly beneficial to SE algorithms.

4   Portfolios

The previous section showed that no single algorithm is optimal for all benchmark groups. Therefore, to maximize the chance of successful verification, it is advisable to use a *portfolio* of different algorithms, i.e., to run several algorithms in parallel until at least one of them succeeds.

We explored all combinations of our five algorithms and identified four portfolios of different sizes that maximize completeness. In this section, we discuss these portfolios and evaluate their performance. It is worth noting that three out of the four winning portfolios contain SE-TR, which we proposed in this paper.

Out of all possible combinations, the smallest set of algorithms needed to get the expected result for *all* examples in our benchmark set is {SE-PS, SE-TR, VCG-TR, VCG-TA}, which is our portfolio $P0$. Since the five algorithms we evaluated have rather diverse sources of incompleteness, most of them are needed to avoid any spurious errors in our benchmark set.

Using a large portfolio is resource intensive and not always justified in practice. There are two portfolios of size three that are complete for all but one example: {SE-PS, SE-TR, VCG-TR} and {SE-PS, SE-TR, VCG-TA}. The examples they fail on seem to be very sensitive to even small changes in the verification algorithms. Each portfolio contains an SE algorithm with partial heaps, an SE algorithm with total heaps, and a VCG algorithm, which demonstrates the complementarity of these approaches. We select the first of these portfolios due to the better average performance of VCG-TR over VCG-TA and name it $P1$.

Reducing the portfolio size further, we can identify two interesting portfolios of size two. The best portfolio of size two, {SE-PS, VCG-TR} ($P2$), is complete for all but six examples. {SE-PS, SE-TR} ($P3$) is complete for all but ten examples, but has the major advantage that it contains only SE algorithms, which reduces the effort of implementing this portfolio substantially. Different SE algorithms can share many parts of the implementation, whereas the implementations of SE and VCG algorithms offer little opportunity for reuse. Consequently, $P3$ provides a relatively easy way for SE tools to improve their completeness by complementing their existing SE-PS algorithm with the new SE-TR algorithm, which only requires re-implementing the heap operations.

Our technical report [25] shows the relative performance of $P1$, $P2$, and $P3$ versus $P0$. While $P1$ mostly performs identical to $P0$, $P2$ has a slight disadvantage for RSL and Ve_C, but performs equally well for all other groups, and thus delivers almost all the benefits of $P0$. Finally, $P3$, due to its lack of a VCG verifier, performs much worse than $P0$ in the previously-identified branch-heavy groups, while delivering good performance for all others.

5 Related Work

The first verification algorithm for separation logic was the SE algorithm for Smallfoot [8]. Its partial heap representation as a collection of heap chunks has been adopted and refined by many separation logic verifiers (such as Caper [17], the Gillian instantiations for C and JavaScript [40], JaVerT [56], SecC [26], VeriFast [32], and Viper's SE-backend), for instance, to support user-defined predicates [32], alternative permission models such as fractional permissions [12] and counting permissions [11], advanced separation logic connectives such as magic wands [58] and iterated separating conjunction [43], and proof search for angelic choice using backtracking [17]. Our evaluation covers those extensions that are implemented in Viper, namely predicates, fractional permissions, magic wands, and iterated separating conjunction.

Gillian [55] is an SE framework that can be instantiated for different input languages and separation logics and lets each instantiation define its own representation of the heap. The existing instantiations for C and JavaScript use an algorithm similar but not identical to SE-PS, but Gillian could also express the other SE algorithms we discuss. Our evaluation can guide developers toward an optimal use of Gillian's expressiveness.

VCG for separation logic was first developed in the context of VeriCool [59] and then extended to concurrency in Chalice [39]. The algorithm there, as well as in Viper's VCG-backend, uses a total-heap representation. While Chalice and Viper use a single total map to represent all heap values, GrassHopper [48] uses a dedicated map for each resource. As we observed in our evaluation, and has previously been shown in the context of VCC [10], this representation can improve performance and completeness by simplifying framing. GrassHopper uses advanced algorithms to automate reasoning about predicates, which were not in scope for our evaluation here.

Existing verifiers support a range of permission logics, including separation logic and implicit dynamic frames [59]. Separation logic is typically defined over partial heaps, whereas the theory of implicit dynamic frames uses total heaps. However, there is a strong connection between both logics [46], and the algorithms discussed in this paper can support both.

There are other approaches to automating verification in separation logic. For instance, Steel [30] is built on top of F* [62], which uses type inference to devise derivations in a dependently typed separation logic. RefinedC [54] automates proof search in Lithium, a fragment of the Iris separation logic [33]. Its verification algorithm is implemented in Coq as a tactic. Such approaches differ substantially from the SE and VCG algorithms discussed in this paper in the degree of automation they provide, their expressiveness, or their ability to devise foundational proofs, which makes a meaningful comparison difficult. Hip/Sleek [15] performs a forward verification similar to SE but operates directly by checking entailments on separation logic formulas and, thus, does not need a heap encoding. To our knowledge, existing separation logic solvers do not support all of the separation logic features (predicates, magic wands and quantified resources, and their combination) supported by the algorithms we considered.

Kassios et al. [34] compared the performance of Chalice's VCG algorithm to an alternative SE-backend most similar to SE-PS, and found a significant performance advantage for the SE-backend throughout. However, their comparison does not include the versions of SE and VCG used in modern tools, does not assess completeness, and does not reflect the diversity of verification problems, with only 29 examples in total being compared.

Finally, choices between explicitly enumerating states (e.g., heap chunks in partial heap models and program paths in SE) and using logical formulas to represent the different options (in total heap models and VCG algorithms) also exist for other ways of automated reasoning. For example, explicit-state model checking enumerates individual states, whereas symbolic model checking represents sets of states via logical formulas, offering different tradeoffs [14].

6   Conclusions and Future Work

We have presented and implemented five algorithms for automated separation logic verification, including two novel algorithms. Our evaluation shows that, across all benchmarks, the prevalent SE-PS algorithm shows the best completeness and performance. However, it is not optimal for all benchmark groups and, thus, should be complemented by other algorithms. We identified algorithm portfolios of different sizes that maximize completeness.

As future work, we plan to extract features from programs that allow us to predict which algorithm will perform best.

Acknowledgement. We are grateful to Sacha-Elie Ayoun, Thomas Dinsdale-Young, and Thomas Wies for discussions about Gillian, Caper, and GrassHopper. We thank Robin Sierra for a first implementation of SE-PC. We thank the ETH Seminar for Statistics consulting service for helpful discussions.

References

1. Armborst, L., Huisman, M.: Permission-based verification of red-black trees and their merging. In: FormaliSE@ICSE, pp. 111–123. IEEE (2021)
2. Arquint, L., Schwerhoff, M., Mehta, V., Müller, P.: A generic methodology for the modular verification of security protocol implementations. In: CCS, pp. 1377–1391. ACM (2023)
3. Astrauskas, V.: Leveraging uniqueness for modular verification of heap-manipulating programs. Ph.D. thesis, ETH Zurich, Zürich, Switzerland (2024)
4. Astrauskas, V., Müller, P., Poli, F., Summers, A.J.: Leveraging rust types for modular specification and verification. Proc. ACM Program. Lang. 3(OOPSLA), 147:1–147:30 (2019)
5. Barbosa, H., et al.: cvc5: a versatile and industrial-strength SMT solver. In: TACAS 2022. LNCS, vol. 13243, pp. 415–442. Springer, Cham (2022). https://doi.org/10.1007/978-3-030-99524-9_24
6. Barnett, M., Chang, B.-Y.E., DeLine, R., Jacobs, B., Leino, K.R.M.: Boogie: a modular reusable verifier for object-oriented programs. In: de Boer, F.S., Bonsangue, M.M., Graf, S., de Roever, W.-P. (eds.) FMCO 2005. LNCS, vol. 4111, pp. 364–387. Springer, Heidelberg (2006). https://doi.org/10.1007/11804192_17
7. Barnett, M., Leino, K.R.M.: Weakest-precondition of unstructured programs. In: PASTE, pp. 82–87. ACM (2005)
8. Berdine, J., Calcagno, C., O'Hearn, P.W.: Smallfoot: modular automatic assertion checking with separation logic. In: de Boer, F.S., Bonsangue, M.M., Graf, S., de Roever, W.-P. (eds.) FMCO 2005. LNCS, vol. 4111, pp. 115–137. Springer, Heidelberg (2006). https://doi.org/10.1007/11804192_6
9. Blom, S., Huisman, M.: The VerCors tool for verification of concurrent programs. In: Jones, C., Pihlajasaari, P., Sun, J. (eds.) FM 2014. LNCS, vol. 8442, pp. 127–131. Springer, Cham (2014). https://doi.org/10.1007/978-3-319-06410-9_9
10. Böhme, S., Moskal, M.: Heaps and data structures: a challenge for automated provers. In: Bjørner, N., Sofronie-Stokkermans, V. (eds.) CADE 2011. LNCS (LNAI), vol. 6803, pp. 177–191. Springer, Heidelberg (2011). https://doi.org/10.1007/978-3-642-22438-6_15
11. Bornat, R., Calcagno, C., O'Hearn, P.W., Parkinson, M.J.: Permission accounting in separation logic. In: POPL, pp. 259–270. ACM (2005)
12. Boyland, J.: Checking interference with fractional permissions. In: Cousot, R. (ed.) SAS 2003. LNCS, vol. 2694, pp. 55–72. Springer, Heidelberg (2003). https://doi.org/10.1007/3-540-44898-5_4
13. Bräm, C., Eilers, M., Müller, P., Sierra, R., Summers, A.J.: Rich specifications for Ethereum smart contract verification. Proc. ACM Program. Lang. 5(OOPSLA), 1–30 (2021)
14. Buzhinsky, I., Pakonen, A., Vyatkin, V.: Explicit-state and symbolic model checking of nuclear i&c systems: a comparison. In: IECON, pp. 5439–5446. IEEE (2017)
15. Chin, W., David, C., Nguyen, H.H., Qin, S.: Automated verification of shape, size and bag properties via user-defined predicates in separation logic. Sci. Comput. Program. 77(9), 1006–1036 (2012)
16. Detlefs, D., Nelson, G., Saxe, J.B.: Simplify: a theorem prover for program checking. J. ACM 52(3), 365–473 (2005)
17. Dinsdale-Young, T., da Rocha Pinto, P., Andersen, K.J., Birkedal, L.: CAPER. In: Yang, H. (ed.) ESOP 2017. LNCS, vol. 10201, pp. 420–447. Springer, Heidelberg (2017). https://doi.org/10.1007/978-3-662-54434-1_16

18. Dross, C., Furia, C.A., Huisman, M., Monahan, R., Müller, P.: VerifyThis 2019: a program verification competition. Int. J. Softw. Tools Technol. Transf. **23**(6), 883–893 (2021)
19. Egli, T.: Translating Pedagogical Exercises to Viper's Go Front-End. Bachelor's thesis, ETH Zürich (2023)
20. Eilers, M.: Modular Specification and Verification of Security Properties for Mainstream Languages. Ph.D. thesis, ETH Zurich, Zürich, Switzerland (2022)
21. Eilers, M., Meier, S., Müller, P.: Product programs in the wild: retrofitting program verifiers to check information flow security. In: Silva, A., Leino, K.R.M. (eds.) CAV 2021. LNCS, vol. 12759, pp. 718–741. Springer, Cham (2021). https://doi.org/10.1007/978-3-030-81685-8_34
22. Eilers, M., Müller, P.: Nagini: a static verifier for Python. In: Chockler, H., Weissenbacher, G. (eds.) CAV 2018. LNCS, vol. 10981, pp. 596–603. Springer, Cham (2018). https://doi.org/10.1007/978-3-319-96145-3_33
23. Eilers, M., Müller, P., Hitz, S.: Modular product programs. ACM Trans. Program. Lang. Syst. **42**(1), 3:1–3:37 (2020)
24. Eilers, M., Schwerhoff, M., Müller, P.: Verification algorithms for automated separation logic verifiers (artifact) (May 2024). https://doi.org/10.5281/zenodo.11218239, https://doi.org/10.5281/zenodo.11218239
25. Eilers, M., Schwerhoff, M., Müller, P.: Verification algorithms for automated separation logic verifiers (2024)
26. Ernst, G., Murray, T.: SecCSL: Security Concurrent Separation Logic. In: Dillig, I., Tasiran, S. (eds.) CAV 2019. LNCS, vol. 11562, pp. 208–230. Springer, Cham (2019). https://doi.org/10.1007/978-3-030-25543-5_13
27. Filliâtre, J.-C., Paskevich, A.: Why3 — where programs meet provers. In: Felleisen, M., Gardner, P. (eds.) ESOP 2013. LNCS, vol. 7792, pp. 125–128. Springer, Heidelberg (2013). https://doi.org/10.1007/978-3-642-37036-6_8
28. Forster, S.: Static Verification of the SCION Router Implementation. Bachelor's thesis, ETH Zürich (2018)
29. Frei, B.: Translating Pedagogical Verification Exercises to Viper. Bachelor's thesis, ETH Zürich (2023)
30. Fromherz, A., Rastogi, A., Swamy, N., Gibson, S., Martínez, G., Merigoux, D., Ramananandro, T.: Steel: proof-oriented programming in a dependently typed concurrent separation logic. Proc. ACM Program. Lang. **5**(ICFP), 1–30 (2021)
31. Heule, S., Kassios, I.T., Müller, P., Summers, A.J.: Verification condition generation for permission logics with abstract predicates and abstraction functions. In: Castagna, G. (ed.) ECOOP 2013. LNCS, vol. 7920, pp. 451–476. Springer, Heidelberg (2013). https://doi.org/10.1007/978-3-642-39038-8_19
32. Jacobs, B., Smans, J., Philippaerts, P., Vogels, F., Penninckx, W., Piessens, F.: VeriFast: a powerful, sound, predictable, fast verifier for C and Java. In: Bobaru, M., Havelund, K., Holzmann, G.J., Joshi, R. (eds.) NFM 2011. LNCS, vol. 6617, pp. 41–55. Springer, Heidelberg (2011). https://doi.org/10.1007/978-3-642-20398-5_4
33. Jung, R., Krebbers, R., Jourdan, J., Bizjak, A., Birkedal, L., Dreyer, D.: Iris from the ground up: a modular foundation for higher-order concurrent separation logic. J. Funct. Program. **28**, e20 (2018)
34. Kassios, I.T., Müller, P., Schwerhoff, M.: Comparing verification condition generation with symbolic execution: an experience report. In: Joshi, R., Müller, P., Podelski, A. (eds.) VSTTE 2012. LNCS, vol. 7152, pp. 196–208. Springer, Heidelberg (2012). https://doi.org/10.1007/978-3-642-27705-4_16

35. Lal, A., Qadeer, S.: Powering the static driver verifier using Corral. In: SIGSOFT FSE, pp. 202–212. ACM (2014)
36. Leino, K.R.M.: This is Boogie 2 (June 2008). https://www.microsoft.com/en-us/research/publication/this-is-boogie-2-2/
37. Leino, K.R.M.: Dafny: an automatic program verifier for functional correctness. In: Clarke, E.M., Voronkov, A. (eds.) LPAR 2010. LNCS (LNAI), vol. 6355, pp. 348–370. Springer, Heidelberg (2010). https://doi.org/10.1007/978-3-642-17511-4_20
38. Leino, K.R.M.: Program Proofs. MIT Press (2023)
39. Leino, K.R.M., Müller, P., Smans, J.: Verification of concurrent programs with chalice. In: Aldini, A., Barthe, G., Gorrieri, R. (eds.) FOSAD 2007-2009. LNCS, vol. 5705, pp. 195–222. Springer, Heidelberg (2009). https://doi.org/10.1007/978-3-642-03829-7_7
40. Maksimović, P., Ayoun, S.É., Santos, J.F., Gardner, P.: Gillian, Part II: real-world verification for JavaScript and C. In: Silva, A., Leino, K.R.M. (eds.) CAV 2021. LNCS, vol. 12760, pp. 827–850. Springer, Cham (2021). https://doi.org/10.1007/978-3-030-81688-9_38
41. de Moura, L., Bjørner, N.: Z3: an efficient SMT solver. In: Ramakrishnan, C.R., Rehof, J. (eds.) TACAS 2008. LNCS, vol. 4963, pp. 337–340. Springer, Heidelberg (2008). https://doi.org/10.1007/978-3-540-78800-3_24
42. Mugnier, E., McLaughlin, S., Tomb, A.: Portfolio solving for Dafny. In: Dafny Workshop (2024), to appear
43. Müller, P., Schwerhoff, M., Summers, A.J.: Automatic verification of iterated separating conjunctions using symbolic execution. In: Chaudhuri, S., Farzan, A. (eds.) CAV 2016. LNCS, vol. 9779, pp. 405–425. Springer, Cham (2016). https://doi.org/10.1007/978-3-319-41528-4_22
44. Müller, P., Schwerhoff, M., Summers, A.J.: Viper: a verification infrastructure for permission-based reasoning. In: Jobstmann, B., Leino, K.R.M. (eds.) VMCAI 2016. LNCS, vol. 9583, pp. 41–62. Springer, Heidelberg (2016). https://doi.org/10.1007/978-3-662-49122-5_2
45. Parkinson, M.J., Bierman, G.M.: Separation logic and abstraction. In: POPL, pp. 247–258. ACM (2005)
46. Parkinson, M.J., Summers, A.J.: The relationship between separation logic and implicit dynamic frames. In: Barthe, G. (ed.) ESOP 2011. LNCS, vol. 6602, pp. 439–458. Springer, Heidelberg (2011). https://doi.org/10.1007/978-3-642-19718-5_23
47. Pereira, J.C., et al.: Protocols to code: formal verification of a next-generation internet router (2024)
48. Piskac, Ruzica, Wies, Thomas, Zufferey, Damien: GRASShopper. In: Ábrahám, Erika, Havelund, Klaus (eds.) TACAS 2014. LNCS, vol. 8413, pp. 124–139. Springer, Heidelberg (2014). https://doi.org/10.1007/978-3-642-54862-8_9
49. Poli, F., Denis, X., Müller, P., Summers, A.J.: Reasoning about interior mutability in rust using library-defined capabilities (2024)
50. Reynolds, J.C.: Separation logic: a logic for shared mutable data structures. In: LICS, pp. 55–74. IEEE Computer Society (2002)
51. da Rocha Pinto, P., Dinsdale-Young, T., Gardner, P.: TaDA: a logic for time and data abstraction. In: Jones, R. (ed.) ECOOP 2014. LNCS, vol. 8586, pp. 207–231. Springer, Heidelberg (2014). https://doi.org/10.1007/978-3-662-44202-9_9
52. Safari, M., Huisman, M.: A generic approach to the verification of the permutation property of sequential and parallel swap-based sorting algorithms. In: Dongol, B.,

Troubitsyna, E. (eds.) IFM 2020. LNCS, vol. 12546, pp. 257–275. Springer, Cham (2020). https://doi.org/10.1007/978-3-030-63461-2_14

53. Safari, M., Huisman, M.: Formal verification of parallel prefix sum and stream compaction algorithms in CUDA. Theor. Comput. Sci. **912**, 81–98 (2022)

54. Sammler, M., Lepigre, R., Krebbers, R., Memarian, K., Dreyer, D., Garg, D.: RefinedC: automating the foundational verification of C code with refined ownership types. In: PLDI, pp. 158–174. ACM (2021)

55. Santos, J.F., Maksimovic, P., Ayoun, S., Gardner, P.: Gillian, part i: a multilanguage platform for symbolic execution. In: PLDI, pp. 927–942. ACM (2020)

56. Santos, J.F., Maksimovic, P., Sampaio, G., Gardner, P.: JaVerT 2.0: compositional symbolic execution for JavaScript. Proc. ACM Program. Lang. **3**(POPL), 66:1–66:31 (2019)

57. Schwerhoff, M.: Advancing Automated, Permission-Based Program Verification Using Symbolic Execution. Ph.D. thesis, ETH Zurich, Zürich, Switzerland (2016)

58. Schwerhoff, M., Summers, A.J.: Lightweight support for magic wands in an automatic verifier. In: ECOOP. LIPIcs, vol. 37, pp. 614–638. Schloss Dagstuhl - Leibniz-Zentrum für Informatik (2015)

59. Smans, J., Jacobs, B., Piessens, F.: Implicit dynamic frames: combining dynamic frames and separation logic. In: Drossopoulou, S. (ed.) ECOOP 2009. LNCS, vol. 5653, pp. 148–172. Springer, Heidelberg (2009). https://doi.org/10.1007/978-3-642-03013-0_8

60. Sprenger, C., Klenze, T., Eilers, M., Wolf, F.A., Müller, P., Clochard, M., Basin, D.A.: Igloo: soundly linking compositional refinement and separation logic for distributed system verification. Proc. ACM Program. Lang. **4**(OOPSLA), 152:1–152:31 (2020)

61. Summers, A.J., Müller, P.: Automating deductive verification for weak-memory programs. In: Beyer, D., Huisman, M. (eds.) TACAS 2018. LNCS, vol. 10805, pp. 190–209. Springer, Cham (2018). https://doi.org/10.1007/978-3-319-89960-2_11

62. Swamy, N., Weinberger, J., Schlesinger, C., Chen, J., Livshits, B.: Verifying higher-order programs with the Dijkstra monad. In: PLDI, pp. 387–398. ACM (2013)

63. Ter-Gabrielyan, A., Summers, A.J., Müller, P.: Modular verification of heap reachability properties in separation logic. Proc. ACM Program. Lang. **3**(OOPSLA), 121:1–121:28 (2019)

64. Vafeiadis, V., Narayan, C.: Relaxed separation logic: a program logic for C11 concurrency. In: OOPSLA, pp. 867–884. ACM (2013)

65. Wolf, F.A., Arquint, L., Clochard, M., Oortwijn, W., Pereira, J.C., Müller, P.: Gobra: modular specification and verification of go programs. In: Silva, A., Leino, K.R.M. (eds.) CAV 2021. LNCS, vol. 12759, pp. 367–379. Springer, Cham (2021). https://doi.org/10.1007/978-3-030-81685-8_17

66. Wolf, F.A., Schwerhoff, M., Müller, P.: Concise outlines for a complex logic: a proof outline checker for TaDA. In: Huisman, M., Păsăreanu, C., Zhan, N. (eds.) FM 2021. LNCS, vol. 13047, pp. 407–426. Springer, Cham (2021). https://doi.org/10.1007/978-3-030-90870-6_22

SMT-Based Symbolic Model-Checking for Operator Precedence Languages

Michele Chiari[1]([⊠]) , Luca Geatti[2] , Nicola Gigante[3] ,
and Matteo Pradella[4]

[1] TU Wien, Treitlstraße 3, 1040 Vienna, Austria
michele.chiari@tuwien.ac.at
[2] University of Udine, Udine, Italy
luca.geatti@uniud.it
[3] Free University of Bozen-Bolzano, Bolzano, Italy
nicola.gigante@unibz.it
[4] Politecnico di Milano, Milan, Italy
matteo.pradella@polimi.it

Abstract. Operator Precedence Languages (OPL) have been recently identified as a suitable formalism for model checking recursive procedural programs, thanks to their ability of modeling the program stack. OPL requirements can be expressed in the *Precedence Oriented Temporal Logic* (**POTL**), which features modalities to reason on the natural matching between function calls and returns, exceptions, and other advanced programming constructs that previous approaches, such as Visibly Pushdown Languages, cannot model effectively. Existing approaches for model checking of **POTL** have been designed following the explicit-state, automata-based approach, a feature that severely limits their scalability. In this paper, we give the first symbolic, SMT-based approach for model checking **POTL** properties. While previous approaches construct the automaton for both the **POTL** formula and the model of the program, we encode them into a (sequence of) SMT formulas. The search of a trace of the model witnessing a violation of the formula is then carried out by an SMT-solver, in a Bounded Model Checking fashion. We carried out an experimental evaluation, which shows the effectiveness of the proposed solution.

Keywords: SMT-based Model Checking · Tree-shaped Tableau · Temporal Logic · Operator Precedence Languages

1 Introduction

Operator Precedence Languages (OPL) [16] are very promising for software verification: as a subclass of context-free languages, they can naturally encode the typical stack-based behavior of programs, without the shortcomings of the better known Visibly Pushdown Languages (VPL), originally introduced as Input-driven languages [5,6,30]. In particular, the main characteristic of VPL is the

© The Author(s) 2024
A. Gurfinkel and V. Ganesh (Eds.): CAV 2024, LNCS 14681, pp. 387–408, 2024.
https://doi.org/10.1007/978-3-031-65627-9_19

one-to-one "matching" between a symbol representing a procedure call and the symbol representing its corresponding return. Unfortunately, this feature makes them ill-suited to model several typical behaviors of programs that induce a many-to-one or one-to-many matching, such as exceptions, interrupts, dynamic memory management, transactions, and continuations.

OPL were introduced through grammars for deterministic parsing by Floyd in 1963, and were re-discovered and studied in more recent works, where containment of VPL and closure w.r.t. Boolean operations were proved [15], together with the following characterizations: automata-based, monadic second order logic [26], regular-like expressions [28], and syntactic congruence with finitely many equivalence classes [22]. OPL are also the biggest known class maintaining an important feature of Regular languages: first-order logic, star-free expressions, and aperiodicity define the same subclass [29]. A temporal logic called OPTL was defined in [11], and a subsequent extension called POTL (on which we focus in this work) was introduced in [12], and then proved to capture the first-order definable fragment of OPL in [13]. The linear temporal logics for VPL CaRet [4] and NWTL [2] were also proved to be less expressive than both OPTL [11] and POTL [13].

POTL contains explicit context-free modalities that interact not only with the linear order of events representing time, but also with the nested structure of function calls, returns, and exceptions. For instance, consider this formula:

$$\Box(\textbf{call} \land \text{qs} \to \neg(\bigcirc^u \textbf{ exc} \lor \chi_F^u \textbf{ exc}))$$

Here $\Box$ is the LTL globally operator, and **call** and **exc** hold respectively in positions that represent a function call and an exception. $\bigcirc^u \textbf{ exc}$ means that the *next* position is an exception (similarly to the LTL next), while $\chi_F^u \textbf{ exc}$ means that a subsequent position, which *terminates* the function call in the current position, is an exception. Thus, the formula means "function qs is never terminated by an exception" (or, equivalently, it never terminates or it always terminates with a normal return).

It is worth to note that VPL were originally proposed for automatic verification, thanks to their nice Regular-like closure properties, but effective Model Checking (MC) tools for them are still not publicly available, in particular supporting logics capable of expressing context-free specifications. This situation improved with the introduction of POMC [8,10,12], a model checker for structured context-free languages based on POTL, but that can be easily adapted to the simpler structure of VPL. POMC's core consists of an explicit-state tableau construction procedure, which yields nondeterministic automata of size at most singly exponential in the formula's length, and is shown to be quite effective in realistic cases in [10,32].

The main shortcoming of explicit-state MC tools is the state explosion problem, i.e. the exponential growth of the state space as the system size and complexity increase, which makes MC infeasible for large and realistic systems. Indeed, as reported in [10], managing longer arrays or variables encoded with a realistic number of bits was problematic. A classical way to address this issue is to use Symbolic Model Checking, which is a variant of MC that represents the system and the specification using symbolic data structures, instead of explicit enumeration of states and transitions. One very successful symbolic technique is Bounded Model Checking (BMC) [7,14], where the model is unrolled for a fixed number of steps and encoded into SAT, i.e. Boolean Satisfiability, to leverage recent efficient SAT solvers, and later the more general Satisfiability Modulo Theories (SMT) solvers, such as Z3 [31].

In this paper we apply BMC to POTL by encoding its tableau into SMT, extending the approach used in the BLACK tool [19]. BLACK is a satisfiability checker and temporal reasoning framework based on an encoding into SAT of Reynolds' one-pass tableau system for classical linear temporal logic [18]. Currently, we consider the future fragment of the temporal logic POTL on finite-word semantics, but we plan to extend the encoding to cover full POTL and ω-words. SMT-based approaches were already introduced for verifying pushdown program models [23,25], but only against regular specifications. To the best of our knowledge, this is the first SMT encoding of a context-free temporal logic, proving that BMC can be beneficial to verification of this class of temporal logics, too.

We applied our tool to a number of realistic cases: an implementation of the Quicksort algorithm, a banking application, and C++ implementations of a generic stack data structure, where our approach is compared with the original POMC. The results are very promising, as our SMT-based approach was able to avoid POMC's exponential increase of the solving time in several cases.

The paper is structured as follows. OPL and the logic POTL are introduced in Sect. 2. Section 3 defines the tree-shaped tableau for POTL, while Sect. 4 presents its encoding into SMT. Section 5 illustrates the experimental evaluation. Last, Sect. 6 draws the conclusions.

2   Preliminaries

2.1   Operator Precedence Languages

We assume that the reader has some familiarity with formal language theory concepts such as context-free grammar, parsing, shift-reduce algorithm [20,21]. Operator Precedence Languages (OPL) were historically defined through their generating grammars [16]; in this paper, we characterize them through their automata [26], as they are more suitable for model checking. Readers not familiar with OPL may refer to [27] for more explanations on their basic concepts.

Let Σ be a finite alphabet, and ε the empty string. We use a special symbol $\# \notin \Sigma$ to mark the beginning and the end of any string. An *operator precedence matrix* (OPM) M over Σ is a partial function $(\Sigma \cup \{\#\})^2 \to \{<, \doteq, >\}$, that, for each ordered pair (a, b), defines the *precedence relation* (PR) $M(a, b)$ holding between a and b. If the function is total we say that M is *complete*. We call the pair (Σ, M) an *operator precedence alphabet*. Relations $<, \doteq, >$, are respectively named *yields precedence*, *equal in precedence*, and *takes precedence*. By convention, the initial $\#$ yields precedence, and other symbols take precedence on the ending $\#$. If $M(a, b) = \pi$, where $\pi \in \{<, \doteq, >\}$, we write $a \, \pi \, b$. For $u, v \in \Sigma^+$ we write $u \pi v$ if $u = xa$ and $v = by$ with $a \pi b$. The role of PR is to give structure to words: they can be seen as special and more concise parentheses, where e.g. one "closing" $>$ can match more than one "opening" $<$. It is important to remark that PR are not ordering relations, despite their graphical appearance.

Definition 1. *An operator precedence automaton (OPA) is a tuple $\mathcal{A} = (\Sigma, M, Q, I, F, \delta)$ where (Σ, M) is an operator precedence alphabet, Q is a finite set of states, $I \subseteq Q$ is the set of initial states, $F \subseteq Q$ is the set of final states, δ is a triple of transition relations $\delta_{shift} \subseteq Q \times \Sigma \times Q$, $\delta_{push} \subseteq Q \times \Sigma \times Q$, and $\delta_{pop} \subseteq Q \times Q \times Q$. An OPA is deterministic iff I is a singleton, and all three components of δ are functions.*

To define the semantics of OPA, we set some notation. Letters $p, q, p_i, q_i, \ldots$ denote states in Q. We use $q_0 \xrightarrow{a} q_1$ for $(q_0, a, q_1) \in \delta_{push}$, $q_0 \dashrightarrow q_1$ for $(q_0, a, q_1) \in \delta_{shift}$, $q_0 \xRightarrow{q_2} q_1$ for $(q_0, q_2, q_1) \in \delta_{pop}$, and $q_0 \overset{w}{\rightsquigarrow} q_1$, if the automaton can read $w \in \Sigma^*$ going from q_0 to q_1. Let $\Gamma = \Sigma \times Q$ and $\Gamma' = \Gamma \cup \{\bot\}$ be the *stack alphabet*; we denote symbols in Γ' as $[a, q]$ or $\bot$. We set $smb([a, q]) = a$, $smb(\bot) = \#$, and $st([a, q]) = q$. For a stack content $\gamma = \gamma_n \ldots \gamma_1 \bot$, with $\gamma_i \in \Gamma$, $n \geq 0$, we set $smb(\gamma) = smb(\gamma_n)$ if $n \geq 1$, $smb(\gamma) = \#$ if $n = 0$.

A *configuration* of an OPA is a triple $c = \langle w, q, \gamma \rangle$, where $w \in \Sigma^* \#$, $q \in Q$, and $\gamma \in \Gamma^* \bot$. A *computation* or *run* is a finite sequence $c_0 \vdash c_1 \vdash \ldots \vdash c_n$ of *moves* or *transitions* $c_i \vdash c_{i+1}$. There are three kinds of moves, depending on the PR between the symbol on top of the stack and the next input symbol:

push move: if $smb(\gamma) < a$ then $\langle ax, p, \gamma \rangle \vdash \langle x, q, [a, p]\gamma \rangle$, with $(p, a, q) \in \delta_{push}$;

shift move: if $a \doteq b$ then $\langle bx, q, [a, p]\gamma \rangle \vdash \langle x, r, [b, p]\gamma \rangle$, with $(q, b, r) \in \delta_{shift}$;

pop move: if $a > b$ then $\langle bx, q, [a, p]\gamma \rangle \vdash \langle bx, r, \gamma \rangle$, with $(q, p, r) \in \delta_{pop}$.

Shift and pop moves are not performed when the stack contains only $\bot$. Push moves put a new element on top of the stack consisting of the input symbol together with the current state of the OPA. Shift moves update the top element of the stack by *changing its input symbol only*. Pop moves remove the element on top of the stack, and update the state of the OPA according to δ_{pop} on the basis of the current state of the OPA and the state of the removed stack symbol. They do not consume the input symbol, which is used only to establish the $>$ relation, remaining available for the next move. The OPA accepts the language $L(\mathcal{A}) = \{x \in \Sigma^* \mid \langle x\#, q_I, \bot \rangle \vdash^* \langle \#, q_F, \bot \rangle, q_I \in I, q_F \in F\}$.

We now introduce the concept of *chain*, which makes the connection between OP relations and context-free structure explicit, through brackets.

Definition 2. *A simple chain $^{c_0}[c_1 c_2 \ldots c_\ell]^{c_{\ell+1}}$ is a string $c_0 c_1 c_2 \ldots c_\ell c_{\ell+1}$, such that: $c_0, c_{\ell+1} \in \Sigma \cup \{\#\}$, $c_i \in \Sigma$ for every $i = 1, 2, \ldots \ell$ ($\ell \geq 1$), and $c_0 < c_1 \doteq c_2 \ldots c_{\ell-1} \doteq c_\ell > c_{\ell+1}$. A composed chain is a string $c_0 s_0 c_1 s_1 c_2 \ldots c_\ell s_\ell c_{\ell+1}$, where $^{c_0}[c_1 c_2 \ldots c_\ell]^{c_{\ell+1}}$ is a simple chain, and $s_i \in \Sigma^*$ is the empty string or is such that $^{c_i}[s_i]^{c_{i+1}}$ is a chain (simple or composed), for every $i = 0, 1, \ldots, \ell$ ($\ell \geq 1$). Such a composed chain will be written as $^{c_0}[s_0 c_1 s_1 c_2 \ldots c_\ell s_\ell]^{c_{\ell+1}}$. c_0 (resp. $c_{\ell+1}$) is called its* left *(resp.* right*) context; all symbols between them form its* body.

	call	ret	han	exc
call	⋖	≐	⋖	⋗
ret	⋗	⋗	⋗	⋗
han	⋖	⋗	⋖	≐
exc	⋗	⋗	⋗	⋗

1 | # ⋖ **call** ⋖ **han** ⋖ <u>**call**</u> ⋗ **exc** ⋗ **call** ≐ **ret** ⋗ **ret** ⋗ #
2 | # ⋖ **call** ⋖ <u>**han** ≐ **exc**</u> ⋗ **call** ≐ **ret** ⋗ **ret** ⋗ #
3 | # ⋖ **call** ⋖ <u>**call** ≐ **ret**</u> ⋗ **ret** ⋗ #
4 | # ⋖ <u>**call** ≐ **ret**</u> ⋗ #
5 | # ≐ #

$$\#[\textbf{call}[[\textbf{han}[\textbf{call}]\textbf{exc}]\textbf{call ret}]\textbf{ret}]\#$$

Fig. 1. OPM $M_{\textbf{call}}$ (left), a string with chains shown by brackets (bottom), and its parsing steps using the OP algorithm (right).

A finite word w over Σ is *compatible* with an OPM M iff for each pair of letters c, d, consecutive in w, $M(c, d)$ is defined and, for each substring x of $\#w\#$ that is a chain of the form $^a[y]^b$, $M(a, b)$ is defined.

Chains can be identified through the traditional operator precedence parsing algorithm. We apply it to the sample word $w_{ex} = \textbf{call han call exc call ret ret}$, which is compatible with $M_{\textbf{call}}$. First, write all precedence relations between consecutive characters, according to $M_{\textbf{call}}$. Then, recognize all innermost patterns of the form $a \lessdot c \doteq \ldots \doteq c \gtrdot b$ as simple chains, and remove their bodies. Then, write the precedence relations between the left and right contexts of the removed body, a and b, and iterate this process until only $\#\#$ remains. This procedure is applied to w_{ex} and illustrated in Fig. 1 (right). The chain body removed in each step is underlined. In step 1 we recognize the simple chain $^{\textbf{han}}[\textbf{call}]^{\textbf{exc}}$, which can be removed. In the next steps we recognize as chains first $^{\textbf{call}}[\textbf{han exc}]^{\textbf{call}}$, then $^{\textbf{call}}[\textbf{call ret}]^{\textbf{ret}}$, and last $^{\#}[\textbf{call ret}]^{\#}$. Figure 1 (bottom) reports the chain structure of w_{ex}.

Let $\mathcal{A}$ be an OPA. We call a *support* for the simple chain $^{c_0}[c_1 c_2 \ldots c_\ell]^{c_{\ell+1}}$ any path in $\mathcal{A}$ of the form $q_0 \xrightarrow{c_1} q_1 \dashrightarrow \ldots \dashrightarrow q_{\ell-1} \overset{c_\ell}{\dashrightarrow} q_\ell \overset{q_0}{\Longrightarrow} q_{\ell+1}$. The label of the last (and only) pop is exactly q_0, i.e. the first state of the path; this pop is executed because of relation $c_\ell \gtrdot c_{\ell+1}$. We call a *support for the composed chain* $^{c_0}[s_0 c_1 s_1 c_2 \ldots c_\ell s_\ell]^{c_{\ell+1}}$ any path in $\mathcal{A}$ of the form $q_0 \overset{s_0}{\leadsto} q_0' \xrightarrow{c_1} q_1 \overset{s_1}{\leadsto} q_1' \overset{c_2}{\dashrightarrow} \ldots \overset{c_\ell}{\dashrightarrow} q_\ell \overset{s_\ell}{\leadsto} q_\ell' \overset{q_0'}{\Longrightarrow} q_{\ell+1}$ where, for every $i = 0, 1, \ldots, \ell$: if $s_i \neq \epsilon$, then $q_i \overset{s_i}{\leadsto} q_i'$ is a support for the chain $^{c_i}[s_i]^{c_{i+1}}$, else $q_i' = q_i$.

Chains fully determine the parsing structure of any OPA over (Σ, M). If the OPA performs the computation $\langle sb, q_i, [a, q_j]\gamma \rangle \vdash^* \langle b, q_k, \gamma \rangle$, then $^a[s]^b$ is necessarily a chain over (Σ, M), and there exists a support like the one above with $s = s_0 c_1 \ldots c_\ell s_\ell$ and $q_{\ell+1} = q_k$. This corresponds to the parsing of the string $s_0 c_1 \ldots c_\ell s_\ell$ within the contexts a, b, which contains all information needed to build the subtree whose frontier is that string.

In [15] it is proved that Visibly Pushdown Languages (VPL) [5] are strictly included in OPL. In VPL the input alphabet is partitioned into three disjoint sets, namely of *call* (Σ_c), *return* (Σ_r), and *internal* (Σ_i) symbols, where *calls* and *returns* respectively play the role of open and closed parentheses. Intuitively, the string structure determined by these alphabets can be represented through an OPM as follows: $a \lessdot b$, for any $a \in \Sigma_c$, $b \in \Sigma_c \cup \Sigma_i$; $a \doteq b$, for any $a \in \Sigma_c$,

$b \in \Sigma_r$; $a \gtrdot b$, for all the other cases. On the other hand, the OPM that we use in this paper cannot be expressed in VPL, because the typical behavior of exceptions cannot be modeled with the limited one-to-one structure of calls and returns.

To sum up, given an OP alphabet, the OPM M assigns a unique structure to any compatible string in Σ^*; unlike VPL, such a structure is not visible in the string, and must be built by means of a non-trivial parsing algorithm. An OPA defined on the OP alphabet selects an appropriate subset within the "universe" of strings compatible with M.

2.2 Precedence Oriented Temporal Logic

POTL is a propositional linear-time temporal logic featuring context-free modalities based on OPL. Here we are only interested in its future fragment, POTL$_f$ (the letter "f" stands for "future"), with the addition of *weak* operators, which are needed for our tableau. In this paper, we focus on the finite words semantics for POTL$_f$.

We fix a finite set of atomic propositions AP. POTL$_f$ semantics are based on OP words, which are tuples $(U, <, M_{AP}, P)$, where $U = \{0, \ldots, n\}$, $n \in \mathbb{N}$, is a finite set of word positions, $<$ a linear order on them, M_{AP} an OPM on $\mathcal{P}(AP)$, and $P : U \to \mathcal{P}(U)$ a labeling function, with $0, n \in P(\#)$. From M_{AP} follows the *chain relation* $\chi \subseteq U^2$, such that $\chi(i,j)$ holds iff i and j are resp. the left and right contexts of a chain. We only define the OPM on propositions in **bold**, called *structural*, and assume that only one of them holds in each position. If $\mathbf{l}_1 \sim \mathbf{l}_2$ for any PR $\sim$ and $i \in P(\mathbf{l}_1)$ and $j \in P(\mathbf{l}_2)$, we write $i \sim j$.

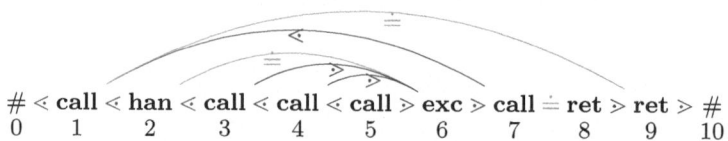

Fig. 2. An example OP word, with the χ relation depicted by arrows, and PRs. First, a procedure is called (pos. 1), which installs an exception handler in pos. 2. Then, another function throws an exception, which is caught by the handler. Another function is called and returns and, finally, the initial one also returns.

POTL$_f$ offers next and until operators based on two different kinds of paths, which we define below, after fixing an OP word w.

Definition 3. *The* downward summary path (DSP) *between positions i and j, denoted $\pi_\chi^d(w, i, j)$, is a set of positions $i = i_1 < i_2 < \cdots < i_n = j$ such that, for each $1 \leq p < n$,*

$$i_{p+1} = \begin{cases} k & \textit{if } k = \max\{h \mid h \leq j \wedge \chi(i_p, h) \wedge (i_p \lessdot h \vee i_p \doteq h)\} \textit{ exists;} \\ i_p + 1 & \textit{otherwise, if } i_p \lessdot (i_p + 1) \textit{ or } i_p \doteq (i_p + 1). \end{cases}$$

We write $\pi_\chi^d(w, i, j) = \varnothing$ if no such path exists. The definition for $\pi_\chi^u(w, i, j)$ is obtained by substituting $\gtrdot$ for $\lessdot$.

DSPs can either go downward in the nesting structure of the χ relation by following the linear order, or skip whole chain bodies by following the χ relation. What this means depends on the OPM: with $M_{\textbf{call}}$, until operators on DSPs express properties local to a function invocation, including children calls. Their upward counterparts, instead, go from inner functions towards parent invocations. For instance, in Fig. 2 we have $\pi_\chi^d(w, 1, 6) = \{1, 5, 6\}$, and $\pi_\chi^u(w, 2, 7) = \{2, 4, 5, 6, 7\}$.

Definition 4. *The* downward hierarchical path *between positions i and j, denoted $\pi_H^d(w, i, j)$, is a sequence of positions $i = i_1 < i_2 < \cdots < i_n = j$ such that there exists $h > j$ such that for each $1 \leq p \leq n$ we have $\chi(i_p, h)$ and $i_p \gtrdot h$, and for each $1 \leq q < n$ there is no position k such that $i_q < k < i_{q+1}$ and $\chi(k, h)$.*
    The upward hierarchical path *$\pi_H^u(w, i, j)$ is defined similarly, except $h < j$ and for all $1 \leq p \leq n$ we have $\chi(h, i_p)$ and $h \lessdot i_p$.*
    We write $\pi_H^d(w, i, j) = \varnothing$ or $\pi_H^u(w, i, j) = \varnothing$ if no such path exists.

Hierarchical paths range between multiple positions in the χ relation with the same one. With $M_{\textbf{call}}$, this means functions terminated by the same exception. For instance, in Fig. 2 we have $\pi_H^d(w, 3, 4) = \{3, 4\}$.
    Let $a \in AP$, and $t \in \{d, u\}$; the syntax of POTL$_f$ is the following:

$$\varphi := a \mid \neg\varphi \mid \varphi \vee \varphi \mid \bigcirc^t \varphi \mid \tilde{\bigcirc}^t \varphi \mid \chi_F^t \varphi \mid \tilde{\chi}_F^t \varphi \mid \varphi\, \mathcal{U}_\chi^t \varphi \mid \varphi\, \mathcal{R}_\chi^t \varphi$$

$$\mid \bigcirc_H^t \varphi \mid \tilde{\bigcirc}_H^t \varphi \mid \varphi\, \mathcal{U}_H^t \varphi \mid \varphi\, \mathcal{R}_H^t \varphi$$

The truth of POTL$_f$ formulas is defined w.r.t. a single word position. Let w be a finite OP word, and $a \in AP$; we set $\sim^d\, = \lessdot$ and $\sim^u\, = \gtrdot$. Then, for any position $i \in U$ of w and $t \in \{d, u\}$:

1. $(w, i) \models a$ iff $i \in P(a)$;
2. $(w, i) \models \neg\varphi$ iff $(w, i) \not\models \varphi$;
3. $(w, i) \models \varphi_1 \vee \varphi_2$ iff $(w, i) \models \varphi_1$ or $(w, i) \models \varphi_2$;
4. $(w, i) \models \bigcirc^t \varphi$ iff $i < |w| - 1$, $(w, i+1) \models \varphi$ and $i \sim^t (i+1)$ or $i \doteq (i+1)$;
5. $(w, i) \models \tilde{\bigcirc}^t \varphi$ iff $i = |w| - 1$ and $(i \sim^t (i+1)$ or $i \doteq (i+1))$ implies $(w, i+1) \models \varphi$;
6. $(w, i) \models \chi_F^t \varphi$ iff $\exists j > i$ such that $\chi(i, j)$, $i \sim^t j$ or $i \doteq j$, and $(w, j) \models \varphi$;
7. $(w, i) \models \tilde{\chi}_F^t \varphi$ iff $\forall j > i$ such that $\chi(i, j)$ and $(i \sim^t j$ or $i \doteq j)$, we have $(w, j) \models \varphi$;
8. $(w, i) \models \varphi_1\, \mathcal{U}_\chi^t \varphi_2$ iff $\exists j \geq i$ such that $\pi_\chi^t(w, i, j) \neq \varnothing$, $(w, j) \models \varphi_2$ and $\forall j' < j$ in $\pi_\chi^t(w, i, j)$ we have $(w, j) \models \varphi_1$;
9. $(w, i) \models \varphi_1\, \mathcal{R}_\chi^t \varphi_2$ iff $\forall j \geq i$ such that $\pi_\chi^t(w, i, j) \neq \varnothing$ we have either $(w, j') \models \varphi_2$ for all $j' \in \pi_\chi^t(w, i, j)$, or $\exists k \in \pi_\chi^t(w, i, j)$ such that $(w, k) \models \varphi_1$ and $\forall j' \leq k$ in $\pi_\chi^t(w, i, j)$ we have $(w, j) \models \varphi_2$;
10. $(w, i) \models \bigcirc_H^u \varphi$ iff there exist a position $h < i$ s.t. $\chi(h, i)$ and $h \lessdot i$ and a position $j = \min\{k \mid i < k \wedge \chi(h, k) \wedge h \lessdot k\}$ and $(w, j) \models \varphi$;

11. $(w, i) \models \tilde{\bigcirc}_H^u \varphi$ iff the existence of a position $h < i$ s.t. $\chi(h, i)$ and $h \lessdot i$ and a position $j = \min\{k \mid i < k \land \chi(h, k) \land h \lessdot k\}$ implies $(w, j) \models \varphi$;

12. $(w, i) \models \bigcirc_H^d \varphi$ iff there exist a position $h > i$ s.t. $\chi(i, h)$ and $i \gtrdot h$ and a position $j = \min\{k \mid i < k \land \chi(k, h) \land k \gtrdot h\}$ and $(w, j) \models \varphi$;

13. $(w, i) \models \tilde{\bigcirc}_H^d \varphi$ iff the existence of a position $h > i$ s.t. $\chi(i, h)$ and $i \gtrdot h$ and a position $j = \min\{k \mid i < k \land \chi(k, h) \land k \gtrdot h\}$ implies $(w, j) \models \varphi$;

14. $(w, i) \models \varphi_1 \, \mathcal{U}_H^t \, \varphi_2$ iff $\exists j \geq i$ such that $\pi_H^t(w, i, j) \neq \varnothing$, $(w, j) \models \varphi_2$ and $\forall j' < j$ in $\pi_H^t(w, i, j)$ we have $(w, j) \models \varphi_1$;

15. $(w, i) \models \varphi_1 \, \mathcal{R}_H^t \, \varphi_2$ iff $\forall j \geq i$ such that $\pi_H^t(w, i, j) \neq \varnothing$ we have either $(w, j') \models \varphi_2$ for all $j' \in \pi_\chi^t(w, i, j)$, or $\exists k \in \pi_H^t(w, i, j)$ such that $(w, k) \models \varphi_1$ and $\forall j' \leq k$ in $\pi_\chi^t(w, i, j)$ we have $(w, j) \models \varphi_2$.

We additionally employ $\land$ and $\rightarrow$ with the usual semantics.

For instance, formula $\top \, \mathcal{U}_\chi^d \, p$ evaluated in a function **call** means that p holds somewhere between the call and its matched return (or exception); formula $\chi_F^u \, p$, evaluated in a **call**, means that p will hold when it returns (this can be used to check post-conditions or, if $p = \mathbf{exc}$, to assert that the function is terminated by an exception). Formula $\top \, \mathcal{U}_H^d \, p$, when evaluated in a **call** terminated by an exception, means that p holds in one of the **calls** already terminated by the same exception. For a more in-depth presentation of POTL, we refer the reader to [13].

3   A Tree-Shaped Tableau for POTL$_f$

In this section, we describe our tableau system for POTL$_f$, that will form the core of our bounded model checking procedure. Let Σ be a set of structural propositions, (Σ, M) an OP alphabet, AP a set of atomic propositions, and φ a formula over $\Sigma \cup AP$. Given $\Gamma \subseteq \mathrm{Cl}(\varphi)$, if $\Gamma \cap \Sigma = \{a\}$, then we define $\mathrm{struct}(\Gamma) = a$. Moreover, for $\Gamma, \Gamma' \subseteq \mathrm{Cl}(\varphi)$ and $\sim \in \{\lessdot, \doteq, \gtrdot\}$, we write $\Gamma \sim \Gamma'$ meaning $\mathrm{struct}(\Gamma) \sim \mathrm{struct}(\Gamma')$.

A tableau for φ is a tree built on top of a set of nodes N. Each node $u \in N$ has four labels: $\Gamma(u) \subseteq \mathrm{Cl}(\phi)$, $\mathrm{smb}(u) \in \Sigma$, $\mathrm{stack}(u) \in N \cup \{\bot\}$, $\mathrm{ctx}(u) \in N \cup \{\bot\}$. Each node u is a *push*, *shift*, or *pop* node if, respectively, $\mathrm{smb}(u) \lessdot \Gamma(u)$, $\mathrm{smb}(u) \doteq \Gamma(u)$, or $\mathrm{smb}(u) \gtrdot \Gamma(u)$.

The tableau is built from φ starting from the root u_0 which is labelled as $\Gamma(u_0) = \{\varphi\}$, $\mathrm{smb}(u_0) = \#$, $\mathrm{stack}(u_0) = \bot$, $\mathrm{ctx}(u_0) = \bot$. The tree is built by applying a set of *rules* to each leaf. Each rule may add new children nodes to the given leaf, while others may *accept* or *reject* the leaf. The construction continues until every leaf has been either accepted or rejected. The tableau rules can be divided into *expansion*, *termination*, *step*, and *guess* rules.

To each leaf of the tree, at first *expansion rules* are applied, which are summarised in Table 1. Each rule works as follows. If the formula ψ in the leftmost column belongs to $\Gamma(u)$, then for each $i \in \{1, 2, 3\}$ for which Γ_i is given in Table 1, a child u_i is added to u, whose labels are identical to u excepting that $\Gamma(u_i) = (\Gamma(u) \setminus \{\psi\}) \cup \Gamma_i$. If multiple rules can be applied, the order in which they are applied does not matter.

Table 1. Expansion rules, where $t \in \{u, d\}$.

$\psi \in \Gamma(u)$	Γ_1	Γ_2	Γ_3
$\alpha \wedge \beta$	$\{\alpha, \beta\}$		
$\alpha \vee \beta$	$\{\alpha\}$	$\{\beta\}$	
$\alpha \, \mathcal{U}_H^u \, \beta$	$\{\alpha, \bigcirc_H^u(\alpha \, \mathcal{U}_H^u \, \beta)\}$	$\{\beta\}$ (only if condition 1 holds)	
$\alpha \, \mathcal{U}_H^d \, \beta$	$\{\alpha, \bigcirc_H^d(\alpha \, \mathcal{U}_H^d \, \beta)\}$	$\{\beta\}$ (only if condition 2 holds)	
$\alpha \, \mathcal{R}_\chi^t \, \beta$	$\{\alpha, \beta\}$	$\{\beta, \tilde{\bigcirc}^t(\alpha \, \mathcal{R}_\chi^t \, \beta), \tilde{\chi}_F^t(\alpha \, \mathcal{R}_\chi^t \, \beta)\}$	
$\alpha \, \mathcal{R}_H^u \, \beta$	$\{\alpha, \beta\}$	$\{\beta, \tilde{\bigcirc}_H^u(\alpha \, \mathcal{R}_H^u \, \beta)\}$	
$\alpha \, \mathcal{U}_\chi^t \, \beta$	$\{\beta\}$	$\{\alpha, \bigcirc^t(\alpha \, \mathcal{U}_\chi^t \, \beta)\}$	$\{\alpha, \chi_F^t(\alpha \, \mathcal{U}_\chi^t \, \beta)\}$
$\alpha \, \mathcal{R}_H^d \, \beta$	$\varnothing$	$\{\alpha, \beta\}$	$\{\beta, \tilde{\bigcirc}_H^u(\alpha \, \mathcal{R}_H^u \, \beta)\}$

(only if condition 2 holds)

condition 1:	the closest step ancestor of u is a *pop* node u_p such that $\Gamma(\text{ctx}(u_p)) \lessdot \Gamma(u_p)$
condition 2:	the closest step ancestor of u is a *push* or *shift* node

When no expansion rules are applicable to a leaf u, and $\Gamma(u) \cap (\Sigma \cup \{\#\}) = \varnothing$, then one child u_a, for each $a \in \Sigma \cup \{\#\}$, is added to u whose labels are the same as u except that $\Gamma(u_a) = \Gamma(u) \cup \{a\}$.

When no expansion rules are applicable to a leaf u and $\Gamma(u) \cup \Sigma \neq \varnothing$, u is called a *step* node. In this case, *termination* rules are checked to decide whether the leaf can be either rejected or accepted. Rejecting rules are described in Table 2. Most rules depend on the type of the leaf node u where they are applied (*i.e.*, it being a push, pop, or shift node), and the type of the closest step ancestor u_s of u. The rule in a given row of the table fires when u and u_s are of the stated type (if any) and where the condition in the last column is met. In this case, u is rejected. We need to set up the following terminology in order to understand some of those rules.

Definition 5 (Fulfillment of a Chain Next Operator). *A $\chi_F^d \, \alpha$ operator is said to be fulfilled in a node u iff $\chi_F^d \, \alpha \in \Gamma(u)$, and there exists a pop node descendant u_p such that $\text{ctx}(u_p) = u$ and:*

1. $\Gamma(u) \lessdot \Gamma(u_p)$ or $\Gamma(u) \doteq \Gamma(u_p)$, and
2. $\alpha \in \Gamma(u_s)$, where u_s is the closest push or shift node descending from u_p.

Replace χ_F^d with χ_F^u and $\lessdot$ with $\gtrdot$ for the upward case.

Definition 6 (Pending Node). *A node u is* pending *iff either:*

1. u is a push node and no pop node u_p exists such that $\text{stack}(u_p) = u$, or
2. u is a shift node and no pop node u_p exists such that $\text{stack}(u_p) = \text{stack}(u)$.

Definition 7 (Equivalent Nodes). *Two nodes u and u' belonging to the same branch are said to be* equivalent *if the following hold:*

1. $\Gamma(u) = \Gamma(u')$;
2. $\mathrm{smb}(u) = \mathrm{smb}(u')$;
3. $\Gamma(\mathrm{stack}(u)) = \Gamma(\mathrm{stack}(u'))$; *and*
4. $\Gamma(\mathrm{ctx}(u)) = \Gamma(\mathrm{ctx}(u'))$.

In contrast to rejecting rules, there is only one simple *accepting rule*: u is accepted when $\Gamma(u) = \{\#\}$ and $\mathrm{stack}(u) = \bot$.

If no termination rules fire on a step node u, the construction can proceed by a *temporal step*. To understand how it works, we need the following notation: given a node u and a unary temporal operator $\odot$, we denote the set of all the formulas that appear as arguments of $\odot$ inside $\Gamma(u)$ as $\mathcal{G}_\odot(u) = \{\alpha \mid \odot \alpha \in \Gamma(u)\}$, and for a set of operators $\{\odot_1, \ldots, \odot_n\}$ we define $\mathcal{G}_{\odot_1,\ldots,\odot_n}(u) = \mathcal{G}_{\odot_1}(u) \cup \ldots \cup \mathcal{G}_{\odot_n}(u)$. The temporal step consists in two parts: the application of one *step* rule, and of one *guess* rule. The step rules, summarised in Table 3, are chosen depending on the type of the leaf at hand, and of its closest step ancestor. Each rule adds exactly one child u' to the leaf u, whose label is described in the table. The child u' is then fed to one of the *guess* rules described in Table 4. The applicability of the guess rules depend on the type of u and some other conditions, in a way such that in each case at most one guess rule is applicable to u'. If any is applicable, the selected rule defines a set of formulas $\mathcal{G}$ as described in the table, and for each $G \subseteq \mathcal{G}$ adds a child u''_G such that $\Gamma(u''_G) = \Gamma(u') \cup G$, $\mathrm{smb}(u''_G) = \mathrm{smb}(u')$, $\mathrm{stack}(u''_G) = \mathrm{stack}(u')$, and $\mathrm{ctx}(u''_G) = \mathrm{ctx}(u')$. After the temporal step is completed, the construction continues with the expansion rules again, and everything repeats.

We can now sketch a soundness and termination argument for the tableau.

Theorem 1 (Soundness). *If the tableau for ϕ has an accepted branch, then ϕ is satisfiable.*

Proof (Sketch). $\mathrm{Cl}(\phi)$ is finite, and so is the number of possible node labels. Thus, unless they are rejected by a rule other than 13, all branches of the tableau must eventually reach a node that is *equivalent* (cf. Definition 7) to a previous one. Then, they are rejected by Rule 13. Thus, once fully expanded, the tableau for a formula ϕ is also finite. Then, soundness of the tableau can be proved by building a word out of any accepted tableau branch, with a mapping from push and shift step nodes of the branch to letters in the word. Chain supports in the word correspond to sequences of step nodes. See [9] for the full proof.

4   SMT Encoding of the Tableau

Our technique for symbolic model checking of POTL$_f$ properties does not directly construct the tableau described in Sect. 3, but rather, it *encodes* it into SMT formulas that can be efficiently handled by off-the-shelf solvers. Iterating over a growing index $k > 1$, at each step our procedure produces an SMT formula that encodes the branches of the tableau of length up to k step nodes, such that

Table 2. Rejecting termination rules.

n°	type of u	type of u_s^1	condition
1.			$\{p, \neg p\} \subseteq \Gamma(u)$
2.			$|\Gamma(u) \cap \Sigma| > 1$
3.			$\{\psi, \#\} \subseteq \Gamma(u)$ and ψ is strong[2]
4.		push/shift	$\Gamma(u_s) \gtrdot \Gamma(u)$ and some $\bigcirc^d \alpha \in \Gamma(u_s)$[1]
		push/shift	$\Gamma(u_s) \lessdot \Gamma(u)$ and some $\bigcirc^u \alpha \in \Gamma(u_s)$[1]
5.		push/shift	$\Gamma(u_s) \lessdot \Gamma(u)$ or $\Gamma(u_s) \doteq \Gamma(u)$, and some $\tilde{\bigcirc}^d \alpha \in \Gamma(u_s)$, but $\alpha \notin \Gamma(u)$
		push/shift	$\Gamma(u_s) \gtrdot \Gamma(u)$ or $\Gamma(u_s) \doteq \Gamma(u)$, and some $\tilde{\bigcirc}^u \alpha \in \Gamma(u_s)$, but $\alpha \notin \Gamma(u)$
6.	pop		$\chi_F^t \alpha$ is *not* fulfilled in u', for some $u' \in G$ such that $\chi_F^t \alpha \in \Gamma(u')$[3], for $t \in \{d, u\}$
7.	push	pop	$\tilde{\chi}_F^d \alpha \in \text{ctx}(u_s)$ and $\alpha \notin \Gamma(u)$
	shift	pop	$\tilde{\chi}_F^t \alpha \in \text{ctx}(u_s)$ and $\alpha \notin \Gamma(u)$, for $t \in \{d, u\}$
	pop	pop	$\tilde{\chi}_F^u \alpha \in \text{ctx}(u_s)$ and $\alpha \notin \Gamma(u)$
8.	pop		$\bigcirc_H^u \alpha \in \Gamma(\text{stack}(u))$ and $\Gamma(\text{ctx}(u)) \not\lessdot \Gamma(u)$
	push	pop	$\bigcirc_H^u \alpha \in \Gamma(\text{stack}(u_s))$ and $\alpha \notin \Gamma(u)$
	push	push/shift	$\bigcirc_H^u \alpha \in \Gamma(u)$
	shift		$\bigcirc_H^u \alpha \in \Gamma(u)$
9.	push	pop	$\tilde{\bigcirc}_H^u \alpha \in \Gamma(\text{stack}(u_s))$, $\text{stack}(u_s)$ is a push node, the closest step ancestor of $\text{stack}(u_s)$ is a pop node, and $\alpha \notin \Gamma(u)$
10.	pop		$\bigcirc_H^d \alpha \in \Gamma(\text{ctx}(u))$ and $\text{smb}(\text{stack}(u)) \doteq \Gamma(u)$
	pop	push/shift	$\bigcirc_H^d \alpha \in \Gamma(\text{ctx}(u))$
	pop	pop	$\bigcirc_H^d \alpha \in \Gamma(\text{ctx}(u))$ and $\alpha \notin \Gamma(\text{ctx}(u_s))$[1]
	pop/shift	pop/shift	$\bigcirc_H^d \alpha \in \Gamma(u_s)$[1]
11.	pop	pop	$\tilde{\bigcirc}_H^d \alpha \in \Gamma(\text{ctx}(u))$, $\text{smb}(\text{stack}(u)) \gtrdot \Gamma(u)$, and $\alpha \notin \Gamma(\text{ctx}(u_s))$
12.	pop/shift	push/shift	$\alpha \mathcal{U}_H^d \beta \in \Gamma(u_s)$
	push/shift	pop	$\alpha \mathcal{R}_H^d \beta$ appears in one of the nodes between $\text{ctx}(u_s)$ and the closest step ancestor of u_s (exclusive)
	pop	pop	$\alpha, \tilde{\bigcirc}_H^d(\alpha \ \mathcal{R}_H^d \ \beta) \notin \Gamma(\text{ctx}(u_s))$, $\alpha, \beta \notin \Gamma(\text{ctx}(u_s))$, and $\alpha \mathcal{R}_H^d \beta$ appears in one of the nodes between $\text{ctx}(u_s)$ and the closest step ancestor of u_s (exclusive)
13.	push/shift		there is a *pending* ancestor u_i of u *equivalent* to u[4]

[1] u_s is the closest step ancestor of u

[2] ψ is strong if it is a positive literal or a strong tomorrow

[3] $G = \{\text{stack}(u)\} \cup \{u' \mid \text{stack}(u') = \text{stack}(u)$ and u' is a shift node$\}$

[4] See Definitions 6 and 7.

Table 3. Step rules

u	u_s^1	$\Gamma(u')$	$\mathrm{smb}(u')$	$\mathrm{stack}(u')$	$\mathrm{ctx}(u')$
push	push/shift	$\mathcal{G}_{\bigcirc^d,\bigcirc^u}(u)$	$\mathrm{struct}(\Gamma(u))$	u	u_s or $\perp^2$
push	pop	$\mathcal{G}_{\bigcirc^d,\bigcirc^u}(u)$	$\mathrm{struct}(\Gamma(u))$	u	$\mathrm{ctx}(u_s)$ or $\perp^2$
shift		$\mathcal{G}_{\bigcirc^d,\bigcirc^u}(u)$	$\mathrm{struct}(\Gamma(u))$	$\mathrm{stack}(u)$	$\mathrm{ctx}(u)$
pop		$\Gamma(u)$	$\mathrm{smb}(\mathrm{stack}(u))$	$\mathrm{stack}(\mathrm{stack}(u))$	$\mathrm{ctx}(\mathrm{stack}(u))$

[1] u_s is the closest step ancestor of u
[2] $\mathrm{ctx}(u') = \perp$ if $\mathrm{stack}(u) = \perp$

Table 4. Guess rules

u	only if	$\mathcal{G}$
push/shift		$\mathcal{G}_{\tilde{\bigcirc}^d}(u_s) \cup \mathcal{G}_{\tilde{\bigcirc}^u}(u_s) \cup \mathcal{G}_{\bigcirc_H^d}(u_s) \cup \mathcal{G}_{\tilde{\bigcirc}_H^d}(u_s)$
pop	$u_c \neq \perp^1$	$\bigcup \begin{cases} \mathcal{G}_{\chi_F^d}(u_c) \cup \mathcal{G}_{\chi_F^u}(u_c) \\ \mathcal{G}_{\tilde{\chi}_F^d}(u_c) \cup \mathcal{G}_{\tilde{\chi}_F^u}(u_c) \\ \mathcal{G}_{\bigcirc_H^d}(u_c) \cup \mathcal{G}_{\tilde{\bigcirc}_H^d}(u_c) \\ \mathcal{G}_{\tilde{\bigcirc}_H^u}(\mathrm{stack}(u_s)) \cup \mathcal{G}_{\bigcirc_H^u}(\mathrm{stack}(u_s)) \end{cases}$

[1] u_s is the closest step ancestor of u and $u_c = \mathrm{ctx}(u_s)$

the formula is satisfiable if and only if an accepted branch of the tableau exists. If not, we increment k and proceed. In this respect, the procedure reminds of classic *bounded model checking* [7,14]. Here we summarize the working principles of the tableau encoding. The full details are available in [9].

The encoding produces formulas whose *models*, when they exist, represent single branches of the tableau. At a given step k, the formulas are interpreted over a restricted form of quantified[1] EUF, over two *finite, enumerated, ordered*[2] sorts: a sort $\mathcal{N}_k$, of exactly $k+1$ elements used to identify the nodes in the branch, and a sort called $\mathcal{S}$ that contains a finite set of symbols used in the encoding to represent the letters of the formula's alphabet. We suppose to have a finite number of constants for the values in $\mathcal{S}$. Among those, we have $p \in \mathcal{S}$ for each $p \in \Sigma \cup AP$. Others will be introduced when needed. We also exploit a fixed arbitrary ordering between elements of $\mathcal{N}_k$, and we abuse notation by denoting the constants for sort $\mathcal{N}_k$ as $0, 1, \ldots, k$, and writing $x+1$ and $x-1$ for an element $x \in \mathcal{N}_k$ to denote its predecessor and successor in this order.

For each proposition $p \in \Sigma \cup AP$, the encoding uses a binary predicate $\Gamma(p, x)$ whose first argument ranges among $\mathcal{S}$ and the second among $\mathcal{N}_k$. The intuitive meaning of $\Gamma(p, x)$ is that $p \in \Gamma(u)$ if u is the x-th step node of the current branch of the tableau. The encoding also uses some function symbols. A unary predicate $\bar{\Sigma}$ ranging over $\mathcal{S}$ tells which symbols from $\mathcal{S}$ are structural symbols. A function

---

[1] Thanks to finite sorts, quantifiers are in fact expanded to disjunctions/conjunctions.
[2] The sort returned by the `Z3_mk_finite_domain_sort()` function of the Z3 C API.

$\text{smb}(x) : \mathcal{N}_k \to \mathcal{S}$ is used to represent the $\text{smb}(u_x)$ symbol. A function symbol $\text{struct}(x) : \mathcal{N}_k \to \mathcal{S}$ represents $\Gamma(u_x) \cap \Sigma$. Two functions $\text{stack}(x) : \mathcal{N}_k \to \mathcal{N}_k$ and $\text{ctx}(x) : \mathcal{N}_k \to \mathcal{N}_k$ represent the corresponding functions in the tableau. When $\text{stack}(u) = \bot$, we denote it as $\text{stack}(x) = 0$, and similarly for $\text{ctx}(x)$.

For any strong or weak *next* or *chain next* temporal formula in the closure of ϕ we also introduce a corresponding *propositional* symbol in $\mathcal{S}$. Specifically, for each formula $\bigcirc^t \psi$, $\chi_F^t \psi$, $\tilde{\bigcirc}^t \psi$ and $\tilde{\chi}_F^t \psi$ in the closure, $\mathcal{S}$ contains the following propositional symbols, which we call *grounded*: $(\bigcirc^t \psi)_G$, $(\chi_F^t \psi)_G$, $(\tilde{\bigcirc}^t \psi)_G$, $(\tilde{\chi}_F^t \psi)_G$, and $(\bigcirc^t \psi)_G$, $(\chi_F^t \psi)_G$, $(\tilde{\bigcirc}^t \psi)_G$, $(\tilde{\chi}_F^t \psi)_G$.

The core building block of the encoding is the following *normal form* for POTL$_f$ formulas.

Definition 8 (Next Normal Form). *Let ϕ be a POTL$_f$ formula. The* next normal form *of ϕ, denoted $\text{xnf}(\phi)$ is defined as follows:*

$$\text{xnf}(p) = p \quad \text{for } p \in \Sigma \qquad\qquad \text{xnf}(\neg p) = \neg p \quad \text{for } p \in \Sigma$$

$$\text{xnf}(\tilde{\bigcirc}^t \psi) = \tilde{\bigcirc}^t \psi \qquad\qquad \text{xnf}(\tilde{\chi}_F^t \psi) = \tilde{\chi}_F^t \psi$$

$$\text{xnf}(\alpha \circ \beta) = \text{xnf}(\alpha) \circ \text{xnf}(\beta) \quad \text{for } \circ \in \{\vee, \wedge\}$$

$$\text{xnf}(\alpha\, \mathcal{U}_\chi^t\, \beta) = \text{xnf}(\beta) \vee \left(\text{xnf}(\alpha) \wedge (\bigcirc^t(\alpha\, \mathcal{U}_\chi^t\, \beta) \vee \chi_F^t(\alpha\, \mathcal{U}_\chi^t\, \beta))\right)$$

$$\text{xnf}(\alpha\, \mathcal{R}_\chi^t\, \beta) = \text{xnf}(\beta) \wedge \left(\text{xnf}(\alpha) \vee (\tilde{\bigcirc}^t(\alpha\, \mathcal{R}_\chi^t\, \beta) \wedge \tilde{\chi}_F^t(\alpha\, \mathcal{R}_\chi^t\, \beta))\right)$$

Intuitively, $\text{xnf}(\phi)$ encodes the *expansion rules* of the tableau (Table 1). Given ϕ and a fresh variable x of sort $\mathcal{N}_k$, we denote as $\text{xnf}(\phi)_G$ the formula obtained from $\text{xnf}(\phi)$ by replacing any proposition p with $\Gamma(p, x)$. Note that $\text{xnf}(\phi)_G$ does not contain temporal operators: it is a first-order formula with a single free variable x.

We can now show the encoding itself. We start by constraining the meaning of the $\bar{\Sigma}$ predicate and the struct and smb functions. We define a formula ϕ_{axioms} that states that the $\bar{\Sigma}$ predicate identifies structural symbols and the $\text{struct}(x)$ and $\text{smb}(x)$ functions only return structural symbols, and we write a formula ϕ_{OPM} that explicitly models the $\lessdot$, $\doteq$ and $\gtrdot$ relations between symbols in $\mathcal{S}$ as binary predicates in the SMT encoding. The predicates range over the whole $\mathcal{S}$ but only the relationship between symbols in Σ will matter. With these in place, we can identify the *type* of each step node depending on the PR between $\text{smb}(x)$ and $\text{struct}(x)$. We encode this by the following three predicates:

$$\text{push}(x) \equiv \text{smb}(x) \lessdot \text{struct}(x) \quad \text{shift}(x) \equiv \text{smb}(x) \doteq \text{struct}(x)$$

$$\text{pop}(x) \equiv \text{smb}(x) \gtrdot \text{struct}(x)$$

A formula ϕ_{init} encodes how the root node of the tableau looks like. In particular, it includes the conjunct $\text{xnf}(\phi)_G(1)$, to say that its label contains ϕ.

We can now encode the step rules of Table 3. For space constraints we only show here the encoding of the step rules concerning *push* nodes (first two lines of Table 3). The encoding of such rules is the following:

$$\text{step}_{\text{push}}(x) \equiv \bigwedge_{\bigcirc^t \alpha \in \text{Cl}(\phi)} \left(\Gamma((\bigcirc^t \alpha)_G, x) \rightarrow \text{xnf}(\alpha)_G(x+1) \right)$$

$$\wedge\, \text{smb}(x+1) = \text{struct}(x) \wedge \text{stack}(x+1) = x$$

$$\wedge\, (\text{stack}(x) = 0 \rightarrow \text{ctx}(x+1) = 0)$$

$$\wedge\, ((\text{stack}(x) \neq 0 \wedge (\text{push}(x-1) \vee \text{shift}(x-1))) \rightarrow \text{ctx}(x+1) = x-1)$$

$$\wedge\, ((\text{stack}(x) \neq 0 \wedge \text{pop}(x-1)) \rightarrow \text{ctx}(x+1) = \text{ctx}(x-1))$$

We can similarly obtain two formulas $\text{step}_{\text{shift}}(x)$ and $\text{step}_{\text{pop}}(x)$. It is worth to note the first line of the above definition, where $\text{xnf}(\alpha)$ is imposed to hold on $x+1$ if a next operator on α is present on x.

Next, we can encode the rejecting rules of Table 2. Since there are so many of them, we only show some examples (see [9] for the full list). What we actually encode is the *negation* of the rejecting rules, that describes what a node has to satisfy to *not* be rejected. We start to note that Rule 1 does not need to be encoded, since it just states that a proposition cannot hold together with its negation, which is trivially implied by the logic. Then, the simplest ones are Rules 2 and 3 of Table 2, and can be encoded as follows:

$$r_2(x) \equiv \forall p\, \forall q (\Sigma(p) \wedge \Sigma(q) \wedge \Gamma(p, x) \wedge \Gamma(q, x) \rightarrow p = q)$$

$$r_3(x) \equiv \Gamma(\#, x) \rightarrow \left(\bigwedge_{\bigcirc^t \alpha \in \text{Cl}(\phi)} (\neg \Gamma((\bigcirc^t \alpha)_G, x)) \wedge \bigwedge_{p \in AP} (\neg \Gamma(p, x)) \right)$$

We similarly have a formula $r_i(x)$ encoding the negation of each block of lines from Rule 4 to 13. With these in place, we define a formula $[\![\phi]\!]_k$ called the *k-unraveling* of ϕ, that encodes all the non-rejected branches of the tableau of up to k step nodes.

$$\phi_{\text{axioms}} \wedge \phi_{OPM} \wedge \phi_{\text{init}} \wedge \forall x \left(x > 1 \rightarrow \bigwedge_{i=2}^{13} r_i(x) \right) \wedge$$

$$\forall x \left[1 \leq x < k \rightarrow \left(\begin{array}{l} (\text{push}(x) \rightarrow \text{step}_{\text{push}}(x)) \\ \wedge\, (\text{shift}(x) \rightarrow \text{step}_{\text{shift}}(x)) \\ \wedge\, (\text{pop}(x) \rightarrow \text{step}_{\text{pop}}(x)) \end{array} \right) \right]$$

The only *acceptance* rule of the tableau is encoded by a formula $e(x)$ defined as $e(x) \equiv \Gamma(\#, x) \wedge \text{stack}(x) = 0$.

Finally, we have the following.

Theorem 2. *If $[\![\phi]\!]_k \wedge e(k)$ is satisfiable for some $k > 0$, then ϕ is satisfiable.*

We exploit this encoding of $\mathsf{POTL_f}$ satisfiability for model checking a formula ϕ through an algorithm that iterates on k starting from $k = 1$. First, we check satisfiability of $[\![\neg \phi]\!]_k \wedge [\![\mathcal{M}]\!]_k$, where $[\![\mathcal{M}]\!]_k$ encodes a length-k prefix of a trace of the program $\mathcal{M}$ to be checked. We automatically translate programs to OPA whose transitions are labeled with program statements in the same way as [3, 10], so that the automaton's stack simulates the program stack. Such *extended* OPA are then directly encoded into SMT in a straightforward manner, using the theories of fixed-size bit vectors and arrays to represent variables (cf. [9]). If this satisfiability check fails, it means no trace of $\mathcal{M}$ of length $\geq k$ violates ϕ, proving that $\mathcal{M}$ satisfies ϕ. Otherwise, we check whether $e(k)$ is satisfied when conjoined with the previous assertions. If it is, then we have found a counterexample trace that violates ϕ. Otherwise, we increase k by 1 and repeat. Since the tableau is finite, we eventually either find a counterexample, or hit a value of k such that Rule 13 rejects all branches, and the initial satisfiability check fails.

5 Experimental Evaluation

We implemented the encoding described in Sect. 4 in a SMT-based model checker that leverages the Z3 SMT solver [31]. We developed it within POMC [8], an explicit-state model checker for POTL developed by the authors of [10].

We compare our SMT-based approach with the explicit-state algorithm powering POMC, which performs the following steps on-the-fly: (i) it builds an OPA $\mathcal{A}_\varphi$ encoding the negation of the formula φ to be checked; (ii) it constructs the synchronized product between $\mathcal{A}_\varphi$ and the model of the system; (iii) it checks the nonemptiness of the product automaton, witnessing a counterexample to the property in the model, in a depth-first fashion.

We ran our experiments on server with a 2.0 GHz AMD CPU and RAM capped at 30 GiB.

5.1 Description of the Benchmarks

We evaluate the two tools on a set of benchmarks adapted from [10], divided in three categories (Quicksort, Jensen, Stack). We modeled all benchmarks in MiniProc, the modeling language of the POMC tool. The checked formulas are reported in Table 5. Below, we give a brief description of each category.

Quicksort. We modeled a Java implementation of the Quicksort sorting algorithm. The algorithm is implemented as a recursive function qs, called by the main function in a `try-catch` block, and is applied to an array of integers that may contain null values, which cause a `NullPointerException`. We vary the length of the arrays from 1 to 5 elements and the width of the elements from 2 to 16 bits. Formulas 1 and 2 both check that the main function returns without exceptions, while 3 checks the same for the qs (QuickSort) function. Formulas 4 (resp., Formula 5) states that the array is sorted when the main function (resp., the qs function) returns without exceptions. Finally, Formula 6 states that either qs throws an exception or the array is sorted (and qs returns normally).

Table 5. Benchmark formulas. The last column states whether they are true (T) or false (F) in each model. $\square$ is the LTL always, which we implemented as in [17].

QuickSort	1	$\chi_F^u(\textbf{ret} \wedge \text{main})$	T
	2	$\textbf{call} \wedge \text{main} \rightarrow \neg(\bigcirc^u \textbf{exc} \vee \chi_F^u \textbf{exc})$	T
	3	$\square(\textbf{call} \wedge \text{qs} \rightarrow \neg(\bigcirc^u \textbf{exc} \vee \chi_F^u \textbf{exc}))$	F
	4	$\chi_F^u \text{sorted}$	F
	5	$\square(\textbf{call} \wedge \text{qs} \rightarrow \chi_F^u \text{sorted})$	F
	6	$\chi_F^d(\textbf{han} \wedge \bigcirc^d(\textbf{call} \wedge \text{qs} \wedge \chi_F^u(\textbf{exc} \vee \text{sorted})))$	T
Jensen	8	$\square(\textbf{call} \wedge \neg P_{cp} \rightarrow \neg(\top \, \mathcal{U}_\chi^d (\textbf{call} \wedge \text{read})))$	T
	9	$\square(\textbf{call} \wedge \neg P_{db} \rightarrow \neg(\top \, \mathcal{U}_\chi^d (\textbf{call} \wedge \text{write})))$	T
	10	$\square(\textbf{call} \wedge ((\text{canpay} \wedge \neg P_{cp}) \vee (\text{debit} \wedge \neg P_{db})) \rightarrow \bigcirc^u \textbf{exc} \vee \chi_F^u \textbf{exc})$	T
	11	$\neg(\top \, \mathcal{U}_\chi^d (\text{balance} < 0))$	T
Stack	12	$\square(\text{modified} \rightarrow \neg(\bigcirc^u \textbf{exc} \vee \chi_F^u \textbf{exc}))$	T/F
	13	$\square(\textbf{call} \wedge (\text{push} \vee \text{pop}) \rightarrow \neg(\top \, \mathcal{U}_H^d \text{modified}))$	T/F
	14	$\square(\textbf{call} \wedge (\text{push} \vee \text{pop}) \wedge \chi_F^d \textbf{ret} \rightarrow$	T/T
		$\neg(\top \, \mathcal{U}_\chi^d (\textbf{han} \wedge \text{Stack} \wedge (\neg\textbf{han} \, \mathcal{U}_\chi^d (\top \wedge \bigcirc^u \textbf{exc})))))$	

Bank Account. This category consists of a simple banking application taken from [24] which allows users to withdraw money or check their balance. The variable representing the balance is protected by a Java AccessController, which prevents unauthorized users from accessing it by raising exceptions. We modeled the balance with an integer variable. Formula 8 (resp., Formula 9) checks that, whenever a function is called without having permission to check the balance (resp., to make a payment), then there is no read-access (resp., write access) to the variable holding the balance. The permission of checking the balance and to make a payment are modeled by the variables P_{cp} and P_{db}, respectively. Formula 10 checks that if the functions that check the balance (canpay) and make a payment (debit) are called without permission, an exception is thrown. Formula 11 checks that the balance never becomes negative, because payments are only made if the account has enough money.

Stack. We model two C++ implementations of a generic stack data structure taken from [33], where constructors of contained elements may throw exceptions. Only one of the two implementations is exception safe. The pop method of the safe implementation does not return the popped element, which must be accessed through the top method, and it performs other operations on a new copy of the internal data structure, to prevent exceptions from leaving it in an inconsistent state. In contrast with [10] which uses a manually-crafted abstraction for the elements in the stack, our model implements the stack with actual arrays of fixed-width integers. Formulas 12 and 13 check *strong exception safety* [1], *i.e.,* that each operation on the data structure is rolled back if any functions related to the element type T throw an exception, leaving the stack in a consistent state. Formula 14 checks *exception neutrality* [1], which means that exceptions thrown by element functions are always propagated by the stack's methods.

5.2   Description of the Plots

We compare the time (measured in seconds) taken by the SMT-based approach (in the plots referred to as SMT) with the time taken by POMC, dividing the plots by the three categories of benchmarks (Quicksort, Jensen, and Stack). For each category, we show a scatter plot (Fig. 3) and a survival plot (Fig. 4).

We first look at the scatter plots in Fig. 3. The x-axis refers to the solving time for the SMT-based approach while the y-axis to the solving time for POMC, both measured in seconds. The blue border lines indicate the timeout (set to 3600 s) for the tools, while the red line denotes the diagonal of the plot.

For all three categories of benchmarks, the scatter plots reveal an exponential blow up for the solving time of the POMC tool; on the contrary, the SMT-based approach does not incur in such a blow up. As an example, we take the scatter plot for the Quicksort category in Fig. 3 (a) and we consider the brown circles in the middle of the plot, corresponding to the Formula 5 of Table 5 checked on an array of size 2 containing numbers of increasing bitvector-size. For the case of numbers of bitvector-size of 3, 4, 5, and 6 bits, the solving time of POMC is of 8, 40, 199, and 956 s, respectively, while the time required by the SMT-based approach is of 13, 18, 16 and 16 s, respectively. Moreover, while for bitvector-size greater than 6 bits POMC reaches always the timeout for Formula 5, the SMT-based approach solves the benchmarks of all bitvector-size (*i.e.,* up to 16 bits) in time always less than 23 s.

A similar consideration can be done for the Jensen and the Stack categories. Take, for example, the blue circles in Fig. 3 (c) corresponding to Formula 14 in Table 5. For this case, the solving times of the SMT-based approach are consistently better than the ones of POMC. The reason may be that this formula contains hierarchical operators, which tend to yield to automata that make more non-deterministic guesses. This, in turn, causes the explicit-state model checker to perform, in general, many steps of backtracking during its depth-first model checking algorithm. Conversely, in the SMT-based approach, this part is managed (efficiently) by the DPLL algorithm inside the SMT-solver.

The exponential trend of POMC is reflected also in the survival plot (Fig. 4). Here, the x-axis represents the time (in seconds) while the y-axis represents the percentage of solved benchmarks. From the blue and yellow lines in Fig. 4, which correspond to the categories Stack and Jensen, respectively, it is clear that the POMC tool gets stuck solving (approximately) the 80% and the 60% of the benchmarks in the corresponding category. Conversely, the SMT-based approach solves all benchmarks in these two categories. If we take a look to the survival plot only for the Quicksort category in Fig. 5 (which reports the absolute number of solved benchmarks), we observe that the POMC tool gets stuck solving (approximately) 330 benchmarks, while the SMT-based approach solves circa 430 benchmarks.

In our benchmarks, we found only one case in which the solving time of POMC is always better than the one of the SMT-based approach. It corresponds to the green squares on the scatter plots in Fig. 3 (c) for the Stack category, corresponding to Formula 12. The reason is that this formula requires

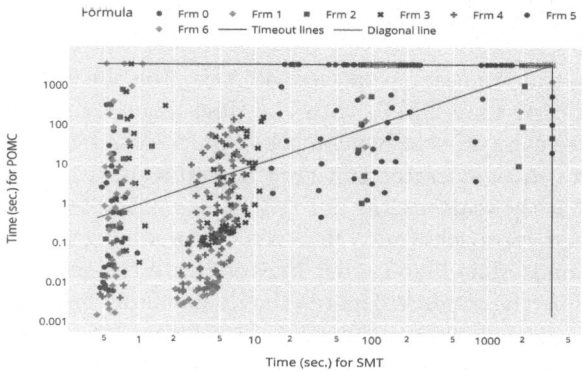

(a) Scatter plot for category Quicksort.

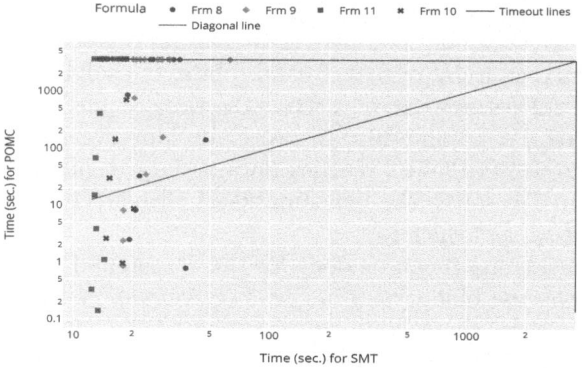

(b) Scatter plot for category Jensen.

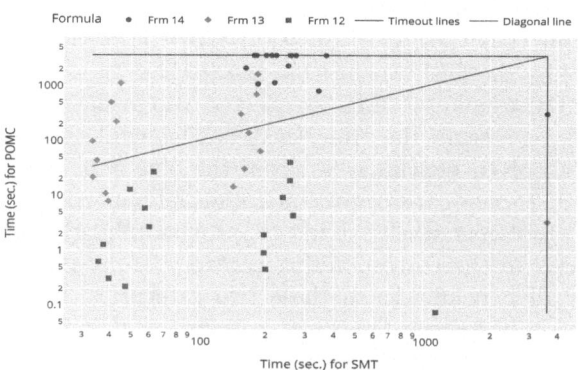

(c) Scatter plot for category Stack.

Fig. 3. Scatter plots

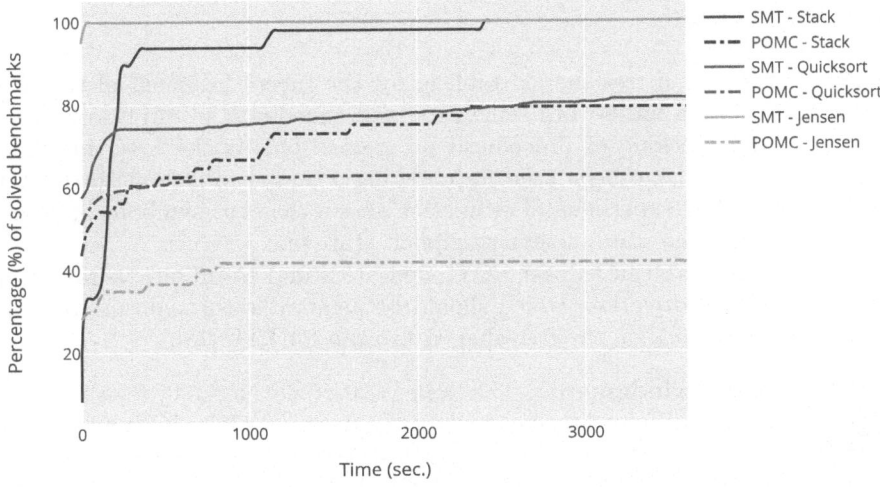

Fig. 4. Survival plot

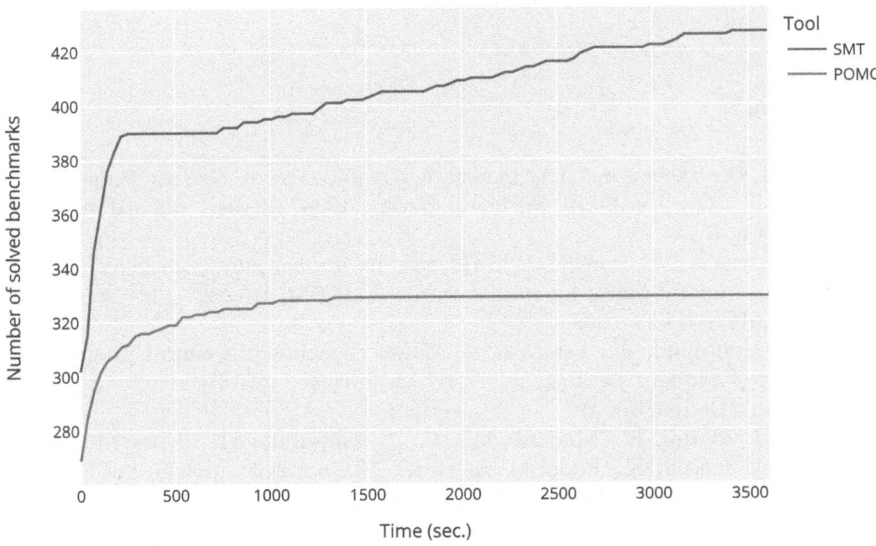

Fig. 5. Survival plot for the Quicksort category.

very few nondeterministic transitions in the explicit-state automaton. This, in turn, makes the search of the state-space a (almost) deterministic step, and thus very efficient for the depth-first algorithm of POMC. On the contrary, the breadth-first algorithm of the SMT-based approach seems to perform worse.

6   Conclusions

We have introduced a tree-shaped tableau for the future fragment of the temporal logic POTL on finite-word semantics, and encoded it in SMT to perform symbolic model checking of procedural programs. This is the first time both of these techniques have been used for checking a temporal logic with context-free modalities. The experimental evaluation shows that our symbolic approach scales better than the state-of-the-art explicit-state one.

Extending the tableau to past POTL operators and to infinite words seems a promising future direction, which should be achievable through an approach similar to related work on the tree-shaped tableau for LTL [18].

Acknowledgments. This work was partially funded by the Vienna Science and Technology Fund (WWTF) grant [10.47379/ICT19018] (ProbInG), and by the EU Commission in the Horizon Europe research and innovation programme under grant agreement No. 101107303 (MSCA Postdoctoral Fellowship CORPORA).

Funded by
the European Union

Disclosure of Interests. The authors have no competing interests to declare that are relevant to the content of this article.

References

1. Abrahams, D.: Exception-safety in generic components. In: Generic Programming. LNCS, vol. 1766, pp. 69–79. Springer, Berlin (1998). https://doi.org/10.1007/3-540-39953-4_6
2. Alur, R., Arenas, M., Barceló, P., Etessami, K., Immerman, N., Libkin, L.: First-order and temporal logics for nested words. LMCS **4**(4) (2008). https://doi.org/10.2168/LMCS-4(4:11)2008
3. Alur, R., Bouajjani, A., Esparza, J.: Model checking procedural programs. In: Handbook of Model Checking, pp. 541–572. Springer (2018). https://doi.org/10.1007/978-3-319-10575-8_17
4. Alur, R., Etessami, K., Madhusudan, P.: A temporal logic of nested calls and returns. In: Jensen, K., Podelski, A. (eds.) TACAS 2004. LNCS, vol. 2988, pp. 467–481. Springer, Heidelberg (2004). https://doi.org/10.1007/978-3-540-24730-2_35
5. Alur, R., Madhusudan, P.: Visibly pushdown languages. In: STOC 2004. pp. 202–211. ACM (2004). https://doi.org/10.1145/1007352.1007390
6. Alur, R., Madhusudan, P.: Adding nesting structure to words. J. ACM **56**(3), 16:1–16:43 (2009). https://doi.org/10.1145/1516512.1516518
7. Biere, A., Cimatti, A., Clarke, E.M., Strichman, O., Zhu, Y.: Bounded model checking. Adv. Comput. **58**, 117–148 (2003). https://doi.org/10.1016/S0065-2458(03)58003-2
8. Chiari, M., Bergamaschi, D., Pontiggia, F.: POMC (2024). https://github.com/michiari/POMC
9. Chiari, M., Geatti, L., Gigante, N., Pradella, M.: SMT-based symbolic model-checking for operator precedence languages. CoRR abs/ arXiv: 2405.11327 (2024)

10. Chiari, M., Mandrioli, D., Pontiggia, F., Pradella, M.: A model checker for operator precedence languages. ACM Trans. Program. Lang. Syst. **45**(3), 19:1–19:66 (2023). https://doi.org/10.1145/3608443

11. Chiari, M., Mandrioli, D., Pradella, M.: Operator precedence temporal logic and model checking. Theor. Comput. Sci. **848**, 47–81 (2020). https://doi.org/10.1016/j.tcs.2020.08.034

12. Chiari, M., Mandrioli, D., Pradella, M.: Model-checking structured context-free languages. In: Silva, A., Leino, K.R.M. (eds.) CAV 2021. LNCS, vol. 12760, pp. 387–410. Springer, Cham (2021). https://doi.org/10.1007/978-3-030-81688-9_18

13. Chiari, M., Mandrioli, D., Pradella, M.: A first-order complete temporal logic for structured context-free languages. Log. Methods Comput. Sci. **18:3** (2022). https://doi.org/10.46298/LMCS-18(3:11)2022

14. Clarke, E.M., Biere, A., Raimi, R., Zhu, Y.: Bounded model checking using satisfiability solving. Formal Methods Syst. Des. **19**(1), 7–34 (2001). https://doi.org/10.1023/A:1011276507260

15. Crespi Reghizzi, S., Mandrioli, D.: Operator precedence and the visibly pushdown property. J. Comput. Syst. Sci. **78**(6), 1837–1867 (2012). https://doi.org/10.1016/j.jcss.2011.12.006

16. Floyd, R.W.: Syntactic analysis and operator precedence. J. ACM **10**(3), 316–333 (1963). https://doi.org/10.1145/321172.321179

17. Geatti, L., Gigante, N., Montanari, A.: A SAT-based encoding of the one-pass and tree-shaped tableau system for LTL. In: Cerrito, S., Popescu, A. (eds.) TABLEAUX 2019. LNCS (LNAI), vol. 11714, pp. 3–20. Springer, Cham (2019). https://doi.org/10.1007/978-3-030-29026-9_1

18. Geatti, L., Gigante, N., Montanari, A., Reynolds, M.: One-pass and tree-shaped tableau systems for TPTL and TPTL$_b$+Past. Inf. Comput. **278**, 104599 (2021). https://doi.org/10.1016/j.ic.2020.104599

19. Geatti, L., Gigante, N., Montanari, A., Venturato, G.: SAT meets tableaux for linear temporal logic satisfiability. J. Autom. Reason. **68**(2), 6 (2024). https://doi.org/10.1007/S10817-023-09691-1

20. Grune, D., Jacobs, C.J.: Parsing techniques: a practical guide. Springer, New York (2008). https://doi.org/10.1007/978-0-387-68954-8

21. Harrison, M.A.: Introduction to Formal Language Theory. Addison Wesley, Boston (1978)

22. Henzinger, T.A., Kebis, P., Mazzocchi, N., Saraç, N.E.: Regular methods for operator precedence languages. In: ICALP 2023. LIPIcs, vol. 261, pp. 129:1–129:20. Schloss Dagstuhl - Leibniz-Zentrum für Informatik (2023). https://doi.org/10.4230/LIPICS.ICALP.2023.129

23. Huang, G., Wang, B.: Complete SAT-based model checking for context-free processes. Int. J. Found. Comput. Sci. **21**(2), 115–134 (2010). https://doi.org/10.1142/S0129054110007179

24. Jensen, T.P., Le Métayer, D., Thorn, T.: Verification of control flow based security properties. In: Proc. '99 IEEE Symp. Secur. Privacy. pp. 89–103. IEEE Computer Society, Oakland (1999). https://doi.org/10.1109/SECPRI.1999.766902

25. Komuravelli, A., Gurfinkel, A., Chaki, S.: SMT-based model checking for recursive programs. Formal Methods Syst. Des. **48**(3), 175–205 (2016). https://doi.org/10.1007/S10703-016-0249-4

26. Lonati, V., Mandrioli, D., Panella, F., Pradella, M.: Operator precedence languages: Their automata-theoretic and logic characterization. SIAM J. Comput. **44**(4), 1026–1088 (2015). https://doi.org/10.1137/140978818

27. Mandrioli, D., Pradella, M.: Generalizing input-driven languages: theoretical and practical benefits. Comput. Sci. Rev. **27**, 61–87 (2018). https://doi.org/10.1016/j.cosrev.2017.12.001
28. Mandrioli, D., Pradella, M., Crespi Reghizzi, S.: Star-freeness, first-order definability and aperiodicity of structured context-free languages. In: Pun, V.K.I., Stolz, V., Simao, A. (eds.) ICTAC 2020. LNCS, vol. 12545, pp. 161–180. Springer, Cham (2020). https://doi.org/10.1007/978-3-030-64276-1_9
29. Mandrioli, D., Pradella, M., Crespi Reghizzi, S.: Aperiodicity, star-freeness, and first-order logic definability of operator precedence languages. Log. Methods Comput. Sci. **19:4** (2023). https://doi.org/10.46298/lmcs-19(4:12)2023
30. Mehlhorn, K.: Pebbling mountain ranges and its application of DCFL-recognition. In: ICALP 1980. LNCS, vol. 85, pp. 422–435 (1980). https://doi.org/10.1007/3-540-10003-2_89
31. de Moura, L., Bjørner, N.: Z3: an efficient SMT solver. In: Ramakrishnan, C.R., Rehof, J. (eds.) TACAS 2008. LNCS, vol. 4963, pp. 337–340. Springer, Heidelberg (2008). https://doi.org/10.1007/978-3-540-78800-3_24
32. Pontiggia, F., Chiari, M., Pradella, M.: Verification of programs with exceptions through operator precedence automata. In: Calinescu, R., Păsăreanu, C.S. (eds.) SEFM 2021. LNCS, vol. 13085, pp. 293–311. Springer, Cham (2021). https://doi.org/10.1007/978-3-030-92124-8_17
33. Sutter, H.: Exception-safe generic containers. C++ Report **9** (1997). https://ptgmedia.pearsoncmg.com/imprint_downloads/informit/aw/meyerscddemo/DEMO/MAGAZINE/SU_FRAME.HTM

On Polynomial Expressions with C-Finite Recurrences in Loops with Nested Nondeterministic Branches

Chenglin Wang$^{(\boxtimes)}$ and Fangzhen Lin

The Hong Kong University of Science and Technology,
Clear Water Bay, Hong Kong
{cwangci,flin}@cse.ust.hk

Abstract. Loops are inductive constructs, which make them difficult to analyze and verify in general. One approach is to represent the inductive behaviors of the program variables in a loop by recurrences and try to solve them for closed-form solutions. These solutions can then be used to generate invariants or directly fed into an SMT-based verifier. One problem with this approach is that if a loop contains nondeterministic choices or complex operations such as non-linear assignments, then recurrences for program variables may not exist or may have no closed-form solutions. In such cases, an alternative is to generate recurrences for expressions, and there has been recent work along this line. In this paper, we further work in this direction and propose a template-based method for extracting polynomial expressions that satisfy some c-finite recurrences. While in general there are possibly infinitely many such polynomials for a given loop, we show that the desired polynomials form a finite union of vector spaces. We propose an algorithm for computing the bases of the vector spaces, and identify two cases where the bases can be computed efficiently. To demonstrate the usefulness of our results, we implemented a prototype system based on one of the special cases, and integrated it into an SMT-based verifier. Our experimental results show that the new verifier can now verify programs with non-linear properties.

Keywords: Program verification · Recurrence analysis · Loop summary

1 Introduction

Loops in computer programs induce inductive behaviors that are difficult to analyze. One method is by recurrence analysis through first extracting recurrences from loops and then solving them for closed-form solutions [11,17,19]. Once the solutions have been computed, they can be used in many downstream tasks such as invariant generation and program verification. So far most recurrence-based methods focus on individual program variables and their recurrences. In practice, due to complex control flow (e.g., nested branches in a loop) and operations

© The Author(s) 2024
A. Gurfinkel and V. Ganesh (Eds.): CAV 2024, LNCS 14681, pp. 409–430, 2024.
https://doi.org/10.1007/978-3-031-65627-9_20

```
while (*) {
    if (*) {
        y = 4*y - 4*x + 2
        x = 2*x + 1;
    } else {
        y = 4*y + 3;
        x = 2*x;
    }
}
```

Fig. 1. Motivated example

(e.g., non-linear operations), individual variables may not have well-defined recurrences. For example, consider the program in Fig. 1. Due to the non-deterministic branches, there are no well-defined recurrences for the variables x and y, not to mention computing closed-form solutions to them. However, if we consider the expression $x^2 + y + 1$, there is a simple c-finite recurrence for it: let $q = x^2 + y + 1$, and $q(k) = x(k)^2 + y(k) + 1$, where $x(k)$ and $y(k)$ denote the values of x and y, respectively, after the kth iteration of the while loop. It is easy to verify that $q(k)$ satisfies the following c-finite recurrence:

$$q(k + 1) = 4q(k),$$

from which one can compute a closed-form solution $q(k) = 4^k q(0)$. This by itself shows an interesting property about the program. It can also potentially be used to prove other properties that can be related to this expression. Furthermore, as shown by Kovács [16], c-finite recurrences and their closed-form solutions can be naturally used as a downstream tool to generate polynomial invariants.

This example shows that although individual program variables may not satisfy any recurrences, expressions made out of them may sometimes have recurrences that can be solved. As mentioned, finding expressions that have solvable recurrences is a useful exercise in itself in program analysis. It can also help program verification as we will see later.

While most works on loops and recurrences have been on individual program variables, there are two recent studies on recurrences arisen from expressions: the work by Amrollahi *et al.* [1] and that by Cyphert and Kincaid [4]. In this paper, we extend the current work by considering a larger program model that allows nested nondeterministic branches:

```
while (*) {
    if (*)        x = p₁(x);
    else if (*)   x = p₂(x);
    :
    else          x = pₘ(x);
}
```

where $\mathbf{x} = \mathbf{p}_i(\mathbf{x})$ is a simultaneous assignments of a tuple of variables $\mathbf{x}$ by a corresponding tuple of polynomials $\mathbf{p}_i(\mathbf{x})$. Given such a program, we consider polynomial expressions and systematically exploring all c-finite recurrences. In comparison, Amrollahi *et al.* [1] considered only simple loops without nested branches, and for limited forms of recurrences. As we shall see, our results in this paper strictly subsumes theirs even for simple loops. While Cyphert and Kincaid [4] also considered nested branches, they are reduced to ones without nested branches by program abstraction which is not guaranteed to be complete. However, their results on simple loops without nested branches are systematic. In fact, for these programs, our results are equivalent to theirs. We will have a more detailed discussion of related work later.

Briefly, our main contributions in this paper are as follows:

1. We propose a sound and semi-complete template-based method for finding polynomials that satisfy c-finite recurrences.
2. We show that the set of polynomials of the bounded degree d that satisfy c-finite recurrences of order r, for any given $d \geq 0$ and $r \geq 0$, forms a finite union of vector spaces. Based on this finding, we propose an algorithm to compute the bases of the vector spaces, and their closed-form solutions.
3. We identify two special cases, (1) $r = 1$ and (2) all $\mathbf{p}_i$'s are linear, where bases of these vector spaces are computed by solving linear equations.
4. We implemented a prototype system for finding closed-form solutions of polynomial expressions for the first special case and integrated it into a program verifier. Our experimental results shows that with this tool, many programs with non-linear properties can now be proved.

The rest of this paper is structured as follows. Section 2 introduces notations and reviews some basic concepts used in this paper. Section 3 introduces the template-based method and shows that the problem of finding polynomials with c-finite recurrences can be reduced to solving a system of quadratic equations. Section 4 shows the polynomials of bounded degree d satisfying c-finite recurrences of order r form a finite union of distinct vector space. Section 5 shows that under some settings, the computation for finite solutions can be easier than that proposed in Sect. 4. Section 6 introduces the implemented system and summarizes the experimental results. Finally, Sect. 7 discusses related work.

2   Preliminaries

In this section, we introduce notations and briefly review some concepts used in this paper.

2.1   Polynomials

A *monomial* in $\mathbf{x} = \begin{bmatrix} x_1, \ldots, x_n \end{bmatrix}^T$ is a product of the form

$$x_1^{\alpha_1} \cdot x_2^{\alpha_2} \cdots x_n^{\alpha_n},$$

where α_i's are nonnegative integers. We simplify the notation for monomials as follows: let $\alpha = (\alpha_1, \ldots, \alpha_n)$ be an n-tuple of nonnegative integers. Then we set

$$\mathbf{x}^\alpha = x_1^{\alpha_1} \cdot x_2^{\alpha_2} \cdots x_n^{\alpha_n}, .$$

The *total degree* of the monomial x^α is denoted $|\alpha| = \alpha_1 + \ldots, \alpha_n$. A *polynomial* p in $\mathbf{x}$ with coefficients in a field $\mathbb{K}$ is a finite linear combination of monomials of form

$$p = \sum_\alpha a_\alpha \mathbf{x}^\alpha,$$

where $a_\alpha \in \mathbb{K}$ and the sum is over a finite number of n-tuples $\alpha = (\alpha_1, \ldots, \alpha_n)$. The set of all polynomials in $\mathbf{x}$ with coefficients in a field $\mathbb{K}$ is denoted by $\mathbb{K}[x_1, \ldots, x_n]$ or $\mathbb{K}[\mathbf{x}]$ for short. The *total degree* of p, denoted $\deg(p)$, is the maximum $|\alpha|$ such that the coefficient a_α is nonzero. By a polynomial p of bounded degree d, we mean the total degree of it is less than or equal to d.

The set of all polynomials of bounded degree d (denoted by $\mathbb{K}_d[\mathbf{x}]$) forms a vector space and all monomials of bounded degree d form a basis. By fixing the order on those monomials, a polynomial p can be represented using coordinate vector whose elements are coefficients of p. For example, let $\left[1, x, y, x^2, xy, y^2\right]^T$ be the basis. Then the coordinate vector of $p = 2 + 3x + 4y^2$ is $[2, 3, 0, 0, 0, 1]^T$.

For a polynomial vector $\mathbf{q} = [q_1, \ldots, q_n]^T$, we have $\mathbf{q}(\mathbf{x}) = \left[q_1(\mathbf{x}), \ldots, q_n(\mathbf{x})\right]^T$. The result of the polynomial composition $(p \circ \mathbf{q})(\mathbf{x}) = p(\mathbf{q}(\mathbf{x}))$ is a polynomial of bounded degree $d_p d_\mathbf{q}$, where d_p is the total degree of p and $d_\mathbf{q}$ is the maximum total degree among total degrees of q_i's. The polynomial composition is distributed over addition. That is, $(p_1 + p_2) \circ \mathbf{q} = (p_1 \circ \mathbf{q}) + (p_2 \circ \mathbf{q})$ for any p_1, p_2, and $\mathbf{q}$. Given another polynomial vector $\mathbf{p} = [p_1, \ldots, p_n]^T$, we have $\mathbf{p} \circ \mathbf{q} = [p_1 \circ \mathbf{q}, \ldots, p_n \circ \mathbf{q}]^T$.

2.2   Eigenvalues and Matrix Polynomials

Given an $n \times n$ matrix M, if a scalar λ and a nonzero vector $\mathbf{a}$ satisfy the equation

$$M\mathbf{a} = \lambda \mathbf{a},$$

then λ is called an *eigenvalue* of M and $\mathbf{a}$ is called an *eigenvector* of M associated with λ. The pair $(\lambda, \mathbf{a})$ is an *eigenpair* for M.

Given a univariate polynomial $p(x) = x^k + a_{k-1}x^{k-1} + \cdots + a_1 x + a_0$ of degree k, the evaluation of it at a square matrix M is well-defined by

$$p(M) = M^k + a_{k-1}M^{k-1} + \cdots + a_1 M + a_0 I.$$

Recall that the following Theorem in [10], which follows the fundamental theorem of algebra, links the eigenpairs of $p(M)$ to those of M in a simple way.

Theorem 1. *Let $p(x)$ be a univariate polynomial of degree k. If $(\lambda, \mathbf{a})$ is an eigenpair of M, then $(p(\lambda), \mathbf{a})$ is an eigenpair of $p(M)$. Conversely, if $k \geq 1$ and if μ is an eigenvalue of $p(M)$, then there is some eigenvalue λ of M s.t. $\mu = p(\lambda)$.*

Example 1. Let $p(x) = x^2 + 3x + 1$ The eigenvalues of $M = \begin{bmatrix} 2 & 3 \\ 4 & 3 \end{bmatrix}$ are 6 and -1.

The eigenvalues of $p(M) = M^2 + 3M + 1 = \begin{bmatrix} 23 & 24 \\ 32 & 31 \end{bmatrix}$ are $p(6) = 6^2 + 3 \cdot 6 + 1 = 55$ and $p(-1) = (-1)^2 + 3 \cdot (-1) + 1 = -1$.

2.3   C-Finite Recurrences

A sequence $\{a(k)\}_{k=0}^{\infty}$ is *c-finite* if it satisfies a *c-finite recurrence* of the following form for some constant $c_i \in \mathbb{Q}$'s and integer $r \geq 1$:

$$a(k + r) = c_1 a(k + r - 1) + \cdots + c_r a(k), \tag{1}$$

where r is the *order* of this recurrence.

The following inhomogeneous c-finite recurrence with an extra constant term c_{r+1} is also considered in this paper:

$$a(k + r) = c_1 a(k + r - 1) + \cdots + c_r a(k) + c_{r+1}. \tag{2}$$

The constant term c_{r+1} is often discarded in the literature because a sequence $\{a(k)\}_{k=0}^{\infty}$ satisfying an inhomogeneous c-finite recurrence (2) of order r must satisfy a homogeneous one (1) of order $r + 1$. We consider the inhomogeneous case because in a setting discussed later, the computation will be easier.

The *characteristic polynomial* p of a c-finite recurrence (1) is a univariate polynomial defined as:

$$p(t) = t^r - c_1 t^{r-1} - \cdots - c_r t.$$

Every c-finite recurrence (1) has a closed-form solution in the following exponential polynomial form [7]:

$$a(k) = \sum_{i=1}^{s} p_i(k) \lambda_i^k, \tag{3}$$

where s is the number of distinct roots of the characteristic polynomial, λ_i's are those distinct roots, and p_i's are polynomials whose degrees are one less than multiplicities of the corresponding roots λ_i's and coefficients are determined by initial values of $a(k)$. Conversely, any sequence admitting a closed-form solution of form (3) is c-finite.

2.4   Program Model and Problem Statement

In this paper, we consider the program model illustrated in Fig. 2. In words, given a set of variables $\mathbf{x} = [x_1, \ldots, x_n]^T$, each iteration of the loop updates the values of these variables non-deterministically by some polynomial transitions $\mathbf{p}_i = [p_{i1}, \ldots, p_{in}]^T$, where $p_{ij} \in \mathbb{Q}[\mathbf{x}]$ and $\mathbf{p}_i(\mathbf{x}) = [p_{i1}(\mathbf{x}), \ldots, p_{in}(\mathbf{x})]^T$. Notice that this class of programs can model nested deterministic branches and nested loops in a natural way - see Sect. 6 for an example.

```
while  (*)  {
     if  (*)        x = p₁(x);
     else  if  (*)  x = p₂(x);
     :
     else           x = pₘ(x);
}
```

Fig. 2. program model

We denote the values of $\mathbf{x}$ after the kth iteration by $\mathbf{x}(k) = [x_1(k), \ldots, x_n(k)]^T$. Given a program in Fig. 2 and some integer $r \geq 1$, we want to find some polynomial expressions $q(\mathbf{x})$ of bounded degree d satisfying the following c-finite recurrence for some $c_i \in \mathbb{Q}$:

$$q(\mathbf{x}(k+r)) = c_1 q(\mathbf{x}(k+r-1)) + \cdots + c_r q(\mathbf{x}(k)). \tag{4}$$

3   Reduction to Solving a System of Quadratic Equations

Given a program as described by Fig. 2, a bounded degree d, and the order r, we want to find polynomials $q \in \mathbb{Q}[\mathbf{x}]$ satisfying c-finite recurrences (4). To consider all possible interleaves of those non-deterministic branches, letting q_i' be the polynomial composition $q_i' = q \circ \mathbf{p}_{w[r-i]} \circ \cdots \circ \mathbf{p}_{w[1]}$, Eq. (4) is equivalent to the following formula:

$$\bigwedge_{w \in W_r} \sum_{i=0}^{r-1} c_i q_i'(\mathbf{x}(k)) = 0, \tag{5}$$

where W_r is the set of all r-tuples over $\{1, \ldots, m\}$ and $c_0 = 1$;

Intuitively, each $w \in W_r$ denotes a possible execution path for any r consequent iterations. So for any $i < r$, the composition $\mathbf{p}_{w[r-i]} \circ \cdots \circ \mathbf{p}_{w[1]}$ denotes the transition after the first i iterations. That is, each $q_i'(\mathbf{x}(k))$ is $q(\mathbf{x}(k+i))$ in recurrence (4) for a possible execution path. Since in the formula (5), w is ranged over all r-tuples over $\{1, \ldots, m\}$, all possible interleaves of those branches are considered. Therefore, this formula is equivalent to the recurrence (4).

To find a polynomial q of bounded degree d satisfying this formula, we set up a template polynomial for it:

$$q(\mathbf{x}) = \sum_\alpha a_\alpha \mathbf{x}^\alpha,$$

where a_α's are unknown and $\mathbf{x}^\alpha$'s are all monomials of bounded degree d. After plugging the template into formula (5), the left-hand side of each conjunct is a polynomial over $\mathbf{x}(k)$. To be zero, all coefficients of this polynomial must be zero. Note that those unknown values c_i's are multiplied with q, whose coefficients are also unknown, so the coefficients of those polynomials on the left-hand side are quadratic expression of these unknown values.

Example 2. Consider the loop in Fig. 1, if $r = 1$ and we want to find polynomial q of bounded degree 2 that satisfies Eq. (1), we set up a template for q as follows:

$$q(x, y) = a_0 x^2 + a_1 xy + a_2 y^2 + a_3 x + a_4 y + a_5.$$

There are two conjuncts in the resulting formula (5). One of them is as follows:

$$(-a_0 c_1 + 4a_0 - 8a_1 + 16a_2)x(k)^2$$
$$+(-a_1 c_1 + 8a_1 - 32a_2 c_1)x(k)y(k)$$
$$+(4a_0 - 16a_2 - a_3 c_1 + 2a_3 - 4a_4)x(k)$$
$$+(-a_2 c_1 + 16a_2)y(k)^2$$
$$+(4a_1 + 16a_2 - a_4 c_1 + 4a_4)y(k)$$
$$+a_0 + 2a_1 + 4a_2 + a_3 + 2a_4 - a_5 c_1 + a_5 = 0$$

By setting all coefficients to be zero, this conjunct produces the following system of quadratic equations:

$$-a_0 c_1 + 4a_0 - 8a_1 + 16a_2 = 0$$
$$-a_1 c_1 + 8a_1 - 32a_2 c_1 = 0$$
$$4a_0 - 16a_2 - a_3 c_1 + 2a_3 - 4a_4 = 0$$
$$-a_2 c_1 + 16a_2 = 0$$
$$4a_1 + 16a_2 - a_4 c_1 + 4a_4 = 0$$
$$a_0 + 2a_1 + 4a_2 + a_3 + 2a_4 - a_5 c_1 + a_5 = 0$$

Together with the equations generated from the other conjunct, each solution to them corresponds to a required polynomial q and the recurrence it satisfies. For this example, $a_0 = 1$, $a_4 = 1$, $a_5 = 1$, $c_1 = 4$, and others are zero is one of the solutions, which corresponds to $q(k) = x(k)^2 + y(k) + 1$ and $q(k + 1) = 4q(k)$. Note that, this is not the only solution to the quadratic equations. For example, $a_0 = \lambda, a_4 = \lambda, a_5 = \lambda, c_1 = 4/\lambda$ is a solution for any $\lambda \neq 0$.

4   Finding Finite Representative Solutions

In the previous section, we achieve a system of quadratic equations, whose solutions correspond to the desired polynomials and the recurrences they satisfy. The number of solutions to such equations may be infinite. But most of them are redundant in the sense that some of them are linear combinations of others. For example, if q_1 and q_2 are polynomials satisfying recurrence (4) for the same c_i's, then any linear combination of them also satisfies this recurrence with the same c_i's. That is, given an assignment to c_i's, the polynomials q satisfying recurrence (4) form a vector space. Since different c_i's may result in different vector spaces for those polynomials, the set of all polynomials satisfying recurrence (4) is a union of vector spaces.

Lemma 1. *Given a loop, a bounded degree d, the order r of the c-finite recurrence, the set of polynomials $q \in \mathbb{Q}_d[\mathbf{x}]$ satisfying recurrence (4) of order r is a union of vector spaces.*

Proof. The zero polynomial must satisfy the recurrence (4) for any assignment to $\{c_1, \ldots, c_r\}$. Suppose both $q_1, q_2 \in \mathbb{Q}_d[\mathbf{x}]$ satisfy the recurrence (4) with the same $\{c_1, \ldots, c_r\}$. That is,

$$q_1(\mathbf{x}(k+r)) = c_1 q_1(\mathbf{x}(k+r-1)) + \cdots + c_r q_1(\mathbf{x}(k)),$$
$$q_2(\mathbf{x}(k+r)) = c_1 q_2(\mathbf{x}(k+r-1)) + \cdots + c_r q_2(\mathbf{x}(k)).$$

Then $k_1 q_1 + k_2 q_2$ for any k_1, k_2 also satisfies the recurrence (4) with the same $\{c_1, \ldots, c_r\}$. So any assignment to $\{c_1, \ldots, c_r\}$ corresponds to a vector space of q. As a result, the set of polynomials q satisfying the recurrence (4) of order r is a union of vector spaces.   □

Lemma 1 shows that the desired polynomials constitute some vector spaces. But distinct vector spaces among them may be infinite, making it impossible to produce finite representative solutions. The following theorem claims that these polynomials form a finite union of vector spaces.

Theorem 2. *Given a loop, a bounded degree d, an order r, the set of polynomials $q \in \mathbb{Q}_d[\mathbf{x}]$ satisfying recurrence (4) of order r is a finite union of vector spaces,*

Proof. By Lemma 1, the set of polynomials $q \in \mathbb{Q}_d[\mathbf{x}]$ is a union of vector spaces. Let B be the set of all basis vectors of these vector spaces. It is known that as a vector space, the dimension of $\mathbb{Q}_d[\mathbf{x}]$ is $\binom{n+d}{d} + 1$, where n is number of program variables. If $|B| > \binom{n+d}{d} + 1$, there is a vector $b \in B$ s.t. b is a linear combination of other vectors in B. Keep removing such vectors in B and denote the resulting set as B'. Then $|B'| \leq \binom{n+d}{d} + 1$ and all vectors in it are linearly independent. In other words, the vector space spanned by B' is the smallest vector space that contains all polynomials in $\mathbb{Q}_d[\mathbf{x}]$ satisfying recurrence (4) of order r. Since each vector q in B' satisfies some recurrence (4) of order r, it must satisfies some exponential polynomial (3). That is, for each vector $q \in B'$, we have

$$q(\mathbf{x}(k)) = \sum_{i=1}^{s_q} p_{q,i}(k)\lambda_{q,i}^k,$$

where $p_{q,i}$ are polynomials and the sum of their total degrees are less than or equal to r. By definition of B', any $q' \in \mathbb{Q}_d[\mathbf{x}]$ that satisfying some recurrence (4) of order r are some linear combination of vectors in B'. Therefore, we have

$$q'(\mathbf{x}(k)) = \sum_{q \in B'} a_q q(\mathbf{x}(k)) = \sum_{q \in B'} a_q \sum_{i=1}^{s_q} p_{q,i}(k)\lambda_{q,i}^k,$$

where $a_q \in \mathbb{R}$. Since it is an exponential polynomial, we can establish the following characteristic polynomial

$$\prod_{q \in B'} \prod_{i=1}^{s_q} (t - \lambda_{q,i})^{d_{q,i}},$$

where $d_{q,i} \in \mathbb{N}$ and the sum of them is r. Any desired $q' \in \mathbb{Q}_d[\mathbf{x}]$ must satisfy some recurrence (4) whose characteristic polynomial is of the above form for some $d_{q,i}$'s. Since the sum of $d_{q,i}$ is r and the number of $\lambda_{q,i}$ is finite (because $|B'|$ is bounded), the number of possible characteristic polynomials and corresponding recurrences are finite. Each recurrence corresponds a vector space, so the number of vector spaces is finite.   □

Note that Theorem 2 is not only applicable to the program in Fig. 2, but applicable to all general loops. In the proof of Theorem 2, a finite set B' is constructed and any polynomial that satisfies some recurrence (4) is a linear combination of vectors in B'. So B' can be used as the representative solutions.

   Given a program in Fig. 2, Algorithm 1 gives the process to compute all polynomial expressions that satisfy recurrence (4). Initially, given the inputs P, d, and r, it sets up a template for the desired polynomial (variable p is the template polynomial and **coeffs** is a vector of the unknown coefficients) and establishes those quadratic equations mentioned in Sect. 3. eqs is the set of quadratic equations and $\mathbf{c}$ is a vector of unknown coefficients c_i's in recurrence (1). The variable bases is initialized as an empty set. $\mathbf{a}$ denotes an assignment to $\mathbf{c}$. θ is a formula recording the remaining possible $\mathbf{c}$ that should be considered. In each iteration, the loop asks for a model of θ, which is an assignment to $\mathbf{c}$. After plugging it into the quadratic equations (Line 7), these equations are reduced to linear ones. Basis $\mathbf{B}$ of these linear equations are then computed and is added to bases. Each element in $\mathbf{B}$ is a solution to **coeffs**, so each corresponds to a desired polynomial. Since in each iteration, a vector space of desired polynomials is computed and the basis is added to bases, bases is a spanning set of the smallest vector space containing all vector spaces computed so far. In future iterations we do not want to consider those $\mathbf{c}$ whose corresponding vector space is contained in the vector space spanned by bases. So variable constraint is the formula that will be added to θ saying that in the future iterations, the computed vector spaces should contain at least one polynomial outside the vector space spanned by bases.

Algorithm 1: Finding polynomial expressions of bounded degree d satisfying recurrence (4) of order r

---

Input : A program P, bounded degree d, order r of the recurrence (4)
Output: basis vectors of those distinct solution vector space.

1 p, **coeffs** $\leftarrow$ template_poly($\mathbf{x}, d$);
2 eqs, **c** $\leftarrow$ build_eqs(P, p, r);
3 bases $\leftarrow \emptyset$;
4 $\theta \leftarrow \bigwedge$_ieqs[$i$];
5 **while** $sat(\theta)$ **do**
6   **a** $\leftarrow$ model($\exists$**coeffs**.θ);
7   cur_eqs $\leftarrow$ eqs.subs(**c**, **a**);
8   **B** $\leftarrow$ solve(cur_eqs);
9   bases = bases $\cup$ **B**;
10   constraint $\leftarrow \exists\lambda_1, \ldots, \lambda_{|\text{bases}|}. \sum_{\mathbf{b}_i \in \text{bases}} \lambda_i \mathbf{b}_i \neq$ **coeffs**;
11      $\theta = \theta \wedge$ constraint;
12 ans $\leftarrow \bigcup_{i=1}^{|\text{bases}|} \{$p.subs(**coeffs**, **b**)$|$**b** $\in$ bases$\}$;
13 **return** ans;

Theorem 3. *Given a program P in Fig. 2, bounded degree d, and the order r, Algorithm 1 terminates with a set of polynomials s.t. all polynomials $p \in \mathbb{Q}_d[\mathbf{x}]$ satisfying recurrence (4) of order r are linear combinations of them.*

Proof. In each iteration, the basis **B** is computed from the quadratic equations established in Sect. 3 with unknown c_i's replaced with some constant **a**. Then it is added to bases, so bases is a spanning set of the smallest vector space containing all vector spaces computed so far. In each iteration, after computing the corresponding basis **B**, a constraint is set up in Line 10, which is then added to θ. Note that the value **a** used to compute a new vector space in each iteration is a valid assignment to θ as shown in Line 6. So the constraint set up in Line 10 states that those desired polynomials in the vector space spanned by bases, which is the smallest vector space containing all computed vector spaces, is found, in later iteration those computed vector spaces should contains at least one vector outside this space. When the loop terminates, θ is unsatisfiable, which means all desired polynomials have been computed. So if it terminates, all desired polynomials are linear combinations of vectors in bases.

We next show the termination. Since in each iteration, at least one polynomial not appeared in the vector space spanned by bases is in the vector space computed in current iteration, the vector space spanned by bases will be enlarged in dimension at least by 1. When dimension of the space spanned by bases reaches the dimension of the smallest vector space containing all desired polynomial, which is upper bounded by $\binom{n+d}{d} + 1$, there is no other vector outside the space, so θ becomes unsatisfiable, which terminates the loop.   □

5   Special Cases Where the Computations Are Easier

In the previous section, we derived an algorithm, which can find finite representative solutions for the quadratic equations set up in Sect. 3. But in each iteration, it asks for a model of a non-linear formula, which requires a powerful SMT solver or algebraic system. In this section, we discuss two special cases, whose computations are much easier. The key observation is that given a polynomial vector $\mathbf{p}$, the polynomial composition $T_{\mathbf{p}}(q) = q \circ \mathbf{p}$ is a linear transformation.

Lemma 2. *Given a polynomial vector $\mathbf{p}$, the polynomial composition $T_{\mathbf{p}}(q) = q \circ \mathbf{p}$ is a linear transformation from $\mathbb{Q}_{d_p}[\mathbf{x}]$ to $\mathbb{Q}_{d_p d_q}[\mathbf{x}]$, $d_q = \deg(q)$ and $d_{\mathbf{p}}$ is the maximum among $\deg(p_i)$;*

Proof. Given any scalars $c_1, c_2 \in \mathbb{Q}$ and polynomials q_1, q_2, we have

$$T_{\mathbf{p}}(c_1 q_1 + c_2 q_2) = (c_1 q_1 + c_2 q_2) \circ \mathbf{p}$$
$$= c_1 q_1 \circ \mathbf{p} + c_2 q_2 \circ \mathbf{p}$$
$$= c_1 T_{\mathbf{p}}(q_1) + c_2 T_{\mathbf{p}}(q_2).$$

□

It is known that a linear transformation can be represented by a transformation matrix, which is constructed by computing the image of each basis element under the transformation and putting coordinates of those images in order.

Example 3. Consider again the program in Fig. 1. Let $\{x^2, xy, y^2, x, y, 1\}$ be the basis of $\mathbb{Q}_2[x, y]$. As in Example 2, let the template polynomial be $q(x, y) = a_0 x^2 + a_1 xy + a_2 y^2 + a_3 x + a_4 y + a_5$, whose coordinate is $\mathbf{a} = [a_0, a_1, a_2, a_3, a_4, a_5]$. For the two transitions in Fig. 1, the transformation matrices are

$$M_1 = \begin{bmatrix} 4 & -8 & 16 & 0 & 0 & 0 \\ 0 & 8 & -32 & 0 & 0 & 0 \\ 0 & 0 & 16 & 0 & 0 & 0 \\ 4 & 0 & -16 & 2 & -4 & 0 \\ 0 & 4 & 16 & 0 & 4 & 0 \\ 1 & 2 & 4 & 1 & 2 & 1 \end{bmatrix}, M_2 = \begin{bmatrix} 4 & 0 & 0 & 0 & 0 & 0 \\ 0 & 8 & 0 & 0 & 0 & 0 \\ 0 & 0 & 16 & 0 & 0 & 0 \\ 0 & 6 & 0 & 2 & 0 & 0 \\ 0 & 0 & 24 & 0 & 4 & 0 \\ 0 & 0 & 9 & 0 & 3 & 1 \end{bmatrix}.$$

Note that $M_1 \mathbf{a}$ and $M_2 \mathbf{a}$ are coordinates of $(q \circ \mathbf{p}_1)(x, y)$ and $(q \circ \mathbf{p}_2)(x, y)$.

5.1   Polynomials Satisfying First Order Inhomogeneous C-Finite Recurrences

In this subsection, given a $d \geq 0$, we consider to find polynomial expressions $q \in \mathbb{Q}_d[\mathbf{x}]$ satisfying a first order inhomogeneous c-finite recurrence of the following form for some c_1, c_2:

$$q(\mathbf{x}(k+1)) = c_1 q(\mathbf{x}(k)) + c_2. \tag{6}$$

There are two cases to be considered:

1. if $c_1 \neq 1$, then for any polynomial q that satisfies Eq. (6), we can construct a new polynomial $q'(\mathbf{x}) = q(\mathbf{x}) + \frac{c_2}{c_1-1}$ s.t. the following equation holds:

$$q'(\mathbf{x}(k+1)) = c_1 q'(\mathbf{x}(k)). \tag{7}$$

2. if $c_1 = 1$, then Eq. (6) becomes

$$q(\mathbf{x}(k+1)) - q(\mathbf{x}(k)) - c_2 = 0,$$

where the left-hand side is a zero polynomial. As a result, all its coefficients must be zero. This forms a system of linear equations, from which a basis can be computed to represent all polynomials that forms the desired recurrence.

Since in the second case, the computation for the desired polynomials is reduced to solve a system of linear equations, which is much easier, so in the rest of this subsection, we focus on the first case.

Similar to Eq. (5), for a program as described by Fig. 2, recurrence (7) is equivalent to the following formula:

$$\bigwedge_{i=1}^{m} (q \circ \mathbf{p}_i)(\mathbf{x}(k)) = c_1 q(\mathbf{x}(k)). \tag{8}$$

Since polynomial composition is a linear transformation and can be represented by a matrix, assuming the basis is ordered by putting monomials with higher degrees in front, formula (8) is equivalent to the following one:

$$\bigwedge_{i=1}^{m} \begin{bmatrix} M_{i1} \\ M_{i2} \end{bmatrix} \mathbf{a} = \begin{bmatrix} 0 \\ c_1 \mathbf{a} \end{bmatrix}, \tag{9}$$

where $M_{i1} \in \mathbb{Q}^{(s-t)\times(t+1)}$, $M_{i2} \in \mathbb{Q}^{(t+1)\times(t+1)}$, $s = \binom{n+dd_\mathbf{p}}{dd_\mathbf{p}}$, $t = \binom{n+d}{d}$, $d_\mathbf{p}$ is the maximum among $deg(p_i)$, $\begin{bmatrix} M_{i1} \\ M_{i2} \end{bmatrix}$ is the transformation matrix of $q \circ \mathbf{p}_i$, and $\mathbf{a}$ is the coordinate for the template polynomial q. There are $(s-t)$ zeros on the right-hand side, because $q \circ \mathbf{p}_i$ may produce terms with higher order than d and they should be zero to ensure formula (8) holds (because there is no terms with degrees higher than d on the right-hand side).

Formula (9) can be further split as follows:

$$\bigwedge_{i=1}^{m} M_{i1}\mathbf{a} = 0, \tag{10}$$

$$\bigwedge_{i=1}^{m} M_{i2}\mathbf{a} = c_1\mathbf{a}. \tag{11}$$

Equations in (10) can be solved using Gaussian elimination. Each equation in formula (11) is the definition of eigenvalues and eigenvectors for a square matrix, so formula (11) says that c_1 must be common eigenvalues of those matrices M_{i2}'s. Because any $n \times n$ matrix has at most n distinct eigenvalues, the number of solutions to c_1 is finite. So to solve the Eq. (11), we just need to enumerate all common eigenvalues of M_{i2}'s and replace c_1 with those eigenvalues. After that, equations in (11) are reduced to linear ones, which can be solved easily.

Theorem 4. *Given a program in Fig. 2 and an integer d, let $d_{\mathbf{p}}$ be the maximum among $deg(p_i)$'s. By ordering all monomials in $\mathbb{Q}_{dd_{\mathbf{p}}}[\mathbf{x}]$ with monomials with higher degree in front, the possible values for c_1 in Eq. (8) are common eigenvalues of lower squared matrices of those transformation matrices of $q \circ \mathbf{p}_i$.*

Example 4. Consider the program in Fig. 1. In Example 3, we computed transformation matrices for both branches as M_1 and M_2. To solve for c_1 and q in Eq. (8), by Theorem 4, c_1 should be common eigenvalues of M_1 and M_2, which are $\{1, 2, 4, 8, 16\}$. For $c_1 = 1$, the solution to q in Eq. (8) is the constant polynomial $q = \lambda$ for all $\lambda \in \mathbb{Q}$, which is trivial. For $c_1 = 2, 8, 16$, the solution to q is zero. For $c_1 = 4$, the solution to q is any multiple of $q(x, y) = x^2 + y + 1$, which is a basis for the solution vector space and used as the representative solution.

5.2   Linear Transitions

In this subsection, we assume all $\mathbf{p}_i$'s in Fig. 2 are linear and try to find all polynomials of bounded degree d that satisfy c-finite recurrences (4) of order r.

If all $\mathbf{p}_i$ are linear transitions, the transformation matrices of them are square. So Eq. (5) is equivalent to

$$\bigwedge_{w \in W_r} (\prod_{i=1}^{r} M_{w[i]} - c_1 \prod_{i=1}^{r-1} M_{w[i]} - \cdots - c_{r-1} M_{w[1]} - c_r I) \mathbf{a} = 0, \qquad (12)$$

where W_r is the set of all r-tuples over $\{1, \ldots, m\}$, M_i's are transformation matrices of $p \circ \mathbf{p}_i$, and $\prod_{i=1}^{s} M_{w[i]} = M_{w[s]} M_{w[s-1]} \cdots M_{w[1]}$.

Formula (12) is hard to solve, because $\mathbf{a}$ lies in the intersection of the nullspaces of the matrices in the parenthesis. Different assignments to c_i's may result in different nullspaces, thus different solutions to $\mathbf{a}$. Our solution is to transform formula (12) into formula (13)–(14) below, where c_i's only appear in matrix polynomials $p(M_1)$ for some univariate polynomials p's:

$$\forall 0 \le l < r. \forall 2 \le i \le m. \bigwedge_{w \in W_{r-l-1}} p_l(M_1)(M_i - M_1)(\prod_{j=1}^{r-l-1} M_{w[j]}) \mathbf{a} = 0 \qquad (13)$$

$$\wedge \, p_r(M_1) \mathbf{a} = 0, \qquad (14)$$

where $p_k(M_1) = M_1^k - \sum_{j=1}^{k} c_j M_1^{k-j}$.

Theorem 5. *Formula (12) is equivalent to formula (13) - (14).*

The proof is given in Appendix A due to page limits. Intuitively, there is a one-to-one correspondence between conjuncts in formula (12) and those in formula (13)–(14). Formula (14) is the conjunct in formula (12) whose $w = [1]^r$. For any other conjunct in formula (12), whose w has l trailing 1's, one can find another one, whose w' has $l + 1$ trailing 1's and has the same prefix of length $r - l - 1$ with w. The difference between them can be simplified into a conjunct in formula (13). Transforming formula (13)–(14) back to formula (12) is done reversely.

Formula (13) and (14) are simpler than Formula (12) in the sense that all c_i's appear in some matrix polynomials $p_k(M_1)$, which makes it easier to be analyzed. In the following, we show how to solve for $\mathbf{a}$ for the following equation, which is a conjunct in formula (13):

$$p_l(M_1)(M_i - M_1)(\prod_{j=1}^{r-l-1} M_{w[j]})\mathbf{a} = 0. \tag{15}$$

Recall that by the fundamental theorem of algebra, a polynomial $p(t) = t^l + c_1 t^{l-1} + \cdots + c_l$ can be factored into $p(t) = \prod_{i=1}^{l}(t - \alpha_i)$, where α_i's are roots of $p(t)$. When this factorization is applied on $p_l(M_1)$ [10], it becomes:

$$p_l(M_1) = \prod_{i=1}^{l}(M_1 - \alpha_i I).$$

Each factor $(M_1 - \alpha_i I)$ is a matrix, whose singularity depends on the value of α_i. If α_i is some eigenvalue of M_1, then this matrix is singular, otherwise it is invertible. The factor $(M_1 - \alpha_i I)$ is called an *eigenvalue factor* of $p_l(M_1)$ if α_i is an eigenvalue of M_1. After this factorization, formula (15) becomes

$$\prod_{j=1}^{l}(M_1 - \alpha_j I)(M_i - M_1)(\prod_{j=1}^{r-l-1} M_{w[j]})\mathbf{a} = 0. \tag{16}$$

Note that the multiplication between those factors $(M_1 - \alpha_i I)$ are mutually commutative. So if some α_i's are not eigenvalues of M_1, then the corresponding factors are invertible and can be canceled, which converts formula (16) into

$$\prod_{j=1}^{s}(M_1 - \lambda_j I)(M_i - M_1)(\prod_{j=1}^{r-l-1} M_{w[j]})\mathbf{a} = 0,$$

where $0 \leq s \leq l$ and λ_j's are eigenvalues of M_1.

This cancellation suggests that it is the eigenvalue factors that determine the solutions set to $\mathbf{a}$. In other words, if $p_l(M_1)$ and $p'_l(M_1)$ have the same set of eigenvalue factors, then $p_l(M_1)(M_i - M_1)(\prod_{j=1}^{r-l-1} M_{w[j]})\mathbf{a} = 0$ and $p'_l(M_1)(M_i - M_1)(\prod_{j=1}^{r-l-1} M_{w[j]})\mathbf{a} = 0$ have the same solution set to $\mathbf{a}$. So solving Eq. (15) can be done by enumerating all possible eigenvalue factor combinations for $p_l(M_1)$. That is, the solution to $\mathbf{a}$ of the following formula is equivalent to that of Eq. (15):

$$\bigvee_{\Lambda \in \Lambda_l} \prod_{\lambda \in \Lambda} (M_1 - \lambda I)(M_i - M_1)\left(\prod_{j=1}^{r-l-1} M_{w[j]} \right)\mathbf{a} = 0, \qquad (17)$$

where Λ_l is the set of all the subsets whose cardinalities are less than or equal to l of the set of eigenvalues of M_1 (i.e., $\forall \Lambda \in \Lambda.|\Lambda| \leq l$). Each disjunct in formula (17) is a linear equation, which can be solved easily. Formula (14) can be solved in a similar way.

Note that the derivation above solves a single equation (15). But solving formula (13)–(14) cannot be simply solving each equation using this approach and then intersecting those solution sets, because all $p_k(M_1)$'s share the same coefficients c_i's, which puts constraints on the choice of eigenvalue factors combinations implicitly. But solving those equations by enumerating all possible eigenvalue factor combinations for those $p_k(M_1)$'s without considering this implicit constraints indeed gets all possible solutions to $\mathbf{a}$, although some may be invalid because of ignoring those constraints. So to solve formula (13) and (14), we adopt the following "generate and check" procedure.

Generate. For each $p_k(M_1)$ in formula (13)–(14), we enumerate all $\Lambda \in \Lambda_l$ and replace $p_k(M_1)$ in formula (13) and (14) with $\prod_{\lambda \in \Lambda} (M_1 - \lambda I)$. Solve the resulted linear equations for a basis, which is a candidate solution to formula (13)–(14).

Check. To validate whether a basis generated in the 'generate' phase represents one of the vector spaces of $\mathbf{a}$, we only need to replace $\mathbf{a}$ with elements in the basis in formula (13) and (14) and see whether the resulting formulas are satisfiable. If it is, the basis indeed corresponds to vector spaces of $\mathbf{a}$. If any element in the basis makes the formulas unsatisfiable, the basis is not valid and is filtered out.

Note that in the 'generate' phase, we only need to compute eigenvalues for some known matrices and in the 'check' phase, the resulting formulas after the substitution are linear. So this procedure is computationally cheaper than Algorithm 1.

Candidate solutions computed in the 'generate' phase are solutions to the formula obtained by ignoring the fact that those p_i's have the same coefficients c_i's, which is a weak version of formula (13) and (14). So each solution to formula (13) and (14) is also a solution generated in the 'generate' phase, which guarantees the completeness. Soundness is guaranteed by the 'check' phase, which those candidate solutions back to formula (13)–(14) and filters out invalid ones.

6 Experimental Evaluation

To evaluate the effectiveness of our proposed methods in program verification, we implemented a prototype system called PExpr on C-like programs based on the algorithm given in Sect. 5.1. The reasons why we choose to implement this algorithm instead of others are as follows: (1) The algorithm in Sect. 5.1 allows polynomial assignments, while the one in Sect. 5.2 can only handle linear ones. And some programs in the benchmark we consider do have polynomial assignments. (2) As it will be seen below that for those programs that cannot be proved by the method in Sect. 5.1, they cannot be proved even if the general Algorithm 1 were used, not to mention the one in Sect. 5.2. And the algorithm in Sect. 5.1 is more efficient than others.

6.1   Implementation

Our system consists of two parts:

- The verifier is built on top of LLVM. C programs are first compiled into LLVM IR, and then the IR is translated into first-order language using a technique similar to the one proposed in [17]. Typically, loops are translated as recurrences and solved using the recurrence solver (see below).
- The core algorithm proposed in this paper is integrated into the recurrence solver proposed in [21], which is capable of solving conditional recurrences. As mentioned above, we only implement the method proposed in Sect. 5.1, which is simple and efficient.

The verifier extracts and feeds recurrences into the recurrence solver, the solver will first try to solve closed-form solutions for each individual variable using the technique proposed in [21]. If it fails, then the method in Sect. 5.1 will be applied. When the first time this method is applied, the polynomial degree is set to be 2. If no non-trivial result is returned, it is set to be 3. The closed-form solutions together with other axioms generated by the verifier is directly fed into SMT solver Z3 [6] to prove the correctness of the program. Nested loops are abstracted using the program model considered in this paper. For example, a loop below (left), whose body consists of two consequent loops, is treated as the one below (right), where A and B are loop-free statements.

$$\textbf{while } (*) \textbf{ do } \begin{cases} \textbf{while } (*) \ A; \\ \textbf{while } (*) \ B; \end{cases} \qquad \textbf{while } (*) \textbf{ do } \begin{cases} \textbf{if } (*) \ A; \\ \textbf{else if } (*) \ B; \end{cases}$$

6.2   Benchmarks and Environment

Our 48 benchmarks programs are adapted from the set of safe programs in the c/nla-digbench set of the Software Verification Competition (SV-COMP) [2]. The original c/nla-digbench consists of 26 classical algorithms. All are annotated with some assertions to be proved in the end and loop invariants in each loop. To make the verification non-trivial, as done in [4], we remove all those loop invariants. Otherwise, the verification will be simply to prove those annotated invariant are indeed invariant and then use them to prove the assertions at the end. Further, since we want to see the effectiveness of our finite representative solutions in verification, programs with multiple assertions to be proved are split into several copies and each copy has one assertion to be proved. By doing so, we can see for each program, what assertions can be proved by simply providing our representative solutions to SMT solvers. As a result, 48 programs are collected as benchmark for the experiment and we call it NLA.

All experiments were conducted on a virtual machine with a guest OS of Ubuntu 22.04 with 8 GB of RAM. The host machine is a MacBook Pro (16-inch, 2019) with 2.3GHz 8-core Intel Core i9. All tools were run with the BENCHEXEC tool [22] using a time limit of 60 s on all benchmarks.

6.3 Comparison Tools

We compared PExpr with USP-Quad [4], VeriAbs [5], ULTIMATE Automizer [9]. And since we integrate the proposed method into the recurrence solver proposed in [21], to see the effectiveness, we also compared with PExpr with the proposed technique disabled (the resulting system is called PRS).

USP-Quad adopts a strategy that given a transition ideal, it computes a solvable one from it and then computes closed-form solutions to polynomial expressions based on the solvable transition ideal (see related works for detailed comparison). As reported in [4], the refinement technique proposed in [3] improves the analysis of USP-Quad, so when running USP-Quad, we enabled the refinement. VeriAbs is the champion in the ReachSafety track in SV-COMP 2023. It is a reachability verifier for C programs that incorporates a portfolio of techniques (e.g., k-induction). ULTIMATE Automizer is the best tool for the c/nla-digbench in SV-COMP 2023, which implements approaches based on automata [8]. PRS applies the technique proposed in [21] to solve conditional recurrence for individual program variables.

6.4 Experimental Results

Table 1 summarizes the comparison results. PExpr is the best among those tools proving 34 programs, of which there are 3 programs can only be proved by PExpr. Programs that PExpr failed to prove are classified as 3 categories:

- *Integer division.* Some loops contain integer division without any guard to guarantee the effect is the same as real division (i.e., rounding occurs). There are 8 programs in this category.
- *Path condition matters.* Our program model ignores all guards of those nested if statements. But some programs' correctness is guaranteed by those guards. PExpr cannot capture this semantics because these guards are discarded. There is 1 program in this category.
- *Non-c-finite recurrences.* PExpr only tries to find polynomial expressions among variables that satisfy c-finite recurrences. So if those expressions are not c-finite, PExpr is not able to find them. 5 programs are in this category.

USP-Quad ranks second. There are 3 programs that it can prove while PExpr failed. Two of them contains integer division which cannot be proved to be equivalent to real divisions by PExpr. The other is the program whose path condition matters when proving its correctness. When facing multi-path loops, USP-Quad tries to find solvable transition ideal in a more semantic way, while PExpr simply discards those guards and treats them as non-deterministic branches.

Table 1. Comparison of tools on the NLA benchmarks. "Number of success" denotes the number of programs that each tool can prove successfully. "Number of timeout" records the number of timeout occurs when running the corresponding tool. "Time" records the amount of time, in seconds, taken by each tool (only cases that are successfully proved are counted). The best result in each category is bolded

	PExpr	USP-Quad	VeriAbs	ULTIMATE Automizer	PRS
Number of success	**34**	23	3	21	20
Number of timeout	**0**	14	42	24	**0**
Time	231	**95.3**	186	447	126

Among those programs proved by VeriAbs, PExpr failed on one of them, whose integer division cannot be handled by PExpr. Both ULTIMATE Automizer and PRS work well on simple loops (loops without nested branches). ULTIMATE Automizer can also prove four more loops with nested branches. One of them belongs to those programs whose expressions do not satisfy c-finite recurrences. Although PRS is able to solve conditional recurrences, those loops with nested branches in the benchmark do not have the periodic property, which is the key for PRS to find closed-form solutions. So PRS only works on simple loops or those whose assertions entailed directly by the loop exiting conditions.

7   Related Works

This work follows up on recurrence-based methods for program verification. The connection between loops and recurrences is widely known. Recently, it was used in Lin's translation [17] from C-like programs to first-order logic. This led to the program verifier VIAP [19] that relies on off-the-shelf tools like Mathematica [23] for solving recurrences. Kincaid et al. [12] also treated loops as recurrences, and proposed algorithms for solving them. Their follow-up works [13,14] consider finding closed-form solutions that can be used directly by SMT solvers. More capable recurrence solvers for multi-paths loops have been studied [20,21].

When recurrences for individual variables either do not exist or cannot be solved, an alternative is to consider expressions of the variables. Lin [18] considered this as an application of automated theorem discovery. Kincaid et al. [14] proposed a method for finding linear expressions with solvable recurrences. As their solvable recurrences are all c-finite, these linear expressions can also be generated by our algorithm. More closely related works are Amrollahi et al. [1] and Cyphert and Kincaid [4]. Below we discuss them in more details.

Amrollahi et al. [1] considered computing polynomial expressions q that satisfy the recurrence $q(\mathbf{x}(n+1)) = cq(\mathbf{x}(n)) + p(\mathbf{v}(n))$, where $c \in \mathbb{R}$, $\mathbf{v}$ are variables that have exponential polynomials as their closed-form solutions, and p a polynomial. Our method can also generate such polynomial expressions because if q satisfies the above recurrence, then it has an exponential polynomial closed-form solution, thus it satisfies a c-finite recurrence. However, there is a polynomial expression that satisfies a c-finite recurrence but not the above recurrence, as pointed out in [4]. Furthermore, the method in [1] is also template-based, and does not consider finite representation of all possible solutions.

Cyphert and Kincaid [4] considered loops as transition ideal and introduced the concept of solvable transition ideals to represent spaces of polynomials with solvable recurrences. Since their solvable polynomial recurrences are equivalent to c-finite recurrences, their results and ours are equivalent if the loop is simple, i.e. when there is no nested branches. For loops with nested branches, they adopt the same method in [15] that looks for linear expressions whose values change by a polynomial loop invariant after an iteration of the loop. As such, they will miss other polynomial expressions that have c-finite recurrences. In comparison, our method is is sound and semi-complete as shown above.

8   Conclusion

Based on the observation that for loops with nondeterministic branches, recurrences for individual program variables may not exist, we have considered the possibility of finding recurrences for expressions. Specifically, for loops with nested nondeterministic branches, we have proposed a sound and semi-complete algorithm for finding polynomial expressions that satisfy some c-finite recurrences. We have also considered in detailed two special cases, one on polynomials that satisfy first-order inhomogeneous c-finite recurrences, and the other on loops with linear transitions, and showed how to compute closed-form solutions more efficiently in these cases. To illustrate the effectiveness of the proposed method, we have implemented our algorithm for the first special case, and showed through experiments that the new technique indeed can be effective in being able to verify more benchmark programs.

A   Proof of Theorem 5

Proof. $\Rightarrow$: For a conjunct in formula (12), if the corresponding $w = [1]^r$, then it is exactly formula (14). Otherwise, if w has l trailing ones (i.e., $w = v + [1]^l$ for some $v \in W_{r-l}$ and $v[r-l] \neq 1$), it can be transformed into a conjunct in formula (13) by finding another conjunct in formula (12) whose corresponding $w' = w[: r - l - 1] + [1]^{l+1}$. The difference between them is

$$\left(\left(\prod_{i=1}^{r} M_{w[i]} - \prod_{i=1}^{r} M_{w'[i]} \right) - \cdots - \left(c_{r-1} M_{w[1]} - c_{r-1} M_{w'[1]} \right) \right) \mathbf{a} = 0. \quad (18)$$

Since w and w' have the same prefix of length $r - l - 1$, we have $\prod_{i=1}^{t} M_{w[i]} - \prod_{i=1}^{t} M_{w'[i]} = 0$ for all $t \leq r - l - 1$. Equation (18) is thus simplified into

$$\left(\left(\prod_{i=1}^{r} M_{w[i]} - \prod_{i=1}^{r} M_{w'[i]} \right) - \cdots - c_l \left(\prod_{i=1}^{r-l} M_{w[i]} - \prod_{i=1}^{r-l} M_{w'[i]} \right) \right) \mathbf{a} = 0. \quad (19)$$

Because w has l trailing 1's, for $s \geq r - l$, we have $\prod_{i=1}^{s} M_{w[i]} = M_1^{s-r+l} \prod_{i=1}^{r-l} M_{w[i]}$, Similarly, for w' we have $\prod_{i=1}^{s} M_{w'[i]} = M_1^{s-r+l+1} \prod_{i=1}^{r-l-1} M_{w'[i]}$, So the difference $\prod_{i=1}^{s} M_{w[i]} - \prod_{i=1}^{s} M_{w'[i]}$ is

$$
M_1^{s-r+l} \prod_{i=1}^{r-l} M_{w[i]} - M_1^{s-r+l+1} \prod_{i=1}^{r-l-1} M_{w'[i]}
$$

$$
= M_1^{s-r+l} \left(M_{w[r-l]} \prod_{i=1}^{r-l-1} M_{w[i]} - M_1 \prod_{i=1}^{r-l-1} M_{w'[i]} \right)
$$

$$
= M_1^{s-r+l} \left(M_{w[r-l]} - M_1 \right) \prod_{i=1}^{r-l-1} M_{w[i]}.
$$

The second equality holds because w and w' have the same prefix of length $r - l - 1$. Applying this conversion on the left-hand side of Eq. (19), we have

$$
\left(M_1^l \left(M_{w[r-l]} - M_1 \right) \prod_{i=1}^{r-l-1} M_{w[i]} \right) - \cdots - \left(c_l \left(M_{w[r-l]} - M_1 \right) \prod_{i=1}^{r-l-1} M_{w[i]} \right).
$$

After factorization, Eq. (19) becomes

$$
p_l(M_1)(M_{w[r-l]} - M_1)(\prod_{i=1}^{r-l-1} M_{w[i]})\mathbf{a} = 0, \tag{20}
$$

where $p_l(M_1) = M_1^l - \sum_{j=1}^{l} c_j M_1^{l-j}$. Since $2 \leq w[r - l] \leq m$, formula (20) is one of conjuncts in formula (13). This completes the proof that each conjunct in formula (12) can be transformed into one conjunct in formula (13)–(14).

$\Leftarrow$: For this direction, we show that each conjunct in formula (12) can be derived from formula (13)–(14). There are two different w in formula (12) and formula (13), to distinguish them we denote w_{12} for the one in formula (12) and w_{12} for formula (13). We prove this by induction on the number l of trailing 1's in w_{12}. For the base case $l = r$, there is only one conjunct whose w has r trailing 1 in formula (12), which is formula (14). For the inductive case, we assume for all conjuncts in formula (12) whose w_{12} has more than l trailing 1's can be derived from formula (13)–(14). Then we need to prove that conjuncts in formula (14) whose w_{12} has l trailing 1 can be derived from formula (13)–(14). For such w_{12}, we have $w_{12} = w_{12}[: r-l]+[1]^l$. We can find another $w'_{12} = w_{12}[: r-l-1]+[1]^{l+1}$, which has more than l trailing ones. So for w'_{12}, its corresponding conjunct in formula (12) can be derived from formula (13)–(14) by the inductive hypothesis. Let $w_{12} = w_{12}[: r - l - 1]$ and $i = w_{12}[r - l]$. Add up the conjunct represented by w'_{12} and (w_{12}, i) in formula (12) and (13) respectively, the result will be the conjunct represented by w_{12}. This completes the proof. $\square$

References

1. Amrollahi, D., Bartocci, E., Kenison, G., Kovács, L., Moosbrugger, M., Stankovič, M.: Solving invariant generation for unsolvable loops. In: Singh, G., Urban, C. (eds.) SAS 2022. LNCS, pp. 19–43. Springer, Cham (2022). https://doi.org/10.1007/978-3-031-22308-2_3
2. Beyer, D.: Competition on software verification and witness validation: sv-comp 2023. In: Sankaranarayanan, S., Sharygina, N. (eds.) Tools and Algorithms for the Construction and Analysis of Systems. Springer, Cham (2023). https://doi.org/10.1007/978-3-031-30820-8_29
3. Cyphert, J., Breck, J., Kincaid, Z., Reps, T.W.: Refinement of path expressions for static analysis. Proc. ACM Program. Lang. **3**(POPL), 45:1–45:29 (2019). https://doi.org/10.1145/3290358
4. Cyphert, J., Kincaid, Z.: Solvable polynomial ideals: the ideal reflection for program analysis. arXiv preprint arXiv:2311.04092 (2023)
5. Darke, P., Agrawal, S., Venkatesh, R.: VeriAbs: a tool for scalable verification by abstraction (competition contribution). In: Groote, J.F., Larsen, K.G. (eds.) Tools and Algorithms for the Construction and Analysis of Systems: 27th International Conference, TACAS 2021, Held as Part of the European Joint Conferences on Theory and Practice of Software, ETAPS 2021, Luxembourg, pp. 458–462. Springer, Cham (2021). https://doi.org/10.1007/978-3-030-72013-1_32
6. De Moura, L., Bjørner, N.: Z3: an efficient SMT solver. In: International Conference on Tools and Algorithms for the Construction and Analysis of Systems, pp. 337–340. Springer (2008)
7. Everest, G., van der Poorten, A.J., Shparlinski, I., Ward, T., et al.: Recurrence sequences, vol. 104. American Mathematical Society Providence, RI (2003)
8. Heizmann, M., et al.: Ultimate automizer with SMTInterpol: (competition contribution). In: Piterman, N., Smolka, S.A. (eds.) Tools and Algorithms for the Construction and Analysis of Systems: 19th International Conference, TACAS 2013, Held as Part of the European Joint Conferences on Theory and Practice of Software, ETAPS 2013, Rome, 16–24 March 2013, pp. 641–643. Springer, Heidelberg (2013). https://doi.org/10.1007/978-3-642-36742-7_53
9. Heizmann, M., Hoenicke, J., Podelski, A.: Refinement of trace abstraction. In: Palsberg, J., Su, Z. (eds.) SAS 2009. LNCS, vol. 5673, pp. 69–85. Springer, Heidelberg (2009). https://doi.org/10.1007/978-3-642-03237-0_7
10. Horn, R.A., Johnson, C.R.: Matrix Analysis. Cambridge University Press (2012)
11. Kincaid, Z., Breck, J., Boroujeni, A.F., Reps, T.: Compositional recurrence analysis revisited. In: Proceedings of the 38th ACM SIGPLAN Conference on Programming Language Design and Implementation (PLDI 2017), pp. 248–262. Association for Computing Machinery, New York (2017). https://doi.org/10.1145/3062341.3062373
12. Kincaid, Z., Breck, J., Boroujeni, A.F., Reps, T.: Compositional recurrence analysis revisited. SIGPLAN Not. **52**(6), 248–262 (2017). https://doi.org/10.1145/3140587.3062373
13. Kincaid, Z., Breck, J., Cyphert, J., Reps, T.: Closed forms for numerical loops. Proc. ACM Program. Lang. **3**(POPL) (2019). https://doi.org/10.1145/3290368
14. Kincaid, Z., Cyphert, J., Breck, J., Reps, T.: Non-linear reasoning for invariant synthesis. Proc. ACM Program. Lang. **2**(POPL), 1–33 (2017)
15. Kincaid, Z., Koh, N., Zhu, S.: When less is more: Consequence-finding in a weak theory of arithmetic. Proc. ACM Program. Lang. **7**(POPL), 1275–1307 (2023)

16. Kovács, L.: Reasoning algebraically about P-solvable loops. In: Ramakrishnan, C.R., Rehof, J. (eds.) Tools and Algorithms for the Construction and Analysis of Systems, pp. 249–264. Springer, Heidelberg (2008). https://doi.org/10.1007/978-3-540-78800-3_18
17. Lin, F.: A formalization of programs in first-order logic with a discrete linear order. Artif. Intell. **235**, 1–25 (2016). https://doi.org/10.1016/j.artint.2016.01.014
18. Lin, F.: Machine theorem discovery. AI Magazine **39**(2), 53–59 (2018). https://www.aaai.org/ojs/index.php/aimagazine/article/view/2794
19. Rajkhowa, P., Lin, F.: VIAP 1.1: (Competition Contribution). In: Beyer, D., Huisman, M., Kordon, F., Steffen, B. (eds.) Tools and Algorithms for the Construction and Analysis of Systems: 25 Years of TACAS: TOOLympics, Held as Part of ETAPS 2019, Prague, 6–11 April 2019, Proceedings, Part III, pp. 250–255. Springer, Cham (2019). https://doi.org/10.1007/978-3-030-17502-3_23
20. Silverman, J., Kincaid, Z.: Loop summarization with rational vector addition systems. In: Dillig, I., Tasiran, S. (eds.) Computer Aided Verification: 31st International Conference, CAV 2019, New York City, 15–18 July 2019, Proceedings, Part II, pp. 97–115. Springer, Cham (2019). https://doi.org/10.1007/978-3-030-25543-5_7
21. Wang, C., Lin, F.: Solving conditional linear recurrences for program verification: the periodic case. Proc. ACM Program. Lang. **7**(OOPSLA1), 28–55 (2023)
22. Wendler, P., Beyer, D.: Bench exec 3.16 (2023). https://github.com/sosy-lab/benchexec
23. Wolfram, S., et al.: The MATHEMATICA® Book, Version 4. Cambridge University Press (1999)

Breaking the Mold: Nonlinear Ranking Function Synthesis Without Templates

Shaowei Zhu$^{(\boxtimes)}$ and Zachary Kincaid

Princeton University, Princeton, NJ 08540, USA
{shaoweiz,zkincaid}@cs.princeton.edu

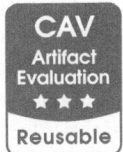

Abstract. This paper studies the problem of synthesizing (lexicographic) polynomial ranking functions for loops that can be described in polynomial arithmetic over integers and reals. While the analogous ranking function synthesis problem for *linear* arithmetic is decidable, even checking whether a *given* function ranks an integer loop is undecidable in the nonlinear setting. We side-step the decidability barrier by working within the theory of linear integer/real rings (LIRR) rather than the standard model of arithmetic. We develop a termination analysis that is guaranteed to succeed if a loop (expressed as a formula) admits a (lexicographic) polynomial ranking function. In contrast to template-based ranking function synthesis in *real* arithmetic, our completeness result holds for lexicographic ranking functions of unbounded dimension and degree, and effectively subsumes linear lexicographic ranking function synthesis for linear *integer* loops.

Keywords: termination · ranking functions · polynomial ranking functions · lexicographic ranking functions · monotone · nonlinear arithmetic

1 Introduction

Ranking function synthesis refers to the problem of finding a well-founded metric that decreases at each iteration of a loop. It is a critical subroutine in modern termination analyzers like Terminator [12], Ultimate Automizer [16], and ComPACT [26]. One could synthesize ranking functions via a *template*, i.e., fixing a particular form of ranking functions to be considered while leaving parameters as free variables, and encoding the conditions for the function to rank the given loop as a logical formula, thereby reducing the synthesis problem to a constraint-solving problem. Provided that the resulting constraint-solving problem is decidable, this method yields a complete procedure for synthesizing ranking functions that match the template. In particular, the template-based method is the basis of complete synthesis of ranking functions for linear and lexicographic linear ranking functions for loops whose bodies and guards can be expressed in linear real or integer arithmetic [3,23]. A limitation of the approach is that it is only complete with respect to template languages that can be defined by finitely

© The Author(s) 2024
A. Gurfinkel and V. Ganesh (Eds.): CAV 2024, LNCS 14681, pp. 431–452, 2024.
https://doi.org/10.1007/978-3-031-65627-9_21

many parameters (e.g., we may define a template for all linear terms or degree-2 polynomials, but not polynomials of unbounded degree).[1]

In this paper, we study the problem of synthesizing polynomial ranking functions for nonlinear loops. There are two apparent obstacles. The first obstacle results from the difficulty of reasoning about nonlinear arithmetic. Nonlinear *integer* arithmetic is undecidable, and so even checking whether a *given* function ranks a loop is undecidable, let alone synthesizing one. While nonlinear real arithmetic is decidable, it has high complexity–prior work has explored *incomplete* constraint-solving approaches to avoid the cost of decision procedures for real arithmetic [1,13], but this sacrifices the completeness property typically enjoyed by template-based methods. The second obstacle is that the set of all polynomials cannot be described as a template language with finitely many parameters, thus precluding complete ranking function synthesis based on the template method.

To tackle the undecidability problem, we adopt a weak theory of nonlinear arithmetic **LIRR** that is decidable [18]. For the infinite template problem, we first compute the finite set of polynomials that are entailed to be *bounded* modulo **LIRR** by the loop, and use them to define a template language with finitely many parameters to describe "candidate terms" for ranking functions. We then show that synthesis of ranking functions consisting of non-negative linear combinations of these candidate terms can be reduced to a constraint-solving problem in linear arithmetic. The adoption of **LIRR** ensures that we do not lose completeness in any of the above steps, i.e., any ranking function modulo **LIRR** can be written as a nonnegative combination of the "candidate terms" in the template. We thus have a procedure for synthesizing polynomial ranking functions that is sound for the reals, and *complete* in the sense that if a polynomial ranking function exists for a formula (modulo **LIRR**), then the analysis will find it. Furthermore, we extend this analysis to one that is sound for the integers and complete relative to lexicographic polynomial ranking functions (modulo **LIRR**).

Using the framework of algebraic termination analysis [26], we extend our termination analysis on loops (represents as formulas) to whole programs (including nested loops, recursive procedures, etc.). The completeness of the proposed procedures leads to *monotone* end-to-end termination analyses for whole programs. Informally, monotonicity guarantees that if the analysis can prove termination of a program P and P is transformed to a program P' in a way that provides more information about its behavior (e.g., by decorating the program with invariants discovered by an abstract interpreter) then the analysis is certain to prove termination of P' as well.

Our experimental evaluation establishes that the procedure based on polynomial ranking function and lexicographic polynomial ranking function synthesis

---

[1] One may imagine using the template paradigm to search for polynomial ranking functions of successively higher degree until one is found; however, this yields a complete *semi-algorithm*, which fails to terminate if no polynomial ranking function exists.

with the background theory of **LIRR** is competitive for SV-COMP termination benchmarks, especially for the nonlinear programs.

2   Background

Linear Algebra and Polyhedral Theory

In the following, we use **linear space** to mean a linear space over the field of rationals $\mathbb{Q}$. Let L be a linear space. A set $C \subseteq L$ is **convex** if for every $p, q \in C$ and every $\lambda \in [0, 1]$, we have $\lambda p + (1 - \lambda)q \in C$. We use $conv(S)$ to denote the **convex hull** of a set $S \subseteq L$, which is the smallest convex set that contains S. A set Q is a **polytope** if it is the convex hull of a finite set. A set $C \subseteq L$ is a (**convex**) **cone** if it contains 0 and is closed under addition and multiplication by $\mathbb{Q}^{\geq 0}$ (nonnegative rationals). For a set $G \subseteq L$, its **conical hull** is the smallest cone that contains G, defined as $cone(G) = \{\lambda_1 g_1 + \cdots + \lambda_m g_m : \lambda_i \in \mathbb{Q}^{\geq 0}, g_i \in G\}$. Given any $A, B \subseteq L$, we use $A + B \triangleq \{a + b : a \in A, b \in B\}$ to denote their Minkowski sum.

A set $P \subseteq L$ is a **polyhedron** if $P = cone(R) + conv(V)$, where R, V are finite sets in L, and use the notation $P = V\text{-}rep(R, V)$. Convex polyhedra are effectively closed under intersection; that is, there is a procedure `intersect` such that for any finite $R_1, V_1, R_2, V_2 \subseteq L$ we have

$$V\text{-}rep(\texttt{intersect}\,(R_1, V_1, R_2, V_2)) = V\text{-}rep(R_1, V_1) \cap V\text{-}rep(R_2, V_2) \ .$$

The Ring of Rational Polynomials

For a finite set of variables X, we use $\mathbb{Q}[X]$ to denote the ring of polynomials over X with rational coefficients, and $\mathbb{Q}[X]^1$ to denote the set of linear polynomials over X. A set $I \subseteq \mathbb{Q}[X]$ is an **ideal** if it contains zero, is closed under addition, and for every $p \in \mathbb{Q}[X]$ and $q \in I$ we have $pq \in I$. For a finite set $G = \{g_1, \ldots, g_n\} \subseteq \mathbb{Q}[X]$, we use $\langle G \rangle \triangleq \{p_1 g_1 + \cdots + p_n g_n : p_1, \ldots, p_n \in \mathbb{Q}[X]\}$ to denote the ideal generated by the elements in G. By Hilbert's basis theorem, we have that every ideal in $\mathbb{Q}[X]$ can be written as $\langle G \rangle$ for some finite set G. Equivalently, for any ascending chain of ideals $I_1 \subseteq I_2 \subseteq \ldots$ in $\mathbb{Q}[X]$, there exists an index j such that $I_j = I_k$ for all $k \geq j$.

Note that $\mathbb{Q}[X]$ is a linear space over $\mathbb{Q}$, and so cones, polytopes, and polyhedra consisting of polynomials are defined as above. We say that a cone $C \subseteq \mathbb{Q}[X]$ is **algebraic** if it is the Minkowski sum of an ideal and a finitely-generated convex cone [18]. For finite sets of polynomials $Z, P \subseteq \mathbb{Q}[X]$, we use

$$alg.cone_X(Z, P) \triangleq \left\{ \sum_{z \in Z} q_z z + \sum_{p \in P} \lambda_p p : q_z \in \mathbb{Q}[X], \lambda_p \in \mathbb{Q}^{\geq 0} \right\}$$

to denote the algebraic cone generated by Z and P; we call Z and P the "zeros" and "positives" of the cone, respectively. When the set of variables is clear, we often omit the subscript and just write $alg.cone(Z, P)$.

For any algebraic cone $C \subseteq \mathbb{Q}[X]$, the set of *linear* polynomials in C forms a convex polyhedron. We use `linearize` to denote the operation that computes this set—that is, for any finite $Z, P \subseteq \mathbb{Q}[X]$, we have

$$V\text{-}rep(\texttt{linearize}\,(Z,P)) = alg.cone\,(Z,P) \cap \mathbb{Q}[X]^1 \ .$$

There is a procedure `inverse-hom` for computing the inverse image of an algebraic cone under a ring homomorphism ([18], Theorem 9). More precisely, let $alg.cone_X(Z,P)$ be an algebraic cone, Y be a set of variables, and $f : \mathbb{Q}[Y] \to \mathbb{Q}[X]$ be a ring homomorphism, then

$$alg.cone_Y(\texttt{inverse-hom}\,(Z,P,f,Y)) = \{p \in \mathbb{Q}[Y] : f(p) \in alg.cone_X(Z,P)\} \ .$$

In this paper it will be useful to define a common generalization algebraic cones and convex polyhedra, which we call a *algebraic polyhedra*. We say that a set of polynomials $R \subseteq \mathbb{Q}[X]$ is an **algebraic polyhedron** if it is the Minkowski sum of an algebraic cone and a convex polytope[2]. An algebraic polyhedron can be represented by a triple $\langle Z, P, V \rangle$ where Z, P, V are finite sets of polynomials; such a triple represents the algebraic polyhedron

$$alg.polyhedron\,(Z,P,V) \triangleq alg.cone\,(Z,P) + conv\,(V) \ .$$

The Arithmetic Theory LIRR and Consequence Finding

We use the following syntax for formulas:

$$F, G \in \textbf{Formula} ::= p \le q \mid p = q \mid Int(p) \mid F \wedge G \mid F \vee G \mid \neg F$$

where p and q denote polynomials with rational coefficients over some set of variable symbols. We regard the reals $\mathbb{R}$ as the standard interpretation of this language, with Int identifying the subset of integers $\mathbb{Z} \subset \mathbb{R}$.

Kincaid et al. [18] defined another class of interpretations for the above language of formulas called *linear integer/real rings*. A linear integer/real ring is a commutative ring equipped with an order and an integer predicate which obeys certain axioms of the theories of linear real and linear integer arithmetic. The standard interpretation $\mathbb{R}$ is an example of a linear integer/real ring. A "nonstandard" example is the ring $\mathbb{Q}[x]$, where $p \le q$ iff p precedes q lexicographically (e.g., $-x^3 < x < x^2 - x < x^2 < x^2 + x$) and $Int(p)$ holds iff p's coefficients are integers.

The fact that the theory **LIRR** of linear integer/real rings (refer to [18] for an axiomatization) admits such nonstandard (and inequivalent) models means that the *theory* is incomplete. Nevertheless it has desirable algorithmic properties that we will make use of in our ranking function synthesis procedures. We discuss the limitations brought by **LIRR** in Example 3.

---

[2] Recalling that a *convex* polyhedron is the Minkowski sum of a *finitely generated convex* cone and a polytope.

Since the reals $\mathbb{R}$ is a model for **LIRR**, if we have $F \models_{\mathbf{LIRR}} G$, we also have $F \models_{\mathbb{R}} G$. However, in this paper we are mostly concerned with entailment modulo **LIRR** rather than the standard model, thus we abbreviate $F \models_{\mathbf{LIRR}} G$ to $F \models G$ by default.

For a formula F and a set of variables X, we use

$$\mathbf{C}_X(F) \triangleq \{p \in \mathbb{Q}[X] : F \models p \geq 0\}$$

to denote the **nonnegative cone** of F (over X). For example, given $X = \{x, y\}$

$$\mathbf{C}_X(x = 2 \wedge y \leq 1) = alg.cone\left(\{x - 2\}, \{1, 1 - y\}\right).$$

$\mathbf{C}_X(F)$ is an algebraic cone, and there is an algorithm for computing it (Algorithm 2 of [18]), which we denote by $\mathtt{consequence}\,(F, X)$. We furthermore have that if $\langle Z, P \rangle = \mathtt{consequence}\,(F, X)$, then $\langle Z \rangle = \{z \in \mathbb{Q}[X] : F \models z = 0\}$.

Transition Systems and Transition Formulas

For a set of variables X, we use $X' \triangleq \{x' : x \in X\}$ denote a set of "primed copies". For a polynomial $p \in \mathbb{Q}[X]$, we use p' to denote the polynomial in $\mathbb{Q}[X']$ obtained by replacing each variable x with its primed copy x'. A **transition formula** over a set of variables X is a formula F whose free variables range over X and X'. We use $\mathbf{TF}(X)$ to denote the set of all transition formulas over X. For a transition formula $F \in \mathbf{TF}(X)$ and real valuation $v, v' \in \mathbb{R}^X$, we use $v \to_F v'$ to denote that $\mathbb{R}, [v, v'] \models F$, where $\mathbb{R}$ denotes the standard model and $[v, v']$ denotes the valuation that maps each $x \in X$ to $v(x)$ and each $x' \in X'$ to $v'(x)$. A **real execution** of a transition formula F is an infinite sequence $v_0, v_1, \cdots \in \mathbb{R}^X$ such that for each i, we have $v_i \to_F v_{i+1}$; we say that $v_0, v_1, \ldots$ is an **integer execution** if additionally each $v_i \in \mathbb{Z}^X$. We say that F *terminates over* $\mathbb{R}$ if it has no real executions, and F *terminates over* $\mathbb{Z}$ if it has no integer executions.

Ranking Functions

Let $F \in \mathbf{TF}(X)$ be a transition formula. We say that $r \in \mathbb{Q}[X]$ is a **polynomial ranking function** (**PRF**) for F (modulo **LIRR**) if $F \models 0 \leq r$ and $F \models r' \leq r - 1$. The set of all polynomial ranking functions of F (modulo **LIRR**) is denoted $\mathbf{PRF}(F)$.

Lemma 1. *If* $\mathbf{PRF}(F) \neq \emptyset$, *then F terminates over* $\mathbb{R}$.

Proof. If $r \in \mathbf{PRF}(F)$, then $\lfloor r(X) \rfloor$ is a ranking function mapping $\mathbb{R}^X$ into $\mathbb{Z}$ that is well-ordered by a relation $\preceq$, defined as $x \preceq y$ iff $x \geq 0 \wedge x \leq y$, where $\leq$ is the usual order on the integers. □

We now consider lexicographic termination arguments. We define a *quasi-polynomial ranking function* (**QPRF**) for a transition formula $F \in \mathbf{TF}(X)$ (modulo **LIRR**) to be a polynomial $r \in \mathbb{Q}[X]$ such that

$$F \models r - r' \geq 0 \wedge r \geq 0 \;.$$

We say that a sequence of polynomials $r_1, \ldots, r_n \in \mathbb{Q}[X]$ is a dimension-n **weak lexicographic polynomial ranking function** (**WLPRF**) for F (modulo **LIRR**) if

$$r_1 \in \mathbf{QPRF}(F)$$
$$r_2 \in \mathbf{QPRF}(F \wedge r_1' = r_1)$$

$$\vdots$$

$$r_n \in \mathbf{QPRF}\left(F \wedge \bigwedge_{i=1}^{n-1} r_i' = r_i\right)$$

$$F \wedge \bigwedge_{i=1}^{n} r_i' = r_i \models \mathit{false} \;.$$

Lemma 3 sketches the proof that the existence of **WLPRF** proves termination of F over $\mathbb{Z}$.

Lemma 2. *Let $F \in \mathbf{TF}(X)$ be a transition formula. If $r \in \mathbb{Q}[X]$ is a quasi-ranking function for F, i.e., $F \models r' \leq r \wedge r \geq 0$, and furthermore $F \wedge r' = r$ terminates over the integers, then so does F.*

Proof. Since quasi-ranking functions are closed under scaling by nonnegative scalars, we may assume that r has integer coefficients without loss of generality. Suppose for a contradiction that F has an infinite integer execution $x_0, x_1, \ldots$. Since $r(x_i) \geq r(x_{i+1})$ for all i, and the range of r is restricted to $\mathbb{Z}^{\geq 0}$, there exists some n such that $r(x_n) = r(x_{n+1}) = \ldots$. But this is impossible since $F \wedge r' = r$ terminates over the integers. $\quad\square$

Lemma 3. *If a transition formula F admits a **WLPRF** (modulo the theory **LIRR**), then F terminates over $\mathbb{Z}$.*

Proof. We prove this by induction on the dimension n of **WLPRF** of F. The base case holds vacuously when $n = 0$ since F is unsatisfiable, and the inductive case holds by Lemma 2. $\quad\square$

Note that Lemma 3 holds only for integer executions. Ben-Amram and Genaim [3] showed that existence of a weak lexicographic linear ranking function (LLRF) for a topologically closed linear formula implies existence of an LLRF for loop with real variables, but the argument fails for *nonlinear* formulas (even modulo **LIRR**). Consider the following **LIRR** transition formula over reals n, z

$$F \triangleq z \geq 0 \wedge n \geq 2 \wedge n' = 2n \wedge z \geq z' \wedge nz' = nz - 1 \;.$$

Then $F \models z \geq 0 \wedge z \geq z'$, and also $F \wedge z = z' \models \mathit{false}$. Thus z does decrease at every iteration of F and its value is bounded from below. However, F does not terminate since the rate at which z decreases diminishes too quickly.

3   Polynomial Ranking for LIRR Transition Formulas

In this section, we consider the problem of synthesizing polynomial ranking functions for transition formulas modulo **LIRR**. Observe that for a transition formula $F \in \mathbf{TF}(X)$, the polynomial ranking functions $\mathbf{PRF}(F)$ of F can be decomposed as $\mathbf{PRF}(F) = \mathit{Bounded}(F) \cap \mathit{Decreasing}(F)$ where $\mathit{Bounded}(F)$ are the bounded and decreasing polynomials of F, respectively:

$$\mathit{Bounded}(F) \triangleq \{p \in \mathbb{Q}[X] : F \models p \geq 0\}$$
$$\mathit{Decreasing}(F) \triangleq \{p \in \mathbb{Q}[X] : F \models p' \leq p - 1\}$$

Thus, one approach to computing $\mathbf{PRF}(F)$ is to compute the sets of bounded and decreasing polynomials, and then take the intersection.

First, we observe that we can use this strategy to synthesize *linear* ranking functions using the primitives defined in Sect. 2[3].

- The convex polyhedron of degree-1 polynomials of $\mathit{Bounded}(F)$ can be computed as `linearize(consequence(`F, X`))`,
- The convex polyhedron of degree-1 polynomials of $\mathit{Decreasing}(F)$ can be computed as follows. Define $f : \mathbb{Q}[X] \rightarrow \mathbb{Q}[X \cup X']$ to be the homomorphism mapping $x \mapsto x - x'$, and observe that

$$\mathit{Decreasing}(F) \cap \mathbb{Q}[X]^1 = \{p \in \mathbb{Q}[X]^1 : F \models f(p) - 1 \geq 0\}$$

We proceed by first computing the polyhedron

$$Q \triangleq \{p + a : p \in \mathbb{Q}[X]^1, a \in \mathbb{Q}.F \models f(p) + a \geq 0\}$$

as `linearize(inverse-hom(consequence(`$F, X \cup X'$`), f))`. Then we intersect Q with the hyperplane consisting of linear polynomials with constant coefficient -1, and then take the Minkowski sum with the singleton $\{1\}$ to get $\mathit{Decreasing}(F) \cap \mathbb{Q}[X]^1$.

The essential difficulty of adapting this strategy to find polynomial ranking functions of unbounded degree is that the function $g : \mathbb{Q}[X] \rightarrow \mathbb{Q}[X \cup X']$ mapping $p \mapsto p' - p$ is not a homomorphism (the function f defined above agrees with g on *linear* polynomials, but not on polynomials of greater degree).

Our method proceeds as follows. As we will later see in Algorithm 2, we can adapt the above strategy to compute the intersection of $\mathbf{PRF}(F)$ with some "template language" $\{a_1 p_1 + \cdots + a_n p_n : a_1, \ldots, a_n \in \mathbb{Q}\}$ for fixed polynomials

---

[3] This is essentially a recasting of the classic algorithms linear ranking function synthesis [3] for LRA, restated in our language.

$p_1, \ldots, p_n$. Our insight is to use the cone generators of $Bounded(F)$ to define $p_1, \ldots, p_n$. This yields a ranking function synthesis procedure that, in general, is sound but incomplete; however, it is complete under the assumption that F is *zero-stable*. In Sect. 3.1 we define zero-stability and show that assuming zero-stability is essentially without loss of generality, and in Sect. 3 we define a procedure for computing $\mathbf{PRF}(F)$ for zero-stable F.

3.1 Zero-Stable Transition Formulas

Consider a transition formula F defined as

$$F \triangleq x = 0 \land y \geq 0 \land (x')^2 = y - y' - 1 .$$

Observe that $F \models x = 0$. F has a PRF $x^2 + y$, but it's hard to find in the sense that it's not a linear combination of the generators of $Bounded(F)$ (x, $-x$, and y). But when $x' \neq 0$, the loop terminates immediately. Thus we can consider the restriction $F \land x' = 0$, which admits the linear ranking function y. The zero-stable restriction process we introduce below formalizes this process.

We define a transition formula $F \in \mathbf{TF}(X)$ to be **zero-stable** if for all polynomials $p \in \mathbb{Q}[X]$ such that $F \models p = 0$, it is the case that $F \models p' = 0$. We give an algorithm for computing the weakest zero-stable transition formula that entails the original formula in Algorithm 1, and we note that the algorithm preserves termination behavior (Lemma 4).

---

1 Function zero-stable-restrict(F)
 Input: A transition formula $F \in \mathbf{TF}(X)$.
 Output: The weakest zero-stable transition formula that entails F.
2 $\langle Z, \_ \rangle \leftarrow$ consequence(F, X);
 /* $\langle Z \rangle = \{p \in \mathbb{Q}[X] : F \models p = 0\}$ */
3 **repeat**
4 $Z' \leftarrow Z$;
5 $F \leftarrow F \land \bigwedge_{z \in Z} z' = 0$;
6 $\langle Z, \_ \rangle \leftarrow$ consequence(F, X);
7 **until** $\langle Z \rangle = \langle Z' \rangle$;
8 **return** F

Algorithm 1: The zero-stable restriction of a transition formula.

Lemma 4. *Let F be an* **LIRR** *transition formula, and*

$$\hat{F} \triangleq \textit{zero-stable-restrict}(F) .$$

1. *Algorithm 1 computes the weakest zero-stable formula that entails F.*
2. *F terminates iff $\hat{F}$ terminates.*

Proof. Let $F^{(k)}$ and $Z^{(k)}$ denote the value of F and Z after the k-th iteration of the loop in Algorithm 1, respectively.

We first prove 1. Clearly, if Algorithm 1 terminates at some iteration n, then $\hat{F} = F^{(n)}$ is zero stable and entails F. It remains to show that (a) $F^{(n)}$ is the *weakest* such formula, and (b) the algorithm terminates.

(a) We show by induction that for any zero-stable formula G that entails F, it is the case that $G \models F^{(k)}$ for all k. The base case holds by assumption, since $G \models F = F^{(0)}$. Now suppose that $G \models F^{(k)}$, and we wish to show that $G \models F^{(k+1)}$. Since for each $z \in Z^{(k)}$ we have $G \models F^{(k)} \models z = 0$, and G is zero-stable, we know $G \models z' = 0$. It follows $G \models (F^{(k)} \wedge \bigwedge_{z \in Z^{(k)}} z' = 0) = F^{(k+1)}$.

(b) We show that Algorithm 1 terminates. Suppose that it does not. Then $\langle Z^{(0)} \rangle \subsetneq \langle Z^{(1)} \rangle \subsetneq \cdots$ forms an infinite strictly ascending chain of ideals of $\mathbb{Q}[X]$, contradicting Hilbert's basis theorem.

For 2, if F terminates then $\hat{F}$ clearly also terminates since $\hat{F} \models F$. To show that if $\hat{F}$ terminates then F must also terminate, we prove by induction that for any $k \geq 0$, $F^{(k+1)}$ terminates implies that $F^{(k)}$ terminates. We show this by arguing that any real execution of $F^{(k)}$ is also one of $F^{(k+1)}$. Let $v_0, v_1, \ldots$ be an execution of $F^{(k)}$. It is sufficient to show that $v_i \rightarrow_{F^{(k+1)}} v_{i+1}$ for all i. Since $v_{i+1} \rightarrow_{F^{(k)}} v_{i+2}$, we must have $z(v_{i+1}) = 0$ for all $z \in Z^{(k)}$, and so since $F^{(k+1)} = F^{(k)} \wedge \bigwedge_{z \in Z^{(k)}} z' = 0$ we have $v_i \rightarrow_{F^{(k+1)}} v_{i+1}$. $\quad\square$

Example 1. Consider running Algorithm 1 on a transition formula F

$$F : x = 0 \wedge y \geq 0 \wedge y' = -(x')^2 + y - 1 + z' \wedge z = x' \ .$$

In the first iteration of the loop, we discover a zero consequence x of F: $F \models x = 0$, and we then constrain the transition formula to be $F \wedge x' = 0$. Now since $F \models z = x'$, we get a new zero consequence z: $F \wedge x' = 0 \models z = 0$. We thus further constrain the transition formula to be $F \wedge x' = 0 \wedge z' = 0$. After adding these constraints, we can no longer find new zero consequences, and the resulting transition formula

$$F \wedge x' = 0 \wedge z' = 0 \equiv x = z = x' = z' = 0 \wedge y' = y - 1 \wedge y \geq 0$$

is zero-stable.

3.2   Complete Polynomial Ranking Function Synthesis

Assuming that a transition formula is zero-stable allows us to ignore polynomials in the ideal $\langle Z \rangle = \{p \in \mathbb{Q}[X] : F \models p = 0\}$ when synthesizing polynomial ranking functions, in the following sense. Suppose there exists $r \in \mathbf{PRF}(F)$ a polynomial ranking function for F, where $\langle Z, P \rangle = \mathtt{consequence}\,(F, X)$. We can write r as $r = z + p$ with $z \in \langle Z \rangle$ and $p \in cone(P)$. Since F is zero-stable, we have $F \models p' \leq p - 1$, thus some polynomial in $cone(P)$ is decreasing. Thus, it is sufficient to search for decreasing polynomials in $cone(P)$. Algorithm 2 computes the complete set of $\mathbf{PRF}$ for zero-stable transition formulas, which is illustrated in the example below.

```
1 Function prf-zero-stable(F)
```
    Input: A zero-stable transition formula $F(X, X')$.

    Output: A tuple Z, R, V such that $alg.polyhedron\,(Z, R, V) = \mathbf{PRF}(F)$ of F.

```
2     ⟨Z, P⟩ ← consequence(F, X);
3     Y ← {yₚ : p ∈ P} be a set of fresh variables;
4     f ← the homomorphism ℚ[Y] → ℚ[X] defined by f(yₚ) = p − p′;
5     ⟨R′, V′⟩ ← linearize(inverse-hom(consequence(F, X ∪ X′), f, Y));
```
    $/^*$ $\langle R_L, V_L\rangle$ *represents the polyhedron of linear terms with positive coefficients for variables and constant coefficient* -1. $^*/$

```
6     R_L ← {y : y ∈ Y}, V_L ← {−1};
7     ⟨R_Y, V_Y⟩ ← intersect(R′, V′, R_L, V_L);
```
    $/^*$ *Translate polyhedron from* $\mathbb{Q}[Y]^1$ *back to* $\mathbb{Q}[X]$, *and add constant* 1. $^*/$

```
8     R ← {r[yₚ ↦ p]ₚ∈P : r ∈ R_Y};
9     V ← {1 + v[yₚ ↦ p]ₚ∈P : v ∈ V_Y};
10    return ⟨Z, R, V⟩
```

Algorithm 2: Computing **PRF** for zero-stable transition formulas. We use notation $p[y \mapsto z_y : y \in S]$ to denote substitution of all variables $y \in S$ with z_y in a polynomial p.

Example 2. Consider running Algorithm 2 on a (zero-stable) transition formula

$$F: \quad nx \geq 0 \wedge n \geq 0 \wedge n' = n \wedge x \geq 0 \wedge z \geq 1$$
$$\wedge ((z' = z - 1 \wedge x' = x) \vee (x' = x - 1 \wedge z' = z + n - 1))\,.$$

The bounded polynomials of F (Line 1) is the algebraic cone defined by $Z = \{\emptyset\}$ and $P = \{nx, x, n, z - 1, 1\}$. Let $Y = \{t_{nx}, t_x, t_n, t_{z-1}, t_1\}$ be a fresh set of variables, let f be the ring homomorphism such that

$$f(t_{nx}) = nx - n'x'$$
$$f(t_x) = x - x'$$
$$f(t_n) = n - n'$$
$$f(t_{z-1}) = (z - 1) - (z' - 1) = z - z'$$
$$f(t_1) = 1 - 1 = 0$$

After Line 5, we obtain the polyhedron of linear polynomials in the inverse image of the nonnegative cone of F under f, which is defined by the rays $R' = \{t_n, -t_n, t_1, -t_1, t_{nx} + t_{z-1} - 1, 1 - t_{nx} - t_{z-1}\}$ and one vertex $V' = \{0\}$. The subset of $V\text{-}rep(R', V')$ of polynomials with nonnegative coefficients for variables and constant coefficient -1 (Line 7), is the polyhedron defined by rays $R_Y = \{t_{nx}, t_x, t_n, t_1\}$, and vertices $V_Y = \{t_{nx} + t_{z-1} - 1\}$. Finally, the algorithm returns the algebraic polyhedron with zeros $Z = \emptyset$, positives $R = \{nx, x, n, 1\}$, and vertices $V = \{nx + z\}$. Thus F has a non-empty set of polynomial ranking function modulo **LIRR** (e.g., it contains $nx + z$), and so we may conclude that F terminates over the reals.

We are then ready to prove the correctness of Algorithm 2.

Theorem 1 (Soundness and completeness of Algorithm 2). *For any zero-stable transition formula F*

$$\mathbf{PRF}(F) = alg.polyhedron\left(\texttt{prf-zero-inv}\left(F\right)\right) .$$

Proof. Let $Z, P, Y, f, R', V', R_L, V_L, R_Y, V_Y, R, V$ be as in Algorithm 2. Let $s : \mathbb{Q}[Y] \to \mathbb{Q}[X]$ be the homomorphism mapping $y_p \mapsto p$ (corresponding to the substitution on lines 8-9). Observe that for any linear combination of the Y variables $q = \sum_{p \in P} a_p y_p$, we have

$$f(q) = \sum_{p \in P} a_p f(y_p) = \sum_{p \in P} a_p (p - p') = \left(\sum_{p \in P} a_p p\right) - \left(\sum_{p \in P} a_p p'\right) = s(q) - s(q)' .$$

By definition (line 5), we have $V\text{-}rep(R_Y, V_Y) = \{q \in \mathbb{Q}[Y]^1 : F \models f(q) \geq 0\}$ and (line 6) $V\text{-}rep(R_L, V_L) = cone(Y) + \{-1\}$. It follows that the intersection of these two polyhedra (line 7) is

$$V\text{-}rep(R_Y, V_Y) = \{q - 1 : q \in cone(Y), F \models s(q) - s(q)' - 1 \geq 0\} .$$

Then by the construction of R and V (lines 7-8) we have

$$V\text{-}rep(R, V) = \{s(q) : q \in cone(Y), F \models s(q) - s(q)' - 1 \geq 0\} .$$

Letting $K = V\text{-}rep(R, V)$, we must show that $\mathbf{PRF}(F) = \langle Z \rangle + K$. We prove inclusion in both directions.

$\subseteq$ Let $r \in \mathbf{PRF}(F)$. Then we have $F \models r \geq 0$ and $F \models r - r' - 1 \geq 0$. Since $F \models r \geq 0$ and $alg.cone\,(Z, P) = \mathbf{C}_X(F)$, we have we have $r = z + p$ for some $z \in \langle Z \rangle$ and $p \in cone(P)$. To show $r = z + p \in \langle Z \rangle + K$, it is sufficient to show $p \in K$.
Write p as $\left(\sum_{t \in P} c_t t\right)$ for some $\{c_t\}_{t \in P} \subseteq \mathbb{Q}^{\geq 0}$. Let $q = \left(\sum_{t \in P} c_t y_t\right)$. Then we have $s(q) = p$ and $q \in cone(Y)$, so it is sufficient to show that $F \models s(q) - s(q') - 1 \geq 0$, or equivalently $F \models p - p' - 1$. Since $F \models z = 0$ and F is zero-invariant, we have $z' = 0$. Since $F \models r - r' - 1 \geq 0$ by assumption, we have $F \models (z + p) - (z' + p') - 1 \geq 0$ and so $F \models p - p' - 1 \geq 0$.

$\supseteq$ Let $r \in \langle Z \rangle + K$. Then we may write r as $z + k$ for some $z \in \langle Z \rangle$ and $k \in K$. By the definition of K, we have $k = s(q)$ for some $q \in cone(Y)$ such that $F \models s(q) - s(q)' - 1 \geq 0 \equiv k - k' - 1 \geq 0$. Since $q \in cone(Y)$ we have $k = s(q) \in cone(P)$ and so $F \models k \geq 0$ and thus $F \models z + k \geq 0$, so r is bounded. Since $F \models k - k' - 1 \geq 0$, $F \models z = 0$, and F is zero-stable, we have $F \models (k + z) - (k' - z') - 1$, so r is decreasing. Since r is bounded and decreasing, $r \in \mathbf{PRF}(F)$. $\square$

Example 3. Even though Algorithm 2 is complete for synthesizing **PRF**s modulo **LIRR**, it does not find all **PRF**s with respect to the standard model. Consider

$$F \triangleq x \geq 1 \wedge y \geq 1 \wedge ((x' = 2x \wedge y' = y/2 - 1) \vee (x' = x/2 - 1 \wedge y' = 2y))$$

which admits the **PRF** xy since $F \models_{\mathbb{R}} xy \geq 1 \wedge x'y' \leq xy - 1$. However the algorithm will not find this **PRF** since we cannot derive $F \models_{\textbf{LIRR}} xy \geq 1$ due to the fact that **LIRR** lacks axioms governing the relationship between multiplication and the order relation [18].

3.3   Proving Termination Through Polynomial Ranking Functions

This section shows how to combine the previous two subsections into a end-to-end termination analysis, which is (1) complete in the sense that it succeeds whenever the input formula has a polynomial ranking function, and (2) monotone in the sense that if $F \models G$ and the analysis finds a termination argument for G, then it can also find one for F.

Our analysis is presented in Algorithm 3, which operates by first computing a zero-stable formula and then invoking Algorithm 2 to check if it has at least one polynomial ranking function.

---

1 **Function** `terminate-PRF`(F)
> **Input:** An **LIRR** transition formula F.
> **Output:** Whether F admits a **PRF**.
2    $\hat{F} = $ `zero-stable-restrict`(F);
3    $_, _, V = $ `prf-zero-stable`($\hat{F}$);
4   **if** $V = \emptyset$ **then**
5 | **return** *unknown*
6   **else**
7 | **return** *true*

Algorithm 3: Proving termination through zero-stable restriction and **PRF** synthesis.

Theorem 2 (Completeness). *If F has a polynomial ranking function (modulo **LIRR**), then Algorithm 3 returns true on F.*

Proof. Suppose F has r as a **PRF**. Since $\hat{F} = $ `zero-stable-restrict`(F) entails F (Lemma 4), r is also a **PRF** of $\hat{F}$. Letting $\langle Z, P, V \rangle = $ `prf-zero-inv`($\hat{F}$), we have $r \in alg.polyhedron(Z, P, V)$ by Theorem 1, and so V is non-empty, and Algorithm 3 returns true. $\square$

Example 4. The reverse of Theorem 2 does not hold. Due to zero-stable restriction, Algorithm 2 can even prove termination of loops that do not admit **PRF**s even in the standard model. For example, it can prove termination of $F \triangleq x = 0 \wedge x' \neq 0$ since its zero-stable restriction is unsatisfiable. To see that F does not admit any **PRF**, suppose for a contradiction that it has r as a **PRF**. But this is impossible since there exists x' such that $r(x') > r(0) - 1$ due to the continuity of r.

The completeness of the ranking function synthesis procedures leads to several desirable properties of behavior of the resulting termination analysis, one of which is *monotonicity*, i.e., if the analysis succeeds on a transition formula G, then it is guaranteed to succeed on a stronger one F. Further, monotone termination analysis on loops can be lifted to monotone whole-program analysis by the framework presented by Zhu et al. [26].

Corollary 1 (Monotonicity). *If $F \models G$ and terminate-PRF (G) returns true, then terminate-PRF (F) returns true.*

4 Lexicographic Polynomial Ranking for Integer Transitions

In this section, we show how to synthesize lexicographic polynomial ranking functions. The strategy (inspired by [3]) is based on the connection between **WLPRF** and quasi-ranking functions. We can describe the set of quasi-ranking functions as the intersection of the sets of bounded and non-increasing polynomials of F:

$$\mathbf{QPRF}(F) = Bounded(F) \cap Noninc(F)$$

where

$$Bounded(F) \triangleq \{p \in \mathbb{Q}[X] : F \models p \geq 0\}$$
$$Noninc(F) \triangleq \{p \in \mathbb{Q}[X] : F \models p \geq p'\} \ .$$

In the following, we first show how to synthesize **QPRF**s (Sect. 4.1), using which we are able to synthesize **WLPRF**s (Sect. 4.2) to prove termination. Similar to Sect. 3, we need to compute zero-stable restriction of transition formulas to make sure that the set of ranking arguments found is complete.

4.1 Synthesizing Polynomial Quasi-Ranking Functions

Algorithm 4 finds all **QPRF**s for a zero-stable transition formula F, using a variation of our strategy for finding **PRF**s.

Theorem 3 (Soundness and completeness of Algorithm 4). *Suppose F is a zero-stable transition formula. Then*

$$\mathbf{QPRF}(F) = alg.cone\left(qprf\text{-}zero\text{-}stable\,(F)\right) \ .$$

Proof. Let Z, P, Y, f, R, V, P_X be as in Algorithm 4. Let $s : \mathbb{Q}[Y] \to \mathbb{Q}[X]$ be the homomorphism mapping $y_p \mapsto p$ (corresponding to the substitution on line 6), and observe that for any linear combination of the Y variables $q = \sum_{p \in P} a_p y_p$, we have $f(q) = s(q) - s(q)'$ (as in Theorem 1). By construction (lines 5-8) we have

$$cone(P_X) = \{s(q) : q \in cone(Y), F \models f(q) \geq 0\} \ ,$$

```
1  Function qprf-zero-stable(F)
       Input: A zero-stable transition formula F ∈ TF(X).
       Output: The algebraic cone of all QPRFs of F.
2      ⟨Z, P⟩ ← consequence(F, X);
3      Y ← {y_p : p ∈ P} be a set of fresh variables;
4      f ← the ring homomorphism ℚ[Y] → ℚ[X] defined by f(y_p) = p − p′;
       /* For any t ∈ cone(R), we have F ⊨ f(t) ≥ 0.                    */
5      ⟨R′, V′⟩ ← linearize(inverse-hom(consequence(F, X ∪ X′), f, Y));
       /* ⟨R_L, V_L⟩ represents the polyhedron of linear terms with positive
          coefficients for variables and constant coefficient 0.       */
6      R_L ← {y : y ∈ Y}, V_L ← {0};
       /* The intersection of V-rep(R′, V′) and V-rep(R_L, V_L) is a cone.  */
7      ⟨R, _⟩ ← intersect(R′, V′, R_L, V_L);
8      P_X ← {r[y_p ↦ p : p ∈ P] : r ∈ R};
9      return ⟨Z, P_X⟩
```

Algorithm 4: Computing **QPRF** for zero-stable transitions.

which by the above observation can be written equivalently as

$$cone(P_X) = \{s(q) : q \in cone(Y), F \models s(q) - s(q)' \geq 0\} \ .$$

Since $\{s(q) : q \in cone(Y)\}$ is precisely $cone(P)$, we have

$$cone(P_X) = \{p \in cone(P) : F \models p - p' \geq 0\}$$

We must show that $\mathbf{QPRF}(F) = \langle Z \rangle + cone(P_X)$. We prove inclusion in both directions.

⊆ Let $r \in \mathbf{QPRF}(F)$. Since $F \models r \geq 0$ and $alg.cone(Z, P) = \mathbf{C}_X(F)$, we must have $r = z + p$ for some $z \in \langle Z \rangle$ and $p \in cone(P)$. It is sufficient to show that $p \in cone(P_X)$. Since F is zero-stable and $F \models z = 0$, we have $F \models z - z' = 0$ and so we must have $F \models p - p' \geq 0$. It follows from the above that $p \in cone(P_X)$.

⊇ Since $\mathbf{QPRF}(F)$ is a cone it is closed under addition, so it is sufficient to prove that $\langle Z \rangle \subseteq \mathbf{QPRF}(F)$ and $cone(P_X) \subseteq \mathbf{QPRF}(F)$. Since F is zero-stable, we have $\langle Z \rangle = \{z \in \mathbb{Q}[X] : F \models z = 0\} \subseteq \mathbf{QPRF}(F)$. Since $cone(P_X) = \{p \in cone(P) : F \models p - p' \geq 0\}$, we have that each $p \in cone(P)$ is both bounded ($p \in cone(P)$) and non-increasing ($F \models p - p' \geq 0$), and thus belongs to $\mathbf{QPRF}(F)$. □

□

4.2 Lexicographic Polynomial Ranking Functions

Given Algorithm 1 for computing zero-stable restrictions and Algorithm 4 for finding **QPRF**s, we present Algorithm 5 for proving termination by finding **WLPRF**s.

```
1  Function terminate-lprf(F)
2  │   Z ← ∅;
3  │   repeat
4  │   │   Z' ← Z;
5  │   │   ⟨Z, P⟩ ← qprf-zero-stable(zero-stable-restrict(F));
6  │   │   F ← F ∧ ⋀_{z∈Z} z' = z ∧ ⋀_{p∈P} p' = p;
7  │   until ⟨Z⟩ = ⟨Z'⟩;
8  │   if 1 ∈ ⟨Z⟩ then
9  │   │   return true /* F is unsatisfiable modulo LIRR iff 1 ∈ ⟨Z⟩      */
10 │   else
11 │   │   return unknown
```

Algorithm 5: Proving termination by synthesizing lexicographic polynomial ranking functions.

Ignoring the effects of zero-stable restriction, Algorithm 5 iteratively computes a sequence of algebraic cones that represent all **QPRF**s, and finally checks if all transitions in F have been ranked.

Example 5. Consider the transition formula

$$F : x - xy \geq 0 \wedge y \geq 0 \wedge ((x' = x \wedge y' = y - 1) \vee (y \geq 1 \wedge x' = x - 1 \wedge y' = y))$$

(which has a dimension-2 **WLPRF** $\langle y, x - xy \rangle$). The following table depicts the execution of Algorithm 5, displaying a (simplified) transition formula F, zero polynomials Z, and positive polynomials P after each iteration of the loop, culminating in $F = false$, which indicates that F terminates.

	F	Z	P
Before	$x - xy \geq 0 \wedge y \geq 0$ $\wedge ((x' = x \wedge y' = y - 1)$ $\vee (y \geq 1 \wedge x' = x - 1 \wedge y' = y))$	$\emptyset$	-
Iter 1	$x - xy \geq 0 \wedge y \geq 0$ $\wedge (y \geq 1 \wedge x' = x - 1 \wedge y' = y))$	$\emptyset$	$\{y\}$
Iter 2	*false*	$\emptyset$	$\{y, x - xy\}$

Theorem 4 (Correctness of Algorithm 5). *Algorithm 5 is a terminating procedure, and for any transition formula F for which **terminate-lprf**$(F) = true$, we have that F terminates over the integers.*

Proof. Let $F^{(k)}, Z^{(k)}, P^{(k)}$ denote the values of F, Z, and P at the beginning of k-th iteration of the loop in Algorithm 5. We first prove termination of the algorithm. Suppose the loop does not terminate, then $\langle Z^{(k+1)} \rangle \supsetneq \langle Z^{(k)} \rangle$ for all iterations k. We have thus obtained an infinite and strictly ascending chain of ideals in the polynomial ring $\mathbb{Q}[X \cup X']$, contradicting Hilbert's basis theorem.

Now we show that if Algorithm 5 returns *true*, all integer executions of F terminate. We prove this by induction on n, the number of times the loop runs in Algorithm 5. The base case holds when $n = 1$ since the zero-stable restriction of F being unsatisfiable modulo **LIRR** implies that F terminates. Suppose that the proposition is true for $n \geq 1$ and we want to prove the case of $(n + 1)$. Consider the first iteration of the loop in Algorithm 5. For convenience, we use F to denote $F^{(1)}$, $\hat{F}$ to denote the zero-stable restriction of F, and F' to denote $F \wedge \bigwedge_{z \in Z^{(1)}} z' = z \wedge \bigwedge_{p \in P^{(1)}} p' = p$. By the inductive hypothesis, F' terminates. Suppose for a contradiction that F does not terminate. By Lemma 4 we know $\hat{F}$ also does not terminate. Define $r = \sum_{p \in P^{(1)}} p$, then $r \in \mathbf{QPRF}(\hat{F})$ due to Theorem 3. By Lemma 2, $\hat{F} \wedge r' = r$ has an infinite integer execution $x_0, x_1, \ldots$ since $\hat{F}$ has one. Let $i \in \mathbb{N}$ be arbitrary. Since $x_i \rightarrow_{\hat{F} \wedge r' = r} x_{i+1}$, we know that $\sum_{p \in P^{(1)}} p(x_{i+1}) - p(x_i) = 0$. This is a sum of nonpositive terms because $p(x_{i+1}) \leq p(x_i)$ holds for any $p \in P^{(1)}$ due to $p \in \mathbf{QPRF}(\hat{F})$. Thus for all $p \in P^{(1)}$, it holds that $p(x_{i+1}) = p(x_i)$. Since $\hat{F}$ is zero-stable, we have that $z(x_{i+1}) = z(x_i) = 0$ for all $z \in Z^{(1)}$. Thus we have $x_i \rightarrow_{F'} x_{i+1}$ and subsequently $x_0, x_1, \ldots$ is an infinite integer execution of F', contradicting the inductive hypothesis that F' terminates. $\square$

The following theorem states that even though we operate modulo **LIRR**, we have a guarantee on the capability of the ranking functions synthesized that it is no less powerful than LLRF modulo the standard linear integer arithmetic, under mild assumptions.

Theorem 5 (Subsumption of LLRFs). *If $F \in \mathbf{TF}(X)$ is a negation-free formula involving only linear polynomials and F has an LLRF modulo linear integer arithmetic (**LIA**), then $F \wedge \bigwedge_{x \in (X \cup X')} Int(x)$ has a **WLPRF** modulo* **LIRR***.*

Proof. We first prove a lemma as follows. Let $F(Y)$ be a ground, negation-free, **LIA** transition formula over variable set Y. Then for any affine term r over Y, if $F \models_{\mathbf{LIA}} r \geq 0$ then $F \wedge \bigwedge_{y \in Y} Int(y) \models_{\mathbf{LIRR}} r \geq 0$. (The proof is similar to Theorem 8 in [18]. Without loss of generality we assume F is a conjunctive formula. Suppose $F \models_{\mathbf{LIA}} r \geq 0$. By [11,24] there is a cutting-plane proof of $r \geq 0$ from F. Since each inference rule in a cutting-plane proof is valid **LIRR**, we have that $F \wedge \bigwedge_{y \in Y} Int(y) \models_{\mathbf{LIRR}} r \geq 0$.)

Suppose that **LIA** formula F admits an LLRF $r_1, \ldots, r_n$ of dimension n, then $F \models_{\mathbf{LIA}} r_i \geq 0$ for each i (bounded), $F \wedge \bigwedge_{j=1}^{i-1} r'_j = r_j \models_{\mathbf{LIA}} r'_i \leq r_i$ for each i (decreasing), and $F \wedge \bigwedge_{j=1}^{n} r'_j = r_j \models_{\mathbf{LIA}} false$ (coverage). Since the left hand side of all the implications listed above contains ground linear formulas without negation and the right hand side all contains linear inequalities (with *false* being interpreted as $0 \leq -1$), these implications also hold modulo **LIRR** by the lemma. Therefore, $r_1, \ldots, r_n$ is a **WLPRF** of F. $\square$

Algorithm 5 is also complete w.r.t. the existence of **WLPRF**s, since it finds a **WLPRF** if there exists one for the transition formula. Moreover, it is optimal in terms of the dimension of the **WLPRF** found.

Theorem 6 (Completeness of Algorithm 5 w.r.t. WLPRF). *If a transition formula F admits a* **WLPRF** *of dimension N, then* `termination-lprf`(F) *returns true and Algorithm 5 terminates in no more than N iterations.*

Proof. Suppose that $r_1, \ldots, r_N$ is a **WLPRF** for F. Let $F^{(k)}$ denote the value of F after the kth iteration of the while loop in Algorithm 5, with the convention that if the loop exits after m iterations then $F^{(m)} = F^{(m+1)} = \cdots$. For any k, let $\langle Z^{(k)}, P^{(k)} \rangle \triangleq$ `qprf-zero-stable(zero-stable-restrict`$(F^{(k)})$`)`.

We prove that $r_i \in alg.cone\,(Z^{(i)}, P^{(i)})$ for all i, by induction on i. For the base case, r_1 is a quasi ranking function for F and so also a quasi ranking function for the zero-stable restriction F, and thus $r_1 \in alg.cone\,(Z^{(1)}, P^{(1)})$. For the inductive step, we have $r_j \in alg.cone\,(Z^{(j)}, P^{(j)})$ for all $j \leq i$, and we must prove $r_{i+1} \in alg.cone\,(Z^{(i+1)}, P^{(i+1)})$. By the inductive hypothesis, we have $r_1, \ldots, r_i \in alg.cone\,(Z^{(i)}, P^{(i)})$. It follows that $F^{(i+1)} \models F^{(i)} \wedge \bigwedge_{j=1}^{i} r'_j - r_j$, so by the (Decreasing) condition of **WLPRF**, r_{i+1} is a quasi ranking function of $F^{(i)}$. It follows that r_{i+1} is a quasi ranking function of `zero-stable-restrict`$(F^{(i)})$, and thus r_{i+1} belongs to $alg.cone\,(Z^{(i+1)}, P^{(i+1)})$.

By the (Coverage) condition of **WLPRF**, we have that $F \wedge \bigwedge_{j=1}^{N} r'_j = r_j$ is unsatisfiable. Since for each j we have

$$r_j \in alg.cone\,(Z^{(j)}, P^{(j)}) \subseteq alg.cone\,(Z^{(N)}, P^{(N)})$$

we must have that $F^{(N)}$ is unsatisfiable, and so $F^{(N)} \models 1 = 0$, and thus `termination-lprf`(F) returns *true*. □

Corollary 2 (Monotonicity of Algorithm 5). *Let F and G be transition formulas with $F \models G$. If* `termination-lprf`$(G) = true$*, then it is guaranteed that* `termination-lprf`$(F) = true$*.*

5   Evaluation

We consider two key research questions in the experimental evaluation. First, how does the proposed technique perform in proving termination of linear or nonlinear programs comparing to existing tools, in terms of running time and the number of tasks solved. We thus compare the proposed techniques with other *sound* and *static* provers for termination. In particular, we compare against Ultimate Automizer [15, 16] and 2LS [9], which are the top two *sound* tools in the **Termination** category in the 12th Competition on software verification (SV-COMP 2023). We also report a qualitative comparison with the dynamic tool DynamiTe [19]. Second, we have shown in Theorem 5 that LPRF subsumes LLRF synthesis for proving termination under certain assumptions, but we would like to understand the performance overhead of our more general procedure. We compare with the LLRF synthesis procedure implemented in ComPACT [26].

Implementation. We implement polynomial ranking functions synthesis (Sect. 3) and lexicographic polynomial ranking function synthesis (Sect. 4) as two mortal precondition operators (i.e., an operator that takes in a transition formula representing a single loop and outputs sufficient terminating conditions for that loop) in the ComPACT termination analysis framework [26], also utilizing the **LIRR** solver, consequence finding, inverse homomorphism, and nonlinear invariant generation procedures from Kincaid et al. [18]. Given any loop, we first try synthesizing polynomial ranking functions, and only attempt to synthesize lexicographic polynomial ranking function upon failure. Our implementation is denoted by "LPRF" in the tables. We have also combined our technique with phase analysis, a technique for improving termination analyzers by analyzing phase transition structures implemented in ComPACT [26].

Environment. We ran all experiments in a virtual machine with Lubuntu 22.04 LTS (kernel version 5.12) with a CPU of Intel Core i7-9750H @ 2.60 GHz and 8 GB of memory. The SV-COMP 2023 binaries of Ultimate Automizer v0.2.2-2329fc70 and 2LS version 0.9.6-svcomp23 are used in the experiments. All tools were run under a time limit of 2 min.

Benchmarks. We collected tasks from the SV-COMP 2023 `Termination` benchmarks. Since the focus of the proposed technique is to prove termination of nonlinear programs, we divide the tasks into two suites according to whether they require nonlinear reasoning. The `linear` suite consists of *terminating* and *nonrecursive* integer programs from the `Termination-MainControlFlow` subcategory in the SV-COMP, excluding the `termination-nla` folder. The `nonlinear` suite contains terminating programs without overflow[4] in the `termination-nla` folder. This suite was originally presented in [19] and contains only integer programs.

Comparing Against Sound and Static Analyses. The results of running all experiments are presented in Table 1. For the `nonlinear` suite, our proposed techniques for synthesizing polynomial ranking functions and lexicographic ranking arguments perform significantly better than the current static analysis tools in terms of both number of tasks proved and running speed. Our technique subsumes linear lexicographic ranking function synthesis for a large class of integer variable programs, and thus remains competitive for the `linear` suite. We see that there is a moderate slowdown comparing to linear lexicographic ranking function synthesis implemented in ComPACT. As a top competitor in the SV-COMP, Ultimate Automizer proves the most tasks in the `linear` suite, while requiring more time to run compared to our techniques (see the cactus plots Figs. 1 and 2).

---

[4] Our technique assumes unbounded integers but 2LS is bit-precise and requires this constraint.

Table 1. Experimental results on termination verification benchmarks comparing our technique (LPRF) with lexicographic linear ranking function (LLRF) synthesis, both techniques with phase analysis (+Φ), as well as ComPACT, Ultimate Automizer, and 2LS. The #c row counts the number of solved tasks, t reports total running time in seconds, excluding timeouts (# timeouts in parentheses).

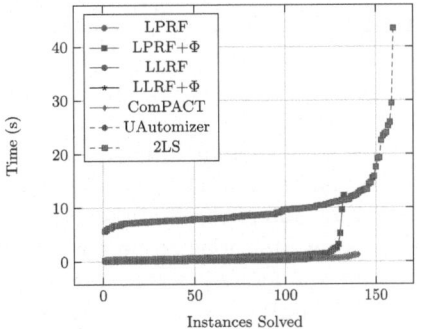

Fig. 1. Linear benchmarks.

#tasks		linear	nonlinear
		171	26
LPRF	#c	118	**17**
	t	333.2 (2)	**47.8** (0)
LPRF+Φ	#c	132	**17**
	t	426.0 (2)	119.5 (0)
LLRF	#c	120	3
	t	**74.6** (0)	161.1 (1)
LLRF+Φ	#c	138	4
	t	98.6 (0)	263.0 (2)
ComPACT	#c	140	4
	t	105.7 (0)	288.8 (2)
UAutomizer	#c	**160**	1
	t	2423.1 (6)	1282.7 (8)
2LS	#c	114	0
	t	5399.1 (43)	2748.7 (20)

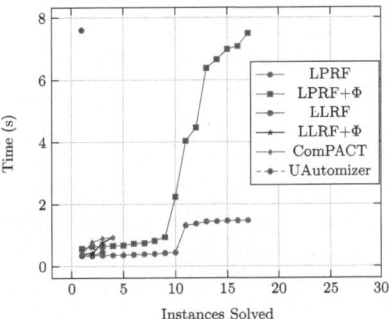

Fig. 2. Nonlinear benchmarks. 2LS cannot solve any task in the suite and is thus omitted in the plot.

Comparing Against DynamiTe. The DynamiTe paper [19] presents a *dynamic* technique that can guess and verify linear or quadratic ranking functions for nonlinear programs and proposes a benchmark suite `termination-nla` for termination of nonlinear programs. Due to hardware constraints, we could not reproduce the original evaluations for DynamiTe in our evaluation environment. Instead, we perform a comparison with the results reported in the paper. Since our tool is automated and sound but can only prove termination, we only count the terminating programs for which DynamiTe can automatically validate the discovered ranking functions. In the `termination-nla` suite, DynamiTe can learn the ranking function for most tasks (23 out of 26) but can only automatically validate 7 of them, whereas our static analysis technique LPRF is able to automatically prove 17. This observation demonstrates that verifying a given ranking function modulo nonlinear integer arithmetic is not only difficult in theory but remains challenging for modern arithmetic theory solvers. This provides additional motivation for the introduction of the weak arithmetic theory **LIRR** in this work.

6   Related Work

Ranking Function Synthesis. For linear loops, there are *complete* procedures for synthesizing particular classes of ranking functions such as linear [3, 23], lexicographic linear [3, 4], multi-phase [2], and nested [20]. For nonlinear loops, it is usually necessary to start with a template, e.g., polyranking functions based on a finite tree of differences between terms [5], or limiting the degree of the polynomial ranking functions to be considered [7, 19]. Other procedures for synthesizing (bounded-degree) polynomial ranking functions rely on semidefinite programming [13] and cylindrical algebraic decomposition [10], but we have not found implementations for these techniques to compare with experimentally. Chatterjee et al. [8] synthesizes polynomial ranking supermartingales for probabilistic programs through Positivestellensatz, which bears some resemblance to our approach based on **LIRR** consequence finding. One key advantage of our work comparing to previous work is the completeness and monotonicity guarantee.

Decision Procedures for Termination. The decision problem for termination of linear loops was introduced by Tiwari [25]. General procedures for loops over the reals was developed by Tiwari [25], over the rationals by Braverman [6], and over the integers by Hosseini et al. [17]. Time complexity for linear and lexicographic linear ranking function synthesis has also been studied [3]. For nonlinear loops, it has been shown that termination of certain restricted classes of single-path polynomial loops over the reals are decidable, e.g., when the guard is compact and connected [21], when the loop is triangular weakly nonlinear [14], when the guard is compact semi-algebraic and the body contains continuous semi-algebraic updates [22]. Additionally, Neumann et al. [22] presents a non-constructive method for reasoning about termination via polynomial ranking functions of unbounded degree. The authors have not found any work that handles polynomial loops over *integers* without assuming real relaxations.

Acknowledgements. This work was supported in part by the NSF under grant number 1942537. Opinions, findings, conclusions, or recommendations expressed herein are those of the authors and do not necessarily reflect the views of the sponsoring agencies.

References

1. Asadi, A., Chatterjee, K., Fu, H., Goharshady, A.K., Mahdavi, M.: Polynomial reachability witnesses via stellensätze. In: PLDI 2021, pp. 772–787. Association for Computing Machinery, New York (2021). https://doi.org/10.1145/3453483.3454076
2. Ben-Amram, A.M., Doménech, J.J., Genaim, S.: Multiphase-linear ranking functions and their relation to recurrent sets. In: Chang, B.-Y.E. (ed.) SAS 2019. LNCS, vol. 11822, pp. 459–480. Springer, Cham (2019). https://doi.org/10.1007/978-3-030-32304-2_22
3. Ben-Amram, A.M., Genaim, S.: Ranking functions for linear-constraint loops. J. ACM **61**(4), 26:1–26:55 (2014). https://doi.org/10.1145/2629488

4. Bradley, A.R., Manna, Z., Sipma, H.B.: Linear ranking with reachability. In: Etessami, K., Rajamani, S.K. (eds.) CAV 2005. LNCS, vol. 3576, pp. 491–504. Springer, Heidelberg (2005). https://doi.org/10.1007/11513988_48
5. Bradley, A.R., Manna, Z., Sipma, H.B.: The polyranking principle. In: Caires, L., Italiano, G.F., Monteiro, L., Palamidessi, C., Yung, M. (eds.) ICALP 2005. LNCS, vol. 3580, pp. 1349–1361. Springer, Heidelberg (2005). https://doi.org/10.1007/11523468_109
6. Braverman, M.: Termination of integer linear programs. In: Ball, T., Jones, R.B. (eds.) CAV 2006. LNCS, vol. 4144, pp. 372–385. Springer, Heidelberg (2006). https://doi.org/10.1007/11817963_34
7. Carbonneaux, Q., Hoffmann, J., Shao, Z.: Compositional certified resource bounds. In: Proceedings of the 36th ACM SIGPLAN Conference on Programming Language Design and Implementation, pp. 467–478. ACM, Portland OR USA, June 2015. https://doi.org/10.1145/2737924.2737955
8. Chatterjee, K., Fu, H., Goharshady, A.K.: Termination analysis of probabilistic programs through positivstellensatz's. In: Chaudhuri, S., Farzan, A. (eds.) CAV 2016. LNCS, vol. 9779, pp. 3–22. Springer, Cham (2016). https://doi.org/10.1007/978-3-319-41528-4_1
9. Chen, H.Y., David, C., Kroening, D., Schrammel, P., Wachter, B.: Bit-precise procedure-modular termination analysis. ACM Trans. Programming Lang. Syst. 40(1), 1–38 (2018). https://doi.org/10.1145/3121136
10. Chen, Y., Xia, B., Yang, L., Zhan, N., Zhou, C.: Discovering non-linear ranking functions by solving semi-algebraic systems. In: Jones, C.B., Liu, Z., Woodcock, J. (eds.) ICTAC 2007. LNCS, vol. 4711, pp. 34–49. Springer, Heidelberg (2007). https://doi.org/10.1007/978-3-540-75292-9_3
11. Chvátal, V.: Edmonds polytopes and a hierarchy of combinatorial problems. Discrete Math. 306(10), 886–904 (2006). https://doi.org/10.1016/j.disc.2006.03.009
12. Cook, B., Podelski, A., Rybalchenko, A.: Termination proofs for systems code. In: Proceedings of the 27th ACM SIGPLAN Conference on Programming Language Design and Implementation, pp. 415–426. ACM, Ottawa, Ontario, Canada, June 2006. https://doi.org/10.1145/1133981.1134029
13. Cousot, P.: Proving program invariance and termination by parametric abstraction, Lagrangian relaxation and semidefinite programming. In: Cousot, R. (ed.) VMCAI 2005. LNCS, vol. 3385, pp. 1–24. Springer, Heidelberg (2005). https://doi.org/10.1007/978-3-540-30579-8_1
14. Hark, M., Frohn, F., Giesl, J.: Termination of triangular polynomial loops. Formal Methods in System Design, pp. 1–63 (2023)
15. Heizmann, M., et al.: Ultimate Automizer and the CommuHash Normal Form: (Competition Contribution). In: Tools and Algorithms for the Construction and Analysis of Systems: 29th International Conference, TACAS 2023, Held as Part of the European Joint Conferences on Theory and Practice of Software, ETAPS 2023, Paris, France, April 22–27, 2023, Proceedings, Part II, pp. 577–581. Springer, Heidelberg (2023). https://doi.org/10.1007/978-3-031-30820-8_39
16. Heizmann, M., Hoenicke, J., Podelski, A.: Refinement of trace abstraction. In: Palsberg, J., Su, Z. (eds.) SAS 2009. LNCS, vol. 5673, pp. 69–85. Springer, Heidelberg (2009). https://doi.org/10.1007/978-3-642-03237-0_7
17. Hosseini, M., Ouaknine, J., Worrell, J.: Termination of Linear Loops over the Integers (Track B: Automata, Logic, Semantics, and Theory of Programming). In: DROPS-IDN/v2/Document/10.4230/LIPIcs.ICALP.2019.118. Schloss-Dagstuhl - Leibniz Zentrum für Informatik (2019). https://doi.org/10.4230/LIPIcs.ICALP.2019.118

18. Kincaid, Z., Koh, N., Zhu, S.: When less is more: consequence-finding in a weak theory of arithmetic. Proceedings of the ACM on Programming Languages **7**(POPL), 1275–1307 (Jan 2023). https://doi.org/10.1145/3571237
19. Le, T.C., Antonopoulos, T., Fathololumi, P., Koskinen, E., Nguyen, T.: DynamiTe: Dynamic termination and non-termination proofs. Proc. ACM Programming Lang. **4**(OOPSLA), 189:1–189:30 (2020). https://doi.org/10.1145/3428257
20. Leike, J., Heizmann, M.: Ranking templates for linear loops. In: Ábrahám, E., Havelund, K. (eds.) TACAS 2014. LNCS, vol. 8413, pp. 172–186. Springer, Heidelberg (2014). https://doi.org/10.1007/978-3-642-54862-8_12
21. Li, Y.: Termination of single-path polynomial loop programs. In: Sampaio, A., Wang, F. (eds.) ICTAC 2016. LNCS, vol. 9965, pp. 33–50. Springer, Cham (2016). https://doi.org/10.1007/978-3-319-46750-4_3
22. Neumann, E., Ouaknine, J., Worrell, J.: On Ranking Function Synthesis and Termination for Polynomial Programs. In: DROPS-IDN/v2/Document/10.4230/LIPIcs.CONCUR.2020.15. Schloss-Dagstuhl - Leibniz Zentrum für Informatik (2020). https://doi.org/10.4230/LIPIcs.CONCUR.2020.15
23. Podelski, A., Rybalchenko, A.: A complete method for the synthesis of linear ranking functions. In: Steffen, B., Levi, G. (eds.) VMCAI 2004. LNCS, vol. 2937, pp. 239–251. Springer, Heidelberg (2004). https://doi.org/10.1007/978-3-540-24622-0_20
24. Schrijver, A.: On Cutting Planes. In: Hammer, P.L. (ed.) Annals of Discrete Mathematics, Combinatorics 79, vol. 9, pp. 291–296. Elsevier, January 1980. https://doi.org/10.1016/S0167-5060(08)70085-2
25. Tiwari, A.: Termination of linear programs. In: Alur, R., Peled, D.A. (eds.) CAV 2004. LNCS, vol. 3114, pp. 70–82. Springer, Heidelberg (2004). https://doi.org/10.1007/978-3-540-27813-9_6
26. Zhu, S., Kincaid, Z.: Termination analysis without the tears. In: Proceedings of the 42nd ACM SIGPLAN International Conference on Programming Language Design and Implementation, PLDI 2021, pp. 1296–1311. Association for Computing Machinery, New York, June 2021. https://doi.org/10.1145/3453483.3454110

Hevm, a Fast Symbolic Execution Framework for EVM Bytecode

Dxo[1], Mate Soos[1]([✉]), Zoe Paraskevopoulou[1], Martin Lundfall[2], and Mikael Brockman[2]

[1] Ethereum Foundation, Berlin, Germany
{dxo,mate.soos,zoe.paraskevopoulou}@ethereum.org
[2] Independent, Berlin, Germany
mikael@brockman.se

Abstract. We present hevm, a symbolic execution engine for the EVM. hevm can prove safety properties for EVM bytecode or verify semantic equivalence between two bytecode objects. It exposes a user-friendly API in Solidity that allows end-users to define symbolic tests using almost the same syntax as they would for their usual unit tests. We evaluate our framework against state-of-the-art tools, using a comprehensive set of benchmarks. Our empirical findings demonstrate that hevm outperforms its counterparts, effectively solving a greater number of problems within competitive time frames.

Keywords: Symbolic Execution · EVM · Smart Contract Verification · Blockchain

1 Overview

Smart contracts running on the Ethereum Virtual Machine (EVM) currently secure assets worth hundreds of billions of dollars [6]. Despite the high impact of failure, losses due to security incidents are still very common (USD 4 billion across the full Web3 ecosystem in 2022 [15]). Symbolic execution is a rigorous method that evaluates a program using *symbolic inputs*, exploring the set of reachable final states. By analyzing these states, one can identify potential security flaws, and enhance the overall robustness of smart contracts.

In this paper, we present hevm, a Haskell implementation of the EVM that supports both symbolic and concrete execution. It symbolically analyzes EVM bytecode, exploring all possible states resulting from (potentially) symbolic inputs, storage, and environmental parameters. hevm enables scalably proving the properties of reachable final states, such as the absence of error states like assertion violations or arithmetic overflows. To prove a property, hevm either statically determines the final state to be unreachable, or generates SMT queries for potentially reachable final states and passes them to an SMT solver (Z3 [10], CVC5 [3], or Bitwuzla [20]) in parallel. The solver can disprove the property, returning a counterexample, prove that it can never be violated, or timeout.

A. Gurfinkel and V. Ganesh (Eds.): CAV 2024, LNCS 14681, pp. 453–465, 2024.
https://doi.org/10.1007/978-3-031-65627-9_22

Additionally, hevm can (dis)prove the equivalence of two final-state sets originating from different EVM bytecode sequences, allowing for equivalence checking between different implementations of the same functionality.

In addition to its command line interface, hevm has a Solidity API that allows users to write symbolic tests in a language with which they are already familiar. This Solidity API, and its associated Solidity library of assertion helpers ds-test [24], has been widely adopted by many tools across the ecosystem and has become the dominant format for testing smart contracts. The format supports standard unit testing, fuzzing, and symbolic execution. In this interface, tests are implemented as public functions on Solidity contracts. By convention, test contracts should inherit from the DSTest contract which provides various assertion helpers. Concrete tests are functions prefixed with test, while symbolic tests have a prove prefix.

As an example, consider a simple Token contract (left) and the corresponding prove_transfer function (right). The contract performs token transfer from the caller's account to a receiver, if the balance suffices and if the amount is not 42. The prove_transfer function checks whether the balance of the sender has been updated correctly, but it does not account for the edge case.

```
contract Token {
  /* account balances mapping */
  mapping(address => uint256) public bal;

  /* Transfer amt from the sender's account to x */
  function transfer(address x, uint256 amt) public {
    /* Check if there's enough balance */
    /* Do not make the transfer if amt equals 42 */
    if (bal[msg.sender] >= amt && amt != 42) {
      bal[msg.sender] -= amt;
      bal[x] += amt;
    }
  }
}
```

```
import "lib/test.sol";
import "src/Token.sol";

contract TokenTest is DSTest {
  Token token;

  function setUp() public {
    token = new Token(); }

  function prove_transfer(address x, uint256 amt)
    public {
    uint256 fromBal= token.bal(msg.sender);
    token.transfer(x, amt);
    assertEq(fromBal - amt, token.bal(msg.sender)); }
}
```

If this test is part of a foundry [27] project, then running hevm test from the root automatically discovers and executes the prove_transfer test, returning the expected counterexample.

```
Failure: prove_transfer(address,uint256)

Counterexample:
  result:   Revert: 0x4e487b710000000000000000000000000000000000000000000000000000000000000001
  calldata: prove_transfer(0x0000000000000000000000000000000000001312,42)
```

hevm uses ABI metadata produced by solc to decode inputs that trigger the assertion violation and displays them in a human-readable format. Optionally, it can also produce a pretty-printed call trace, including log output from the ds-test assertion library.

In the rest of this paper, we do a short survey of related work (Sect. 2), give an overview of the internals of hevm (Sects. 3, 4 and 5), and evaluate hevm against other state-of-the-art tools (Sect. 6).

2   Related Work

Symbolic execution, introduced in the 1970s to check for property violations of software [5,13,16], has garnered significant attention across various domains of software analysis. In this section, we focus on its aspects related to blockchain security, and refer the interested reader to [2] for an excellent survey of symbolic execution in general.

In the broader landscape of blockchain security, prior research has primarily focused on using symbolic execution to validate the reachability of potential issues detected via static code analysis, as done by Oyente [18], sCompile [7], and Mythril [19]. These systems analyze Solidity and EVM bytecode for common vulnerabilities through static code analysis and use symbolic execution to filter out (some) false positives in order to present higher-quality results to their users. These symbolic engines tend not to be complete. For example, Oyente specifically does not fully model the EVM and the underlying blockchain and is known to report false positives even after filtering through its symbolic execution engine[1]. In general, when these symbolic engines cannot prove that a path is unreachable, they fail-safe by allowing the static code analysis to present a potentially false positive to the user.

Within the realm of symbolic execution on blockchain platforms, significant contributions have been made in adapting the technique to the EVM. Notable examples include the Certora Prover [4,14], EthBMC [11], halmos [23], and KEVM [12]. These tools all employ a variation of the principles of S^2E [8] in that they perform execution inside a virtual environment at a specific EVM state and attempt to accurately symbolically execute it wherever possible. These tools all make use of some over-approximations (e.g. in the SMT encoding of cryptographic hash functions like SHA3).

Symbolic execution frameworks make extensive use of SMT solvers (e.g. CVC5 [3], Z3 [10], and Bitwuzla [20]) to determine the reachability of a given branch of the execution tree. Recently there have been significant advances made in SMT bit-vector theory solving, with the introduction of local search [21], and the use of integer reasoning for large bit-width formulas [22].

3   Symbolic Interpreter for the EVM

The EVM. The Ethereum Virtual Machine (EVM) is a stack machine designed for verifiable, deterministic execution over a shared state. A so-called *consensus protocol* is usually used to provide a globally unique ordering of transitions over this shared state. The EVM state is segmented into accounts. Each account has a unique 20-byte identifier (i.e. address), and can be controlled by a private key, or by some EVM bytecode (so-called contract account). Each account has a balance in Ether (the native currency of Ethereum), and contract accounts each have their own region of persistent storage. During contract execution, calls to other contracts generate call frames. Each call frame has its own isolated memory region (a mutable byte array). The `calldata` and `returndata` regions are used to pass data between parent and child callframes. Gas, a unit for measuring computational effort, limits and monetizes executions to prevent network abuse.

---

[1] see page 10 regarding the `Validator` at [18].

The Interpreter. The core of the symbolic interpreter is the VM record, holding the machine state at each execution step with individual state items stored as terms of hevm's internal representation: Expr (Sec. 4). The interpreter will fully evaluate concrete subcomputations, ensuring that terms remain as concrete as possible.

The interpreter executes by repeatedly applying the exec1 function to update the VM record within Haskell's State monad. This function processes the opcode at the pc value in the input state and returns an updated state. For efficiency in resource-intensive tasks, the St [17] monad is used for in-place memory mutation when hevm can be sure that all relevant state entries are fully concrete.

Branching And Eager Exploration. At potential branch points (usually the conditional jump instruction JUMPI), hevm clones the VM state and explores both possible branches. Each branch is executed in parallel using Haskell's asynchronous runtime. Once the end of execution is reached in each branch, they are summarized into Expr End's, retaining only the final externally observable effects of each branch. hevm skips almost all SMT queries during exploration. This results in the exploration of provably unreachable paths. Since SMT queries are usually more costly than path exploration, we have found this to be a performance optimization in most cases. Before SMT-based reachability analysis, hevm applies static simplification passes (constant folding, partial evaluation, etc.) that are comparatively very cheap to execute, in order to eliminate unreachable branches during exploration.

Loops, Recursion, and Loop Heuristics. EVM loops are implemented using the JUMPI instruction and are unrolled by hevm during exploration. A naive application of our eager approach to exploration would cause infinite loops (even in loops with a fixed iteration count), as both branches of a JUMPI would always be explored. hevm tackles this potential issue in the following two ways. **(1) User-supplied maximum iteration bound.** In this approach, loops are unrolled only up until some user-defined depth. This approach guarantees termination even with unbounded loops, but can lead to incompleteness of exploration (for which a warning is printed). **(2) Automated detection of bounded loops.** In this approach, a loop detection heuristic is applied and whenever the loop is about to be executed again, an SMT call is made to determine branch condition satisfiability. If the SMT solver can determine that the loop cannot run one more time (e.g. because its condition is always falsified after k iterations), the loop is exited. This approach retains the completeness of exploration while guaranteeing termination for bounded loops only.

EVM control flow, which implements both branching and looping via JUMPI, complicates loop detection. A naive approach, classifying repeated visits to the same JUMPI as a loop, can misidentify repeated branches as loops. hevm overcomes this by recording the stack content at each JUMPI visit. A subsequent encounter with the same JUMPI leads to a comparison of valid jump destinations on the stack. A change in these destinations indicates a branch, while consistency suggests a loop. This heuristic, based on the assumption that reused basic blocks have differing return locations, is effective for most Solidity-generated code.

Gas. In the context of symbolic analysis of EVM programs, gas accounting is not usually relevant for assessing most safety properties. The primary concern is potential branching on the result of the GAS opcode, which allows introspection into the remaining gas. hevm incorporates a precise gas model for concrete execution. For symbolic execution, we implement an abstracted gas model. When executing symbolically, precise gas tracking is omitted. Instead, executing the GAS opcode introduces a unique symbolic value on the stack to represent the remaining gas.

Remote State and RPC Calls. hevm supports symbolic execution against a concrete state from a blockchain node adhering to the Ethereum RPC interface [1]. This enables execution against the live state of networks like Ethereum. In this mode, when executing the SLOAD/CALL opcodes, hevm makes an RPC call to a user-defined node to fetch storage values and contract code from the node. Execution against remote state can be very valuable when testing since it allows users to easily write tests that exactly mirror the production environment that their code is planned to be deployed into.

4 Expr, hevm's Internal Representation

The result of symbolic execution is represented using hevm's internal representation, Expr, that encodes final states and the path conditions leading to them. hevm leverages Haskell's type system and indexes Expr with the type of expression it represents, using a so-called generalized algebraic data type (GADT). This allows hevm to build terms that are well-typed by construction. An expression *e* has a type Expr a, where a can be any of the types Byte, EWord, Storage, Buf, EAddr, EContract, and End, which we explain below.

Expr End: *Top-level expressions.* At the top-level, an expression is a tree with if-then-else statements as branches, representing branching points of execution, and final states as leaves. Final states can be either a successful *final state*, a *failed state*, or a *partial execution state*.

```
ITE      :: Expr EWord {-- branch condition --} -> Expr End -> Expr End -> Expr End
Success  :: [Prop] {-- path conditions --} -> Expr Buf -> Map (Expr EAddr) (Expr EContract) -> Expr End
Failure  :: [Prop] {-- path conditions --} -> EvmError -> Expr End
Partial  :: [Prop] {-- path conditions --} -> PartialExec -> Expr End
```

A Success node represents a successful final state and contains the return-data (of type Expr Buf) and the resulting EVM state, which is a contract map from (potentially symbolic) contract addresses to the contract's state (type Map (Expr EAddr) (Expr EContract)). The state of a contract is a record consisting of its bytecode, storage (of type Expr Storage), balance, and nonce.

```
C :: { code :: ContractCode, storage :: Expr Storage, balance :: Expr EWord, nonce :: Maybe W64 }
   -> Expr EContract
```

Partial nodes represent cases where hevm prematurely halted execution, either due to an unsupported execution state (e.g. a symbolic JUMPDEST, or a call into an address with unknown code), or the loop unrolling bound being reached.

Each final state is annotated with a list of logical propositions of type [Prop], representing the path conditions leading there. The tree structure can be flattened to a list of final symbolic states, accumulating the if-then-else conditions as path conditions in the final state nodes. For example the term

```
ITE c1 (Success [] b1 st1) (ITE c (Success [] b2 st2) (Failure [] (Error Revert)))
```

is flattened down to the list:

```
[Success [PNeg (PEq c1 (Lit 0x0))] b1 st1, Success [PEq c1 (Lit 0x0), PNeg (PEq c2 (Lit 0x0))] b2 st2,
Failure [PEq c1 (Lit 0x0), PEq c2 (Lit 0x0)] (Error Revert)]
```

Expr Byte *and* **Expr Word***: Bytes and 256-bit words.* Words can be concrete or symbolic. Operations on words include arithmetic, boolean, and bitwise operations. Bytes can be concrete literals or symbolic expressions but hevm does not have symbolic byte variables. **Expr** has specific abstract values representing the block, transaction, or frame context.

```
Lit             :: W256 -> Expr EWord {-- literal words --}
Var             :: Text -> Expr EWord {-- symbolic words --}
LitByte         :: Word8 -> Expr Byte {-- literal bytes --}
IndexWord       :: Expr EWord -> Expr EWord -> Expr Byte
-- Arithmetic operations
Add             :: Expr EWord -> Expr EWord -> Expr EWord
... {-- Sub, Mul, Div, SDiv, Mod, SMod, AddMod, MulMod, Exp, SExp, Min, Max --}
-- Boolean operations
LT              :: Expr EWord -> Expr EWord -> Expr EWord
... {-- LT, GT, LEq, GEq, SLT, SGT, Eq, IsZero --}
-- bitwise operations
And             :: Expr EWord -> Expr EWord -> Expr EWord
... {-- Or, Xor, Not, SHL, SHR, SAR --}
-- Context
TxValue         :: Expr EWord
Origin          :: Expr EWord
Balance         :: Expr EAddr {-- contract address --} -> Expr EWord
...
```

Expr Buf*: Buffers.* Memory, calldata, and returndata are all represented as buffers. A base buffer is either a concrete buffer, represented as a byte string, or a symbolic buffer variable. Operations on buffers include reading and writing bytes and words, copying slices, getting the length, and computing the Keccak cryptographic hash.

```
ConcreteBuf     :: ByteString -> Expr Buf
AbstractBuf     :: Text -> Expr Buf
ReadWord        :: Expr EWord {- offset -} -> Expr Buf {- buffer -} -> Expr EWord
ReadByte        :: Expr EWord {- offset -} -> Expr Buf {- buffer -} -> Expr Byte
WriteWord       :: Expr EWord {- offset -} -> Expr EWord {- value -} -> Expr Buf -> Expr Buf
WriteByte       :: Expr EWord {- offset -} -> Expr Byte {- value -} -> Expr Buf -> Expr Buf
CopySlice       :: Expr EWord {- src offset -} -> Expr EWord {- dst offset -} -> Expr EWord {- size -}
                -> Expr Buf {- src buffer -} -> Expr Buf {- dst buffer -} -> Expr Buf
BufLength       :: Expr Buf -> Expr EWord
Keccak          :: Expr Buf -> Expr EWord
```

Expr Storage*: Storage.* An individual contract's storage maps word-sized *storage addresses* to words. Base storage values are either a concrete map or an abstract variable annotated with the address of the contract it belongs to.

```
ConcreteStore :: (Map W256 W256) -> Expr Storage
AbstractStore :: Expr EAddr -> Expr Storage
SLoad         :: Expr EWord {- key -} -> Expr Storage {- storage -} -> Expr EWord {- result -}
SStore        :: Expr EWord {- key -} -> Expr EWord {- value -} -> Expr Storage -> Expr Storage
```

Expr EAddr*: Addresses.* An *account address* (not to be confused with a storage address) is a 160-bit unique identifier created when a new account is added to the state. For soundness, hevm asserts that all symbolic contract addresses that are present in the the contracts map are pairwise distinct. the aliasing of symbolic addresses must be prevented.

```
SymAddr        :: Text -> Expr EAddr
LitAddr        :: Addr -> Expr EAddr
WAddr          :: Expr EAddr -> Expr EWord {-- conversion to words --}
```

Prop: *Assertions.* Various assertions, such as path conditions, are represented in Haskell with the `Prop` datatype. The datatype includes boolean connectives, polymorphic equality, and comparison operators over hevm words. This is distinct from the EVM level boolean operations, which operate on, and return 256-bit Words.

```
data Prop where
  PBool :: Bool -> Prop
  PAnd :: Prop -> Prop -> Prop
  PEq :: forall a. Expr a -> Expr a -> Prop {-- polymorphic equality --}
  PLT :: Expr EWord -> Expr EWord -> Prop
  ... {-- PNeg, PAnd, PImpl, PLEq, PGT, PGEq --}
```

4.1 Expr Simplification

The `Expr` generated by the symbolic interpreter can be verbose with many opportunities for simplification. To simplify it, the following set of rewrite rules are applied: **(1) Constant folding** is a technique that replaces an expression with its concrete value, if it can be computed e.g. via applying arithmetic operations such as addition modulo 2^{256}. **(2) Canonicalization** is performed, making sure that wherever possible, the first argument of a 2-argument operator is always a constant. This helps improve the effectiveness of the following steps. **(3) Partial Evaluation** is performed wherever possible. For example `Max (Lit 0) (Var"a")` is evaluated to `Var "a"`. **(4) Arithmetic simplifications** are applied, to reduce the overhead of execution. For example, `Sub (Add x y) y` is rewritten to `x`. **(5) Write simplifications** help eliminate a memory write in case there is no corresponding read to the affected memory region or the write has been overwritten by a subsequent write.

Sets of assertions, expressed as list of `Prop`'s can also be simplified. Hence, hevm performs **(6) Equivalence propagation**, a technique where if e.g. an `Expr` forces `Var "a"` to `Lit 5`, then `Var "a"` can be safely replaced in every other `Expr` with `Lit 5`. To make the final expression easier to deal with, hevm also applies **(7) Trivial constraint deletion** to remove all constant true constraints, and remove all constraints but the constant false, in case a constant false is found.

4.2 Example Program in Expr

Figure 1 shows how a simple Solidity program looks in `Expr` once the `Expr` has been simplified. The end-states of the program are represented in orange and the branch conditions in green. Solidity inserts a reverting end-state when Ether is sent to the function (i.e. `TxValue` is larger than zero) since the function is not marked as `payable`. The next end-state is due to the `require` statement that forces a revert in case the condition `val1 < 10` doesn't hold. Finally, the `assert` forces either a revert or a success depending on whether `val1` can overflow.

5   SMT Encoding

The core function used for verification in hevm is `assertProps` which takes a list of `Prop`'s (the data type of propositions) and turns it into an SMT2 script to check its validity. It first declares any necessary symbolic variables (buffers, stores, addresses, words, EVM context) mentioned in the input and then asserts the propositions translating `Expr` and `Prop` into SMT2. We discuss some subtle points of this encoding below.

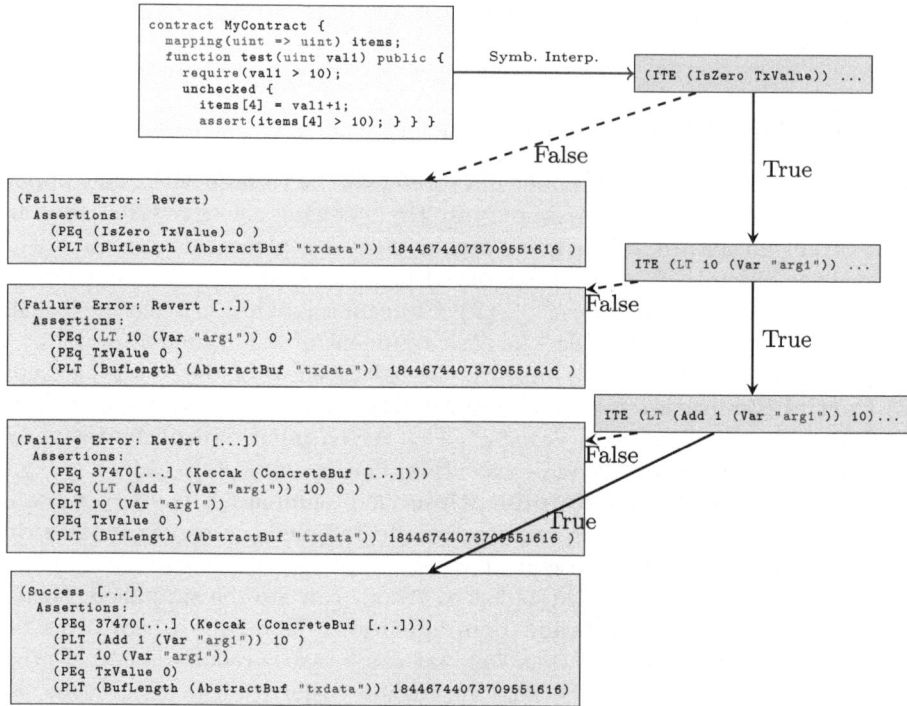

Fig. 1. The result of symbolically executing the call `test(uint val1)`.

Keccak. Solidity uses the Keccak hash function to adapt its high-level storage model to the EVM's flat storage structure. For example, for the mapping data type the value of key k is located at the storage slot `keccak256`$(k||p)$, where p is a compile-time constant [28] and $||$ is concatenation. The security of this scheme relies on the hash function being collision-free. For example, in the following Solidity contract, absence of injectivity can cause a collision in the storage slot of `a1` and `a2`.

```
contract C {
    mapping (address => bool) public map;
    function withdraw(address a1, address a2) public {
        require(a1 != a2);
        map[a1] = false; map[a2] = true;
        assert(map[a1] != map[a2]); // assertion violation is reachable without assuming injectivity }
}
```

In the SMT encoding, Keccak is an uninterpreted function. To encode injectivity without using quantifiers, hevm gathers all buffers onto which Keccak is applied and for each possible pair (b1, b2), adds the assertion b1 != b2 → Keccak(b1) != Keccak(b2). We also need to assert that the "gap" between two Keccak calls is large enough (currently it is arbitrarily set to be at least 256). This is important for avoiding collisions between Solidity arrays.

Storage Decomposition. While the encoding above is accurate, the usage of uninterpreted functions has been empirically identified as a bottleneck in SMT query execution. A key optimization in hevm is the analysis of storage accesses to reconstruct the original high-level Solidity storage layout, an idea originally implemented by halmos. The required analysis is done without making any additional trust assumptions, i.e. hevm does not utilize the storage layout metadata made available as part of the compiler output. The inferred structure is used in SMT queries, assigning separate SMT arrays to each logical storage region and eliminating Keccak calls in the generated SMT. This optimization is executed through rewrite rules on Expr, applied only when safe. The current implementation supports 1-dimensional mappings and arrays, with plans to expand to more complex nested structures.

Abstraction-Refinement. Abstraction-refinement [9] is a method used to improve the performance of SMT solvers. Select (often more complicated) parts of the formula are abstracted into a fresh new variable(s) and satisfiability is checked. If this new formula is UNSAT, then the original formula must have been UNSAT too since abstraction only weakened it. If the new formula is SAT, the solver may have encountered a spurious counterexample. In such cases, hevm performs so-called refinement to constrain the fresh variables to be (closer to) the original value.

hevm performs two kinds of abstraction-refinement, one for complex arithmetic operations, and one for EVM memory operations. In both cases, hevm does not perform counterexample-guided refinements. Instead it refines all abstracted-away elements in one go.

Fuzzing over the Symbolic Endstate. Some common properties of interest, such as those involving complex non-linear arithmetic, can be very hard for an SMT solver to analyze. If unsafe, counterexamples to these properties can often be found with little effort via fuzzing. hevm by default applies a short round of fuzzing over the symbolic endstate of interest before passing it to the solver.

6   Evaluation

Correctness. hevm is tested to pass the standard EVM test suite [26], which is a set of test vectors to validate the conformance of an EVM client to the expected semantics. This gives confidence in the concrete part of hevm's semantics. In addition, hevm comes with a differential fuzzing harness against geth, the most popular EVM concrete execution client. This fuzzing framework exercises

Table 1. Performance and correctness of different symbolic analysis tools on the benchmark set [25]

	Correct	Unknown	False Positives	False Negatives
hevm-bitwuzla	**134**	54	10	1
hevm-z3	129	60	9	1
halmos	114	75	9	1
kontrol	73	61	63	2

both the concrete and symbolic parts of hevm's semantics. It randomly generates a bytecode sequence, symbolically executes it, concretizes any abstract variables, and simplifies it down to a fully concrete result. This concrete result is then checked against the result produced by geth. Finally, hevm contains a set of SMT-based semantic fuzzing harnesses to check the various simplification steps, making sure the semantic meaning of Expr terms is not changed through simplification.

Performance. To validate the performance of hevm, we collaborated with the authors of competitive symbolic analysis tooling halmos [23] and KEVM [12] to produce a set of shared benchmarks publicly available on GitHub [25]. We hope this benchmark set can become a useful standard that future tooling can use to validate performance, as well as an interface for feedback from users to tool developers. It currently contains 199 benchmarks: a mix of conformance tests (focused on the correctness of a specific EVM feature or opcode) and performance tests that mimic real-world use cases (ERC20 and ERC721A tokens, the beacon chain deposit contract, and various CTF challenges). Test harnesses are currently implemented for hevm, halmos [23], and KEVM (through kontrol [29]), the tools that support the ds-test format. kontrol and halmos were run with default settings, hevm was run with both the default settings (using z3) and with its bitwuzla backend. Each tool was given a 300 s time limit and 110GB memory limit for each benchmark. The benchmarks were run on an AMD 5950x with 128GB RAM (Table 1).

Results. All tools reported false positives, indicating a counterexample for tests marked as safe. In the case of kontrol, the majority resulted from differences in revert handling: kontrol treats all reverts as test failures, while halmos and hevm only consider reverts from assertion violations as failures. Newer versions of kontrol have added a mode to align with the hevm and halmos semantics. For hevm and halmos, the false positives were caused by the various overabstractions utilized by each tool, e.g. in the SMT encoding of Keccak.

Each tool also reported false negatives, where a test was marked as safe but should have shown a counterexample. For hevm, this was due to a now-fixed bug. Another false positive was reported by both halmos and kontrol: both tools pass concretely sized calldata to the top level test method, meaning they missed assertions in branches that could only be reached if the input calldata had an abstract size. After discussion with the authors of `halmos` and `kontrol`, we have agreed to standardize on concrete calldata size. `kontrol` had an additional false positive due to differences in the concreteness of test inputs (callvalue and test contract balance). We have not yet reached a consensus on which approach should be standard in this case.

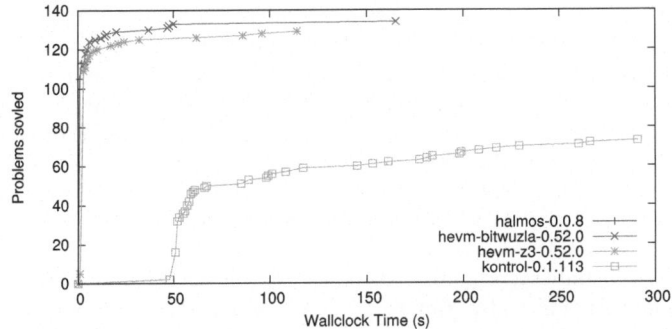

Fig. 2. CDF plot of the results. False negatives/positives are excluded.

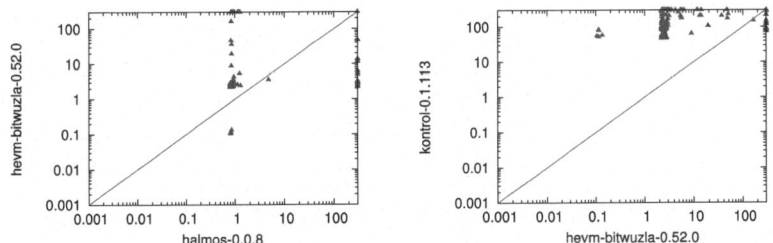

Fig. 3. Pairwise comparison of `hevm`, `halmos`, and `KEVM`. In comparison to `halmos`, hevm solves more instances, although can sometimes be slower. In comparison to `KEVM`, hevm is both faster and solves more instances.

References

1. JSON-RPC API, Ethereum Development Documentation. https://ethereum.org/en/developers/docs/apis/json-rpc (2022)
2. Baldoni, R., Coppa, E., D'Elia, D.C., Demetrescu, C., Finocchi, I.: A survey of symbolic execution techniques. ACM Comput. Surv. **51**(3), 50:1–50:39 (2018). https://doi.org/10.1145/3182657
3. Barbosa, H., et al.: cvc5: a versatile and industrial-strength SMT solver. In: TACAS 2022. LNCS, vol. 13243, pp. 415–442. Springer, Cham (2022). https://doi.org/10.1007/978-3-030-99524-9_24

4. Bernardi, T., et al.: Finding bugs automatically in smart contracts with parameterized invariants. WIP, Retrieved July from arxiv (2020)
5. Boyer, R.S., Elspas, B., Levitt, K.N.: SELECT - a formal system for testing and debugging programs by symbolic execution. In: Shooman, M.L., Yeh, R.T. (eds.) Proceedings of the International Conference on Reliable Software 1975, Los Angeles, California, USA, April 21-23, 1975, pp. 234–245. ACM (1975). https://doi.org/10.1145/800027.808445
6. Brunny.eth: The market cap of the ethereum ecosystem. https://mirror.xyz/brunny.eth/-0Jn0dD5868h_WshCirxJPyjBD6hQvqPL18blZrEbsU (2022)
7. Chang, J., Gao, B., Xiao, H., Sun, J., Cai, Y., Yang, Z.: sCompile: critical path identification and analysis for smart contracts. In: Ait-Ameur, Y., Qin, S. (eds.) ICFEM 2019. LNCS, vol. 11852, pp. 286–304. Springer, Cham (2019). https://doi.org/10.1007/978-3-030-32409-4_18
8. Chipounov, V., Kuznetsov, V., Candea, G.: The S2E platform: design, implementation, and applications. ACM Trans. Comput. Syst. **30**(1), 2:1–2:49 (2012). https://doi.org/10.1145/2110356.2110358
9. Clarke, E., Grumberg, O., Jha, S., Lu, Y., Veith, H.: Counterexample-guided abstraction refinement. In: Emerson, E.A., Sistla, A.P. (eds.) Computer Aided Verification, pp. 154–169. Springer, Berlin, Heidelberg (2000). https://doi.org/10.1007/10722167_15
10. de Moura, L., Bjørner, N.: Z3: an efficient SMT solver. In: Ramakrishnan, C.R., Rehof, J. (eds.) TACAS 2008. LNCS, vol. 4963, pp. 337–340. Springer, Heidelberg (2008). https://doi.org/10.1007/978-3-540-78800-3_24
11. Frank, J., Aschermann, C., Holz, T.: ETHBMC: a bounded model checker for smart contracts. In: Capkun, S., Roesner, F. (eds.) 29th USENIX Security Symposium, USENIX Security 2020, August 12-14, 2020, pp. 2757–2774. USENIX Association (2020). https://www.usenix.org/conference/usenixsecurity20/presentation/frank
12. Hildenbrandt, E., et al.: KEVM: a complete formal semantics of the ethereum virtual machine. In: 31st IEEE Computer Security Foundations Symposium, CSF 2018, Oxford, United Kingdom, July 9-12, 2018, pp. 204–217. IEEE Computer Society (2018). https://doi.org/10.1109/CSF.2018.00022
13. Howden, W.E.: Symbolic testing and the DISSECT symbolic evaluation system. IEEE Trans. Software Eng. **3**(4), 266–278 (1977)
14. Hozzová, P., Bendık, J., Nutz, A., Rodeh, Y.: Over approximation of non-linear integer arithmetic for smart contract verification. In: Proceedings of 24th International Conference on Logic, vol. 94, pp. 257–269 (2023)
15. Immunefi: Immunefi crypto losses report. https://immunefi.com/research/ (2022)
16. King, J.C.: A new approach to program testing. In: Shooman, M.L., Yeh, R.T. (eds.) Proceedings of the International Conference on Reliable Software 1975, Los Angeles, California, USA, April 21-23, 1975, pp. 228–233. ACM (1975). https://doi.org/10.1145/800027.808444
17. Launchbury, J., Jones, S.L.P.: Lazy functional state threads. In: Sarkar, V., Ryder, B.G., Soffa, M.L. (eds.) Proceedings of the ACM SIGPLAN'94 Conference on Programming Language Design and Implementation (PLDI), Orlando, Florida, USA, June 20-24, 1994, pp. 24–35. ACM (1994). https://doi.org/10.1145/178243.178246
18. Luu, L., Chu, D., Olickel, H., Saxena, P., Hobor, A.: Making smart contracts smarter. In: Weippl, E.R., Katzenbeisser, S., Kruegel, C., Myers, A.C., Halevi, S. (eds.) Proceedings of the 2016 ACM SIGSAC Conference on Computer and Communications Security, Vienna, Austria, October 24-28, 2016, pp. 254–269. ACM (2016). https://doi.org/10.1145/2976749.2978309

19. Mueller, B., Luca, D.: Advances in automated EVM smart contract vulnerability detection and exploitation. In: Proceedings of HITBSecConf2018 (2018)
20. Niemetz, A., Preiner, M.: Bitwuzla at the SMT-COMP 2020. CoRR abs/2006.01621 (2020). https://arxiv.org/abs/2006.01621
21. Niemetz, A., Preiner, M., Biere, A.: Precise and complete propagation based local search for satisfiability modulo theories. In: Chaudhuri, S., Farzan, A. (eds.) CAV 2016. LNCS, vol. 9779, pp. 199–217. Springer, Cham (2016). https://doi.org/10.1007/978-3-319-41528-4_11
22. Niemetz, A., Preiner, M., Reynolds, A., Zohar, Y., Barrett, C., Tinelli, C.: Towards bit-width-independent proofs in SMT solvers. In: Fontaine, P. (ed.) CADE 2019. LNCS (LNAI), vol. 11716, pp. 366–384. Springer, Cham (2019). https://doi.org/10.1007/978-3-030-29436-6_22
23. Park, D., et. al: Halmos, a symbolic testing tool for EVM smart contracts. https://github.com/a16z/halmos
24. The Dapphub Team: ds-test (2024). https://github.com/dapphub/ds-test/
25. The Eth SC Comp Authors: Ethereum smart contract analysis benchmarks (2024). https://github.com/eth-sc-comp/benchmarks/
26. The Ethereum Project: Ethereum tests (2023). https://github.com/ethereum/tests
27. The Foundry Project: foundry (2024). https://github.com/foundry-rs/foundry
28. The Solidity Authors: Mappings and dynamic arrays in solidity (2023). https://docs.soliditylang.org/en/latest/internals/layout_in_storage.html#mappings-and-dynamic-arrays
29. Verification, R.: KEVM based symbolic execution of foundry tests. https://github.com/runtimeverification/kontrol?tab=readme-ov-file

SolTG: A CHC-Based Solidity Test Case Generator

Konstantin Britikov[1], Ilia Zlatkin[2], Grigory Fedyukovich[2(✉)],
Leonardo Alt[3], and Natasha Sharygina[1]

[1] University of Lugano, Lugano, Switzerland
{konstantin.britikov,natasha.sharygina}@usi.ch
[2] Florida State University,, Tallahassee FL, USA
iz20e@fsu.edu, grigory@cs.fsu.edu
[3] Ethereum Foundation, Berlin, Germany
leo@ethereum.org

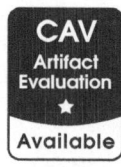

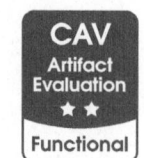

Abstract. Achieving high test coverage is important when developing blockchain smart contracts, but it could be challenging without automated reasoning tools. In this paper, we present SolTG, an automated test case generator for Solidity based on constrained Horn clauses (CHC). SolTG exhaustively enumerates symbolic path constraints from the contract's CHC representation and makes calls to the Satisfiability Modulo Theories (SMT) solver to find input values under which the contract exhibits the corresponding behavior. Test cases synthesized by SolTG have the form of a sequence of function calls over concrete values of input parameters which lead to a specific execution scenario. The tool supports multiple Solidity-specific features and is capable of exhibiting a high coverage for industrial-grade Solidity code. We present a detailed architecture of SolTG based on the existing translation of smart contracts into a CHC representation. We also present the experimental results for test generation on the regression and industrial benchmarks.

1 Introduction

Constrained Horn clauses (CHC) provide a logic-based format for automated verification which has an advantage over other solutions since it separates modeling from solving and makes it suitable for various application domains and reusable across different verification tasks. The CHC-based solutions focus on one hand on the development of a front-end for the translation of the source code into the language of logic constraints and on the other hand on the implementation of the back-end for solving logical queries constructed from the encoding. Various CHC solvers have been applied to solve verification problems in different domains (e.g., SeaHorn [10], Korn [8] and TriCera [9] for C, JayHorn for Java [17], RustHorn for Rust [13], SolCMC [2] and SmartACE [18] for Solidity).

K. Britikov and I. Zlatkin—The authors contributed equally.

A. Gurfinkel and V. Ganesh (Eds.): CAV 2024, LNCS 14681, pp. 466–479, 2024.
https://doi.org/10.1007/978-3-031-65627-9_23

Recently the CHC-based approach called HORNTINUUM was proposed for the exhaustive test case generation for an imperative language without recursion [19]. Given a CHC-encoding of a program, this approach systematically explores various control-flow paths represented by CHC unrollings and relies on an off-the-shelf SMT solver to produce exact input values to the program. The approach is exhaustive in the sense that it terminates only when each branch of the original program either has a test case or has been proven to be unreachable (using an automatically generated invariant).

In this paper, we demonstrate the evolution of the ideas described in [19] for programs in a contract-oriented language, namely Solidity. It relies on a CHC representation of a smart contract generated by a recent Solidity compiler's model checker, SoLCMC [2]. The logic encoding of a contract is different from the encoding of an imperative program, due to the presence of functions that can be invoked in any order. This complicates the trace enumeration process which is necessary for the exhaustive test case generation. In our approach, we explore contract behaviors gradually, from shorter ones to longer ones, and we keep track of functions and branches that have already been covered.

We present SoLTG, a new fully automated tool for Solidity test generation. SoLTG receives a Solidity source file(s), extracts the compiler metadata and the CHC representation from SoLCMC, computes multiple CHC unrollings, and communicates with the Z3 solver [14] to receive values of function parameters to compute a test case. Each test case is compiled into a human-readable test file following the format for a well-known FOUNDRY[1] framework to build, test, fuzz, debug and deploy Solidity smart contracts. Thus it becomes immediately useful for contract engineers who receive the test coverage reports based on the contract execution, which cannot be obtained by the other tools, e.g. [18].

SoLTG generates tests for real-world contracts fully automatically. We evaluated the tool on the benchmarks both from the SoLCMC repository [2] and industrial contracts. All the tests were executed by FOUNDRY on smart contracts as they were running in the actual blockchain. Our experimentation demonstrates that SoLTG provides a high level of test coverage. Specifically, it reached 71% branch coverage, 81,2% line coverage, and 90,9% function coverage on average. Furthermore, for 35% of benchmarks, SoLTG achieved 100% test coverage within 5 s of running time. Overall, the evaluation demonstrates the practicality of SoLTG since it provides contract-specific feedback in a small amount of time.

2   Tool Overview

SoLTG[2] supports most of the Solidity features, it can process smart contracts with constructors, multiple fields and functions, polymorphism, inheritance of other contracts or interfaces, etc. It can also handle Solidity-specific constructs

---

[1] https://book.getfoundry.sh.

[2] The tool is available as a Python module and can be installed via `sudo pip3 install solTg`. The code is available at https://github.com/BritikovKI/aeval/tree/tg-nonlin (back-end) and at https://github.com/BritikovKI/solidity_testgen (front-end).

like inherent transaction data, a current state of blockchain, contract state variables, and a full set of standard Solidity datatypes.

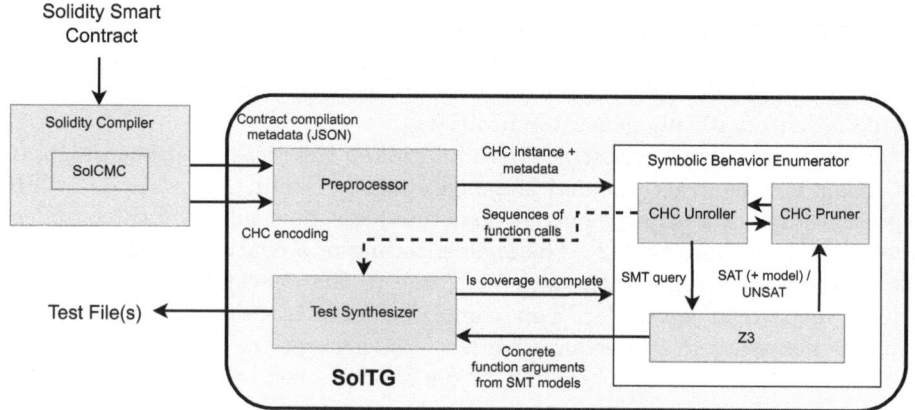

Fig. 1. Architecture of SOLTG.

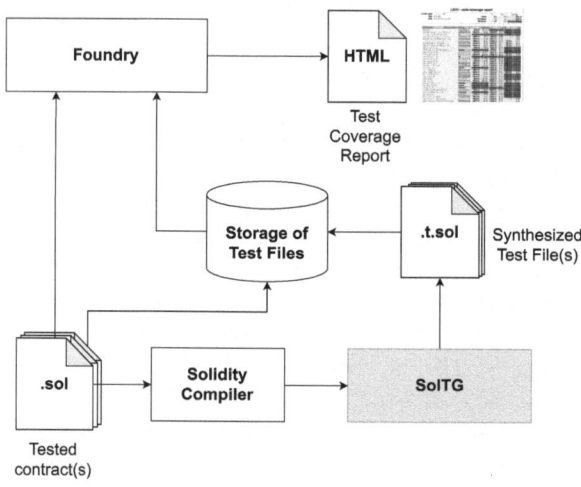

Fig. 2. Role of SOLTG in the testing workflow.

Figure 1 gives an overview of the architecture of SOLTG. The input is a source file with a Solidity smart contract, and the output is a set of test files for FOUNDRY, a framework to build, test, fuzz, debug, and deploy Solidity smart contracts. The tool relies on the external modules: **Solidity Compiler** to obtain the compilation metadata, **Solidity Compiler Model Checker**, to get the CHC encoding, and an SMT solver **Z3** to actually extract concrete values for test cases.

Figure 2 gives an overview of a higher-level testing process monitored by engineers, where SoLTG plays the central role. The generated test files are human-readable and are kept until the contract under test has been updated and are thus used for testing. The test reports in the HTML format are generated by FOUNDRY that compiles the contracts being tested and executes the test cases. The internal components of SoLTG are defined below.

Preprocessor is responsible for parsing and analyzing the input data. It receives compilation metadata and the CHC encoding of the Solidity contract. The preprocessor then parses the compiler's metadata, determining the complete list of the contract's public and external (testable) functions, constructors and their required inputs. Preprocessor encodes the full set of constructors, functions, and input variables. It then provides them as input together with the CHC encoding to Symbolic Behavior Enumerator to discover possible execution scenarios.

Symbolic Behavior Enumerator (see details in Sect. 3) synthesizes sequences of function calls over tuples of concrete values for function parameters. Overall SoLTG exhaustively enumerates symbolic representations of different paths through the contract's functions and relies on an SMT solver (in our case, Z3) to extract values of those parameters, until either all branches are covered with tests or a timeout is reached.

Test Synthesizer receives a set of concrete function arguments for the tests from the SMT models and corresponding sequences of function calls which are provided by Symbolic Behavior Enumerator. It processes the inputs and generates a set of tests stored as a test file for FOUNDRY.

FOUNDRY compiles, executes, performs coverage analysis, and generates a report for the synthesized test files. Coverage analysis uses classical test coverage metrics such as line/branch/function coverage which are commonly used by contract engineers. The distinguishing feature of our framework is that the reported results reflect the exact blockchain response to the tested function calls.

Limitations. Currently SoLTG does not support inline assembly code and uses approximate reasoning about dynamically sized byte arrays and strings. SoLTG does not model the gas consumption during the function execution, and thus it may generate test cases for some unreachable blocks of source code due to this.

3   Test Case Generation from CHC Encoding

Although SoLTG targets smart contracts in Solidity, our test case generation approach can be lifted to other contract-oriented languages given an encoder for them to constrained Horn clauses.

3.1   CHC Preliminaries

A *constrained Horn clause* (CHC) over a set of uninterpreted predicate symbols $R = \{r_1, \ldots, r_n\}$, is a universally quantified first-order formula that matches the following regular expression:

$$\forall \vec{x}, \vec{y}.\left((r_1 \mid \ldots \mid r_n)(\vec{x}) \wedge \right)^* \varphi(\vec{x}, \vec{y}) \implies ((r_1 \mid \ldots \mid r_n)(\vec{y}) \mid false)$$

where $\vec{x}, \vec{y}$ are vectors of variables, $*$ is Kleene star, the left side of the implication (called *body*) may have multiple occurrences of any symbol from R but φ does not have occurrences of any symbol from R. For readability reasons, we omit writing $\forall \vec{x}, \vec{y} \ldots$ In the following formulas, we introduce indexes (e.g., in $\vec{x_1}$ or $\vec{x_2}$) whenever we need to introduce fresh variables.

CHCs are used as an intermediate representation for procedural and object-oriented programs and allow the verification tools to symbolically enumerate program behaviors. To formally introduce the process, we define the notion of CHC *unrolling* as follows. Given a CHC system S over uninterpreted predicates R and a rule $r_1(\vec{x_1}) \wedge \varphi \implies r_0(\vec{x_0})$ where $r_0, r_1 \in R$, an *unfolding* of r_1 is another CHC rule $\psi(\vec{x_1}, \vec{x_2}) \wedge \varphi \implies r_0(\vec{x_0})$ such that:

- for some $\vec{x_3}$ and $\vec{x_4}$, $\psi(\vec{x_3}, \vec{x_4}) \implies r_1(\vec{x_3})$ is a CHC in S, and
- $\vec{x_2}$ is a vector of fresh variables that does not overlap with $\vec{x_1}$ and $\vec{x_0}$.

For a given CHC, an *unrolling* is an output of any number of consecutive unfoldings of that rule that does not have uninterpreted predicates in the body. There could be multiple possible unrollings for a single CHC instance, and we illustrate it in the next subsection.

3.2 Solidity Smart Contracts to CHCs

We begin with a brief intuitive overview of the CHC encoding employed by SOLTG which is inspired by SolCMC. For demonstration reasons, we simplify the encoding principles, but we highlight the main ingredients. Each test case-generation target may operate over the application binary interface and cryptographic functions, transaction data, the blockchain state, balances, and storage for every contract. We denote their logic representation as $\vec{s}$ and assume there is a fully interpreted formula $init(\vec{s})$ that describes how $\vec{s}$ is instantiated *before* an instance of the contract under test has been created. We assume the contract under test has a vector of fields $v_1, \ldots, v_n$ that is symbolically encoded into some $\vec{v}$ that does not overlap with $\vec{s}$. Throughout the lifecycle of an instance of the contract, it could undergo a (possibly unbounded) number of changes made by calling the contract's functions. These are modeled with the help of an auxiliary uninterpreted predicate fc. Intuitively, it corresponds to a *contract transition system* (we will use this notation later) that has two logic rules, for the initiation and consecution respectively:

$$init(\vec{s}) \implies fc(\vec{s}, \vec{v}) \tag{1}$$

$$fc(\vec{s}, \vec{v}) \wedge summ(\vec{s}, \vec{s'}, \vec{v}, \vec{v'}) \implies fc(\vec{s'}, \vec{v'}) \tag{2}$$

For the second rule, we assume a set of defined functions F. An uninterpreted predicate *summ* stands for a *summary* of an arbitrary function over two vectors of logic variables $\vec{v}$ and $\vec{v'}$ that represent symbolic values of contract's fields before and after each function call, respectively.

Each $f \in F$ has a CFG (V_f, E_f), where V_f is a set of basic blocks and E_f is a set of control-flow edges, each one connecting two basic blocks. The dedicated basic block en_f is the only one with no incoming edge in E_f, and the dedicated basic block ret_f is the only one with no outgoing edge in E_f. We also assume there exists an encoding function $\tau : E_f \rightarrow \textit{Prop}$ that translates each $(b_1, b_2) \in E_f$ into an SSA form and further to a logic formula over $\vec{s}, \vec{s'}, \vec{v}, \vec{v'}, \vec{in}, \vec{loc}$, where $\vec{in}$ is a vector of input variables to f and $\vec{loc}$ is a vector of fresh local variables (and auxiliary SSA variables created during the encoding). This formula encodes symbolically the basic block b_1 and the condition under which the control transitions to basic block b_2. The CHC encoding has then a set of rules for f:

For each control-flow edge (b, ret_f), the CHC encoding uses an uninterpreted predicate b:

$$\tau(b, ret_f) \implies b(\vec{s}, \vec{s'}, \vec{v}, \vec{v'}, \vec{in}, \vec{loc}) \tag{3}$$

Then for each control-flow edge (b_1, b_2) where $b_2 \neq ret_f$, the CHC encoding uses uninterpreted predicates b_1 and b_2:

$$b_2(\vec{s}, \vec{s'}, \vec{v}, \vec{v'}, \vec{in}, \vec{loc}) \wedge \tau(b_1, b_2) \implies b_1(\vec{s}, \vec{s'}, \vec{v}, \vec{v'}, \vec{in}, \vec{loc}) \tag{4}$$

Lastly, to connect the entry to function f with its summary, it uses uninterpreted predicates en_f and sum (which is in turn used to connect f with the contract transition system via rule (2)):

$$en_f(\vec{s}, \vec{s'}, \vec{v}, \vec{v'}, \vec{in}, \vec{loc}) \implies summ(\vec{s}, \vec{s'}, \vec{v}, \vec{v'}) \tag{5}$$

We illustrate this encoding using the following example contract with one field a, a constructor, and two other functions.

```
1  contract A{
2    uint a;
3    constructor(uint in) {a = in;}
4    function reset() public {a = 0;}
5    function f(uint x, uint y) public {
6      if (a < x) reset();
7      else a += y;}
8  }
```

The CHC encoding is as follows. Field a (resp. inputs in, x, and y) is represented in CHCs by logic variable a (resp. in, x, and y). For simplicity, we let $\vec{s}$ to be empty and $init$ to be $true$. The entry points to the constructor and two functions are represented using predicates en_{con}, en_{reset}, and en_f, respectively. The CFG of the constructor (similarly, function reset) is trivial, so it needs one CHC of form (3) and one of form (5). Since function f contains a conditional statement, its CFG has basic blocks b_1 and b_2, and its CHC encoding makes uses of predicates b_1 and b_2 in the CHCs of form (3) and (4). For readability, formula $\tau(en_f, b_1)$ (resp. $\tau(en_f, b_2)$) is colored purple (resp. blue) and placed in the box. Lastly, note that $\tau(\mathbf{b}_1, \mathtt{ret}_f)$ has an occurrence of predicate en_{reset} which corresponds to calling function $\mathtt{reset}$.

$$true \implies fc(a)$$
$$fc(a) \wedge summ(a, a') \implies fc(a')$$
$$\boxed{a' = in} \implies en_{con}(a, a', in)$$
$$en_{con}(a, a', in) \implies summ(a, a')$$
$$\boxed{a' = 0} \implies en_{reset}(a, a')$$
$$en_{reset}(a, a') \implies summ(a, a')$$

$$en_{reset}(a, a') \implies b_1(a, a', x, y)$$
$$\boxed{a' = a + y} \implies b_2(a, a', x, y)$$
$$b_1(a, a', x, y) \wedge \boxed{a < x} \implies en_f(a, a', x, y)$$
$$b_2(a, a', x, y) \wedge \boxed{a \geq x} \implies en_f(a, a', x, y)$$
$$en_f(a, a', x, y) \implies summ(a, a')$$

The boxed formulas are the building blocks to be used in the test-code generation as described in the next subsection. Purple (resp. blue) color emphasizes that the formula is used to symbolically encode the **then**-branch (resp. the **else**-branch) of f's behavior, black color in the box – the code of the constructor.

3.3   Algorithmic Enumeration of Contract Behaviors

SOLTG generates tests by symbolic enumeration of the possible behaviors of the contract under test. Each test case begins with creating an instance of the contract c (by calling its constructor). Suppose then we wish to observe the behavior of certain function f which will be expressed as c.f(...) in the test. If f uses an input, the test case should specify one of the possible concrete values. A test could have a sequence of multiple functions under certain inputs, each of which contributes to updating the fields. For the example above, when we wish to test function f's behavior, we could (manually) create a test c = A(0); c.f(0,0). This would however be not enough to test the **then**-branch of the conditional in f's body. For this reason, another test, e.g., c = A(0); c.f(1,0) would be needed. In general, finding these sequences of function calls and concrete inputs is challenging. Our tool effectively generates sequences of function calls by enumeration over permutations of available functions, and it generates concrete inputs from the models of satisfiable logic formulas that correspond to distinct unrollings of CHCs. Specifically, our enumeration has three nested loops (denoted respectively **A**, **B**, and **C**).

A: *Enumerating the lengths of tests* At the higher level, the tool sequentially considers *unfoldings* of the contract transition system (1)-(2), that allows it to eventually consider test cases of various lengths. That is, an unrolling of length one would yield only test cases with constructors, an unrolling of length two – test cases with a constructor and one function call, etc. More formally, at this level, the tool performs an unfolding of fc in CHC $fc(v) \wedge summ(v, v') \implies fc(v')$ but keeps $summ$ uninterpreted. For a length n, the tool unfolds fc exactly $n+1$ times, for which it uses the consecution rule n times and then the initiation rule once. As a result, we get a new CHC (called C_n) with n distinct occurrences of $summ$ in the body.

B: *Enumerating the functions* At the middle level, i.e., for an unrolling of a fixed length n, the tool considers a sequence of n functions (possibly, with repetitions), where the first function is necessarily a constructor. Specifically, given the output from the outer loop, i.e., a CHC C_n with n distinct occurrences of *summ* in the body, the tool considers a set of n-tuples F^n and computes $|F|^n$ tuples of uninterpreted predicates $T = \{en_f \mid f \in F\}^n$. It finally computes $|F|^n$ distinct CHCs, each one by the pairwise replacement of the n-tuple of *summ* predicates in C_n by an n-tuple from T (with introducing fresh variables for *in* and *loc* whenever needed).

C: *Enumerating behaviors for each function* At the inner level, for each n-th function that we wish to test, the tool considers all paths through its CFG. That is, it receives one of the CHCs constructed at the middle level, and it computes all possible *unrollings* by recursively eliminating all uninterpreted symbols. Algorithmically, an unrolling of each function is similar to the approach of [19], and the tool repeats it n times, for each high-level function call (i.e., that it synthesizes in the test file). This loop gives a set of logic formulas, each of which is sent to an SMT solver. Lastly, to enumerate inputs for each function call, we rely on an SMT solver. Given a formula, the solver targets finding a satisfying assignment from which the desired input values are extracted.

Pruning test case enumeration Because of the exhaustiveness of enumeration, the complexity of steps **A**, **B**, and **C** grows exponentially with the number of contract functions and the points of control-flow divergence. We attempt to mitigate it using optimizations to prune the search space of the test cases, which is similar to [19]. First, the initial function to be called in a test case should always be the constructor of the contract under test. Second, assume there is a subset $F' \subseteq F$ of functions that have already full coverage (thanks to the already synthesized test cases). Then, given that we need to synthesize a new test case as a sequence n function calls, in step **B**, instead of enumerating $|F|^n$ possibilities, we can only enumerate $|F|^{n-2} * |F \setminus F'|$ possibilities (i.e., any function from $f \in F'$ could only be called in either 1-st, 2-nd, ..., or $n-1$-th position).

Synthesizing tests Each test case is synthesized from two components: a sequence of functions created at the end of step **B**, and a sequence of tuples of concrete values extracted from an SMT model at the end of step **C**. In general, the tool has to create an unrolling of the following CHC, for some $f_1, f_2, \ldots \in F$:

$$en_{f_1}(\vec{s}, \vec{s'}, \vec{v}, \vec{v'}, \vec{loc}, \vec{in}) \wedge en_{f_2}(\vec{s'}, \vec{s''}, \vec{v'}, \vec{v''}, \vec{loc'}, \vec{in'}) \wedge \ldots \implies fc(s^{(n)}, v^{(n)})$$

Note that the ultimate unrolling still has the occurrences of variables $\vec{in}$ and $\vec{in'}$ but no predicates en_{f_1}, en_{f_2}, ... Thus, if satisfiable, the SMT solver returns a tuple of values in_1, in_2, ... for $\vec{in}$, a tuple of values in'_1, in'_2, ... for $\vec{in'}$, etc. The final test case is then constructed as follows:

$$f_1(in_1, in_2, \ldots); \ f_2(in'_1, in'_2, \ldots); \ldots$$

We illustrate the whole process in our example. The formula encoding calls to the constructor and function f under the **then**-branch has the following unrolling:

$$a' = in \wedge \qquad (\texttt{constructor} - \text{first call})$$
$$a' < x \wedge \qquad (\texttt{f(x, y)} - \text{second call}, \texttt{then}\text{-branch})$$
$$a'' = 0 \qquad (\texttt{reset()} - \text{nested call})$$

It is satisfiable with a model $in \mapsto 0, x \mapsto 1, y \mapsto 0 \ldots$ Parsing this model and determining that in represents an input to the constructor and x represents an input to f gives us the test case c = new A(0); c.reset().

A formula encoding the same function calls but another branch is as follows:

$$a' = in \wedge \qquad (\texttt{constructor} - \text{first call})$$
$$a' \geq x \wedge a'' = a' + y \qquad (\texttt{f(x, y)} - \text{second call}, \texttt{else}\text{-branch})$$

It is satisfiable with a model $in \mapsto 0, x \mapsto 0, y \mapsto 0 \ldots$ which gives us test case c = new A(0); c.f(0,0).

These test cases now can be used for the generation of a Solidity test file:

```
1   contract A_Test is Test {
2     A a0; A a1;
3     function setUp() public { a0 = new A(0); a1 = new A(0); }
4     function test_A_0() public { a0.f(1, 0); }
5     function test_A_1() public { a1.f(0, 0); } }
```

The test file consists of multiple functions, the naming convention for which follows the FOUNDRY[3] standards. SetUp is used to prepare a testing environment by FOUNDRY. Functions test_A_0 and test_A_1 incorporate test cases generated by SOLTG above. The test file is human-readable and reusable: it can be used to generate test coverage right away and/or stored for regression testing later.

4   Evaluation

We evaluated SOLTG on 59 benchmarks from the SOLCMC repository [2] and industrial smart contracts which exhibit different Solidity-specific features. All experiments were conducted on a machine with a 2.3GHz 8-core Intel Core i9 processor and 16 GB RAM running on macOS 13.4. Test coverage data was collected from the Foundry test reports.

For the given set of benchmarks, SOLTG provided a high level of test coverage. In particular, on average, it achieved 71% branch coverage, 81,2% line coverage, and 90,9% function coverage for a 60-second timeout. A correlation of the coverage and the chosen timeout for each benchmark is shown in Fig. 3. The cactus plot has a range of timeouts from 0.1 sec to 60 sec on the x-axis and the corresponding coverage on the y-axis. Each curve represents multiple

---

[3] https://book.getfoundry.sh/forge/writing-tests.

behaviors of SoLTG on a single benchmark w.r.t. different timeouts. The rapid growth of many curves demonstrates that 1) the prepossessing and initial enumeration steps are very fast, and 2) SoLTG often needs just a few seconds to produce many test cases. In fact, SoLTG generates the majority of tests within the first 10 s of the execution. For 21 benchmarks SoLTG generated tests that report on 100% line coverage within the first 5 s. Further, with the increase of time, SoLTG finds additional test cases, but the production expectedly becomes costlier.

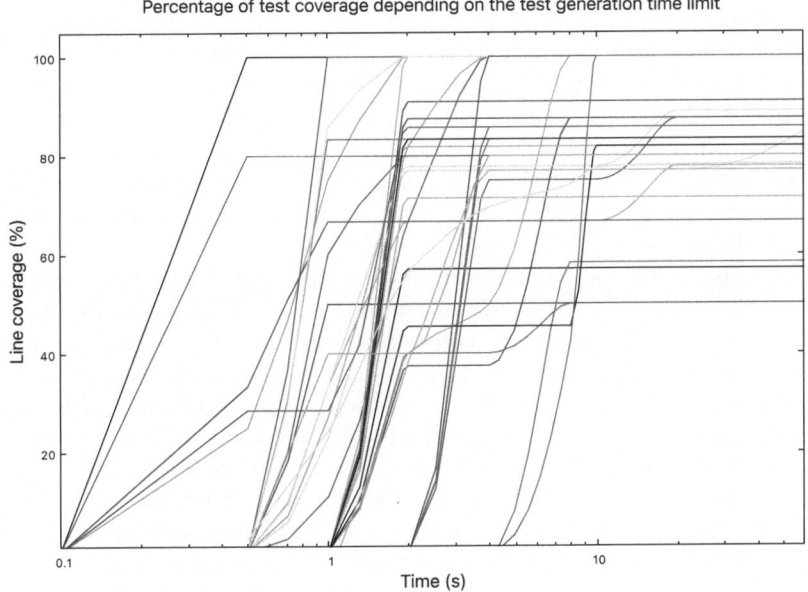

Fig. 3. SoLTG performance for the benchmark set with different timeouts.

We investigated the cases when SoLTG did not report the full test coverage within the 60-second timeout. One reason as expected was due to the complexity of the control structures of the contracts, resulting in less efficient test case generation. Remarkably, the other reason is the discrepancies between the CHC encoding and the actual semantics of the contracts.

We evaluated SoLTG on multiple industrial Ethereum contracts (e.g., Weth.sol, ERC20.sol, VestingWallet.sol), and it exhibited similar performance as for SoLCMC benchmarks. For example, for Weth.sol[4] SoLTG generated tests that produce 100% line and branch coverage within 120 s timeout. Overall, the results demonstrate the practical value of SoLTG in the contract development process.

---

[4] https://etherscan.io/token/0xc02aaa39b223fe8d0a0e5c4f27ead9083c756cc2.

5   Related Work

The principles of the CHC encoding of smart contracts that SOLTG relies on originate from [12]. Previously, they enabled the development of the SOL-CMC [2] model checker built into the Solidity compiler. SOLCMC, however, is not designed to generating test cases for each branch of each function of a given contract which requires an exhaustive enumeration of path conditions. On the other side, SOLTG does not rely on external CHC solvers and has its own approach towards the exhaustiveness of the enumeration.

Automated reasoning about Solidity is also enabled by LLVM-based frameworks SMARTACE [18] and SKLEE [11]. SMARTACE uses an existing infrastructure for model checking, symbolic execution, and fuzzing [5,10], and it does not translate tests from LLVM back to Solidity. SKLEE targets the detection of certain types of bugs rather than maximizing the function, branch, or line coverage. Both tools reason about an LLVM binary which is semantically different from the original contract in Solidity. By contrast, SOLTG guarantees that behavior demonstrated by the generated tests corresponds to the actual blockchain behavior.

Existing tools for test case generation for Solidity [7,15] follow genetic algorithms and traditional fuzzing. These methods may struggle with corner cases because they extensively modify some initial random test cases, producing a significant amount of superfluous tests, e.g., ones that cover the same branch. By contrast, SOLTG is driven by exploitation of the program's structure, and specifically, it attempts to cover blocks of code that have not been tested yet.

There exist multiple SMT-based test generation tools like KALI [3], CAVI-TEST [16] for Java, FUSEBMC [1], SYMBIOTIC [6], KLEE [4] for C and other languages. Many of them produce test cases after some communication with an SMT solver, but neither of them is based on CHCs. The closest tool to SOLTG is the only CHC-based test case generator, HORNTINUUM [19], which is, however, not tailored for smart contracts and assumes that the CHC representation is linear (i.e., all function calls have to be inlined). HORNTINUUM alternates invariant generation and test case generator, and it accelerates the enumeration process by exploiting the invariants discovered so far. In the future, we would like to adopt this strategy in SOLTG as well.

6   Conclusion

We have presented SOLTG, a fully automated Solidity test case generator based on CHC encoding capable of generating tests for industry-grade smart contracts. SOLTG analyzes the system of nonlinear CHCs provided by SOLCMC and synthesizes test cases as a result of exhaustive enumeration of contract behavior and SMT models, thus avoiding fuzzing. The compiled tests are supported by the widely used FOUNDRY framework. Our evaluation demonstrates that the tool is effective in generating test cases on a range of Solidity contracts and can be fully integrated into the development process. In the future, SOLTG could benefit from a tighter connection with invariant generation techniques to accelerate its enumeration process.

Acknowledgments. The USI authors were supported by the Swiss National Science Foundation grant 200021_185031. The FSU authors were supported by the National Science Foundation grant 2106949 and by a gift from the Ethereum Foundation.

References

1. Alshmrany, K.M., Menezes, R.S., Gadelha, M.R., Cordeiro, L.C.: FuSeBMC: a white-box fuzzer for finding security vulnerabilities in C programs. CoRR (2020). https://arxiv.org/abs/2012.11223
2. Alt, L., Blicha, M., Hyvärinen, A.E.J., Sharygina, N.: Solcmc: Solidity compiler's model checker. In: Shoham, S., Vizel, Y. (eds.) Computer Aided Verification - 34th International Conference, CAV 2022, Haifa, Israel, August 7-10, 2022, Proceedings, Part I. Lecture Notes in Computer Science, vol. 13371, pp. 325–338. Springer (2022). https://doi.org/10.1007/978-3-031-13185-1_16
3. Bombarda, A., Gargantini, A., Calvagna, A.: Multi-thread combinatorial test generation with SMT solvers. In: Hong, J., Lanperne, M., Park, J.W., Cerný, T., Shahriar, H. (eds.) Proceedings of the 38th ACM/SIGAPP Symposium on Applied Computing, SAC 2023, Tallinn, Estonia, March 27-31, 2023, pp. 1698–1705. ACM (2023). https://doi.org/10.1145/3555776.3577703
4. Cadar, C., Dunbar, D., Engler, D.R.: KLEE: unassisted and automatic generation of high-coverage tests for complex systems programs. In: Draves, R., van Renesse, R. (eds.) 8th USENIX Symposium on Operating Systems Design and Implementation, OSDI 2008, December 8-10, 2008, San Diego, California, USA, Proceedings, pp. 209–224. USENIX Association (2008). http://www.usenix.org/events/osdi08/tech/full_papers/cadar/cadar.pdf
5. Cadar, C., Nowack, M.: KLEE symbolic execution engine in 2019. Int. J. Softw. Tools Technol. Transf., 867–870 (2021). https://doi.org/10.1007/S10009-020-00570-3
6. Chalupa, M., Novák, J., Strejcek, J.: Symbiotic 8: parallel and targeted test generation - (competition contribution). In: Guerra, E., Stoelinga, M. (eds.) Fundamental Approaches to Software Engineering - 24th International Conference, FASE 2021, Held as Part of the European Joint Conferences on Theory and Practice of Software, ETAPS 2021, Luxembourg City, Luxembourg, March 27 - April 1, 2021, Proceedings. Lecture Notes in Computer Science, vol. 12649, pp. 368–372. Springer (2021). https://doi.org/10.1007/978-3-030-71500-7_20
7. Driessen, S.W., Nucci, D.D., Tamburri, D.A., van den Heuvel, W.: Solar: automated test-suite generation for solidity smart contracts. Sci. Comput. Program. **232**, 103036 (2024). https://doi.org/10.1016/J.SCICO.2023.103036
8. Ernst, G.: Korn - software verification with horn clauses (competition contribution). In: Sankaranarayanan, S., Sharygina, N. (eds.) Tools and Algorithms for the Construction and Analysis of Systems - 29th International Conference, TACAS 2023, Held as Part of the European Joint Conferences on Theory and Practice of Software, ETAPS 2022, Paris, France, April 22-27, 2023, Proceedings, Part II. Lecture Notes in Computer Science, vol. 13994, pp. 559–564. Springer (2023). https://doi.org/10.1007/978-3-031-30820-8_36

9. Esen, Z., Rümmer, P.: Tricera: Verifying C programs using the theory of heaps. In: Griggio, A., Rungta, N. (eds.) 22nd Formal Methods in Computer-Aided Design, FMCAD 2022, Trento, Italy, October 17-21, 2022, pp. 380–391. IEEE (2022). https://doi.org/10.34727/2022/ISBN.978-3-85448-053-2_45

10. Gurfinkel, A., Kahsai, T., Komuravelli, A., Navas, J.A.: The seahorn verification framework. In: Kroening, D., Pasareanu, C.S. (eds.) Computer Aided Verification - 27th International Conference, CAV 2015, San Francisco, CA, USA, July 18-24, 2015, Proceedings, Part I. Lecture Notes in Computer Science, vol. 9206, pp. 343–361. Springer (2015). https://doi.org/10.1007/978-3-319-21690-4_20

11. Jain, N., Kaneko, K., Sharma, S.: SKLEE: A dynamic symbolic analysis tool for ethereum smart contracts (tool paper). In: Schlingloff, B., Chai, M. (eds.) Software Engineering and Formal Methods - 20th International Conference, SEFM 2022, Berlin, Germany, September 26-30, 2022, Proceedings. Lecture Notes in Computer Science, vol. 13550, pp. 244–250. Springer (2022). https://doi.org/10.1007/978-3-031-17108-6_15

12. Marescotti, M., Otoni, R., Alt, L., Eugster, P., Hyvärinen, A.E.J., Sharygina, N.: Accurate smart contract verification through direct modelling. In: Margaria, T., Steffen, B. (eds.) Leveraging Applications of Formal Methods, Verification and Validation: Applications - 9th International Symposium on Leveraging Applications of Formal Methods, ISoLA 2020, Rhodes, Greece, October 20-30, 2020, Proceedings, Part III. Lecture Notes in Computer Science, vol. 12478, pp. 178–194. Springer (2020).https://doi.org/10.1007/978-3-030-61467-6_12

13. Matsushita, Y., Tsukada, T., Kobayashi, N.: RustHorn: CHC-based verification for rust programs. ACM Trans. Program. Lang. Syst. **43**(4), 15:1–15:54 (2021). https://doi.org/10.1145/3462205

14. de Moura, L.M., Bjørner, N.S.: Z3: an efficient SMT solver. In: Ramakrishnan, C.R., Rehof, J. (eds.) Tools and Algorithms for the Construction and Analysis of Systems, 14th International Conference, TACAS 2008, Held as Part of the Joint European Conferences on Theory and Practice of Software, ETAPS 2008, Budapest, Hungary, March 29-April 6, 2008. Proceedings. Lecture Notes in Computer Science, vol. 4963, pp. 337–340. Springer (2008). https://doi.org/10.1007/978-3-540-78800-3_24

15. Olsthoorn, M., Stallenberg, D.M., van Deursen, A., Panichella, A.: SynTest-Solidity: automated test case generation and fuzzing for smart contracts. In: 44th IEEE/ACM International Conference on Software Engineering: Companion Proceedings, ICSE Companion 2022, Pittsburgh, PA, USA, May 22-24, 2022, pp. 202–206. ACM/IEEE (2022). https://doi.org/10.1145/3510454.3516869

16. Peña, R., Sánchez-Hernández, J., Garrido, M., Sagredo, J.: SMT-based test-case generation and validation for programs with complex specifications. In: López-García, P., Gallagher, J.P., Giacobazzi, R. (eds.) Analysis, Verification and Transformation for Declarative Programming and Intelligent Systems - Essays Dedicated to Manuel Hermenegildo on the Occasion of His 60th Birthday. Lecture Notes in Computer Science, vol. 13160, pp. 188–205. Springer (2023). https://doi.org/10.1007/978-3-031-31476-6_10

17. Rümmer, P.: Jayhorn: a java model checker. In: Murray, T., Ernst, G. (eds.) Proceedings of the 21st Workshop on Formal Techniques for Java-like Programs, FTfJP@ECOOP 2019, London, United Kingdom, July 15, 2019. p. 1:1. ACM (2019). https://doi.org/10.1145/3340672.3341113

18. Wesley, S., Christakis, M., Navas, J.A., Trefler, R.J., Wüstholz, V., Gurfinkel, A.: Verifying solidity smart contracts via communication abstraction in smartace. In: Finkbeiner, B., Wies, T. (eds.) Verification, Model Checking, and Abstract Interpretation - 23rd International Conference, VMCAI 2022, Philadelphia, PA, USA, January 16-18, 2022, Proceedings. Lecture Notes in Computer Science, vol. 13182, pp. 425–449. Springer (2022). https://doi.org/10.1007/978-3-030-94583-1_21
19. Zlatkin, I., Fedyukovich, G.: Maximizing branch coverage with constrained horn clauses. In: TACAS 2022. LNCS, vol. 13244, pp. 254–272. Springer, Cham (2022). https://doi.org/10.1007/978-3-030-99527-0_14

Interactive Theorem Proving Modulo Fuzzing

Sujit Kumar Muduli(✉)📍, Rohan Ravikumar Padulkar📍, and Subhajit Roy📍

Department of Computer Science and Engineering,
Indian Institute of Technology Kanpur, Kanpur, India
smuduli@cse.iitk.ac.in

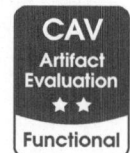

Abstract. Interactive theorem provers (ITPs) exploit the collaboration between humans and computers, enabling proof of complex theorems. Further, ITPs allow extraction of provably correct implementations from proofs. However, often, the extracted code interface with external libraries containing real-life complexities—proprietary library calls, remote/cloud APIs, complex models like ML models, inline assembly, highly non-linear arithmetic, vector instructions etc. We refer to such functions/operations as *closed-box components*. For such components, the user has to provide appropriate *assumed* lemmas to model the behavior of these functions. However, we found instances where these assumed lemmas are inconsistent with the actual semantics of these closed-box components. Hence, even *correct-by-construction* code extracted from an ITP may still behave incorrectly *when interfaced with such closed-box components*.

To this end, we propose STARFUZZ, that allows the F* interactive theorem prover to provide better end-to-end assurance on the application—*even when interfaced with the closed-box components*. Under the hood, STARFUZZ rides on SĀDHAK, an SMT solver that combines fuzz testing to allow satisfiability checking over closed-box components. On the F* library that includes external implementations in OCaml, STARFUZZ discovered four bugs—one bug that revealed an error on the assumed lemmas for a closed-box function, and three bugs in the external implementations of these components.

1 Introduction

Interactive theorem provers (ITPs) have been immensely successful in assisting/checking mathematical proofs, including those pertaining to properties of complex hardware/software systems. ITPs benefit from a synergistic human-computer collaboration: humans provide the necessary "intuitions" about the problem (eg. invariants) while the computer attempts to complete and check the proof. This allows ITPs to solve problems that are beyond automated theorem provers (like SMT solvers). In recent years, ITPs have been effective in building large-scale verified systems, such as secure TLS1.3 record layer [4], secure parser [22], compilers [17,18], and OS microkernels [14]. Not only do such verified

© The Author(s) 2024
A. Gurfinkel and V. Ganesh (Eds.): CAV 2024, LNCS 14681, pp. 480–493, 2024.
https://doi.org/10.1007/978-3-031-65627-9_24

systems assure robustness in deployment, they also provide important guarantees on the system implementation.

Interactive theorem provers allow a human user to interactively complete a proof with machine assistance. Further, if one can prove the validity of a specification, ITPs allow the extraction of *provably correct* implementations. Modern ITPs provide code backend for a variety of target languages: Coq allows extraction to OCaml, Haskell or Scheme language; F^* allows extraction to OCaml, $F^\#$, C, Wasm or assembly.

For verification of programs, ITPs need the complete formal semantics for all program components. However, real-life programs often contain program components whose semantic definitions are not available. For example, an implementation may use proprietary library calls, remote/cloud APIs, complex models like ML models, inline assembly, non-linear arithmetic, vector instructions, and external function calls where the implementation of certain operations/functions are either not available or too complex to be handled by the verifier. However, these components can be *executed*, and hence, available as *oracles*—one can pose an input query and observe their responses. We refer to such components as *closed-box components*.

Currently, closed-box components are handled with the user *assuming* relevant lemmas about them. However, the assumed lemmas may be inconsistent with the actual implementation, leading to two possible problems:

- the *assumed specification* of the closed-box components (in form of the admitted lemmas) can be incorrect: as the prover's proof is based on the assumed lemmas, the proof is, then, invalid;
- the *implementation* of the closed-box box components (that is not available to the ITP) is faulty: in this case, the implementation extracted from the ITP will be faulty when linked and executed with the closed-box components.

In this work, we propose STARFUZZ as a framework that allows an Interactive Theorem Prover to construct *almost correct* proofs over the end-to-end application (including closed-box libraries). STARFUZZ uses the F^* prover [25] to interactively construct proofs over the program components whose definitions are available. For the closed-box components, STARFUZZ constructs a relevant *verification condition* including the closed-box components, and uses a fuzzing-enabled SMT solver, SĀDHAK [19], to reason over such *closed-box* functions. Hence, STARFUZZ attempts to provide guarantees beyond what conventional ITPs provide—that the implementation extracted from the ITP will (most likely) demonstrate the expected behavior *even after being linked to the required closed-box components*.

We have used STARFUZZ to validate F^* specifications for many library calls that are used in proofs; for each of these calls, certain lemmas were assumed to construct the proofs. These library calls are heavily optimized implementations. The code extracted from F^* proofs is finally linked against these libraries to build the final applications. STARFUZZ could discover 4 violations in these libraries and proofs: one of them a case of an incorrect specification for a closed-box function, in the other three cases, the implementation of the closed-box components was faulty. Three of these bugs were unknown bugs.

This work makes the following contributions:

- We propose that fuzz engines should be integrated within ITPs to validate the assumed lemmas over closed-box components;
- We build STARFUZZ, a framework that uses a synergy of proofs and tests for almost-correct verification of applications with closed-box components;
- We have used STARFUZZ on F* libraries and have been able to discover multiple, hitherto unknown, faults.

2   Overview

2.1   Introduction to F*

F* [25] is a general purpose proof-oriented functional programming language that is used to write pure functional and effectful programs. Theorems and program specifications can be written in F* using dependent, refinement types.

Syntax. F* follows an OCaml-like syntax structure for defining functions (proofs). Functions can be typed via the arrow-type: `val incr: int -> int`; here, the function `incr` takes a value of the `int` type and, also, returns an `int` value. The `let` binding can be used to write named expressions, e.g., `let incr = fun (x: int) -> x + 1`.

Further, refinement predicates can be added to existing types to allow a refined specification. For example, in `val incr : x:int{x > 0} -> y:int{y > 1}`, (x > 0) and (y > 1) are type refinements for parameters x and y over base type `int`. One may also interpret these type refinements over input and outputs of a function as pre- and post-conditions of the function `incr`. F* also provides syntactic sugar, the keyword `Lemma`, to specify properties or proof obligations. For example, `inc_lemma` below uses the `requires` and `ensures` predicates to describe a lemma.

```
1  val incr_lemma: (x:int) -> (y:int) ->
2                  Lemma ((requires (x > 0)) (ensures (y > 1)))
```

Code Extraction. F* allows the extraction of verified code from F* proofs to target languages like OCaml, F#, Wasm, or C. For code extraction, one can invoke F* with the target language name passed with `-codegen` command-line argument.

```
1  module Incr
2  let incr (x: int {x > 0}) : (y: int {y = x + 1}) = x + 1
```

Listing 1.1. F* implementation of `incr` along with the specification.

```
1 open Prims
2 let (incr : Prims.int -> Prims.int) = fun x -> x + Prims.int_one
```

Listing 1.2. OCaml code extracted from Listing 1.1 after verification. Prims OCaml module is provided by F* which can be linked to the program to run.

2.2   F* with Closed-Box Functions

Functions that are only available in some external modules or are too complex for verification, can still be used in F* proofs. However, we need to assume the necessary specification of such functions to be able to complete the proofs. For example, in Listing 1.4, char_of_int is an external function that is used within the F* function load_string; a lemma that summarizes the behavior of this function is shown in Listing 1.5. Such *closed-box* functions may have bugs, either in their specification (i.e. assumed lemmas in F*), or in their implementation (in the external module). Hence, verification of a module within F* does not necessarily imply that the verified code is indeed correct *after it it linked with the external module with the closed-box functions.*

We discuss some bugs that STARFUZZ was able to uncover in the F* library.

Example 1. (Bug in Specification). Listing 1.4[1] is taken from the F* library. The function load_string reads a string of fixed length from a buffer, and uses the *closed-box* function Char.char_of_int. The lemma assumed about the implementation of this closed-box function is shown in Listing 1.5: it says that the Char.char_of_int function would work correctly for all integers less than 2^{21}, and must generate a UTF-8 char value in an unsigned 32-bit integer.

STARFUZZ uncovered a bug in this specification. Investigating further, we found that the char_of_int implementation eventually ends up calling a external OCaml module batUChar[2] which is outside of the F* library. As we can see from the batUChar module code snippet in Listing 1.3, a valid UTF character should be in the range [U+0000, U+D7FF] to [U+E000, U+10FFFF]. However, the given allowed range of the input [0, 2^{21}] in Listing 1.5 is beyond the valid range.

Understandably, as F* *believes* the lemmas provided by the users, it was unable to detect this issue. Further, any proofs that used this lemma were invalid (as the lemma was invalid). Clearly, the refinement type for the input (i.e., precondition) in Listing 1.5 is weak. To fix the problem, this precondition can be strengthened (shown in Listing 1.6).

The F* proofs completed successfully with the new lemma (Listing 1.5 replacing Listing 1.6) for char_of_int, now providing assurance that not only is the

---

[1] https://github.com/FStarLang/FStar/blob/e4cdebfa1d7aa45404650108b177dac3 37251d12/examples/old/tls-record-layer/crypto/Crypto.Test.fst#L116.

[2] https://github.com/ocaml-batteries-team/batteries-included/blob/ 77bd2aace3e16499ec71bf544270e169656c3c23/src/batUChar.ml#L51-L55=.

```
1  ...
2  (* valid range: U+0000..U+D7FF and U+E000..U+10FFFF *)
3  let chr n =
4    if (n >= 0 && n <= 0xd7ff)  (n >= 0xe000 && n <= 0x10ffff)
5    then n
6    else raise Out_of_range
7  ...
```

Listing 1.3. OCaml code snippet from batUChar shows the valid range of UTF-8 character code. If the input is not in valid range, then throws `Out_of_range` exception.

```
1  let rec load_string l buf =
2  if l = 0ul then "" else
3  //16-09-20 we miss String.init, proper refinements, etc
4  let b = UInt8.v (Buffer.index buf 0ul) in
5  let s = String.make 1 (Char.char_of_int b) in
6  let t = load_string (l -^ 1ul) (Buffer.sub buf 1ul (l -^ 1ul)) in
7  String.strcat s t
```

Listing 1.4. Code that leads to error for `char_of_int` specification. This example code is taken from F* Crypto.Test.fst of F* GitHub repo. `char_of_int` is closed-box function whose definition is not available.

implementation that is exposed to F* safe, but it is also higly likely to interface well with the functions in the external libraries (eg. `batUChar`). It is extremely hard for verification engineers to come up with a *good enough* specifications for such instances and such interfacing issues with external libraries is quite common, thereby motivating the use of STARFUZZ for specification validation of external libraries. This example was taken from an older version of F*; the same fix (Listing 1.6) appears in a subsequent commit.

```
1  val char_of_int: (i: nat{i < pow2 21}) -> Tot char
```

Listing 1.5. Weak specification for `FStar_Char.char_of_int`.

```
1  val char_of_int : (i: nat{(i < 0xd7ff) \/
2                            (i >= 0xe000 /\ i <= 0x10ffff)}) -> Tot char
```

Listing 1.6. Strengthened `FStar_Char.char_of_int` specification.

```
1 val  shift_left : v:int -> i:nat -> Tot (res:int{res = v * (pow2 i)})
```

Listing 1.7. Specification of closed-box function `shift_left` from `FStar.Math.Lib`.

```
1 let (shift_left : Prims.int -> Prims.nat -> Prims.int) =
2 fun v -> fun i -> v * (Prims.pow2 i)
```

Listing 1.8. OCaml code for closed-box function of `shift_left` which has to be linked.

Example 2. (Bug in Implementation). Listing 1.7 is the lemma assumed for the closed-box function `shift_left` in the F* library. The implementation of this function is in OCaml and is available in Listing 1.8. While the specification seems to capture the expected behavior of this function, STARFUZZ discovers an interesting test input, `(0, 549755813888)`, for which the function is expected to be produce 0 after evaluation, but it fails with an *out-of-memory* error.

The verified-by-construction code extracted from F*, when linked with this implementation of `shift_left`, is susceptible to crashing due to `shift_left`. In this case, though the specification is correct, the implementation of the function in the external module is faulty; again, F* cannot detect this problem as the implementation is outside the scope of F*.

This issue, reported by STARFUZZ, was an unknown bug in the F* library that had not been discovered earlier. STARFUZZ found multiple other, hitherto unknown bugs, that we discuss in Sect. 4.

3   Tool Architecture and Operation

3.1   Invoking StarFuzz

STARFUZZ accepts as input F* files with additional annotations for each closed-box functions. We assume that the closed-box components are functional, i.e. given a closed-box component f and two inputs a, b in its domain, $(a = b) \implies f(a) = f(b)$. Given an F* program, we can prepare it for STARFUZZ by annotating all closed-box (CB) functions with the `@starfuzz` annotation, followed by the names of the libraries that contain implementations of these closed-box and other functions that the closed-box functions depend on. This annotation must be followed by the F* type of the closed-box function. The syntax of the `@starfuzz` annotation is as follows:

```
1 @starfuzz: <cb-func-name> [lib1, ..., libN]
2 <cb-func-name> <fstar-type>
```

```
1  @starfuzz: shift_left [FStar_Math_Lib]
2  val shift_left: v:int -> i:nat -> Tot (res:int{res = v * (pow2 i)})
3  @starfuzz: pow2 [Prims]
4  val pow2: x:nat -> y:pos
```

Listing 1.9. A closed-box function annotated file as given to STARFUZZ as input.

STARFUZZ uses this annotation to identify the closed-box functions whose specification must be validated. For example while validating the closed-box function `shift_left` in Listing 1.7 we need to provide the input as shown in Listing 1.9. The `pow2` method used in type refinement of `shift_left` function is defined in the `Prims` module which has to be linked to create the executable.

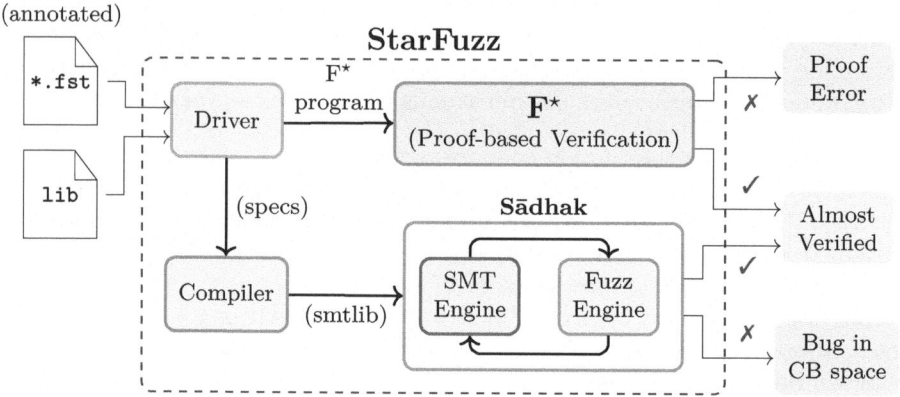

Fig. 1. Overview of the STARFUZZ architecture.

3.2 Architecture

Figure 1 shows the architecture of STARFUZZ: the annotated F* file(s) and the libraries of the closed-box functions are fed to the STARFUZZ driver, that dispatches two queries:

- The @starfuzz annotations are stripped to create a "pure" F* file which can be sent to F*;
- The @starfuzz annotations are extracted and passed to our logic compiler.

The logic compiler compiles the F* types into first-order logic formulae. The compilation process guarantees that the closed-box functions are *type-safe* if and only if the resulting formula φ is unsatisfiable; we refer to this formula as the *verification condition*. Next, the verification condition is checked with an SMT solver that is capable of handling closed-box constraints, with the associated libraries made available to it to enable fuzz-based search.

We made a conscious decision to maintain a loose coupling between F* and STARFUZZ: no code changes were needed within F* to integrate it within STAR-FUZZ. It offers two advantages: firstly, it was easier to develop and will be easier to maintain STARFUZZ across changing F* versions. Secondly, this loose coupling allows other theorem provers (like Agda [1], Iris [12] etc.) to be plugged into STARFUZZ with little change to the STARFUZZ implementation. We have plans of extending STARFUZZ to support other ITPs in the future.

3.3   Constructing Verification Conditions

Consider an F* type: $\tau_1 \to \tau_2 \to \ldots \to \tau_n$. Each meta-variable τ in the above expression either represents a F* primitive type or a refinement type. Primitive types could be `int`, `char`, etc. The refinement types are in the form $\boxed{(x : t\{\varphi\})}$, where x is to name the parameter, t is a type and φ is a predicate for type refinement which defines the set of values that x belongs to. In other words an expression e belongs to the refined type $(x : t\{\varphi\})$ iff e is of type t and $\varphi[e\backslash x]$ is a valid formula. STARFUZZ also also supports sub-types of `int` from F* such as `type nat = x:int{x >= 0}` and `type pos = x:int{x > 0}`. The type refinement predicate φ for `nat` and `pos` are kept implicit.

In the STARFUZZ's compiler we have provided rules to translate the above type annotation of any function to an appropriate SMT constraints, which is inspired from F* to SMT encoding discussed in [2]. The type annotation $\tau_1 \to \tau_2 \to \ldots \to \tau_n$ is translated to the logic expression shown in Eq. (1) (where $\mathcal{T}$ denotes the translation procedure),

$$\mathcal{T}(\tau_1) \wedge \mathcal{T}(\tau_2) \wedge \ldots \mathcal{T}(\tau_{n-1}) \wedge \neg \mathcal{T}(\tau_n) \tag{1}$$

Along with refinement types user can also write the `Lemma` statements in F* using `requires` (pre) and `ensures` (post) conditions for each function. The `Lemma` statement is of form $\boxed{\text{Lemma (requires } \vartheta) \text{ (ensures } \varphi)}$, then we would like to find violation for the `ensures` condition by assuming `requires` i.e. the satisfiable assignment for the expression: $\mathcal{T}(\vartheta) \wedge \neg \mathcal{T}(\varphi)$.

Lemmas can also be defined without the `requires` keyword, simply as $\boxed{\text{Lemma } (\varphi)}$; then, we test for violation in $\mathcal{T}(\varphi)$.

To encode the closed-box functions, we use the recently proposed closed-box logic fragment [19] that allows us to solve first-order logical formula over closed-box functions supported by the SĀDHAK [19] SMT solver. SĀDHAK needs the closed-box functions to be declared as closed-box sorts using the keyword `declare-cb` in the extended SMTLIB format. For example, the declaration of closed-box functions `shift_left` and `pow2` in Listing 1.7 is shown below,

```
1  (declare-cb shift_left ((_ BitVec 64) (_ BitVec 64)) (_ BitVec 64))
2  (declare-cb pow2 ((_ BitVec 64)) (_ BitVec 64))
```

3.4   Solving Verification Conditions

The verification condition constructed above cannot be solved by regular SMT engines due to the presence of the closed-box functions. For this purpose, we use the SĀDHAK SMT solver that is capable of solving constraints over such logic fragments.

SĀDHAK employs the CDFL (*Conflict-drive Fuzz Loop*) algorithm to combine SMT solving and Fuzzing. SĀDHAK dispatches the set of constraints that contain closed-box terms to the fuzz engine, while the remaining constrained are sent to the SMT engine. The closed-box terms are represented simply as uninterpreted functions within the SMT engine. The fuzz engine in SĀDHAK generates a partial model from its constraints and dispatches it to the SMT solver. The SMT solver searches for a completion of this partial model such that the resulting model is consistent with its own set of constraints. If such a model is found, the set of constraints are deemed satisfiable. Otherwise, SĀDHAK performs a conflict analysis on the constraints in the SMT solver to discover the reason for unsatisfiability; the terms participating in the conflict are sent to the fuzz engine for it to generate a better partial model. At the same time, the SMT engine caches the input-output relations over the closed-box functions from the partial model it had received from the fuzz engine. The fuzz engine, now, prepares a new partial model that it consistent with its augmented constraint set, and communicates it back to the SMT engine. This process is repeated, both the SMT solver and the fuzz engine learning new lemmas in each iteration, till they converge to a model. SĀDHAK is sound but not complete—that is, if it terminates with a model, it is guaranteed to be a solution to the provided constraints, but it may not be able to find a model or a proof of unsatisfiable due to the presence of a fuzzer in the loop.

To run the CDFL loop, SĀDHAK translates logic constraints to program which is then compiled down to a binary target to be fuzzed after linked with the libraries of the closed-box functions. Because it uses a fuzzer, SĀDHAK is sound but not complete, and termination may not be guaranteed.

For interfacing with F*, we enhance SĀDHAK with a novel OCaml code generation backend to the existing C code backend. Generated OCaml code can be interfaced with closed-box functions that are defined in external OCaml modules and are called from F* programs. The generated OCaml code is instrumented with **afl-instrument** and **Crowbar** packages. The binary fuzz target is generated after linking the external modules containing the closed-box functions. Finally, the generated target binary is then fuzzed with AFL++ [9] fuzzer.

A satisfiying model from SĀDHAK is reported as a violation of a F* closed-box function specification under consideration. The user will, then, have to do the triage to isolate the specification defects by evaluating the closed-box function against the corresponding specification.

4   Evaluation

We evaluate STARFUZZ on 56 specifications from F* library that are used as external function calls. We validate these specifications against corresponding OCaml implementations; verified code extracted from F* are linked against these implementations. Our benchmark suite contains specifications dealing with both integer and string data types, implemented either as refinement types or lemmas in F*. The evaluation was performed on Intel Core i7-8700 CPU @3.2 GHz machine running Ubuntu 18.04 (x86-64) with a timeout of 300 s.

The third violation was found in the `concat_length` lemma:

```
1  val concat_length: s1:string -> s2: string ->
2                Lemma ( (length (s1 ^ s2)) = (length s1) + (length s2))
```

In our evaluation of these 56 benchmarks we found around four violations. Out of these, two have already been discussed in Example 1 and Example 2 of Sect. 2.2, respectively.

This lemma defines distributive property of the `length` function from `FString_String` module: the sum of the lengths of two input string should always be equal to the length the concatenated string. However, STARFUZZ was able to find a violation for this lemma for the current implementation of the function: invoking `FStar_String.length` (`"{\163"` ^ `"\004"`) produces output 2, while the expected output is 3—since the string length of `"{\163"` and `"\004"` is 1 and 2, respectively.

The fourth violation was found in the lemma `string_of_list_of_string`, which fails for the input `"\225"`.

```
1  val string_of_list_of_string: (s:string) ->
2                Lemma ((string_of_list (list_of_string s)) = s)
```

Invoking (`list_of_string "\225"`) returns the character list `['\225']` and converting the resulting output back to a string with (`string_of_list ['\225']`) returns the string `"\225\128\128"`. The lemma `string_of_list_of_string` expects `string_of_list` to be the inverse of `list_of_string`, however STARFUZZ was able to find this violation for the lemma.

5   Related Work

Reasoning programs with external function calls has been a challenging task. COLOSSUS [20], ACHAR [15], DELPHI [21] and SĀDHAK [19] use constraint solving for reasoning with closed-box functions. COLOSSUS [20] uses fuzzing to solve path constraints containing closed-box functions calls to recover lost coverage in symbolic execution. ACHAR [15] uses fuzzing along with SMT solving to find inductive loop invariant for programs which may contain CB functions, using fuzzing to validate program paths containing closed-box functions and SMT solving for the rest. DELPHI [21] uses SMT solver by interpreting the closed-box function calls as *uninterpreted functions* to find a candidate solution, and then, validates the candidate solution by calling an oracle for the closed-box function. SĀDHAK [19] combines both SMT solving and fuzzing to find out satisfiable solution for a given constraint in first-order logic. In contrast to COLOSSUS, SĀDHAK uses a lazy approach called *conflict-driven fuzz loop* (CDFL) when invoking fuzzer from the SMT solver. STARFUZZ uses these ideas to propose a solution for handling closed-box functions in context of verification-oriented programming such as F*.

Angelic verification [7,8,11,16] use heuristics to suppress false alarms due to overapproximation of the external functions, but they risk missing real bugs. Multi-abduction [3] attempts to infer maximal permissive specifications of closed-box functions. HORNSPEC [23] also tries to synthesize maximal specifications for closed-box (undefined) functions appearing in constrained horn clauses and ensures non-vacuity. AMURTH [13] can infer a sound and maximally precise (in a provided DSL) *abstract* specifications of library functions in a provided abstract domain from concrete specifications. The technique proposed in [10] can infer maximal refinement types for higher-order functional programs.

6   Conclusion and Future Work

In this work, we enable interactive theorem provers to provide better end-to-end assurance on programs that contain closed-box components. We demonstrate the applicability of this proposal by building a tool, STARFUZZ, that integrates the F* interactive theorem prover with the SĀDHAK solver. SĀDHAK is capable of combining SMT solving and fuzzing to reason on constraints that may contain closed-box functions. We evaluated STARFUZZ on 56 specifications from the F* library that includes external implementations in OCaml, to discover four bugs; three of these bugs were unknown.

In the future, we are interested in applying STARFUZZ on more libraries and applications of F*. Further, as STARFUZZ couples with F* quite loosely, we are also interested in extending the support of such *almost verification* to other interactive theorem provers as well. Finally, we would also like to invest in integrating SĀDHAK with other verification methodologies, like bounded model checking [5,6,24]. In summary, we believe satisfiability modulo fuzzing is an exciting technology with potential for solving many other real-world software engineering problems.

References

1. Agda Development Team: The Agda wiki. Chalmers University of Technology (2007–2021). http://wiki.portal.chalmers.se/agda/pmwiki.php/
2. Aguirre, A.: Towards a provably correct encoding from F* to SMT. Master's thesis, Université Paris, vol. 7 (2016)

3. Albarghouthi, A., Dillig, I., Gurfinkel, A.: Maximal specification synthesis. In: Proceedings of the 43rd Annual ACM SIGPLAN-SIGACT Symposium on Principles of Programming Languages, POPL 2016, pp. 789–801. Association for Computing Machinery, New York (2016). ISBN 9781450335492. https://doi.org/10.1145/2837614.2837628

4. Bhargavan, K., et al.: Implementing and proving the TLS 1.3 record layer. Cryptology ePrint Archive, Paper 2016/1178 (2016). https://eprint.iacr.org/2016/1178

5. Chatterjee, P., Meda, J., Lal, A., Roy, S.: Proof-guided underapproximation widening for bounded model checking. In: Shoham, S., Vizel, Y. (eds.) CAV 2022. LNCS, vol. 13371, pp. 304–324. Springer, Cham (2022). https://doi.org/10.1007/978-3-031-13185-1_15

6. Chatterjee, P., Roy, S., Diep, B.P., Lal, A.: Distributed bounded model checking. In: Formal Methods in Computer Aided Design (FMCAD), pp. 47–56 (2020). https://doi.org/10.34727/2020/isbn.978-3-85448-042-6_11

7. Das, A., Lahiri, S.K., Lal, A., Li, Y.: Angelic verification: precise verification modulo unknowns. In: Kroening, D., Păsăreanu, C.S. (eds.) CAV 2015, Part I. LNCS, vol. 9206, pp. 324–342. Springer, Cham (2015). https://doi.org/10.1007/978-3-319-21690-4_19

8. Das, A., Lal, A.: Precise null pointer analysis through global value numbering. In: D'Souza, D., Narayan Kumar, K. (eds.) ATVA 2017. LNCS, vol. 10482, pp. 25–41. Springer, Cham (2017). https://doi.org/10.1007/978-3-319-68167-2_2

9. Fioraldi, A., Maier, D., Eißfeldt, H., Heuse, M.: AFL++: combining incremental steps of fuzzing research. In: 14th USENIX Workshop on Offensive Technologies (WOOT 2020). USENIX Association (2020)

10. Hashimoto, K., Unno, H.: Refinement type inference via horn constraint optimization. In: Blazy, S., Jensen, T. (eds.) SAS 2015. LNCS, vol. 9291, pp. 199–216. Springer, Heidelberg (2015). https://doi.org/10.1007/978-3-662-48288-9_12

11. Joshi, S., Lahiri, S.K., Lal, A.: Underspecified harnesses and interleaved bugs. In: Field, J., Hicks, M. (eds.) Proceedings of the 39th ACM SIGPLAN-SIGACT Symposium on Principles of Programming Languages, POPL 2012, Philadelphia, Pennsylvania, USA, 22–28 January 2012, pp. 19–30. ACM (2012). https://doi.org/10.1145/2103656.2103662

12. Jung, R., et al.: Iris: monoids and invariants as an orthogonal basis for concurrent reasoning. In: Proceedings of the 42nd Annual ACM SIGPLAN-SIGACT Symposium on Principles of Programming Languages, POPL 2015, pp. 637–650. Association for Computing Machinery, New York (2015). ISBN 9781450333009. https://doi.org/10.1145/2676726.2676980

13. Kalita, P.K., Muduli, S.K., D'Antoni, L., Reps, T., Roy, S.: Synthesizing abstract transformers. Proc. ACM Program. Lang. 6(OOPSLA2) (2022). https://doi.org/10.1145/3563334

14. Klein, G., et al.: Sel4: formal verification of an OS kernel. In: Proceedings of the ACM SIGOPS 22nd Symposium on Operating Systems Principles, SOSP 2009, pp. 207–220. Association for Computing Machinery, New York (2009). ISBN 9781605587523. https://doi.org/10.1145/1629575.1629596

15. Lahiri, S., Roy, S.: Almost correct invariants: synthesizing inductive invariants by fuzzing proofs. In: Proceedings of the 31st ACM SIGSOFT International Symposium on Software Testing and Analysis, ISSTA 2022, pp. 352–364. Association for Computing Machinery, New York (2022). ISBN 9781450393799. https://doi.org/10.1145/3533767.3534381

16. Lahiri, S.K., et al.: Angelic checking within static driver verifier: towards high-precision defects without (modeling) cost. In: 2020 Formal Methods in Computer Aided Design, FMCAD 2020, Haifa, Israel, 21–24 September 2020, pp. 169–178. IEEE (2020). https://doi.org/10.34727/2020/isbn.978-3-85448-042-6_24

17. Leroy, X.: Formal certification of a compiler back-end or: programming a compiler with a proof assistant. In: Conference Record of the 33rd ACM SIGPLAN-SIGACT Symposium on Principles of Programming Languages, POPL 2006. Association for Computing Machinery, New York (2006). ISBN 1595930272.https://doi.org/10.1145/1111037.1111042

18. Leroy, X.: Formal verification of a realistic compiler. Commun. ACM **52**(7), 107–115 (2009). ISSN 0001-0782. https://doi.org/10.1145/1538788.1538814

19. Muduli, S.K., Roy, S.: Satisfiability modulo fuzzing: a synergistic combination of SMT solving and fuzzing. In: Proceedings of the ACM on Programming Languages, OOPSLA2. Association for Computing Machinery, New York (2022). https://doi.org/10.1145/3563332

20. Pandey, A., Kotcharlakota, P.R.G., Roy, S.: Deferred concretization in symbolic execution via fuzzing. In: Proceedings of the 28th ACM SIGSOFT International Symposium on Software Testing and Analysis, ISSTA 2019 (2019). https://doi.org/10.1145/3293882.3330554

21. Polgreen, E., Reynolds, A., Seshia, S.A.: Satisfiability and synthesis modulo oracles. In: Finkbeiner, B., Wies, T. (eds.) VMCAI 2022. LNCS, vol. 13182, pp. 263–284. Springer, Cham (2022). https://doi.org/10.1007/978-3-030-94583-1_13

22. Ramananandro, T., et al.: EverParse: verified secure zero-copy parsers for authenticated message formats. In: 28th USENIX Security Symposium (USENIX Security 2019), pp. 1465–1482. USENIX Association, Santa Clara, CA (2019). ISBN 978-1-939133-06-9. https://www.usenix.org/conference/usenixsecurity19/presentation/delignat-lavaud

23. Prabhu, S., Fedyukovich, G., Madhukar, K., D'Souza, D.: Specification synthesis with constrained horn clauses. In: Freund, S.N., Yahav, E. (eds.) PLDI 2021: 42nd ACM SIGPLAN International Conference on Programming Language Design and Implementation, Virtual Event, Canada, 20–25 June 2021, pp. 1203–1217. ACM (2021). https://doi.org/10.1145/3453483.3454104

24. Solanki, M., Chatterjee, P., Lal, A., Roy, S.: Accelerated bounded model checking using interpolation based summaries. In: Finkbeiner, B., Kovács, L. (eds.) TACAS 2024. LNCS, vol. 14571, pp. 155–174. Springer, Cham (2024). https://doi.org/10.1007/978-3-031-57249-4_8

25. Swamy, N., Hriţcu, C., et al.: Dependent types and multi-monadic effects in F*. In: Proceedings of the 43rd Annual ACM SIGPLAN-SIGACT Symposium on Principles of Programming Languages, POPL 2016. Association for Computing Machinery, New York (2016). https://doi.org/10.1145/2837614.2837655

Author Index